Sinclair on
Warranties and Indemnities on
Share and Asset Sales

Sinclair on
Warranties and Indemnities on
Share and Asset Sales

Eighth Edition

General Editor
Robert Thompson

SWEET & MAXWELL

THOMSON REUTERS

Fifth Edition 2001
Sixth Edition 2005
Seventh Edition 2008
Eighth Edition 2011

Published in 2011 by
Sweet & Maxwell Limited of
100 Avenue Road, London, NW3 3PF,
part of Thomson Reuters (Professional) UK Limited
(Registered in England & Wales, Company No 1679046.
Registered Office and address for service:
Aldgate House, 33 Aldgate High Street, London EC3N 1DL)

For further information on our products and services, visit
http://www.sweetandmaxwell.co.uk

Typeset by Interactive Sciences Ltd, Gloucester
Printed in the UK by CPI William Clowes Beccles NR34 7TL

No natural forests were destroyed to make this product:
only farmed timber was used and replanted.

British Library Cataloguing in Publication Data

A CIP catalogue record for this book
is available from the British Library

ISBN 9780414043169

Preface to the Eighth Edition

The last edition of this work was published in January 2008. This eighth edition reflects the changes in law, convention and practice since then.

There have been major changes to the Taxation Warranties and the Tax Covenant following the implementation of the Income Tax Act 2007 and the Corporation Tax Acts of 2009 and 2010 as part of the tax law rewrite project. As these changes have just been made, where relevant both the old references and the new are stated as many practitioners have not yet updated their precedents to reflect these changes.

In the last edition some of the provisions of the Companies Act 2006 had not come into effect. That process is now complete in respect of the principal provisions so only the new references have been included in this work. The Bribery Act 2010 was due to be implemented in April 2011, but this has now been delayed. Nonetheless, the relevant warranties on anti-corruption anticipate the coming into effect of this piece of legislation by way of alternative drafting. This should enable practitioners to ensure that their drafting and understanding of the issues remains current.

The warranties have been overhauled to reflect not only changes in law since the last edition but also changes in convention and approach. Substantial changes have been made on key focus areas to reflect this including pensions, data protection, employment and social media. Chapter 8 which deals with asset rather than share deals has been expanded to incorporate the latest trends on indemnities and warranties applicable to these sort of transactions. The latest position on TUPE is reflected here with detailed commentary on recent case law.

Chapter 11 now includes a brief discussion on warranty and indemnity insurance which in some circumstances can be used to broker an impasse between the vendors and the purchaser where they have been unable to agree an appropriate risk apportion basis between themselves. On larger deals it is occasionally possible to have the entire risk underwritten by insurance from either a buy or sell perspective. In auction situations this can give a purchaser a significant commercial advantage where it does not require the vendors to underwrite the risk through appropriate warranties and indemnities.

The aim of the book has not changed. It is primarily a practitioners' guide designed to assist in the preparation and negotiation of suitable sale and purchase documentation. Given the current economic climate it is not uncommon to find that deals fail for a myriad of extraneous factors beyond the practitioner's control. As most deals will involve an element of compromise in terms of either parties' ideals it beholds us as practitioners to ensure that we have a sufficient understanding of the issues and alternative perspectives to a given problem to enable suitable solutions to be found wherever possible.

As always, the views expressed in this work as to the appropriateness or otherwise of any of the warranties or indemnities, or the suggested amendments to any of them from either perspective are subjective, although in most cases they reflect current thinking. Aside from my own work I am indebted to my partners and their responsible fee earners throughout the firm for their respective contributions. Of particular mention: Paul Christian for tax, Alex Cox for property, Dr Tristan Mander for pensions, Judy Baker for IP/IT, Jim James for insolvency and my assistant, Tom Pollard, who has been invaluable throughout.

The law is stated as at January 1, 2011.

Robert Thompson
January 2011

Introduction

The book is largely organised around precedents of clauses and documents, accompanied by commentary. In the precedents, words which begin with a capital letter are assumed to be defined terms; the definitions in either Ch.4.1 or the Tax Covenant have been adopted. The words and phrases which are included in square brackets in the precedents are, in the main, suggested amendments for the benefit of the party to whom the first draft, which would not usually include any of the bracketed additions, is presented. Where relevant and for ease of interpretation, the clauses have been highlighted in bold to differentiate the wording of these from the accompanying commentaries and explanations.

The precedents deal primarily with the sale of shares of a company but, without overloading the text with obvious variations, the amendments which are applicable to the sale of a business have generally been indicated. In the text, the company which is being sold is referred to as "the target company". The vendors of the shares are described as such throughout the book, and it is assumed that they are also the persons giving the warranties. When they are not, it would be appropriate to differentiate between them in the sale and purchase agreement and in the Tax Covenant by reference to vendors and warrantors. The word "covenantors" is used in circumstances where there is reference to a separate tax deed.

To assist readers who wish to make use of, or be reminded about the precedents, these are collected together in the Appendices. In particular, Appendix 8 contains the various clauses discussed in Chs 1 to 4, whilst Appendix 4 repeats the warranties by the vendors which are examined in Chs 5 to 7. A short form version of the warranties contained in Appendix 4 can be found at Appendix 9. In addition, Appendix 10 contains a disclosure letter precedent.

The following initials are used in relation to particular statutes:

CA	Companies Act
CAA	Capital Allowances Act
CTA	Corporation Tax Act
FA	Finance Act
ICTA	Income and Corporation Taxes Act
IHTA	Inheritance Tax Act
IT(EP)A	Income Tax (Earnings and Pensions) Act
ITA	Income Tax Act
LPA	Law of Property Act
LPMPA	Law of Property (Miscellaneous Provisions) Act
TCGA	Taxation of Chargeable Gains Act
TIOPA	Taxation (International and Other Provisions) Act
TMA	Taxes Management Act

TUPE	Transfer of Undertakings (Protection of Employment) Regulations 2006
VATA	Value Added Tax Act

The initials "VAT" refer to Value Added Tax, the initials "SDLT" refer to Stamp Duty Land Tax, the initials "ACT" refer to Advance Corporation Tax and the initials "ESC" refer to an HMRC Extra Statutory Concession.

The chapters are arranged into a logical chronology beginning with the history and function of warranties and indemnities. The book then considers the various parties to the sale and purchase agreement, and some of the nuances between them. There is then a chapter explaining the rights and liabilities that arise from a breach of warranty, and the particular issues that need to be considered in relation to this. Subsequently, there are three successive chapters containing in depth analysis of taxation warranties, property warranties and general long-form commercial warranties that are likely to be of application in a share sale. Warranties and indemnities applicable to the sale of a business are then separately considered before moving on to a detailed review of disclosure letters, their purpose and effect. The next chapter then focuses on the form of Tax Covenant (in its modern format) and relevant limitations. This is followed by a chapter dedicated to limitation provisions that might be applicable to warranty and/or indemnity claims. Finally there are two further chapters dealing with completion accounts and valuation, so as to give the reader an insight into how the negotiation of warranties and indemnities may be affected by completion accounts, where a transaction includes these, and to put the warranties and indemnities in context by reference to how the target company or business was valued.

Contents

Page

APPENDICES

Table of Cases

Table of Statutes

Table of Statutory Instruments

Table of European Legislation

CHAPTER 1

History and Function of Warranties and Indemnities

PURPOSE OF WARRANTIES

The purchaser of the share capital or business and assets of a company receives very little protection under the law, if the bargain turns out to be not what was expected, unless there has been misrepresentation or fraud by the vendors. The concept is embodied in the somewhat dated Latin tag *caveat emptor*, which effectively means that it is for the purchaser to decide what protection it requires, and that it is not for the law to provide it. In both types of purchases, the effect is to leave the purchaser generally at risk that the assets which it thinks it is acquiring (either directly in the case of the purchase of a business or indirectly in the case of the purchase of share capital), are less than it believed, or subject to unexpected defects. In the case of the purchase of shares, the purchaser has the further risk that the company is subject to unknown or unduly onerous liabilities which it may not have been possible to unearth in any due diligence. **1–01**

This difference between the two alternative ways of acquiring a business arises because, in general, the liabilities of a company are unaffected by changes in the identity of its owners and the purchaser effectively acquires all assets, rights and liabilities of the company by acquiring its share capital. Where the transaction relates to the purchase of assets, however, it is most unusual for the purchaser to become subject to liabilities of the business, unless they are expressly taken over by it in the sale agreement. A notable exception to this general rule is that the purchaser will take on employment liabilities if the Transfer of Undertakings (Protection of Employment) Regulations 2006 apply.

It is therefore customary for the purchaser of a private company or a business to receive some form of assurances from the vendors as to the assets of the company or the business and, where the acquisition is of the shares of a company, as to the liabilities which attach to the target company. Over the years there has been a steady expansion in the scope and nature of the assurances that purchasers require—the agreements tend to be very extensive, with a large part being in the nature of warranties and indemnities. **1–02**

It is sometimes suggested that a major purpose of the extensive warranties in a sale agreement is to bring to the attention of the vendors (by way of disclosure) the points which are likely to be of concern to the purchaser. The process of checking the warranties for the purposes of disclosing against them is designed to bring out all potential problems, enabling the parties to negotiate before the sale, as to what impact these should make on the transaction. In this way, the chances of acrimonious disputes arising after completion are reduced. Where the transaction involves completion accounts, disclosure of a liability against the warranties may not be the end of the matter. See Ch.12 for further discussion of this.

1–03   It should never be forgotten though, that the main purpose and effect of the warranties is to impose legal liability upon the vendors, and to provide the purchaser with a remedy if statements made about the company prove to be incorrect, and the value of it reduced. In effect, the warranties allocate risk, as between the vendors and the purchaser, in relation to the target company whose assets or shares are being purchased. To the extent that warranties *are* given, the *vendors* accept the potential liability if the warranties are breached; in so far as warranties are *not* given, are restricted in their scope or disclosed against, the *purchaser* takes the risk. The negotiation of the warranties is often referred to as the "battle of the risks" for this reason. The "risk" can also be addressed through indemnities or adjustments being made to the price through a completion accounts or similar mechanism.

There are nevertheless normally some warranties which in practice will not entitle the purchaser to any damages in the event of a breach. In practice, the only purpose of including these warranties is to perform a checklist function against which any relevant disclosures are required to be made. Examples of such warranties are those which are invariably rendered ineffective by the disclosure letter (see cl.1.10.1 in para.7–21, relating to the memorandum and articles of association of the target company, and general disclosure (i) in para.9–23), or those where a breach would not normally mean that the purchaser suffers any loss (see cl.3.3.1 in para.7–58, relating to bank accounts). In relation to the acquisition of the shares in a company, it is current convention for any breach of warranty to be assessed on a normal damages basis (as opposed to an indemnity basis). This will usually require an assessment of overall loss in the context of the acquisition of the target company as a whole. Often the result of this is that an individual breach of warranty may not give rise to compensation in favour of the purchaser. Where, therefore, there is a particular concern over any potential liability or defect that will often be addressed through a specific indemnity or for those particular warranties to be subject to on an indemnity basis of damages.

1–04   Although the principle of caveat emptor applies equally to acquisitions of listed shares and shares of private companies, it has nevertheless been generally accepted by bidders for listed companies that they do not receive warranties. In cases where there is a recommended offer, the bidder may be given the opportunity of undertaking some due diligence although it would be rare for information provided to be warranted in any way. Occasionally, if there is a large controlling shareholding, the bidder may receive some kind of limited protection, but in general the bid is made blind. There is no real logic why a purchaser of a listed company should be prepared to take on board the risk of deficiencies in the assets or the existence of undisclosed liabilities, whilst not being prepared to do so if it is purchasing a private company or a business, however that is the accepted practice.

It might be considered that one reason for the difference in approach arises from the fact that many private companies are operated in a somewhat more casual manner than public companies, but this view would not explain why it is that, for example, the purchaser of a wholly-owned subsidiary of a listed company would expect the full warranties that apply on any purchase of a private company, or why the purchaser of a business from a listed group requires warranty protection. It is also difficult to explain the difference on the grounds that more information is available in relation to listed companies as, unless circulars have had to be sent out by the listed company which give more detail than would appear in the accounts, there is usually no greater access to information concerning the affairs of a listed group than of a private group. The reason is more often likely to be a practical one, namely that the shareholders of a listed company are generally not included in the management or control of the company, and are therefore unlikely to accept any warranty liability in relation to the affairs of it, even though, on a risk apportionment basis, the provision of appropriate warranties might be justified.

Conversely it is very rare for the vendors of an unlisted company or business **1–05** to avoid the provision of extensive warranties, but it is reasonable for the vendors to require the purchaser to justify each warranty that is sought, rather than their having to demonstrate that the deletion or qualification of the warranty is fair. In striking contrast to the widespread acceptance of the obligation to give vendor warranties is the fact that it is unusual for the vendors to seek warranties from the purchaser, when the purchase consideration is satisfied wholly or partly by the allotment of shares in the purchaser. If the consideration shares constitute a significant proportion of the purchaser's total capital, the vendors should consider the provision of appropriate warranties to underpin the worth of the consideration shares. An indication of warranties that might be suitable for this purpose is provided in Appendix 3.

THE ORIGIN OF INDEMNITIES

The concept of warranties is that the purchaser should receive compensation for **1–06** any loss of bargain it may suffer as a result of a breach of the warranties. In effect, the warranties give rise to an adjustment in the purchase price, and therefore concern only the vendors and the purchaser. In the case where there is a sale of shares, the target company itself is not directly involved.

While historically this was generally considered satisfactory, it was recognised some years ago that there were two particular types of liabilities where, on a share sale, the target company rather than the purchaser should receive the benefit of an indemnity from the vendors. These related to statutory liabilities for taxation, which were imposed upon a company in respect of benefits derived or liabilities avoided by a shareholder, in respect of which the company was therefore required to discharge a taxation liability which was really nothing to do with it, without having a corresponding statutory right of recovery or reimbursement from the relevant shareholder.

The first of these provisions was FA 1940 s.46, which in certain circumstances imposed a liability to estate duty on the death of a person who had, during his lifetime, transferred property to the company. The company could be liable to estate duty in respect of benefits derived by the deceased, but it had no right to recover the estate duty from his estate. The second case arose under the Income Tax Act 1952 s.245 in respect of liability arising from surtax assessments. In that case, if a closely held company did not pay adequate dividends, an assessment in respect of surtax (being the equivalent of higher rate tax) could be made on the company, based upon the surtax that would have been paid by the shareholders if full dividends had been distributed. Again, no statutory right of recovery existed for the company.

1–07   In both cases, therefore, as the company could incur a liability which should really have fallen upon another party, it is perfectly reasonable for the purchaser to require the vendors to provide an indemnity in respect of those liabilities. It is consistent with this analysis that the question of indemnities in favour of the purchaser of a company's business has never arisen, as the purchaser does not take over the tax liabilities of the vendor in these transactions. The convention was to provide a specific indemnity in respect of these liabilities, and for that indemnity to be in favour of the target company rather than the purchaser.

Over the years, this simple principle became obscured, and what began as an indemnity against specific secondary taxation liabilities where there was no right of recovery, gradually became extended so that until relatively recently it applied to all taxation liabilities of the target company.

The concept of the vendors indemnifying the target company against such tax liabilities became outmoded a few years ago, principally because of the potential for the target company to have to pay tax on the receipt of any payment made to it by the vendors, with the consequence that the vendors were required to pay a greater amount than the relevant liability, so as to cover the tax that the target company had to pay. The simple way to avoid the issue was to ensure that the indemnity was in favour of the purchaser, rather than the target company, as this removed the need to gross up any payment to reflect the receipt, as the payment was instead treated as an adjustment to the consideration.

Indemnities in respect of taxation have now been simplified further by the widespread abolition of a separate tax deed and the inclusion instead of a tax covenant within the sale agreement. See Ch.10 for a further discussion of this.

On a more general basis, indemnities also arose in circumstances where damages for breach of warranty might not have put the purchaser in a position to rectify the problem without cost to itself; for example, if the defect in one of the acquired assets did not affect the overall value of the company, an indemnity, which gives rise to an automatic right to payment in prescribed circumstances might be more appropriate.

1–08   In the event of a claim under an indemnity, the court will assess whether the specified event has occurred and how much should be paid to fix the problem by reference to the terms of the indemnity itself, which are, in the main, more favourable to the claimant than the position would otherwise be at common law. There is usually no need to prove a link between the liability and the value of the company, and the indemnity clause will commonly provide for recovery of costs and expenses, including legal fees, on a far more extensive basis than might otherwise be recoverable. Indemnities are therefore often used where a specific problem has been identified, and it is agreed that the risk will be borne by the vendors.

An additional point which is sometimes made to justify the use of indemnities as an alternative, or in addition to the warranties, concerns the effect of the purchaser's knowledge on its right to damages for breach of a warranty. In recent years the generally accepted position has been that if the purchaser is aware when it enters into the sale agreement that a warranty is incorrect, its entitlement to damages is likely to be reduced accordingly (see *Eurocopy Plc v Teesdale* [1992] B.C.L.C. 1067 and para.4–24). Where a purchaser chooses to act through an agent for the purpose of an acquisition, the actual knowledge of the agent, to the extent that it is knowledge within the scope of the purpose for which the agent is acting, will be treated as the knowledge of the purchaser (see *Infiniteland Ltd v Artisan Contracting Ltd* [2004] EWHC 955 Ch. D.). However, it should be noted that the *Eurocopy* decision was a ruling on a preliminary matter only, and not a final decision on the effectiveness of a clause that seeks to prevent the knowledge of a purchaser from prejudicing a claim made by it under the warranties where it has actual knowledge of facts, but they are not disclosed to the appropriate standard in the disclosure letter. In *Infiniteland*, the High Court rejected the argument that, as a general rule, if the purchaser knew something and still completed the deal, it could not claim for breach of warranty no matter what the terms of the agreement, although in that case, as the purchaser had the requisite actual knowledge the reference in the agreement to actual knowledge of the purchaser limiting the extent of the warranties defeated the warranty claim. Notwithstanding the *Infiniteland* decision, in view of *Eurocopy*, where a purchaser has knowledge of facts that would constitute a breach of warranty, it should not be assumed that it will automatically have a claim for breach of warranty if the relevant facts are not stated in the disclosure letter. The safest course of action will be to cover the issue of what will and what will not defeat a warranty claim in the sale agreement. Following the *Infiniteland* decision it has become common for the purchaser to include a clause such as cl.4M in the sale agreement in an attempt to preserve its ability to make warranty claims even where it had knowledge of the relevant facts that constituted the breach. See para.4–24 for a further discussion of this.

These issues do not arise in relation to indemnities, as knowledge of the purchaser is irrelevant and in the absence of agreement to the contrary, which would be very unusual, the extent of the actual loss suffered by the purchaser is irrelevant. The indemnity will usually provide on its terms the degree of losses, liabilities, costs and expenses.

If a liability has been disclosed against a particular warranty, it is not possible to undo that knowledge by seeking to delete the disclosure. As suggested above, the way to address the risk in favour of the purchaser is for the vendor to provide an appropriate indemnity in respect of the matter. A purchaser may seek to provide that all warranties are given on an indemnity basis, but this should always be resisted by vendors, as such a basis potentially allows an unscrupulous purchaser to profit from its bargain, given that many of the matters that are covered by warranties will not have been remotely relevant to its initial valuation of the target company, but on an indemnity basis may give rise to a claw-back of consideration.

OVERLAP OF WARRANTIES AND INDEMNITIES ON SHARE SALES

1–09 Although the concepts of warranties and indemnities have developed along rather different routes, they inevitably overlap to some extent. The warranties given to the purchaser will deal with numerous matters covering all aspects of the target company including, in particular, taxation liabilities of it. The tax liabilities will also generally be covered by the tax indemnity or tax covenant (as it is more usually termed).

In addition, there may then be further indemnities to cover the risk of either disclosed matters where the purchaser is not prepared to accept the risk, or matters of concern to the purchaser that have arisen during due diligence.

Currently, the tax warranties are almost exclusively used for the purposes of requiring disclosure of specific tax issues or liabilities. Once such disclosures have been made, then subject to them meeting the agreed standard of disclosure, the relevant warranty will be rendered ineffectual. However, the tax covenant will provide that the relevant disclosed tax liability is required to be paid to the purchaser effectively on an indemnity basis.

Recognising the current convention of having the tax covenant as an integral part of the sale and purchase agreement (usually as one of the schedules) the traditional distinction between a "tax loss" being treated differently from any other loss has become eroded and it is increasingly common to see financial deductibles applying equally to the tax covenant as to the warranties. Where tax was historically dealt with separately it was far easier for the hypothetical distinction between a tax loss and any other to be maintained.

The sale agreement will make it clear as to which, if any, of the various warranty protections will apply to the tax covenant.

PREPARATION OF THE SALE AGREEMENT

1–10 Historically it has been normal practice for the sale agreement to be drafted in the first instance by the solicitors acting for the purchaser. However, if the share capital or business of the target company is being sold by way of an auction process, which is becoming increasingly common where there is likely to be significant interest in the target company or business, the vendors' solicitors will often provide the first draft agreement as part of the bid process. Where there is an inequality of resources or expertise between the advisors acting for either the purchaser or vendor then practicalities may dictate that traditional drafting conventions are disregarded. Often at the early stages of a transaction, the solicitors have limited information available to them concerning the target company or business and there is sometimes a tendency to prepare the agreement using a standard form which may be inappropriate to the actual circumstances.

However, this should not be the case in an auction process, where any draft should be carefully tailored to reflect the business or target company being sold and provide a balance of risk apportionment in terms of the warranties and indemnities offered. Ideally, any draft should be prepared on the basis of detailed information regarding the target company or business, and this may be obtained either from an accountant's due diligence report, if one is available, or, more usually, from a legal due diligence questionnaire, substantially in the form set out in Appendix 1, which should ideally be sent to the vendors or their solicitors and replied to before drafting starts.

CHAPTER 2

Parties

THE VENDORS

2–01   In the case of the sale of shares of a company, the vendors will be the owners of the shares. The main continuing liability for the vendors will arise in relation to the warranties and indemnities, although there are likely to be other provisions, such as restrictions on the activities which they may carry on in the period immediately following the sale, that continue to affect them.

In the case of a sale of shares, the purchaser at least has the comfort that the vendor will receive the proceeds of sale subject only to any related taxation liability, and as such the proceeds of sale should be traceable in the event of a warranty or indemnity claim (unless the vendors are planning or have already relocated to a different jurisdiction). In the case of the sale of a business, however, the position is quite different. The vendor, which will be the company whose business is being sold, will dispose of the assets of the business, but remain subject to its liabilities. Indeed, the vendor may have no net assets when the liabilities are taken into account and, even where there are net assets, it may be expected that these will rapidly be extracted by the shareholders of the company if the effect of the sale is to leave it as a non-trading shell. See para.2–02 for further discussion of this.

CORPORATE VENDORS

2–02   When accepting warranties and indemnities from a corporate vendor, the purchaser should consider not only the vendor's initial covenant status, but also the extent to which it can deplete its assets and reduce the worth of its covenant by the payment of dividends. When determining the funds available for distribution by way of dividend, it is not necessary for the company to make provision for contingent liabilities, such as those which might arise under the warranties, unless there is reason to believe that the liability is likely to accrue (CA 2006 s.836). The purchaser could thus find itself with a warranty claim against a vendor which has substantially reduced its net worth by the payment of dividends. As such, if a corporate vendor's assets are largely in the form of distributable reserves, the purchaser should consider the desirability of imposing a restriction upon the vendor, in relation to the making of distributions during the warranty period. The form of such a restriction would follow that suggested in relation to trustee shareholders in para.2–06, but it will be of limited value unless the target company's net assets are of the same order as the amount that could be involved in a warranty claim. An alternative or additional approach would be to seek a parent company or other shareholder guarantee, or to insist that some of the proceeds are placed into an escrow or retention account as security for any claims.

The directors of a corporate vendor will need to be satisfied that it has the necessary powers under its articles of association to enter into the transaction and to give the warranties. Generally this will not be a matter of doubt as, if the vendor has the power to hold the shares of the target company or, as the case may be, to carry on the business with the assets which are the subject matter of the sale, then it will also have the power to sell the shares or assets and to enter into such commitments as are a normal attribute of such a sale. The purchaser need not concern itself at all with this question as it will be protected by CA 2006 ss.39 and 40. **2–03**

With a view to obtaining further protection, purchasers sometimes seek warranties to the effect that the vendor has the power to enter into the sale agreement. This is an ineffective approach since if the vendor does not have power to enter into the agreement it will not have power to give the warranty. There is a further discussion of this in para.7–04 in relation to cl.1.1.1.

EXECUTIVE SHAREHOLDERS

In determining who should give the warranties on a share sale, and how the liability should be divided among the vendors, the most straightforward case arises where the vendors are also executives of the target company. In that event, the persons accepting responsibility for the warranties are those who are also receiving the benefit of the sale. It is generally appropriate in such a case that normal joint and several or, at any rate, pro rata liability should apply. However, as indicated in para.3–15, it may be desirable to modify this broad principle in special cases, for example, where liability under the warranties is attributable to benefits received by *one* of the shareholders, and not by the others. **2–04**

The position becomes more complicated if there is a difference between the persons who are the vendors and those who have knowledge about the affairs of the target company. The extreme example of this would arise where a subsidiary—which operates entirely independently—is sold by a corporate vendor, and the management remains with the subsidiary. It is in circumstances such as this that the real function of warranties—which is to impose liability upon the vendors and not merely to extract information about the target company—is shown at its clearest. When considering the warranties, the vendors will doubtless request information from the executives of the target company, but it would be unreasonable in practice to impose financial risk upon them in relation to their replies, as they obtain no corresponding financial benefit.

In between these two extreme cases arises the common situation where some of the vendors are passive investors, such as trustees, while others are active executives. If some of the vendors are venture capitalists, it is usually the case that they will resist giving any warranties at all, other than those relating to their own share ownership leaving the executive vendors with the greater burden of risk. While this might be thought fair in principle, as they have the means of **2–05**

verifying generally whether the warranties are likely to be breached, it is
suggested that this view is flawed, as if an unexpected liability arose, then all of
the shareholders of the target company would have suffered a diminution in the
value of their investment if they had not sold the target company. By analogy,
therefore, they should each bear pro rata the loss arising if the liability results in
a breach of warranty. In practice, a purchaser will usually accept a lower claims
maximum against the executive vendors so that they cannot be made liable for
more than they in aggregate receive. Where the price to be paid for the shares is
adjusted by reference to completion accounts, venture capitalists will usually
agree that they will participate in this and share the risk of any diminution or
addition to the amount they receive. This is somewhat at odds with their standard
position on warranties. However, it might be explained by the speed with which
any adjustments which are to be made by reference to completion accounts will
be known, as opposed to the often long-winded and drawn out process of
warranty claims.

While the concept of sharing liability seems to be justified where the
warranties are in an absolute form, it is often the case that some of the warranties
are qualified so that they apply only if there is an undisclosed liability of which
one or more of the vendors was aware. In such a case, it might sometimes be
appropriate that the party who was aware of the liability but deliberately failed
to disclose it should alone be penalised, although he might argue that, by failing
to disclose the liability, he has avoided a possible renegotiation of the sale terms
by the purchaser. This question is considered further in para.4–19. Deliberate
non-disclosure is likely to be a high-risk strategy as it often removes the benefit
of any warranty limitation provisions that have been negotiated in favour of the
vendors and can give rise to the commission of a criminal offence, for example
under the Financial Services and Markets Act 2000 or under the Fraud Act 2006.
(See para.9–35 for further discussion of this.)

TRUSTEE VENDORS

2–06   Similar principles to those which apply to corporate vendors of shares arise in the
case of sales by trustees or personal representatives, although in a more extreme
form. A purchaser from a corporate vendor at least has the comfort that, in the
absence of special circumstances, the paid-up share capital cannot be distributed,
but no similar restrictions exist in relation to trusts. The purchaser might wish to
restrain the trustees or personal representatives from making distributions during
the warranty period, but this is unlikely to be acceptable to them. An alternative
approach is to require that, in the event of a distribution being made, it must be
on terms that the recipient of the distribution accepts pro rata responsibility under
the warranties and indemnities. A suitable clause for this purpose follows, it
being assumed that "Trust" and "Trustees" are defined terms:

[1A] Restrictions on distributions by trustee Vendors

2–07   **The liability of the Trustees under the Warranties is limited to the net value
from time to time of the capital of the Trust, after deduction of sums due to**

the Taxation Authority and costs and fees properly chargeable against the capital of the Trust. The Trustees may not distribute capital of the Trust, other than for the payment of those sums, costs and fees, whilst a claim under the Warranties is outstanding or prior to the expiration of the time limit for making a claim, unless an undertaking in favour of the Purchaser is obtained from a beneficiary, in a form satisfactory to the Purchaser, by which the beneficiary accepts joint and several liability with the Trustees to the extent of the value of the distribution.

Trustees will often prefer to amend this restriction so that they will be released from warranty liability to the extent that the recipient of a capital distribution agrees to be bound by the warranties. They will also normally seek to remove or restrict the liability of a trustee who retires or dies and to restrict the liability to a defined period, normally not exceeding six years.

The remaining vendors may wish to protect themselves from suffering, as a result of this limitation, a larger proportion of any claim than is fairly attributable to their shareholding. For further discussion of this point see para.2–20.

An additional matter for trustee vendors to consider is whether they can give warranties and indemnities without incurring personal liability to the beneficiaries. Where an express power to give the warranties and indemnities is granted by the trust instrument, this will prevent any liability being imposed on the beneficiaries. Such an express power would normally be included in trusts based upon modern precedents, but older trust deeds or those less comprehensively drafted may not contain such administrative provisions.

It may be argued that no implied power to give the warranties and indemnities exists, but it is suggested that this approach fails to have regard to the true purpose of warranties. In effect, they operate to adjust the purchase price, and there can be no real doubt that trustees who have power to sell can negotiate a price which is adjusted according to the true value of the asset sold. The point is perhaps less clear in relation to the indemnities, and trustees might be well advised to decline to give indemnities or to obtain a court order under the Trustee Act 1925 s.57 before doing so.

A separate potential problem for purchasers from trustees arises under the Insolvency Act 1986. For further details, reference should be made to the discussion of cl.1.2.4 in para.7–08.

MANAGEMENT BUY-OUTS

This is another situation where there is normally a separation between ownership **2–08** on the one hand and knowledge on the other. It might be thought that the management who are buying the target company will know the most about its affairs, and accordingly should not have the benefit of warranties from a vendor who ultimately will rely upon them to provide the very information which is warranted. It is suggested, however, that the correct way to proceed under these circumstances is to divide the normal warranties into two broad categories.

First, there are the warranties which relate to matters independent of the activities of the management. These would include, in particular, the title of the target company to its assets, the title of the vendor to the shares, taxation liabilities, and possibly the accuracy of the accounts.

The second group of warranties would be those which concern the management of the target company, such as the target company's contractual and trading relationship, employees and day-to-day trading matters. Although there may be difficulty in determining whether a particular warranty falls into one category rather than the other, it is suggested that in principle the vendors should accept responsibility for the first group of warranties but not the second. The management should be made aware that any party providing funding for the acquisition will itself require warranties from them which will inevitably go far beyond those given by the vendors.

RECEIVERS AND ADMINISTRATORS

2–09 When an administrator or an administrative receiver is appointed in respect of a company, the administrator or receiver may, on occasion, hive-down the assets and continuing activities into a new subsidiary for the purpose of trading. This is most common in hotel and retail businesses, where it is damaging to customer confidence for the customers to be aware that the business is in administration or receivership. When a hive-down has occurred the administrator or receiver may, on occasion, sell the new subsidiary—as opposed to the assets—themselves. In these circumstances, the administrator or receiver will not be prepared to provide any significant warranties in relation to the shares or the trading of the subsidiary. The only warranties which would normally be available would relate to the title of the shares being sold, the authorised (if applicable) and issued share capital of the target company (including any options outstanding), and compliance with statutory obligations in relation to the formation of the target company. A purchaser should also request a general warranty that the target company is not carrying on any activities other than those pursuant to the hive-down agreement. On occasion the administrators or receivers will, as a matter of policy, refuse to provide even these warranties, and will offer instead vague assurances, sometimes only of a verbal nature, the benefits of which are negated by various exclusions in the sale agreement. Many administrators or receivers pride themselves on their ability to sell "fresh air" as they term it. Buying from administrators or receivers therefore is high risk, particularly, as the only limited comfort that can be obtained is through due diligence rather than any warranty or indemnity cover.

SUBSCRIPTION FOR SHARES

2–10 Different principles arise where there is a subscription for, rather than a sale of, shares. In the event of a subscription, the shareholders who existed before the injection of new capital receive no direct benefit from the payment for the new shares. Indeed, if the subscription price is a fair market value for the new shares, then the existing shareholders will not even receive any indirect benefit. The subscriber for the new shares is entitled to be satisfied that the price attributed to the new shares is correct, and will therefore wish to receive the normal warranties. The most logical party to give the warranties in this case will be the target company which is issuing the shares, as it will have received the consideration paid by the subscribers. If there are undisclosed liabilities then the subscription price will have been overstated, and a refund should be made to the subscriber.

While this may seem to provide a straightforward solution, the subscriber may find itself in a dilemma. Ordinarily, an issue of new shares takes place in circumstances where the money is required by the target company for its business activities, and there could be serious implications if the expected funds prove not to be available. The subscriber could therefore find that it suffers both from the unexpected liability which makes the value of the shares for which it subscribed less than they initially appeared, and from the disadvantage of prejudicing the target company, in which it now has a stake, by causing it to pay back what may be much needed resources. A further point which must be considered by the subscriber is that the target company will be able to refund only such part of the subscription money as constitutes a premium on the nominal value of the shares, as a greater refund would mean that the target company was allotting its shares at a discount.

It would seem that, in practice, where funds are provided by an institutional **2–11** investor, logic is ignored and the existing shareholders are required, as a term of the finance being made available, to give warranties in favour of the investor. The taxation position arising from a claim in these circumstances appears to be unsatisfactory for the shareholders, as they will receive no relief for the payment made; in particular it is suggested that the payment will not be taken into account in computing their capital gains tax liability on an eventual disposal of their own shareholdings, as none of the headings for computing allowable expenditure under TCGA 1992 s.38 will apply. Similarly, such a payment may prove to be unsatisfactory for the subscriber, in that the payment is not treated as by a vendor to a purchaser, the payment may be treated as a capital receipt arising on a disposal of the right to receive it (see para.3–18).

SUBSEQUENT DISPOSALS BY THE PURCHASER

The warranties are given to the purchaser, and it may happen that the purchaser **2–12** itself disposes of all or part of the target company or the business which it has purchased, before learning that it has a claim for a breach of warranty. The question will then arise as to whether the purchaser has suffered any loss as a result of the breach. It is considered that, where there has been a sale of the target company by the purchaser and the circumstances of that sale are such that there is no corresponding liability upon the purchaser in respect of the breach of warranty, then the purchaser cannot claim from the original vendors as it will have suffered no loss from the breach.

If, however, the purchaser has itself given warranties to its sub-purchaser, as would be usual, then it is suggested that, in the absence of special provision, the liability of the original vendors would be equal to the lesser of the loss which the purchaser would have suffered if it had retained the target company and the loss which it has to make good to the sub-purchaser, by reason of the warranties given on the sub-sale. If the sale agreement expressly provides that the warranties shall enure for the benefit of the purchaser's successors in title to the shares of the target company itself, or for the benefit of a sub-purchaser of the business, it is considered that the liability of the vendors will remain unaltered even if the purchaser ceases to own the target company or the acquired business.

2–13   This principle may well be unacceptable to the vendors, who might take the view that the warranties which they give are not to be treated as assets capable of being sold by the purchaser. In general, a prohibition against assignment will be effective, although in cases where the parties can be taken to have contemplated that a subsequent sale of the shares or assets might occur, the purchaser may be taken to have acquired the warranties for the benefit of its successors in title (*Linden Gardens Ltd v Lenesta Sludge Disposals Ltd* [1994] 1 A.C. 85).

The position is complicated further by the Contracts (Rights of Third Parties) Act 1999, by virtue of which, if the sale agreement expressly provides that a term may be enforceable by a third party, then the relevant term will be enforceable by that party or, if a term purports to confer a benefit on a third party, there will be a rebuttable presumption that the relevant term will be enforceable by that third party. A purchaser contemplating an onward sale of the target company or acquired business might consider use of the Act. However, since rights under the Act are generally less satisfactory than rights conferred directly, it is in the interests of both the purchaser and, if third parties are not to be entitled to warranty protection, the vendors, to make the position totally clear. In reality, application of the Contracts (Rights of Third Parties) Act 1999 is in the vast majority of instances excluded from transactions. Clause 1D provides suitable wording for achieving this. Without such an exclusion, not only will a third party be able to enforce relevant terms of the sale agreement (subject to the provisions of the Act), but there would seem to be nothing in principle to stop it assigning those rights. If the Contracts (Rights of Third Parties) Act 1999 is not to be excluded and there are relevant provisions in the sale agreement, this right of assignment should be excluded.

If assignment by the purchaser is to be prohibited, the following clause should be included:

[1B] No assignment of Warranties

2–14   **The Purchaser shall not be entitled to assign the Warranties and shall not be taken to hold the benefit of the Warranties for its successors in title to [the Shares] [the Assets].**

If assignment of the benefit of the agreement is permitted, the vendors should seek to ensure expressly that their liability under the warranties cannot be increased. A suitable qualification to the assignment clause is:

[1C] Liability of Vendors to assignee

If the benefit of the Warranties is assigned, the liability of the Vendors shall   2–15
be no greater than it would have been had the Purchaser remained the
owner of [the Shares] [the Business] and retained the benefit of the
Warranties.

If this approach is accepted, the vendors may wish to make it clear that they will
be entitled to avail themselves of any defences and rights of set-off that would
otherwise be available to them in the event that a claim for breach of warranty
is made. In these circumstances they should consider the insertion of the words
"and the Vendors shall be entitled to rely upon the defences and to exercise the
rights that would have been available to the Vendors" prior to the words "had the
Purchaser remained" in cl.1C. From the purchaser's point of view, the principle
involved would appear to be reasonable, although practical difficulties can
arise.

Where the damages resulting from a breach of warranty are not clearly
quantifiable, a claim under the warranties may necessitate both the plaintiff and
the original purchaser having to prove the damage they have suffered or, in the
case of the original purchaser, would have suffered, if the shares or business had
been retained. Apart from this, the sub-purchaser will not usually have the means
to compel the purchaser to quantify its notional loss, unless the sub-sale
agreement expressly includes an obligation to do so. The sub-purchaser would
generally prefer, therefore, not to take an assignment of the warranties, but
instead to seek to impose full liability on its vendor (see also para.4–11).

The position in relation to indemnities on share sales is different in those cases   2–16
(which used to be the normal position but are increasingly less common) where
the benefit of the indemnities belongs to the target company itself. If there is a
sub-sale of the target company, the obligations under the tax deed (on the
assumption a separate tax deed in favour of the target company was entered into)
will remain unaffected. In view of this, the covenantors may wish to consider
whether they should restrict their liabilities, so that the indemnity lapses in the
event of a change of control of the target company. From the covenantors' point
of view, this is not an unreasonable request. The outcome of disputes between the
target company and HMRC may well depend upon the view that HMRC takes of
the shareholders of the target company and, if the target company comes into the
hands of an unsavoury purchaser, the covenantors could be prejudiced. This is
not likely to be a relevant consideration in most cases given current convention
as far as tax covenants are concerned.

Unless the parties have specifically agreed that the Contracts (Rights of Third   2–17
Parties) Act 1999 is to apply to the transaction, a provision excluding its
application should be included in the sale agreement as follows:

[1D] Exclusion of the Contracts (Rights of Third Parties) Act 1999

A person which is not a party to this Agreement has no right under the   2–18
Contracts (Rights of Third Parties) Act 1999 to enforce any of its terms but

this does not affect the rights or remedies of a third party which exist or are available apart from or pursuant to that Act.

CHANGES IN CONTROL OF THE PURCHASER

2–19 Although the circumstances are different, the vendors should also have regard to their position if there should be a change in control of the purchaser. They may consider that, whereas they were happy to give the warranties and indemnities in circumstances involving a specific known purchaser, they would not be content to rely upon the way that these would be enforced by an unknown party who took over control of the purchaser.

A second point arises from the fact that the warranties and indemnities, while primarily imposing liabilities upon the vendors, will also impose certain obligations upon the purchaser. These relate to such matters as giving the conduct of litigation to the vendors and reimbursing the vendors with any repayments of tax following a successful appeal. The vendors may therefore be concerned that the financial status of the purchaser and its ability to perform its obligations might be reduced following a change of control.

Accordingly, it is understandable if the vendors should wish to provide that their liability should cease if there were a change of control of the purchaser. In general, the purchaser would not be prepared to accept this restriction, as it is irrelevant to the purchaser itself who controls it. However, the question is one that may have to be debated with the owners of the purchaser. In practice, most commercial purchasers will resist any attempt to negate the worth of the warranties on a change of control as it effectively devalues the investment that they have made in circumstances where they have an intention to sell the target company during the currency of the warranties or indemnities.

CONFLICTS OF INTEREST BETWEEN VENDORS AND COVENANTORS

2–20 In the case of a sale of a business there is, in the vast majority of cases, one clear vendor, and no problem of conflict should arise. The position will often be different where there is a share sale and, although it is usual to look upon the vendors as a single composite body who can readily be advised by one solicitor, this may not be the case for a variety of reasons. Some of those are dealt with above, and relate primarily to cases where there are differences between the financial benefits which are derived from the transaction and the information which is available for dealing with the warranties.

Vendors may also be concerned where there are trustee vendors whose liability is restricted to the trust assets and, between themselves, the vendors may wish to provide for special treatment of liabilities arising from warranties and indemnities which are in some way related to benefits which have been enjoyed by members of the company. Typical examples relate to indemnities in respect of employee benefits or loans to participators (ICTA 1988 s.419). In these circumstances, where the vendors have agreed to accept joint and several liability, they may wish, amongst themselves, to consider including in the sale agreement the following provision:

[1E] Sharing of liability between Vendors

Without affecting their joint and several liability under this Agreement, the Vendors agree that, as between themselves, any one person shall bear only his appropriate part of a liability which arises in relation to the Warranties. For this purpose "appropriate part" means: 2–21

> **[1E.1] in the case of a liability which is fairly attributable to, or which arises by reason of, income or benefits received by, or the act or default of, that person or persons connected with him (not themselves being any of the Vendors): the whole liability; and**

> **[1E.2] in any other case that proportion of the liability that the number of the Shares sold by him bears to the total number of the Shares.**

This clause assumes that the sale agreement includes a suitable definition of "connected", such as that contained in CTA 2010 s.1122.

A similar provision could also be included in relation to the tax covenant. In extreme cases of a conflict of interest between the parties, they should consider the desirability of separate professional representation. See also the discussion of joint and several liability in para.3–15.

A purchaser may, however, prefer for such matters to be dealt with in a separate contribution deed prepared by the respective vendors' advisors so as to avoid any confusion on the otherwise clear basis of liability between itself and the relevant vendors. Often the vendors will also prefer this approach so that the purchaser is not aware of any private arrangements between themselves in relation to the division of their liability.

CHAPTER 3

Rights and Liabilities

BREACH OF WARRANTY OR MISREPRESENTATION

3–01 Where the purchaser finds that the company or business is not as it anticipated, the entitlement to claim damages for breach of contract will depend on the scope of the warranties implied or expressly given to it. The contractual remedy for a breach will generally be damages or, rather exceptionally, rescission. Both of these are discussed below.

As an alternative remedy, the purchaser might be able to claim rescission or damages on the grounds of misrepresentation by the vendors. The purchaser is fully protected against fraudulent misrepresentation, but the position is more complicated if the misrepresentation, is either wholly innocent or, whilst not fraudulent, is the result of negligence by the person making it. The rights of the purchaser are governed by the Misrepresentation Act 1967, and a detailed analysis can be found in any of the standard books on contract law. There are, however, certain points which need to be considered in the context of a transaction where there is a detailed legal agreement between the parties, which includes specifically prepared and negotiated warranties.

3–02 Under the Misrepresentation Act 1967, if the misrepresentation was negligent, the purchaser, as an alternative or in addition to rescission, has a right to damages, computed on the same basis as if the misrepresentation had been fraudulent (s.2(1)). In the case of an innocent misrepresentation, damages may be awarded in place of rescission (s.2(2)).

As the purchaser, who has the benefit of warranties in an acquisition agreement, is in principle protected by the agreement, it might be thought that, in the absence of fraud, the purchaser would not have the right to seek relief for a breach of warranty by claiming, instead, for misrepresentation. This, however, is not the case as the rights under the contract and under the Misrepresentation Act 1967 are cumulative and the latter may be excluded only to the extent that the exclusion satisfies the test of reasonableness (s.3).

There are two particular implications for the vendors which arise from the concurrent rights under the contract and under the Act:

(1) The measure of damages is different in the two cases.

(2) The provisions of the contract limiting the time within which claims for breach of warranty may be brought (see para.11–02) and imposing floors and ceilings on the claims (see paras 11–04 and 11–07) will not

apply to claims for misrepresentation unless expressly stated otherwise. If the restrictions were extended to claims for misrepresentation they might be rendered invalid by s.3.

In the past, attempts have been made to exclude liability for misrepresentation **3–03** by incorporating into the contract a clause to the effect that the contract represents the whole agreement between the parties in relation to the subject matter of the transaction, and that the purchaser acknowledges that it has not relied on any representations which are not included as warranties. Such a clause is often termed an "entire agreement clause". The effect of such a clause was considered in *Thomas Witter Ltd v TBP Industries Ltd* [1996] 2 All E.R. 573. There, it was held that an entire agreement clause was ineffectual in excluding the right of the purchaser to make a claim based upon misrepresentation, even though the representations in question were included as express warranties. In particular, the clause was unreasonable within the meaning of s.3 because it purported to exclude claims based on misrepresentation even where there was fraud. However, in *EA Grimstead & Son Ltd v McGarrigan* [1998–99] Info. T.L.R. 384 the Court of Appeal found obiter that an entire agreement clause that did not carve out fraudulent misrepresentation from the exclusion was reasonable in the context in which it was used, this being in circumstances of a commercial contract between experienced parties of equal bargaining power, where the parties had entered into the arrangement with (most importantly) the benefit of professional advice. (Chadwick L.J.'s reasoning in that case was that it was reasonable to assume that the parties desired commercial certainty, that the bargaining between them would be found in the documents that they had signed and that the price to be paid reflected the commercial risk which each party was prepared to accept. It was legitimate and commercially desirable that both parties should be able to measure the risk and agree the price on the basis of the warranties that had been given and accepted.) This is an approach that was supported by the High Court in *Government of Zanzibar v British Aerospace* [2000] W.L.R. 2333 and the Court of Appeal in *Watford Electronics Ltd v Sanderson CFL Ltd* [2001] EWCA Civ 317. However, notwithstanding that judicial thinking in these cases would tend to suggest that where parties have entered into arrangements with the benefit of professional advice, the approach in *Thomas Witter* would no longer be followed, in the interests of certainty, it is nonetheless common practice for the entire agreement clauses to include a carve out for fraudulent misrepresentation. A properly drafted and reasonable entire agreement clause which deals with this point should effectively operate to exclude innocent or negligent misrepresentation claims.

RESCISSION

The circumstances in which a right to rescind the sale agreement will arise are **3–04** complex, and it is not the purpose of this discussion to provide a detailed analysis of them. In practice, however, rescission is primarily a remedy against misrepresentation, and is generally of limited value in the context of a share sale or a business sale where the company or business is to be carried on as a going concern following its acquisition. The essential requirement is that the parties should be capable of being restored substantially to their original position. This will often not be possible once completion of the sale has taken place. In addition, the purchaser will lose its right of rescission if, once it discovers the misrepresentation, it nevertheless takes action which effectively affirms the contract. Ordinarily the purchaser will continue the running of the target company or the acquired business whilst it is considering its rights, and thus is likely to be deemed to have affirmed the contract. In practice, therefore, rescission is not a realistic option once completion has taken place, and there is usually no harm in the purchaser's advisers agreeing a specific provision in the sale agreement to exclude this remedy.

Rescission is, however, a significant and practical remedy where there is an interval between contract and completion. In that event, it is customary by the use of *interregnum* provisions to restrict the method of conducting the businesses of the target company, or the business that is being acquired, so that the interests of the vendors and the purchaser are adequately recognised during the intervening period. An example of clauses which might be adopted in this situation are set out in Appendix 2 and, although they are drafted in the context of a share purchase, they may be readily adapted to a purchase of assets. If, prior to completion, it is found that the warranted circumstances do not exist, either because they never did or because of a change which occurs in relation to the target company or the business, it is normal for the purchaser to be given an express right to rescind in terms such as the following:

[2A] Right to rescind prior to Completion

3–05   **The Purchaser may rescind this Agreement by notice in writing to the Vendors or the Vendors' solicitors if prior to Completion:**

> **[2A.1] it appears that the Warranties were not or have ceased to be accurate [in all material respects]; or**
>
> **[2A.2] an act or event occurs which, had it occurred on or before today's date, would have had the effect that there would have been a [material] breach of the Warranties; or**
>
> **[2A.3] there is a [material] breach or non-fulfilment of the Warranties which (being capable of remedy) is not remedied prior to Completion.**

Although in practice it should be possible to achieve an effective rescission prior to completion without too much difficulty, in some cases the vendors may prefer to complete the sale and suffer a reduction in the sale price as a result of a warranty claim. This could be the case, for example, if the simple act of announcing the exchange of contracts had such an unsettling effect on staff, suppliers or customers that the business could not readily be resumed under the original ownership if the sale did not proceed. If a right of rescission is accepted, cl.2A should be amended by the vendors by the addition of the words in square brackets, although materiality would usually be defined by reference to financial criteria. This might be by reference to the same financial deductibles that applied to the warranties to be given at completion. A purchaser will often try and resist this approach although it is difficult to see why.

To avoid the argument that the failure by the purchaser to exercise a right of rescission amounts to a waiver of its right to claim for damages, it is helpful to include an express denial of waiver as in cl.3S. Sometimes a vendor may seek to resist a provision such as that which effectively gives the purchaser a choice as to whether to rescind or complete and claim damages, on the basis that it gives the purchaser too much bargaining power should an event entitling this arise. In such circumstances, the purchaser is often forced to choose whether it wishes to rescind or complete, but in the latter case on the basis that it waives its entitlement to make any claim for damages. There is little logic to such a position. For a further discussion as to the circumstances in which the remedy is available and the effect of a rescission, reference should be made to any of the leading works on contract law.

DAMAGES

The remedy which is normally sought by a purchaser where there is a breach of **3–06** warranty is compensation by the payment of damages. The measure of damages will be determined on the normal principles of contract law or, if the claim is based on misrepresentation, on the rules relating to claims in tort. The standard textbooks should be consulted for a detailed analysis of the principles involved in determining the quantum of damages in any particular case. The basic rule in contract is that the purchaser should be compensated for its loss of bargain; in the case of a claim in tort, the damages will be such as will put the purchaser back in the same position that it would have been in if the representation had not been made. Normally the measure of damages will be the same whether the purchase has been affected for cash or for shares of the purchaser.

A considerable complication arises in the case of a business sale if the sale agreement adopts the normal practice of allocating the purchase consideration amongst the various categories of assets being sold. It is often advantageous for the purchaser's tax position to attribute the minimum acceptable amount to the goodwill (see the comments in para.3–20). If the breach of warranty is of such a nature that the value of the goodwill is diminished, it is difficult as a general principle to see how the purchaser can claim a loss greater than the amount allocated to it. The purchaser would have to argue that the values attributed to the other assets, such as stocks, are valid only if the company is in a sound commercial position. If the breach of warranty has an adverse effect on the business as a whole, it might be the case that a different valuation should have been applied to the other assets. To assist the purchaser in arguing that proposition, it could seek to include the following clause (for the purposes of which the definitions of "Goodwill" and "Assets" in Pt 1 of Appendix 5 are used):

[2B] Purchaser's loss on breach of Warranty

3–07 **If a Warranty does not relate to the value, or to anything affecting the value, of the Assets other than the Goodwill, the loss suffered by the Purchaser as a result of a breach of the Warranty shall be determined as if the value of each of the Assets (other than the Goodwill) was not that stated in clause [   ] but the lesser value that they would have had if the sale of the Business had been a forced sale and the reduction in the value of those Assets was additional consideration given for the Goodwill. If the parties are unable to agree to the adjustments to be made under this clause, the matter shall be referred to an independent firm of accountants nominated by the President of the Institute of Chartered Accountants in England and Wales for their determination as independent experts [and not as arbitrators and the Arbitration Act 1996 shall not apply] and, in the absence of manifest error, their determination shall be final.**

Apart from this special consideration in relation to business sales, the agreement will often provide expressly as to how damages are to be quantified in circumstances where a specific basis of valuation has been used to value the target company or business, and a particular basis of damages lends itself to most appropriately compensating the purchaser (recognising the basis of valuation) in the event of any claims. However, sometimes a shrewd purchaser may seek to impose a specific basis of damages simply to improve its own position, rather than in circumstances where the basis sought correlates to that of its valuation. The vendors will need to be wary of this.

An example of a specific damages clause is the following:

[2C] Measure of damages for breaches of Warranty

3–08 **Without limiting the rights of the Purchaser or its ability to claim damages on any basis if there is a breach of Warranty or any of the Warranties is untrue or misleading, if [the Company incurs or becomes subject to a liability or an increase in any liability which it would not have incurred or been subject to had the breach not occurred or] the value of any asset of the Company is less or becomes less than the value would have been had the breach not occurred then the Vendor[s] undertake to the Purchaser to pay to the Purchaser (as the Purchaser elects) in cash on demand a sum equal to the [liability or increased liability, or the] reduction in the value of the asset [(as appropriate), or the reduction in the value of the Shares caused by the breach].**

This clause effectively gives the purchaser the right to choose between the normal measure of damages for breach of contract and the indemnity basis of damages. If normal damages would exceed the amount paid by way of indemnity, the purchaser's right to the additional compensation is preserved. The vendors will usually wish for a damages basis to apply, while a purchaser will sometimes favour an indemnity basis. Current convention follows a damages basis in most circumstances. Usually the sale agreement is silent on the measure of damages to apply which preserves the common law basis of damages. In the context of a company sale, it is the measure of overall loss to the purchaser that needs to be proven. In assessing damages, a court is likely to take account of how the parties valued the company or business, so if the valuation had been undertaken by reference to an EBITDA multiplier (see later commentary in Ch.13 for further discussion of this) or by reference to the level of net assets, or a combination of the two, it is likely that the court would be persuaded to adopt a similar approach in assessing the appropriate level of damages.

The clause may be used in the case of the purchase of a business although, in that case, some of the words in square brackets will not be relevant. (The reference to "undertake" will need to be changed to "undertakes".) **3–09**

Where the consideration for the acquisition is the allotment of shares of the purchaser, the effect of a payment of damages is somewhat obscure. The consideration for the allotment will be the transfer of the shares of the target company or the business of the vendor company. If, in the event, the value of the target company or the business proves to be less than the par value of the consideration shares, then it might be thought that the purchaser will be in the rather unfortunate position of having allotted its shares for a consideration of less than par which, of course, is not permitted. It is suggested that in practice this should not give rise to a difficulty, as if the directors of the purchaser company, acting bona fide and on the basis of a valuation of the target company or the business, have allotted shares which they thought were for a consideration at least equal to par, then there can be no criticism if it proves to be the case that the consideration was less than par. A further protection in practice arises under CA 2006 s.593 which requires non-cash consideration for the issue of shares of a public limited company to be valued before the allotment takes place.

So far as the vendors are concerned, the consideration which they receive will be in the form of securities of the purchaser which have a variable value. If compensation has to be paid under the warranties and, at the time that the claim is made, the consideration shares have fallen in value, the vendors might wish to take advantage of the provisions of CA 2006 Pt 18, which permit a company to purchase its own shares. The vendors might suggest that, in the event of a warranty claim arising, the claim should be satisfied by the purchaser re-purchasing an appropriate number of the consideration shares for a nil purchase price. In this way, the vendors will be put in the same position as if the target company had been correctly valued in the first instance and the number of the consideration shares reduced accordingly. **3–10**

The vendors will wish the purchaser to limit its claim for damages on a breach of warranty to the net loss it suffers, taking into account any unexpected benefits which the target company or business enjoys. It might well seem reasonable that the purchaser should not complain about the bad without giving credit for the good, and a possible clause in the case of a share sale is the following:

[2D] Credit for improvements

The liability of the Vendors under the Warranties shall be reduced by: **3–11**

[2D.1] an amount equal to the value or additional value of any fixed assets (apart from the Properties and goodwill) owned at Completion

which were not included in the Accounts or were included at less than market value after deducting (in the case of assets acquired after the Balance Sheet Date) their cost of acquisition [and Taxation which would arise on their disposal at those values];

[2D.2] the amount of or by which Taxation for which the Company is accountable is extinguished or reduced as a result of the claim giving rise to the liability;

[2D.3] the amount by which a provision for Taxation [not being a provision for deferred Taxation], bad or doubtful debts or contingent or other liabilities contained in the Accounts proves after Completion to have been excessive, except by reason of a reduction in Taxation rates [or as a result of an event occurring, or action taken by the Purchaser or the Company,] after Completion;

[2D.4] the amount of debts paid which had been previously written off [less attributable Taxation];

[2D.5] the amount of credits, recoveries or other benefits which have been or will be received or obtained by the Company by reason of the matters giving rise to the liability.

3–12   Only the first of the above sub-paragraphs might be relevant in relation to a business sale depending upon the actual terms agreed. (In such circumstances "Goodwill" should be a defined term. The definition of "Goodwill" in Pt 1 of Appendix 5 would be suitable for these purposes.)

The concept of this clause is not particularly fair if the purchase price for the shares has been calculated otherwise than on the basis of the asset value of the target company. Very rarely is this the only basis. Even in that event, it is difficult to see how the reduction can be quantified in any but the simplest case. This in itself is not an adequate reason to reject it, as an arbitration procedure (for example permitting the target company's auditors to certify the adjustment) can be included. Most purchasers will be reluctant to accept provisions such as these without further definition and care over the precise terms. The vendors might reasonably argue that clauses such as this are no more than a contractual recognition of the need to prove overall loss in the context of a company acquisition where no specific basis of damages has been agreed. If the purchaser accepts the clause, it should add the words in square brackets to make a rather crude adjustment for the tax implications and to avoid the vendors benefiting from reductions in taxation liability which were not attributable to circumstances existing before completion. In relation to this last point, the vendors would not normally be entitled to savings which result from a retrospective reduction in the corporation tax rate or the carry-back by the target company of subsequent losses. Similarly, the adequacy of a provision for deferred taxation will depend on later events, and should not affect the liability of the vendors whether it proves to be excessive or inadequate. It would be unusual to see a clause such as this in practice. To the extent that the purchaser is willing to agree to the vendors having contractual rights to the benefit of any "upside" arising in connection with breaches of the warranties, these will usually be included in the warranty limitation provisions. See Ch.11 for details and a discussion of some of the standard warranty limitation provisions that the vendors might seek to include in the sale agreement.

SECURITY IN RELATION TO THE WARRANTIES

The vendors will have a potential liability to the purchaser for perhaps the whole **3–13** amount of the consideration which they receive, and this liability might remain a contingent risk for a number of years. This is particularly so in the case of the obligations under the tax covenant which customarily continue for at least six years, and more usually seven. The purchaser should review the ability of the vendors in the case of a share sale, or the vendor in the case of a business sale to meet claims which might be quantified only after a considerable period of time. This is of particular concern where some or all of the vendors may be looking to retire abroad. Where the transaction involves the sale of a business, the ability of the vendor company to meet warranty claims needs particular attention, as the liabilities retained by the vendor will invariably, and often drastically, reduce the net assets which it has available.

The purchaser might wish to consider whether it should require security for these liabilities. In relation to the tax covenant, it is impossible in practice for the purchaser to require the covenantors to provide any significant amount of security for the whole of the six or seven year period unless perhaps a significant potential tax liability has been identified, in which circumstances it may be appropriate to provide for a proportion of the sale proceeds to be retained in an escrow or retention account. There is, however, a possibility that the vendors will agree to provide security for the duration of the warranties if the period in respect of which they apply is sufficiently short. In these circumstances, it is not unusual in the case of a share sale, but less likely on a business sale, for part of the purchase price to be retained in an escrow or retention account for some period to enable the purchaser to determine whether warranty claims are in fact likely to arise. Typically, this might be for one or two years. This is usually appropriate where there is a risk that the sale proceeds are likely to be difficult to trace.

If the consideration is in the form of shares of the purchaser, the most suitable **3–14** security is a charge on those shares. This, however, cannot be given in favour of the purchaser if it is a public limited company (CA 2006 s.670). Historically, in the case of private companies, it has been common for the articles to amend reg.11 in Table A of the Companies (Table A to F) Regulations 1985 (SI 1985/805) so that the company has a lien on the shares held by a member in respect of all sums which he owes to the company. There is no equivalent provision in the model articles under CA 2006 since they have been drafted on the assumption that shares in private companies are issued fully paid, as is most often the case. To take advantage of the same principle for securing warranty claims, it would be possible for the purchaser to sub-sell the shares and assign the warranties to a subsidiary, which would take a charge or lien to secure potential claims. This solution is not free from difficulties and reference should be made to para.2–12.

While it is obvious that the purchaser has a risk in respect of these unsecured liabilities, it is often overlooked that the vendors are also at risk in respect of the obligations of the purchaser under the warranties and the tax covenant. This point arises, particularly, under the tax covenant where it is not unusual for a tax liability to arise because of a decision of a lower court, only to find that this is reversed on appeal to a higher court. In those circumstances, the payments under the tax covenant may pass backwards and forwards between the vendors and the purchaser during the currency of the tax covenant.

JOINT AND SEVERAL LIABILITY

3–15   In the absence of express provisions to the contrary, where two or more parties undertake the same obligation they are considered to have assumed liability jointly with each other (*White v Tyndall* (1888) 13 A.C. 263). This presumption can be rebutted by an express statement in the sale agreement, and in the case of the sale of shares, it is almost invariable for the purchaser to request that the warranties and the tax covenant are given on a joint and several basis by the vendors and, if different, the covenantors.

The broad effect of this is well known. The purchaser, having the benefit of the warranty or indemnity, can recover against any one of the vendors or covenantors leaving him to exercise his right to obtain a contribution from the other vendors or covenantors. This right of contribution is given under the Civil Liability (Contribution) Act 1978 and entitles the court to determine a just and equitable basis for allocating the liability amongst the vendors and the covenantors. More commonly the liability is shared between the vendors or covenantors by a specific deed of contribution drawn up by their advisors and reflecting what has been agreed as just and equitable between them. Purchasers, or their advisers, commonly set great store by the apparent advantage of joint and several liability, since it offers the purchaser the flexibility to sue all or some of the vendors or covenantors for the full amount. In the usual case, however, the ultimate effect is to shift from the purchaser to the vendors the risk that, if a claim is made, a vendor may not be traceable or may not be able to meet his share of the liability.

3–16   If, as is commonly the position, the vendors and covenantors are one and the same and the consideration is paid to them pro rata to their shareholdings, the statutory concept of liability sharing will give rise to no difficulty. The following are some examples of cases where complications arise:

> (1) If some of the vendors are not required to give the warranties and indemnities or different maximum claim levels apply, as frequently happens in the case of trustee shareholders (see para.2–06). While in that event, it may normally be the case that the liability will be apportioned among those vendors who do give the warranties, or who

are not able to take advantage of a reduced maximum claim level, in proportion to the consideration which they receive, this may be unfair. If, for example, the target company is owned by two families and one of the families holds a large number of their shares through a trust, then the family for whose benefit the trust exists should accept responsibility for liability which would have fallen upon the trustees if they had given the warranties.

(2) If the share capital of the target company consists of preference shares and ordinary shares. It would normally be appropriate for liability under the warranties to be borne only by the ordinary shareholders. Preference shares usually have a fixed value and beyond their fixed value do not ordinarily participate in the overall equity value.

(3) If the claim under the warranty results from benefits received by one of the vendors, such as a distribution from the target company. In that event, it would normally be appropriate for the liability under the warranty to be borne by the shareholder who has received the corresponding advantage.

Accordingly, where the sale is not a straightforward case of all the vendors giving the warranties and indemnities, the vendors should come to an agreement amongst themselves determining how liability should be apportioned. Whilst the contribution agreement may be included in the sale agreement so as to bind the purchaser, it is almost always in a separate document as the purchaser will not wish to be a party to the arrangements for the reasons noted at para.2–21. A clause which partly deals with this is suggested in that paragraph, and this may suffice where the position is not particularly complicated. If, however, there are significant differences in the interests of the parties or, for example, one shareholder is willing to accept liability under the warranties in respect both of his or her own holding and those of other members of his family or his trustees, then the clause will have to be altered.

It will also be necessary in a complicated case to determine how any **3–17** provisions relating to a floor for claims should apply (see para.11–04). In the absence of a special arrangement, it would seem that the floor for claims would operate for the benefit of the parties who are liable in relation to the first claim which happens to be made. A fairer arrangement would be for the vendors to agree amongst themselves that the benefit of any floor should apply pro rata to the liabilities which they incur. Even this may not be wholly satisfactory in cases where, for example, a warranty liability arises specifically because of a benefit which has been received by one shareholder, and where the other shareholders have had nothing to do with it.

If the vendors are successful in making inroads into the basic concept of joint and several liability, there are two approaches which they might adopt. The more extreme is to provide that each vendor is liable only for an appropriate proportion of any claim—normally being the proportion which he receives of the total purchase price. A more modest alternative would be to provide that the total liability of each vendor has a ceiling, which would usually be the amount of the sale proceeds which he actually receives. It is a matter for negotiation to determine whether one of these approaches, and if so which, should apply.

TAXATION TREATMENT OF PAYMENTS UNDER WARRANTIES AND INDEMNITIES IN CONNECTION WITH SHARE PURCHASES

3–18 In general, the vendors will hold the shares of the target company as a capital asset and the proceeds of sale will be brought into account in a capital gains tax computation. A partial recognition of the taxation implications is contained in TCGA 1992 s.49. This provides that, in the first instance, no account is taken of any contingent liability in respect of a warranty or representation made on a sale of property other than land. If and when a liability materialises, a retrospective adjustment is made.

Accordingly, a payment under a warranty operates retrospectively to effect a reduction in the purchase consideration. The vendor's chargeable receipt is decreased and a corresponding reduction is made to the purchaser's base cost with, on an eventual sale of the shares, a related increase in its chargeable gain at that time. This is clear enough if the consideration is cash, but the position is more obscure if the disposal is wholly or partly by way of exchange for shares or other securities of the purchaser. In such circumstances, it is suggested, and understood to be the view of HMRC, that:

(1) Where the vendors receive wholly securities of the purchaser, the warranty payment is treated as additional consideration given for those securities under TCGA 1992 s.128(1), being the section giving a roll-over on a capital reorganisation.

(2) Where the vendors receive a mixture of securities and cash, the payment will be apportioned pro rata and dealt with partly under s.128(1) and partly under s.49.

It is considered that in the rather unusual case of the shares of the target company being held by the vendors as trading stock, a warranty payment will be treated as a revenue expense.

Different principles would apply to payments under the tax covenant in circumstances where it was structured such that the benefit of it was in favour of the target company rather than the purchaser. (It would be very unusual to have a tax covenant structured in this way these days.) The legal position, which derives from the decision in *Zim Properties Ltd v Procter* [1985] S.T.C. 90, has been recognised by HMRC as giving rise to some unintended results. In that case, it was held that a right to compensation arising from the negligence of a solicitor constituted an asset. The receipt of the compensation resulted in a disposal of the asset for the amount received. By analogy, it would seem that the contingent right to receive an indemnity payment is an asset of the target company of which disposal is made when the payment is received.

As the right would have been acquired for no consideration and without a **3–19** corresponding disposal, no allowable expenditure can be brought into account to reduce the chargeable gain (TCGA 1992 s.17). The whole payment is thus taxable. On December 19, 1988 the Inland Revenue (as it then was) published a concession (ESC D33) to the effect that payments made by the vendor, whether under a warranty or an indemnity, to the purchaser (or, at its direction, to the target company) will be dealt with under TCGA 1992 s.49. However, ESC D33 does not deal specifically with payments to the target company in its own right and therefore such payments may be treated as giving rise to a gain, on the disposal of the right, which is not exempt from capital gains tax.

Although this concession removes a potential liability arising from payments to the purchaser made under indemnities, payments to the target company are not of themselves within the concession and will generally be subject to corporation tax on the full amount of the payment without any deduction for the cost of acquiring the right to the payments. Furthermore, the covenantors will receive no tax relief for the indemnity payments made to the target company.

It is therefore generally in the interests of all the parties, so far as tax is concerned, that a claim should be made by the purchaser under the warranties or indemnities and not by the target company. In most cases this will not be an issue as indemnities are rarely now given in favour of the target company for these reasons and in the vast majority of transactions the tax covenant is an integral part of the sale agreement with any payments required pursuant to it being made to the purchaser.

TAXATION TREATMENT OF PAYMENTS UNDER WARRANTIES IN CONNECTION WITH BUSINESS SALES

A major difference between share and business purchases is that while the former **3–20** involves the acquisition of a single category of assets, the latter relates to a mixture of assets with widely differing commercial and tax characteristics. Certainly for tax purposes, and probably also for balance sheet reasons, both the vendor and the purchaser will have to allocate the price amongst the assets which are sold. Although it is not essential that they should adopt the same allocation, the agreement of HMRC will be more readily forthcoming if the purchase price is attributed to the different assets by the sale agreement. HMRC will not normally dispute the allocation in the sale agreement unless it is manifestly unreasonable and is excessively motivated by tax considerations.

For the purchaser it will usually be advantageous to minimise the part of the price paid for goodwill and to maximise the part of the consideration that is apportioned to stocks as this will reduce the taxable profits on the eventual sale of the stocks. The vendor has a more difficult tax analysis as much will depend upon the base cost for the purpose of chargeable gains of the goodwill sold by it. If the base cost is high, the vendor may prefer the purchase price to be attributed to the goodwill as this could result in a lower tax bill than if the price is dealt with as a profit on the sale of trading stock.

3–21   Where a payment has to be made in respect of a warranty claim, it will not always be obvious which of the purchased assets is affected. A number of warranties—such as those relating to trading relationships and employees—clearly affect the value of the goodwill, and it is likely that this is true of most of the warranties which do not specifically concern particular assets. The impact of this on the amount of damages that can be claimed on a breach of warranty is discussed in para.3–06.

If the warranty payment relates to a capital asset, the taxation implications will arise under the legislation in respect of corporation tax on chargeable gains and will be similar to those applicable to share sales as discussed in the preceding section. There is a difficulty, however, if the warranty payment exceeds the amount of the purchase price allocated to the asset involved. This will often arise if the claim affects the value of the goodwill of the business and the common practice of allocating a nominal value to the goodwill has been adopted. In that case, no relief will be obtained by the vendor for the excess of the amount of the claim over the allocated price.

3–22   Where the claim concerns trading assets such as stock, the tax liability will be determined in accordance with the normal rules for corporation tax purposes. The taxable profits will initially be determined on the basis of the allocation of the purchase consideration set out in the sale agreement, unless it is clearly unrealistic, and no deduction will be made at that stage for contingent liabilities under the warranties unless the likelihood of a claim being made is so great that normal accountancy practice would require the making of a provision. If by the time the claim is made and settled, the vendor has ceased to trade, the warranty payment will be made otherwise than for the purposes of a trade and accordingly will not carry tax relief.

The above tax analysis is an additional reason for the vendor to seek a very short warranty period where there is the sale of a business (see also the discussion in para.11–02). If the claim can be quantified before the accounts for the period in which the sale takes place are adopted, it may be possible to adjust the accounts to provide for the claim.

CHAPTER 4

General Points Relating to Warranties

DEFINED TERMS

To facilitate the drafting of the warranties, it is usual to make use of a number of   **4–01**
defined terms. In this book, the term "Company" (meaning the target company)
is used generally in the draft clauses.

Typical examples of further definitions are set out below, and these definitions
are used in the warranties and indemnities and draft clauses discussed throughout
the book. Definitions which relate to tax matters are, as explained in Ch.10, often
contained in a separate tax schedule and these are, where relevant, discussed in
Ch.10. The definitions intended for the tax covenant are contained within it or
referred to by reference to those definitions outlined in the sale agreement.

[3A] Definitions

In this Agreement, the following expressions have the meanings stated   **4–02**
namely:

"Accounts" the audited financial statements of the Company as at and to
the Balance Sheet Date including the balance sheet, profit and loss account
together with the notes on them, the cash flow statement and the auditor's
and directors' reports.

In the case of a business sale, this definition should be amended so that it refers
to the accounts of the vendor.

It should be borne in mind by the vendors that, by virtue of this definition, the
accounts warranty will also cover the directors' report.

"Accounting Standards" SSAPs, FRSs, UITF Abstracts, SORPs and all
other generally accepted accounting principles applied to a United Kingdom
company [at the date hereof] [at the Balance Sheet Date] (excluding
International Accounting Standards and International Financial Reporting
Standards issued by the International Accounting Standards Board).

This definition essentially encapsulates UK GAAP, excluding International
Accounting Standards. The definition will need to be amended if they are
relevant. It will need to be considered which is the appropriate applicable date for
determining which accounting standards are to apply. For the purposes of the

warranties that relate to the last statutory accounts, it will be by reference to the Balance Sheet Date as that will have been the last date to which the accounts were made up. In the case of completion accounts, the accounting standards in force as at completion may be the most appropriate, although if they have changed since the Balance Sheet Date that may result in inconsistent accounting between the two. Depending upon the circumstances, this may be an issue. In relation to earn out accounts which might relate to two or three financial periods after completion, it may be appropriate to refer to the accounting standards then in force at the time of preparation of each set of earn out accounts, although this might give rise to a lot of uncertainty for the vendors, and in some cases might have an unanticipated or adverse effect upon the earn out. Careful thought needs to be applied to ensure an outcome satisfactory to both the vendors and the purchaser.

"Agreement" this agreement [and the schedules hereto] for the sale and purchase of the Shares.

If the general interpretation clauses do not make it clear that schedules are included as part of the agreement, then the wording in brackets should be added to this definition.

"Associate" in relation to any person, a person who is connected with that person within the meaning of CTA 2010 s.1122.

"Associated Person" in relation to a company, a person (including an employee, agent or Subsidiary) who performs or has performed services for or on that company's behalf.

This definition should be included with effect from the implementation of the BA 2010. The definition derives from BA 2010 s.8 and is designed to include both those which are associated with the target company at completion and those which were formerly associated with the target company.

"Balance Sheet Date" [   ] 200[   ] (being the date as at and to which the Accounts were prepared).

"BA 2010" the Bribery Act 2010.

This definition should be included with effect from the implementation of the BA 2010.

"Business Day" 9.00 am to 5.00 pm on any day other than Saturdays and Sundays and bank holidays during which clearing banks are open for business in the City of London.

This definition is usually only relevant if there is a gap between contracts and completion where conditions are to be satisfied and completion is expressed to take place on the next "Business Day" following satisfaction of the conditions. The definition may also be used where deferred payments are to be made to ensure that such payments are made on business days when banks are open for business.

"CA 1985" the Companies Act 1985.

"CA 2006" the Companies Act 2006.

"Civil Sanction" any of the sanctions referred to in the Regulatory Enforcement and Sanctions Act 2008 s.36(1).

Under the Regulatory Enforcement and Sanctions Act 2008, the Environment Agency has been given new powers to impose "civil sanctions", including fixed and variable monetary penalties. Using these powers, the Environment Agency can in effect impose fines (and determine the amount) without going through the courts. Other civil sanctions that are open to the Environment Agency include: (i) issuing compliance notices and stop notices which can affect how and what a company is permitted to do; (ii) issuing a restoration notice, requiring remedial action to be taken; and (iii) accepting enforcement undertakings from companies—these are "voluntary" agreements to take corrective actions. Failing to comply with an enforcement undertaking is a criminal offence, hence they are voluntary only in the sense that they are offered voluntarily; once accepted by the Environment Agency, they effectively have the force of law.

"Companies Acts" CA 2006 and CA 1985, as amended, and in each case, in so far as the same are in force at the date of this Agreement or in force at the time of the relevant event for the purposes of the Warranties.

This definition goes further than being simply a consolidating definition since it seeks to apply the relevant companies act to the relevant point in time for the purposes of the warranties.

"Completion" completion of the sale and purchase of [the Shares] [the Business].

"Computer Systems" all hardware, handheld devices, firmware, peripherals, communication links, storage media, back up systems, networking equipment and other equipment used by or on behalf of the Company together with all software [and all source, object and executable codes], databases and websites used by or on behalf of the Company.

As most businesses are increasingly reliant on their information technology and computer systems, it is usual to include specific warranties relating to them. Such warranties are included in para.7–248. The vendors are unlikely to want to give any warranties in relation to their information technology infrastructure to the extent that information technology is shared with others, for example if it is provided by third party service providers. However, the purchaser will still expect information to be provided in relation to this area during the due diligence process, even if no warranties are given in relation to it. The wording in square brackets should be included where the software has been written by or specifically for the target company. Without the source code and object code libraries, the purchaser will not be able to continue to develop the software. In the case of a business sale this definition should be amended so that it refers to the vendor as opposed to the company.

"Confidential Business Information" all or any information relating to the following (details of which are not in the public domain) existing in any form:

> **(1) the business methods, corporate plans, management systems, finances, new business opportunities or development projects of the Company;**
>
> **(2) the marketing or sales of any present or future product of the Company including, without limitation, customer names and lists and other details of customers, prospects, sales targets, sales statistics, pricing information, market research reports and surveys and advertising or other promotional material; and**
>
> **(3) any trade secrets or other information relating to the provision of any product or services of the Company which is of a confidential nature or in respect of which the Company owes an obligation of confidence to any third party.**

This is an extremely wide definition, the primary function of which is to provide expansive warranty cover, however, it is equally applicable to the usual non-compete restrictions that are generally contained in the sale agreement. In the context of a business sale, definitions such as "Confidential Business Information" and "Intellectual Property Rights" are usually relevant for the purposes of identifying the assets that are to be the subject of the sale. In the case of a business sale, this definition should be amended so that it refers to the vendor as opposed to the company.

"Control" has the same meaning as in CTA 2010 s.1122.

Various statutory definitions of "control" may be adopted—s.1122 is reasonable, in that it covers the ability, whether through voting power or otherwise, to control the conduct of affairs. As noted above, a virtually identical definition of control is contained in the Income Tax Act 2007 s.995.

"Criminal Property" shall be defined by reference to the Proceeds of Crime Act 2002 s.340(3) (but disregarding paragraph (b) of that section).

The definition is derived from the interpretation section of the Proceeds of Crime Act 2002 and relates to money laundering offences. The disregard of para.(b) excludes knowledge or suspicion from the definition of criminal property (the primary defence in cases of inadvertent receipt of criminal property) so as to make the definition, absolute. Given the far-reaching nature of this definition, vendors should take great care in the consideration and negotiation of the relevant warranties.

"Disclosed" disclosed with sufficient information or particularity in the Disclosure Letter to enable a reasonable purchaser to make an informed assessment of the impact upon the Company of the matter disclosed [after taking appropriate advice upon the matter and the relevant disclosure].

This is an attempt at defining the more or less established common law principle of "fair disclosure". A purchaser may seek to change the objective reference to a reasonable purchaser to the subjective "Purchaser" and may find the concept of having to take advice upon the subject matter and the terms of the disclosure itself unacceptable. In most cases, where the vendors and the purchaser are well advised, this simply reflects reality. In the case of a business sale this definition should be amended so that it refers to the vendor as opposed to the company.

"Disclosure Letter" the disclosure letter (together with all documents attached or appended to it), having the same date as this Agreement, from the Vendors to the Purchaser and delivered to the Purchaser immediately prior to execution of this Agreement.

As to the form and content of the disclosure letter, see Ch.9.

"Encumbrance" any mortgage, charge, debenture, assignment or assignation by way of security, guarantee, indemnity, hypothecation, restriction, right to acquire, right of pre-emption, option, right of conversion, pledge, declaration of trust, lien, right of set off or counterclaim, combination of accounts, retention of title arrangement, third party right or equity or any other security interest, encumbrance or preferential arrangement whatsoever, howsoever created or arising and any agreement or arrangement to create any of the above.

"Environment" includes any or all of the following media: air, water and land and the medium of air includes the air within buildings and the air within other natural or man-made structures above or below ground and the medium of water includes ground water and aquifers.

"Environmental Claim" any actual, pending or threatened claim, notice of violation, prosecution, demand, action, official warning, abatement or other order or notice (conditional or otherwise) relating to any Environmental Matters or Environmental Liabilities and any other notification or order requiring compliance with the terms of any Environmental Permit or Environmental Laws.

"Environmental Damage" any pollution, contamination, degradation, damage or injury caused by, related to or arising from or in connection with the presence, generation, use, handling, processing, treatment, storage, transportation, disposal or release of any Hazardous Substance.

"Environmental Laws" any Official Requirements relating to the protection of the Environment or the control or prevention or remedying of Environmental Damage or the control of Hazardous Substances.

"Environmental Liabilities" any liabilities, responsibilities, claims, losses, costs (including remedial, removal, response, abatement, clean-up, investigative and/or monitoring costs), damages, expenses, charges, assessments, liens, penalties and fines which are incurred by, asserted against or imposed upon a person as a result of or in connection with any violation of or non-compliance with Environmental Laws (including the failure to procure or violation of any Environmental Licence required by Environmental Laws); or any Environmental Damage.

"Environmental Matters" means any of the following:

(1) any generation, deposit, keeping, treatment, transportation, transmission, handling or manufacture of any Hazardous Substances;

(2) damage to property, nuisances, noise, defective premises health and safety at work or elsewhere;

(3) the carrying out of a development (as defined in the Town and Country Planning Act 1990 s.55(1)); and

(4) the pollution, conservation or protection of the Environment whether relating to man or any living organisms supported by the Environment or any other matter whatsoever affecting the Environment or any part of it.

The environmental definitions are extremely wide, and great care should be taken by the vendors when reviewing them for the purposes of the warranties. Where the purchaser requires an indemnity in respect of a specific, or all environmental matters, then these definitions will double for that. In the case of a business sale this definition should be amended so that it refers to the vendor as opposed to the company. For further discussion on the Environmental warranties please refer to para.7–157.

"Environmental Permit" any permit, licence, authorisation, consent, registration, exemption or other approval obtained or which ought to have been obtained pursuant to any Environmental Laws at any time by either the Company and/or in relation to the business carried on by the Company.

"FA" the Finance Act.

"FRS" a financial reporting standard adopted or issued by The Accounting Standards Board Limited or such other body or bodies as are prescribed for the purposes of CA 2006 s.464.

The Accounting Standards Board Limited is the prescribed body for the issue of United Kingdom statements of standard accounting practice for the purposes of "CA 2006 s.464".

"Hazardous Substances" any solid, liquid, gas, noise and any other substance or thing which causes or may cause harm (alone or in combination with any other substance) to the Environment or any structure, thing or living organism within the Environment including any substance regulated under any Environmental Laws.

"HMRC" HM Revenue & Customs.

This definition is used in conjunction with the definition of "Taxation Authority".

"ICTA 1988" the Income and Corporation Taxes Act 1988.

"Intellectual Property" all copyright and related rights, moral rights, design rights, registered designs, database rights, [semiconductor topography rights,] patents, rights to inventions, [utility models,] business names, trade marks, [service marks,] trade names, domain names, [rights in get-up,] know-how, trade secrets and rights in confidential information, rights to goodwill or to sue for passing off or unfair competition, and any other intellectual property rights or rights of a similar nature (in each case whether or not registered) and all applications for any of them which may subsist anywhere in the world.

As this definition will form the basis of numerous intellectual property warranties, the vendors should consider whether its scope is unduly wide and whether certain of the rights referred to are inappropriate, for example semiconductor topography rights. In particular, the general words "and any other intellectual property rights or rights of a similar nature . . . which may subsist anywhere in the world" may be unacceptable if the target company carries on business in a number of foreign jurisdictions. Conversely, in the context of a business sale the purchaser will want to ensure that it acquires all relevant intellectual property rights existing anywhere in the world and warranty protection in relation to all such rights whether the sale is of a business or shares. The term "unfair competition" is included since under the 1883 Paris Convention for the Protection of Industrial Property, the UK is bound to assure its nationals effective protection against unfair competition. Whilst the courts have preferred to consider cases under the narrower tort of passing off rather than recognising a general tort of unfair competition, the purchaser will want to acquire any such rights, and will need to do so where the target company conducts business in a jurisdiction which has "unfair" competition laws such as the US, Australia or many European countries.

"Intellectual Property Rights" all Intellectual Property owned or used by the Company or in relation to its business.

In the case of a business sale, this definition should be amended so that it refers to the vendor as opposed to the company.

"ITA 1984" the Inheritance Tax Act 1984.

"IT Contracts" all arrangements and agreements under which any third party provides any element of, or services relating to, the Computer Systems, including without limitation leasing, hire purchase, licensing, subscription, supply, escrow, maintenance, support and services agreements.

It may be necessary to list in a schedule to the sale agreement any such IT contracts that are in place. This is because IT systems are an essential but often a significant cost to a business. There are specific risks, such as underlicensing (not having enough software licences in place), associated with poor management of IT contracts. Asking the vendors to list the IT contracts will give the purchaser an overview of the arrangements in place, and will help to indicate issues at an early stage. For example, there may be obvious gaps in the list, indicative of underlicensing or poor management—such as a lack of an escrow agreement for a key software application; there may be issues of compatibility and therefore integration with the purchaser's own systems; the list may even indicate an opportunity for cost savings where a "SaaS" (software as a service) solution would be much cheaper than the incumbent "installed" software.

"IT(EP)A 2003" the Income Tax (Earnings and Pensions) Act 2003.

"LPMPA 1994" the Law of Property (Miscellaneous Provisions) Act 1994.

See para.4–08 for a discussion of the covenants that are implied under the Act into an instrument effecting a disposition of assets where the disposition is expressed to be made "with full title guarantee" or "with limited title guarantee".

"Licence" a licence, permit, certificate, consent, approval, filing of notifications, reports and assessments, registrations or authorisations required by law for operation of the Company's business, its ownership, use, possession or occupation of any asset or the performance of this Agreement.

This is a consolidating definition which is designed to cover all types of licences, consents etc. which a target company is required to have in order to operate its business. In the case of a business sale this definition should be amended so that it refers to the vendor as opposed to the company.

"Management Accounts" the unaudited balance sheet of the Company as at [ ] and the unaudited profit and loss account of the Company for the period ended on [ ] copies of which are attached to the Disclosure Letter.

The period of the management accounts should run from the date of the last audited accounts to the date of the most recent management accounts. In the case of a sale of part of the business of a company, it may not be possible to extract relevant information from the last accounts, in which case the purchaser will be reliant upon management accounts produced in respect of the business to be acquired. In these circumstances, the purchaser may require that the management accounts cover a longer period, for example, two or three years. In the case of a business sale this definition should be amended so that it refers to the vendor as opposed to the company.

"Non-Taxation Warranties" those warranties other than the Taxation Warranties.

The definition is included in order to differentiate between the non-taxation and taxation warranties. In the context of a share sale, the taxation warranties are now typically included in a tax schedule that deals with the taxation covenant, the taxation warranties and the limitations that are to apply to them. See Ch.10 for further details of the tax schedule. Even where there is not a separate tax schedule, it is customary to distinguish between the taxation and non-taxation warranties, as there are usually different limitation provisions that apply to them.

"Official Requirement" any law, statute, ordinance, pact, decree, treaty, code, rule, regulation, directive, order, notice or official published plan or policy with legal or actual force in any geographical area and/or for any class of persons.

The vendors will undoubtedly be asked to provide a "compliance with all laws" type warranty, and this definition will form the basis of that warranty. The definition is wide ranging, and the vendors are likely to wish to reduce the scope of it. See para.7–119 for a discussion of approaches that the vendors should consider when reviewing and negotiating the "compliance with all laws" warranty in the context of a share sale. In the context of a business sale this is likely to be less of an issue as liabilities will generally remain with the vendor.

"Planning Acts" the Town and Country Planning Act 1990, the Planning (Listed Buildings and Conservation Areas) Act 1990, the Planning

(Hazardous Substances) Act 1990 (as amended) and the Planning and Compensation Act 1991.

"Political Cause" includes political parties, election committees, party affiliated organisations, party aligned research bodies, pressure and lobby groups.

This definition is used in conjunction with the definition of "Sensitive Payments". With effect from the implementation of BA 2010 this definition should be deleted.

"Political Contributions" any payments to support a Political Cause which may include, but is not limited to, donations, loans, gifts, provisions of services, advertising and/or promotional expenditure.

This definition is used in conjunction with the definition of "Sensitive Payments". Political contributions could amount to offences of bribery, as they may be used as a subterfuge by companies to obtain or retain a business advantage. This definition is wide and is designed to capture any payment made to any political organisation. With effect from the implementation of BA 2010 this definition should be deleted.

"Properties" the [leasehold and freehold] properties briefly described in Schedule [   ] and reference to a "Property" include a reference to each of the individual Properties.

"Scheme(s)" [details of disclosed pension scheme(s) to be inserted].

A target company or business may have one or more pension schemes or death in service schemes in operation, or similar benefit schemes such as income replacement or permanent health insurance arrangements. Where the target company has more than one scheme, it will be necessary to consider the nature of the schemes and the issues arising from this so as to precisely link the appropriate scheme to the appropriate warranty or indemnity.

The pension warranties and indemnities set out in Chs 7 and 8 fall broadly into three categories: those that apply to all schemes, those that apply only to defined benefit schemes and those that apply to defined contribution schemes. Depending on the results of due diligence, it may be necessary to have several definitions. For example, it may be necessary to define "the Group Personal Pension" or "GPP" or "the Stakeholder Plan" on the one hand, and "the Final Salary Scheme" on the other, and refer all of these definitions back to the overall definition of "the Schemes". Other definitions may be envisaged, such as "the Open Scheme", "the Closed Scheme", "the Directors' Scheme", "the Unregistered Scheme", etc. Such precision is necessary to ensure that the scheme(s) is/are adequately defined and that the warranties provide appropriate comfort and risk apportionment.

In order to precisely define a pension scheme, the draftsman should seek to ascertain the scheme's full legal name from the scheme documents, the pension scheme registration number or PSR (for occupational schemes), the HMRC approval number, or the name and reference number of the scheme administrator from annual renewal documentation (for contract-based arrangements such as group personal pensions and stakeholder plans).

"Sensitive Payments" means:

(1) **Political Contributions;**

(2) **commercial bribes, bribes or kickbacks paid to any person including central or local government officials, trade union officials or employees;**

(3) **amounts received with an understanding that rebates or refunds will be made in contravention of the laws of any jurisdiction either directly or through a third party;**

(4) **payments or commitments (whether made in the form of commissions, payments or fees for goods received or otherwise) made with the understanding or under circumstances that would indicate that all or part thereof is to be paid by the recipient to central or local government officials or as a commercial bribe, influence, payment or kickback; and**

(5) **any payment deemed illegal under the Prevention of Corruption Acts 1889 to 1916.**

With effect from the implementation of BA 2010 this definition should be deleted.

"Shares" the fully paid up shares in the capital of the Company to be and comprising the whole of the issued and allotted share capital of the Company.

This definition will be relevant only on a share sale, and the reference to "allotted" shares is unnecessary unless shares have been allotted—perhaps on provisional allotment letters—but without the allottees having been entered in the register of members (*National Westminster Bank Plc v Inland Revenue Commissioners* [1994] 3 W.L.R. 159).

This definition would not be relevant for a business sale.

"Social Media" all social networking sites, blogs, microblogs, wikis or other forms of social media used by or on behalf of the Company for business purposes.

Companies increasingly use social media to promote their businesses. This definition is designed to cover all relevant activity carried out by the target company. Please refer to para.7–275 for discussion of the concerns the relevant warranty will seek to address. In the case of a business sale, this definition should be amended so that it refers to the vendor as opposed to the company.

"Subsidiary" a subsidiary undertaking as defined in CA 2006 s.1162 save that a company shall be treated, for the purposes of the membership requirement contained in subss.1162(2), as a member of another company even if its shares in that other company are registered in the name of: (a) another person (or its nominee) whether by way of security or in connection with the taking of security, or (b) its nominee.

It was held in *Enviroco Ltd v Farstad Supply A/S* [2009] EWCA Civ 1399 that if, a definition for "Group", "Subsidiary" or "Holding Company" is by reference to CA 2006 s.1159 or CA 1985 s.736, and a bank or other entity is registered in the register of members in respect of a company's shareholding in another, by way of taking security over those shares, then that company could, for the purposes of the definition, not be classed as a subsidiary. Consequently, it is advisable, pending the outcome of the appeal to the Supreme Court, which has been scheduled to take place on January 19, 2011, that the definition of "Subsidiary" or equivalent should be defined by reference to the definition of "subsidiary undertakings" in CA 2006 s.1162. This definition is unlikely to be required on a business sale.

"SORP" a statement of recommended practice issued by The Accounting Standards Board Limited or such other body or bodies as are prescribed for the purposes of CA 2006 s.464.

"SSAP" a statement of standard accounting practice published by the accounting standards committee of CCAB Limited and adopted by The Accounting Standards Board Limited.

Although new accounting standards are now identified as FRSs, the use of the acronym SSAP is still required as many of the standards identified by a SSAP number are extant.

"Taxation or Tax" all forms of taxation, duties, imposts, governmental charges (whether international, national or local) and levies whatsoever and whenever created, enacted or imposed and whether of the United Kingdom or elsewhere and without prejudice to the generality of that expression includes:

> **(1) income tax, corporation tax, capital gains tax, capital transfer tax, inheritance tax, stamp duty, stamp duty reserve tax, stamp duty land tax rates, VAT, customs and other import duties, insurance premium tax, national insurance contributions, amounts for which the Company is liable to account under PAYE and any payment whatsoever which the Company may be or become bound to make to any Taxation Authority or any other person as a result of any enactment relating to taxation and any other taxes, duties or levies supplementing or replacing any of the above; and**

(2) all costs, charges, interests, fines, penalties and expenses incidental or relating to any taxation, duties, imposts, charges and levies whatsoever (including without limitation any such described above).

The wide scope of the definition of "Taxation" can have unexpected results, particularly in relation to the more general warranties such as cl.1.1 in para.5–04. This is discussed in more detail in relation to the specific tax provisions at para.10–16.

In the case of a business sale the definition should be amended so that it refers to the vendor as opposed to the company.

"Taxation Authority" HMRC or any statutory or governmental authority or body (whether in the United Kingdom or elsewhere) involved in the collection or administration of Taxation.

"Tax Covenant" the covenant contained in Part 3 of Schedule [3].

The tax covenant is discussed in detail in Ch.10. This is not applicable in relation to a business sale.

"Tax Warranties" the warranties in Part B of Schedule [3].

A definition referring specifically to those of the warranties dealing with taxation will be required if, as suggested in Ch.10, the limitations applicable to the tax warranties are different from the limitations applying to the warranties generally.

"TCGA 1992" the Taxation of Chargeable Gains Act 1992.

"TMA 1970" the Taxes Management Act 1970.

"UITF Abstract" an abstract issued by the Urgent Issues Task Force of The Accounting Standards Board Limited or such other body or bodies as are prescribed for the purposes of CA 2006 s.464.

"VATA 1994" the Value Added Tax Act 1994.

"Warranties" the warranties[, representations and undertakings] of the Vendors contained in [this Agreement] [clause [   ] and] Schedules [   ] and the Tax Warranties and "Warranty" means anyone of them.

It is assumed that the warranties discussed in the following chapters are contained in a schedule. This is the usual and most convenient way of dealing with them.

This definition needs careful attention. The agreement will invariably contain a clause similar to cl.3C which imposes an obligation on the vendors in relation to "the Warranties" which is of considerable importance. A general definition such as the above, if the words in brackets on the first line are included, as is often the case, obscures the commitments which are undertaken. When it is being reviewed, the following points should be taken into account:

(1) The warranty obligations accepted by the vendors will apply not only to warranties as normally understood, but also to wider matters which might amount to representations or undertakings assuming that the wording in brackets in the first line is included. It would be usual therefore for well-advised vendors to ensure that this wording is deleted so that the obligations only extend to the intended warranties.

(2) The final draft of the sale agreement, after it has been amended by the vendors' solicitors, will usually include restrictions on the period within which claims for breach of the "Warranties" must be brought and on the amounts which can be claimed (see paras 11–02 to 11–09). The definition of "Warranties" set out above would extend, for example, to the obligations on the vendors under covenants restricting the activities they can carry on after completion of the sale if, unusually, the wording in brackets on the first line were retained and the reference on the second line was to the agreement. This is not usually intended or likely to be acceptable to the purchaser. The purpose of seeking to suggest that the statements contained in the relevant clause or schedule (which to all intents and purposes is intended to be the warranties) are also expressed as representations is to seek to have the benefit of alternative remedies under the Misrepresentation Act 1967 as well as a conventional damages claim for breach of contract. Please refer to Ch.3 for a discussion of the available remedies and their appropriateness or otherwise in the context of a share sale or a business and assets sale. In most cases well-advised vendors will restrict their liability to contractual damages by exclusion of the reference to such statements being given as representations and in practice most purchasers will be sympathetic to this approach in the interests of achieving certainty. If a tortious basis of damages is intended, then the more direct way to achieve this is with an appropriately worded damages clause rather than seeking to rely on the applicability of the Misrepresentation Act 1967.

(3) Any given problem may entitle the purchaser to alternative remedies either for breach of contract or for misrepresentation (see para.3–01).

Most vendors will wish to exclude liability for non-fraudulent misrepresentation and with a carefully drafted entire agreement clause (which does not purport to exclude fraudulent misrepresentation—see para.3–03 for further discussion of this) that should be perfectly possible. In most cases both the purchaser and the vendors will want to achieve certainty in relation to the warranties and the limitations that are to apply to them. The use of the definition without the words in brackets achieves this by ensuring that the limitation provisions only apply to the warranties themselves rather than other parts of the agreement. Care also needs to be taken to ensure that the fundamental title warranties are not eroded by the warranty protection provisions and that is why reference should be made to a specific schedule of the sale agreement which will contain the non-taxation warranties but, importantly, not the fundamental warranties which will be contained separately in a clause in the main body of the sale agreement.

"Warranty Claim" any claim made by the Purchaser for breach of any of the Warranties.

In addition to the definitions suggested above, the following are often included: **4–03**

"month" a calendar month.

the singular includes the plural and vice versa.

the masculine includes the feminine and vice versa.

Express definitions are in fact not required as they are contained in Law of Property Act 1925 s.61 and apply, unless excluded, for the purpose of documents executed after the commencement of the Act. Section 61 also provides that "person" includes a corporation but does not expressly include partnerships (see the Interpretation Act 1978 Sch.1). Where this could be a matter of concern, it would be appropriate to add:

"person" includes a firm or other body of persons.

STATUTORY REFERENCES

It is usual to find a definition concerning the statutory provisions referred to in the warranties and indemnities substantially in the following form: **4–04**

[3B] Statutory references

References to any statute, or to any statutory provision, statutory instrument, order or regulation made thereunder, includes that statute, provision, instrument, order or regulation as amended, modified, consolidated, re-enacted or replaced from time to time, whether before or after the date of this Agreement and also includes any previous statute, statutory provision, instrument, order or regulation, amended, modified, consolidated, re-enacted or replaced by such statute, provision, instrument, order or regulation. **4–05**

As drafted, this clause would cause the vendors to bear the risk of retrospective legislation causing, or increasing, a liability under the warranties or indemnities. This is generally inconsistent with the principle that, as from the exchange of contracts (or at any rate, completion), the business of the target company (or the business which is being acquired) is conducted at the risk of the purchaser. Another circumstance in which an unexpected result can arise is where liability under a warranty, which depends on a statutory reference, may arise only a considerable time after the date of the sale agreement. An example is in the case of a warranty as to contamination which may state that there is no liability in regard to the target company arising from environmental laws. If this reference to laws is deemed to incorporate changes enacted after the date of the sale agreement, then the vendors may find that the scope of their liability is greatly increased as a result of legislative developments. The vendors should therefore amend this definition by reversing the phrases in brackets (re-enactments applying only if they do not modify the original legislation) and modifications being effective only if the relevant provisions are enacted before the date of the sale agreement.

An alternative way of limiting the effect of retrospective legislation is for the vendors to add the following words to the end of the above clause:

" ... except to the extent that an amendment, modification, consolidation, re-enactment or replacement enacted after today's date would extend or increase the liability of the Vendors under the Warranties or the Tax Covenant."

The purchaser should take into account that it is not unusual for legislation to take effect from an earlier date, being the date upon which a public announcement was made of the intention to bring in the legislation in question. This is particularly common with taxation matters and, indeed, the Finance Act each year will for the most part operate retrospectively to the date of the relevant budget speech and, in the case of tax anti-avoidance measures, will often apply from the date on which the proposal to introduce legislation was announced. The purchaser should consider amending the suggested alternative wording so that it refers to legislation taking effect, rather than being enacted, after the date of the agreement.

THE WARRANTY OBLIGATION

4–06   It is convenient, and normal practice, for the warranties to be set out in a separate schedule, as will be seen from the definition of "Warranties" in para.4–01. The schedule would be adopted by a clause in the body of the sale agreement as follows:

[3C] The Warranties

4–07   **The Vendors [jointly and severally] warrant and [represent] to the Purchaser that, save as Disclosed, the Warranties are true in all respects.**

It is now convention to agree the warranties without seeking to amend the terms of them by reference to factual matters which are known to conflict with them. Qualifications to the warranties which are not intended simply to alter the drafting are collected together in the disclosure letter. Clause 3C accordingly provides for the warranties to be read subject to the disclosures. The use of the defined term "Disclosed" seeks to adopt current thinking at what ought reasonably to constitute fair disclosure in relation to exceptions to the warranties.

In addition, cl.3C, by inclusion of the word "represent", provides for the warranties to constitute representations as well as warranties. This provides the purchaser with additional remedies for breach of warranty at common law and under the Misrepresentation Act 1967, if the relevant representations have been relied upon see Ch.3 for the remedies available in cases of misrepresentation. In practice, however, rescission is unlikely to be available by the time the representation has been found to be wrong, in which case the purchaser's remedy will be to seek damages—the same as if the warranties were not also representations. The vendors will nonetheless wish to delete references to representations, and to include an entire agreement clause excluding liability for representations made (see Ch.3). Please refer to the definition of "Warranties" for further discussion on this point.

In a case where there is doubt about the abilities of the target company or the purchaser to continue in business, the vendors might wish to qualify the warranty by adding the words:

" . . . and all the Warranties are given on the basis that [the Company will carry on its business as a going concern] [the Business will be carried as a going concern]."

The purpose of this addition is to avoid any possibility that the vendors should bear extra liabilities which arise only by reason of a cessation of business—such as redundancy payments to employees or balancing charges in respect of plant and equipment—and should be acceptable to the purchaser.

IMPLIED WARRANTIES AS TO TITLE

The LPMPA 1994 provides for certain covenants to be implied in an instrument **4–08** effecting a disposition of assets where the disposition is expressed to be made "with full title guarantee" or "with limited title guarantee". In both cases the implied covenants may be limited or extended by the instrument itself.

The covenants implied by using the formula "with full title guarantee" are that:

(1) the person making the disposition has the right to dispose of the asset as he purports to (s.2(1));

(2) he will at his own cost do all that he reasonably can to give the person to whom he disposes of the asset the title he purports to give (s.2(2)); and

(3) the disposer is disposing of the asset free from all charges and encumbrances and from all other rights exercisable by third parties other than rights which the disposer does not and could not reasonably be expected to know about (s.3(1)).

The first two of these covenants are also implied by the words "with limited title guarantee". The third covenant adds that the disposer has not since the last disposition for value:

(1) charged or encumbered the asset by means of a charge or encumbrance which subsists when he makes the disposition; or

(2) granted third party rights in relation to the asset which subsist; or

(3) suffered the asset to be charged or encumbered or subjected to third party rights; and that he is not aware that anyone else has done so since the last disposition for value (s.3(3)).

With both types of title guarantee, the covenants do not apply to anything of which the person to whom the disposition is made is actually aware when the disposition is made, or which is a necessary consequence of the facts which are then actually known by him (s.6(2)).

4–09   The covenants implied by the limited title guarantee are unlikely to be sufficient for most purchasers but the full title guarantee may be acceptable. If the words are used the following points arise:

(1) The covenants are impliedly given by the vendors. While this is appropriate in the case of a business sale, it may not be correct in relation to a share sale if the vendors and the parties giving the warranties are not the same.

(2) Warranties by the vendors as to title, such as cll.1.2.1 and 1.2.2 in paras 7–05 and 7–06 will not be required.

(3) The purchaser will wish to amend the implied covenants by excluding the reference to the knowledge of the disposer which appears in s.3(1) and the exception in respect of matters of which the purchaser is aware which is provided by s.6(2). A suitable clause for this purpose is the following:

[3D] Restriction on implied covenants

4–10   **The express assurance in clause [   ] as to freedom from encumbrances and the covenants implied in that clause by ss.2 and 3 of the LPMPA 1994 shall apply to anything falling within the scope of such assurances and covenants notwithstanding that the Vendors do not know or could not reasonably be expected to know about it, or, at the time of transfer, it is within the actual knowledge, or is a necessary consequence of facts then within the actual knowledge of the Purchaser, and the operation of the covenants implied by**

ss.2 and 3 of the LPMPA 1994 shall be deemed to be extended so as not to exclude the liability of the Vendors thereunder in any of such circumstances.

An alternative way of dealing with this (and one that reflects current convention) is to amend the clause containing the express assurance such that it reads "sell with [full][limited] title guarantee free from Encumbrances"—by selling "free from Encumbrances", the vendors will be selling free from those that it did and did not know about, and then to deal with the exclusion of the purchaser's knowledge in a separate clause, similar to that at cl.3M. The wide ranging definition of "Encumbrance" is used.

From the point of view of both parties it will often be preferable to omit the implied covenants entirely and to rely instead on express warranties which take account of the circumstances relevant to the particular transaction. In practice most sale agreements contain both.

RESTRICTION OF WARRANTIES TO PERIOD OF OWNERSHIP

The form of many warranties is such that there could be a breach however long **4–11** ago the occurrence of the relevant event. An example, is a warranty that all statutory returns have been properly made and filed (see para.7–25, cl.1.11.1). If the period of ownership or involvement of the vendors has been short, they may wish to seek to avoid liability for defects attributable to an earlier period and the following provision might be appropriate in these circumstances.

[3E] Application of Warranties to past events

The Vendors shall not be liable, in relation to a breach of the Warranties, if **4–12**
and to the extent that the breach is primarily attributable to anything which
occurred prior to [   ].

Although the vendors may seek to justify the principle underlying this clause on the basis that they cannot warrant the correctness of statements where they have no means of knowing whether or not they are accurate, this argument, which is based on the checklist function of the warranties, is flawed. Either the vendors or the purchaser must accept the risk of inaccuracy and, if neither of them has knowledge of the applicable facts, they must decide by negotiation where the risk is to lie. If the purchaser accepts the principle, the wording of cl.3E is more likely to be approved if "primarily" is omitted or replaced by "wholly". In addition, the purchaser should require the vendors to assign to it, or to enforce for its benefit, any warranties in relation to the target company or business which were obtained when the vendors made their acquisition (see para.2–12). In practice most purchasers would expect the vendors to bear the risk in these circumstances.

The vendors may also wish to restrict the warranties so that liability will not arise if a breach of warranty results from the combined effect of events both before and after completion.

[3F] Effect of post-Completion events

4–13   **The Vendors shall not be liable for a claim under the Warranties which would not have arisen but for anything occurring after Completion.**

A purchaser will usually want to ensure that such a clause does not negate any warranty claim which arises as a result of a combination of circumstances occurring before and after completion when those that occurred after completion are either in the ordinary course of the business or were contractually committed to prior to completion.

DATE OF APPLICATION OF WARRANTIES

4–14   Although completion may follow immediately upon the exchange of the contracts for the purchase of the target company or business, it is sometimes the case that there is an interval between contracts and completion. This may arise, for example, because certain consents are required, or where the consideration is to be satisfied by a placing of shares. Where an interval exists, the target company or business will usually continue to be run by the vendors although normally this will be for the benefit, and at the risk, of the purchaser.

The purchaser may therefore wish to include provisions in the sale agreement which restrict the way in which the business of the target company or the acquired business may be conducted in the intervening period (*interregnum* provisions) (see Appendix 2 which contains an example of generic provisions that would be suitable in such circumstances). In addition, the purchaser will wish the warranties contained in the sale agreement to apply both at the date of the exchange of contracts and at completion and perhaps even at every moment in between. The first of these dates is relevant as the purchaser will, in part, be relying upon the warranties in deciding to enter into the sale agreement. It is also appropriate, from the purchaser's point of view, for the warranties to be extended to completion as the purchaser will wish to protect itself so far as possible against any changes occurring after contracts by passing the risk of them to the vendors.

As the vendors will generally control the target company or business until completion, it is difficult for them to resist some extension of the warranties to completion. It is likely that the vendors will be presented with clauses to cover these aspects similar to those which follow in this section. Great care needs to be taken by the vendors in extending the warranties to completion as that will substantially erode the usual basis that the company or business is carried on after exchange of contracts at the purchaser's risk.

[3G] Events occurring prior to Completion

4–15   **[Each of the Vendors] [The Vendor] will promptly disclose in writing to the Purchaser any [material] circumstance which arises, or becomes known to [him] [her] [it], prior to Completion and is inconsistent [in a material respect] with any of the Warranties or the matters Disclosed[, or which**

might be material to be known by a purchaser for value of [the Shares] [the Business]].

The purchaser will be justified in seeking to include this clause where it has a right to rescind the contract if a breach of warranty occurs or is identified prior to completion. The purchaser might also wish to retain the clause in any case on the basis that, if difficulties arise before completion, notification should be given to it so that it can plan appropriate corrective action. Whilst this argument has some validity, the vendors might reasonably object to putting themselves in a position where a failure to comply with the clause could give rise to a claim for damages. Furthermore, they should not underestimate the considerable practical difficulty of keeping constantly in mind in the period up to completion the wording of lengthy and technical warranties.

The purchaser will probably insist that any disclosure under this provision is in writing, so that there can be no dispute afterwards as to whether the disclosure has taken place. The vendors should therefore ensure that a written record is made of any relevant discussions which take place with the purchaser between contracts and completion. It would be usual if there were any relevant matters for a supplementary disclosure letter containing details of them to be prepared and provided at completion.

The clause as drafted refers to all the warranties and the vendors should consider each warranty specifically to determine whether or not the obligations imposed by the clause should extend to that warranty. The vendors should also consider inserting the references to materiality that are included in square brackets.

The suggested wording would require a disclosure of information which is in **4–16** the public domain and which does not relate specifically to the target company or business. Thus, for example, during the interval between contracts and completion, there might be an announcement of new legislation to be introduced with effect from the date of the announcement. This could render a warranty incorrect, but the vendors should not be required to make a disclosure of the announcement. It is therefore suggested that the vendors should consider qualifying the clause by adding the words:

" . . . being a circumstance relating specifically to [the Company] [the Business]."

The vendors would also wish to consider carefully whether the words "or which might be material to be known by a purchaser for value of [the Shares] [the Business]" are acceptable, as they have no way of knowing what might affect a purchaser in general rather than the actual purchaser. Even to amend the clause so that it applies only to matters which might be material to be known by the actual purchaser may not be acceptable, as the vendors may have little information about the purchaser's reasons for acquiring the target company or business.

A second clause which the purchaser would wish to include in cases of deferred completion, in addition to any express restrictions such as are contained in Appendix 2, would be to the following effect:

[3H] Conduct of the Company pending Completion

4–17   **The Vendors shall procure that, save as may be necessary to give effect to this Agreement, the Company shall not, before Completion, without the prior written consent of the Purchaser [knowingly] do, procure or allow anything which might constitute or result in a [material] breach of the Warranties, or make any of them inaccurate or misleading, if they were given at Completion.**

The equivalent wording in the case of a business sale would be:

"Save as may be necessary to give effect to this Agreement, the Vendor shall not, before Completion, without the written consent of the Purchaser [knowingly] do, procure or allow anything which might constitute or result in a [material] breach of the Warranties, or make any of them inaccurate or misleading, if they were given at Completion".

The purpose of this provision is to apply the warranties on a continuing basis throughout the interval between exchange of contracts and completion. It is accordingly an onerous clause, to be viewed with caution by the vendors. If they accept it in principle, they should at least make sure that extraordinary transactions are avoided during the period between contracts and completion. It would also be reasonable for the vendors to qualify the clause by adding the following wording:

"[The Vendors] [The Vendor] shall not, however, be liable under this clause for a breach which arises from the ordinary and proper course of [business of the Company] [the Business]."

An example of an event which would come within this sentence is a routine change in the identity of named employees (for example, cl.6.1.1 in para.7–166). The vendors should also consider whether the word "might" should be replaced by "would" or "would be likely to". The third clause which the purchaser will require, whether the interval between contracts and completion is short or long, is along the following lines:

[3I] Warranties to apply at Completion

4–18   **Each of the Warranties shall be deemed to be repeated, with any necessary modification, immediately before the time of Completion, with reference to the facts then existing.**

This clause differs from cl.3G in that it takes no account of whether any change has been caused by the vendors or was within their control. It is inconsistent with the concept, which is standard in conveyancing practice, that the risk of adverse events occurring which are outside the control of the vendors passes to the purchaser on exchange of contracts, a concept which is usually heavily eroded on share transactions by the combined effect of the interregnum provisions and the repetition of the warranties up to the point of completion. Clause 3G is as far as the vendors would normally wish to go.

Even if this clause is accepted, it is desirable to consider each warranty individually to determine whether or not it is appropriate for it to be extended in this way.

VENDORS' KNOWLEDGE

It is usual for certain of the warranties requested by the purchaser to be qualified **4–19** so that they apply only to the best of the knowledge and belief of the vendors, or only so far as the vendors are aware of the relevant facts or circumstances, and it is common practice for the vendors' solicitors to try to amend the warranties, either generally or to a significant extent, in this way. This is probably unnecessary, as it would appear from *William Sindall Plc v Cambridgeshire CC* [1994] 1 W.L.R. 1016 that, if there is a duty on the vendors to make disclosures, a statement that the vendors are not aware of something implies that they have made such investigation as might reasonably be expected to be made by or under the guidance of a prudent vendor. Nevertheless, to ensure that appropriate enquiry is made by the vendors before expressing their knowledge and belief it is useful to add a specific provision to the following effect:

[3J] Enquiry by the Vendors

Where a Warranty refers to the knowledge, information, awareness or belief **4–20** **of the Vendors, each of the Vendors undertakes that they have made full enquiry into the subject matter of the Warranty and it shall not be a defence that the Vendors did not appreciate the relevance of any particular matter.**

The last part of this clause is intended to make it clear that the lack of knowledge is determined objectively. The vendors should replace "full enquiry into the subject matter of the Warranty" with either "due and careful enquiry" or "such enquiry into the subject matter of the Warranty as is reasonable in the context of the sale of the [Shares] [Business]". Unless the wording is qualified in the latter way, the clause could mean, for example, that before warranting that there is no investigation planned by the taxation authorities, the vendors should request the authorities to confirm that this is so.

Often the vendors' advisors will wish to achieve certainty in relation to the level of enquiry the vendors have to make in order to satisfy the relevant standard. This is often done by stating the persons or entities of whom enquiry has to be made (for example solicitors, accountants, insurance brokers, surveyors, bankers and the like together with a defined list of executives and/or employees). If this course is acceptable to a purchaser, it will need to be satisfied that the relevant entities or persons are sufficient to obtain all relevant information from. Usually an objective standard without reference to a defined list will be the purchaser's preference.

4–21   A problem arises where the relevant knowledge is that possessed by a company. This occurs most generally in the case of a business sale where the vendor, and the only party giving the warranties, will invariably be a company. The point can also exist in relation to share sales, particularly if the target company is a wholly owned subsidiary. Although it is not possible to provide a simple rule for identifying the individual whose knowledge is treated in a particular case as being that of the selling company, certain broad principles can be identified. What has to be determined, by applying the usual canons of interpretation, is whose knowledge for the particular purpose was intended to count as that of the company (*Meridian Global Funds Management Asia Ltd v Securities Commission* [1995] 2 B.C.L.C. 116). In the Meridian case, the knowledge of some senior investment managers was treated as being that of the company. The Court of Appeal in *El Ajou v Dollar Landholdings Plc (No.1)* [1994] 1 B.C.L.C. 464 held that it is necessary to identify the person having actual management and control in relation to the particular act. The clearest technique for resolving the matter is to specify the individuals whose knowledge is attributed to the company and it may also be appropriate to state the warranties in relation to which named individuals are treated as having relevant knowledge. It might be reasonable, for example, to state that the knowledge of any director is taken into account for all the warranties, but that senior executives who are not directors are treated as relevant only in relation to those areas for which they have executive responsibility. A clause to that effect is the following:

[3K] Knowledge of the Vendor

4–22   In determining whether the Vendor has the knowledge referred to in a Warranty it shall be treated as knowing:

> **[3K.1] anything which is known to any of its directors; and**

> **[3K.2] anything which is known to the persons listed in Schedule [   ] but, in respect of each of the individuals named, only in relation to those of the Warranties which are specified against his name in that Schedule.**

This clause deals only with the knowledge of the vendor. While the concept of belief sits rather awkwardly with a corporate vendor, if it is to be included cl.3K it should be extended to cover the attribution to the company of the beliefs of the specified individuals.

Other difficult questions can arise in the case of a sale of shares where *one* of the vendors is in default in this respect, because of deliberate concealment, oversight or negligent failure to make due enquiry, but the remaining vendors are not. The normal form of this qualification to the warranties would result in all the vendors in such a case being in breach.

If the purchaser accepts a warranty qualified in this manner, then essentially it is seeking to protect itself against deliberate concealment or negligence by the vendors in reviewing the affairs of the target company in relation to the warranty.

If, therefore, only one vendor has access to the relevant information, the purchaser's objective is to prevent him being fraudulent or negligent. For clarity, the purchaser might prefer to add the following clause:

[3L] Awareness of one of the Vendors

If one of the Vendors is or could reasonably have been aware that there was   4–23
a breach of a Warranty which refers to the knowledge, information, awareness or belief of the Vendors, he shall be liable for a fraction of the Purchaser's loss arising from that breach equal to the fraction of the Shares which are sold by him.

The effect of cl.3L on the minimum level for making claims (see para.11–04) should be considered carefully. The purchaser would wish to add the following to cl.3L:

"In determining whether claims exceed the amount specified in clause 11B, the whole of the loss, and not just the fraction, shall be taken into account."

EFFECT OF INVESTIGATION

In most transactions, financial and legal due diligence will be undertaken on the   4–24
target company. It is usual for the purchaser to request that the factual replies to enquiries submitted as part of the due diligence process be warranted as true and accurate. Most vendors will be reluctant to warrant the accuracy of the due diligence reports themselves, even if they have been disclosed, as they will often contain the subjective views of those who undertook the due diligence which the vendors would not wish to underwrite.

The purchaser will normally wish to include the following clause:

[3M] Effect of investigation or waiver of liability

The remedies of the Purchaser in respect of a breach of the Warranties shall   4–25
not be affected by any investigation made, or to be made, by or on behalf of the Purchaser into [the affairs of the Company] [the Business], or by the Purchaser rescinding, or failing to rescind, this Agreement or anything else other than a specific and duly authorised written waiver or release.

It is questionable whether the exclusion will be effective to protect a purchaser who had knowledge of the relevant circumstances when entering into the sale agreement (*Eurocopy Plc v Teesdale* [1992] B.C.L.C. 1067) either itself or through its agent (*Infiniteland Ltd v Artisan Contracting Ltd* [2004] EWHC 955—although see commentary at para.1–08 in relation to this) and the knowledge would make it difficult for the purchaser to show that it suffered damage as a result of the breach. The vendors, nevertheless, cannot fairly object to this clause as it is normally in the interests of both parties that qualifications to the warranties should be in writing in the disclosure letter. The vendors might reasonably require that the words "duly authorised" are omitted as it may in practice be difficult to ascertain whether due authority has been obtained.

If there is to be a purchaser's warranty confirming that outside of those matters contained in the disclosure letter the purchaser has no actual knowledge of any matters that as at completion would entitle it to make a warranty claim then the warranty needs to be amended to reflect this and ensure consistency. See para.4–37 for the wording of a purchaser's warranty.

PARTLY-OWNED SUBSIDIARIES

4–26 If the target company has subsidiaries, one of which is partly owned, then the purchaser's entitlement to damages where a breach of warranty occurs in relation to that subsidiary will be adjusted automatically. It would not normally be necessary, therefore, to make any special provision in relation to the warranties to cover partial ownership unless—exceptionally—the partly-owned subsidiary is under the control of a third party and not of the purchaser, perhaps because of special voting rights.

A different position arises in respect of the taxation covenant. If no special arrangement is made, then the vendors will have to compensate the purchaser in full, even though the purchaser effectively derives only a proportionate part of the benefit. The dilemma can be resolved by making the taxation covenant relate to an appropriate proportion of any claim that is made.

EJUSDEM GENERIS RULE

4–27 The following clause is quite frequently to be found in share sale (and, indeed, other) agreements:

[3N] *Ejusdem generis* rule

4–28 In construing this Agreement the so-called "*ejusdem generis* rule" does not apply and accordingly the interpretation of general words is not restricted by:

> **[3N.1] being preceded by words indicating a particular class of acts, matters or things; or**

> **[3N.2] being followed by particular examples.**

This rule originates from the decision of Tenterden C.J. in *Sandiman v Breach* (1827) 7 B & C 96 who said "Where general words follow particular ones, the rule is to construe them as applicable to persons *ejusdem generis*". The rule has not been consistently applied, particularly in modern times, but care is needed where a list of examples precedes a general word, or a general word is followed by specific examples. These qualifications will be unnecessary except in the rare cases where there is a real doubt as to whether it is intended that the general operation of the wording is to be restricted. As a matter of drafting technique, it is better to ensure that the doubt does not arise, by issuing a clause such as the above. Qualifying "including" by a phrase such as "but without limitation", provides an alternative approach.

FOREIGN COMPANIES OR BUSINESS

Where the target company or business has limited overseas activities, the **4–29** warranties considered in Chs 7 and 8 will generally be suitable. If, however, there is a material overseas involvement, it is desirable for local advice to be obtained as to the equivalent matters to be covered by the warranties so far as they relate to the overseas jurisdictions. For this purpose it should be borne in mind that the law in Scotland is not the same as in England and Wales.

A somewhat shorthand approach which may reasonably be adopted if the overseas involvement is slight is to include the following clause:

[3O] Overseas companies or businesses

The Warranties apply, with any necessary modification, to [that part of the 4–30 Company's business as is carried on] [any part of the Business carried on] outside England and Wales, and for the purpose of construction:

> **[3O.1] a reference to a statutory provision enacted, or accounting principle applying, in England and Wales includes a reference to the corresponding provision in the local legislation and (where relevant) to a generally accepted accounting principle; and**

> **[3O.2] a reference to a governmental, or administrative, authority or agency includes a reference to the equivalent local governmental, or administrative, authority or agency.**

This is very much a broad brush approach and will be unlikely to provide the purchaser with suitable protection if the overseas activities are more than minimal.

EXCLUSIONS

It will normally be agreed that the warranties do not apply, for example, to **4–31** matters disclosed in or reasonably apparent from the target company's or, in the case of a business sale, the vendor's accounts or on file at the Companies House Registry. These qualifications to the warranties can be set out in the sale agreement but it is more usual to list them in the disclosure letter together with other relevant ones (see cl.3C and Ch.9).

Another circumstance which could operate to exclude liability for a breach of warranty is where the purchaser has failed to act in accordance with the instructions of the vendors in relation to the conduct of disputes relating to the subject matter of the warranty. This is discussed further in Ch.11.

GENERAL CLAUSES

4–32   Where, on a sale of shares, the vendors are not closely involved in the management of the target company, they will normally base their reaction to the draft warranties, and the preparation of the disclosure letter, on information provided to them by the company's management. If this information is negligently prepared, and as a result the purchaser is able to mount a successful claim under the warranties or for misrepresentation, then the vendors may have a counter-claim against either the target company or the directors of the target company for negligence in providing the relevant information. Such a claim would operate to the detriment of the purchaser (as it would either be against the target company or its employees) and it is therefore usual for the purchaser to exclude that right. A clause dealing with this point is as follows:

[3P] Information supplied to Vendors

4–33   **Information supplied by the Company or its professional advisers to the Vendors, or their agents, representatives or advisers, in connection with the Warranties and the Disclosure Letter, or otherwise in relation to the business and affairs of the Company, is not deemed to be a representation by the Company to the Vendors as to its accuracy, and the Vendors may not make a claim against the Company, its officers or employees or its professional advisors in respect of that information.**

Although the waiver may not be effective as far as the target company is concerned, it not being a party to the sale agreement, in the event of a claim being made the purchaser would be able to sue for breach and claim damages if loss could be established. An alternate way of dealing with this (and the approach that currently seems to be favoured) is to amend the clause that deals with the waiver of third party rights (see cl.1D) such that there is a caveat so that the target company and the others that have provided information for the purposes of the warranties and the disclosure letter can rely on and enforce this clause.

Another clause of general relevance is:

[3Q] Warranties independent

4–34   **Each of the Warranties is independent of other Warranties [and undertakings] and, unless the contrary is expressly stated, no clause in this Agreement limits the extent or application of another clause.**

Inevitably, there will be a degree of overlap in the warranties and the purpose of the first part of this clause is to eliminate any suggestion that might otherwise exist to the effect that a qualification to one warranty operates to reduce the scope of an overlapping warranty. The vendors should treat each warranty on its own merits and make amendments to them on that basis. In view of the overlap that occurs between warranties, the vendors will wish to ensure that the disclosures contained in the disclosure letter are not interpreted as being limited to specific warranties but qualify the warranties generally (see Ch.9).

The second half of the clause, even with the words between the commas, is unnecessary and potentially harmful to the vendors. There will in most instances be clauses in the sale agreement that intentionally limit the extent or application of other clauses. They should therefore delete this.

[3R] Warranties to survive Completion

Each of the Warranties, other than a Warranty fully performed at Completion, shall remain in full force and effect notwithstanding Completion.   4–35

The purpose of this provision is to avoid the concept of merger of a contract into the completion document. If an executory contract is to be implemented by a subsequent deed, the general principle is that the real completed contract is to be found in the deed and the contract ceases to be relevant except for the purpose of construing the deed (*Leggott v Barrett* (1880) L.R. 15 Ch. D. 306). This rule is subject to the qualification that those terms of the contract which are not intended to be performed by the deed are not merged with it (*Knight Sugar Company Ltd v The Alberta Railway Irrigation Co* [1938] 1 All E.R. 266).

As there is no deed with which the sale agreement can merge, the principle would seem to be inapplicable to share sales although it is possible that by analogy the courts may apply it to completion of a share sale. There is a greater possibility of its applying to a business sale. Furthermore, the whole tenor of the warranties is that they should survive, and be enforceable after completion. While it could therefore be argued that cl.3R is strictly superfluous, given the fact that it is possible that the courts may apply the principle to a share sale a prudent purchaser would be well advised to incorporate it. While it is primarily the terms relating to enforcement of the warranties that the purchaser will be concerned with, given that there are likely to be other unperformed terms of the sale agreement at completion the purchaser ought to consider amending the clause to cover the whole of the sale agreement and not just the warranties. The following wording would be suitable for this:

"The provisions of this Agreement, in so far as the same have not been fully performed at Completion, shall remain in full force and effect notwithstanding Completion."

[3S] Delay in enforcing Warranties

A failure by the Purchaser to exercise, or a delay by it in exercising, a right in respect of a Warranty shall not operate as a waiver of the right or Warranty, and a single or partial exercise of a right shall not preclude another or further exercise of the right or the exercise of another right.   4–36

This provision might be unduly favourable to the purchaser in a case where the warranties have no significant time limit as the purchaser might then be entitled to raise a claim many years after it became aware of it. If, as is normal, a reasonable time limit is imposed within which claims must be brought, then the clause has little practical significance.

[3T] Purchaser's Warranty

4–37   **The Purchaser has not already formulated, and does not presently have any actual knowledge (save as Disclosed) of any circumstances which it knows would presently entitle it to make, a Warranty Claim.**

The use of this warranty by vendors' advisers has been more popular since *Eurocopy Plc v Teesdale* [1992] B.C.L.C. 1067. The warranty is designed to put the common law position under *Eurocopy* into contractual effect. There are many alternative forms of this warranty but the wording used here is likely to be acceptable to both the vendors and the purchaser. The provision or otherwise of this warranty is a question of bargaining position between the parties. Most purchasers will be wary of conceding the warranty while most vendors will want the comfort of it. Where there has been significant due diligence undertaken then an alternative approach, to achieving a similar outcome, is to ensure that any due diligence reports are generally disclosed even where the vendors have not had actual sight of them. See Ch.9 for a more detailed discussion of this. The phrase "actual" in respect of knowledge is designed to contrast with constructive or imputed knowledge. The recognition, by reference to the provisions in brackets, makes it clear that the purchaser does have actual knowledge of matters "Disclosed" i.e. those that have been fairly disclosed in accordance with the terms of the definition but not to matters that may be inadequately referred to or annexed to the disclosure letter but do not meet the required contractual standard of "Disclosed".

CHAPTER 5

Taxation Warranties

INTRODUCTION

A large number of the warranties normally required by the purchaser of a **5–01** company relate to tax. Whilst it would be possible to deal with all taxation matters in a few general paragraphs (as in the short form warranties set out in Appendix 9), it is particularly in relation to taxation that the value of the checklist concept of warranties demonstrates itself. By listing all taxation sections which it considers to be relevant, the purchaser assists the vendors in checking systematically whether any circumstances have arisen which ought to be brought to its attention.

A more recent trend is for tax warranties to be shorter than was previously the case and to be focused on warranties designed to elicit information rather than protect against liability—the vendors will usually be liable under the tax covenant in any event.

Disclosure of any relevant matters will usually negate any warranty claim. However, the tax covenant will still catch any tax liability that the target company has in relation to the warranted matters. Disclosures rarely operate to take effect against the tax covenant, and the purchaser's knowledge will be irrelevant to any claim made under it.

Even where warranty claims can be made for tax matters they will rarely be **5–02** made if the matter is covered by the tax covenant, as under the tax covenant there is neither a need to prove loss (as will often be the case for a breach of warranty) nor a need to overcome the "suite" of warranty protection provisions that there will usually be including, in particular, the financial deductibles. In most cases these will not apply to the tax covenant.

As noted in Ch.10 the current convention for incorporating tax warranties in the sale agreement is to put them in a schedule dealing with all tax issues, rather than including them in the general warranty schedule. However, wherever the tax warranties are incorporated, the substance of the warranties will be the same.

In this chapter we set out and discuss the tax warranties which might be required if an active trading company is being purchased. The following is a list of the headings which are covered:

Clause	Title
1	**Returns and clearances**
2	**PAYE and other deductions at source**
3	**Penalties**
4	**Claims, elections, liabilities and reliefs**

ANALYSIS OF INDIVIDUAL WARRANTIES

5–03   As a result of inertia, standard form documents often continue to include warranties relating to specific tax liabilities long after the relevant legislation has been abolished. An indication of the more common examples and of a number of special taxes which are not reviewed in detail in this chapter appear in para.5–106.

In considering the tax warranties, the vendors' solicitors and the target company's auditors will need to work closely together. A review of tax computations and returns for the past six years is normally desirable.

As a result of the tax law rewrite project, many of the statutory references in the tax warranties have recently changed, particularly with the introduction of ITA 2007, CTA 2009 and CTA 2010. Some practitioners have not yet updated their precedents and still have the old references, others have completely updated and others refer to both the new and the old statutory provisions. This last approach is the one adopted in this edition, both to assist those who may not be as familiar with the new references and to make the commentary easier to apply when reviewing warranties which have not been updated.

The warranties considered below adopt the definitions in para.4–02 and Ch.10.

1 Returns and clearances

1.1 All returns, notifications, computations and payments which should have **5–04**
been made or given by the Company for a Taxation purpose were made or
given within the requisite periods and were [in all material aspects] up-to-
date, correct and on a proper basis; and none of them is, or [(so far as the
Vendors are aware)] is likely to be, the subject of a [material] dispute with
HMRC or other Taxation Authorities.

Apart from the returns which have been required under FA 1998 Sch.18, Pt II (Company tax return) since July 1, 1999 when self-assessment became operative the principal returns relate to income tax deducted from payments which must be returned under ITA 2007 Pt 15 Ch.15 (Collection: Deposit-Takers, Building Societies and Certain Companies) (formerly ICTA 1988 Sch.16) non-qualifying distributions, within 14 days of the accounting period under CTA 2010 s.1101 (Non-Qualifying distributions etc.: returns and information) (formerly ICTA 1988 s.234) employees' earnings (such as forms P11D) under TMA 1970 s.15 (Return of employees' earnings, etc.) and the Income Tax (Pay As You Earn) Regulations 2003 and reportable events in relation to employment securities (including the acquisition of securities and chargeable events relating to restricted and convertible securities) under IT(EP)A 2003 s.421(J).

Accounts and returns generally have to be filed 12 months after the end of the accounting period to which they relate (FA 1998 Sch.18, para.14 (Filing Date)).

Other taxation returns include, in particular, those relating to VAT. For example, a change in the particulars registered for VAT purposes must be notified within 30 days (Value Added Tax Regulations 1995 (SI 1995/2518) reg.5(2), as amended).

The vendors should be cautious about giving this warranty as it is unlikely in **5–05**
practice that all returns will have been made precisely within the statutory time limits. This is, nevertheless, a matter of some relevance to the purchaser in view of the onerous interest charges and penalties which are imposed as a result of late payment of tax. Furthermore, the target company may have made special arrangements regarding certain returns such as P11Ds. These arrangements should either be disclosed or excluded from the warranty. The vendors must bear in mind the width of the defined term "Taxation". If, for example, the uniform business rate falls within the definition, it will be necessary to make a disclosure of any dispute with the rating authorities.

The reference to returns not being "likely" to be the subject of a dispute needs care. In view of the approach taken by the courts in relation to tax avoidance arrangements, it might be anticipated that any arrangements which have been entered into on an artificial basis, or which have been largely motivated by tax avoidance reasons, will be possible targets for HMRC attack, however firm the theoretical basis upon which they rest.

The vendors may wish, in any event, to qualify the warranty by the addition of the words in square brackets.

5–06   **1.2 All particulars furnished to the Taxation Authorities, in connection with an application for consent or clearance on behalf of the Company, or affecting the Company, fully and accurately disclosed everything material to their decision; the consent or clearance is valid and effective; and the transactions for which the consent or clearance was obtained have been carried into effect (if at all) only in accordance with the terms of the application and the consent or clearance.**

The primary consent referred to was that required under ICTA 1988 s.765 (Migration, etc. of companies). This section related to the migration of companies, transfers of businesses abroad and the issue of shares or debentures by a foreign subsidiary, but was repealed in relation to the first two categories by FA 1988 and as to the remainder by FA 2009.

Clearances are given on various matters under CTA 2010 s.1091 (Advance clearance of distributions) (formerly ICTA 1988 s.215) in relation to demergers; CTA 2010 s.1044 (Advance clearance of payments by Commissioners) (formerly ICTA 1988 s.225) in respect of purchases of own shares; CTA 2010 s.748 (Application for clearance of transactions) (formerly ICTA 1988 s.707) and ITA 2007 s.701(Application for clearance of transactions), in respect of transactions in securities; ITA 2007 Pt 13, Ch.3 (Transactions in Land) and CTA 2010 Pt 18 (Transactions in Land) (formerly ICTA 1988 s.776); TCGA 1992 s.138 (Company reconstructions and amalgamations: Procedure for clearance in advance) and s.139 (Reconstruction involving transfer of business) in relation to capital gains tax on company reconstructions.

Apart from the statutory clearances, it is sometimes possible to obtain informal rulings from HMRC either on general points or on the specific facts of a particular case. It should be emphasised that these rulings cannot be relied upon, and that the relevant departments do not consider themselves bound by them. The vendors should not therefore be expected to accept responsibility for the effectiveness of any informal clearance obtained in this way.

As this warranty relates only to applications made by the target company, it is largely a question of fact whether a breach could arise. The warranty will accordingly present little difficulty for the vendors in normal circumstances, although it would be a sensible precaution to limit the warranty to the preceding six years or some shorter period. This warranty has increased importance from the purchaser's perspective following *R. v Inland Revenue Commissioners, Ex p. Matrix Securities Ltd* (1994) S.T.C. 272 (HL) which showed that incomplete information will invalidate a HMRC clearance or consent.

5–07   **1.3 The Company has not taken any action which has had, or might have, the result of altering or prejudicing for a period commencing after the Balance Sheet Date an arrangement or agreement which it has with a Taxation Authority.**

In practice, the taxation authorities frequently agree to arrangements which are designed to operate on a broadly equitable basis and do not require that a strict detailed application of the legislation is adopted. Examples arise in relation to the treatment of expenses, benefits to directors and employees, valuation of stocks and depreciation of assets. Arrangements of this kind may be terminated at any time but it is important for the purchaser to be aware of any changes which have occurred after the end of the last accounting period. Alternatively, the purchaser may want disclosure of all such arrangements so that it can take a view on them.

The vendors should consider carefully whether the clause should be limited so that it is restricted to actions which, to their knowledge, have altered such arrangements, and the word "might" should be replaced by "will". They should also seek to restrict the warranty to arrangements agreed with HMRC.

1.4 There has been no determination under FA 1998 Sch.18, Pt V   5–08
(Revenue determinations and assessments) of the amount of tax payable by the Company.

Schedule 18 of FA 1998 allows the Inspector to make a determination as to the amount of corporation tax payable or as to the amount of any element which goes into the calculation of tax liability, including, for example, profits, sets-offs and reliefs. The time limit for such a determination is six years from the end of the relevant accounting period.

As the warranty covers a factual question in relation to which the purchaser will have a legitimate interest, the vendors might reasonably be expected to accept the warranty.

1.5 The Company is not obliged to pay corporation tax in quarterly   5–09
instalments under the provisions of the Corporation Tax (Instalment Payments) Regulations 1998 (SI 1998/3175) and TMA 1970 s.59E.

Under the corporation tax, self assessment regime companies (and groups) whose tax liabilities exceed a certain level are required to make payments of their corporation tax liabilities in instalments. Payments are made on an estimate of the actual liability and any excess or shortfall in relation to the amount which should have been paid (determined when the tax return for the accounting period is submitted) attracts interest until such time as it is correct.

1.6 The Company has not entered into any group payment arrangements   5–10
under TMA 1970 ss.59F–59H (formerly FA 1998 s.36).

If the target company is part of a group payment arrangement, it is important to ensure that the arrangement is amended when the target company comes out of the vendors' group, and that payment arrangements are made in relation to the purchaser's group.

2 PAYE and other deductions at source

5–11 **2.1 The Company has properly operated the PAYE system, by duly deducting tax from all payments made, or treated as made, to its employees or former employees, and accounting to HMRC for all tax deducted by it and for all tax chargeable on benefits provided for its employees or former employees.**

This warranty applies not only in relation to the normal PAYE system which operates under IT(EP)A 2003 s.684 (PAYE Regulations) in relation to employment income of employees, but also in relation to certain benefits in kind, such as cash vouchers and readily convertible assets, and the special charges on employment related securities. This is all dealt with in IT(EP)A 2003 Pt 11. The PAYE system also applies to certain workers engaged through agencies (IT(EP)A 2003 s.688 (Agency Workers)). A number of special provisions apply dealing with a variety of unusual cases, including those where payments are made by intermediaries or to employees of non-United Kingdom employers (IT(EP)A 2003 ss.687 and 689 respectively).

Sections 703–707 IT(EP)A 2003 provide a statutory procedure to enable employers to adopt a simplified method for settling the liability of employees in respect of tax on certain benefits.

Although the purchaser is entitled to be satisfied that PAYE requirements have been properly carried out and are up to date, it will in practice often be the case that minor infringements of the regulations have occurred. Furthermore, the last part of the clause, which refers to tax chargeable on employees' benefits, is unlikely to be satisfied in practice. The vendors may wish to qualify the warranty by providing that no significant failures to operate the system have occurred but, if a floor to claims has been agreed as described in para.11–04, then the purchaser might reasonably take the position that this adequately protects the vendors against trivial claims being made under the warranty without a qualification also being necessary.

5–12 **2.2 The Company has complied fully with all its obligations relating to Class 1 and Class 1A National Insurance Contributions, both primary and secondary.**

Since Class 1A National Insurance Contributions have been made applicable to most benefits not otherwise subject to National Insurance, and National Insurance avoidance schemes have become increasingly common, it has become important to obtain this kind of warranty.

5–13 **2.3 The Company has made all deductions and retentions of or on account of Taxation as it was obliged or entitled to make and has made all such payments of or on account of Taxation as should have been made to any Taxation Authority in respect of such deductions or retentions.**

In certain circumstances, a company has to deduct an amount on account of tax from certain payments. A non-exhaustive list includes:

(a) ITA 2007 ss.901 and 963 (formerly ICTA 1988 ss.349 and 350): these sections provide a withholding tax system in relation to interest and annual and certain others payments. ITA 2007 s.930 which gives a broad exemption from such withholdings for payments between companies if the payer reasonably believes the payee is United Kingdom resident for tax purposes.

(b) ITA 2007 s.910 (formerly ICTA 1988 s.524): this relates to payment of the proceeds of sale of a United Kingdom patent to a person resident outside the United Kingdom. The exemption at ITA 2007 s.930 also applies to deductions under this section.

(c) ITA 2007 s.906 (formerly ICTA 1988 s.536): this relates to payment of copyright royalties to a person resident outside the United Kingdom.

(d) ITA 2007 ss.965–970 (formerly ICTA 1988 ss.555–558): basic rate income tax must be deducted from payments made to non-resident entertainers or sportsmen for United Kingdom appearances.

(e) CTA 2009 s.413 (formerly ICTA 1988 s.582): this relates to funding bonds issued in lieu of interest.

(f) ITA 2007 s.944 (formerly ICTA 1988 s.777): where ITA 2007 Pt 13 Ch.4 (Sales of Occupation Income) (formerly ICTA 1988 s.775) or ITA 2007 Pt 13, Ch.3 (Tax Avoidance: transaction in land) (formerly ICTA 1988 s.776) applies, HMRC may direct that tax should be withheld.

2.4 The Company is not and has not been a contractor for the purposes of FA 2004 Pt 3, Ch.3 (Construction Industry Scheme). 5–14

If the target company is a contractor for the purposes of the construction industry scheme, it has to deduct tax from certain payments to subcontractors, and there are various administrative requirements. A "contractor" is not necessarily a builder in the normal sense and care must be taken whenever a company has carried out extensive construction works.

2.5 No liability to National Insurance Contributions or obligation to account for income tax under the PAYE system could fall on the Company as a result of a chargeable event (within the meaning of IT(EP)A 2003 Pt 7) before, at or after Completion in respect of securities and interests in securities made available or securities options granted to an employee or director prior to Completion. 5–15

Part 7 of IT(EP)A 2003 provides a regime in relation to employment related restricted securities and convertible securities (and interests in such securities), under which an income tax charge may arise in respect of various chargeable events. Generally the target company will be liable to account for the income tax under PAYE and pay National Insurance Contributions. Under the regime it is possible to make various elections which mitigate the future income tax relating to such securities and take future gains or losses into the capital gains regime.

5–16   **2.6 No officer or employee of the Company participates in any scheme approved under IT(EP)A 2003, Schs 2 (Approved share incentive plans), 3 (Approved SAYE option schemes), or 4 (Approved CSOP schemes) or has any unapproved options (whether under IT(EP)A 2003, Sch.5 (Enterprise Managing Incentives) or otherwise).**

Employee participation schemes have become a common part of the remuneration packages offered by companies of all sizes. This warranty can be used for fact-finding but further examination of any scheme will be required.

3 Penalties

5–17   **3.1 The Company has not paid or, since the Balance Sheet Date, become liable to pay a penalty or interest under any statute relating to Taxation.**

The prime examples of penalties or interest in relation to the corporation tax self-assessment regime arise under FA 1998 s.117 and Sch.18 paras 17 and 18. The most common penalties arise in relation to failing to make proper returns, making incorrect returns or paying tax after the due date. Stringent penalty provisions apply in relation to VAT under VATA 1994 s.63 (Penalty for misdeclaration or neglect resulting in VAT loss for one accounting period equalling or exceeding certain amounts), s.64 (Repeated misdeclarations) and s.67 (Failure to notify and unauthorised issue of invoices). Stamp duty penalties can arise for late stamping under Stamp Act 1891 s.15 (Penalty upon stamping instruments after execution). FA 2003 Sch.10 (SDLT: returns, enquiries, assessment and appeals) provides for penalties in relation to SDLT.

It is important that the width of the definition of "Taxation" (when referring to payments due under any statute relating to Taxation) should be taken into account by the vendors and they might wish to restrict the warranty to corporation tax penalties. Penalties relating to VAT are covered in cl.28.

The vendors may want to restrict this to the last (for example) six years to make disclosure less onerous.

5–18   **3.2 The Company has not been the subject of an investigation, discovery or access order by or involving a Taxation Authority and there are no circumstances which make it likely that an investigation, discovery or order will be made.**

The Inspector of Taxes can make a "discovery" under TMA 1970 s.29 (Assessment where loss of tax discovered) within six years unless the point has been agreed under s.54 (Settling of appeals by agreement). If there has been fraud or wilful default, a "back-duty" investigation can be made for up to 20 years under FA 1998 Sch.18, para.46 (Fraudulent or negligent conduct). The time periods as from April 1, 2010, subject to transitional provisions, are four years, six years in the case of careless default and 20 years in the case of deliberate default. An access order permitting the removal of documents may be made under VATA 1994 Sch.11, para.11 (Order for access to recorded information etc.).

The vendors might reasonably object to this warranty on the basis that it is irrelevant, in so far as it relates to past investigations. Although there is some justification for the purchaser requesting a warranty about future enquiries, the wording is so wide that the vendors should be most cautious in accepting it. It is common to qualify the wording of this warranty in relation to routine PAYE and VAT inspections.

4 Claims, elections, liabilities and reliefs

4.1 The Disclosure Letter contains full details of all matters relating to   **5–19**
Taxation in respect of which the Company (either alone or jointly with another person) is, or at Completion will be, entitled:

    4.1.1 to make a claim (including a supplementary claim) for, disclaimer of or election for relief under any statute relating to Taxation;
    4.1.2 to appeal against an assessment to or a determination affecting Taxation;
    4.1.3 to apply for the postponement of Taxation.

It is important that the purchaser should be aware of any outstanding rights that exist in relation to the target company to make claims, elections, appeals or applications as described so that the necessary action can be taken before any time limits expire. Clause 4.1.1 refers specifically to supplementary claims, which may be made under FA 1998 Sch.18, para.56 (Supplementary claim or election) if a claim has already been made and a mistake is discovered. Disclaimers arise, for example in relation to capital allowances as mentioned below. Appeals can not only cover assessments, but also numerous other matters relevant to taxation liability, such as the existence of a group structure for corporation tax or VAT purposes, or whether a company is trading or carrying on an investment business.

Generally, in relation to corporation tax, claims, etc. may be made at any time   **5–20** within six years after the relevant event or accounting period or within four years with effect from April 1, 2010, subject to transitional provisions. The main provisions which impose shorter time limits are the following:

Claims

    (a) Appeals: generally a 30-day limit applies.

    (b) Capital allowances: claims for capital allowances which are available primarily against a specified class of income to be set-off against other income must be made within two years from the end of the relevant accounting period (CAA 2001 ss.259–260 (Special Leasing)). Under corporation tax self-assessment, claims for capital allowances must be included in a company tax return. Claims may normally be made, amended or withdrawn up to the first anniversary of the filing date for the relevant company tax return (FA 1998 Sch.18, Pt IX).

(c) Capital gains: if the value of an asset becomes negligible, a claim may be made for the asset to be treated as if it had been sold and reacquired at market value. The claim may be made retrospectively to an accounting period which ended not more than 24 months before the date of the claim (TCGA 1992 s.24(2) (Disposals where assets lost or destroyed, or become of negligible value)).

(d) Group relief: claims must be included in the relevant company tax return (FA 1998 Sch.18, Pt VIII).

(e) Loan relationships: non-trading deficits on a company's loan relationships may be treated in a variety of different ways as provided by CTA 2009 ss.456 et seq. (Non-trading deficits). Claims must be made within two years of the end of the relevant period or within such further period as HMRC may allow.

(f) Losses on unquoted shares in trading companies: a claim may be made by an investment company to apply against its income a loss on shares subscribed by it within two years after the end of the accounting period in which the loss occurs CTA 2010 s.68 (Share loss relief).

(g) Trading losses: a claim to set-off losses incurred in a trade against other profits of the same accounting period, or to carry the losses back to the preceding three accounting periods, must be made within two years of the end of the accounting period in which the loss is made CTA 2010 Pt 4, Ch.2 (Trade losses).

(h) VAT bad debt relief: if VAT is accounted for on a debt which is written off by the creditor, it may, on a claim being made, be recovered provided a period of six months has elapsed since the supply (VATA 1994 s.36 (Bad debts)). The effect of the warranty is to cover cases where a debt has actually been written off; cl.28.2 deals with those debts which, being at least six months old, could be written off, thereby giving rise to a right to claim relief.

Elections

(a) Advance corporation tax and shadow advance corporation tax: since the abolition of ACT with effect from April 6, 1999 companies pay dividends without accounting for ACT, and so an election to do so is no longer necessary. While a company with unrelieved surplus ACT as at April 6, 1999 will fall within the shadow ACT regime (the Corporation Tax (Treatment of Unrelieved Surplus ACT) Regulations 1999), companies may opt out of the shadow ACT system (regs 4 and 5).

(b) Corporation tax: see the commentary on cl.5 in relation to unremittable income. Two companies in a group may, by giving notice to the Inspector before the refund has been made, elect that a tax refund to which one of them is entitled is surrendered to the other (CTA 2010 s.963 (Power to surrender tax refund)).

(c) Capital allowances: CAA 2001 s.569 (Election to treat sale as being for alternative amount) gives the transferor and transferee in relation to sales of equipment the right in certain cases to elect that the assets are treated for capital allowances purposes as transferred at their written down values and not market values. The election must be made within two years of the transfer. A similar election on a transfer of trade may be made under s.266 (Elections where predecessor and successor are connected persons). An election may be made for certain equipment to be treated as short-life assets, thereby enabling capital allowances to be computed as if those assets were used for a separate notional trade. The election must be made not later than two years after the end of the period in which the expenditure was incurred (CAA 2001 s.85 (Election for short-life assets treatment: procedure)).

If an equipment lessor incurs expenditure on fixtures and the lessee has an **5–21** interest in the relevant property so that he would have been entitled to claim capital allowances under CAA 2001 s.176 (Persons who are treated as owners of fixtures: person with interest in relevant land having fixtures for purposes of qualifying activities) had he himself incurred the expenditure, the lessor and lessee may elect that the fixtures should be treated as belonging to the lessor. The effect of this will be to entitle the lessor to the capital allowances. The election must be made within two years of the end of the period in which the lessor incurs the expenditure (CAA 2001 s.177 (Equipment lessors)). Where machinery or plant has become a fixture and the lessor grants a lease under which the lessee incurs expenditure on fixtures in relation to which, had the lessor incurred the expenditure, it would have been entitled to allowances, the lessor and lessee may elect for the fixture to be treated as if it belonged to the lessee. The election must be made within two years from the grant of the lease (CAA 2001 s.183 (Incoming lessee: where lessor entitled to allowances)).

(a) Capital gains: if an asset was acquired before April 6, 1965, an election may be made within two years of its disposal (or within such further period as HMRC may by notice allow) to have the gain or loss based on its market value at that date and not determined by applying straight-line growth (TCGA 1992 Sch.2, para.17 (Election for valuation at April 6, 1965)). An election may be made under TCGA 1992 s.35 (Assets held on March 31, 1982 (including assets held on April 6, 1965)) to have the capital gains and losses on assets held on March 31, 1982 determined by reference to their value at that date without regard to the original acquisition cost. The election may be made within two years of the end of the period in which the first relevant disposal occurs (see also cl.21.2). An election may be made under TCGA 1992 Sch.4 (Deferred charges on gains before March 31, 1982) for certain rolled-over or postponed capital gains to be halved. The election must be made within two years of the end of the accounting period in which there is a disposal, or deemed disposal, of the relevant asset.

(b) Capital losses: TCGA 1992 s.171A allows two group members to elect to be treated as if an asset had been transferred between them immediately, prior to its disposal to a third party. This election can only be made if the company making the disposal could have made a no gain/no loss transfer to the other group company at that time (see cl.17.1). The election must be made less than two years after the end of the relevant accounting period.

(c) VAT: an election may be made to opt to tax land in respect of value added tax in relation to certain property transactions (see cl.28.4).

Postponement

(a) If a company believes it is being overcharged by an amendment of a self assessment, it may within 30 days of the issue of the amendment apply for payment to be postponed pending hearing of the appeal. The 30-day period can be extended where there is a change of circumstances which is believed to have caused the overcharge (TMA 1970 s.55 (Recovery of tax not postponed)). The short time scale applicable in most cases makes it unlikely that a right to apply for postponement will, in practice, ever need to be disclosed.

A claim to postpone the taxation on chargeable gains arising on a transfer of the trade of a United Kingdom company, which is carried on abroad, to a non-resident in exchange for securities may be made under TCGA 1992 s.140 (Postponement of charge on transfer of assets to non-resident company) or s.140C (Transfer or division of non-UK business) if both parties to the transfer are resident in member states (see cl.26.1). If a company which is resident in one member state transfers a United Kingdom trade to another company which is resident in another member state in exchange for securities of the transferee, they may jointly claim that the transferee takes over the base cost of the transferor (TCGA 1992 s.140A (Transfer or division of UK business)).

This warranty is so widely drawn, both in its express terms and by reason of the definition of "Taxation", that it will often be difficult for the vendors to ensure compliance. They should seek to limit the warranty so that it applies to specified statutory provisions only.

5–22   **4.2 The Company has not made a claim under TCGA 1992 s.24(2) (Disposals where assets lost or destroyed, or become of negligible value) or exercised an option to pay tax by instalments under s.280 (Consideration payable by instalments).**

If a capital asset becomes negligible in value, the owner may claim under s.24(2) to be treated as if the asset had been sold and immediately reacquired at that value. Section 280 applies where the purchase consideration on a disposal is payable over a period exceeding 18 months. At the option of the person making the disposal, the tax may be paid by instalments over a period of up to eight years. Clause 4.1 covers entitlements to make claims whereas this warranty deals with claims which have already been made.

The purchaser will have an interest in knowing about these claims, but the vendors may wish to limit the application of the clause to claims within the previous six years or to cases where the asset in relation to which a s.24 claim was made is still owned or where instalments remain outstanding under s.280.

4.3 The Company is not, nor will it become, liable to pay, or to reimburse or indemnify another person in respect of Taxation in consequence of the failure by any other person (not being the Company) to discharge the Taxation, where the Taxation relates to a profit, income or gain arising or deemed to have arisen or anything occurring or deemed to have occurred (whether wholly or partly) prior to Completion.   **5–23**

There are several statutory provisions whereby a company can be liable for the payment of corporation tax or VAT which is the primary responsibility of another company. The main ones are the following.

(a) CTA 2010 s.710 (formerly ICTA 1988 s.767A) (Recovery of unpaid corporation tax for accounting period beginning before change): if the ownership of a company changes after November 30, 1993 and corporation tax for a period which began before the change remains unpaid six months after the date of the corporation tax assessment, the tax may be collected from a person who during the three years preceding the change of ownership had control of it or from a company controlled by that person. For the section to apply, there must have been either a major change in the activities of the company which owes the tax associated with a transfer of assets to a connected party or a cessation of the company's trade. The person required to pay the tax has a right of recovery from the company which owed it (s.717 (Effect of payment in pursuance of assessment under ss.710 or 713)).

(b) TCGA 1992 s.137(4) (Restriction on application of ss.135 and 136): s.135 (Exchange of securities for those in another company) and s.136 (Scheme of Reconstruction involving issue of securities) provide a roll-over for capital gains tax purposes on certain company reconstructions and amalgamations. Section 137 restricts the relief so that it is not available if the transaction was carried out mainly for the purpose of avoiding tax. If s.137 applies and the transferor fails to pay the resulting tax within six months of the due date, it may be assessed at any time within two years on a holder of the securities which acquired them by intra-group transfer.

(c) TCGA 1992 s.139 (Reconstruction involving transfer of business): a bona fide reconstruction involving a transfer of one company's business to another can be disregarded. If, however, the transfer was not effected for bona fide commercial reasons, the tax arising from the transfer can be recovered from the transferee.

(d) TCGA 1992 s.189 (Capital distribution of chargeable gains: recovery of tax from shareholder): this is discussed in relation to cl.12.3.

(e) TCGA 1992 s.190 (Tax recoverable from another group company or controlling director): this relates to circumstances where a chargeable gain has accrued to a company when it is a member of a group. If the company does not pay the corporation tax within six months of the due date it can be recovered from the principal company of the group or any other company which, at any one time within two years ending with the disposal, was another member of the group and owned the relevant asset. This liability will accordingly be relevant only if the company primarily responsible for the payment of the taxation is not a member of the target company's group of companies. A controlling director of the company may also be liable in certain circumstances.

(f) Section 190 further provides that if the United Kingdom corporation tax liability of a non-resident company remains unpaid more than six months after the due date, corporation tax may be recovered from:

(1) the principal company of the group;

(2) any other company which, at any time during the 12 months before the gain accrued, was a member of the group and owned all or part of the asset (or an underlying asset); and/or

(3) any person who is a controlling director of the taxpayer company or a company controlling the taxpayer company, or was such a controlling director during the 12 months before the gain accrued.

CTA 2010 ss.973–980 provides that if the United Kingdom corporation tax liability of a non-resident company remains unpaid more than six months after the due date, that corporation tax liability may be recovered from other companies with which it is (or was) related. HMRC can recover the outstanding tax liability from a company within the same group, a member of a consortium which owned the non-resident company at any time in the relevant period or a member of the same group as a company which was a member of a consortium which owned the non-resident company at any time in the relevant period.

5–24   Where there is a clawback of stamp duty where relief under FA 1930 s.42 or FA 1986 s.76 is withdrawn pursuant to FA 2002 ss.111 and 113, the stamp duty which then becomes payable can be recovered under FA 2002 Schs 34 and 35 from the transferor company, any company which at the relevant time was a member of the same group as the transferee company and was above it in the group structure and any controlling director of the transferee company. Similar provisions apply in relation to SDLT under FA 2003 Sch.7.

(a) VATA 1994 s.43 (Groups of companies): companies in a group for which there is a group registration are jointly and severally liable for the group's VAT, which is primarily payable by the representative member of the group.

The purchaser has a real interest in this warranty only if there is no statutory right of reimbursement or if the covenant of the person against whom the right exists is of doubtful strength. The vendors should include an obligation on the purchaser to procure that the target company pursues any right of recovery which it has against third parties. The vendors should also consider whether the extension of the warranty to future events, arising from the phrase "will become", is acceptable. Finally, the warranty should fairly be restricted to taxation in the usual narrow sense.

4.4 No relief from Taxation has been claimed by or given to the Company,   **5–25** **or taken into account in determining the provision for Taxation in the Accounts, which could be withdrawn, postponed or restricted as a result of anything occurring after Completion [which is not a deliberate act or omission, or a circumstance deliberately created, by the relevant Company after Completion for the purpose of effecting the withdrawal, postponement or restriction].**

The purpose of this warranty is to cover the very unusual case where relief available before completion may be at risk because of action occurring after completion. This could occur if within the three years preceding the sale of the target company to the purchaser there had been another change of ownership.

If the purchaser allows a major change to occur in the nature or conduct of the trade of the target company before the three years expire, losses carried forward from a period prior to the first alteration in ownership could be prejudiced by the operation of CTA 2010 s.674 (Disallowance of trading losses) (formerly ICTA ss.768 and 768A). Inland Revenue Statement of Practice SP10/91 explains the basis on which the Inland Revenue interprets the term "a major change in the nature or conduct of a trade".

While the purchaser would wish to be covered against the withdrawal of past reliefs as an inadvertent result of transactions occurring after completion, the vendors might fairly consider that it is up to the purchaser to ensure that no such circumstances arise. To cover this, the words in square brackets could be added. Furthermore, the warranty is reasonable only if the loss of the relief results in an immediate liability to taxation. The withdrawal of relief should otherwise not be the subject of a warranty unless a representation has been made that reliefs would remain available.

It may be necessary to consider the interplay of this warranty, if given, with any general provision dealing with liabilities which are the result of events both before and after completion (see, for example, paras 4–12 and 4–13).

5 Unremittable income and capital gains

5.1 The Company has not received or become entitled to income which is   **5–26** **"unremittable income" within the meaning of CTA 2009 s.1274 (Unremittable income: introduction) (formerly ICTA 1988 s.584) or a gain to which TCGA 1992 s.279 (Foreign assets: delayed remittances) could apply [and which has not been remitted to the United Kingdom].**

Income is unremittable for the purposes of s.1274 if it cannot be brought to the United Kingdom, because of the laws of the territory in which the income has arisen, executive action of the government of that territory or the impossibility of obtaining foreign currency in the territory. In those circumstances, the taxpayer may apply by notice, given before the relevant assessment has become final and conclusive, for the United Kingdom tax liability on the income to be held over until it becomes remittable. TCGA 1992 s.279 applies similar rules in relation to chargeable gains accruing from the disposal of assets in foreign territories where the gains cannot be remitted.

The purchaser will wish to ensure not only that it is notified of any claims which have been made, and which therefore give rise to a contingent liability when remittance occurs or could occur, but also that claims have been made where the legislation permits them. The vendors may wish to qualify the warranty by the words in square brackets to cover cases where claims were made in the past but the gains were subsequently remitted and the tax paid. It will also be noted that the warranty effectively relates not only to cases where claims have been made but also to circumstances where they could have been made. The vendors may wish to restrict the clause so that they merely warrant that no claims have been made.

If the vendors accept that the warranty applies to cases where there is an unexercised right to make a claim, they should, in the case of a target company which has overseas business activities, ensure that any extension of the warranties to completion does not cover this part of the clause.

6 Tax avoidance

5–27 **6.1 The Company has not, since the Balance Sheet Date, engaged in, or been a party to, a scheme or arrangement of which the main purpose, or one of the main purposes, was the avoidance of, or a reduction in liability to, Taxation.**

While it might be possible for the vendors to satisfy themselves as to whether or not the target company has engaged in transactions intended to avoid taxation, they would not normally be able to give a warranty in relation to a reduction of tax liability. Many ordinary commercial transactions are structured in a way that will minimise the taxation impact and it would be reasonable for the vendors to require the purchaser to specify the circumstances in which it is interested. The warranty is particularly dangerous as a result of the very wide definition of "Taxation" adopted by para.4–02. The sections listed in cl.6.2 can be argued to deal comprehensively with all relevant anti-avoidance legislation and to provide the purchaser with adequate protection.

5–28 **6.2 The Company has not been a party to, or otherwise involved in, a transaction to which any of the following could apply:**

ICTA 1988 s.56 (Transactions in deposits with and without certificates or in debts);

CTA 2010 s.52 (Dealing in commodity futures) (formerly ICTA 1988 s.399);
CTA 2010 s.53 (Leasing contracts and company reconstructions) s.154 (Arrangements for transfer of group of companies etc.) s.960 (Restrictions on use of reliefs) and s.961 (Non-trading profit and losses) (formerly ICTA 1988 ss.395, 410 and 116);
CTA 2010 Pt 16 Ch.1 (Transfers of Income Streams);
CTA 2010 Pt 16 Chs 2 and 3 (Finance Arrangements);
CTA 2010 Pt 17 Chs 2 to 4 (Manufactured Dividends);
CTA 2009 Pt 6 Ch.10 (Repos);
CTA 2010 ss.710 and 713 (Recovery of Unpaid Corporation Tax) (formerly ICTA 1988 s.767A);
ICTA 1988 s.774 (Transactions between dealing company and associated company);
CTA 2010 ss.834–848 (formerly ICTA 1988 s.779) (Payments connected with transferred land);
CTA 2010 ss.870–886 (Leased Assets: Capital Sums) (formerly ICTA 1988 s.781);
CAA 2001 Pt 2, Ch.17, ss.218, 221–224, 232(1), 241–243 or 246(1) (Anti Avoidance);
CAA 2001 s.5 (When capital expenditure is incurred); and
TCGA 1992 s.29 (Value shifting: General provisions).

The following gives a brief indication of the scope of the provisions listed in this warranty.

(a) ICTA 1988 s.56: this section taxes as income the profit on the disposal of deposits unless the property is taxable as a trading receipt.

(b) CTA 2010 s.52: this section counteracts certain artificial arrangements for obtaining tax relief by dealing in commodities, financial futures or traded options.

(c) CTA 2010 ss.53, 154, 960, 961: this series of anti-avoidance provisions prevents the surrender of group relief where there is a partnership of companies and one partner receives a benefit in relation to its share of the losses of the partnership (ss.960 and 961), where leasing contracts may be transferred (s.53) or where arrangements exist which could cause a group structure to be broken (s.154).

(d) CTA 2010 Pt 16, Ch.1: this relates to the sale of the income from a security without the security itself being sold (other than under a sale and repurchase contract).

(e) CTA 2010 Pt 16, Chs 2 and 3: this relates to financing arrangements which in substance equate to loans but are structured in such a way as to give tax relief in respect of repayment of the principal as well as interest.

(f) CTA 2010 Pt 17, Chs 2 to 4: where there is a transfer of securities and one party pays to the other an amount representing a dividend both parties are taxed as though it were a payment of dividend.

(g) CTA 2010 Pt 6, Ch.10: this treats certain sale and repurchase contracts which in substance are secured loans as loans.

(h) CTA 2010 ss.710 and 713: this section is briefly summarised in the commentary on cl.4.3. The purpose of the provision is to prevent the abuse arising from the purchase of companies with tax losses which could be used to shelter the profits of the purchaser, followed by the extraction of funds from the loss making company. Although the reduction of the assets of the company will have taken place quite properly, the effect would be to leave the company without any funds to discharge the tax liability arising from the transaction if HMRC were to be successful in challenging its effectiveness.

(i) ICTA 1988 s.774: where there are transactions between a dealing company and an associated company which is not a dealing company, certain deductions, which are allowed for the dealing company but would otherwise not be taxed in the hands of the associated company, will be treated as taxable income of the associated company.

(j) CTA 2010 ss.834 et seq.: this limits the tax deduction allowed in relation to a sale and leaseback transaction to a commercial rent for the premises.

(k) CTA 2010 ss.870 et seq.: this section applies where a tax deduction is available in respect of payments under a lease of an asset and the payer receives a capital sum under the lease or the lessor's interest belongs to an associate of the payer who has received the capital sum.

(l) CAA 2001 Pt II, Ch.17: qualifying expenditure for the purposes of claiming writing down allowances can be restricted by anti-avoidance provisions where, in particular, sale and leaseback transactions occur.

(m) CAA 2001 s.5: capital expenditure is treated as incurred when the obligation to pay becomes unconditional. If, however, the obligation arises on a date earlier than that which accords with normal commercial usage and the sole or main benefit of the arrangement was to ensure that the capital allowances were available in an earlier period, the relevant date is the date for payment and not the date of obligation.

(n) TCGA 1992 s.29: a disposal occurs for capital gains tax purposes where a person exercises control to pass value out of shares in a company into other shares in the company.

The vendors should be cautious about accepting any liability in relation to the matters covered by this warranty. Many of the sections will clearly not apply to normal trading companies and should be deleted. Those sections which could, in the particular circumstances of the target company, have some relevance should be retained only if the terms of the sale are such that it is fair for the vendors to accept the risk of liabilities arising.

6.3 The Company has not, since the Balance Sheet Date, been a party to   5–29
a transaction to which any of the following provisions have been, or could
be, applied other than transactions in respect of which all necessary consents
or clearances were obtained:

> **CTA 2010 ss.731–751 (Transactions in Securities) (formerly ICTA 1988**
> **ss.703–709;**
> **ICTA 1988 s.765 (Migration, etc., of companies);**
> **CTA 2010 ss.815–833 (Transactions in Land) (formerly ICTA 1988**
> **s.776 Transactions in land: taxation of capital gains);**
> **TCGA 1992 ss.135–138 (Company reconstructions); or**
> **TCGA 1992 s.139 (Reconstruction involving transfer of business).**

The above sections all relate to anti-avoidance measures and provide clearance procedures. They are of necessity extremely complex and the following is only a very broad summary of their scope:

(a) CTA 2010 ss.731–751: this is a very onerous group of provisions which enables tax advantages arising from transactions in securities to be counteracted. Clearances may be obtained under s.748.

(b) ICTA 1988 s.765: it was a criminal offence for a United Kingdom resident company to permit the issue of shares or debentures by, or to transfer shares or debentures of, a non-resident subsidiary of a United Kingdom resident company, unless Treasury consent was obtained. This has been repealed for transactions on or after July 1, 2009.

(c) CTA 2010 ss.815–833: this relates to transactions involving a disposal of assets representing the value of land where a capital gain would otherwise arise. There is a limited right to obtain a clearance under s.831.

(d) TCGA 1992 ss.135–138: these sections provide roll-over relief for capital gains tax purposes where there is a reconstruction. Clearance can be obtained under s.138.

(e) TCGA 1992 s.139: the purpose of s.139 is to disregard for taxation purposes a reconstruction which involves the transfer of the whole or part of a company's business to another company for a consideration involving only the transfer of liabilities. The section will not apply, however, if the reconstruction was effected otherwise than for bona fide commercial reasons or with a view to avoiding tax. Subsection (5) provides that a clearance may be obtained under s.138 (Procedure for clearance in advance).

Although these anti-avoidance provisions are widely drawn, particularly those contained in ss.731–751 and ss.815–833, the vendors should generally be in a position to determine whether the warranty can be given. If, however, there is any doubt as to whether any of the sections apply, it would be appropriate for the vendors to make a full disclosure and for the purchaser to be required to assess the likelihood of an infringement having occurred.

7 Depreciatory transactions and value shifting

5–30   **7.1 No allowable loss, which may accrue on the disposal of an asset by the Company, is likely to be reduced by reason of TCGA 1992 s.176 (Depreciatory transactions within a group) or s.177 (Dividend stripping).**

Section 176 of TCGA 1992 relates to depreciatory transactions within a group where a disposal of assets takes place at less than market value. If the effect of the transaction is to reduce the value of the shares of the company, any allowable loss for capital gains tax purposes occurring on a disposal of the shares within the following six years will be reduced by an amount reflecting the depreciatory transaction. Section 177 extends this concept to dividend stripping where a dividend is paid and, as a result, a loss would arise on a disposal of the shares in the company paying the dividend.

The only effect of those sections in the present context is to restrict the allowable loss that would otherwise occur. While in principle it would seem fair that the purchaser should not suffer if the sections apply, nevertheless the vendors might reasonably argue that, unless the arrangements relating to the sale of the target company specifically envisaged that allowable losses would occur on disposals of assets, the purchaser will not suffer if an allowable loss is restricted.

5–31   **7.2 No chargeable gain or allowable loss arising on a disposal by the Company is likely to be adjusted under TCGA 1992 s.30 (Tax-free benefits).**

Section 30 provides for an adjustment to the consideration received on a disposal of an asset where an arrangement exists whereby the value of the asset has been materially reduced and the person disposing of it receives a tax-free benefit. Under s.30(2), where a parent company disposes of shares in a subsidiary a reduction in the value of certain assets other than those shares may be taken into account in determining the chargeable gain or allowable loss arising on the disposal. The relevant assets are those owned by a member of the parent's group and the circumstances must be such that their reduction in value causes a material decrease in the value of the shares.

This provision is of a narrow scope and, provided the vendors carefully review any transactions which might fall within this section, they should have no difficulty in agreeing the warranty. Nevertheless, the vendors might reasonably consider that the warranty should apply only in so far as s.30 gives rise to an increased chargeable gain and not to a reduction in an allowable loss.

5–32   **7.3 No reduction in the value of the shares of the Company has occurred as a result of:**

7.3.1 **the payment of a dividend after March 13, 1989 out of chargeable profits within the meaning of TCGA 1992 s.31 (Distributions within a group followed by a disposal of shares) as extended by TCGA 1992 s.31A (Asset-holding company leaving the group); or**

7.3.2 **a transfer of an asset in circumstances within TCGA 1992 s.32(2) (Disposals within a group followed by a disposal of shares).**

Section 31 provides that the provisions referred to in cl.7.2 apply where there is a group dividend and the dividend is paid out of "chargeable profits", being primarily accounting profits which are non-taxable because they result from either an intra-group transfer or a re-valuation of assets.

Section 31 does not apply unless the asset with enhanced value is no longer owned, immediately after the disposal, by the company that has made the disposal or by an associated company of it. TCGA 1992 s.31A provides for a charge to tax if, at any time within the six years following the first disposal of the asset, the company owning the asset in question leaves the group of which it was a member at the time of the disposal or ceases to be a 75 per cent subsidiary, or an effective 75 per cent subsidiary, of a member of that group.

Section 32 applies the value shifting rules to a sale of shares where the value of the shares has been reduced by an intra-group transfer of an asset for a consideration which is less than both market value and original cost. The section does not apply if the transfer was for bona fide commercial reasons and not as part of a scheme to avoid tax.

This warranty will only be material in circumstances where the target company has subsidiaries and will be relevant on a disposal of the target company's shares in a subsidiary. In such circumstances the vendors will be entitled to resist the warranty if either the purchase price for the target company has not been determined with regard to the potential tax liability if a subsidiary is sold off or no disposal of any subsidiaries is contemplated.

8 Disallowance of deductions

8.1 No rents, interest, annual payments or other sums of an income nature paid, or payable, since the Balance Sheet Date by the Company or which the Company is under an obligation to pay are, or may be, wholly or partially disallowable as deductions in computing profits or as charges on income, for the purposes of corporation tax. 5–33

The purpose of this provision is to protect the purchaser against unexpected circumstances in which the profits of the target company earned since the balance sheet date and shown, for example, in interim or management accounts are less than the taxable profits because of the disallowance of deductions. It also covers the possibility that there are payments to be made under a contractual liability which it might reasonably expect to be, but which in the event are not, deductible for taxation purposes. The warranty is restricted to payments made after the balance sheet date as earlier payments are adequately covered by other warranties, such as cl.2.1.2.7 in para.7–39.

The provisions which are most likely to be relevant are as follows.

(a) CTA 2009 s.54: this sets out the basic rule that expenses are not deductible unless wholly and exclusively for the purposes of the trade. The following sections deal with various specific items incurred.

(b) CTA 2009 s.1301: an anti-avoidance provision intended to attack the so-called reverse annuity schemes. An annual payment is deductible only if the consideration for which it is made is taxable as income.

(c) TIOPA 2010 Pt 6 (formerly s.770A and Sch.28AA ICTA): provides for the substitution of market prices for actual prices where transactions take place on non-arm's length terms between parties, one of whom participates in the management, control or capital of both. Such participation may be direct or indirect. It will normally result in an increase in the amount treated as received but might occasionally give rise to a reduction.

(d) CTA 2010 s.838: if land is subject to a sale and lease-back, the rent is not deductible to the extent that it exceeds a commercial amount.

(e) CTA 2010 ss.874 et seq.: if a trader makes deductible payments for the use of an asset leased to him, any capital sum received by him under the lease will be taxed under Sch.D, Case VI to the extent of the deduction.

(f) CTA 2009 Pt 5, Ch.15: this contains anti-avoidance provisions under the loan relationship rules whereby certain deductions are not allowed in specified circumstances, including where the loan relationship has an unallowable purpose and where interest is artificially high.

While this warranty is unlikely to require substantial disclosure for most companies, care is needed, particularly in relation to s.54 as often companies will have some expenditure which is non-deductible on general principles such as entertainment expenditure. Accordingly vendors will sometimes seek to exclude small items of expenditure from the scope of this warranty to reduce the burden of disclosure.

9 Transactions not at arm's length

5–34 **9.1 The Company has not [since the Balance Sheet Date] carried out, or been engaged in, a transaction or arrangement to which TIOPA 2010 Pt 4 (Transfer Pricing) (formerly ICTA 1988 s.770A and Sch.28AA) has been or may be applied.**

TIOPA 2010 Pt 4 applies to transactions on non-arm's length terms between persons, one of whom participates in the management, control or capital of the other, or where the same person or persons participate in the management, control or capital of both. Such participation may be direct or indirect. The term "transactions" is very broadly defined. It includes arrangements, understandings and mutual practices, whether or not intended to be legally enforceable. There can be a series of transactions between two persons even if, for example, there is no transaction to which both those persons are parties. Under corporation tax self-assessment there is a risk of substantial penalties in this area.

There is a broad exemption for small and medium sized enterprises. Taxpayers can make Advance Pricing Agreements with HMRC to secure confidence as to the tax treatment of their pricing policies (TIOPA ss.218–230). The transfer pricing rules also affect excessive debt financing of companies which was previously dealt with by thin capitalisation rules. All adjustments made under the transfer pricing rules are made in the self assessment tax returns of the taxpayers involved (both sides of the transaction) and the usual penalties apply for fraud or negligence in completing those returns.

This is a wide warranty but in principle there is no reason, under corporation tax self-assessment, why this warranty should not be given. It would be reasonable for the vendors to limit this clause to events after the balance sheet date, as earlier transactions will be effectively covered by a warranty such as cl.2.1.2.7 in para.7–39.

9.2 The Company has not disposed of or acquired an asset in such circumstances that TCGA 1992 s.17 (Disposals and acquisitions treated as made at market value) could apply.   5–35

The basic effect of s.17 is to substitute market value for the actual consideration where an asset is acquired or disposed of otherwise than by a bargain made at arm's length unless there was no corresponding disposal (as where shares of a company are subscribed).

As regards assets acquired, the vendors may argue that the purchaser's only interest is to ensure there is no unexpected tax charge on the disposal of the assets on the basis that the acquisition cost for capital gains tax purposes is less than the cost appearing in the last accounts. This is already covered by the warranty set out at cl.21.1 and similar considerations to the ones detailed there will apply.

10 Disallowance of losses

10.1 There has not been in the past three years a major change in the nature or conduct of the trade or business of the Company such as might prevent the carry forward or back of trading losses or excess management expenses by reason of the application of CTA 2010 s.674 (Disallowance of trading losses) (formerly ICTA 1988 ss.768 and 768A) or CTA 2010 ss.679 to 684 (Restrictions on relief) (formerly ICTA 1988 s.768B).   5–36

The sections referred to in this warranty are among several provisions of the tax legislation where the concept of a major change in the nature or conduct of a trade or business is relevant. The effect of the sections referred to is as follows:

(a) CTA 2010 s.674(1): restricts the carry back of losses to an earlier accounting period under CTA 2010 s.37 (Relief for trade losses against total profits) and s.42 (Ring fence trade: further extension of period of relief) if, in any period of three years, there is both a change in the ownership of the company and a major change in the nature or conduct of its trade.

(b) CTA 2010 s.674(2): this applies a restriction in relation to the carry forward of a trading loss under s.45 (carry forward of trade loss against subsequent trade profits) in the same circumstances.

(c) CTA 2010 ss.679–684: this prevents excess management expenses from a period before the change of ownership being deducted in determining the taxable profits for a later period if, in a period of six years beginning three years before the change in ownership, there is both a change in the ownership of the company and a major change in the nature or conduct of its trade.

The vendors should resist giving this warranty unless the negotiations relating to the sale of the target company have taken into account the availability of losses. If the vendors do agree to the clause, they should bear in mind that the loss of the relief may be the result of a gradual series of events taking place over the period spanning the sale of the shares. The vendors would therefore wish to confine the warranty to a loss of relief which is solely attributable to events occurring prior to completion and to replace "might" with "will". Furthermore, it may be desirable to include a specific provision as to how the purchaser's loss in the event of a disallowance is to be computed (see para.3–06).

11 Loan relationships

5–37   **11.1 The Company is not a party to a loan relationship (within the meaning of CTA 2009 s.302 "loan relationship", "creditor relationship", "debtor relationship") formerly FA 1996 s.81):**

     11.1.1   **where there is or was previously a connected companies relationship between the parties as defined in CTA 2009 s.348 (Introduction: meaning of "connected companies relationship");**

     11.1.2   **to which CTA 2009 s.444 (Transactions not at arm's length: general) applies or may apply;**

     11.1.3   **to which CTA 2009 Pt 6, Ch.6A (Shares accounted for as liabilities) or Ch.7 (Shares with guaranteed returns etc.) applies.**

In general, loan relationships are treated for tax purposes in the same way as they are treated in accordance with generally accepted accounting practice—CTA 2009 s.307(2). The purchaser will want to know of any loan relationship where the tax treatment does not necessarily follow the accounting treatment. This warranty identifies three particular areas:

(a) CTA 2009 s.349: this provides that where there is a connection between the parties loans must be accounted for on an amortised cost basis. Connection is, in outline, determined by reference to control.

(b) CTA 2009 s.444: this substitutes arm's length terms for transactions not on arm's length terms, subject to certain exceptions.

(c) CTA 2009 Pt 6 Chs 6A and 7: this deals with shares which have the characteristics of a loan.

In general, the vendors should be aware of any such situations and be able to disclose details of them against these warranties and so will not usually have an issue with giving the warranties.

11.2 The Company is not subject to a restriction as to the amount of the   5–38
loss that it may bring into account in respect of a loan relationship by virtue
of CTA 2009 s.327 (Disallowance of imported losses etc.).

The purpose of this paragraph is to restrict relief that is available where the losses in question relate to periods when the loan relationship was not subject to United Kingdom taxation. For this purpose, the loss is referable to such a period if the company which is seeking to benefit from the loss would not have been subject to tax on a profit or gain arising from the loan relationship.

The circumstances giving rise to a restriction under this paragraph are sufficiently unusual that the vendors should be fully aware if the paragraph could apply. Nevertheless, it would be reasonable for them, as an alternative to giving a warranty, to make a full disclosure of the circumstances and to leave it to the purchaser to evaluate the potential exposure. In any case, unless the purchase has been negotiated on the basis that the purchaser is expecting to benefit from the availability of the losses arising from the relationship, it is unlikely that the purchaser would suffer any loss as a result of the restriction being applied.

11.3 The Company has not acquired or disposed of rights or liabilities in   5–39
respect of a loan relationship where the company from which it made the
acquisition or to which it made the disposal was a member of the same group
of companies within the meaning of CTA 2009 s.336 (Transfer of loans on
group transactions).

If the rights or liabilities under a loan relationship are transferred within a group, the transaction is ignored for the purposes of the loan relationship legislation. The transferee company takes over the entitlement to debits and credits arising from the relationship.

Accordingly, if the target company has been a party to the transfer of a loan relationship, the taxation treatment might work unfairly so far as it is concerned. A disposing company may have incurred tax liabilities without receiving these subsequent taxation benefits and the converse may occur where there is the acquisition of the debt. The purchaser is entitled to be informed of circumstances where a transaction has occurred which could give rise to disadvantages to the target company under this paragraph but the vendors may reasonably feel that, if such transaction has occurred, the correct way to deal with any potential problems is for a disclosure to be made to the purchaser which can then evaluate the potential tax risk.

5–40   **11.4 The Company has not been a party to a loan relationship which had an unallowable purpose within the meaning of CTA 2009 s.442 (meaning of "unallowable purpose").**

This is an anti-avoidance provision which deals with cases where the purposes for which a loan relationship was entered into included a purpose which was not among the business or commercial purposes of the company. If the paragraph applies, the effect is to exclude relief for debits which result from the transaction.

This paragraph gave rise to considerable debate at the time it was enacted. Even though the final form of the provision is much narrower than was originally proposed, it is still uncertain in its scope and exposes borrowers to risk of non-deduction. Whether this risk should be borne by the vendors or the purchaser is a matter for negotiation between them.

12 Distributions

5–41   **12.1 The Company has not repaid, or agreed to repay, or redeemed, or agreed to redeem, any of its shares, or capitalised, or agreed to capitalise, in the form of redeemable shares or debentures, any profits or reserves.**

Repayments of share capital are treated as distributions under CTA 2010 s.1000(1)B (meaning of "distribution") to the extent of any premium over the amount paid up on the shares. A bonus issue of redeemable share capital or securities is treated as a distribution under CTA 2010 s.1000(1)C. If a company has repaid share capital since April 6, 1965, and subsequently issues new shares by way of bonus, the amount treated as paid up on the new shares is, to the extent of the capital repayment, treated as a distribution (CTA 2010 s.1022 (Bonus issue following repayment of share capital treated as distribution)). The provisions relating to bonus issues do not apply after a period of ten years except in the case of closely held companies or where redeemable share capital is involved (CTA 2010 ss.1023(1) and 1026(3)).

5–42   **12.2 No security, within the meaning of CTA 2010 s.1117 ("Other Interpretation") of the Company was issued in such circumstances that the interest payable on it, or any other payment in respect of it, falls to be treated as a distribution under CTA 2010 s.1000 (meaning of "distribution").**

A security comes within the definition contained in CTA 2010 s.1117 even if no security is created or evidenced by it. Various circumstances are specified in s.1000 as a result of which interest and other payments on securities are treated as a distribution. In particular, the consideration given for the use of the principal money secured is a distribution to the extent that it exceeds a reasonable commercial return.

12.3 The Company has not received a capital distribution to which TCGA   **5–43**
1992 s.189 (Capital distribution of chargeable gains: recovery of tax from
shareholder) could apply.

Section 189 has a limited impact as it relates to capital distributions by a company which are not treated as income of the recipient. There are few such distributions which are not caught by (meaning of "distribution"). The effect of s.189 is that, if the target company has received a capital distribution from a connected company which represents the proceeds of a disposal giving rise to a chargeable gain, then corporation tax on the chargeable gain of the distributing company may be recovered from the target company to the extent that the gain is represented by the distribution. As the target company has a statutory right of reimbursement, it is questionable whether the vendors should ever be expected to accept this liability unless the distributing company is one which is controlled by them. In any event, the vendors should provide that the target company should pursue its right of recovery and, in an appropriate case, assign the benefit of it to the vendors (see para.11–12).

13 Close companies

13.1 The Company is not, nor was it at any time during the six years ended   **5–44**
on the Balance Sheet Date, a close company as defined in CTA 2010 s.439
("Close Company") (formerly ICTA 1988 s.414).

The purchaser will wish to be satisfied that the target company does not have any outstanding liabilities attributable to a period of close company status. If the warranty can be given in this simple form, it will avoid the necessity for more detailed warranties covering the specific provisions relating to close companies. If this warranty is not appropriate, the alternative warranties set out in the following clauses will have to be considered.

13.2 No distribution within CTA 2010 s.1064 (Certain expenses of close   **5–45**
companies treated as distribution) (formerly ICTA 1988 s.418) has been
made by the Company [since the Balance Sheet Date].

Section 1064 treats as a distribution by a close company expenses incurred in providing benefits in kind for participators and their associates which are not otherwise taxed. The value of the benefits will be non-deductible for taxation purposes. If the clause is accepted by the vendors, they should consider restricting its application to an appropriate period, such as the broken period following the balance sheet date.

This clause will rarely apply, as the benefit will normally be taxable as income of the recipient under IT(EP)A 2003 Pt 3 (Employment Income: Earning and benefits, etc. treated as earnings). As any liability which does not arise will be attributable to benefits which have been enjoyed by participators in the target company, it is difficult for the vendors to resist the warranty. It may, however, be appropriate for the vendors to agree among themselves that, if the liability is attributable to the benefits received by one of them, he alone should be responsible for liability under the warranty (see para.3–15).

5–46   **13.3 No loan or advance within CTA 2010 Pt 10, Ch.3 (Charge to tax in case of loan to participator) (formerly ICTA 1988 Pt XI, Ch.II) has been made [and remains outstanding], or agreed to, by the Company [and the Company has not, since the Balance Sheet Date, released or written off the whole or part of the debt in respect of such a loan or advance].**

Chapter 3 comprises ss.455–464. A loan by a close company to an individual who is a participator or his associate, otherwise than in the ordinary course of a lending business, gives rise to a tax charge equal to 25 per cent of the loan under s.455 (Charge to tax in case of loan to participants). The tax is recoverable when the loan is repaid or if the debt in respect of the loan is written off.

Although the section primarily relates to loans to individuals, it is extended to apply also to loans made to companies in a fiduciary capacity (s.55(6)). Indirect loans are covered by s.459. Section 460 (Loan treated as made by close company) is an anti-avoidance provision which prevents s.455 being circumvented by indirect loans through controlled companies. If the debt attributable to a loan or advance which falls within s.455 is to any extent released or written off, the amount released or written off is treated as income of the debtor under s.463 (Taxation of debtor on release of loan to trustees of settlement which has ended) or, in the case of individuals, s.415 of the Income Tax (Trading and Other Income) Act 2005. If that is relevant, the additional words in brackets should be added to the warranties to flush out any relevant transactions.

The vendors cannot reasonably resist giving this warranty, but they should consider the desirability of an agreement between themselves that, where the offending loan has been enjoyed by only one of the vendors, or his associates, he should bear the ultimate responsibility for the warranty (see para.3–15). Furthermore, a provision should be inserted in the sale agreement requiring the purchaser to make a refund if and when the tax is recovered on the repayment of the loan.

The part of the warranty relating to the release or writing-off of the debt is, however, irrelevant to the purchaser as the resulting tax liability falls only upon the debtor.

It should be noted that the purchaser will not in fact be prejudiced if the loan was made at a date prior to the balance sheet date as any tax payment will have been made or shown as a liability. The right of recovery of the tax paid will thus constitute a windfall benefit for the purchaser, unless it has been specifically taken into account. Far from warranting that no such loan has been made, the vendors may wish to provide that they alone should benefit as and when the tax recovery is received. Different principles will apply if the loan was made after the balance sheet date, since the payment of tax under the section will not then have been apparent to the purchaser.

14 Sale and leaseback of land

14.1 The Company has not, since the Balance Sheet Date, entered into a   5–47
transaction to which the provisions of CTA 2010 ss.850 to 862 (New Lease of
Land after assignment or surrender (formerly ICTA 1988 s.780)) have been,
or could be, applied.

The effect of ss.850–862 is to tax as income part of the sale consideration received where a short lease, having less than 50 years to run, is sold on a leaseback for a term not exceeding 15 years. The warranty is restricted to transactions occurring after the balance sheet date as any earlier transaction will be shown in the tax provision. In these circumstances, the vendors should have no difficulty in agreeing to the warranty.

15 Intangible Assets

Legislation contained in CTA 2009 Pt 8 (formerly FA 2002 Sch.29) treats   5–48
expenditure on the creation or acquisition of intellectual property fixed assets as revenue expenditure if it is treated as such in the target company's profit and loss account. Research and development expenditure is specifically excluded.

FRS 10 generally requires expenditure on intangible assets to be written off when incurred when it is expenditure on internally generated intellectual property. Internally generated intellectual property is therefore rarely capitalised. In these circumstances a tax deduction normally arises in the accounting period in which the expenditure is written off (s.728). For many companies, therefore, the warranties will be of little relevance. For other companies the warranties may be very important and, in such circumstances, additional warranties to the ones here should be considered.

15.1 No election has been made by the Company pursuant to CTA 2009   5–49
s.730 (Writing down at fixed rate: election for fixed rate basis) (formerly FA
2002 Sch.29, para.10).

An intangible fixed asset can be written down for tax purposes on either an accounting basis or, if an election is made, on a fixed-rate basis (CTA 2009 s.726). This warranty is an information gathering warranty to allow the purchaser to determine the future tax position of the target company. As it is a matter of fact whether an election has been made, the vendors should in principle not have any objection to it.

15.2 The Company has not made any claim for relief under CTA 2009   5–50
ss.754 to 763 (Rollover relief in case of realisation and reinvestment)
(formerly FA 2002 Sch.29, Pt 7).

CTA 2009 ss.754–763 allows for profits on the sale of intangible fixed assets to be rolled over into new intangible fixed assets in certain circumstances. The effect of a rollover will be to reduce the cost for tax purposes of the acquisition of the new asset. The purchaser will want to know that the cost as stated in the accounts in respect of intangible fixed assets is the same as the tax cost. Generally the vendors should be aware of this and able to give the warranty, however they may object on the grounds that it is not envisaged that the intangible fixed assets will be disposed in circumstances where that is the case.

5–51   **15.3 No intangible fixed asset of the Company was acquired on a tax neutral basis pursuant to CTA 2009 s.775 (Transfers within a group) (formerly FA 2002 Sch.29, para.55).**

CTA 2009 s.775 provides for intra-group transfers to be tax neutral, in a similar way to transfers of capital assets under TCGA s.171. A purchaser will want to know that the accounts cost and the tax cost is the same. Similar considerations apply as in relation to cl.15.2.

5–52   **15.4 No intangible fixed asset of the Company was transferred to the Company by a related party within the meaning of CTA 2009 s.845 (Transfers between company and related party treated as being at market value) (formerly FA 2002 Sch.29, para.92(1)).**

CTA 2009 s.845 treats transfers between related parties (not being members of a group) as being at market value. Similar considerations apply as in relation to cl.15.2.

5–53   **15.5 The Company has not within the last six years acquired any intangible fixed asset from another company at a time when that other company was a member of the group of companies (as defined in CTA 2009 Pt 8, Ch.1) of which the Company is or was within the last six years, a member.**

Although this warranty to some extent covers the same issues as cl.15.3, it serves as a reminder that CTA 2009 s.780 applies a degrouping charge to intangible fixed assets similar to that in TCGA s.179.

16 Group relief and group surrenders

5–54   This section, s.7 and part of s.17 are only relevant when the target company has been or is part of a group of companies. Although this is not expressed to be the case for the target company referred to throughout the book, it was considered useful to include these to cover a group situation. A suitable definition for "Group Companies" might be the Company and Subsidiaries of the Company, "Subsidiary" already having been defined. In certain circumstances it would also be appropriate to include a holding company of the Company in the definition as well.

16.1 The Group Companies comprise a group for the purposes of CTA 2010 s.99 (Surrendering of losses and other amounts) (formerly ICTA 1988 s.402) and there is nothing in CTA 2010 s.154 or s.155 (Arrangements for transfers of companies (formerly ICTA 1988 s.410) which precludes a Group Company from being regarded as a member of the group.   5–55

For group relief purposes, companies comprise a group where there is a common shareholding of not less than 75 per cent of the ordinary share capital (CTA 2009 s.152).

CTA 2009 s.151 (meaning of "75% subsidiary" and "90% subsidiary") lays down requirements for ensuring that a true 75 per cent relationship exists in relation to dividend rights and rights on a winding-up. In determining rights to dividends and on a winding-up, the interests of "equity holders" are taken into account and these include not only shareholders but also certain classes of loan creditors.

Even where a group appears to exist, the anti-avoidance provisions contained in s.154 could result in one or more of the companies being treated as not being members of the group. The provision is extremely complex but broadly operates as follows. If there is an arrangement which could result in one of the companies leaving the group and becoming related to another company, or where a third company takes over the trade of one of the companies, the companies will not be treated as a group from the time of the arrangement. The term "arrangement" is not defined other than to state that it includes "arrangements of any kind (whether in writing or not)" s.156(2). It is clear that arrangements do not need to be legally enforceable (see Inland Revenue Statement of Practice 3/93) but that in the context of negotiations for the disposal of shares, although they do not need to be binding, they must be capable of taking effect, such as a non-binding agreement made subject to contract (see *Scottish and Universal Newspapers Ltd v Fisher (Inspector of Taxes)* [1996] S.T.C.(S.C.D.) 311). Furthermore, if the disposal requires shareholder approval, "arrangements" will not arise until the approval is given or the directors become aware that it will be forthcoming. However, the courts have held that the group relief relationship is broken only for the period while the "arrangements" for the target company to leave the group exist (see *Shepherd (Inspector of Taxes) v Law Land Plc* [1990] S.T.C. 795).

Section 155 applies similar rules for consortium companies. Notwithstanding the difficulties of interpretation which exist in relation to these provisions, the vendors should generally be able to see clearly whether any member of the target company's group of companies may be treated as not being a member of the group for group relief purposes. Care will have to be taken if unusual loans have been made to a member of the target group by a non-member or if there have been any arrangements to sell off one of the members of the group separately from the other members.

Nevertheless, the vendors might reasonably question the appropriateness of giving this warranty to the purchaser unless surrenders of group relief amongst the members of the target group are contemplated.

5–56   **16.2 The Company has not, since the Balance Sheet Date, made or agreed to make, otherwise than to or from another Group Company a surrender of, or claim for, group relief under CTA 2010 Pt 5 (Group Relief) (formerly ICTA 1988 Pt X, Ch.IV).**

A member of a 75 per cent group may surrender its losses to other members of the group, and the losses thus surrendered are deducted from the taxable profits of the claimant companies. Claims for group relief must be made within two years from the end of the surrendering company's accounting period to which the claim relates. It is therefore possible for surrenders or claims to have been made since the balance sheet date in respect of the last two complete accounting periods of the target company.

The purchaser will wish to know about any surrenders or claims since the balance sheet date as these will not necessarily appear in the latest accounts. It should be noted that because of the anti-avoidance provisions of CTA 2010 s.154, referred to above, if the negotiations relating to the sale of the target company commenced prior to the balance sheet date, the actual accounting period will be treated as consisting of two notional periods respectively ending and commencing when the arrangements came into existence. This could prevent a full surrender of group relief for the last accounting period.

5–57   **16.3 No Group Company is liable to make or entitled to receive a payment for group relief otherwise than to or from another Group Company.**

If a company having excess losses is a member of a group and surrenders its losses to another company—the claimant company—it is usual for the claimant company to pay for the surrender. A payment for group relief is disregarded for tax purposes, so long as it does not exceed the amount of the losses surrendered CTA 2010 s.183 (Payments for group relief). A liability or entitlement will be relevant only if it involves a company outside the target group, such as a corporate vendor. If it is the target group which is entitled to receive the payment, the vendors may wish to consider the question of security.

5–58   **16.4 The Company has not made or received a payment for group relief (otherwise than to or from another Group Company), which may be liable to be refunded in whole or in part.**

If a surrender of group relief proves ultimately to be ineffective, perhaps because losses which were thought to exist are not in fact available or because of a defect in the group structure, the surrendering company will normally be required to repay, in whole or in part, the payment made for the surrender. Accordingly, until the surrender has been agreed with HMRC, the surrendering company is contingently liable to make a refund and, if this liability is to a company which is not a member of the target group, the purchaser will wish to know about it. The vendors should have no difficulty with the warranty in relation to payments made or received but may wish to redraft it as follows:

"All claims for group relief by any Group Company either have been agreed with HMRC or are detailed in the Disclosure Letter".

An alternative warranty covering the same point in relation to group relief is:

"All claims for group relief made by each Group Company [(otherwise than as a result of a surrender of group relief by another Group Company)] were valid and have been, or will be, allowed by way of relief from corporation tax".

This wording is likely to be acceptable in so far as it relates to past claims, but the vendors should seek the deletion of "or will be".

16.5 If any member of the Group Company only became a member after the Balance Sheet Date, the apportionment of profits and losses will be made under CTA 2010 ss.138 to 142 (General limitation on amount of group relief given) (formerly ICTA 1988 s.403B) on a time basis according to the respective lengths of the component accounting periods. 5–59

If a member of the target group joined the group after the balance sheet date, there is a restriction under ss.138–142 on the losses that may be surrendered and the profits that may be sheltered in respect of the joining company and any other member of the group. Only a proportion of the losses of the surrendering company may be surrendered and only a proportion of the profits of the claimant company may be sheltered. In each case, the basic rule is that the proportion should be determined on a time apportioned basis according to the fraction of each company's accounting period which overlaps the other. However, s.141(3) provides that, instead of apportionment on a time basis, such other method shall be used as appears just and reasonable, if it appears that time apportionment would work unreasonably or unjustly.

This warranty will, accordingly, be relevant only if there is a member of the target group which became a member after the balance sheet date. Even in that event, the purchaser would not be entitled to the warranty unless it was part of the agreement between the parties that group relief would be surrendered or claimed by the company which joined the target group in respect of the overlapping accounting period.

16.6 The Company is not restricted in relation to the surrendering of group relief by CTA 2010 s.109 (Restriction on losses etc. surrenderable by dual resident) (formerly ICTA 1988 s.404). 5–60

Section 109 is designed to prevent the exploitation of tax losses in more than one jurisdiction ("double-dipping"). A company could be simultaneously resident in two countries because of different criteria adopted by those countries in determining residence. A loss arising in one country could give tax relief in both. As s.109 applies to specific—usually contrived—circumstances of an unusual nature, the vendors will generally know whether the warranty can be given, although they might fairly question why the purchaser should be entitled to it.

5–61   **16.7 The Company has not agreed to surrender, otherwise than to another Group Company, any right to receive a tax refund under CTA 2010 s.963 (Power to surrender tax refund) (formerly FA 1989 s.102).**

Under the pay-and-file system, there is a liability to pay interest on tax underpaid and a corresponding right to receive interest on tax overpaid. As, however, the rate of interest to be paid will be higher than the rate to be received, it may be in the interests of a group to take advantage of s.963, whereby one member of a group will be able to surrender its right to receive a repayment to another member which has underpaid its tax. For a surrender to be made, both companies have to be members of a 75 per cent group, for the purposes of group relief, throughout the relevant accounting period. Notice must be given jointly by both companies specifying the amount of the refund which is to be surrendered. When a valid notice has been given, the recipient company will be treated as having paid an amount of corporation tax for the relevant accounting period equal to the part of the prospective refund which has been surrendered.

This warranty is unlikely to give any difficulty to the parties but will operate as a useful reminder to ensure that the benefit of any refund is properly taken into account when analysing the asset value of the target company.

17 Acquisitions from group members

5–62   **17.1 The Company does not own an asset which was acquired from another company [not being a Group Company], which was, at the time, a member of the same group of companies (as defined in TCGA 1992 s.170 (Groups of companies: interpretation of ss.170–181)) as the relevant Group Company, and which owned that asset otherwise than as trading stock within TCGA 1992 s.173 (Transfers within a group: trading stock).**

Section 170 defines a group as comprising a principal company and its 75 per cent subsidiaries. The specified percentage relates to ordinary share capital as defined in CTA 2010 s.1154, and the group may include non-resident companies.

Where an asset held as a capital asset is transferred between members of a group, the transfer will be deemed to have taken place at the base cost for capital gains tax purposes of the transferor company (TCGA 1992 s.171 (Transfers within a group: general provisions)). If the transferor held the asset as a capital asset and the transferee acquires it as trading stock, then the transferee is entitled to choose either to treat as an immediate chargeable gain an amount equal to the change in value between the date of acquisition by the transferor and the date of transfer or, by election, to avoid the corporation tax liability on the chargeable gain but to have its eventual trading profits or losses computed as if its acquisition cost was equal to the purchase price originally paid by the transferor company (thus creating a no gain/no loss transfer). If the transferee has made the election in circumstances where the asset has increased in value, thereby having avoided an immediate liability to tax at the cost of a deferred but potentially greater liability, the company will have a hidden additional liability to taxation against which the purchaser is entitled to the benefit of a warranty. If, on the other hand, the asset has decreased in value when the transfer takes place, the election may convert what would otherwise be a capital loss into a more flexible trading loss. Since April 1, 2000 a transfer of an asset between two members of a group has been a no gain/no loss transfer only if the relevant asset is, and as a result of the transfer remains, within the scope of United Kingdom corporation tax. Significantly, the incorporation of a United Kingdom branch of a non-resident company which is achieved by the transfer of the assets of the branch to a United Kingdom resident subsidiary company in exchange for an issue of new shares by the United Kingdom subsidiary to the non-resident company, will be treated as a no gain/no loss transfer. Consequently, TCGA 1992 s.172, under which it was possible to elect for such treatment, has been repealed. The current regime, however, allows no right of election, and as a result the incorporation of a branch in the manner described will always potentially give rise to a degrouping charge if the United Kingdom subsidiary subsequently leaves the group.

The vendors cannot reasonably resist giving this warranty but it may be difficult to ensure that no assets are held by a member of the target group which were not originally acquired from another company which was previously in the same group. The vendors may accordingly prefer to insert the bracketed words which exclude from the warranty transfers between members of the target group, although the purchaser will wish to know about group transfers so that it can avoid inadvertently triggering a liability under TCGA 1992 s.179 (Company ceasing to be member of group: post-appointed day cases), as described in relation to cl.17.2. The vendors may reasonably consider that, in the absence of special circumstances, the purchaser is nevertheless not entitled to the protection of a warranty.

17.2 The execution or completion of this Agreement will not result in profit or gain being deemed to accrue to the Company for Taxation purposes, whether under TCGA 1992 s.179 (Company ceasing to be member of group: post-appointed day cases) or otherwise. 5–63

The effect of s.179 is to impose a liability to corporation tax on chargeable gains where a company, which has acquired a capital asset from another group company, ceases to be a member of the same group while still owning the asset. The company leaving the group is treated as having, immediately it left, disposed of and reacquired the asset at its then market value. The section applies only if the ending of the group structure occurs within six years of the transfer of the asset. The degrouping charge will generally operate so as to claw back relief given in respect of intra-group no gain/no loss transfers within the previous six years. However, the relevant asset need not be transferred to the company leaving the group by way of intra-group transfer, and it will be sufficient that the transferee company leaves the same group of which the transferor company was a member at the time of transfer.

This warranty will not normally be relevant, unless there is a corporate vendor, as the sections do not apply if the transferor and transferee of the asset are both members of the target group.

The words "or otherwise" which appear at the end of this warranty may need special consideration. The purchaser will wish to include these words to cover any possible liability which might arise by a termination of the group structure, such as contractual arrangements between one or more members of the vendor group which come to an end on the sale of the target company and which, by so doing, give rise to tax liability. These circumstances would be quite exceptional and it would not be possible for the purchaser to know of the circumstances unless they were specifically disclosed to it. The vendors, however, should reasonably be expected to be aware of any taxation implications which can arise by virtue of any unusual arrangements which exist between the target company and other companies.

The vendors should take account of the possibility that, owing to the wide definition of "Taxation" in para.4–02, a liability could arise in an overseas jurisdiction.

18 Demergers and purchase of own shares

5–64   **18.1 The Company has not been engaged in, or been a party to, any of the transactions set out in CTA 2010 ss.1073–1099 (Demergers) (formerly ICTA 1988 ss.213–218) nor has it made or received a chargeable payment as defined in CTA 2010 s.1088 (meaning of "chargeable payment") (formerly ICTA 1988 s.214).**

Sections 1073–1099 provide for certain types of demergers to be exempt from treatment as distributions. Essentially, exempt distributions are those arising from a transfer by a company to its members of the shares of one or more of its 75 per cent subsidiaries or the transfer by a company of its trade, or of one or more of its 75 per cent subsidiaries to another company in exchange for shares issued to its members. Exemption will be lost if within five years there is a chargeable payment, namely a non-taxable payment, made in connection with its shares otherwise than for bona fide commercial reasons. Provision is made for obtaining advance clearance (see also cl.1.2).

If a demerger has occurred to which the sections apply, the vendors should be able to argue that they should nevertheless not be liable for any tax resulting from the demerger or a subsequent chargeable payment as the purchaser, being aware of the transaction by reason of disclosure, would be able to ensure that no liability subsequently occurred.

5–65   **18.2 The Company has not redeemed, repaid or purchased or agreed to redeem, repay or purchase, any of its own shares.**

CTA 2010 ss.1033–1043 (Purchase of own shares) provide that a purchase of its own shares by an unquoted company which is a trading company or the holding company of a trading group does not give rise to a distribution if the purpose is to benefit the company's trade. Section 1044 (Advance clearance of payments by Commissioners) provides a clearance procedure.

The purchaser will wish to ensure that a purchase of its own shares by the target company was not a distribution giving rise to a liability to advance corporation tax if occurring prior to April 6, 1999. The vendors will normally have the benefit of a clearance in which case the warranty will amount to a representation that the clearance was properly obtained (see cl.1.2). If no clearance was obtained in relation to any of the transactions falling within the warranty, the vendors will need to consider very carefully whether the exemption conditions in ss.1033–1043 were satisfied.

19 Stock dividends

19.1 The Company has not issued share capital to which the provisions of   5–66 CTA 2010 s.1049 (Stock Dividends) (formerly ICTA 1988 s.249) or TCGA s.142 (Capital gains on stock dividends) could apply and the Company does not own any such share capital.

The purpose of s.1049 is to avoid the tax advantages which would otherwise derive from arrangements whereby shareholders, who did not wish to receive unearned income on their shares, were offered the opportunity to take bonus shares in substitution for, and of equal value to, the dividends they would otherwise have received on the shares. Section 1049 effectively treats bonus issues received in this way as taxable income, but only higher rate tax is payable. TCGA 1992 s.142 allows the amount taxed in this way to be treated as expenditure on the bonus shares acquired. As the tax liability affects only individuals, the warranty is substantially irrelevant except in so far as there is an administrative obligation upon the company to make appropriate returns. In view of the curious drafting of s.1049, which could apply to normal bonus issues, the vendors may find it difficult to give the warranty with absolute confidence if the target company has issued bonus shares in the past. As the purchaser will be aware, from its searches and the other warranties, of the capital history of the target company, it should be prepared to accept the risk of s.1049 applying as the only disadvantage relates to the administration involved in making the appropriate returns.

20 Capital allowances

20.1 All expenditure which the Company has incurred or may incur under   5–67 a subsisting commitment on the provision of machinery or plant has qualified or will qualify (if not deductible as a trading expense of a trade carried on by the Company) for writing-down allowances under CAA 2001 Pt 2, Ch.5 (Allowances and charges).

Expenditure on machinery and plant incurred by a person carrying on a trade for the purpose of the trade qualifies for writing-down allowances. These were, prior to April 2008, usually at the rate of 25 per cent of the excess of qualifying expenditure over disposal value for the relevant accounting period. However, first year allowances in excess of this are available on certain types of expenditure, particularly expenditure by small and medium-sized enterprises.

Changes were introduced to the capital allowances regime from April 1, 2008. The principal changes were:

(a) the separate classification of integral fixtures to which a 10 per cent rate applies;

(b) the introduction of a new annual investment allowance;

(c) a reduction in the main rate of allowances on plant and machinery from 25 per cent to 20 per cent; and

(d) an increase in the rate applicable to long life assets from 6 per cent to 10 per cent.

It is currently proposed that as from April 1, 2012:

(a) the main rate of allowances on plant and machinery will reduce to 18 per cent;

(b) the rate on integral fixtures and long life assets will reduce to eight per cent; and

(c) the maximum annual investment allowance will reduce to £25,000.

Special rules which may restrict or exclude the availability of capital allowances apply to lessors, particularly where the lessee is non-resident (CAA 2001 Pt 2, Ch.11 (Overseas Leasing)).

In general, the vendors will be able to accept this warranty unless the target company claims allowances by virtue of being equipment lessors. Nevertheless, unless the availability of allowances has been a factor in settling the purchase price, they might reasonably take the view that they should not be required to guarantee future tax reliefs.

5–68   **20.2 No event has occurred since the Balance Sheet Date which may be treated as a notional sale by the Company of machinery or plant pursuant to CAA 2001 ss.61 (Disposal events and disposal values) or 72 (Disposal values).**

If a company discontinues its trade or sells its equipment at less than market price (unless between connected persons) or the equipment ceases to be used for the purposes of trade, it is deemed to have sold the equipment at market value. Any balancing charge or allowance is determined on that basis. The purchaser is entitled to ensure that tax will not be calculated on the basis of notional rather than actual proceeds and the vendors should readily be able to ascertain if these sections could apply. The warranty can be limited to events since the balance sheet date as the accounts for completed periods should cover any adjustment by an appropriate tax provision.

20.3 No capital allowances made or to be made to the Company in respect   5–69
of capital expenditure already incurred or to be incurred under a subsisting
commitment arise from special leasing (as defined in CAA 2001 s.19) or
qualifying non-trade expenditure (as defined in CAA 2001 s.469) on
patents.

Generally, capital allowances are given effect by allowing them as an expense of
the trade. In the two situations referred to in the clause allowances can only be
set against income from that specific asset. Special leasing is leasing otherwise
than in the course of a qualifying activity and qualifying non-trade expenditure
is expenditure on patents otherwise than for the purposes of a trade.

20.4 Since the Balance Sheet Date the Company has not done, or omitted   5–70
to do, or agreed to do, or permitted to be done, an act as a result of which
a balancing allowance or a balancing charge may be brought into account
for capital allowances purposes, or there may be a recovery of excess relief
under CAA 2001 s.111 (Excess allowances: standard recovery
mechanism).

In general, capital allowances are available on a pool basis. If a company's
qualifying expenditure in an accounting period (being expenditure on which
writing-down allowances arise) is less than the disposal value which is to be
brought into account for that period, a balancing charge arises on the amount of
the difference. A disposal value arises if the equipment ceases to belong to the
company or the company permanently ceases the trade for which the equipment
is used. A different basis applies in relation to short-life assets (essentially those
with a useful life of less than four years) where an election is made under CAA
2001 s.83 (meaning of "short-life asset"). In that event each asset is treated as
comprising a separate pool and a balancing charge or allowance arises on the
disposal of the individual asset.

CAA 2001 s.109 (Assets leased outside the United Kingdom) provides that
assets are eligible for writing-down allowances at the reduced rate of 10 per cent
on machinery and plant if during the requisite period (in this case, 10 years from
when the asset is brought into use) they are let on a long-term basis to foreign
lessors who do not carry on a United Kingdom trade. Excess relief can arise on
assets initially leased in the United Kingdom if, during the requisite period, the
equipment is leased to a non-resident. Section 111 treats the excess as if it were
a balancing charge.

The vendors should normally have no difficulty in knowing if this warranty
would be infringed.

20.5 The Company is not in dispute with any person as to any entitlement   5–71
to capital allowances under CAA 2001 Pt 2, Ch.14 (Fixtures) and at the date
of this Agreement as far as the Vendors are aware there are no
circumstances which might give rise to such a dispute.

CAA 2001 Pt 2, Ch.14 (Fixtures), sets out rules for determining entitlement to
capital allowances on expenditure on fixtures among parties having different

interests in land. As disputes can arise, the tribunal can determine whether or not equipment has become a fixture. The parties affected by the decision are entitled to take part in the hearing.

Although the vendors will generally be in a position to know whether a dispute can arise in relation to claims for allowances on expenditure on fixtures, they may nevertheless consider that, unless the anticipated relief has been a factor in the sale negotiations, the purchaser is not entitled to the protection of this warranty.

21 Base values and acquisition costs

5–72   **21.1 If each of the capital assets of the Company was disposed of at Completion for a consideration equal to its book value in, or adopted for the purpose of, the Accounts, no liability to corporation tax on chargeable gains and, on the assumption that the expenditure on each asset was incurred for the purpose of a separate trade, no balancing charge under CAA 2001 would arise; and, for the purpose of determining the liability to corporation tax on chargeable gains, there shall be disregarded reliefs and allowances available to the Company other than amounts falling to be deducted under TCGA 1992 s.38 (Acquisition and disposal costs etc.).**

TCGA 1992 s.38 defines the categories of allowable expenditure which are deductible in determining the amount of a chargeable gain. The purpose of the last part of this clause is to require deductions which are not allowable expenditure, such as carry-forward losses, to be disregarded in determining whether the disposal would give rise to a chargeable gain.

The value of the capital assets of the target company as shown in its last accounts may exceed the value for capital gains tax or capital allowances purposes, for example because the value has been written up in the books, or because of transfers from connected persons (TCGA 1992 s.18 (Transactions between connected persons)); deemed disposals under s.24 (Disposals where assets lost or destroyed, or become of negligible value); roll-over under ss.126–136 (Reorganisation of share capital, conversion of securities etc.), reconstruction (s.139 (Reconstruction involving transfer of business)); transfers of a trade within s.140 (Postponement of charge on transfer of assets to non-resident company); or group transfers (s.171 (Transfers within a group: general provisions)).

Other relevant provisions are TCGA 1992 s.39 (Exclusion of expenditure by reference to tax on income), which excludes from the allowable expenditure for capital gains tax purposes sums which are deductible as a trading expense; s.42 (Part disposals), which apportions the original expenditure between the part disposed of and the part retained on the occasion of a part disposal; and s.43 (Assets derived from other assets) which provides that an "appropriate proportion" of the allowable expenditure incurred on the original asset shall be treated as having been incurred on a new asset whose value is derived from the original asset. The vendors might fairly require that the indexation allowance, which adjusts the allowable expenditure by changes in the retail prices index under TCGA 1992 s.53 (the indexation allowance and interpretative provisions), should not be disregarded.

Balancing charges arise under CAA 2001 ss.318–320 (Calculation of **5–73** balancing adjustments), in respect of industrial buildings, and under s.56 (Amount of allowances and charges), where machinery or plant in respect of which capital allowances have been obtained are disposed of or cease to be used for trading purposes. The consideration brought into account will be the market value of the equipment or, if there is an arm's length disposal, the proceeds of sale. The warranty will apply if the book value exceeds the balance of qualifying expenditure available for writing-down allowances. Particular care may be required if a target company owns machinery or plant which was acquired from a connected company. In that event, an election may have been made to apply CAA 2001 s.266 (Election where predecessor and successor are connected persons) so that, for capital allowances purposes, the transfer was effectively disregarded.

The vendors should generally have no difficulty, in principle, in checking on the matters covered by this clause, although a substantial amount of work may be involved. They might nevertheless reasonably consider that, unless the sale of the target company was negotiated with regard to the taxation results of a sale of fixed assets, the purchaser is not entitled to the protection of this warranty.

If the purchaser insists on retaining the clause, it might be appropriate to provide that a breach of warranty arises only if an increased liability is incurred on a disposal, within a limited period of perhaps one year, of an asset to which the warranty applied.

21.2 The Company has not made an election under TCGA 1992 s.35 **5–74** **(Assets held on March 31, 1982 (including assets held on April 6, 1965)) for capital gains and losses on all the assets held by it on March 31, 1982 to be computed by reference only to their market value on that date.**

A general rebasing for capital gains tax purposes to March 1982 was introduced in 1988. All the target company's assets will be treated for computing capital gains as if they were sold and reacquired for their market value on that date. Unless the company elects otherwise, rebasing does not take place if it would result in a gain in place of a smaller gain or a loss, or if it would result in a loss and there would otherwise have been a smaller loss or a gain. The election had to be made by April 1990 or within two years of the end of the accounting period in which the first relevant disposal occurs and must relate to all assets which were held in March 1982. An election is irrevocable. In relation to companies within a 75 per cent group, the election may be made only by the principal company (TCGA 1992 Sch.3, para.8 (Elections under s.35(5): group of companies)).

This warranty has a valuable information function for the purchaser but the vendors might reasonably object to accepting the commitment which the warranty imposes, even though it will usually be a clear matter of record as to whether an election has been made. This warranty is often included by the purchaser even when wholly irrelevant, for example because the target company was incorporated after 1982. In such circumstances it should be deleted.

5–75   **21.3 The Company has not since the Balance Sheet Date engaged in a transaction in respect of which there may be substituted, for Taxation purposes, a different consideration for the actual consideration given or received by it.**

This warranty is intended to cover cases where the actual profit or gain made by the target company on a transaction differs from the taxable profit. In general, this will not be material for transactions which have been completed prior to the balance sheet date, as the taxation position will be reflected in the accounts. For transactions occurring after that date, the purchaser will wish to know that there will not be a liability to tax on a profit or gain of a greater amount than that which has actually accrued.

The vendors should insist on the deletion of this provision and require the purchaser to rely on the warranties which specifically deal with those statutory provisions that enable actual considerations paid or received to be replaced by notional amounts (see particularly cll.9 and 21.4). If the warranty stands, it should be limited to "taxation" in a narrower sense than the definition in para.4–03.

5–76   **21.4 In determining the liability to corporation tax on chargeable gains in respect of any asset which has been acquired by the Company, or which the Company has agreed to acquire (whether conditionally, contingently or otherwise):**

> **21.4.1**   **the sums allowable as a deduction will be determined solely in accordance with TCGA 1992 ss.38 (Acquisition and disposal costs etc.) and 53 (The indexation allowance and interpretative provisions);**
>
> **21.4.2**   **the amount or value of the consideration, determined in accordance with s.38(1)(a), will not be less than the amount or value of the consideration actually given by the Company for the asset; and**
>
> **21.4.3**   **the amount of any expenditure on enhancing the value of that asset, determined in accordance with s.38(1)(b) will not be less than the amount or value of all expenditure actually incurred by the Company on the asset.**

In determining liability to capital gains tax, a deduction is made for allowable expenditure, determined in accordance with s.38. This expenditure comprises the consideration given wholly and exclusively for the acquisition of the asset or, where the asset was not acquired, consideration wholly and exclusively incurred in providing the asset, expenditure wholly and exclusively incurred in enhancing the value of the asset or preserving title to it, and costs incidental to the disposal. Section 53 provides for the unindexed gain or loss to be adjusted by taking into account an indexation allowance. This is broadly equal to the actual expenditure multiplied by the rise in the retail prices index over the period of ownership.

Numerous provisions in the capital gains tax legislation provide for the substitution of a deemed acquisition cost for the true cost or for the disallowance of certain expenditures.

While on the face of it, it might appear reasonable for the purchaser to require a warranty that the gain on a disposal of a capital asset will not, for capital gains tax purposes, exceed the true gain, it is doubtful in fact whether the requirement is fair. The purchaser will be affected only if and when a disposal of the asset occurs and, unless its disposal has been specifically contemplated in the course of the negotiations leading to the purchase of the target company, the vendors might reasonably consider that the possibility of a disposal should be disregarded. In any case, a disposal may not take place for a considerable time, and the purchaser should not be entitled to a claim under the warranties if no loss would result to it in the foreseeable future. Indeed, under general principles relating to the quantification of damages for breach of warranty, it is doubtful whether the purchaser could make a significant claim unless the contemplation of the parties was that a disposal would take place within a foreseeable time.

21.5 No asset owned, or agreed to be acquired, by the Company (other than plant and machinery in respect of which it is entitled to capital allowances) is a wasting asset within TCGA 1992 s.44 (meaning of "wasting asset").   5–77

The significance of this warranty is that the allowable expenditure on a wasting asset, being plant or machinery or substantially any other asset with a predictable life not exceeding 50 years, is reduced over the expected life of the asset. Accordingly the chargeable gain arising on the disposal will exceed the actual gain (TCGA 1992 s.46 (straightline restriction of allowable expenditure)). This provision does not apply to assets qualifying for capital allowances (TCGA 1992 s.47 (wasting assets qualifying for capital allowances)).

As with the previous warranty, it is unreasonable in general for the purchaser to require this warranty in cases where the parties have not expressly contemplated that a disposal of the assets in question would take place. If such a disposal is in mind, it would be appropriate for a more precise agreement to be reached between the parties as to how any increased taxation liability resulting from an asset being a wasting asset should be borne.

21.6 The Company has not joined in the making of a claim under TCGA 1992 s.140A (Transfer of a UK trade) in relation to the transfer to it of the whole or part of a trade carried on within the United Kingdom.   5–78

A United Kingdom company which transfers the whole or part of the trade carried on by it in the United Kingdom to a company resident in another member state, in exchange for securities of the transferee, may elect jointly with the transferee for roll-over relief. The effect of the relief is that the transfer is deemed to take place at the base cost of the transferor. The transferee accordingly has a greater prospective liability to corporation tax on chargeable gains arising on a subsequent disposal than it would incur if the consideration paid by it were treated as its base cost.

The purchaser is entitled to know of circumstances where there is a hidden potential liability to tax. The vendors should have no difficulty in giving the warranty in cases where no acquisition of the kind covered by the section has taken place, particularly as the purchaser is unlikely to suffer loss even if the warranty is breached unless the parties had in mind a disposal of the acquired business.

22 Replacement of business assets

5–79   **22.1 The Company has not made a claim under TCGA 1992 ss.23 (Receipt of compensation and insurance money not treated as a disposal), 152 (Replacement of business assets: Roll-over relief), 153 (Assets only partly replaced), 154 (New assets which are depreciating assets), 175 (Replacement of business assets by members of a group) or 247 (Roll-over relief on compulsory acquisition) which would affect the amount of the chargeable gain or allowable loss which would, but for the claim, have arisen on a disposal of any of its assets.**

Roll-over relief for capital gains tax purposes in relation to disposals of assets, which are replaced by qualifying business assets within a period of one year before the disposal and three years afterwards, is given under TCGA 1992 ss.152–154. The consideration received on the disposal of the old asset is treated as being reduced, so as to give rise to neither a gain nor a loss and the consideration given on the acquisition of the new assets as being reduced to an equal extent. There are, however, special rules where depreciating assets are involved (s.154).

Section 247 extends the relief in relation to land disposed of as a result of a compulsory acquisition. Under s.175 all the trades carried on by a group of companies are treated as a single trade.

Section 23 provides a form of roll-over, where compensation or insurance proceeds arising on the loss of or damage to an asset are applied in restoring or replacing the asset.

The vendors should have no difficulty in giving this warranty as the information will be a matter of record. They might, nevertheless, wish to consider whether the purchaser would ever expect to incur any increased liability by reason of a roll-over as, in the case of an expanding business, there might be no reason to suppose that a recapture would ever occur.

23 Chargeable gains: special cases

5–80   **23.1 The Company is not owed a debt (not being a debt on a security), upon the disposal or satisfaction of which a liability to corporation tax on chargeable gains will arise under TCGA 1992 s.251 (Debts: General provisions).**

A debt does not normally constitute a chargeable asset although, as discussed in relation to cl.23.2, certain qualifying loans can give rise to an allowable loss.

Accordingly, in the exceptional event of a disposal or satisfaction of the debt giving rise to a gain, there will not be a tax liability unless the gain constitutes income. The general rule does not, however, apply to a debt on a security or a debt where the creditor was not the person to whom the liability was first incurred. The meaning of a debt on a security is obscure as the somewhat circular definition, which is in TCGA 1992 s.132 (Equation of converted securities and new holding), provides that security includes loan stock of a company, whether or not secured.

If, therefore, a target company owns a debt which has the characteristics of a security or a debt which was acquired by it from the original creditor, a liability to corporation tax on capital gains could arise which would not be anticipated by the purchaser. The clause should present no difficulty for the vendors. Although it may be doubtful which debts are debts on a security for the purpose of this clause, it will rarely be possible for a debt in respect of which a target company is the original creditor to give rise to a gain. In so far as the warranty relates to debts owing to a target company in circumstances where it was not the original creditor, it will generally be clear if a potential liability exists.

23.2 The Company has not claimed nor is it entitled to claim under TCGA 1992 s.253 (Relief for loans to traders) that an allowable loss has accrued in respect of a loan made by it. 5–81

As is indicated above, debts normally fall outside the scope of the capital gains tax legislation. Exceptions are made in respect of "qualifying loans", that is loans to United Kingdom traders who use the loans for the purposes of trade. If the loan becomes to any extent irrecoverable and it is still owned by the original creditor, an allowable loss may be claimed. If, after a s.253 claim, a recovery is made, a chargeable gain accrues equal to so much of the allowable loss as corresponds to the amount recovered.

It may be difficult for the vendors to know whether a claim can be made in relation to an outstanding loan. In any case, as the effect is to give rise to an allowable loss, the vendors could reasonably maintain that they should not be responsible for ensuring that the purchaser can obtain the benefit of it unless the sale terms have contemplated otherwise. Conversely, the purchaser is entitled to know whether recovery of a bad debt would result in a tax charge, although the vendors could argue that, if an unanticipated recovery is made, there should be no objection to it being taxed.

On this basis the vendors should at least delete "is entitled to claim" and possibly seek to exclude the whole warranty.

23.3 The Company does not own rights, or an interest in rights, under a policy of assurance or contract for a deferred annuity on the life of any person of which it is not the original beneficial owner. 5–82

A disposal of a life assurance policy or deferred annuity does not give rise to a chargeable gain unless the disposal is by a person who is not the original owner, and acquired the rights for actual consideration (TCGA 1992 s.210 (Life assurance and deferred annuities)). The warranty is intended to protect the purchaser from an unexpected tax liability but, unless specific representations were made that such an asset existed and would generate a tax-free gain, the vendors should reject the clause.

5–83   **23.4 No part of the consideration given by the Company for a new holding of shares (within the meaning of TCGA 1992 s.126 (Reorganisation or reduction of share capital: Application of ss.127–131) will be disregarded by virtue of s.128(2) (Consideration given or received by holder).**

The broad effect of s.128 is to treat consideration given by a person on acquiring a new holding of securities as a result of a reorganisation as being part of the cost of acquiring the original holding of shares. If, however, the transaction is not at arm's length, the new consideration is taken into account only in so far as it does not exceed the increase in the value of the new holding as compared with the value of the original holding immediately prior to the reorganisation. The implications of this qualification can be widespread and would have an unexpected effect where, for example, a minority shareholder takes up a rights issue, since the resultant increase in the value of his shareholding is unlikely to match precisely the consideration put up for the new shares.

While the purchaser is entitled to be satisfied that no expenditure will be disallowed for capital gains tax purposes, the vendors should treat this provision with the utmost care and an analysis of the possible impact of s.128(2) on any rights issues that have involved the target company should be made. The vendors might also reasonably consider that the purchaser should not be entitled to compensation for a breach of this warranty unless the parties specifically contemplated a disposal of the shares concerned.

5–84   **23.5 No asset owned by the Company has been the subject of a deemed disposal under TCGA 1992 Sch.2 (Assets held on April 6, 1965), so as to restrict the extent to which the gain or loss, over the period of ownership, may be apportioned by reference to straightline growth.**

If a capital asset, not being a quoted security or land reflecting development value, was owned on April 6, 1965, when capital gains tax was introduced, the taxpayer can normally elect to have the ultimate gain or loss arising on a disposal determined in one of two ways. The straightline growth method treats the gain or loss as having accrued steadily over the whole period of ownership and only that part attributed to the post-April 1965 period is brought into the computation. Alternatively, the asset is deemed to have been sold and repurchased at market value on April 6, 1965.

The straightline apportionment method, which will be advantageous if the rate of growth has increased, is lost when a part disposal occurs (TCGA 1992 Sch.2, para.16(8) (Apportionment by reference to straightline growth of gain or loss over period of ownership)), or if there is a reorganisation of share capital which gives rise to a holding of shares of a different class (para.19 (Reorganisation of share capital, conversion of securities, etc.)), or if assets are transferred to a close company by a person having control over it, in so far as the value of the shares of the close company on a subsequent transfer reflects a profit on the assets transferred (para.21 (Assets transferred to close companies)).

The significance of the right to time apportionment has been greatly reduced by the rebasing of capital gains tax to 1982. Even where the loss of the right to time apportionment is disadvantageous, it is generally unreasonable to require this warranty to be given, unless a disposal of assets, which were acquired by a target company before April 6, 1965, is in the contemplation of the parties, and the purchaser has reasonably relied upon the availability of the apportionment method.

Again this warranty is often irrelevant as the target company will often not have capital assets acquired before April 6, 1965.

24 Capital losses

24.1 The Company has not incurred a capital loss to which TCGA 1992 s.18(3) (Transactions between connected persons) is applicable.   5–85

This section applies to a capital loss arising on a disposal of an asset to a connected person. The loss can be set-off only against chargeable gains arising on a disposal of chargeable assets to the same connected person.

The vendors should resist this warranty unless the purchase price for the target company reflects the value of expected losses.

25 Gifts involving group companies

25.1 The Company has not received assets by way of gift as mentioned in TCGA 1992 s.282 (Recovery of tax from donee).   5–86

Section 282 entitles HMRC to recover from a donee the capital gains tax which should be paid by the donor on the making of a gift. The donee has a statutory right of recovery from the donor. Although the purchaser is entitled to protect itself against an unexpected liability under this section, the vendors should ensure that they are given the benefit of the right of recovery. See also cl.29.1 regarding the inheritance tax implications.

26 Foreign businesses

26.1 The Company has not made a claim under TCGA 1992 s.140 (Postponement of charge on transfer of assets to non-resident company) or s.140C (Transfer of a non-UK trade) in relation to the transfer of the whole or part of a trade which it carried on outside the United Kingdom through a branch or agency.   5–87

Section 140 applies where a United Kingdom resident company carrying on a trade outside the United Kingdom transfers all or part of it to a non-resident company in exchange for shares or loan stock of the non-resident company. Provided the United Kingdom resident company controls at least one quarter of the ordinary share capital of the transferee, the transferor may make a claim for the gains and losses to be aggregated. The net gain is then deemed to arise on a single transaction, and the chargeable gain is rolled over until the transferor disposes of the shares it acquires or the transferee disposes of the relevant assets. There is thus a contingent additional liability to tax which will arise if and when there is a disposal of the securities, or if there is a disposal of the assets within six years.

Section 140C provides similar alternative relief where a United Kingdom resident company transfers to a company resident in another member state the whole or part of a trade carried on by the transferor outside the United Kingdom but within the EU.

This kind of transaction is perhaps becoming more common given the tendency of EU law to reduce discrimination between residents of different member states. The warranty will not, however, be relevant in a transaction where there is no cross-border aspect.

5–88 **26.2 No notice under ICTA 1988 s.747 (Imputation of chargeable profits and creditable tax of controlled foreign companies) has been received by the Company, no application has been made under ICTA 1988 s.751A (Reduction in chargeable profits for certain activities of EEA business establishments) and [so far as the Vendors are aware] no circumstances exist which would entitle HMRC to apportion profits of a controlled foreign company to the Company under ICTA 1988 s.752 (Apportionment of chargeable profits and creditable tax) as extended by ICTA 1988 ss.752A (Relevant interests), 752B (Section 752(3): the percentage of shares which a relevant interest represents) and 752C (Interpretation of apportionment provisions).**

A controlled foreign company is one that is resident outside the United Kingdom, but controlled by persons resident in the United Kingdom, and which is subject to a level of taxation in the country of its residence which is less than a specified fraction of the corresponding level of taxation in the United Kingdom. An apportionment of the profits of the company may be made amongst United Kingdom residents according to their interests in the company unless either the company distributes by way of dividend at least half of its trading profits or it is engaged in specified exempt activities. When this legislation was introduced, the rate of corporation tax in the United Kingdom was 45 per cent and the fraction was one-half. Following the reduction in the corporation tax rate that has occurred since then, the fraction was increased to three-quarters by FA 1993 s.119 (Controlled foreign companies).

Following the ECJ judgment in *Cadbury Schweppes Plc v IRC* [2006] S.T.C. 1908, which found certain aspects of the controlled foreign companies ("CFC") legislation to be contrary to European law, the law was amended from December 6, 2006 to allow an application to be made to HMRC for genuine economic activities in EEA countries to be disregarded for CFC purposes (ICTA 1988 s.751A). Various proposals were made and discussions held regarding changing the CFC tax rules. Following the change in government, it was announced in the

June 2010 Budget that new CFC rules would be introduced in Spring 2012, with interim rules in Spring 2011 and proposals have been put out to consultation. Although the vendors will have no difficulty with the first two parts of this clause, which relate to the factual question of whether notices have been received, the third part is more problematic for the vendors and they will prefer to have it subject to their awareness by including the wording in brackets.

27 Residence

27.1 The Company is and has at all times been resident in the United Kingdom for the purposes of all Taxation laws and has not at any time been resident outside the United Kingdom or had a permanent establishment outside the United Kingdom for the purposes of any Taxation law or any double Taxation arrangement. The Company has never paid tax on income profits or gains to any Tax Authority in any other country.   5–89

The substance of the warranty is fairly self explanatory. The vendors should be able to give such a warranty and it would be unreasonable for them to refuse.

28 Value added tax

28.1 In relation to value added tax the Company: 5–90

28.1.1   has duly registered and is a taxable person;

A taxable person is one who makes or intends to make taxable supplies of goods or services in the United Kingdom, other than exempt supplies (VATA 1994 s.4 (Scope of VAT on taxable supplies)). The level of taxable supplies at which registration becomes necessary is specified in VATA 1994 Sch.1 (Registration in respect of taxable supplies) and is updated frequently. There should in general be no difficulty in determining whether registration is required and has been effected.

28.1.2   has complied, in all material respects, with all statutory requirements, orders, provisions, directions and conditions;   5–91

There are extensive regulations controlling the operation of VAT, and the vendors may find difficulty in satisfying themselves that all of them have been followed. Nevertheless, the purchaser is entitled to be sure that no unexpected liability to VAT will arise and ultimately it is a question of where the risk should lie, as between the parties, of any VAT return being incorrect or not having been properly made.

28.1.3   maintains complete, correct and up-to-date records as required by the applicable legislation;   5–92

The obligations to keep records are set out with reasonable clarity in VATA 1994 Sch.11, para.6 (Duty to keep records) and Notice No.700. The vendors should not have difficulty in accepting this warranty.

5–93   **28.1.4   has not been required by HMRC to give security;**

HMRC is entitled, under the provisions of VATA 1994 Sch.11, para.4(2) (Power to require security and production of evidence), to require that security is given of such amount and in such manner as they may determine. Clearly the purchaser will be extremely concerned if security has been required, as it will reflect badly either on the way that the target company has conducted its value added tax payments in the past, or, alternatively, on its credit standing.

5–94   **28.1.5   has not applied for treatment as a member of a group which includes another company; and**

A group of companies may elect for treatment as if they were a single entity under VATA 1994 s.43 (Groups of companies). It is important to bear in mind that a consequence of group registration is that each member of the group is jointly and severally liable for all VAT payable in respect of the activities of the group. The purchaser will therefore wish to know whether the target company has at any stage been a member of a group for VAT purposes. Companies can form VAT groups only if each company is established or has a fixed establishment in the United Kingdom and one company controls the other (within the terms of CA 2006 s.1159 and Sch.6) or one person (which may be one individual or a number of individuals in partnership) controls all of them (VATA 1994 s.43A(1) (Groups: eligibility)).

5–95   **28.1.6   is not, nor has it agreed to become, an agent (for the purposes of VATA 1994 s.47 (Agents etc.)) for the supply of goods for a person who is not a taxable person.**

The effect of s.47 is to make an agent liable for VAT if his principal is a non-taxable person in two circumstances. These are that:

(1) goods are acquired from another member state by the non-taxable person and the agent acts in relation to the acquisition and supplies the goods in his own name for his principal; or

(2) goods are imported from a place outside the member states and supplied by the agent in his own name.

As the agent incurs liability for his or her principal, it is reasonable for the purchaser to require that the vendors give this warranty. Since the subject matter is a question of fact, the vendors will normally have no difficulty in determining whether the warranty could be infringed.

5–96   **28.2 The Disclosure Letter sets out accurate and complete particulars of claims for bad debt relief which have been made and remain outstanding, or which may be made, by the Company under VATA 1994 s.36 (Bad debts) and of any debts which, if written off, would give a right to claim relief.**

Value added tax has to be paid over to HMRC following the rendering of an invoice regardless of whether payment is then received. If payment is never received, the VAT may be recovered under s.36. A number of requirements have to be satisfied, principally that the debt has been written off as bad and that at least six months have elapsed from the time of the supply. The purchaser has a limited interest in claims for relief which have been made but is concerned to make due application where a debt could be written off but no action has been taken. The vendors should be cautious about warranting that all claims which can be made are disclosed as they may have no ready means of knowing whether the required circumstances exist.

28.3 The Company has not, during the past 12 or 24 months respectively, received a surcharge liability notice under VATA 1994 s.59 (The default surcharge) nor may it be liable to a penalty under FA 2007 Sch.24 (Penalties for Errors). 5–97

A default surcharge notice may be served on a taxable person if he fails to furnish a return for a prescribed accounting period, or to pay the VAT shown on the return. The surcharge is a specified percentage—varying between two per cent and 15 per cent according to the number of periods for which there is a default—of the outstanding VAT.

Under FA 2007 Sch.24, a penalty may be imposed if there is an inaccuracy in a return which is careless or deliberate. The penalty may be up to 100 per cent of the potential lost revenue depending on culpability.

It is clearly reasonable that the purchaser should be informed if either category of notice has been received by a target company or if there have been defaults which could result in liability to penalties.

28.4 No option to tax in relation to any of the Properties has been made by the Company or a predecessor in title under VATA 1994 Sch.10, para.2 (Election to waive exemption). 5–98

A number of transactions in relation to land are exempt from VAT under VATA 1994, Sch.9, Group 1 (Exemptions—Land). The "option to tax", enables input tax to be recovered in circumstances where it would otherwise be lost as a result of the partial exemption provisions. In general, the exercise of the option is irrevocable and the purchaser will be entitled to the information.

As it is a question of fact whether the option has been exercised, the vendors should have no difficulty with the warranty but, as an alternative, they may seek to obtain confirmation from HMRC as to whether there has been an exercise of the option in relation to each of the target company's properties (though HMRC will often be unable to give confirmation).

29 Inheritance tax

29.1 The Company has not made a transfer of value (as defined in IHTA 1984 s.3 (Transfers of value)) [otherwise than for the purposes, or in the course, of its business]. 5–99

A transfer of value by a target company will be relevant only if it is a close company in which case the provisions of IHTA 1984 s.94 (Charge on participators), could apply. Under that section, the amount transferred by the close company, less the amounts received by the participators in the company, is apportioned amongst the participators according to their respective rights and interests and the company has the primary liability for any resulting inheritance tax.

Broadly speaking, liability arises under this section only if the gift has been made otherwise than to the participators. There are many ex gratia payments which may be made by a company for bona fide commercial reasons, and the vendors might reasonably consider that they should not be penalised if they have had no benefit themselves and if the liability arises as a result of actions carried out for the benefit of the target company. To cover this point, the vendors might wish to add the bracketed words, although this will not protect them from their statutory secondary liability which arises if the target company, which is primarily liable, fails to pay.

The purchaser is unlikely to accept the additional words on the ground that any such liability should entitle it to a reduction in the purchase consideration paid for the target company.

5–100   **29.2 No HMRC charge for unpaid inheritance tax (as provided by IHTA 1984 ss.237 (Imposition of charge) and 238 (Effects of purchases) exists over an asset of the Company or in relation to any shares in the capital of the Company.**

HMRC's entitlement to a charge for unpaid inheritance tax is not only relevant to close companies. HMRC is entitled to a charge on any property (still referred to in legislation as the Inland Revenue charge despite the merger of the Inland Revenue and HM Customs and Excise to form HMRC) involved in a transfer (s.237), and this could attach to assets owned by a target company. A purchaser of property subject to a charge takes free of the charge if he is not aware of it (s.238) and, while this would normally result in the purchaser taking free of any charge on the shares which are being sold, it would not assist in relation to assets of the target company which were charged. If the warranty cannot readily be given, it may be appropriate for the purchaser to require that, before exchange of contracts, the vendors obtain a certificate of discharge under IHTA 1984 s.239 (Certificates of discharge).

30 Stamp duty and stamp duty land tax

5–101   **30.1 The Company has not within the past three years made a claim for relief or exemption under FA 1930 s.42 (Relief from transfer stamp duty in case of transfer of property as between associated companies), FA 1995 s.151 (Leases etc. between associated bodies corporate) or FA 1986 ss.75–77 (Acquisitions: reliefs).**

FA 1930 s.42, as amended by FA 1995 s.149 (Transfer: associated bodies), provides relief from stamp duty on a conveyance or transfer where assets are transferred within a group where at least 75 per cent of the share capital of the companies concerned is in common ownership. Although there is no obligation to maintain the group relationship for any specific period, the relief will be withdrawn if it appears that it was not the intention of the transferor and the transferee to remain associated (FA 1967 s.27 (Conveyances and transfers on sale: reduction of duty, and amendment of provisions for exemption)). FA 2000 s.123 (Transfer of property between associated companies: Great Britain) introduced changes such that relief for intra-group transfers will be available only if the parent company has a substantial economic interest in its subsidiary, the existence of which will be assessed by reference to CTA 2010 Pt 5, Ch.6.

FA 1995 s.151 essentially provides a similar relief for leases between companies in common ownership. FA 1986 ss.75–77 provide for relief from stamp duty on certain reorganisations of companies and their businesses. As these reliefs were being used to avoid stamp duty, legislation was introduced in FA 2002 ss.111–113. These sections provide that where there was a transfer to which one of the reliefs applied and the transferee company left the transferor's group within three years of the transfer, the relief would be effectively clawed back and stamp duty become payable.

For the purchaser, it will be important to know that any disposal after completion or where the vendor is itself a company, completion itself will not trigger a clawback of stamp duty relief. It should be relatively easy for the vendors to obtain the necessary information to disclose, however, the vendors may object in principle to this warranty if post acquisition disposals are not expressly contemplated.

30.2 All documents in the possession of the Company, or which the Company is entitled to require the production of, and which confer any right upon the Company or are necessary to establish the title of the Company to any asset, have been stamped and any applicable stamp duties or charges in respect of such documents have been accounted for and paid, and no such documents which are outside of the United Kingdom would attract stamp duty if they were brought into the United Kingdom.   5–102

It is now quite common to require an all-encompassing warranty from the vendors in relation to the stamping of documents. By virtue of FA 1999, FA 2003 and FA 2004, stamp duty has been abolished in the transfer of all assets other than shares, marketable securities and certain partnership interests. SDLT applies to transactions in land.

When stamp duty applied to land and certain other assets, it was not uncommon for documentation to be executed and held outside the UK. Stamp duty is only then payable when the documents are brought back into the UK. Therefore there is a contingent liability to stamp duty.

30.3 Stamp duty land tax has been paid in full in respect of all estates or interests in land acquired on or after December 1, 2003 by the Company. The Company has not made any application to defer payment of stamp duty   5–103 land tax pursuant to FA 2003 s.90 and there are no contingent liabilities or requirements to submit a further land transaction return in relation to:

30.3.1   properties acquired as a going concern for the purposes of VATA s.49 (Taxation of going concerns);

30.3.2   unascertainable future consideration;

30.3.3   transactions capable of being treated as linked for the purposes of FA 2003 s.108 (Linked transactions);

30.3.4   turnover leases;

30.3.5   leases subject to a rent review within five years of grant;

30.3.6   leases the assignment of which would be deemed to be the grant of a new lease; or

30.3.7   any other arrangement capable of giving rise to a further charge to stamp duty land tax.

It is quite common for the purchaser to seek a warranty to the effect that SDLT has been properly administered. This is particularly important given that the payment of it is obligatory.

A further feature of SDLT which was not part of the stamp duty regime is that there is in certain circumstances an obligation to file further returns after the initial return has been filed. These situations are listed above at cll.30.3.1–30.3.7. It is important for the purchaser to know what future returns may be necessary, not only so that it can assess any contingent liability but also so that it can ensure that the target company will not breach any of the administration requirements.

5–104   **30.4 The Company has not claimed relief from stamp duty land tax under FA 2003 Sch.7, Pts 1 or 2 (Stamp Duty Land Tax: Group Relief and Reconstruction and Acquisition Reliefs) in relation to any estate or interest in land that has been transferred to it.**

The comments at cl.30.1 apply equally to the position in relation to group relief and reconstruction and acquisition relief under the SDLT regime.

31 Disclosure Requirements

5–105   **31.1 The Company has not entered into any notifiable arrangement for the purposes of FA 2004 Pt 7, any notifiable contribution arrangement for the purpose of the National Insurance (Application of Pt 7 of the Finance Act 2004) Regulations 2007 (SI 2007/785) or any notifiable schemes for the purposes of VATA Sch.11A and there are no circumstances in which any such disclosure should have been made by the Company.**

Following the introduction of disclosure requirements in FA 2004, it is important to now obtain this kind of warranty in order to find out what, if any, schemes have been disclosed and also to cover the situation where a scheme should have been disclosed but has not been.

OBSOLETE PROVISIONS AND LIMITED APPLICATION TAXES

The convenience of standard forms is such that warranties continue to make their **5–106** appearance in relation to obsolete taxation matters long after any liability or dispute can arise. The following are taxes and taxation provisions which have ceased to be relevant:

(a) Estate duty: the predecessor of inheritance tax in respect of deaths prior to March 1975;

(b) Capital transfer tax: now redesignated as inheritance tax;

(c) Special charge: a one off surcharge on 1967/68 investment income;

(d) Selective employment tax: imposed upon employers until 1973;

(e) Purchase tax: replaced in 1973 by value added tax;

(f) Development gains tax: applied to certain developments which took place before August 1976;

(g) Development land tax: abolished in relation to disposals occurring after March 1985; and

(h) Capital duty: abolished from March 1988.

Reliefs which have been withdrawn include:

(a) Stock relief: withdrawn for accounting periods beginning after March 1984; and

(b) Relief from transfer stamp duty on the amalgamation of companies under FA 1927 s.55 (replaced by narrower reliefs under FA 1986 ss.75 (Acquisitions: reliefs) and 77 (Acquisition of target company's share capital)).

From 1973 to 1999, companies paying dividends were required to pay part of their corporation tax liability at the same time ("ACT"). The ACT paid during the year was then available to be set against their corporation tax liability at the normal time for payment of that liability. This regime was withdrawn with the introduction of corporation tax self assessment instalment payments. It was possible to build up surplus (unrelieved) ACT by paying ACT on dividends in excess of the tax liability for the period; there were various restrictions on the use of surplus ACT. In order to allow relief of the surplus ACT which companies were carrying forward, a "shadow ACT" system was introduced which allows set off of surplus ACT broadly in the same way as before the ACT regime was abolished. However, companies are no longer required to pay tax at the time of paying dividends. Large companies may have surplus ACT carried forward for some time to come.

Until 1988, close companies were liable to "apportionments" if insufficient **5–107** dividends were paid in accordance with the ICTA 1988 Pt XI, Ch.III and Sch.19.

These provisions were repealed in relation to accounting periods which began after March 31, 1989 and, in the absence of fraud, will now no longer be relevant. They entitled the Inland Revenue to recover amounts equivalent to higher rate income tax and advance corporation tax if, without good cause, a close company failed to make a distribution of its investment or estate income. If distributions of the required level were not made, the best protection that could be given against an assessment was a clearance. This was binding upon the Inland Revenue only if the information accompanying the request for the clearance and any further particulars furnished to the Inspector of Taxes made full and accurate disclosure of all facts and considerations which were material to be known.

A number of taxes have very limited application and are not considered separately in this book. It should nevertheless be borne in mind that the wide definition of "Taxation" adopted in para.4–02 and in relation to the tax covenant in Ch.10 will have the effect that all these taxes are automatically covered by many of the tax warranties and by the tax indemnity. The taxes which are not discussed include:

(1) Air passenger duty;

(2) Excise duties, other than VAT;

(3) Insurance premium tax;

(4) Landfill tax;

(5) Petroleum revenue tax; and

(6) Aggregate levy.

CHAPTER 6

Property Warranties

PURPOSE IN THE CASE OF BUSINESS AND SHARE PURCHASES

In the case of the purchase of a business, the procedures adopted in relation to properties included in the assets which are being purchased will be no different from those of a property purchase which is not connected with a business sale. The usual surveys and searches should take place and the contract and completion documents should conform to normal conveyancing practice. It is possible that warranties will be sought which would not normally be relevant to a simple property purchase if there are aspects of the properties which impact on the value of the goodwill of the business. The warranties that might be considered are included in Appendix 5, which provides precedents of the warranties appropriate for the purchase of a business. In general, however, it would be unusual in the case of the purchase of a business for the purchaser to seek or the vendor to give substantial property warranties. **6–01**

The practice in relation to a share purchase, in a case where the assets of the target company include properties, is rather different as are the remedies. The general concept of property warranties is to support the assumption made by the prudent purchaser that the target company's title to its property is good and marketable. How this will apply in any given case depends on a variety of factors, but will usually revolve around the issues of saleability—can the target company sell, let or otherwise dispose of it?; value—will the target company be able to dispose at a price equal to a proper valuation placed upon it, or obtain loan finance at expected levels upon the security of the property?; and use and enjoyment—in the normal course of events will the target company be able to carry on its business there?

These issues overlap substantially. If there are factors preventing or hampering a sale, the value otherwise ascribed to the property will be reduced. If the property is required as a place of business, it may well lose its ascribed value if its use as such cannot be continued, and so on. Nevertheless, the emphasis of the warranty protection which is sought may, in appropriate circumstances, be concentrated on one or more, rather than all, of these issues and, while the purchaser may request, and accept if it is offered, wide-ranging property warranty protection, the vendors will wish to limit their liability. In any event the vendors should be concerned to offer no more than the purchaser reasonably requires, having regard to the purposes for which the property is intended to serve the target company under the ownership of the purchaser and the extent to which the value or use of the property has been a factor in determining the price paid by the purchaser. A fuller understanding of some of the principles of valuation may be obtained by reference to Ch.13.

TYPES OF PROTECTION ON TITLE TO PROPERTY

6–02   There are three conventional ways in which the purchaser of shares may wish to be satisfied that the target company has a good and marketable title to its properties. It may, through its own solicitor, carry out an investigation of title; rely upon warranty protection; accept a certificate of title from the target company's solicitor; or rely upon a combination of all three.

A full set of property warranties obtained from the vendors can serve as a substitute for an investigation of title to the properties made by the solicitor acting for the purchaser. However, if the purchaser has the opportunity to make an investigation of title itself, why should it also seek the protection of property warranties? If the target company's solicitor is in a position to give a certificate of title, what need then for property warranties or an investigation of title?

There is, of course, no general answer to these questions, for circumstances will vary in every case, but it is pertinent to examine the functions of property warranty protection, investigation of title and certificates of title, and the issues involved in deciding which measures or mix of measures to adopt. In most cases a mix of at least two of the three options will best protect the purchaser and meet the provisions of timescale and costs faced by both parties. Each is dealt with in turn below.

WARRANTY PROTECTION

6–03   In the case of full property warranties, the principal function will be to provide to the purchaser, by way of damages, protection against the presence of factors in relation to the properties which were not known to the purchaser at the time of the acquisition of the target company, and which detrimentally affect it. Provided that the vendors have the financial substance to support the warranty liability, the purchaser has recourse through the warranties for any loss arising from breach subject to ensuring that the particular loss suffered on the property is recoverable perhaps on an indemnity basis. Please refer to Chs 1 and 3 for discussions relating to the difference between recovering loss for breach of warranty on a standard basis and on an indemnity basis.

There is another, practical, function; if warranties are given, the purchaser may be relieved wholly or partly of the need to investigate title, but there are other practical considerations which are examined below.

INVESTIGATION OF TITLE

6–04   The purchaser, through its solicitor, will carry out the same investigative conveyancing procedures as it would if it were to acquire the properties as such rather than the target company, and will satisfy itself on all relevant matters. It will not enjoy the same protection in damages against the vendors since, in the absence of property warranties, it would not even enjoy the benefit of normal covenants for title implied by a vendor selling the property with full title guarantee (see para.4–08). There is no purchase of the property, only the purchase of shares. There may be some responsibility placed on the vendors by a general warranty with respect to disclosure, so that liability is incurred by the vendors for failure to bring to the attention of the purchaser material matters (if such a warranty were given), or a warranty that such information as has been disclosed is accurate and complete. Liability for breach of those warranties would then be similar to liability for damages for misrepresentation by a vendor of property in answer to preliminary enquiries. Indeed, even without such general warranties, there may be liability for damages for misrepresentation under the Misrepresentation Act 1967 (see para.3–01) although in most cases this will now be limited to fraudulent misrepresentation by effective use of entire agreement clauses (see para.3–03). For this reason, a purchaser should seek to avoid this by qualifying such provisions to concede reliance on the representations made by the vendor in the form of written replies in line with good conveyancing practices in a pure property transaction. Alternatively, vendors should be asked even in circumstances when only limited warranty protection is being given, to warrant the accuracy and completeness of all such representations made by it (see para.6–27 for the forms of warranty suggested).

The function of an investigation of the target company's title to its properties, in isolation, is to allow the purchaser the opportunity of doing the job thoroughly for itself, through its own professional adviser, whom it knows and trusts. Most purchasers prefer to deal with the matter in this way where time and budgets permit, but it may have no choice if the vendors refuse to give any property warranties or give only limited property warranties. In the absence of the warranties, the purchaser will be particularly anxious to ensure, through its solicitor, that the vendors give comprehensive replies to preliminary enquiries and warrant their accuracy and completeness.

CERTIFICATE OF TITLE

A certificate of title may be given by the target company's solicitor and, if **6–05** properly drawn, covers similar ground as a full set of property warranties or the subject matter of a report of the purchaser's solicitor if he had investigated title. The purchaser therefore relies on the certificate of the target company's solicitor and not on its own solicitor. The purchaser's protection is based on a right of action for negligence against the solicitor. Generally, the target company and the vendors would not be liable for the negligence of the target company's solicitor in the absence of some general warranty given in support, but the target company or the vendors might well be joined as co-defendants in an action for negligence, since the relevant part of the certificate may have been based upon inaccurate information provided by the vendors amounting to misrepresentation. In practice, when relying on a certificate of title from the target company's solicitor, the purchaser should as a minimum insist on a warranty from the vendors as to the accuracy and completeness of the information supplied by the vendors for the purposes of the certificate, and as to the accuracy of the certificate, to the best of the vendors' knowledge and belief.

The function of a certificate of title is to cover the subject matter of an investigation of title, and to relieve the purchaser of the need to make one. Whilst the availability of a certificate of title may well be attractive to a purchaser—avoiding a time consuming and potentially costly title investigation by its own solicitor—it can have drawbacks of its own. Negotiation of the form of the certificate can sometimes become protracted and the resultant certificate may leave the purchaser with limited protection. Additionally, each certificate must be reviewed by the purchaser's solicitor and will invariably require a commentary from him for the purchaser's benefit, as it is the function of such certificates to state relevant matters of fact, and not to comment on their significance or offer potential solutions for issues which they reveal.

In recent years it has become increasingly common for vendors, purchasers, lenders and their respective solicitors to agree on the use of one of the current forms of certificate issued by the City of London Law Society. The Long Form Certificate of Title (6th edn) is effectively the "industry standard" certificate of title, and has been largely successful in its objective of reducing negotiation of the form of the certificate to a minimum and of providing a comprehensive certificate that fairly balances the interests of the recipients and the provider. The certificate is particularly beneficial where the target company's solicitor is prepared to address it to the purchaser's lender, therefore avoiding the need for the purchaser's solicitor to prepare a separate certificate for the lender. The purchaser should carefully note, however, the qualifications to which the certificate is subject, such as the exclusion of a physical inspection of the property, no consideration of environmental assessments and reports and no investigation of what insurance may be in force in respect of the property. Often these are fundamental matters related to the value or use of the property and will need to be addressed either through separate enquiry, warranty or indemnity.

WARRANTIES, INVESTIGATION OR CERTIFICATE?

6–06 In terms of content, there should in principle be little difference between a full set of property warranties, an unqualified certificate of title and the report of the purchaser's solicitor following an investigation of title. However, there are differences with each in terms of the nature and effect of the protection they afford to a purchaser. Which factors then determine the choice between them, and would it be appropriate to combine or mix them? How comprehensive should their content be? This decision should be influenced by a number of considerations which are set out below.

REMEDIES AND PROTECTION PROVIDED

In a single choice between warranties, investigation of title and a certificate of **6–07** title, the purchaser probably achieves the greatest legal protection from a full set of property warranties. If the vendors have the financial substance to discharge any liability arising from breach, then the purchaser obtains something akin to insurance. However, it would not generally be prudent for the purchaser to ignore the perils of litigation in pursuing warranty claims, nor to indulge the belief that the vendors will always be able to pay or that any damages awarded will always fully compensate the purchaser for all losses arising from a breach, nor more generally to disregard the adage "prevention is better than cure". Far better, therefore, for the purchaser to combine full warranty protection with its own solicitor's investigation of title, giving it the benefit of knowledge of any property issues before it has committed to the purchase. Depending on the nature and significance of any issues revealed, a purchaser can then consider, having been fully advised on the issue, whether still to proceed or will have the opportunity to seek to tackle the issues in warranties, indemnities, price adjustment or a combination of them. Conversely, the vendors will wish to avoid—so far as they may do in the circumstances—assuming any liability. If there is a balance of negotiating power between the parties and all other factors are equal, then the vendors' best position is to require the purchaser to investigate title, and only to warrant that the information given in replies to enquiries made by the purchaser's solicitor in the course of investigation is, to the best of the knowledge and belief of the vendors, true and accurate. In that way, there is a fair division of responsibilities between the parties, a balance between the need for prudent enquiry and an obligation to answer fully and accurately. This balanced approach is appropriate provided that the purchaser obtains sufficiently detailed and comprehensive information through the enquiry process. It also presupposes that, as would be the case on a pure property transaction, the conveyancing process of raising pre-contract enquiries is adopted as an integral part of a purchaser's solicitor's investigation on title.

Traditionally, purchaser's solicitors would use their own forms of enquiries when raising pre-contract enquiries about a property but in recent years a suite of standard documents have been prepared by the London Property Support Lawyers Group (and endorsed by the British Property Federation) and these "Commercial Property Standard Enquiries" have now become the industry-standard, adopted by practitioners on most transactions. Where this approach becomes more difficult would be in situations where vendors only give limited information in the replies to pre-contract enquiries raised. In such circumstances, a purchaser may then seek to reintroduce further warranty protections to deal with any deficiencies.

Timing will, however, also usually play an important part, and may interfere with the ideal position from the vendors' (and indeed also the purchaser's) point of view. Often the purchaser's solicitors will be unable to undertake a full investigation of title in the available time and therefore the vendors will have to "fill in the gaps" by appropriate warranty protection.

6–08   The offer or availability of a certificate of title from the solicitor to the target company is usually determined by considerations of timing and convenience, but, dealt with in this setting, the purchaser is simply substituting the report of the target company's solicitor for that of its own solicitor following an investigation. Its remedy for a defective report from its own solicitor, or inaccuracies in the certificate of title from the target company's solicitor, is an action for negligence. In practice, the target company's solicitor will usually endeavour to qualify the certificate by incorporating certain exemptions and even disclaimers. As previously mentioned, the purchaser should require a warranty from the vendors confirming the accuracy and completeness of the certificate of title and, where the certificate is qualified, specific warranty protection to cover the gaps which it leaves. In that way, the purchaser has the double protection of the warranty from the vendors and the solicitor's insurance cover against negligence.

Similar considerations apply to investigations of title. The purchaser's solicitor will obviously not seek to exempt himself from liability as such, but will point out any areas which are not satisfactory. Warranty protection should be sought from the vendors on these specific matters. It is considered that an investigation of title is a more satisfactory protection to a purchaser than a certificate of title. The purchaser's own solicitor can be as thorough and searching as the purchaser requires and will represent the purchaser as such. The purchaser and its solicitor, between them, set the depth of investigation. The target company's solicitor, in producing a certificate of title, is not answerable to the purchaser in the same way and does not act for it. Furthermore, not every inaccuracy or mistake in a certificate of title is necessarily the result of a failure by the target company's solicitor to take reasonable care, giving rise to liability for negligence.

In addition, a certificate of title is likely to be limited in comparison to a report provided by a prudent purchaser's solicitor. As mentioned above, the function of a certificate of title is essentially to state relevant matters of fact. Whilst a certificate may identify issues or potential defects with the legal title to a property, it is unlikely to provide any advice as to how the identified issue or deficit will or may impact on the ongoing use and enjoyment of the property or its marketability nor will it offer any solutions or practical advice as to how a particular issue or deficit could be resolved. The consequence of this is that even with the offer or availability of a certificate of title, a purchaser may still need to instruct its solicitors to undertake investigations of title in order to properly advise the purchaser on issues or deficits identified, which may then have a knock on effect on both timing and cost.

6–09   It is common for the sale agreement to limit the period for claims for breach of warranty to significantly less than the statutory limitation periods that *would* usually apply to a certificate of title or the purchaser's solicitor's report on title. Additionally, it is usual for de minimis provisions, floors and a suite of warranty limitation provisions to apply to the warranties. Certificates of title and reports on title seldom, if ever, contain similar provisions, and whilst they may contain a cap on liability, this would normally be set at a level that would give the purchaser full protection, save in the most exceptional circumstances. Provided the solicitor giving the certificate or making the report is adequately insured (which the purchaser will need to check) a purchaser may well put more reliance on recovery from that source than on a warranty claim.

IMPORTANCE OF THE PROPERTY

The transaction, in form, is a purchase of shares—the acquisition of the target **6–10** company. The properties may, at one end of the scale, be the only assets of substance (as they would be on the acquisition of a property investment company), or at the other, merely one group of assets of scant importance (for example surplus premises held on an unprotected lease due to expire within a short period). A useful guide as to the properties' importance in the transaction is whether the price for the target company is calculated by reference to the net asset value of the target company, or is determined according to its profitability. If the former, the significance of the properties would probably be greater. However, it should not be forgotten that a property of little capital value (say one held upon a lease at a full market rental) may nevertheless be vital to the running of the business of the target company, or conversely a property which is unimportant to the business may nonetheless harbour substantial liabilities arising from such things as dilapidations or environmental issues. It would therefore, be dangerous for a purchaser to simply ignore any property which it considers to be of limited or no importance to the operation of the business of the target company. A substantial dilapidations claim arising out of leasehold premises which are of little operational significance could have a significant impact on the business of the target company.

In any case where the properties are of substantial importance and where all other factors are equal, it is recommended that the purchaser should carry out an investigation of title, and should seek such warranty protection from the vendors as it can get, settling for no less than warranties or indemnities dealing with the areas of defect or uncertainty unearthed by the investigation, plus a general warranty that all information given to the purchaser's solicitor upon such investigation is accurate and complete.

TIMING AND CONVENIENCE

Often, all other considerations have to give way to the timing of a transaction; **6–11** with the urgency such that it dictates what can be done in the time allotted. If the target company's solicitor can give a certificate of title in time, and it is convenient for him to do so, then that course may well be quicker than the making of an investigation of title, although both are equally subject to delays in the search process. Where timing will not allow for the usual search process but a purchaser is concerned as to the vendors' ability to meet a warranty claim, a further option, where a property is of significant importance, might be for a purchaser's solicitor to combine its title investigations with the purchase of an appropriate indemnity insurance policy. On many occasions, it will not be convenient for a certificate of title to be given or practicable for an investigation to be carried out. In such circumstances, a full set of property warranties comes into its own; the parties are forced to fall back on that route by the practicalities of the deal.

The choice between the certificate of title and the investigation of title is often grounded on issues of convenience alone, although it is rare that questions of timing are not also involved. The complexity of title, coupled with the familiarity with the properties and the knowledge of the target company's solicitor, may make the offer of a certificate of title appropriate, particularly, if the properties are not of crucial importance.

Cost

6–12 An investigation of title can be a costly process, as is the preparation and negotiation of a certificate of title. Again, if the significance of the properties is only incidental, it may be satisfactory to save cost, and to rely on warranty protection only. Where there are properties of varying significance to both parties, the purchaser may elect to undertake a full investigation in respect of key properties, and to undertake a limited investigation or no investigation of the remainder, and to seek a comprehensive set of property warranties for those properties where a full investigation is not undertaken.

Bargaining Power

6–13 In many cases, the determining factor will be simply the relative bargaining strengths of the parties. Reluctant vendors, much courted by an anxious purchaser, can afford to give less away in warranties than in a case where there are both willing vendors and a willing purchaser. At the other extreme, hard pressed vendors anxious to unload the target company on to a cautious purchaser may assume all sorts of liability under stringent warranties for the short-term benefits of disposing of the target company, taking on the risk of long-term liability if all is not what it appears to be in relation to the properties.

Scope of Warranty Protection

6–14 It has been stated that the purpose of property warranties is to support the assumption made by the prudent purchaser that the target company's title to its property is good and marketable. The meaning of "good and marketable title" has now to be examined.

A vendor of land will be expected to show good title. He must prove that he is entitled to and is selling the legal estate in land for the appropriate tenure (i.e. freehold or leasehold), free from encumbrances or defects which will or may impact the use and enjoyment of the property for the purpose for which it is intended to be used save as is otherwise provided or disclosed. In the case of registered land, the vendor must show that he is registered as the proprietor of the property with absolute title and that he is beneficially entitled to it. If title to the property is unregistered, he must be able to deduce a chain of title to the legal estate commencing not less than 15 years earlier with a good root—that is a document of title which deals with the legal and beneficial ownership of the property, identifies the property, and contains nothing to cast doubt on the title of the disposing party. Anything less, or any qualification, must be provided for or disclosed.

The inclusion of the words "and marketable" involves a separate requirement, by implying that there is an absence of other factors relating to the property, either rendering it commercially unsaleable or impairing its saleability. The limited nature of the requirement to show good title is thus opened out to general aspects of marketability. By analogy with the sale of land, the purchaser is concerned with much more than mere title upon an investigation. It will have the property surveyed in order to be advised upon its state and condition (both above and below ground). It will, through its solicitor, make searches in the Register of Local Land Charges and enquiries of the local authority to ascertain, for example, whether the property will be, or is likely to be, compulsorily acquired and to find out information on planning matters, highway rights and obligations, compliance or non-compliance with statutory requirements in relation to the property, and the like.

It will submit through its solicitor preliminary pre-contract enquiries to the **6–15** vendors on a large and wide range of issues and its solicitor will, if the circumstances are appropriate, make additional searches both of the index map held and maintained by the Land Registry and in the registers of common land and town or village greens. It may also enquire with the Coal Authority to find out about the presence of mining activity in the area and subsidence and may also make further enquiries and searches which are considered appropriate in the context of the relevant transaction, for example, searches of the relevant statutory utilities undertakings for the area in which the relevant property is located. For the most part, these procedures deal with issues and matters which have little to do with title as such; they are designed to ascertain information about the property generally, so that the purchaser will be able to assess the value of the property for the purposes of the purchase or for obtaining mortgage finance, the likelihood of imminently having to carry out repairs and maintenance, the suitability of the land for the purchaser's requirements and the problems that might arise on resale. An investigation of title is in practice, therefore, not limited to matters of ownership, and is much more extensive. It is submitted that all these matters are encompassed by the expression "good and marketable title".

It follows that, if as a substitute for an investigation of title, the purchaser is offered a full set of property warranties, those warranties should cover the matters which would have been dealt with on an investigation of title by the purchaser of the target company; that is an exercise in parallel with the investigation that is carried out by a purchaser of land. Indeed, if title is warranted as good and marketable, the circle is completed.

The protection afforded by a full set of property warranties will also need to be assessed against the nature of any general disclosures vendors might seek to make. General disclosures against property warranties are likely to transfer risk back to the purchaser, necessitating investigations and enquiries in relation to the matters that are the subject of a general disclosure. Where the approach being adopted on a transaction is one where it is agreed that the purchaser will be given and rely upon a full set of property enquiries the use of general disclosures would largely deflect the usefulness of the warranties so should be resisted. On the other hand, general disclosures may be appropriate when the purchaser is relying upon its own investigations. As to the effect of general disclosures please refer to Ch.9.

PURCHASE OF SHARES AND PURCHASE OF LAND

6–16 The scope of a full set of property warranties is purposely set as widely as possible, not only to confer requisite protection, but also to compel disclosure of information by the vendors beforehand in order to avoid liability which they might otherwise incur. In such circumstances, the purchaser is given the opportunity to review relevant information about the property of the target company before the point of legal commitment, to acquire the target company and, if appropriate, may withdraw or renegotiate. Once contracts are exchanged, the purchaser's only remedy is in damages or rescission. The purchaser of land with registered title has the additional benefit of procedural protections, afforded by a title pre-completion search at the Land Registry which will give the purchaser of land priority for a specified period within which to register its transfer. With this priority, the purchaser of land is then protected against any other transaction not similarly protected by an earlier search. It will also allow the purchaser of land the opportunity to raise with the vendors, and address before completion the existence of any adverse entries submitted to the Land Registry for registration, and not previously disclosed by the vendors. Notwithstanding there will be no dealing with the property, a pre-completion Land Registry search is still recommended (albeit without priority) on a purchase of shares when the purchaser is relying upon its own title investigations on or as near as practicable to the date that the purchaser will commit to the acquisition. Whilst on a purchase of shares no priority protection can be obtained, such a search ought to be undertaken to check that there have been no adverse changes to the registers of title since the changes to initial title investigations were completed and the date the purchaser will commit to the purchase. A purchaser of land will also expect a transfer with full or limited title guarantee giving him the benefit of the covenants implied by the LPMPA 1994 (see paras 4–08 to 4–10).

ANALYSIS OF WARRANTIES

6–17 The warranties in this chapter are prepared in connection with a share purchase and, although many of them may be of interest to a purchaser of a business, it is less usual in such transactions for extensive property warranties to be requested or given. Nonetheless, where time or other factors do not permit a full investigation of title, the provision of a fairly full set of warranties may be appropriate to supplement such search protection and implied covenants for title, as are available.

If, in the case of a share sale, the properties are not of significant importance, short form warranties may be appropriate as set out in Appendix 9. The rest of this chapter deals with long form warranties. The full set of property warranties is so designed as to cover the complete range of circumstances in which any property asset of the target company may be utilised from pure investment to occupation, for the purposes of the target company's business. Each warranty is drafted to deal with a single issue, or group of issues, so that, if it is inapplicable to a particular transaction, it may usually be deleted without repercussion in relation to any other warranty. The issue raised by each warranty may be substantive and provide specific protection to the purchaser, or its primary purpose may be to draw forth necessary information and to give general protection to the purchaser against the absence of—or inaccurate—disclosure.

The form of the property warranties presupposes that, by way of appropriate schedules, each property is described, the principal terms of leases under which the target company holds the property or of tenancies to which the target company holds the reversion are itemised, and details of encumbrances and latent defects in title given. Accordingly, a number of warranties are in negative form so that their presence will elicit the disclosure of important information which might otherwise not be forthcoming. That aspect will be of even greater importance when the commercial purpose of the purchaser in acquiring the target company is not primarily directed to its property assets, and little or no investigation of title or enquiry about them has been made.

Some suggestions are made as to how the vendors may modify the full severity **6–18** of certain warranties. As the protection sought from warranties runs in parallel with an investigation of title which would be made on a purchase of land, the view is taken in general that if information would reasonably be expected to be obtained from the vendors in that context, then the equivalent warranty protection should be provided by the vendors.

Where warranty protection is being combined with certificates of title and/or the purchaser's own investigations or is being used only to fill in the gaps left by a full investigation, then the view taken is that it would be reasonable for vendors to resist any of the warranties when a purchaser would in the normal course of an investigation of title obtain the information or comfort it is seeking by other means. The warranties discussed in the following paragraphs are as follows:

Clause	Title
1	**Title**
2	**Encumbrances**
3	**Planning matters**
4	**Statutory obligations**
5	**Adverse orders**
6	**Condition of the Properties**
7	**Insurance**
8	**Leasehold properties**

9   Tenancies

The clauses set out below adopt the definitions appearing in para.4–02.

1 Title

6–19   The warranties grouped under this heading deal principally with matters of ownership and tenure. They are intended to cause the vendors to provide full information about the properties in the target company's portfolio under the sanction of liability for damages for failure to disclose and inaccurate disclosure.

1.1 The Properties comprise all the properties owned, occupied or otherwise used by the Company in connection with its business and the Company does not have any right of ownership, rights of use, rights options, rights of first refusal or obligations to purchase or take purchase or acquire, or any other legal or equitable estate or interest in or in relation to any land or buildings other than the Properties.

This warranty is provided as a checklist to ensure that every property owned, occupied or used by the target company is identified. It is unlikely that the purchaser will have an entitlement to damages if the warranty is incorrect, unless the undisclosed properties carry liabilities, for example under repairing covenants or under any mortgage secured thereon or in respect of any environmental liabilities relating to prior occupation. Similarly the purchaser will want to establish whether the company is subject to obligations to acquire any property interests that could be onerous.

Ownership means that the freehold interest in, or a lease of the property, is held. The right to occupy or use a property may be an incident of holding either the freehold or leasehold interest, or may be enjoyed under a licence granted by the owner. A licence creates no interest, as such, in a property but merely permits the licensee to occupy or to use and enjoy it according to the terms laid down in the licence.

The information required to be given should be readily available and the purchaser is entitled to it.

6–20   **1.2 Those of the Properties which are occupied or otherwise used by the Company in connection with its business are occupied or used by right of ownership or under lease or licence, the terms of which permit the occupation or use.**

In contrast with the warranty in cl.1.1, which is concerned with identifying all of the properties, the issue here is lawful use and occupation. Use or occupation which is not permitted may amount to trespass and be actionable in damages. Title may be in the course of being acquired by adverse possession. The purchaser requires, and should insist upon, protection against circumstances in which such occupation or use may be unexpectedly terminated by persons having a better title to the property.

1.3 The Company is the sole legal and beneficial owner of the Properties   **6–21**
[and, where any of the Properties are leasehold, the unexpired residue of the
term granted by each lease is vested in the Company and is valid and
subsisting against all persons, including any person in which any superior
estate or interested is vested].

Ownership of the freehold or a leasehold interest may be vested in a nominee for
the absolute benefit of another, or held upon certain other express or implied
trusts for another party. In either case the beneficial ownership would be vested
in that other party. The purchaser must therefore be assured that the property of
the target company is held beneficially. In addition, on a sale of land, the
beneficial ownership passes to the purchaser as from the date of contract.
Protection against the undisclosed presence of beneficial interests which are not
held by the target company, and the possibility of onerous trust obligations
attached to the legal interest in property, is an extension of the general principle
that a vendor of land is required to give good title free from undisclosed
encumbrances.

When dealing with unregistered leasehold property, the purchaser must be
assured that the residue of the term granted by the lease is vested in the target
company. The wording in brackets covers this point when relevant.

1.4 The information contained in Schedule [ ] as to the tenure of each of   **6–22**
the Properties, the principal terms of the leases or licences held by the
Company and the principal terms of the tenancies and licences subject to
and with the benefit of which the Properties are held, is true, complete and
accurate.

"Tenure" means a freehold or leasehold estate in land but does not include a
licence.

Possession of a property usually connotes either the right of use and
occupation or the receipt of rents and profits (LPA 1925 s.205) and this clause
follows that concept.

The information to be provided under this clause is fundamental but will rarely
be difficult to obtain.

1.5 The Company has a good and marketable title to each of the   **6–23**
Properties.

The meaning of "good and marketable" title has already been considered (see
para.6–14). The purpose of a full set of property warranties is to ensure that the
purchaser is protected against a bad or unmarketable title of the target company
to its properties. This warranty, which is all embracing, not only duplicates the
protection provided by other more specific warranties but also "sweeps up" other
areas of liability which may not be covered by the aggregate effect of the
particular liability imposed by other individual warranties.

The vendors may properly seek to limit the wide and unlimited ambit of the
use of "marketable". They may point to the presence of large numbers of other

warranties dealing with specific aspects of marketability which, they might argue, give adequate protection. If "marketable" is not to be omitted, then a more limited form of warranty might be acceptable, such as:

"The Company has good title to the Properties and, so far as the Vendors are aware, there is nothing which renders the Properties unmarketable."

In this way, the protection against unmarketable property is narrowed to those circumstances which are known, or constructively known, to the vendors.

6–24   **1.6 [The Company is the proprietor of the Properties registered at the Land Registry with absolute title.] [None of the Properties are registered at the Land Registry.]**

These alternative forms of warranty are primarily for the purposes of information, and will require adaptation to accord with the circumstances. Both forms may be applicable. They are intended to serve in place of an official certificate of a search of the index map at the Land Registry, such a certificate states whether the land is registered and, if registered, whether as freehold or leasehold land (or otherwise as the case may be).

A transfer for value of freehold land, or of a lease having more than seven years unexpired, or the grant of a lease for more than seven years, which are not already registered at the Land Registry, must be registered within two months, failing which the title of the owner to the legal estate in the land becomes void. The Chief Land Registrar has a discretion, however, to extend the period of registration (Land Registration Act 2002 s.6(5)).

A person may be registered as proprietor with absolute title or possessory title (depending upon the circumstances) and, in the case of leaseholds only, there is an additional category of good leasehold title. It is beyond the scope of this commentary to explore the differences between these forms of title. However, there is no better registered title than absolute. With absolute title, the property is vested in the proprietor subject only to entries on the register and to overriding interests (one of the most important overriding interests being a lease for a term of seven years or less).

The use of the first alternative form will cause the vendors to disclose title which is possessory or qualified (and, in the case of a lease, a good leasehold title), and which may have adverse implications for value or disposability.

6–25   **1.7 Each lease of the Properties granted for more than seven years is either registered at the Land Registry with absolute title or not registered because it was not registerable at the time of grant and no event has occurred in consequence of which first registration of title should have been effected.**

This warranty provides, in relation to leasehold properties, similar protection to that afforded under cl.1.6. A lease granted for more than seven years must be registered at the Land Registry. Failure to do so within two months renders the legal estate created by the lease void, although the Chief Land Registrar has a discretion to extend the period of registration (Land Registration Act 2002 s.6(5)).

1.8 The Company is in possession and actual and exclusive occupation of the whole of each Property and no third party has acquired or is in the course of acquiring any rights to occupy or enjoy any of the Properties nor has the Company granted, or agreed to grant, any right of occupation or enjoyment in respect of any of the Properties to any third party.   6–26

This warranty will require the vendors to disclose when the target company is not in occupation of the whole or part of a property. It also gives protection against (or disclosure of) any third party acquiring the right to occupy whether through a formal grant of rights or adverse possession.

1.9 All [written] replies given by or on behalf of the Vendors or their solicitors in response to any [written] enquiries raised by or on behalf of the Purchaser or its solicitors in relation to the Properties were true, complete and accurate when given and remain so.   6–27

This warranty should be included (in the absence of a warranty elsewhere which would provide the same protection) in circumstances where the vendors have answered enquiries in respect of the properties raised by or on behalf of a purchaser. The reason for this is explained at para.6–06 above.

1.10 The Company has in its possession and control and has disclosed copies of all the title deeds and documents necessary to prove good and marketable title to the Properties and (where any of the Properties are leasehold) have further disclosed in relation to each lease evidence of the reversioner's title to the lease, all consents required under the lease, copies of all assignments of the lease and evidence of the current annual rent payable under the lease and the documents of title to be delivered to the Purchaser at Completion shall be the original documents, properly stamped with stamp duty and registered, where required.   6–28

Where any of the Properties are unregistered the purchaser will need to know that the original title deeds will be handed over completion as this will be the target company's evidence of title. In addition, the purchaser will want to ensure the deeds to be handed over will be sufficient to prove title. Even where the properties are registered, any original title deeds (particularly if the property is leasehold) ought to be handed over and this warranty therefore still ought to be included, albeit in a more limited form.

1.11 Where title to any of the Properties is not registered at the Land Registry, there is no caution against first registration of title and [to the best of the knowledge and belief of the Vendors] no event has occurred in consequence of which a caution against first registration of title could be effected.   6–29

This warranty should be included where any of the properties are unregistered although where a purchaser has time it can verify the first element of this itself through its own searches. In these circumstances vendors should resist giving this warranty or at least the first part of it. If the vendors are to give the warranty, they should seek the insertion of the wording in brackets.

6–30   **1.12 There is no circumstance that could render any transaction affecting the title of the Company to any of the Properties liable to be set aside under the Insolvency Act 1986.**

The purpose of this warranty is primarily to establish that the target company has not acquired any of the properties at an undervalue, leaving a potential risk that the purchase could in certain circumstances be set aside under the Insolvency Act 1986. The vendors ought to be able to give this warranty.

2 Encumbrances

6–31   **2.1 The Properties are free from mortgages, debentures, charges, rent charges, liens or other encumbrances.**

This clause is principally directed to encumbrances which secure upon land some financial liability, either of the target company itself or of some other party.

A mortgage connotes a document or deed which transfers a legal or equitable interest, with a provision for redemption so that, upon repayment of a loan or performance of some other obligation, the transfer becomes void or the interest is re-transferred. It is distinguished from a common law lien, which is the right to retain possession of the property or the deeds of the property, and which confers no right upon the holder to sell or otherwise deal with it. An equitable lien may in certain circumstances result in a court ordering a sale of land upon the application of the holder, and is therefore less effective in comparison to the powers of enforcement vested in a mortgage. A charge is a species of mortgage, but transfers nothing; the chargee nevertheless holds an interest in the property conferring upon him the power of sale or other forms of enforcement, according to the circumstances. A debenture is a comprehensive term for a document issued by a company evidencing an indebtedness, which is normally, but not necessarily, secured by a charge over property. A rent charge does not secure repayment of money, but is an annual or periodic payment secured on the charged land. It allows the chargee to enforce the burden of positive covenants against the owner for the time being of the charged land, which otherwise would not run with the land, or to secure payment for the cost of services provided by the chargee without the creation of a lease.

The various terms used in this clause substantially overlap therefore, and are intended principally to cover all circumstances where the land may be taken in order to enforce the security.

The circumstances in which any encumbrance may be created or arise are numerous. They range, for example, from an ordinary mortgage, given to secure a loan, to a charge imposed by statute to secure property taxes. This warranty applies equally to a rent charge or annuity issuing out of land, as it does to a charge by the target company to secure a guarantee given for the benefit of a third party. Nevertheless, the vendors should be aware of all relevant information and a purchaser is entitled to the protection afforded in order to obtain the equivalent of good title.

2.2 The Properties are not subject to outgoings, other than business rates, water and sewerage charges and insurance premiums and additionally, in the case of leasehold properties, rent and service charges. 6–32

The term "outgoings" covers all forms of recurring and non-recurring liability incidental to land ownership or occupation. They will usually arise under statute. It includes, for example, an obligation of a frontager to contribute to the cost of making up a road for dedication as a public highway and unoccupied property rate. The outgoings specifically referred to in the warranty may be regarded as being usual; all others, being unusual, should be disclosed. This information is normally requested in, and given in reply to, preliminary enquiries preparatory to a purchase of land.

In relation to leasehold properties, rent and service charges are usual and, therefore, do not need to be disclosed in this limited context. However, they are of vital importance in relation to value and are dealt with in cll.8 and 9.

2.3 The Properties are free of restrictive covenants, stipulations, easements, profits à prendre, wayleaves, licences, grants, restrictions, overriding interests or other similar rights vested in third parties or other encumbrances (whether of a private or public nature and whether legal or equitable) which restrict or conflict or may resist or conflict with the existing use of any of the Properties or are of an onerous or unusual nature or affect the value of the Properties. 6–33

This clause is primarily addressed to non-financial encumbrances over land which are commonly encountered. They are of a kind which enable parties in whom they are vested either to use the land owned by another or to prevent its use in some manner by the owner.

A restrictive covenant may prevent the owner of land from using or enjoying his land in some specified way. The burden of an enforceable covenant runs with the land in equity, and affects the current owner at any time. It may be enforceable by injunction by the owner of the land which enjoys the benefit. A covenant not to use land for a particular trade or business could be of vital importance to the purchaser of the target company wishing to change or expand its business conducted on the land in breach of the restriction. A covenant not to build would present a major obstacle to a purchaser needing to develop the land of the target company.

Easements are rights which one landowner holding the "dominant" land may exercise over the "servient" land of another which is adjoining or nearby. The most common examples of easements are rights of way, rights for services and rights of light. The acquisition of the target company with a view to the development of its properties may give rise to important questions on these issues. The presence of a right of way or of light over land may prevent or restrict the land's development. Conversely, a right of access may be essential to use of land without which its value would be heavily reduced. A wayleave is a right enjoyed by permission of the owner which is usually granted to a public utility to authorise, for example, the passage of cables, pipes or conduits through or over land, for which a nominal rent is often paid. A licence, in this context, is a permission to use or occupy land.

All other terms used in this warranty involve some minor extension of, or difference from, these concepts which encumber land. The reference to "other similar rights" would normally include options over land although these are specifically dealt with in cl.2.5.

Certain encumbrances will be specifically noted on the title to a property, and the vendors will have no difficulty in disclosing their presence. That is not true, however, of all such matters and it is customary on the sale of land for a vendor to endeavour to limit liability for non-disclosure of or inability to define all such burdens. Typical examples are the passage of services in, on, or under land, and drainage rights. By analogy, it is legitimate for the vendors to endeavour to limit their liabilities in the same way. They may argue that they should only be fairly responsible for restrictions which inhibit existing use.

6–34 **2.4 Where any of the matters referred to in clauses [2.1, 2.2 and 2.3] are disclosed in the Disclosure Letter, the obligations and liabilities imposed and arising under them have been performed and discharged, no payments in respect of them are outstanding and no notice of any alleged breach or failure to perform or discharge any of them has been received by the Company.**

The presence of such third party rights may, of course, be perfectly acceptable to the purchaser, and have been taken into account. Nevertheless the purchaser will be concerned to be protected against the failure of the target company to discharge its obligations and liabilities in relation to those rights.

While this protection may properly be sought by the purchaser, the vendors should endeavour to restrict liability to material matters. In its unrestricted form, the clause allows the purchaser to claim redress on minor matters except in so far as trivial claims are excluded by a clause imposing a floor on claims (see para.11–04).

6–35 **2.5 The Properties are free of options, estate contracts or rights of pre-emption.**

An option or other agreement to purchase a property, or to take up a lease, creates an equitable interest in land which requires registration as a land charge in the case of unregistered land, or noting on the charges register relating to the title to registered land, in order to secure full protection to the option-holder. The protection provided by this warranty overlaps with that provided under cl.2.6. A right of pre-emption, or right of first refusal, however, does not create a registerable interest in land (at least not before it is exercised and, indeed, will not become exercisable unless and until the vendor ever decides to sell). They are conveniently dealt with together, even though their technical character and consequences in conveyancing terms are different.

This information should be known to the vendors and the purchaser is entitled to it.

2.6 There are no local land charges, land charges, cautions, inhibitions or notices registered against the Properties and there is nothing which is capable of registration against them.   6–36

These are matters which would be covered by searches in the Register of Local Land Charges maintained by local authorities, the Land Charges Registry in the case of unregistered title to land, and the Land Registry where the title to land is registered. The principal purpose of this warranty is to provide protection in a case where the purchaser has not had time to make the usual searches.

The matters referred to either create charges over land or are procedural devices to protect certain rights of third parties against it. For example, an option or restrictive covenant is registerable as a land charge in the case of unregistered land, or is protected by notice or caution if title is registered. Without such registration, the option or restrictive covenant would be void against a purchaser of the legal estate in the land. The emphasis of the warranty is therefore concentrated upon the procedures to protect encumbrances.

The scope of this warranty is so wide that the vendors will be reluctant to give it in all but exceptional cases, and only then if the property is not of great importance. The vendors should do so only against the background of recent searches made by them, or on their behalf, so that they will be able to avoid liability by making full disclosure of that which searches by the purchaser would themselves reveal. In any event, it will be legitimate for the vendors to limit liability to their actual or constructive knowledge and to information of which they ought reasonably to be aware.

The vendors should be careful to omit "local land charges" from any renewal of the warranty at completion if there is an interval between contracts and completion; the purchaser would otherwise be placed in a better position than a purchaser of land.

3 Planning matters

Planning matters are creatures of statute and could logically be included in the group of warranties which appear under the heading "statutory obligations"; they have separate treatment in this arrangement of headings as being of fundamental importance. The value of property depends on how it may lawfully be used. This grouping accords to planning matters their proper significance, and compels the vendors to consider them individually.   6–37

3.1 Each of the Properties are used by the Company only for the specific purposes set out in Schedule [   ] and the use of each of the Properties is the permitted use for the purposes of the Planning Acts.   6–38

The first element of this warranty is concerned with identifying the current actual use of each of the properties (whether or not this may be lawful). The second, and more important element, concentrates on the lawfulness of such use.

A permitted use is one which is authorised by the grant of planning permission, or for which planning permission is deemed to have been granted. The potential consequences of an unauthorised use which leads to the property being discontinued, even if only temporarily, could be serious for the purchaser. The ensuing disruption to the business could give rise to significant costs and liabilities over and above the potential impact or the value on the property. The object of this clause is to protect the purchaser not only from the inconvenience arising from enforcement proceedings taken by a planning authority to terminate an unauthorised use, but also against the loss of value to a property if its existing use has to be discontinued. Careful consideration as to the adequacy of this warranty will need to be given, particularly, if a material breach is known to the purchaser. A claim under the warranty might be limited and any damages awarded insufficient to actually cover all losses sustained as a result. Combining this warranty with a specific indemnity may therefore be necessary.

"Permitted use" should be distinguished from "lawful use", a term introduced by the Planning and Compensation Act 1991, which replaced "established use". Lawful use is one which has not been authorised by planning permission, but has been rendered immune from enforcement proceedings by the passage of time (in the case of commercial uses continuous use for 10 years since the breach of planning control began) and through a successful application for a certificate of Lawful Use or Development. The penalty for giving this warranty recklessly may be very severe. However, the vendors should have the relevant information available to them and they would be expected to give it in answer to preliminary enquiries were they vendors of land. If the vendors are in any doubt, they should either make full disclosure of the circumstances or seek to limit their liability in an appropriate manner.

6–39 **3.2 Planning permission has been obtained, or is deemed to have been granted, for the purpose of the Planning Acts with respect to all development at and of the Properties; no planning permission has been suspended or revised and no application for planning permission has been called in or is otherwise awaiting a decision; no planning permission is temporary or personal and there is no planning permission which is subject to conditions any of which are not fully satisfied.**

This clause overlaps with the warranty in cl.3.1, since it would by itself cover issues of permitted user, but its emphasis is upon development of the target company's properties.

"Development" is defined by the Town and Country Planning Act 1990 s.55 which, broadly speaking, is divided into two categories. The first is the carrying out of building, engineering, mining or other operations in, on, over or under land. The second category is the making of a material change in the use of buildings or land. Planning permission is required for all such development, unless it is deemed to have been granted by the Town and Country Planning

General Permitted Development Order 1995 (SIs 1995/418 and 419 (as amended)) or the Town and Country Planning (Use Classes) Order 1987 (SI 1987/764 (as amended)). The General Permitted Development Order lays down a number of different classes of development for which planning permission is automatically granted, provided that these rights have not been removed, and various criteria met. Certain developments within the curtilage of a dwellinghouse, the erection of certain gates and fences, the erection of temporary buildings and uses in connection with the carrying out of other development are examples of classes of permitted development under the Order. Under the Use Classes Order, there are now some 12 categories of use. Planning permission is deemed to be granted for any change of use to another within the same class, and also for changes to other classes in certain instances, again subject to the rights not having been removed.

Under planning law it is possible for a planning application for which there is a resolution to approve to be called in or to be suspended. The wording of the clause has been extended to cover these potentially damaging circumstances, although their occurrence is comparatively rare. The clause, which for the most part concentrates upon substantive protection for the purchaser, changes course by adding that no application for planning permission is awaiting a decision; this is essentially for information only.

This information would normally be revealed in searches in the Register of **6–40** Local Land Charges, but such is its importance that preliminary enquiries on the subject are also usually addressed to a vendor of land.

Planning permissions are almost invariably granted subject to compliance with conditions, and any permission for substantial development is likely to have endorsed on it a large number of such conditions, some of which may be framed to require that they are discharged prior to the development being commenced, or before the development is brought into use. The purchaser shall be rightly anxious to ensure either that such conditions have been discharged, or that any outstanding conditions are disclosed. A failure to comply with certain pre-development conditions can render the entire development unlawful.

The vendors cannot easily resist the inclusion of a warranty in this form, since the target company should have accurate records of any development which it has carried out, or of detailed enquiries made upon the acquisition of a property if it was developed before it came into the target company's ownership. Disclosure of circumstances casting doubt is particularly important.

3.3 Building regulation and all other statutory consents and certificates **6–41**
have been obtained (including without limitation a building regulations final
completion certificate) with respect to all development of and alterations and
improvements to the Properties.

This is not strictly speaking a planning matter, but it relates to development and is conveniently grouped with the other warranties under this heading.

Building regulation consents must be obtained for most building operations under numerous statutes and by-laws, some of which may apply only in the locality of the property. This not only extends to major development of a property, but also to comparatively minor alterations and improvements. Alterations and improvements to properties not requiring planning permission may nevertheless require building regulation consents. The expressions used connote differences of scale and "development" should be construed as applying to forms of development other than mere alterations and improvements to properties. Alterations are distinguished from improvements as being building activities which do not add anything to property. For example, the demolition of an outhouse and the bricking up of a wall would be alterations; the addition of a new storey to an existing building would be an improvement.

The purchaser is entitled to this protection. By analogy, a purchaser of land would require the information.

6–42   **3.4 The Company has complied and is complying with all planning permissions and statutory consents orders and regulations with respect to and applicable to the Properties.**

This clause overlaps substantially with the ground covered by previous warranties under this heading, but the emphasis of this clause is upon compliance, not only with consents which have been obtained, but also with requirements of the law. As such, it provides substantial protection for the purchaser. It does not, however, deal with outstanding requirements under these consents.

The vendors should think carefully before giving this warranty, since it is in absolute and general terms. They would be well advised, even if they are confident that no major breach or non-observance on the part of the target company has taken place, to introduce qualifying words to limit its scope. A purchaser would normally accept compliance "in all material respects" as being sufficient for its purposes.

6–43   **3.5 The Company has complied and is complying with all agreements and all obligations made in respect of the Properties under s.52 of the Town and Country Planning Act 1971, s.106 of the Town and Country Planning Act 1990, s.18 of the Public Health Act 1936, s.104 of the Water Industry Act 1991, s.33 of the Local Government (Miscellaneous Provisions) Act 1982 and any other legislation relating to the condition and use of the Properties or any services or access servicing or adjoining the Properties.**

Irrespective of the powers to control development by granting or withholding planning permission, or imposing conditions upon the grant of planning permission, a planning authority may also enter into agreements with landowners, restricting or regulating the development of land either permanently or for temporary periods. These agreements are enforceable against successors in title to the land.

The agreements have now become commonplace on large or important developments, and planning permissions often contain a condition that such an agreement must be entered into particularly in order to secure planning gain (i.e. some additional but related gain to the community, subject to a qualification that it must relate to the proposed development and be necessary to the grant of planning permission). A common example is the provision of car parking accommodation for members of the public.

Frequently, and in particular with reference to housing estate development, the Local Authority requires that a new road be made up and, once it has been completed and maintained for a period to the satisfaction of the Highway Authority, it will be declared a highway repairable by the public. Under agreements pursuant to the Highways Act 1980 s.38 a specification for the road, the manner of construction and its maintenance to the satisfaction of the Highway Authority are generally laid down. Security from the developer is usually required in the form either of a deposit of cash or of a performance bond provided by a financial institution. Full disclosure of such obligations on the part of the target company is obviously of administrative and financial importance to the purchaser.

Similarly agreements under the Water Industry Act 1991 s.104 (formerly dealt with under the Public Health Act 1936 s.18) deal with commitments to make up sewerage infrastructure and offer it for adoption by the statutory sewerage undertaker.

The vendors would not normally be justified in resisting the giving of this warranty where applicable, since it relates to information which they should have readily available and would be required to provide were they vendors of land.

3.6 None of the Properties is listed as being of special historic or architectural importance or located in a conservation area.

6–44

This information would be revealed by a search in the Register of Local Land Charges. The Secretary of State for Culture, Media and Sport approves lists of buildings of special architectural or historic interest (which are then administered by English Heritage). It is an offence to demolish, alter or extend a listed building without a listed building consent or to damage such a building. While a building may not be so listed, it may be within a conservation area—that is an area of special architectural or historic interest with a character or appearance which ought to be preserved, and which is designated as such an area by the Local Planning Authority. No building in such an area may be demolished without consent and trees in the area are protected as if they were subject to a tree preservation order.

These issues can be of critical importance if the target company is being acquired for the purpose of the redevelopment of its properties. In such an event, however, the vendors should require the purchaser to make an investigation of title, since the property assets of the target company will be of fundamental importance. Therefore the warranty will usually be deleted or omitted. Furthermore, if the disclosure letter treats as being disclosed all matters which would be revealed in a search (see, for example, sub-para.(h) of the disclosure letter discussed in para.9–22), then this warranty will be valueless. Nonetheless if time or other circumstances do not permit the obtaining of appropriate search results by the purchaser, it should insist upon the warranty and refuse to accept disclosure of the hypothetical search.

4 Statutory obligations

6–45   **4.1 The Company has complied and is complying with all applicable statutory and by-law requirements with respect to the Properties including the Public Health Acts, the Occupiers Liability Act 1957, the Offices, Shops and Railway Premises Act 1963, the Fire Precautions Act 1971, the Health and Safety at Work etc. Act 1974, the Environmental Protection Act 1990, the Sunday Trading Act 1994, the Construction (Design and Management) Regulations 1994, the Environment Act 1995, the Disability Discrimination Act 1995, the Control of Asbestos Regulations 2006, the Regulatory Reform (Fire Safety) Order 2005, the Construction (Design and Management) Regulations 2007 and any other legislation current or previous currently affecting the Properties and any other [applicable or] relevant orders, regulations, rules or directions and delegated legislation of a competent authority affecting the Properties.**

These are essentially checklist items, but impose potentially substantial liability upon the vendors for failure to disclose or inaccurate disclosure. The listing of individual statutes is not necessary.

In contrast with the reference to compliance with the building regulation consents and by-laws raised under the "planning matters" group of warranties, compliance with statutory and by-law requirements in this clause is intended to relate to use and enjoyment of the properties and not to their development, although the wording is wide enough to cover development obligations. The statutes specifically mentioned in this warranty lay down regulations as to how certain properties may be used and enjoyed. They are largely concerned with safety precautions and good working conditions.

Specific reference is made to some of the more recent acts and regulations, because they are relatively recent and in some instances, less likely to have been fully complied with. Their inclusion gives the vendors a reminder to consider compliance with them and to disclose or remedy any non-compliance, as appropriate.

As with all warranties which state generally that "compliance has been made", the liability is virtually limitless. If the warranty is to be given, the vendors should seek to limit it to those matters of which they are aware. This is another example of a warranty which should be given only where the properties are not of great importance or issues of timing or the strength of the purchaser's bargaining power allow the vendors little freedom to manoeuvre. In all other circumstances, it should be for the purchaser to satisfy itself.

6–46   **4.2 There is no outstanding or unperformed obligation with respect to the Properties, compliance with which is necessary to satisfy the requirements (whether formal or informal) of a competent authority exercising statutory or delegated powers.**

This warranty overlaps with the protection given under cl.4.1. However, that clause is essentially directed to the application of the general law to property, whereas this warranty relates to specific requirements which competent authorities in exercise of their powers have laid down in respect of the properties of the target company. It is one thing to infringe the requirements of the general law, and another to fail to comply with the requirements of competent authorities exercising their powers specifically in relation to a property. These requirements ought to be known to the vendors and the protection sought by the purchaser is sufficiently specific not to be resisted. The vendors might properly seek to limit the scope of the warranty by reference to materiality.

4.3 No licences are required in relation to any of the Properties.　　6–47

This warranty is intended to cause disclosure to be made of licences required with respect to any particular use of property, or to the business carried on upon property. It essentially duplicates cl.4.14.1 in para.7–123 and, unless the activities carried out on the premises are such as to require special licensing, it need not be repeated here.

5 Adverse orders

The two warranties appearing under this heading could logically be allocated to "encumbrances" and "planning matters". It is considered, however, that this grouping is more convenient and draws better attention to their subject matter.　　6–48

5.1 There are no compulsory purchase notices, orders or resolutions affecting the Properties and [to the best of the knowledge and belief of the Vendors] there are no circumstances likely to lead to any being made.　　6–49

This warranty relates to matters which would be revealed in the Register of Local Land Charges in answer to the standard CON 29 enquiries invariably submitted as part of the Local Authority search. Accordingly, the warranty would be rendered inoperative by most disclosure letters (for example sub-para.(g)(1) in para.9–22). The warranty is in two parts. Since the second part relates to circumstances which may lead to such notices, orders or resolutions being made, it should be limited by the addition of the words in square brackets.

If the purchaser has time to make searches, the vendors should be reluctant to give this warranty other than as to the vendors' knowledge of the likelihood of notices and the like being made.

5.2 There are no closing, demolition or clearance orders, enforcement notices or stop notices affecting the Properties and [to the best of the knowledge and belief of the Vendors] there are no circumstances likely to lead to any being made.　　6–50

Closing, demolition and clearance orders are mainly to do with safety regulations and slum clearance under the Public Health Acts. Enforcement notices and stop notices are procedures under the Planning Acts to prevent infringements of planning control. An enforcement notice can require the demolition or alteration of buildings or works, the discontinuance of any use of land or the carrying out on land of any building operations or other operations. An enforcement notice may be accompanied by a stop notice, the effect of which is to prohibit any person on whom it is served from carrying out or continuing any specified operations on land.

The existence of such orders or the service of such notices should be information known or available to the vendors, but they are matters upon which the purchaser should make searches and, if there is time for that to be done, the vendors should resist giving this warranty. If the vendors are to give the warranty, they should seek the insertion of the wording in brackets.

6 Condition of the Properties

6–51   On a purchase of land, the purchaser usually has no remedy against the vendor for any grievance arising out of the state and condition of the property acquired and the legal principle of caveat emptor will normally apply. The prudent purchaser will therefore carry out a survey of the property, prior to entering into a contract to acquire it. It may make preliminary enquiries about the state and condition of the property, which are customarily parried by the vendor's solicitor who ordinarily answers that the purchaser must rely upon its own inspection. The group of warranties under this heading gives the purchaser of the target company protection which it would not usually be able to obtain if it were to buy land. Their inclusion ought therefore to be resisted by the vendors, save in exceptional and appropriate circumstances, usually only when timing is such that the purchaser will be unable to undertake appropriate surveys of the properties.

6–52   **6.1 The buildings and other structures on the Properties are in good and substantial repair and fit for the purposes for which they are used.**

The standard of repair required by this warranty adopts the formula often seen in leases, and is often described as a full repairing obligation. Certainly there would be a breach of the warranty if any but the most minor repairs are required to be done.

The warranty is likely to be acceptable only if the purchase price of the target company reflects a value of the properties depending upon their being in good condition and the opportunity for full inspection and survey is not open to the purchaser for confidentiality or other reasons.

Care needs to be taken with this warranty when dealing with leasehold properties. The target company might well be bound with a full repairing obligation but may have made provision for potential dilapidation liabilities in its accounts. Provided this provision is sufficient, it may therefore be the case that this potential liability is dealt with and taken into account in the purchase price. When dealing with new buildings it may be that the target company has the benefit of protection in the form of appropriate collateral warranties and guarantees. In such circumstances, the vendors should also resist this warranty as the benefit of the collateral warranties and guarantees will stay with the target company.

6.2 No structure on the Properties has been affected by structural damage   6–53
or electrical defects or by timber infestation or disease.

These circumstances would normally be investigated on the survey of land. The vendors should therefore resist the inclusion of this warranty but, if it is retained, it should be limited to a reasonable period in the past and to the vendors' knowledge.

6.3 No structure at the Properties contains any materials which do not   6–54
comply with relevant regulations, standards and codes of practice or which
are generally regarded as deleterious to health, safety or the durability of
buildings or structures.

In the post-war period, a number of building substances were used by the construction industry which have since proven unsound, and which have rendered certain larger constructions susceptible to collapse. Some have also since proven to be harmful to public health and the environment. They are usually the subject of a preliminary enquiry to a vendor of land. Rather than list examples of prohibited substances, the warranty employs a general reference to deleterious materials, which is the approach now favoured by most construction lawyers.

If the target company has built the properties, then the vendors should have the relevant information. If the target company acquired them, it may have replies to preliminary enquiries made on its behalf at the time of acquisition. In those circumstances, the vendors may feel themselves able to give the warranty, but in all other circumstances they should resist doing so. With more modern buildings, the target company may, as mentioned above, already have protection in the form of appropriate collateral warranties and guarantees, and so, even when the vendors should have the relevant information, the vendors should still resist this warranty.

6.4 There are no disputes with a neighbouring owner with respect to   6–55
boundary walls and fences, or with a third party with respect to easements
or rights over or benefiting the Properties.

In the purchase of land, a standard preliminary enquiry is made on these matters. Support may be required for a boundary wall, and disputes over rights of way, rights of light and access to the property are often key issues when development proposals are about to be implemented.

The vendors cannot easily resist giving this warranty since it is information which should be available to them, save perhaps, by limiting to the extent of their own awareness.

6.5 The principal means of access to the Properties are over roads which   6–56
have been taken over by the local or other highway authority and which are
maintainable at the public expense, and such roads immediately abut the
boundary of the legal title to the Properties at each of them where access is

granted, and no means of access to the Properties is shared with another party or subject to rights of determination by another party.

The purchaser will want to know whether the properties have sufficient legal rights to enable the properties to be accessed and further whether there is any liability to repair and maintain any road on to which a property abuts and whether there is any potential liability to the cost of making up the road, in order that it should be adopted by the highway authority. The second part of the warranty is concerned with whether a right of access may be lost.

The wording used is an amalgamation of enquiries which are normally directed to the Local Land Charges Department and raised by way of preliminary enquiries on the purchase of land.

6–57   **6.6 Each of the Properties enjoys the mains services of water, drainage, electricity and gas.**

This is normally the subject of a preliminary enquiry on the purchase of land. The vendors should give this information.

6–58   **6.7 [To the best of the knowledge and belief of the Vendors] none of the Properties are located in an area or subject to circumstances particularly susceptible to flooding.**

These circumstances would normally be investigated on the survey of land and by enquiry of the Environment Agency. The vendors should endeavour to qualify the warranty by adding the wording in brackets.

6–59   **6.8 The Properties are not subject to rights of common.**

This warranty is usually only applicable to land in country areas. An example is the right to pasture cattle on the land. This would be dealt with on a purchase of land by a search in the registers of common land and town or village greens.

6–60   **6.9 None of the Properties is subject to registration as a town or village green and [to the best of the knowledge and belief of the Vendors] there are no circumstances which could give rise to the registration of any of the Properties as a town or village green.**

Whilst on a purchase of land, the existence of a town or village green will be disclosed by a search of the registers of town and village greens, the Commons Act 2006 provides that anyone can apply to register land as a town or village green where a significant number of the inhabitants of any locality, or of any neighbourhood within a locality, have indulged as a right in lawful sports and practices on the land for a period of at least 20 years and it continues to be so used at the time of the application, or where the use has ceased before the application:

(i) the cessation was before April 6, 2007 and the application is made within five years of the cessation; or

(ii) the cessation was after April 6, 2007 and the application is made within two years of the cessation.

The uncertainties that these provisions have created for purchasers of land are not to be underestimated. Land which is not subject to a relevant registration at the time of purchase, and on which no lawful sports and pastimes are being undertaken by inhabitants of the locality, may nonetheless be capable of being registered as town or village green on the strength of an application made up to five years after that use ceased. A purchaser of land for development accordingly now expects very firm assurances from the vendor that such circumstances do not apply, and a purchaser of shares will expect a warranty in these terms, which the vendors will find it difficult to resist. The impact of a successful registration could be significant as effectively any development on the registered land is prohibited. Consequently, the liability under such a warranty could be very large and the vendors will need to consider carefully what disclosure needs to be made against it. They may well wish to moderate it by reference to their knowledge and period of ownership.

6.10 [To the best of the knowledge and belief of the Vendors] the Properties are not affected by mining activity. 6–61

A prudent purchaser of land in areas which are, or might be affected by subsidence due to mining activity can make a search with the Coal Authority which will certify, or otherwise give information as to, mining activity, past present and, as at the date of the search, any known future proposals in the area, and whether or not the property could be affected by subsidence. The vendors should endeavour to exclude this warranty, or to qualify it by introducing the wording in brackets.

7 Insurance

Although the question of proper insurance is of particular significance in relation to properties, the following clauses overlap the warranties in cl.8.4 in para.7–223. The vendors should seek to eliminate the duplication. 6–62

7.1 The Properties are covered by insurance of a type usually available in the United Kingdom insurance market against a comprehensive range of risks (including subsidence and terrorism) in their full reinstatement values and against third party and public liabilities and professional fees to an adequate extent and, where any of the Properties are let, for not less than three years' loss of rent or such greater period as may be specified in the tenancies affecting the Properties. 6–63

Reinstatement value is based upon the cost of rebuilding the buildings or structures insured. It is customary to insure for loss of rent from premises for a period long enough to allow for the reconstruction of buildings which have been totally destroyed. These amounts are measurable according to current building costs and rental values. Third party and public liability insurances cover injury or damage to personal property, and as such the cover to be provided should be adequate.

If the purchaser has had time and opportunity to consider these questions, the vendors may properly resist giving the warranty.

6–64   **7.2 All premiums due in respect of insurance policies relating to the Properties have been duly paid and, where the Properties are let, the premiums are recoverable in full from the tenants pursuant to the tenancies affecting the Properties and nothing has arisen which would vitiate the policies or permit the insurers to avoid them.**

The warranty in cl.7.1 deals with the cover afforded by the policies; this clause is concerned in part with the payment of premiums and additionally with the validity of the policies. This last matter is not always easily determined and that element of the clause may reasonably be resisted by the vendors although understandably a purchaser will want to secure as much protection as possible on this. A balance might be achieved by limiting the last matter to the vendors' awareness.

6–65   **7.3 The information in the Disclosure Letter with respect to insurance policies is complete and accurate.**

This clause presupposes that insurance details will have been supplied by the vendors which it ought to have been. The vendors should have no difficulty with the clause provided that the relevant information is purely factual.

8 Leasehold properties

6–66   The warranties under this heading relate to leases held by the target company. A lease creates a tenancy, but the expression "tenancies" has been used for the heading for the warranties in cl.9 which relate to leases subject to and with the benefit of which the properties are held so that income is derived from them. It is emphasised that this distinction is neither technical nor even proper; it is merely a convenient way, in this context, of labelling them.

On an assurance of leasehold land by a vendor conveying with full title guarantee, further covenants are implied in addition to the covenants as to right to convey, further assurance and freedom from undisclosed encumbrances. These are that the lease is subsisting, that there are no breaches of the tenant's covenants (although breach of the repairing covenants will frequently be excluded), and that there is nothing rendering the lease liable to forfeiture. The warranties under this heading are based on, and expand upon those covenants.

Details of the leases held by the company will have been given, and are referred to in cl.1.4.

8.1 The Company has paid the rent and performed [in all material 6–67
respects] the covenants on the part of the tenant and the conditions
contained in any leases (which expression in this clause [8] includes
underleases) under which the Properties are held, the last demands for rent
(or receipts, if issued) were unqualified and all the leases are in full force.

The expression "leases" is extended to underleases so that it includes all
derivative underleases.

The clause borrows the assumption made in the LPA 1925 s.45(2) that on the
sale of a lease, the production of the receipt for the last payment of rent due under
the lease before the date of actual completion of the purchase causes the
purchaser to assume, unless the contrary appears, that all the covenants and
provisions of the lease have been duly performed and observed up to the date of
actual completion of the purchase. This provides a mechanism for completion of
the purchase of land to take place, notwithstanding that there may in fact be a
breach of such covenants. Following on from that procedure, it used to be
customary, and is still good estate management practice, for any known breach
of covenant to be recorded on a receipt for rent given by the landlord or his agent.
The production of an unqualified receipt for rent is therefore some, but limited,
comfort that there is no material breach of covenant outstanding.

The vendors cannot easily resist giving this warranty, but may properly
endeavour to qualify it by introducing the words in square brackets. A purchaser
in a stronger bargaining position may require a tougher warrant to the effect that
the target company has not received any notice or communication alleging any
breach of any of the tenant's covenants and conditions.

One particular aspect of this warranty does, however, necessitate specific
consideration: by giving this warranty, vendors may also effectively be
warranting the state and condition of the premises depending upon the nature of
the repairing covenant in the lease. It may therefore be necessary to specifically
carve out from this warranty compliance with covenants relating to repair and the
state and condition of the properties where it has already been agreed between the
parties either that this liability will not fall on the vendors or is to be dealt with
by other means.

8.2 All licences, consents and approvals required from the landlords and 6–68
any superior landlords under leases of the Properties have been obtained,
and the tenant's covenants therein have been performed [in all material
respects].

Leases invariably contain tenant's covenants which involve the obtaining of the
prior consent or approval of the landlord. The most common instances are
assignments and sublettings of the premises demised by the lease, the making of
alterations to the premises and a change in the user of the premises. Licences
granting permission in respect of such matters usually contain additional tenant's
covenants. The purchaser of the target company will be equally concerned that
additional covenants imposed by such licences and approvals have been
performed. As minor breaches can easily occur, the vendors should seek to

qualify this warranty by the addition of the words in square brackets or along the same lines recommended at para.6–61 above.

6–69   **8.3 There are no rent reviews in progress under leases of the Properties held by the Company and no rent can be reviewed for at least a year after Completion.**

In general, time is not of the essence for a rent review unless it is expressly or impliedly made so. It is therefore possible for rent reviews to take place long after their appointed date. The warranty will give the purchaser the reassurance that there are no outstanding or unimplemented reviews in relation to any lease and the vendors should be prepared to give it and disclose against it if necessary.

6–70   **8.4 No obligation necessary to comply with a notice or other requirement [properly] given by the landlord under a lease of any of the Properties is outstanding and unperformed.**

The scope of this clause overlaps with the protection provided under cll.8.1 and 8.2, but its emphasis is concentrated upon notices which have been given by the landlord. It has in contemplation, primarily, notices given under the LPA 1925 s.146, which are a procedural prerequisite to forfeiture of a lease for breach of covenant, other than in the case of non-payment of rent. The landlord must serve a notice on the tenant specifying the particular breach complained of, and whether the breach is capable of remedy requiring the tenant to remedy the breach, and in any case requiring the tenant to make compensation in money for the breach. If the tenant fails within a reasonable time to remedy a breach which is capable of remedy to the landlord's satisfaction and to make reasonable monetary compensation, the landlord is entitled to exercise its right of re-entry or forfeiture, subject to the powers of the court to award relief. The vendors might reasonably require the insertion of the word "properly" as indicated.

6–71   **8.5 There is no obligation to reinstate any of the Properties by removing an alteration made to it by the Company or a predecessor in title to the Company and all such alterations are to be disregarded on any review of the rent payable under each lease of the Properties.**

It is good estate management practice for a landlord to require in the grant of a licence permitting alterations that the premises should, if the landlord so requires, be reinstated at the expiration or earlier determination of the lease. The origins of this requirement are in the Landlord and Tenant Act 1927 Pt I, which allows a tenant to claim compensation for improvements to premises in appropriate cases by complying with the very cumbersome procedure laid down by the Act. The imposition of covenants requiring the reinstatement of the premises enabled the landlord to avoid paying compensation for improvements in appropriate cases. While this part of the Act is now seldom used, the practice of requiring reinstatement has been continued as a practical, useful tool in the hands of a landlord who may not wish to retain the "improvement" even if issues of compensation are not also involved.

The second part of this warranty gives the purchaser confirmation that on review, additional rent will not be payable to reflect the cost of alterations undertaken by the target company or its predecessors.

8.6 The Company has not entered into an authorised guarantee agreement under the Landlord and Tenant (Covenants) Act 1995 s.16 in respect of any property. 6–72

Section 16 was introduced in connection with the abolition by that Act of the doctrine of privity of contract in relation to leases granted on or after January 1, 1996. Under s.16, the landlord may require the tenant, in accordance with the terms of the lease, to enter into an authorised guarantee agreement when assigning the lease. While the Act provides for the release of a tenant on an assignment it allows, in specified circumstances, the entering into of an authorised guarantee agreement by the tenant guaranteeing the performance of the tenant's covenants by the assignee. The guarantee may relate only to the performance of the immediate assignee and may subsist only for the period during which the lease remains vested in the immediate assignee.

The purchaser will be able to ascertain whether any of the leases of properties held at the date of the share sale contain a provision relating to an authorised guarantee agreement, but it has no ready means of determining the position in relation to leases which have already been assigned. As it will be a question of fact whether the target company has entered into an agreement, the vendors should have no difficulty in giving the warranty although, in appropriate cases, they would wish to restrict the application of the warranty to assignments which have taken place while the company has been in their ownership.

8.7 The Company has not had the right to call for an overriding lease of any property under the Landlord and Tenant (Covenants) Act 1995 s.19. 6–73

Section 19 provides that a former tenant or its guarantor which has incurred liability under the tenant's covenants in a lease as a result of a default by the assignee may, on discharging the liability, call for an overriding lease to be granted to it, subject to and with the benefit of the existing lease. It could be an important matter for the purchaser to be aware of but, as the vendors may not know that circumstances exist entitling the target company to call for the lease, the warranty should be qualified so that it applies only to the best of their knowledge.

8.8 The Company has not entered into an agreement with the lessor of any of the Properties specifying circumstances in which it would be reasonable for the lessor to withhold its consent to an assignment in accordance with the Landlord and Tenant Act 1927 s.19(1A). 6–74

Section 19(1A) was inserted into the Landlord and Tenant Act 1927 by the Landlord and Tenant (Covenants) Act 1995 s.22 to lessen the impact on landlords of the abolition of privity of contract in leases granted on or after January 1, 1996. The section permits a landlord to agree with the tenant, either in the lease or in a separate document, permitted circumstances in which the landlord may reasonably withhold consent to an assignment. The circumstances which may be specified are restricted so that, for example, it may not include matters which are to be determined by the landlord unless there is a reasonableness test.

The purchaser will be particularly concerned about the existence of such an agreement which is separate from the lease itself and the vendors should generally be able to give the warranty without difficulty.

9 Tenancies

6–75   **9.1 The Properties are held subject to and with the benefit of the tenancies (which expression in this clause [9] includes subtenancies) as set out in Schedule [   ] and no others.**

The principal terms of the tenancies will have been specified; cl.1.4 compels such disclosure.

6–76   **9.2 With respect to the tenancies, the Disclosure Letter contains particulars of:**

> **9.2.1   the rent and any rent reviews and, with respect to rent reviews, the date for giving notice of exercise of the reviews and the operative review date;**
> **9.2.2   the term and rights to break or renew the term;**
> **9.2.3   the obligations of the landlord and tenant in respect of outgoings, repairs, insurance, services and service charges;**
> **9.2.4   options or pre-emption rights;**
> **9.2.5   the user required or permitted;**

The information disclosed in cll.9.2.1–9.2.5 is essential for administrative and management purposes. As an alternative and recommended from the vendors' point of view, the vendors could produce to the purchaser copies of the relevant leases and warrant them to be accurate.

Where the properties are held for investment purposes, this information will be crucial. The maintenance and potential growth of value in a property centres upon the right to review rent and the full recovery from tenants of the cost of repair, maintenance, insurance and the provision of services.

6–77   **9.2.6   the entitlement of a tenant of the Properties to compensation either on quitting the premises, for improvements or otherwise;**

A tenant of business premises will be entitled under the Landlord and Tenant Act 1954 s.37 (as amended) to compensation on quitting the premises in certain circumstances. For example, if the landlord terminates the business tenancy at the appropriate time and opposes the grant of a new tenancy on the grounds that it requires the premises for its own business, or that upon the termination of the current tenancy it intends to demolish or reconstruct the premises, then the right to such compensation accrues. The procedure for obtaining compensation for improvements under the Landlord and Tenant Act 1927 Pt I has already been mentioned. The purchaser will be entitled to know of any potential liability of the target company for such compensation.

9.2.7   any unusual provisions; and   6–78

Usual covenants in a lease are those which "occur in ordinary use" and depend on the facts of each particular case. In an open contract for the grant of a lease containing usual covenants, the court will allow evidence of what is current practice in leases of premises of that type and in that locality. The purpose of this information is to place the onus upon the vendors to bring to the attention of the purchaser any provisions which are not in accordance with current practice. The vendors might object to its indeterminate nature and refuse to give it if the purchaser has time to investigate. The alternative is for the vendors to produce the leases to the purchaser, which can then evaluate the provisions for itself.

9.2.8   short particulars of subtenancies derived out of the tenancies [of   6–79
which the Vendors are aware].

This information is particularly important in determining the existence of business tenancies under the Landlord and Tenant Act 1954 Pt II. A subtenant in occupation of the premises for the purposes of his business enjoys rights of renewal as conferred by the Act but a tenant, having sublet and not occupying any part of the premises, has no such security of tenure. A landlord usually has this information, but it would be proper for the warranty to be qualified by the addition of the words in square brackets.

9.3 The Vendors are not aware of a material or persistent breach of   6–80
covenant by a tenant of the Properties.

This information is of importance to a purchaser and enables it to assess the covenant strength of the tenant and its effect on the value of the property. In addition, persistent delay in paying rent or other substantial breaches of covenant by the tenant constitute grounds of opposition by the target company to the grant by the court of a new tenancy under the Landlord and Tenant Act 1954 Pt II.

9.4 The Company has not at any time: 6–81

9.4.1   surrendered any lease, licence or tenancy to the landlord without
first satisfying itself that the landlord had good title to accept such surrender and without receiving from the landlord an absolute release from all liability arising under such lease, licence or tenancy;

9.4.2 assigned, or otherwise disposed of, any lease, licence or tenancy without receiving a full and effective indemnity from the assignee or transferee in respect of its liability under such lease, licence or tenancy;

9.4.3 been a guarantor of a tenant's liability under any lease, licence or tenancy or otherwise given any guarantee or indemnity for any liability relating to any of the Properties, any property or any other land or buildings previously owned; or

9.4.4 assigned or otherwise disposed of dealt with or held any property in such a way that it retains any other residual liability (whether actual or contingent) in respect thereof.

This clause is designed to flush out any residual liability that the target company may have in respect of any premises formerly occupied or owned by it or in which it otherwise had an interest and to protect the purchaser against any that are unknown, or not disclosed. In practice it is unlikely to cause the vendors any difficulty and will simply require disclosure of any relevant matters.

CHAPTER 7

Typical Long Form Commercial Warranties on Share Sales

INTRODUCTION

The form that warranties may take where the shares of an active trading company **7–01** are purchased is infinitely variable, and no standard set of warranties can be entirely suitable for every deal. In selecting which warranties are appropriate for a particular transaction, it is helpful to have a comprehensive standard form available which can be suitably edited to deal with the particular circumstances of the target company or deal. Vendors will not appreciate receiving an agreement that contains extensive warranties on areas that are of little or no relevance to the target company, or on areas where there is already a mechanism in the agreement for addressing the potential risk that the warranties are designed to cover. For example, in circumstances where there is to be a stock valuation exercise carried out and the purchase price adjusted based on the outcome of that, vendors will generally resist giving warranties about the quality of the stock.

For a systematic approach, it is essential, as well as being good practice, for the warranties to be grouped into sections dealing with related subject matters. The following is an example of the headings which might usefully be considered other than in relation to taxation and properties (which are dealt with separately in Chs 5 and 6), each paragraph being analysed in some detail further on in this chapter. The warranties themselves are repeated in Appendix 4, with the omission of the amendments which are included within square brackets and which are put forward to assist and protect the vendors.

Clause	*Title*
1	**PRELIMINARY**
1.1	**Capacity and authority of the Vendors**
1.2	**Ownership of Shares**
1.3	**Share capital**
1.4	**Details of the Company**
1.5	**Directors and shadow directors**
1.6	**Subsidiaries and branches**
1.7	**Options over the Company's capital**
1.8	**Commissions**
1.9	**Elective resolutions**
1.10	**Constitutional documents, statutory books and resolutions**
1.11	**Documents filed**

Short Form Warranties

7–02   If the target company's affairs are comparatively simple or if the consideration for the company is modest, the use of extensive warranties may not only be inappropriate but actually counter-productive. A shorter set of warranties would be suitable in such cases and a precedent is contained in Appendix 9. The precedent essentially takes the long-form warranties and condenses them down into a set of warranties which, while much shorter, cover for the most part the same areas. The effect of this is to put the burden on the vendors and their advisers to consider fully the potential scope of each of the warranties, as the warranties themselves will not direct their minds specifically to all relevant areas. The purchaser will enjoy a similar level of cover as if long-form warranties had been used, but save the costs of negotiating long-form warranties and, to unsuspecting vendors, the purchaser may appear to be more reasonable.

While the warranties in Appendix 9 would be particularly useful in a low value transaction where little is known of the target company, in circumstances where details are known and the target company's affairs are relatively simple, consideration should be given as to whether it would be preferable to tailor the long-form warranties to cover relevant areas to try to ensure that the vendors' attention when making disclosures is focused on all of the pertinent areas and that the purchaser is provided with details of all relevant matters which it can carefully consider.

Analysis of Individual Warranties

7–03   In the following detailed analysis of typical warranties it is assumed that the vendors and warrantors are one and the same, that the purchase relates to the shares of a trading company and that the purchaser is a company. The definitions in para.4–02 are adopted, and defined terms are printed with a capital first letter. Where words are included in square brackets it is assumed, in most cases, that the warranty is prepared by the purchaser's solicitors without those words and that the vendors might wish to add them.

1 Preliminary

1.1 Capacity and authority of the Vendors

7–04   **1.1.1 Each of the Vendors has the necessary power and authority to enter into and perform this Agreement and all other documents to be executed by**

them at or before Completion in accordance with this Agreement which constitutes or will when executed constitute binding and enforceable obligations on each of the Vendors

Lack of power, authority or incapacity, can arise in the case of infants, bankrupts, trustees, persons of unsound mind and companies which do not have appropriate provisions in their articles of association. Where a vendor is a foreign entity, it is standard practice to obtain an opinion letter from a lawyer qualified in the relevant jurisdiction as to the existence of the required capacity.

Where there is a sole vendor who is also the warrantor, the warranty has no function except to operate by way of a reminder to the purchaser's advisers to check the capacity of the vendor, which they should do as a matter of course. If the vendor lacks capacity to enter into the agreement, he/it will also lack capacity to give the warranty, and so it will provide no protection to the purchaser. The provision has legal value in practice only where there are a number of vendors and each vendor accepts responsibility for any incapacity of another vendor, or where the vendors and warrantors differ. If there is any risk attached to this matter, it seems appropriate that it should fall upon the vendors who are, in principle, obtaining the benefit of the sale of the target company rather than the purchaser. The vendors should have no need to amend or seek to resist the warranty, if they do then the purchaser will need to be careful to ensure that the vendors are in fact entitled to do what they are purporting to do.

1.2 Ownership of Shares

1.2.1 The Shares are fully paid or credited as fully paid and will, at   7–05 Completion, constitute the whole of the issued and allotted share capital of the Company.

Issued shares are shares in respect of which an entry has been made in the register of members. Allotted shares are shares which have been allotted by a company and are held on letters of allotment, but have not been registered. Shares are fully paid if they are subscribed for in cash, and are credited as paid if allotted for a non-cash consideration, including in particular a capitalisation of reserves. Shares in a private company can be allotted partly or fully paid. In the case of a public company, they must be paid up at least one quarter of their nominal value and the whole amount of any premium. If shares are not fully paid, there is a contingent liability under the Insolvency Act 1986 s.74 upon holders and certain past holders to pay up the shares on an insolvency. The warranty may also have particular relevance in relation to a target company which is a public limited company, as CA 2006 s.586 requires the shares of a public company to be paid up to the extent of at least one quarter of their nominal value. Again, other than where it is not the entire issued share capital of the target company that is being sold (in which circumstances the warranty will need to be amended to refer to the share capital that is in fact being sold), the vendors should not seek any amendment to or resist giving the warranty.

7–06   1.2.2 The Vendors have the right to transfer to the Purchaser (without the consent of any third party) and will on Completion transfer the legal and beneficial title to the Shares.

It is only the legal ownership, that is the ownership conferred by entry in the register of members, of the shares of the target company, that is strictly relevant. This is because the persons entered in the register are defined to be the members of the company (CA 2006 s.112). The subscribers to the memorandum become members on registration of the company even if their names are not entered in to the register of members (CA 2006 s.112(1)). The reference to beneficial ownership will often be inappropriate, for example if the vendors include trustees or the target is a wholly owned subsidiary and one of the vendors is the nominee for the holding company. If for good reason the vendors wish to omit the reference to beneficial ownership, the purchaser should not be concerned. This warranty will be superfluous if the vendors are expressed to sell with full title guarantee (see para.4–08) unless the vendors and the warrantors are not the same persons.

7–07   1.2.3 There is not now existing nor is there any agreement to create any Encumbrance on or affecting the Shares or any unissued shares or securities of the Company.

"Encumbrance" is defined to include not only those matters that would normally be considered to be encumbrances in the ordinary English meaning of the word, but also more esoteric matters which might arguably not ordinarily amount to an encumbrance. There are minor, and largely irrelevant, differences between the various types of encumbrances in the way that they might apply to shares. If share certificates are handed over for the purpose of securing a debt, the transaction strictly gives rise to a pledge. A lien exists where the certificates are held by a person to whom a debt is owed, such as a banker who happens to be holding the certificates on behalf of a customer indebted to the bank, without a formal charge being created. In relation to a bank, it would appear to be correct to confine the concept of a lien to a right which attaches to documents coming into the bank's possession otherwise than directly in relation to the indebtedness. A lien on the shares held by a vendor may also exist if he is indebted to the target company and its articles of association provide for a lien even where the shares are fully paid.

The 1985 version of Table A reg.8 provides for a lien over shares that are not fully paid. For companies incorporated under CA 2006 they use the model articles set out in The Companies (Model Articles) Regulations 2008 which presume that shares in a private company will be fully paid (as is most often the case). As such they do not include provisions relating to liens (or other mechanisms dealing with partly paid shares) as they are not necessary in those circumstances.

A charge or other encumbrance on shares is not registerable under CA 2006 s.860, unless given for the purpose of securing an issue of debentures, and the normal rules applicable to bona fide purchasers without notice will therefore apply. If the purchaser is to take free of such a charge of which it did not have actual notice, it must be able to show that the lack of notice was bona fide and this warranty will assist it in doing so. Furthermore, from a practical point of view, the purchaser will wish to ensure that the vendors are reminded to check whether the shares are charged so that arrangements can be made to deliver the shares, free of encumbrances, at completion. Whilst overlapping with cl.1.1.1 in this regard, this warranty will also require the vendors to check and confirm to the purchaser that there are no encumbrances, or arrangements to create the same, which might apply in respect of a future issue of unissued shares (or other securities) in the capital of the target company. The vendors cannot reasonably resist the warranty and would in practice gain nothing by doing so.

If the shares were the subject of a "chargeable transfer" under IHTA 1984 and tax arising on the transfer remains unpaid, the shares will be subject to a charge to secure the tax (see the comments on cl.29.2 in para.5–100).

The vendors will generally be required to sell their shares with full title guarantee (as defined in the LPMPA 1994) and free from "Encumbrances". Selling with such title implies that: the vendors own the property and are not trying to dispose of something that they do not own; the vendors can dispose of the property in the way they say they are going to; the vendors will do all that they reasonably can to give the title that they purport to give (at their own cost); and that the title is free from all charges, encumbrances and adverse rights, other than any which the vendors do not know or could not reasonably be expected to know (i.e. free from all known encumbrances). The additional wording relating to freedom from "Encumbrances" is added to ensure that the buyer gets a clean title (as it is not subject to knowledge). As such the warranty is not strictly required in relation to the shares being sold as the position is already covered. It is becoming almost universal practice, however, to now include one.

1.2.4 None of the Shares was, or represents assets which were, the subject **7–08** **of a transfer at an undervalue (within the meaning of the Insolvency Act 1986 ss.238 or 339) within the past five years.**

If an asset is transferred at an undervalue "at a relevant time" and the transferor becomes bankrupt, or goes into liquidation or administration, the court may order, amongst other remedies, the asset to be revested in the transferor (Insolvency Act 1986 s.241 in relation to companies and Insolvency Act 1986 s.342 in relation to individuals).

The "relevant time" for a company is two years prior to the liquidation, the filing of a notice of intention to appoint an Administrator or the making of an application to court to appoint an Administrator (where an Administrator is appointed pursuant to the filing of that notice or application) (Insolvency Act 1986 s.240). The provisions in relation to Insolvency Act 1986 s.238 will not apply if the company transferring the shares was not insolvent at the time it transferred the shares and did not become insolvent as a result of the transfer of the shares. Where the shares were transferred to a connected party as defined in the Insolvency Act 1986 ss.249 and 435 insolvency is presumed unless the contrary can be shown.

The relevant time for a bankrupt is five years prior to the date of the bankruptcy petition upon which the bankruptcy order is subsequently made. If the transaction took place between two and five years before the date of the bankruptcy petition then it is necessary to show insolvency at the time the transaction occurred. However, if the transfer was to an "associate" within the meaning of the Insolvency Act 1986 s.435 it is assumed by the court that the transferor was insolvent unless the contrary can be shown. If the transfer was within two years of the bankruptcy order then it is not necessary to show that the transferor was insolvent at the time.

The court has the power to make orders against any person, whether or not that person was a direct recipient of the transaction at an undervalue. However, an order cannot be made against an owner of the asset who acquired the asset in good faith and for value. If the buyers are associates of, or connected with, the person who has made the transfer at an undervalue then it will be presumed that the transaction was other than in good faith unless the contrary can be shown. A similar presumption arises if the purchaser of property which has been the subject of a transfer at an undervalue knew that the initial transaction was a transaction at an undervalue and that the initial transferor was, subject to insolvency proceedings at the time of the second transfer.

There remains a small risk to a purchaser, for a period of two years after a transfer has been made for example to trustees or any other person as a gift by an individual, that the transferor may have or will become bankrupt and steps taken to set the transfer aside. Purchasers should also be wary of, for example, the target company having been formerly a subsidiary which was then transferred to associated parties of the former shareholder. As the purchaser who is genuinely purchasing for value and in good faith is safe if it did not know of both the transaction at an undervalue and of the insolvency proceedings, the warranty helps to demonstrate that it did not have the requisite knowledge if the acquisition should be contested. A purchaser will, however, be vulnerable if notwithstanding he is able to show he did not have actual knowledge of the transaction at an undervalue and the relevant proceedings there is other evidence that the transaction was not in "good faith". This might be found if, for example, the purchaser was a mere nominee of the initial transferor or transferee or one of their associates and attempting to put distance between the shares and a possible insolvency appointment. From the point of view of the vendors, there may be some concern about each of them having to accept responsibility in relation to the history of the previous transfers of the shares unless they are all well known to each other. Purchasers should, however, be alert to the fact that as a result of due diligence they may become aware or may be held to be on notice of these issues notwithstanding the warranty.

7–09   1.2.5 None of the Shares was allotted at a discount.

Under CA 2006 s.580 there is a prohibition on the allotment of shares at a discount, that is for a consideration of less than par. Allotment at a discount is unlikely to have occurred if the shares were allotted for cash, but if the consideration was the transfer of assets or provision of services, the possibility of a breach is more real. The purchaser will avoid liability to make good any shortfall under CA 2006 s.588 if it is a bona fide purchaser without notice (CA 2006 s.588(2)) and the warranty will help to establish this defence should it be required.

1.3 Share capital

1.3.1 No share or loan capital has been issued or allotted or agreed to be   7–10 issued or allotted by the Company since the Balance Sheet Date.

This warranty is designed to elicit disclosure of any share or loan transactions which have occurred since the last annual accounts were prepared as the purchaser will be basing its assessment of the target company on the position stated in the accounts and will want to know whether the position in them has changed. The warranty brings the position in respect of shares and loan capital up to date as at completion.

1.3.2 The Company has not at any time [during the last [   ] years] repaid,   7–11 redeemed or purchased any or its own shares, reduced its share capital or capitalised any reserves or profits (or agreed to do the same).

The purchaser will wish to check that prior transactions have been properly undertaken in order to ensure that there is no risk arising from any of them, and that the vendors have good title to the shares they are purporting to sell. For instance, a prior buy back of shares which was not properly undertaken in accordance with the requirements of CA 1985 or CA 2006 is likely to be void. The consequence of this is that the prior owners of the relevant shares will still be the owners of the shares and the company will have paid out money for no benefit. This can cause significant complications, particularly, if the prior owners cannot be located or are not co-operative, as their involvement will inevitably be needed in correcting the position and no prudent purchaser will want to enter into a transaction with the vendors unless it is satisfied that they do in fact have good title to sell all of the relevant shares. Where the vendors have not owned the shares since incorporation of the target company, they will prefer to limit the warranty to their period of ownership (by adding the wording in brackets) on the basis that they will not necessarily know what the company did prior to then. The purchaser is unlikely to agree to this and will argue that that is a risk that should fairly lie with the vendors. They would have had the opportunity to obtain confirmation of the position at the time of their acquisition of the shares.

As with all of the warranties relating to the share capital and other constitutional matters, the purchaser will need to be careful to ensure that it is not deemed to have knowledge of illegal buybacks or other issues (in circumstances where the vendors have not made any disclosures of such matters) by virtue of, for example, accepting the general disclosure of information available in respect of the target company at the Companies House Registry. If the purchaser is going to accept general disclosure of relevant searches, it should undertake its own investigations and ask further questions of the vendors in the event of any inconsistency between the results of its investigations and the information provided by the vendors so as to get a clear understanding (so far as possible) of the actual position.

7–12   **1.3.3 The Company has not at any time [during the last [   ] years] provided financial assistance pursuant to CA 1985 ss.151 and 158 or CA 2006 ss.678 or 679.**

Since October 1, 2008 private limited companies have been permitted to give financial assistance without any restrictions being imposed, save for where the company is a subsidiary of a public company and the assistance is being given in connection with an acquisition of the shares in the public company, as a result of the implementation of CA 2006.

The purchaser will wish to ensure that the procedures were properly followed in respect of transactions undertaken prior to October 1, 2008 under CA 1985 (and after that time where the target company has been re-registered from being a public company since October 1, 2008 or has been a subsidiary of a public company during that time) as the consequences of breach or failure to follow them will mean that the provision of the financial assistance was unlawful, any agreement or charge given as part of the financial assistance will potentially be void, and the directors of the company may be guilty of a criminal offence. Again where the vendors have not owned the shares since incorporation of the target company they will prefer to limit the warranty to their period of ownership by adding the wording in brackets but this is unlikely to be acceptable to the purchaser for the reasons stated at cl.1.3.2.

1.4 Details of the Company

7–13   **1.4.1 The information relating to the Company in Schedule [   ] is accurate and complete [in respect of the matters dealt with].**

Information which it is appropriate to include in the schedule would be details of the company number, date of incorporation, authorised (if applicable), issued and allotted share capitals, registered office, directors, secretary (if applicable), auditors and accounting reference date. Cautious vendors might reasonably object to the statement that the information is "complete" on the ground that it is for the purchaser to specify precisely what particulars are required and should consider including the additional words in brackets which would give them comfort in this regard.

1.5 Directors and shadow directors

7–14   **1.5.1 The Company has no liability to a former member, officer or shadow director or any person nor are there any circumstances in which such liability could arise.**

The vendors should bear in mind that the definition of "director" in CA 2006 s.250 includes a person occupying the position of a director by whatever name called and so is not just confined to people who have been formally appointed as directors of the target company and whose names appear in the register of directors in the company's statutory books and at the Companies House Registry (the so called de jure directors) but would also include de facto and shadow directors. Shadow directors are discussed at cl.1.5.2. De facto directors were distinguished from shadow directors in *H Laing (Demolition Building Contractors) Ltd, Re* [1998] B.C.C. 561. De facto directors are "insiders" of the company, such as shareholders, and senior employees who effectively are directors, whereas shadow directors are often "outsiders", for example who direct the de facto or de jure directors. (It should be noted that the definition of "director" is also relevant for the purposes of the various obligations that are imposed on directors with respect to disclosing interests and other matters under CA 2006).

1.5.2 No person is or has been a shadow director (within the meaning of the Companies Acts) of the Company but not treated as one of its directors for all the purposes of the Companies Acts. 7–15

A shadow director of a company is a person who is not a director but in accordance with whose instructions the directors of the company are accustomed to act. Section 251(3) CA 2006 expressly excludes a parent company from falling within the definition for most purposes. In practice, therefore, a shadow directorship is most likely to occur in family companies and, as noted above, the purchaser will wish to be aware of arrangements giving rise to a shadow directorship so that they may be terminated.

1.6 Subsidiaries and branches

1.6.1 The Company: 7–16

1.6.1.1 is not the holder or beneficial owner of nor has it agreed to acquire, share or loan capital of a body corporate; and

An agreement to acquire an asset will be relevant if it results in an outstanding liability. In any other case it might be thought that a purchaser will not be concerned if, in the event, the target company has more subsidiaries than were disclosed. However, the purchaser will often be subject to group borrowing restrictions and a heavily geared new subsidiary could have an important impact on the purchaser's gearing ratios. There may also be other cases where such additional companies would be objectionable. Thus, for example, the undisclosed companies might be engaged in activities which are not consistent with other activities of the purchaser, or be in serious financial difficulty so that the purchaser might then face the embarrassment of inadvertently becoming the owner of insolvent companies. Two further examples are where the undisclosed shares are only partly paid or are shares in an unlimited company.

1.6.1.2 has not outside the United Kingdom a branch, agency or place of business, or a permanent establishment (as that expression 7–17

is currently defined in the relevant double taxation relief order).

The term "permanent establishment" is used in most double tax treaties but the definitions vary. In general, a permanent establishment exists if there is a fixed place of business and will usually include a branch or office or an agency where the agent has, and habitually exercises, power to conclude contracts on behalf of his principal.

This provision is relevant for a number of reasons. Clearly if the warranty is incorrect, there is a potential taxation liability in the overseas jurisdictions concerned and, if significant activities are involved, it would be prudent to obtain local advice as to the precise implications. However, in addition to taxation matters, any overseas branch will involve a consideration of the regulations applying in the overseas jurisdiction to business activities carried on by foreigners, including such matters as registration requirements and work permits. A foreign branch may also be subject to local exchange control restrictions which would prevent or inhibit repatriation of profits (see also cl.4.4.2).

1.7 Options over the Company's capital

7–18 **1.7.1 Apart from this Agreement, there are no agreements or arrangements which provide for the issue, allotment or transfer of, or grant a right (whether conditional or otherwise) to call for the issue, allotment or transfer of share or loan capital of the Company. No claim has been made by any person to be entitled to any of the foregoing.**

It might be thought sufficient to refer to outstanding "agreements" to acquire shares or loan capital but the purchaser would nevertheless wish to extend the warranty to cover arrangements. This is because unilateral obligations, such as the grant of an option, may be said not to constitute agreements. Equally preemption rights (where shareholders agree to sell shares to each other on a first refusal basis) are often set out in the articles of association of a company and it is not usual to regard the articles as an agreement. This point could be met by replacing "agreements or arrangements" with "obligations". The warranty expressly excludes the sale agreement as otherwise the agreement to sell the target company itself would strictly conflict with the warranty, although it is difficult to see how a breach of the warranty in that respect could give rise to a claim for damages.

1.8 Commissions

7–19 **1.8.1 No one is entitled to receive from the Company a finder's fee, brokerage or other commission in connection with the sale and purchase of the Shares under this Agreement.**

Although CA 1985 s.151 has now been repealed (it formerly made it illegal for a company to give financial assistance in connection with the purchase of its own shares or the shares of its holding company) this warranty should be retained as it is relevant in other contexts. For example, in transactions involving local authorities, it is possible that payment of commission could involve corruption and the warranty would minimise any possibility of the purchaser being implicated in that. (Clause 4.24.1 below deals specifically with the issue of "sensitive payments".) This warranty also serves the practical function of reducing the chances of a subsequent dispute as to who is liable for any broker's fees and is quite often extended to cover legal fees to ensure that no personal fees of the shareholders are being met by the target company.

1.9 Elective resolutions

1.9.1 The Company has not passed an elective resolution under CA 1985 s.379A which remains in force. 7–20

The purpose of this warranty is to ascertain details of any elective resolutions passed by the target company. This is in order for the purchaser to ensure that they were passed in accordance with the requirements of CA 1985 and to identify whether any remain in force (as a result of falling under the scope of transitional or saving provisions introduced by the various Commencement Orders brought in following the implementation of CA 2006).

The elective regime under CA 1985 s.379A was intended to deregulate certain aspects of private companies to try and simplify the administrative burden placed upon them. Further simplification has been adopted under CA 2006 as the elective regime is now the default position for private companies.

Prior to the implementation of CA 2006, there were the following five elective resolutions which could be adopted by private companies:

(1) Amending the duration of directors to allot securities (CA 1985 s.80A) (repealed with effect from October 1, 2009).
   (The provisions of CA 2006 regarding authority to allot shares did not take effect until October 1, 2009 and therefore the ability to pass an elective resolution under s.80A was retained up until that date. As a result of The Companies Act 2006 (Commencement No.8, Transitional Provisions and Savings) Order 2008 Sch.2 para.45 (Eighth Commencement Order) an authorisation in force prior to October 1, 2009 also has effect on and after that date as if it were passed pursuant to CA 2006 s.551.)

(2) Dispensing with the requirement to present accounts and reports before the members in general meeting (CA 1985 s.252) (repealed with effect from October 1, 2007).
   (Following the repeal of CA 1985 s.252, private companies are no longer required to lay their accounts and reports before the general meeting. This therefore rendered the elective regime and elective resolutions passed in this regard prior to October 1, 2007 redundant.)

(3) Dispensing with the requirement to hold annual general meetings (CA 1985 s.366A) (repealed with effect from October 1, 2007).

(4) Although s.366A was repealed on October 1, 2007, this did not affect any provision of a private company's memorandum or articles of association that expressly requires the company to hold an AGM. If there was an elective resolution under s.366A in force prior to October 1, 2007, however, then this shall remain valid and so the company shall not to be treated as one whose articles expressly require it to hold an AGM (The Companies Act 2006 (Commencement No.3, Consequential Amendments, Transitional Provisions and Savings) Order 2007 Sch.3 para.32(4) (Third Commencement Order)) altering the majority required to authorise the holding of a meeting at short notice and the passing of a resolution at short notice be reduced from 95 per cent to a lower figure but not less than 90 per cent (CA 1985 ss.369(4) and 378(3)) (repealed with effect from October 1, 2007).

(5) If a private company has passed an elective resolution, to specify a percentage of 90 per cent to consent to short notice or specifying a percentage between 90 per cent and 95 per cent, and it remained in force immediately before October 1, 2007, such elective resolution will remain valid (The Companies Act 2006 (Commencement No.6, Saving and Commencement Nos 3 and 5 (Amendment)) Order 2008 Sch.3 para.2(1) and (2) (Sixth Commencement Order)). Any provision of the company's articles of association that specifies a different percentage will be disregarded where such provision(s) of the articles of association were adopted prior to October 1, 2007. This saving provision does not apply in relation to provisions of the company's articles adopted on or after October 1, 2007 dispensing with the requirement to appoint auditors annually (CA 1985 s.386) (repealed with effect from October 1, 2007).

Where a private company has passed an elective resolution under CA 1985 s.386, and the election was in force immediately prior to October 1, 2007, such auditors may be deemed re-appointed under CA 2006 (The Companies Act 2006 (Commencement No.3, Consequential Amendments, Transitional Provisions and Savings) Order 2007 Sch.3 para.44). This saving provision takes precedent over CA 2006 s.487(2)(a) which provides that there is no deemed re-appointment of auditors that have been appointed by the directors of the company. In addition to this particular exception, where an elective resolution has been passed under CA 1985 s.390A fixing the remuneration of the company's auditors, and that resolution was expressed as continuing so long as an elective resolution under CA 1985 s.386 was in force, the resolution will continue to have effect after October 1, 2007 notwithstanding the repeal of CA 1985 s.386 (The Companies Act 2006 (Commencement No.3, Consequential Amendments, Transitional Provisions and Savings) Order 2007, Sch.3 para.45).

1.10 Constitutional documents, statutory books and resolutions

7–21   **1.10.1 The copy of the memorandum and articles of association of the Company attached to the Disclosure Letter is accurate and complete and has**

embodied in it, or attached to it, a copy of every resolution and agreement required to be annexed to or incorporated in these documents by any applicable laws.

Under CA 2006 s.36, there must be incorporated in or accompanying the articles of association the following documents:

(1) special resolutions;

(2) elective resolutions and resolutions revoking an elective resolution;

(3) resolutions or agreements which have been agreed to by all the members but which, if not so agreed to, would not have been effective unless passed as special or extraordinary resolutions;

(4) a copy of any resolution or agreement relating to the company which CA 2006 Pt 3A Ch.3 applies;

(5) where the company has been required to give notice to the Companies House Registry under CA 2006 s.34(2) (notice where company's constitute altered by enactment), a statement that the enactment in question alters the effect of the company's constitution;

(6) where the company's constitution is altered by special enactment as defined in CA 2006 s.34(4), a copy of the enactment; and

(7) a copy of any order required to be sent to the Companies House Registry under CA 2006 s.35(2)(a) (order of court or other authority altering the company's constitution).

Prior to the implementation of CA 2006 s.36, CA 1985 s.380 required that there must be incorporated in or accompanying the articles of association the following documents:

(1) special resolutions;

(2) extraordinary resolutions;

(3) elective resolutions and resolutions revoking an elective resolution;

(4) resolutions or agreements which have been agreed to by all the members but which, if not so agreed to, would not have been effective unless passed as special or extraordinary resolutions;

(5) resolutions or agreements which have been agreed to by all the members of a class of shareholders but which, if not so agreed to, would not have been effective unless passed by some particular majority or otherwise in some particular manner, and all resolutions that effectively bind all of the members of any class of shareholders though not agreed to by all those members;

(6) a directors' resolution to change the company's name following a direction of the Secretary of State;

(7) resolutions creating, varying, revoking or renewing the authority of directors to allot shares;

(8) a directors' resolution altering the company's memorandum on the company ceasing to be a public company following acquisition of its own shares;

(9) resolutions creating, varying, revoking or renewing a s.166 authority (market purchase of own shares);

(10) resolutions requiring the company to be wound up voluntarily;

(11) resolutions to re-register old public companies; and

(12) directors' resolutions allowing title to a public company's shares to be evidenced and transferred without written instrument.

The purchaser will normally have made a search at the Companies House Registry against the company but it remains a possibility that the memoranda and articles of association which are shown on the files are not correct. This could be as a result of a failure to file resolutions or arise from the fact that the resolutions do not have to be filed before a lapse of 15 days from the date of passing. There is therefore always the possibility that a company's file at the Companies House Registry will not be up to date.

It will be noted that the warranty requires the copies of the memoranda and articles of association to be annexed to the disclosure letter so that there is no question as to the copies which are warranted. If the disclosure letter contains the normal exclusion from the scope of the warranties of matters which appear on the file at the Companies House Registry (see, for example, sub-para.(c) in para.9–18), the first half of this warranty will for all practical purposes be rendered inoperative.

In respect of companies incorporated under CA 2006, it will no longer be necessary for a copy of the memorandum of association to be attached to the Disclosure Letter as the version of it shown on the file will be correct. The new form of memorandum of association is not subject to subsequent change as it reflects a "snapshot" of the company at the time of incorporation. However, in respect of pre-CA 2006 companies, a copy of the memorandum of association that was in force at the time of implementation of CA 2006 s.28 should be required to be attached to the disclosure letter. This is because at that time the provisions in the company's memorandum of association, which are not the kind that are to be contained in the new style memorandum (as in CA 2006 s.8) will be treated as provisions of the company's articles of association and the purchaser will want to know that it has all the correct details of the provisions that are in the articles of association.

7–22   **1.10.2 The register of members and other statutory books of the Company have been properly kept [in accordance with all applicable laws] [in accordance with the Companies Acts] and contain an accurate and complete record of the matters with which they should deal.**

The statutory books of a company are the register of members (CA 2006 s.113 formerly CA 1985 s.352), overseas branch register (if one is kept) (CA 2006 s.131 formerly CA 1985 s.362), index of members where the number of members exceed 50 (CA 2006 s.115 formerly CA 1985 s.354), register of debenture holders (CA 2006 s.743 formerly CA 1985 s.190) (if one is kept), register of charges (CA 2006 s.876 formerly CA 1985 s.407), register of directors and secretary (if applicable) (CA 2006 s.162 formerly CA 1985 s.288) in respect of directors and CA 2006 s.275 (formerly CA 1985 s.288) in respect of secretaries and register of interests in shares (CA 2006 s.808 formerly CA 1985 s.213). As it is quite possible that minor/irrelevant inaccuracies exist in the statutory books, for example in listing other directorships of a past director, the vendors might wish to qualify the warranty so that immaterial errors are excluded. However, in practice it is most unlikely that such errors could entitle the purchaser to make a claim and the vendors should therefore be able to leave the warranty unchanged without undue concern. To avoid potential ambiguity, the vendors might wish to remove the wording in brackets "in accordance with all applicable laws" and replace it with the other wording in brackets "in accordance with the Companies Acts" to make it clear that it is only compliance with CA 1985 and CA 2006 requirements that is being warranted and nothing outside of that.

1.10.3 No notice or allegation has been received that the statutory books of the Company are incorrect or should be rectified. 7–23

Powers of rectification of the registers of members and charges exist under CA 2006 ss.125 and 873. Although the purchaser is substantially protected by the warranties as to charges and in respect of title to the shares (and, where relevant, ownership of any subsidiaries), it is also of importance to the purchaser that the registered particulars are not in dispute. As the warranty relates to notices or allegations received the vendors should know or be able to easily ascertain the position and so should be relatively comfortable in giving the warranty.

1.10.4 Since the Balance Sheet Date, no alteration has been made to the memorandum or articles of association of the Company and no resolution has been passed by its shareholders. 7–24

The copies of the memoranda and articles of association of the target company whose accuracy is warranted under cl.1.10.1 should reveal most relevant resolutions passed by them and the dates on which they were passed. Nevertheless the purchaser is entitled to be specifically satisfied that no change has taken place in the memoranda and articles of association since the last accounts were prepared as in certain cases a change could affect the treatment of the accounts. For example, an amendment to the memorandum of association of an investment company to make it into a trading company could alter the tax treatment of its fixed assets. It is also possible for an ordinary resolution to have been passed, for example giving approval to substantial property transactions involving directors under CA 2006 s.190, where there is no obligation to file the resolution.

1.11 Documents filed

7-25   1.11.1 All returns, particulars, resolutions and documents required by CA 2006 [or other legislation] to be filed with the Registrar of Companies [or other authority] in respect of the Company have been [duly] filed and were accurate and complete.

The filing obligations imposed by CA 2006 are extensive and it is not realistic to attempt to list all of them. While the purchaser is entitled to be satisfied that these obligations have been fully performed, to ensure both freedom from default penalties and that the searches against the target company will be complete, the actual wording of the warranty is quite onerous. It is not unusual for filing of annual returns and accounts to be late but the vendors should be able to disclose all recent cases of late filing.

The extension of the warranty to filing obligations under legislation other than CA 2006 and the reference to "other legislation" are so wide in their scope that they are unlikely to be acceptable to the vendors. Indeed, the warranty could be interpreted as applying even to the filing of tax returns. This is a reasonable position for the vendors to take in an effort to achieve certainty as to the scope of the warranty. If the purchaser is concerned about the position in respect of certain other filings then it should include specific warranties in relation to them. Deletion of the word "duly" would remove the need for the vendors to disclose details of late filings. If this is to be accepted the purchaser should consider the insertion of the following:

"No notice has been received that any such filings were out of time that remains unresolved and all filings made within the last [30] days have been made within the requisite time periods".

7-26   1.11.2 All charges in favour of the Company have (if appropriate) been registered in accordance with the provisions of the Companies Acts.

Most, but not all, charges created by a company (or to which property acquired by a company is already subject) must be registered with the Companies House Registry within 21 days to be effective. Sections 860 to 877 of CA 2006 (formerly CA 1985 ss.395–409) relates to registration of charges by companies registered in England and Wales; CA 2006 ss.878–892 (formerly CA 1985 ss.410–424) contain similar provisions for companies registered in Scotland. Sections 874 and 889 of CA 2006 (formerly CA 1985 ss.395 and 410) provide that a registerable charge which is not duly registered is void against a liquidator or administrator and any creditor of the company, and any money secured by the charge becomes immediately payable. Furthermore, if a registerable charge is not registered within the prescribed time limits, the company and each officer of the company is liable to a default fine. (Charges over certain types of property such as land, will also need to be registered at the specialist registries for those types of property.)

The effect of CA 2006 ss.1046 and 1052 (formerly CA 1985 ss.409 and 424) is to extend the filing obligation to charges on property in the United Kingdom which are created, and to charges on property in the United Kingdom which is acquired by an overseas company with an established place of business in the United Kingdom. In *Slavenburg's Bank NV v Intercontinental Natural Resources Ltd* [1980] 1 All E.R. 955, it was decided that the obligation to register a charge created over an asset in England, of a kind described in CA 1985 s.395, applied to all overseas companies having a place of business in England, and that lack of registration under the predecessor of CA 1985 Pt XXIII (which relates to registration of overseas companies) was not conclusive as to the existence of a place of business. Following this decision the cautious view has been to register charges over United Kingdom property created by unregistered overseas companies, the Registrars maintaining the information in the "Slavenburg register".

1.12 Possession of documents

1.12.1 All the title deeds relating to the assets of the Company, an executed copy of all [subsisting written] agreements to which the Company is a party and the original copies of all other documents [which are in force or otherwise relevant to the Company and] which are owned by, or which ought to be in the possession of, the Company are in its possession [or under its control]. All documents are, where relevant, stamped with the correct amounts of stamp duty. 7–27

In practice this warranty would normally require modification or the making of disclosures as documents are frequently held by solicitors and bankers as well as by the company itself; alternatively, the final words in brackets could be added to the clause. From an administrative point of view it is obviously important for the purchaser to know where relevant documents are held but there could also be a legal significance in the warranty in that documents held by a third party could give rise to a lien, for example for unpaid fees. The vendors would probably wish to restrict this warranty in relation to documents which are not title deeds, either by deleting the reference to "other documents" or by limiting the warranty so that it applies only to documents of material importance to the assets or business of the target company. The words in square brackets are additional amendments which are worth consideration by the vendors in order to limit the scope of this warranty and the associated disclosure bundle.

1.12.2 There is no document held outside the United Kingdom which, if brought within the United Kingdom, would result in the Company incurring a liability to pay stamp duty. 7–28

When stamp duty applied to land and certain other assets, it was not uncommon for companies to execute and hold outside the UK documentation which if brought into the UK would trigger a contingent liability to stamp duty. The purpose of this warranty is therefore to elicit information regarding any contingent stamp duty liability of the target company.

By virtue of FA 1999, FA 2003 and FA 2004, stamp duty has now been abolished in the transfer of all assets other than shares, marketable securities and certain partnership interests.

1.13 Investigations

7–29   1.13.1 No investigation or enquiry by, or on behalf of, a governmental or other body in respect of the affairs of the Company is taking place or pending and the Vendors are not aware of any fact or matter that could lead to any such investigation or enquiry.

The most important form of investigation would be under the powers of the Competition Commission or the EU's European Commission. The vendors may not know whether an enquiry is pending and as such that part of the warranty should either be deleted or be qualified by reference to the vendors' knowledge or notice of such investigation or enquiry having been received.

1.14 Information disclosed to the Purchaser is correct

7–30   1.14.1 All [material] [written] information given by any of the Vendors or any director of the Company, the Vendors' professional advisors or the Company's auditors to the Purchaser, the Purchaser's solicitors or the Purchaser's accountants in the course of negotiations leading to this Agreement and relating to the business, affairs, assets and liabilities of the Company was and is true, accurate and complete [in all material respects] and not misleading and opinions, expectations and beliefs included in the information are honestly held and have been arrived at on a reasonable basis after full enquiry.

The purchaser will wish to achieve the greatest possible cover from this clause by including all information, whether or not committed to writing. If the vendors are willing to provide a warranty in respect of such information, they will be interested in maximising certainty by restricting the warranty to the replies to legal due diligence enquiries supplied by their solicitors. (The vendors' solicitors will have prepared the replies submitted by them on a basis that takes into account the fact that they may be required to be warranted and tailored them accordingly so as to reduce the vendors' potential exposure. If the vendors have supplied information direct themselves they are unlikely to have appreciated the potential implications of the terms of some of their replies.) They should, in addition, be very cautious about accepting responsibility for information provided by their other professional advisers. If the vendors are to agree to extend the scope of the warranty beyond the replies to legal due diligence enquiries then any information that is to be warranted should be collated, reviewed by the vendors' solicitors (so that any potential issues can be identified and either appropriately disclosed against or the warranty amended) and agreed with the purchaser's solicitors.

Although the vendors will also wish to confine the warranty to material matters, for example, by making the amendments in square brackets, the purchaser might reasonably maintain, if there is a floor to warranty claims as described in para.11–04, that this provides adequate protection for the vendors against trivial claims. Additionally the vendors should consider whether the word "affairs" is reasonable, in that its very breadth can give rise to difficulties in interpretation, and whether it is for them or the purchaser to be responsible for determining whether the information was complete. (The vendors will be reluctant to warrant that the information provided is "complete" given the difficulties in assessing what constitutes a complete disclosure.)

The second part of the warranty relating to opinions, expectations and beliefs places a heavy burden upon vendors not involved in the day-to-day running of the company. However, it is not unreasonable for the purchaser to seek protection in respect of matters which are not purely factual. The vendors might seek to restrict the nature and extent of the enquiry undertaken (see cl.3K).

As the warranty relates to information provided by any of the vendors, they should also consider obtaining a mutual confirmation, perhaps in an agreement of the kind described in para.3–16, that each of them is satisfied that the warranty is correct in relation to information given by him. In view of the wide ranging nature of this warranty it will often be restricted to the formal replies to the legal due diligence questionnaire. This can be achieved by amending the warranty appropriately. Well-advised vendors would usually require anything that the purchaser required to be warranted be dealt with in a specific warranty on the issue.

Whilst the purchaser will routinely include a warranty in respect of information supplied by the vendors and their advisors in their first draft of the sale agreement, there is a strong argument against any such warranty being given in view of the purpose for which such information was prepared and supplied. It could, for example, include the Information Memorandum which the vendors' financial advisors prepared as a selling document but not to be warranted as being true and accurate. The information will have been supplied for the purposes of providing the purchaser with enough information about the target company to enable it to make an assessment of it and whether, and on what basis, it wanted to proceed with the acquisition, not with the intention that it be warranted. Where the vendors have supplied information direct, there is likely to have been information supplied that would not usually be the subject of warranties and, as such, if the replies are warranted there is a risk that the vendors will warrant matters that they would not ordinarily be willing to, increasing their potential exposure to warranty claims. It is common practice for the purchaser's solicitors to seek to use the due diligence exercise as a means for obtaining warranties on areas that would not ordinarily be agreed to by the vendors' solicitors in the sale agreement and care needs to be taken to ensure that this does not happen. Often there will be detailed warranties on some of the information provided such as management accounts or copies of statutory accounts. Such warranties will usually have been negotiated to an acceptable standard recognising the subject matter of the warranty. A "true and accurate" warranty of information supplied (which might include the relevant financial information) cuts across this and may expose the vendors to a tougher warranty than was ever intended. Great care needs to be taken with the terms of these warranties and what they are intended to cover.

7–31   **1.14.2 [So far as the Vendors are aware] there are no material facts or circumstances in relation to the assets, business or financial condition of the Company which have not been Disclosed and which, if Disclosed, might reasonably have been expected to affect the decision of the Purchaser to enter into this Agreement on the terms set out herein.**

This is the infamous sweeping-up warranty which is intended to cover any matters not specifically dealt with by the detailed warranties. Whether or not the vendors will agree to give such a warranty depends entirely on the commercial position of the parties as the objective is to impose upon them the risk of any residual problems not dealt with by the specific warranties. As previously indicated, although warranties serve a valuable purpose as a checklist, their primary function from a legal point of view is to ensure that the risk that adverse factors relating to the target company, which were unknown or had not been disclosed, lies on either the vendors or the purchaser on an agreed basis. It will be a matter for negotiation to determine how this residual risk should be borne or shared. At the very least, the vendors will wish to avoid giving an absolute warranty by adding the words in square brackets. The parties should carefully consider whether it is more appropriate to refer to the decision of "the Purchaser" or "a purchaser" to provide for either a subjective or objective view. By use of the defined term "Disclosed" an objective standard is used to determine the fairness of such a disclosure. The second reference to the "Purchaser" makes the decision as to the reference of the disclosed matter a subjective one. The vendors will be reluctant to give the warranty on a subjective basis as they will not be in a position to know what precise factors have influenced the purchaser's decision to acquire the target company and what the purchaser's plans for it are. Even on an objective standard they would expose themselves to potential arguments about what an objective purchaser would have wanted to know about. If there was information that came to light after completion that resulted in any loss, the purchaser would no doubt seek to argue that it was something that an objective purchaser would have wanted to know about. In most cases where there are full warranties dealing specifically with all areas of importance to a purchaser, this warranty, even in amended form, will not be given by the vendors and it is difficult in such circumstances for the purchaser to justify its inclusion.

2 Accounts

2.1 The Accounts

7–32   **2.1.1 The Accounts were prepared in accordance with the historical cost convention and with the requirements of all relevant statutes and Accounting Standards; and on the same bases and policies of accounting as adopted for the purpose of preparing the audited accounts of the Company in respect of the preceding three accounting periods.**

Although the accounts will include a statement as to the accounting policies adopted in their preparation, it is appropriate for a warranty to be given that this is a correct statement. The warranty requires that the accounts (which will usually be the most recent audited accounts, or the most recent annual accounts where the target company's accounts are not required to be audited, and the ones upon which some or all of the financial valuation will have been based) are warranted as having been prepared in accordance with the historical cost convention and more particularly the Accounting Standards (as defined) which is wide ranging and includes SSAPs, FRSs, UTIF Abstracts and SORPs and that the three prior sets of accounts have been produced consistently. The accounts warranties in this section have been prepared on the assumption that the target company has not chosen to prepare its accounts in accordance with international accounting standards. If it has then the warranties will need amending to reflect that.

2.1.2 The Accounts: 7–33

2.1.2.1   give a true and fair view of the [assets and liabilities and] state of affairs of the Company at the Balance Sheet Date and the profits or losses [and cash flow] of the Company for the period ended on that date;

It is sometimes suggested that the wording of this warranty should be to the effect that the accounts are "true and accurate". This would not be an acceptable form of the warranty for the vendors, as the statutory obligation under CA 2006 s.396 is that the accounts should give a true and fair view of the state of affairs of the company as at the end of the financial year and of the profit or loss of the company for that year. The vendors should seek to delete the wording in brackets as it is not a requirement that the accounts show a true and fair view of the assets and liabilities or cash flow of the company. No accounts can claim to provide an "accurate" view and a warranty that the accounts are accurate would be unrealistic. The vendors should endeavour to follow the precise wording that appears in the auditors' reports and might prefer to replace "give" by "gave".

The interpretation of "true and fair view" has recently been considered by the Court of Appeal in the case of *Macquarie Internationale Investments Ltd v Glencore UK Ltd* [2010] EWCA Civ 697. This decision involved the analysis of whether a breach of this particular warranty could occur on its terms even though under normal accounting procedures the relevant liability that caused the accounts not to show a true and fair view was undiscoverable at the point the accounts were signed off. The Court of Appeal held that the vendor was not in breach of warranty on the basis that the existence of the unknown liability could not have been reasonably discovered at the relevant time and the accounts had been prepared in accordance with the relevant accounting standards.

In light of this case, it is likely that astute legal practitioners acting for the purchaser will propose amendments to the standard form of this warranty so as to impose liability on the vendors irrespective of whether a liability could have been discovered at the point of finalisation of the accounts. That said, it is clear from the terms of the judgement that simply adding clarifying words within the context of the accounts warranties themselves may not be sufficient to put the matter beyond doubt as there is a risk that additional words could be interpreted within the terms of the overall accounts warranties. In addition, the terms of CA 2006 would not necessarily ground a liability for breach of warranty.

If, as in this case, an unknown or undiscoverable liability came to light post-completion it would be hoped that a thorough completion accounts exercise might have unearthed the liabilities and then provided for a corresponding price adjustment in respect of the diminution in net assets of the target company (please refer to Ch.12 for further discussion regarding completion accounts). The alternative approach, however, is to seek to address the issue through specific warranties which attempt to underpin the actual levels of net assets or liabilities and make it clear that the existence or otherwise of unknown or undiscoverable liabilities shall be taken into account in determining the accuracy of the warranty even if they only come to light subsequently.

7–34   **2.1.2.2 comply with the requirements of CA 2006;**

The accounts of a company must be prepared in accordance with CA 2006 Ch.4.

7–35   **2.1.2.3 comply with current Accounting Standards;**

The reference to "Accounting Standards" includes all UK FRSs, SSAPs, SORPs and UITF Abstracts.

SSAPs were the forerunners of FRSs, the latter being developed by the Accounting Standards Board (the "ASB"). Some SSAPs have been replaced by FRSs, others remain in force. A list can be found on the FRC web site at *http://www.frc.org.uk/asb*. Ordinarily, the accounts would specify where they do not comply with the FRSs but a warranty of compliance is desirable. The vendors should have no difficulty in obtaining from the auditors of the target company details of all necessary disclosures if there has not been full compliance with them, although they should amend the warranty to read:

" . . . complied with all the Accounting Standards which were at the relevant time applicable to a United Kingdom company."

The UITF Abstracts set out the consensus reached by the UITF (a sub-committee of the ASB) on significant accounting issues where unsatisfactory or conflicting interpretations of an existing standard or legislative requirement have developed or appear likely to develop. The UITF Abstracts do not amend or override the accounting standards or other statements adopted or issued by the ASB and are read in conjunction with them. Although the UITF Abstracts are not envisaged by the Companies Acts, it is the expectation of the Consultative Committee of Accountancy Bodies, the ASB and the accountancy profession that they will be observed and it is, therefore, reasonable for a purchaser to require a warranty as to compliance.

SORPs are generally issued on subjects on which it is not decided appropriate to issue an accounting standard at that time. They usually relate to auditing specific areas of industry. They do not have mandatory status but are considered "best practice" when they apply. If the target company is in one of the specialist sectors where SORPs are relevant then the warranty will obtain confirmation of compliance or disclosure of non-compliance.

If the vendors wished to achieve greater certainty on cl.2.1.2 they could delete cll.2.1.2.2 and 2.1.2.3 and add in at the end of cl.2.1.2.1:

" . . . and comply with the requirements of all relevant statutes and generally accepted accounting practices".

2.1.2.4 are not affected by extraordinary, exceptional or non-recurring items; 7–36

Although there is no statutory definition of "extraordinary items", they were defined in SSAP 6 as being derived from events or transactions outside the ordinary activities of the business which were both material and expected not to occur frequently or regularly. They did not include an item which, although exceptional in size or incidence and therefore requiring separate disclosure under CA 1985 Sch.4, para.57(3), derived from the ordinary activities of the business. "Exceptional items" were defined in SSAP 6 as deriving from events and transactions which fell within the ordinary activities of the company but which, because of their size or incidence, needed to be disclosed in order to present a true and fair view. This distinction was changed by FRS 3, which has replaced SSAP 6. Extraordinary items now require "a high degree of abnormality" and, as a result, will in future be extremely rare.

As the warranties will invariably include provisions along the lines of cll.2.1.2.1 and 2.1.2.3, this clause adds nothing of value to the purchaser. Indeed, the subjective nature of the concepts referred to in the clause make it difficult for the vendors to accept the clause in its absolute form without amendment.

2.1.2.5 fully disclose all the assets of the Company on the Balance Sheet Date [including reflecting any events or matters that are discovered after the Balance Sheet Date which, if known at the Balance Sheet Date, would have been included in the Accounts]; 7–37

Accounts will not necessarily show all assets, for example goodwill which has accrued but has not been shown in the accounts. It would be appropriate for the vendors to qualify this warranty by stating that assets are disclosed to the extent required by CA 2006 and the appropriate FRS and to delete the word "fully". In any event, the purchaser is unlikely to have valid ground for complaint if the warranty proves to be incorrect. Following the *Macquarie Internationale Investments Ltd v Glencore UK Ltd* [2010] EWCA Civ 697 decision, well-advised purchasers may wish to consider including the wording in brackets in relation to this and the subsequent warranty, cl.2.1.2.6, in order to seek to impose liability on the vendors where applicable. Obviously, a loss is more foreseeable in respect of the subsequent warranty than in relation to the warranty in hand as in most cases the omission of an asset is not likely to give rise to a loss whereas in relation to cl.2.1.2.6 the converse is true. Whilst it might be prudent to include the wording in brackets, as can be seen from the *Macquarie* case, clarifying wording such as this may not of itself be sufficient to impose liability. Please refer to para.7–33 for a discussion of the *Macquarie* decision.

This warranty overlaps, to some extent, the provisions of cl.8.1.1.

7–38   **2.1.2.6   [to the extent required by CA 2006 and the relevant FRSs] provide or reserve in full for all liabilities and capital commitments of the Company outstanding at the Balance Sheet Date, including contingent, unquantified or disputed liabilities [including reflecting any events or matters that are discovered after the Balance Sheet Date which, if known at the Balance Sheet Date, would have been included in the Accounts]; and**

Provisions for liabilities and charges must be shown as a separate main heading in the balance sheet. These provisions are defined in CA 2006 Pt 15 as any amounts retained as reasonably necessary for the purpose of providing for a liability or loss which is either likely to be incurred, or certain to be incurred but uncertain as to amount or as to the date on which it will arise. Capital commitments must be noted under CA 2006 Pt 15, if they are contracted for.

FRS 12, which has replaced SSAP 18, has completed the process of moving United Kingdom accounting practice from a decision-based to a commitment-based approach to making provisions. The standard aims to ensure that appropriate recognition criteria and measurement bases are applied to provisions and to contingent assets and liabilities and that disclosure in respect of their nature, timing and amount is sufficient. A contingency is defined as a condition which exists at the balance sheet date where the outcome will be confirmed only on the occurrence of one or more uncertain future events. A material contingent loss should be accrued in the accounts where it is probable that a future event will confirm a loss which can be estimated with reasonable accuracy. Any other material contingent loss should be noted unless the possibility of loss is remote.

As the accounts will of necessity show commitments and liabilities only to the extent required by CA 2006 and the relevant FRS, it would be appropriate for the vendors to amend the warranty by the addition of the bracketed words in the first line of the warranty and the deletion of "in full".

Please refer to para.7–37 for a discussion as to when the wording in brackets at the end of the warranty should be included.

7–39   **2.1.2.7   provide or reserve [to the extent required by CA 2006 the relevant FRSs and], in accordance with the principles set out in the notes included in the Accounts, for all Taxation liable to be assessed on the Company, or for which it may be**

accountable, in respect of the period ended on the Balance Sheet Date.

FRS 16 has superseded SSAP 8, which became outdated with the abolition of advanced corporation tax (ACT) early in 1999. It requires that current tax is recognised in the profit and loss account except to the extent that it relates to gains or losses that have been recognised directly in the statement of total recognised gains and losses. The standard is mandatory for accounting periods ending on or after March 23, 2000 and there are transitional arrangements for unrelieved ACT. FRS 19 superseded SSAP 15 for accounting periods ending on or after January 23, 2002. FRS 19 requires that deferred taxation be provided for on a "full provision" basis as opposed to the "partial provision" basis previously required under SSAP 15. The new requirements are designed to bring United Kingdom accounting practice more in line with international requirements although conceptual differences remain.

While the purchaser will wish to ensure that the taxation provisions in the accounts have been accurately prepared, the vendors may prefer to delete this warranty on the basis that the purchaser should rely on the lengthy, detailed tax warranties. If the warranty is given, the vendors should bear in the mind the wide definition of "Taxation" and should include the wording in brackets so that the warranty reflects the fact that the provisions or reserves will have been made in accordance with the applicable FRS. As with cl.2.1.2.6 the warranty will need to be amended to refer to the Companies Act under which the accounts were prepared.

2.1.3 The amount included in the Accounts in respect of each asset, whether fixed or current, does not exceed its purchase price or production cost or (in the case of current assets) its [estimated] net realisable value at the Balance Sheet Date.   7–40

The reference to the net realisable value of the assets should be qualified by the vendors by the addition of the word "estimated", as indicated.

2.2 Valuation of stock in trade and work in progress

2.2.1 In the Accounts and in the accounts of the Company, the stock in trade and work in progress of the Company was valued at the lower of cost or net realisable value. Cost represents materials and appropriate proportion of direct labour and overheads.   7–41

SSAP 9 provides a comprehensive statement as to the determination of the value for accounts purposes of stocks and work in progress. The basic requirement is that these should be stated at the lower of cost and net realisable value of the separate items concerned or of groups of similar items. Long-term contract work in progress is valued at net cost less foreseeable losses and progress payments on account. As there is a subjective element involved in these requirements, the purchaser would generally have difficulty in proving a breach unless the accounts were clearly prepared negligently or on the basis of values which no reasonable person could have thought to be correct.

7–42   2.2.2 In the Accounts slow-moving stock in trade was written down as appropriate and redundant, obsolete, obsolescent and defective stock was wholly written off.

Appendix 1 to SSAP 9, dealing with practical considerations in relation to the valuation of stocks and work in progress, provides that the main circumstances in which the net realisable value is likely to be less than cost are where there is an increase in costs or fall in selling price, physical deterioration, obsolescence, a decision to manufacture or sell at a loss, or errors in production or purchasing. If stocks are unlikely to be sold within the normal turnover period, the resulting increased likelihood of deterioration or obsolescence should be taken into account. Although the last accounts should therefore have taken into consideration the factors mentioned in this clause, the vendors should resist the warranty on the grounds that it involves highly subjective judgments and that the purchaser is adequately protected by cl.2.2.1.

7–43   2.2.3 In valuing work in progress in the Accounts no value was attributed in respect of eventual profit and adequate provision was made for such losses as were at the time of signature of the Accounts by the directors of the Company foreseeable as arising or likely to arise on completion and/or realisation thereof.

This warranty focuses on the work in progress dealt with in cl.2.2.1. It is designed to flush out early attributions of profit and adequate provision for losses on work in progress.

2.3 Depreciation of fixed assets

7–44   2.3.1 In the Accounts the fixed assets of the Company were depreciated in accordance with FRS 15.

FRS 15, which has superseded SSAP 12, deals with the accounting treatment required to provide for depreciation of tangible fixed assets, other than investment properties. The standard seeks consistency in the initial measurement, valuation and depreciation of fixed assets and introduces some new requirements aimed at precluding perceived abuses. Broadly speaking, tangible fixed assets are initially recorded at cost and then depreciated on a systematic basis over their useful economic lives. A significant change is that FRS 15 introduces a formal framework for revaluation, which must be carried out on a periodic basis.

2.4 Deferred Taxation

7–45   2.4.1 Full provision or reserve for all Taxation which has been or may be assessed or for which the Company may become accountable in respect of any act, omission or event (whether of the Company or any other person) up

to and including the Accounts Date and for any contingent or deferred liability provided for in the Accounts.

For a short summary of FRS 19, which deals with deferred taxation, see the commentary on cl.2.1.2.7.

2.5 Accounting reference date

2.5.1 The accounting reference date of the Company is, and has always been,   **7–46**
[ ].

The accounting reference date of a company is defined by CA 2006 s.391, being the date in the calendar year on which the accounting reference period of the company is to be treated as coming to an end. There are complicated provisions defining the circumstances in which an accounting reference date may be changed and these may be of significance in taxation matters. In principle, an accounting period for taxation purposes ends when the accounting period ends in accordance with CA 2006. If, however, the period of the accounts is for more than 12 months, the first 12 months are treated as one accounting period for taxation purposes and the balance of the period as another (ICTA s.12). As it may be essential for taxation purposes to extend or shorten an accounting period to ensure that profits or losses arise in the appropriate period, the restrictions contained in CA 2006 s.391 could be important. The vendors should ask the purchaser for a clear statement of the reason why it requires this warranty so that a determination can be made of the resulting exposure which they would incur.

2.6 Management Accounts

2.6.1 The Management Accounts have been prepared [in accordance with   **7–47**
accounting policies consistent with those used in the preparation of the
Accounts,] with all due care and on a basis consistent with the management
accounts of the Company prepared in the preceding [year].

The wording of this warranty is likely to be the subject of much negotiation between the vendors and the purchaser. As with the last accounts, the vendors will be very reluctant to warrant the management accounts as "accurate" for the reasons given with respect to cl.2.1.2.1 and further because the procedures used in their preparation are likely to be less rigorous than those at audit. The aim of the wording at the start of the warranty which refers to consistency with the last accounts is to flush out, by disclosure, differences between the accounting policies adopted in the management accounts and those in the last accounts which will in most instances have been audited. If the vendors are to agree to the inclusion of the wording in the first set of brackets then they should bear in mind that the requirement of CA 2006 s.386 which requires a company to keep accounts which disclose with reasonable accuracy, at any time, the financial position of the company at that time.

The vendors might seek to avoid giving any warranties with regard to the management accounts, beyond confirmation of compliance with CA 2006 s.386 (see cl.2.7.1.4), particularly when completion accounts are to be prepared in respect of the period from the Balance Sheet Date to completion.

The purchaser might argue with some justification that the "materiality" qualification is unnecessary if the agreement includes de minimis provisions.

Given that the management accounts will usually be annexed to the disclosure letter, the vendors will need to be careful that they do not indirectly warrant their accuracy by virtue of general wording in the disclosure letter of the type discussed in Ch.9.

2.7 Books and records

7–48   ### 2.7.1 The accounting and other records of the Company:

2.7.1.1   are in its exclusive ownership and direct control;

Section 388 of CA 2006 requires that the accounting records of a company are kept at its registered office or at such other place as the directors think fit. If the records are kept abroad, the company must send certain accounts and returns to be kept in the United Kingdom.

The purpose of this warranty is primarily as a reminder, to ensure that the purchaser will obtain possession of all the books and records of the target company. An example of circumstances where this might otherwise be overlooked is where the target company is a subsidiary of a corporate vendor and the books of the target company are maintained, perhaps on a computer, by the parent company which is not being sold.

The reference to "other records" should be considered carefully by the vendors in view of its potentially wide reaching scope. It may also be appropriate to restrict the warranty to accounts and other records of not more than a certain age, particularly as CA 2006 s.388 requires private companies to preserve their accounting records for only three years, as compared with six years for public companies.

7–49   #### 2.7.1.2   have been fully, properly and accurately kept and completed;

On the face of it this is an onerous warranty in that it is most unlikely in practice that any records will be entirely free from deficiencies. On the other hand, if these are of a minimal nature they will in practice not result in any liability under the warranty as the purchaser will suffer no loss.

7–50   #### 2.7.1.3   are accurate in all material respects;

Even with the qualification "in all material respects", this is an onerous warranty. Accuracy is a concept that is difficult to apply to financial statements on any basis. Concepts of "true and fair view" are generally more appropriate.

2.7.1.4   show a true and fair view of its trading transactions and its   7–51
financial, contractual and trading position.

Section 386 of CA 2006 requires that the accounting records which every
company is obliged to keep should disclose with reasonable accuracy, at any
time, the financial position of the company at that time. As the books will provide
on a daily basis a less comprehensive picture than the true and fair view of the
annual accounts, it is apparent that the statutory obligation is less onerous than
the requirements of this warranty. The vendors should seek to limit this warranty
to the requirements of CA 2006 s.386.

   The vendors will need to be careful that by agreeing to warranties under the
"books and records" heading, they are not indirectly warranting financial records
of the company to a higher standard than the position agreed in relation to the
main accounts warranties. The warranty of the statutory books has already been
dealt with at cl.1.10.2. The vendors should seek to amend the warranties to
address such issues. The warranty given in respect of the accounts, management
accounts and statutory books should be limited to that at cl.2.7.1.1.

3 Finance

3.1 Capital commitments

3.1.1 No commitments on capital account were outstanding at the Balance   7–52
Sheet Date and, since then, the Company has not [to any material extent]
made, or agreed to make capital expenditure, incurred or agreed to incur
capital commitments, or disposed of or agreed to dispose of capital assets (or
any interest in them).

Unless qualified by the reference to materiality as indicated in square brackets,
this clause will normally be unduly onerous. Although the purchaser might argue
that the purpose of the warranties de minimis (see para.11–04), if there is one, is
to avoid the necessity of qualifying the warranty in this way, the vendors might
reasonably maintain that the warranty, if unqualified, would result in unfair and
inappropriate inroads being made into the cushion provided by the floor. If the
warranty is amended, it would be as well, in cases of doubt, to clarify what is
intended by "material". This will not usually give rise to difficulty but, where
there is a programme of capital purchases, it may be as well to insert a specific
sum per item and an aggregate limit below which disclosure is not required.

3.2 Bank and other borrowings

3.2.1 Particulars of all money borrowed by the Company are set out in the   7–53
Disclosure Letter. The Company does not have any bank borrowings which
exceed applicable overdraft limits (and has not had any that have done so
during the last 12 months).

The purchaser will want to know details of all money borrowed by the target
company, not least to ensure that the company does not have any borrowings that
it is not already aware of.

It is important for the purchaser to know whether a temporary accommodation has been given to the company by its bankers allowing it to exceed its normal facilities. It will, however, be appreciated that overdrafts are invariably repayable on demand and a facility can normally be withdrawn at any time. It is accordingly unlikely that the purchaser could prove any loss if the warranty was breached as, in general, the only sanction for the bank would be to exercise the right it has in any case to call for immediate repayment. The last part of the clause is designed to elicit details of prior excesses and should allow the purchaser to determine whether current facilities are sufficient.

7–54   **3.2.2 The total amount borrowed by the Company (as determined in accordance with the provisions of the relevant documents) does not exceed any limitation on borrowing powers contained in its articles of association or in a debenture or other document to which it is subject.**

In practice, a breach of borrowing limits imposed by a loan stock or debenture trust deed has more serious implications than a breach of borrowing limits contained in the articles of association. Most trust deeds contain a provision entitling the lenders or trustees to call in the loan immediately in the event of an infringement of the borrowing restrictions. If there is particular concern about this, the purchaser should examine any such restrictions to satisfy itself, so far as possible, that no breach has occurred. If there has been a breach and the right to call in a loan or debenture is exercised as a result, the compensation for breach of warranty is unlikely to provide much satisfaction, and as such in circumstances where the vendors are unable to satisfy the purchaser of the position, the purchaser should consider seeking an indemnity against such an eventuality or on a more practical basis requiring the vendors to obtain a financial waiver.

7–55   **3.2.3 The Company does not have outstanding nor has it agreed to create or issue any loan capital nor has it factored or discounted its debts or engaged in financing of a type which would not require to be shown or fully reflected in the Accounts.**

Debt factoring or invoice discounting involves the sale of debts and, where it has taken place, it would be appropriate to ensure that the target company has not given a warranty that the debts will be recoverable in full or to any specified extent. Factoring is a method of financing which may be off-balance sheet, and the purchaser will be entitled to ensure that all financing arrangements by the target company have been fully disclosed.

7–56   **3.2.4 The Company has not since the Balance Sheet Date repaid or become liable to repay any loan or other indebtedness in advance of its stated maturity.**

This warranty should present little difficulty to the vendors and, as the continuing availability of facilities may be of some importance to the purchaser, there will normally be no reasonable basis for objecting to it.

3.2.5 The Company has not received notice (whether formal or informal) **[which remains outstanding] from any lenders of money, requiring repayment or intimating the enforcement of security which it holds over assets of the Company; and [so far as the Vendors are aware] there are no circumstances likely to give rise to such a notice.**   7–57

The purchaser is entitled to ensure that financial facilities apparently available to the target company have not been withdrawn but, without the qualifications of the words in square brackets, the vendors might reasonably consider the clause to be too onerous. If the purchaser will not agree to the inclusion of the wording in the first set of brackets (the purchaser will probably argue that it needs details of all notices, not just those that remain outstanding, as they may be indicative of recurrent breaches or other issues), then the vendors should seek to limit the period to which the warranty relates.

3.3 Bank accounts

3.3.1 Statements of all the bank accounts of the Company, showing their **balances as at a date not more than one day before today's date, have been supplied to the Purchaser.**   7–58

Historically the purchaser would require the bank statements to be provided as at a few days prior to completion, so that the purchaser could carry out reconciliations of them with the financial statements that had been provided to it. More recently, however, there has been a move to require the vendors to deliver bank statements (as at the day prior to completion) and reconciliations of them as a completion requirement. The purchaser may also seek to have such documents warranted (as envisaged by cl.3.3.2). The warranty serves little purpose as it is unlikely that a breach would entitle the purchaser to any damages.

3.3.2 Since the date of each statement, there have been no payments out of **the account to which the statement relates, except for payments in the normal course of business; and the balances on current accounts are not substantially different from the balances shown in the statements.**   7–59

In so far as this provision relates to transactions which have occurred up to the date of the sale agreement, it is not difficult for the vendors to check the accuracy of the warranty although they will need to consider carefully what payments are within the normal course of business. Nevertheless, the vendors might reasonably consider that this is not a matter upon which the purchaser is entitled to a warranty if there are clauses in the agreement corresponding to cl.4.1 which covers in some detail the activities which have occurred between the balance sheet date and the date of the agreement. Furthermore, if the warranty is extended so that it applies also at completion (when there is a gap between contracts and completion) and there is a delay of any significance between the date of the signing of the contract and the date of completion, this will amount in effect to a cash flow warranty. In the case of a normal trading company where a material interval is involved, it would be unreasonable to expect the vendors to give a warranty as to the precise cash position at completion since this will depend upon a variety of arbitrary events. Where the transaction involves completion accounts, cash in hand will simply form part of the overall net assets. The cash position may be far more important where the transaction has been structured on a "debt and cash free" basis. In these circumstances the gross price that has been agreed will be adjusted by reference to the level of debt (as a deduction off the price) and by the addition of "excess cash" which would normally be determined by reference to any excess over normal working capital requirements. An example of this is contained in Ch.13.

3.4 Continuation of facilities

7–60   **3.4.1 The Disclosure Letter sets out full details of (and there are attached to it accurate copies of all documents relating to) all debentures, acceptance credits, loans or other financial facilities outstanding or available to the Company (referred to in this clause as the "Facilities") and of any limits or restrictions to which they are subject.**

Although the purchaser should require production of copies of all documents relating to material financing facilities, the vendors should not expect simply by producing the documents to avoid an obligation, under a warranty corresponding to cl.4.15.1, to disclose to the purchaser specifically provisions in the facility documents of a particularly onerous nature. It is not clear that the purchaser would normally have any remedy if the disclosure omitted a facility.

7–61   **3.4.2 [So far as the Vendors are aware] There has been no contravention of, or non-compliance with, the terms of the Facilities.**

In practice it is not always possible to avoid minor infringements of the extensive restrictions which are to be found in some facility documents and the vendors and the purchaser will need to negotiate as to which of them carries the ultimate risk that a minor infringement gives a creditor the right to terminate a facility or call in a loan. The vendors will prefer to include the wording in brackets so as to pass the risk of an unknown technical breach to the purchaser. Alternatively or in addition they may wish to include reference to "materiality" to avoid the need to disclose trivial technical breaches.

7–62   **3.4.3 No steps for the early repayment of sums outstanding under the Facilities have been threatened or [so far as the Vendors are aware] taken and [so far as the Vendors are aware] no circumstances have occurred which give rise to an obligation to make, or would permit the calling for, early repayment.**

This provision will need qualification if a threat has been made in the past but withdrawn; in that event it would be appropriate to add the words "and not withdrawn" after "threatened" and "which remain outstanding" after "occurred". The vendors may wish to limit the warranty by adding the words in the second set of brackets given its wide ranging nature and to add the words in the first set as the vendors will not know whether a third party has taken any steps unless they have been notified of this. A purchaser may be unsympathetic to such an approach on a risk apportionment basis.

3.4.4 There have not been and are no circumstances known to the Vendors   7–63
whereby the continuation of any of the Facilities might be prejudiced or
their terms altered.

This warranty is drafted so that the knowledge of the vendors is stated to relate to the circumstances and not to the impact that the circumstances will have on the continued availability of the facilities. The vendors may wish to consider altering the wording so that it reads:

"There have been and are no circumstances which, so far as the Vendors are aware, are likely to prejudice the continuation of any of the Facilities or to give rise to an alteration in their terms".

3.4.5 None of the Facilities is dependent on the guarantee or indemnity of,   7–64
or security provided by, a third party.

This provides an important reminder to both parties. The vendors will wish to ensure that any guarantee or security given by a third party is released when the sale takes place while the purchaser will require details of any such circumstances so that it can consider what alternative arrangements should be made. The vendors should not have a problem with giving the warranty as they will be able to check the position relatively easily.

3.5 Debts

3.5.1 No part of the amounts included in debtors in the Accounts, or   7–65
subsequently recorded in the books of the Company as owing by a debtor, is
overdue by more than 90 days, or, has been released on terms that the debtor
pays less than the full book value of his debt, or has been written off, or has
had a credit issued against it or has proved to be, or is regarded as, wholly
or partly irrecoverable.

This is substantially a straightforward factual matter in so far as it relates to the position of debtors at the date of the exchange of the sale agreement but careful consideration will be necessary if there is a general clause in the agreement which extends the warranties to the completion date. In such a case, the vendors should, if possible, provide that the extension does not apply to this warranty. Alternatively, they should ensure that the length of the period which is specified in the warranty, as being the maximum period for which debtors are overdue, takes into account the anticipated duration of the interval between contracts and completion when there is to be a gap between the two.

7–66   **3.5.2 The amounts due from [trade] debtors as at Completion [(less the amount of any relevant provision or reserve, determined on the same basis as that applied in the Accounts and Disclosed)] will be recoverable in full, in the normal course of business, and in any event not later than 60 days after Completion; and none of the debts is subject to a right of counterclaim or set-off, or withholding or other deduction except to the extent of the provision or reserve.**

This warranty is unusual in that it extends to events that will be determined only after completion, when the vendors will no longer have control over the target company. The collection of debts after completion is largely in the hands of the purchaser and, if the target company continues to trade with a slow payer, there may be disputes as to whether a payment by the debtor relates to any particular debt. The vendors might wish to provide that, unless a debtor appropriates a payment to a specific debt, then payments by the debtor are treated as discharging older rather than more recent debts.

The warranty is unlikely to be acceptable to the vendors as it amounts to a guarantee of outstanding debts, and will not be appropriate unless in some manner the purchase price for the target company was determined on the basis that the debts would be good. If the vendors agree to give the warranty, they should consider restricting it to trade debtors if there are other debts, such as loans, outstanding. They might also require that in relation to any warranty claim that is made the debt the subject matter of the claim is assigned to them, so that they have the opportunity of chasing and collating the debt themselves if they have to pay out for it on the warranty claim. If, following the assignment, the debt proves to be bad, it is likely that the vendors will be entitled to an allowable loss for capital gains tax purposes since they would not be the original creditors in relation to the debt.

The vendors should be entitled to qualify the warranty by the addition of the words in the second pair of brackets.

7–67   **3.5.3 Complete and accurate details, including repayment terms and maturity dates, of loans made by the Company which remain outstanding at, and immediately after, Completion are set out in the Disclosure Letter and all the loans will be repaid in full by their maturity dates.**

The first part of this warranty has little more than informational value but the second part effectively amounts to a guarantee by the vendors and is unlikely to be acceptable to them. If the concept is agreed, the wording should at least be qualified by wording such as "provided that no time or indulgence is granted to the debtors" by reference to the vendors' knowledge.

7–68   **3.5.4 The Company has not to or with made a loan or quasi-loan or entered into a credit transaction (as defined in CA 2006 s.202) to a director**

of the Company or any holding company or persons connected to such directors contrary to the Companies Acts.

Following the implementation of CA 2006, loans to directors of private companies are permitted (provided that member's approval is obtained) (CA 2006 s.197) and the restriction on private companies (provided they are not associated with a public company) giving quasi-loans has been removed. A quasi-loan, which is defined in CA 2006 s.199, arises if the target company agrees to pay a sum to a third party for the benefit of a director who is then himself liable to reimburse the target company. If a private company is associated with a public company (CA 2006 s.198), for example, because its parent company happens to be a public company, then member's approval must be obtained where a quasi-loan has been made to a director. If the target's group of companies does not contain any company which is a public company or any of the companies are associated with a public company, the reference to quasi-loan could be replaced by a warranty that no company in the target company's group of companies is a public company or a company associated with a public company for the purposes of CA 2006 s.198(1).

3.5.5 The Company has not made a loan, which remains outstanding, on terms entitling it to receive either a rate of interest varying with, or a share of, the profits of a business.   7–69

A loan to a person engaged in a business on the terms described in this clause is prima facie evidence of a partnership (Partnership Act 1890 s.2). Unless the loan agreement is in writing signed by all the parties, the lender's right of recovery is postponed to all other creditors of the borrower. The implications of a loan of this nature for the purchaser are obvious and it is reasonable for the purchaser to seek protection. If the terms of a loan are such that it is unclear whether it could fall within s.2, the details should be disclosed to the purchaser and the parties could then negotiate as to who should take the risk of difficulty.

3.6 Liabilities

3.6.1 The Company has no outstanding liabilities (including disputed or contingent liabilities) other than the liabilities disclosed in the Accounts or incurred, in the normal course of business [since the Balance Sheet Date].   7–70

A liability is outstanding so long as it remains in existence and the vendors will wish to consider carefully what liabilities could be covered by this warranty. It will be noted that the exclusion for transactions in the normal course of business relates only to those which were incurred since the last accounts date. The vendors should delete the wording in brackets so that all liabilities incurred in the normal course of business are excluded, whenever they arose (although see the discussion in relation to cl.4.1.1.1).

3.6.2 The Company has not been at any time the tenant of, or a guarantor in respect of, a leasehold property which is not one of the Properties.   7–71

If a target company was the original lessee of premises under a lease granted before January 1, 1996, it will remain contingently liable to the lessor by virtue of the privity of contract between them, notwithstanding a subsequent assignment. Even if it were not the original lessee it will normally, upon taking the assignment of the lease, have given covenants for indemnity to its predecessor in title. There is therefore a contingent liability in the event of the current tenant defaulting under the lease. In the case of leases granted on or after January 1, 1996, the original tenant or assignee of a lease ceases to be liable following an authorised assignment of the lease, except to the extent of any liability arising under an authorised guarantee agreement (Landlord and Tenant (Covenants) Act 1995; see also cl.8.6 in para.6–67).

If a disclosure has to be made under this warranty in relation to a substantial lease, the purchaser may wish to consider the quality of the covenant of the present tenant so that an analysis can be made of the likelihood of a default which would involve the target company.

7–72   **3.6.3 There has been no exercise, purported exercise or claim for any Encumbrance over any of the assets of the Company and there is no dispute directly or indirectly relating to any assets.**

"Encumbrance" is widely defined and as such the vendors should ensure that all relevant matters have been considered. They might also consider imposing a time period to which the warranty relates to save the need to disclose historical issues and the risk of not disclosing them, although such matters would be unlikely to result in claims. The purchaser will be concerned to ensure that there is no claim over or dispute in respect of any of the assets of the target company.

3.7 Working capital

7–73   **3.7.1 Having regard to the Facilities (as defined in clause [3.4.1]), the Company has sufficient working capital to carry on its business, in its present form and at its present level of turnover, for 18 months after Completion and to carry out, in accordance with their terms, all outstanding commitments.**

The first part of this warranty follows broadly the statement that has to be given by directors of a company when making certain public issues, and the vendors must carry out a careful cash flow analysis if they are to give it. (Most vendors will reasonably object to the warranty given its forward looking nature. Where the purchaser has undertaken financial due diligence it will have had the opportunity to analyse the position.) The vendors might require that a definition of working capital is included, such as "debtors, prepayments and stock, less creditors and accruals". The second part of the warranty will depend on events after completion, including the way the purchaser procures that the target company fulfils its subsisting obligations, and is not something to which the vendors should readily agree. Although the warranty is onerous, it must be recognised that a purchaser will have difficulty in ever showing a breach of warranty unless it can demonstrate that the assumptions made in preparing the cash flow statement were, or should have been, known by the vendors to have been incorrect. In assessing whether such a warranty has been breached, in circumstances where the actual outcome differs from the projected figures, the court will ask whether the forecast in question was a reasonable interpretation of the relevant information. If it concludes that it was, then there will have been no breach of warranty (see *Lion Nathan Ltd v CC Bottlers Ltd* [1996] 2 B.C.L.C. 371). It would also be appropriate for the vendors to include a statement of the assumptions upon which the cash flow statement is believed to be correct, such as no major insolvencies among customers, no significant changes in tax rates and no events occurring of a general nature which would cause a properly prepared cash flow forecast to be rendered inaccurate.

3.8 Dividends and distributions

3.8.1 Since the Balance Sheet Date, no dividend or other distribution (as   7–74 defined in ICTA 1988 Pt VI and s.418) has been, or is treated as having been, declared, paid or made by the Company.

ICTA 1988 Pt VI (and particularly s.209) contains extensive definitions of "distributions" which include not only dividends but also any distributions out of assets and such special cases as issues of bonus redeemable shares. Section 418 brings within the definition expenditure incurred in providing benefits for shareholders in close companies.

The purpose of this warranty is to protect the purchaser against deliberate reductions in shareholders' funds occurring in the period between the end of the last accounting period and contracts. Often a purchaser will require a certain level of net assets at completion. This warranty would require disclosure of any "distributions" in favour of the shareholders since the end of the last accounting period, allowing the purchaser to check that the likely level of net assets will be as expected.

Although the warranty is intended to deal with dividends as understood for Companies Act purposes, it is nevertheless convenient, for the purchaser, to extend the concept of dividends to include the wide tax definition of distributions. The vendors might prefer to amend the warranty so that it relates only to dividends and distributions within the meaning of CA 2006. The purchaser cannot reasonably object to such an amendment as the taxation implications of other distributions will be covered by the detailed tax warranties.

3.8.2 All dividends and distributions declared, made or paid by the   7–75 Company were declared, made or paid in accordance with its articles of association and the applicable provisions of the Companies Acts and in accordance with any agreements or arrangements between the Company, its shareholders or any third party regulating the payment or declaration of dividends.

If a dividend has been improperly paid, it will normally be recoverable by the paying company. In general a purchaser will not be concerned about this aspect, since any defect in a dividend payment by a target company can operate only to the benefit of that company. The warranty will, however, be of significance to a purchaser if, for example, there are different classes of shares, as a shareholder who has not received the appropriate payment could have a claim against the target company. Similarly, if dividends have been paid improperly by reference to a shareholders' agreement, that could result in a claim against the company, it often being a party to such arrangements.

The clause, as expressed, applies to the whole term of existence of the target company and, unless the target company is comparatively newly formed, the vendors should consider restricting the warranty to a reasonable past period.

3.9 Government grants

7–76 **3.9.1 The Company has not in the last six years applied for, or received, a grant, subsidy or financial assistance from any government department or agency, or a local or other authority.**

Many grants are repayable if certain conditions are not fulfilled and the vendors should have no difficulty in determining whether this warranty applies. The purchaser will wish to know what conditions remain outstanding so that it can review its plans for the target company with them in mind. There are also certain taxation implications which can arise in relation to grants. Thus, for example, if the grant is made in connection with the acquisition of plant or machinery generally capital allowances will be obtained only on the net amount (CAA 2001 s.532).

4 Trading and contracts

4.1 Changes in business activities and financial position since the Balance Sheet Date

7–77 **4.1.1 Since the Balance Sheet Date:**

> **4.1.1.1** **the business of the Company has been continued in its normal course [as regards the nature, extent and manner of carrying it on] with a view to maintaining the business as a going concern and without entering into any transaction assuming any liability or making any payment which is not provided for in the Accounts or which is not in the normal course of its business;**

The purchaser is entitled to be sure that the target company has carried on its business in the normal manner since the balance sheet date and will also wish to ensure that it continues to do so up to completion. To refer to continuing in "the ordinary course of business" would provide the purchaser with little protection as it is clear from such cases as *Borax Company, Re* [1901] 1 Ch. 326 that almost any transaction within the powers of a company, short of a disposal of its whole business, can be in the ordinary course. It is therefore desirable from the purchaser's point of view to refer to "normal" or "ordinary and proper". For the vendors these concepts are not clear and, unless the target company has acted in a purely routine manner since the balance sheet date, they would need to satisfy themselves that there is no problem in identifying what constitutes the "normal" course of the business. They may also wish to add the words in square brackets which limit the scope of the warranty, although each of the words "nature", "extent" and "manner" would need to be considered carefully if they are to be added.

Purchasers will be looking for reassurance through this warranty that, in particular, the target company has been carrying on business in accordance with its restricted objects. Until September 30, 2009, all private companies were required to state their objects in their memorandum of association and were restricted to pursuing its stated objects only. Following the implementation of CA 2006 on October 1, 2009 the objects clause of all existing companies automatically became a provision of their articles of association (CA 2006 s.28), from which the restrictions may be deleted by special resolution unless it is subject to a provision of entrenchment. All companies formed on October 1, 2009 or later will not have a restricted objects clause unless specifically included in their articles of association.

4.1.1.2   there has been no deterioration in the turnover[, or financial   **7–78**
or trading position] [or prospects, of the Company] [except as
a result of factors generally affecting similar businesses] [to a
similar extent];

While there should be little difficulty in practice in determining whether turnover has been maintained and as such the vendors should be willing to accept the first part of the warranty, greater difficulty may be experienced in warranting the financial and trading position of the target company in view of the vagueness of these concepts and the fact that the accuracy of the warranty would be very dependent on events occurring after completion. "Prospects" would rarely be warranted by the vendors given its forward looking nature. It would usually be appropriate where the warranty extends beyond turnover for the vendors to add the words in the third pair of square brackets, in which case the purchaser should add a qualification such as that in the fourth pair.

4.1.1.3   the Company has not by doing, or omitting to do, anything   **7–79**
[materially] prejudiced its goodwill;

This warranty, which may at first sight seem to be comparatively innocuous, is in fact potentially very onerous. If goodwill is a measure of the ability to generate profits, then a warranty as to the maintenance of goodwill amounts to a warranty as to the ability to maintain profitability. In addition, in an active business many routine transactions may, in the event, have unexpected repercussions. The clause is accordingly unlikely to be acceptable to the vendors, even with the addition of "materially". If the vendors are compelled to give a warranty along these lines, they should try to limit the clause so that it relates only to things done and not to things omitted.

7–80   **4.1.1.4   the Company has not entered into any capital transaction as seller, purchaser, lessor or lessee or otherwise undertaken any material commitment [that is of a value in excess of £[   ]] on its capital account;**

This warranty requires disclosure of capital transactions arising after the balance sheet date which are likely to be of interest to the purchaser. The vendors would not normally have an issue with this warranty, although they will probably want to add the wording in brackets to clarify what is regarded as material.

7–81   **4.1.1.5   of the plant, machinery, fixtures, fittings, equipment, vehicles, furniture, property, materials and other assets (not being included in the current assets) included in the Accounts or acquired by the Company since the Balance Sheet Date:**

         4.1.1.5.1   none has been sold or disposed of at a figure lower than book value or an open market arm's length value whichever is the higher; and

         4.1.1.5.2   none has been or has been agreed to be let on hire or hire purchase or sold on deferred terms.

These warranties are targeted at eliciting details of any transactions involving the assets included in the accounts or those that have been acquired since then, which it would not be routine for the company to dispose of. Normally the warranty would not give rise to concern for the vendors and would simply require disclosure of relevant transactions.

7–82   **4.1.1.6   the Company has paid its creditors in accordance with their respective credit terms; and there are no amounts owing by it which have been due for more than [60] [90] days.**

The first half of this warranty would imply an analysis of the credit terms of every supplier with whom the target company has dealings. The vendors may prefer to amend the wording so as to provide that creditors have been paid in accordance with the normal practice of the target company. This would be a reasonable approach for the vendors to take, although the purchaser may want to extend the warranty such that the vendors are required to confirm that no claims have been made or are pending under the Late Payment of Commercial Debts (Interest) Act 1998, which incorporates into business supply contracts an implied term that overdue debts carry fixed statutory interest. The second half of the warranty relating to outstanding amounts is purely factual and, while there may be difficulty in checking every small item, this problem will be minimal if a sufficiently long period is specified.

4.1.2 The value of the net realisable assets of the Company is not less than   7–83
at the Balance Sheet Date.

Although "net realisable assets" is not defined and no method for determining "value" is provided, in effect the warranty amounts to a statement that the target company has not made losses or suffered a reduction in the value of its fixed assets since the balance sheet date. In practice the purchaser would have great difficulty in verifying whether this warranty had been breached but, nevertheless, unless the purchase of the target company has been negotiated on the basis that a representation is made as to the net asset position of the target company at the date of contracts or completion, the vendors should not accept the clause. Generally, where the price has been agreed on the basis of a representation of net assets there will be completion accounts in the sale agreement to test the position and so the warranty will not be required. If there are not to be completion accounts then such a warranty may be appropriate, although if it is accepted, the vendors should ensure that the terms mentioned above are clearly defined.

4.2 Vendors' other interests and liabilities

4.2.1 The Vendors and their Associates are not, directly or indirectly,   7–84
interested in any business, other than that now carried on by the Company, which is or is likely to be competitive with the business of the Company, apart from interests in securities [normally] listed on the Official List of the UK Listing Authority and admitted to trading to the main market of the London Stock Exchange Plc, or dealt in on its Alternative Investment Market, and in respect of which the Vendors, with their Associates, are interested in less than three per cent of any class of the securities in that company.

The warranty refers to the vendors but, in cases where the warrantors are not the same persons as the vendors, consideration will have to be given to the question of precisely what interest the purchaser is trying to protect. The body of the sale agreement will normally contain a restrictive covenant which will prohibit the vendors from carrying on competing activities within a specified area and for a specified period. The vendors might reasonably consider that, if a restrictive covenant is given, the purchaser derives as much protection as it is entitled to receive against possible competitive activities under that provision. This warranty, while covering similar ground to the normal restrictive covenant, is also wider in its scope and the vendors should particularly give careful consideration to the acceptability of the reference to "Associates" given the wide range of people that the defined term covers and the use of the words "are likely to be". It will be preferable from the vendors' perspective for the relevant activities to be specified. In addition, the insertion of the word "normally" as indicated in square brackets would be a desirable precaution for the vendors to cover the case where an investment in a listed company falls outside the strict wording of the warranty by reason of a temporary suspension of the listing. From the purchaser's point of view it will have a legitimate interest in finding out about any potentially competing activities prior to completion so that it can address them in the restrictions it seeks or otherwise as part of the negotiations.

7–85   **4.2.2 None of the Vendors, or their Associates, is indebted to the Company.**

The purpose of this warranty is primarily to provide a reminder that the purchaser would normally expect all indebtedness of the vendors and their associates to the target company to be cleared. The vendors may wish to amend this clause so that it provides instead that any such indebtedness will be discharged by completion and as with cl.4.2.1 the previous warranty will need to give careful consideration to the range of people caught by the term "Associates". It may be noted that a breach of the warranty would not usually give rise to a loss provided that the debtor is able to meet the liability.

4.3 Effect of sale of Shares

7–86 **4.3.1 The Vendors are not aware, and have no grounds for believing, that after Completion (whether by reason of an existing agreement or arrangement or as a result of the acquisition of the Company by the Purchaser):**

    4.3.1.1   **a [material] supplier [for the purposes of this warranty being a supplier that in the 12 months prior to Completion dealt with or supplied the Company] of the Company will cease, or be entitled to cease, supplying it or may substantially reduce its level of supplies;**

    4.3.1.2   **a [material] customer [for the purposes of this warranty being a customer that in the 12 months prior to Completion dealt with or was supplied with goods or services by the Company] of the Company will cease, or be entitled to cease, to deal with it or may substantially reduce its level of business;**

    4.3.1.3   **a [material] supplier or customer (as defined in Warranty 4.3.1.1 and 4.3.1.2) of the Company will seek to impose or negotiate materially different terms of trading from those currently enjoyed by the Company;**

    4.3.1.4   **the Company will lose a right of benefit which it enjoys; or**

    4.3.1.5   **any officer or senior employee of the Company will leave its employment.**

While the purchaser will generally wish to know if the purchase of the target company is likely to have an adverse effect on relationships with suppliers and customers, the vendors may wish to qualify the warranty by adding in the wording in brackets and limiting it to suppliers and customers which are material to the company either by virtue of the type of goods involved or because of the percentage of total supplies or sales which the group obtains from that supplier or makes to that customer. Often materiality for these purposes will be defined further by reference to the percentage levels of supplies or sales so as to achieve certainty as to the ambit of the warranty. The vendors would usually wish to limit the effect of the warranty further by making it clear that no actual enquiry has been made of the customers, suppliers or employees by adding:

" . . . (but without having made any actual enquiry of any supplier, customer or employee)"

after "The Vendors are not aware". This would not be unusual given the need to preserve confidentiality with most transactions until they are completed.

4.3.2 Compliance with this Agreement will not: 7–87

4.3.2.1   breach or constitute a default under an agreement or arrangement to which the Company is a party or any undertaking to or order of any court or governmental agency or regulatory body or any provision of the memorandum or articles of association of the Company, or any security interest, lease, contract or order, judgment, award, injunction, regulation [or [so far as the Vendors are aware] other restriction or obligation of any kind] affecting the Company;

Save in respect of banking and finance documentation (which will often contain a change of control provision) it would be unusual for the change in control of the target company to give rise, of itself, to a breach of an agreement binding the target company. A corporate vendor may find that it will breach a trust deed if it sells the target company without the appropriate approvals but such a breach should not affect the target company. The only provisions of a normal sale agreement which may require attention in the context of this warranty would usually be an obligation for directors to retire (which may involve a wrongful dismissal by the target company) or terms which adversely affect employees' pension rights. The vendors should be cautious about the reference to "any other restriction or obligation of any kind". If there is anything that the purchaser is concerned about, then it should be asked to specify it. If the purchaser will not agree to this, then the vendors should seek to have the latter part of the warranty subject to their knowledge by inserting the wording in the first set of brackets. In reality there are likely to be very few matters that will not already have been caught by the first part of the warranty.

4.3.2.2   relieve any person from any [material] obligation to the 7–88 Company (whether contractual or otherwise), or enable any person to determine any such obligation [or any right or benefit enjoyed by the Company, or to exercise a right in respect of the Company];

The purchaser is entitled to a warranty that no significant agreements will, by reason of the change of control of the target company, be terminable. The vendors should, however, delete the words in the second set of brackets given its vague and very wide ranging nature and restrict the warranty to material contractual obligations.

7–89   **4.3.2.3   result in any present or future indebtedness of the Company becoming, or becoming capable of being declared, due and payable prior to its stated maturity or loan facilities being withdrawn;**

The vendors should have no difficulty in checking all facility letters and loan agreements to ascertain whether a change in control would cause an early repayment obligation to arise. The most common circumstance would be where there is a corporate vendor which has guaranteed the indebtedness, although this is already covered by cl.3.4.5. It is unlikely that, apart from the sale itself of the target company, any other provision of the sale agreement would be relevant. See also cl.3.2.5.

7–90   **4.3.2.4   result in the creation, imposition, crystallisation or enforcement of any Encumbrance on any of the assets of the Company; or**

To some extent this overlaps with cl.4.3.2.1 although there is a technical difference. In practice it is not likely to be an issue in the context of change of control when any relevant matters will be required to be disclosed and, if material, appropriate consents obtained.

7–91   **4.3.2.5   result in a breach of a Licence or result in losing the benefit of a Licence.**

Although on the face of it this looks like a fairly innocuous warranty given the definition of "licence" it is extremely wide. Well-advised vendors may therefore ask the purchaser to justify its inclusion or limit it to matters pertinent to the target company.

4.4 Business conducted lawfully

7–92   4.4.1 The Company has carried on business and conducted its affairs in compliance [in all material respects] with the Companies Acts, the terms of any Licences, its memorandum and articles of association, and all other documents to which it is, or has been, a party and all other statutory obligations applicable to it.

While the vendors might reasonably accept responsibility for conduct of affairs in accordance with the memorandum and articles of association of the target company, they should be extremely cautious about agreeing to represent that all "Companies Acts" and all "other statutory obligations" and obligations arising under all "Licences" (as widely defined) and "other documents" have been properly performed. If the purchaser has particular concerns regarding a specific document or transaction, then the vendors could reasonably require that the document or transaction in question is identified in the warranty and that others are excluded.

Alternatively, the warranty could be restricted to certain specific categories of documents, such as loan agreements or leases or amended to include the wording in brackets. If there is not an individual de minimis in respect of warranty claims then the vendors may want to include reference to materiality so as to try and avoid claims being made by the purchaser in respect of a series of minor breaches. No company is "perfect" and a purchaser which undertakes a post-completion audit will inevitably find areas of non-compliance in respect of which it can seek to bring warranty claims.

The vendors will need to ensure that in giving a general warranty such as this one, they are not inadvertently agreeing to warrant matters in respect of which they have negotiated a different standard elsewhere in the warranty schedule of the sale agreement, for example, it is likely that the vendors will have negotiated the property warranties such that they are not required to warrant that they have complied with all of the terms of applicable leases on an absolute basis. Accepting this warranty in its proposed form would override that. The vendors should also consider whether it would be appropriate to restrict the application of the warranty to the reasonably recent past, although this is unlikely to be acceptable to the purchaser as it will not want to have responsibility for historic problems. The vendors can take some comfort from the fact that any historical issues are likely to have materialised already.

4.4.2 The Company has the power and authority to carry on business in all jurisdictions in which it carries on business.   7–93

While this warranty is reasonable in principle, the vendors should be careful in considering the phrase "carries on business". If, for example, the target company has overseas distributors, they might under local law be deemed to be carrying on business in the countries where the distributors operate. In cases of doubt the vendors could seek to exclude business activities which are limited to dealing with distributors and agents. Alternatively, the warranty could be brought more closely into line with cl.1.6.1.2.

If the overseas activities of the target company are significant, the purchaser should consider extending this warranty by also specifying the particular overseas requirements with which it is primarily concerned. Local advice will usually be required to identify these.

4.5 Joint ventures and partnerships

4.5.1 The Company is not, nor has it agreed to become, a party in or member of a joint venture, consortium, partnership or other unincorporated association or other profit or income sharing arrangement [(other than recognised trade associations)].   7–94

Membership of a partnership will be relevant because of the exposure that arises from the joint and several liability for the obligations of the other partners. Although joint and several liability should be unusual in the case of a joint venture or consortium, care should be taken with contractual or unincorporated joint ventures because agreement by the joint venturers to share either profits or losses will be prima facie evidence of a partnership. It is also possible that there could be a joint venture or consortium operating outside the United Kingdom in jurisdictions where joint and several liability exists even though there is no partnership. Additionally, the terms of a joint venture could include a surrender of rights by the target company, for example by granting control to another participant in the venture. The inclusion of reference to trade associations is a convenient way of avoiding the necessity of making a specific disclosure if such memberships exist.

4.6 Agency agreements and agreements restricting business

7–95   **4.6.1 The Company is not a party to an agency, distributorship, marketing, purchasing, manufacturing or licensing agreement or arrangement, or a restrictive agreement or arrangement, under which part of its business is carried on or which restricts its freedom to carry on its business as it thinks fit.**

In so far as the warranty refers to agreements, it is largely an administrative task to review existing agreements to see whether any relevant restrictions exist. It is reasonable for the purchaser to require this review to be undertaken by the vendors who will, or should, have the information necessary to enable them to ensure that the review is comprehensive. Difficulty will arise if agreements have not been properly documented and exist either in the form of correspondence or as a result of a course of conduct. In such cases, however, the existence of a relevant restriction would be most unusual. The vendors should carefully consider whether reference to the different types of agreements is appropriate in the context of the target company and should, in the event of any doubt, require the purchaser to clarify the precise nature of agreements that the warranty is intended to contain.

The vendors should carefully consider whether the references to "arrangement" are acceptable, as they might take the view that an unenforceable arrangement would not adversely affect the purchaser. However, from the purchaser's point of view commercial prudence may make it important to adhere to informal arrangements and a suitable compromise might be to include only those arrangements which are material to the businesses of the target company.

The vendors may prefer to omit agreements or arrangements for the licence of third party intellectual property rights to members of the target company's group of companies as many, if not all, of the licences, will include restrictions as to the use of the licensed intellectual property rights. If this is the case, the words:

" . . . (other than any agreement or arrangement relating to the use of any Intellectual Property Rights)"

should be added after the word "arrangement" on the second line. However, such an amendment is likely to be resisted by the purchaser who will want to understand the nature of any restrictions upon the conduct of the business.

4.6.2 The Company is not subject to any order, judgment, undertaking or assurance which it has given to a court or government agency which is still in force.   7–96

The importance of court undertakings is self-evident. Undertakings given to government agencies are rare in practice in the United Kingdom although they may be given for the purpose of obtaining a grant or other assistance (see cl.3.9). Different considerations will arise if material business activities are conducted outside the United Kingdom, in which case undertakings to government agencies may be commonplace but nonetheless important.

4.7 Unfair trade and restrictive practices

4.7.1 The Company is not nor has it been a party to or concerned in any agreement, practice or arrangement (whether legally binding or not) which is or was: 7–97

4.7.1.1   in contravention of the Trade Descriptions Act 1968;

The Trade Descriptions Act 1968 makes it an offence to apply to goods, in the course of a trade or business, a false or misleading trade description. The warranty will be inappropriate for a company which does not manufacture or market goods.

4.7.1.2   in contravention of the Fair Trading Act 1973 Pt XI, as amended by the Trading Schemes Act 1996;   7–98

The Fair Trading Act 1973, Pt XI deals with "pyramid selling". Essentially this involves methods of selling otherwise than on business premises where inducements are given to the sellers for introducing other participants or meeting certain targets. There should be little difficulty in determining whether the activities of the target company are such as might fall within the scope of this legislation but, if they do, detailed consideration will have to be given to the precise wording of the legislation, which is complex and obscure in many aspects.

4.7.1.3   in contravention of the Consumer Credit Act 1974 (as amended);   7–99

The Consumer Credit Act 1974 essentially deals with credit agreements which involve a personal credit not exceeding £25,000 and hire agreements which do not require the hirer to make payments exceeding £25,000. Part III of the Act establishes a system of licensing consumer credit businesses and consumer hire businesses. Part IV regulates advertisements and Pt V deals with the formalities which are to be complied with when regulated credit and hire agreements are entered into. If the target company does deal in consumer credit or consumer hire transactions, it will be necessary for the vendors to review its activities to ensure that the statutory formalities have been met. Although the Consumer Credit Act 2006 has now been implemented this does not replace the terms of the 1974 Act in its entirety but simply amends and repeals certain sections. Therefore, convention now dictates that the "(as amended)" wording is included.

7–100   **4.7.1.4   in contravention of or invalidated (in whole or in part) by the Competition Act 1998;**

The Competition Act 1998 repealed the Restrictive Trade Practices Acts 1976 and 1977, the Restrictive Trade Practices Court Act 1976, the Resale Prices Act 1976 and the anti-competition provisions of the Competition Act 1980 (which allowed investigation by the old Monopolies and Mergers Commission of certain anti-competitive practices). The Act contained transitional provisions allowing agreements and practices which had complied with those repealed Acts to be immune from investigation but these transitional provisions have all ceased to have effect. The Act replaced this legislation with two prohibitions based closely on EU law; namely, a prohibition on anti-competitive agreements and arrangements that have or are capable of having an effect on trade within the United Kingdom (based on art.81 (formerly art.85) of the Treaty of Rome, now art.101 of the Treaty on the Functioning of the European Union ("TFEU")); and, a prohibition against the abuse of a dominant position that has or is capable of having an effect on trade within the United Kingdom (based on art.82 (formerly art.86) of the Treaty of Rome, now art.102 TFEU). Under the Act the Office of Fair Trading, under the Director General of Fair Trading was given substantial new enforcement powers (which have been strengthened by subsequent legislation), including the ability to conduct "dawn raids" and to impose significant fines of up to 10 per cent of global group turnover upon infringing undertakings. This liability for fines remains with the undertaking responsible for the infringement even if it has undergone changes of control and ownership subsequent to the infringements. Parties who have suffered loss due to infringement of the Act are entitled to damages from the infringing undertakings. The Office of Director General of Fair Trading was abolished by the Enterprise Act 2002 (for further details of which please see commentary below). The Act is capable of enforcement not only by the Office of Fair Trading, but also a variety of sectoral regulators in respect of the industries they regulate (for example; Ofcom, Ofwat, Ofgem, Postcomm and the Rail Regulator). The Act compels all United Kingdom authorities involved in its application to ensure, so far as is possible, that questions arising under the Act are dealt with in a manner consistent with the way in which arts 101 and 102 have been and are interpreted by the European Court of Justice and the European Commission.

The Act excludes from its remit mergers as defined in the Fair Trading Act and the provisions of the Enterprise Act 2002 which replaced that Act and also concentrations, which fall within the exclusive jurisdiction of the EU

Commission under the EC Merger Regulations (the current version of which is Regulation 139/2004).

4.7.1.5   in contravention of the Enterprise Act 2002;   7–101

The Enterprise Act 2002 repealed the monopoly and merger provisions of the Fair Trading Act 1973, introduced new systems of merger control, market studies and market investigations (giving the successor to the Monopolies and Mergers Commission, the Competition Commission the power to make final decisions on merger and market investigations) and changed the institutional framework of United Kingdom competition authorities (replacing the Director General of Fair Trading with the Office of Fair Trading (having a variety of functions under the Competition Act 1998 and the Enterprise Act 2002) and establishing the Competition Appeal Tribunal to which appeals/reviews of the decisions of the Competition Commission, Office of Fair Trading, Secretary of State (whose powers in relation to competition law matters are significantly reduced by the Enterprise Act), and sectoral regulators can be made). The Act also introduced a criminal cartel offence for individuals who had been involved in price-fixing, market sharing and bid-rigging activities as well as granting the Office of Fair Trading the power to seek disqualification of directors of companies which had infringed the Competition Act 1998 for up to 15 years.

4.7.1.6   in contravention of [arts 101 and 102 of] the Treaty on the   7–102
Functioning of the European Union;

Articles 101 and 102 (formerly arts 81 and 82 and prior to that 85 and 86 of the Treaty of Rome) render void various agreements which may affect trade between Member States and which have the object or effect of preventing, restricting or distorting competition in the EU. Any abuse by one or more undertakings having a dominant position within the EU is prohibited in so far as it may affect trade between Member States. The detailed provisions are extremely complex and subject to ongoing development (for example, the procedural application of arts 101 and 102 was fundamentally changed on May 1, 2004 when Council Regulation 1/2003 (the EC Modernisation Regulation) came into force including providing national competition authorities, such as the Office of Fair Trading in the UK, with the power to apply them) and as such specialist works dealing with EU Competition Law should be consulted. The vendors should in any event amend this warranty by adding the words in brackets so that it refers only to arts 101 and 102 as there are other provisions, such as arts 34 and 35 (dealing with free movement of goods), arts 107 and 108 (dealing with State Aids) and the rules on anti-dumping, which could be covered by not restricting the warranty to arts 101 and 102.

4.7.1.7   or in contravention of any regulations, orders, notices or   7–103
directions made thereunder, or otherwise registerable,
unenforceable or void or renders the Company or any of its
officers or employees liable to administrative, civil or criminal

proceedings under any anti-trust, anti-monopoly or anti-cartel, trade regulation or similar legislation or regulation in any jurisdiction where the Company carries on business.

This broad provision is intended primarily to deal with competition legislation in jurisdictions outside of the EU. If the target company carries out a substantial part of its business outside of the EU a well-advised purchaser should include specific warranties in this regard. If the target company does not engage in business in jurisdictions outside of the EU the vendors might reasonably decline to give this warranty. The vendors should bear in mind the implications of the words "carries on business"—see comments at cl.4.4.2 for a discussion of this.

The legislation on competition law is complex and as such reference should be made to specialist works dealing with competition law, or appropriate specialist advice taken, if there is a possibility that the target company and any of its officers and employees may be involved in anti-competitive practices.

4.8 Litigation

7–104   **4.8.1 Neither the Company nor any person for whose acts or defaults the Company is or may be vicariously liable are engaged in litigation, mediation, arbitration, administrative or criminal proceedings or other proceedings or hearings before any statutory or governmental body, department, board or agency [except for debt collection in the normal course of business]; there are no proceedings pending or threatened, either by or against the Company or such persons; and [so far as the Vendors are aware] there is nothing which is likely to give rise to such proceedings.**

The vendors should have no difficulty in confirming that the target company is not engaged in litigation or similar procedures. The purpose of the exclusion of small debt collecting is to avoid lengthy disclosures for minor debt collecting matters. The vendors should, however, consider carefully the implications of the part of the warranty which refers to circumstances likely to give rise to proceedings. At the very least, the vendors might wish to qualify this part of the warranty by the inclusion of awareness as suggested by the words in brackets but, furthermore, the vendors may feel, in a complex business, that it is not realistic for them to express a view as to whether litigation is likely. Many vendors are concerned by the extension of the warranty to threats of litigation. In many businesses, such threats are common but rarely give rise to litigation. Finally, as currently drafted the warranty would arguably catch, for example, litigation that employees were involved in a personal capacity, in respect of which the target company would not be vicariously liable. Whilst in such circumstances the company would be unlikely to suffer a loss (as it would have no vicarious (or other) liability), the proceedings may be such that they impact on the target company, for example if any employee is convicted of a serious criminal offence that is published in the national press and impacts on the company's reputation. If the warranty is to be left in its current form then the vendors should seek to have it subject to their knowledge in respect of matters involving the employees that are not work related. See also cl.4.10.1.

4.8.2 The Company is not subject to any order or judgment given by any court or governmental agency (local or national).   7–105

The vendors will usually have no difficulty in confirming these matters as they are largely factual and should be known to the target company.

4.8.3 There are no claims pending or threatened or [so far as the Vendors are aware] capable of arising against the Company by an employee or workman or third party in respect of any accident or injury.   7–106

This warranty needs to be reviewed carefully by the vendors. The vendors would be wise to separate the warranty into several elements. The first should deal with actual notice of any such claims which should be straightforward. The second would be that the vendors have no actual knowledge of any circumstances which might give rise to a claim

4.8.4 There is no dispute with any government (local or national) or agency or body acting on behalf of such government or other authority in the United Kingdom or elsewhere in relation to the affairs of the Company and [so far as the Vendors are aware] there are no facts or circumstances which may give rise to such a dispute.   7–107

The first part of the warranty is factual and should not be an issue for the vendors. Please see comments above at cl.4.8.1 in relation to the vendors' position on warranties which refer to circumstances likely to give rise to proceedings which will apply equally here in relation to the last part of this clause. The second part of the warranty could be moderated by the vendors by the inclusion of an awareness qualification by including the wording in brackets.

4.8.5 Neither the Company nor any current or former employee, officer or agent of the Company has been convicted of an offence in relation to the Company and [so far as the Vendors are aware] no employee or officer has been convicted of an offence that reflects upon the reputation of the Company or their suitability for holding the position that they hold in the Company.   7–108

With the suite of legislation that can give rise to criminal offences that can be committed by a target company or its officers or directors (common examples are breach of data protection, working time regulations, environmental legislation and financial assistance), the purchaser will have a legitimate interest in seeking any relevant disclosure. In relation to previous conduct the purchaser will be interested to see the level of fines that the target company has paid and whether the conduct is likely to be a continuing issue. On change of control the purchaser's directors and officers will usually assume the position of the target company's directors and officers and will be concerned to ensure that there is no continuing criminal exposure for them. The vendors might wish to qualify the latter part of the warranty that relates to officers and employees and extends beyond convictions for offences in relation to the target company by reference to knowledge by including the wording in brackets.

4.9 Winding-up

7–109   **4.9.1 The Company is not insolvent or unable to pay its debts within the meaning of the Insolvency Act 1986 s.123 (the references in that section to proving to the satisfaction of the court being disregarded).**

There is no single definition of "insolvency", but a company will generally be taken to be insolvent if either it is unable to pay its debts as they fall due (Insolvency Act 1986 s.123(1)(e)) or there is an excess of liabilities over assets (s.123(2)). A rather odd feature of these definitions is that they strictly seem to require that the court is satisfied that the relevant circumstances exist. The purpose of the words in brackets at the end of the warranty is to avoid the argument that neither of these two tests can be met unless a court ruling has actually been obtained. In addition, s.123 provides a number of special cases which result in a company being deemed unable to pay its debts, including non-payment for 21 days after a statutory notice is served by a creditor who is owed more than £750.

The purchaser will be most concerned if a target company is likely to be insolvent. If an insolvency procedure has commenced, and shares in the target company or some or all of its assets are among the assets to be realised in the administration, liquidation or other insolvency procedure the purchaser will be keen to ensure that the transaction is valid and that it will receive good title. If a procedure has not begun but may be imminent, any sale may be liable to adjustment or avoidance under the Insolvency Act 1986. The warranty is, therefore, a reasonable one. Inability to pay debts is one of the most common grounds for a court to grant a winding-up order and the vendors should have little difficulty in deciding whether the warranty could possibly be infringed. It would be otherwise if the warranty were rephrased so as to refer, instead, to the likelihood of the target company becoming insolvent.

7–110   **4.9.2 No order has been made, petition presented or resolution passed for the winding-up of the Company; no distress, execution or other process has been levied and remains undischarged in respect of the Company; and there is no outstanding judgment or court order against the Company in connection with the same nor has any application been made for the making of an administration order or notice of intention to appoint an administrator been filed at court, or served on a creditor with the benefit of a floating charge.**

"Distress" is a summary remedy by which a person is entitled, without legal process to take possession of another person's goods, "execution" involves the enforcement of a court judgment or order, "process" is anything other than distress or execution and includes any document which is served or executed in connection with the purposes of any court. These are all important matters of fact which can readily be checked by the vendors.

4.9.3 No steps have been taken for the appointment of an administrator or **7–111** **administrative receiver or receiver or liquidator or provisional liquidator over the whole or any part of the Company's assets or undertaking.**

This is usually not an issue for the vendors as it is very unlikely that a sale of shares would take place in these circumstances. Nonetheless, the vendors should consider making the warranty subject to their knowledge in respect of steps that might have been taken by a third party as they would not necessarily know what had or had not been done.

4.9.4 No meeting of the Company's creditors, or any class of them, has **7–112** **been held or summoned and no proposal has been made for a moratorium, composition or arrangement in relation to any of the Company's debts, or for a voluntary arrangement in relation to any of its debts, or for a voluntary arrangement under Pt 1 of the Insolvency Act 1986.**

The warranty does not just include formal meetings for the proposal of a voluntary arrangement but informal meetings of creditors or a class of creditors. Composition and arrangement covers a wide variety of debt rescheduling. It is not uncommon for companies in financial difficulty to have informal meetings with particular classes of creditors for the purpose of agreeing the rescheduling of debts. Vendors should ascertain whether any meeting of this nature has taken place in the past.

4.9.5 In relation to each of the Vendors: **7–113**

4.9.5.1 no statutory demand has been served or attempted to be served on any of them nor are there any grounds for believing that they are unable to pay any debts within the meaning of the Insolvency Act 1986 s.268 (as amended);

An individual is insolvent within the meaning of s.268 if: (i) a statutory demand has been served and at least three weeks have passed without the demand having been satisfied or set aside; or (ii) execution of a judgement debt has been returned unsatisfied.

4.9.5.2 no petition has been presented and no order made for the **7–114** **bankruptcy of any of them or for the appointment of a receiver over any of their assets;**

The term receiver refers to any type of receiver, for example, the appointment of a receiver under the LPA 1925 in respect of land or other charged property. It also can include the appointment of a receiver by the court over assets to enforce a judgement.

7–115   **4.9.5.3   no Encumbrance has been enforced and no distress, execution or other process has been levied, on or over any of the Shares or any assets held by the Vendors; and**

Although encumbrances over shares are often registered in the target company's records this does not always occur. Without disclosure it would not be possible to ascertain whether such an encumbrance exists.

7–116   **4.9.5.4   no proposal has been made in respect of an individual voluntary arrangement, or interim order applied for the purpose of making a proposal of an individual voluntary arrangement pursuant to the Insolvency Act 1986 (as amended).**

The purpose of the above warranties is to obtain confirmation that there is no possibility of a third party avoiding the sale of the shares or making a claim that the proceeds of sale should not be paid to the vendors but to a third party.

7–117   **4.9.6 No event analogous to those described in clauses [4.9.2] or [4.9.3 or 4.9.5] has occurred outside England.**

A purchaser might seek to include this warranty if the company is established overseas. Given the importance of the solvency of the target company, the vendors should be prepared to give such a warranty.

7–118   **4.9.7 No floating charge created by the Company has crystallised and [so far as the Vendors are aware] there are no circumstances likely to cause such a floating charge to crystallise.**

Events of "crystallisation" are usually myriad and it is possible that the target company may have inadvertently triggered one or more. It would be unusual for these to give rise to a loss unless the holder of the charge sought to enforce their rights. The vendors would usually seek to qualify the warranty by the addition of the words in brackets. If necessary, a letter of non-crystallisation can be obtained on completion from any floating charge holder.

4.10 Compliance with statutes

7–119   **4.10.1 Neither the Company nor [so far as the Vendors are aware] any of its officers, agents or employees (during the course of their duties), have done or omitted to do anything, the doing or omitting of which is, or could be, in contravention of a statute, regulation or the like giving rise to a penalty, default proceedings or other liability [which could have a material adverse effect on the business of the Company].**

This clause is extremely widely drawn and would cover even such matters as parking offences relating to a vehicle belonging to the target company or driven by an employee of the target company. (It overlaps to an extent with cl.4.8.1 and care will need to be taken by the vendors to ensure that the warranties are consistent in terms of the standards that the vendors are subject to.) The vendors should certainly seek to exclude trivial matters, perhaps by putting a minimum level on any fine or penalty below which a breach of warranty will not occur. The purchaser might well reply to any proposed exclusion, if a floor for warranty claims has been agreed as discussed in para.11–04, that the floor protects the vendors from trivial claims and that it is accordingly not necessary to also amend the warranty. The vendors should, in addition, alter the clause so that it relates only to the position at the date of the agreement and not also to the past. The vendors may also wish to limit the warranty by reference to their knowledge given the extension of its scope to the target company's officers, agents and employees. The vendors should also consider carefully whether the words "or could be" are acceptable. Most vendors would be reluctant to accept them on the basis that the purchaser is adequately covered by the other wording.

An alternative form of the warranty, which is likely to be more acceptable to the vendors, would be:

"The Company has conducted and is conducting its business in all [material] respects in accordance with all applicable Official Requirements."

This position is, however, already substantially covered by cl.4.4.1 save that the definition of "Official Requirements" goes a little further. The vendors may refuse to give warranties such as those above unless the purchaser specifies the legislation in respect of which it requires warranty cover. A blanket risk approach is unlikely to find much favour.

4.11 Business names

4.11.1 The Company does not make use of any name other than its corporate name.   **7–120**

Under the Business Names Act 1985 a company cannot, without approval, carry on business in Great Britain under a business name which includes certain words and expressions. The list of words and expressions is contained in the Companies and Business Names Regulations 1981 (SI 1981/1685) which also specify which government department must be approached to obtain approval in any particular case. In addition the law of passing off can give a right of action to a party whose proprietary interest in a name is infringed.

The purchaser has reasonable grounds for satisfying itself that all business names can be used without risk and, as the warranty merely invites disclosure of business names used and does not require the vendors to state that no statutory obligations or proprietary rights are infringed, it should be acceptable to the vendors.

It should be noted that the definition of "Intellectual Property Rights" in para.4–02 includes business names and this should be borne in mind when considering cl.8.7.

4.12 Transactions involving directors

7–121   **4.12.1 The Company has not been a party to a transaction to which CA 1985 ss.320 or 330 [or CA 2006 ss.190 or 197] might apply.**

The broad effect of CA 2006 s.190 (formerly CA 1985 s.320) is quite clear and is intended to prohibit substantial property transactions between a company and its directors which are not sanctioned by the shareholders. Where a substantial property transaction has been entered into without the approval of shareholders, or it was entered into without being on the condition of such approval of the members being obtained (CA 2006 s.190(1)), the agreement may be avoided by the company (other than in limited circumstances). Such avoidance is not available where the transaction has been affirmed within a reasonable period (CA 2006 s.196). Certain exclusions exist for transactions below a minimum size (a de minimis of £2,000 applied under CA 1985 which has been increased to £5,000 under CA 2006) but the difficulty of the section arises not under its direct impact but in relation to transactions which do not obviously fall within its scope. In particular, the section applies to transactions entered into between a company and a person connected with a director of the company. The wide definition of "connected persons" contained in CA 2006 s.252 (formerly CA 1985 s.346) has the effect that a director is connected with a company in which he and his family (including trustees of family settlements) are interested in more than 20 per cent of the share capital. The CA 2006 definition of "connected persons" extends the definition beyond CA 1985 position to include persons with whom the director lives as a partner in an enduring family relationship (CA 2006 s.253). The section could be very important, therefore, if a target company had engaged in a transaction with another company and a director of that other company was "connected" with a significant proportion of the shareholders in the target company. Approval is not required, however, for a substantial property transaction between a company and a person in his character as a member of that company, or between a holding company and its wholly-owned subsidiary, or between two wholly-owned subsidiaries of the same holding company (CA 2006 s.192).

The vendors will want to amend the warranty to exclude those transactions for which approval has been obtained in accordance with the provisions of the section by amending the warranty as follows:

"The Company has not been a party to any transaction that has been in breach of CA 1985 ss.320 or 330 or CA 2006 ss.190 or 197".

In addition, the warranty is relevant only if the other party to a transaction with a target company might, by reason of the infringement, have a right to avoid the contract.

Section 330 CA 1985 formerly imposed a general restriction (subject to limited exceptions) on the making of loans by a company to its directors or the directors of its holding company. Section 197 CA 2006 now permits them provided that members' approval is obtained. Any such members' approval must be in the form of an ordinary resolution but cannot be passed before a memorandum is made available to the members setting out the nature of the transaction and the amount of the loan and purpose for which it is required. The section extends to guarantees of loans to directors and to indirect loans where a third party makes the loan which is then taken over by the company. The part of the warranty relating to these sections should not give the vendors any difficulty.

4.13 Powers of attorney and authorities

4.13.1 No powers of attorney or authorities (express or implied) by which a person may enter into a contract or incur an obligation on behalf of the Company are subsisting [other than by reason of the ostensible or implied authority of directors or employees to enter into routine contracts in the normal course of their duties].   7–122

The purpose of this warranty is to ensure that the purchaser is aware of outstanding powers given to third parties enabling them to bind the target company. A breach of the warranty is, however, unlikely to give rise of itself to a claim for damages.

The vendors will normally have no difficulty in giving this warranty in relation to powers of attorney which are in the form of independent documents. A special point arises, however, where a power of attorney is contained as a provision of a longer document such as a debenture or lease. In such cases, the power of attorney is normally limited to matters relating to the execution of documents and implementation of transactions arising from the debenture or lease itself and therefore should give little concern to the purchaser. As such, the vendors may wish to qualify this warranty so that it does not apply to powers of attorney contained in other documents as merely an incidental provision. With regard to other authorities, if the vendors add the words in square brackets or confine the warranty's scope to express authorities, the warranty will apply only to unusual cases which should be readily capable of being identified and disclosed to the purchaser.

4.14 Licences and consents

4.14.1 The Company has all necessary Licences required for the proper carrying on of its business in the manner in which the business is now carried on (short particulars/copies of each such licence being set out in the Disclosure Letter).   7–123

Although most businesses carried on in the United Kingdom do not require any specific licences, there is nevertheless a very large number of activities for which licences are required. In particular, excise licences are required for the carrying on of many trades, for example, the manufacture or sale of intoxicating liquors, and various gaming activities. Licences are also required by employment agencies and in connection with certain offensive and dangerous trades.

As drafted, this clause could cover licences to exploit patents and other intellectual property rights. It is preferable for these to be dealt with expressly, as, for example, in cl.8.7. If this approach is adopted, the wording should be amended by adding after "Licences" the words "(other than in respect of Intellectual Property Rights)".

The warranty is deliberately drafted in general terms as the purchaser would reasonably be entitled to take the view that the vendors are in a far better position than the purchaser to know whether licences are required for any particular aspect of the target company's activities. If, as for most companies, no licences are required, the vendors may prefer this warranty to be in the following form:

"The Company does not require a Licence for the proper carrying on of its business."

In considering this warranty, the vendors should have particular regard to licences or authorities which are required outside the United Kingdom if the target company has material overseas activities.

7–124   **4.14.2 The Company is not in breach of any of the [material] terms and conditions of any Licence; all Licences are effective and there is nothing [known to the Vendors and relating to the Company] that might prejudice the continuation or renewal of a Licence on the same terms as currently held.**

This warranty will be inappropriate if a warranty is given in the alternative form suggested above in relation to cl.4.14.1. However, if there are licences or consents in existence, the vendors should consider whether the form of this warranty is unduly onerous as immaterial breaches often take place which are of no practical importance and should consider seeking to include reference to materiality by inserting the wording in the first set of brackets. (See cll.1.14.1 and 4.4.1 for comments on the inclusion of such a caveat). The purchaser's concern is that there should be no penalties from such a breach and that breaches do not bring the licence or consent to an end or prejudice the prospects of its renewal. This latter point is dealt with in the second half of the clause although the wording may be too wide for the vendors. They will prefer to restrict the second half either by inserting the words in square brackets or by amending the provision so that it applies only to breaches of the terms or conditions of the licences or consents which are likely to render the licence or consent terminated or prevent its renewal. The vendors should appreciate that the implications of a breach of this warranty could be very serious, since the refusal to continue a licence could have a major impact on the goodwill of the target company. If licences relating to intellectual property rights are excluded from cl.4.14.1, this clause should be amended by adding after references to "a Licence" the words "falling within clause [4.14.1]".

4.14.3 The Company does not carry on investment business or regulated activities within the meaning of the Financial Services and Markets Act 2000.   7–125

If a company carries on regulated activities in the United Kingdom, it is required under the Financial Services and Markets Act 2000 to obtain permission to do so from the Financial Services Authority (FSA), or otherwise be regulated by a designated professional body (DPB) as an exempt professional firm, under the Financial Services and Markets Act 2000 Pt XX. Regulated activities are very widely defined in various Regulated Activities Orders and it is frequently difficult to be sure that particular activities do not fall within the definition even though they would not normally be thought to comprise a regulated activity. If the target company does in fact carry on regulated activities, it would be appropriate for the warranty to be in the following form:

"The Company has either been granted permission by the Financial Services Authority, or is regulated by a designated professional body as an exempt professional firm, and [so far as the Vendors are aware] is complying and has complied with the rules of the appropriate regulator in relation to its conduct of business."

The rules issued by the FSA and DPBs are extremely complex and it is consequently difficult for any member to be absolutely sure that no infringement has occurred. The vendors might therefore prefer, if there is scope for doubt, to disclose to the purchaser precisely what activities are carried on and to provide a copy of their Scope of Permission Notice (if applicable), so that the purchaser can reach its own view as to whether an infringement might have occurred. Alternatively, they may wish to qualify the warranty by awareness although given the potential implications for a breach this is unlikely to be satisfactory to the purchaser.

4.15 Subsisting contracts

4.15.1 The Company is not party to any agreement or arrangement which: 7–126

    4.15.1.1   **is of an unusual nature or was entered into outside the normal course of business;**

    4.15.1.2   **is of a long-term nature (that is unlikely to have been fully performed, in accordance with its terms, within six months after the date on which it was entered into);**

    4.15.1.3   **is incapable of termination by it in accordance with its terms on not more than 60 days' notice;**

    4.15.1.4   **is of a loss-making nature;**

4.15.1.5   **cannot readily be performed by it on time without undue or unusual expenditure or application of money, effort or personnel;**

4.15.1.6   **involves payment by it by reference to fluctuations in the index of retail prices, or other index, or in the rate of exchange for a currency;**

4.15.1.7   **involves an aggregated outstanding expenditure by it of more than £[   ];**

4.15.1.8   **involves, or is likely to involve, the supply of goods or services the aggregate sales value of which will be more than 10 per cent of its turnover for the preceding financial year;**

4.15.1.9   **is a contract for hire or rent, hire purchase or purchase by way of credit sale or periodical payment;**

4.15.1.10   **can be terminated as a result of a change in the control of the Company; or**

4.15.1.11   **involves, or is likely to involve, other obligations or liabilities which ought reasonably to be made known to an intending purchaser of the Shares.**

This list is intended to be by way of guidance only for a purchaser. The business activities of the target company should be reviewed carefully by both the purchaser and the vendors to see whether these provisions are all relevant and whether any others ought to be included. The vendors will need to be mindful of the fact that the introductory wording to the clause refers not only to agreements but also to arrangements and should also bear in mind the disclosure burden that may be imposed on them if there are numerous contracts that will have to be reviewed. In circumstances where the purchaser has been provided with copies of all contracts as part of the legal due diligence process it would be reasonable for the vendors to, for example, decline to give certain elements of the warranty on the basis that the purchaser will be easily able to ascertain the position itself from its own review of the disclosed contracts. The purchaser should, if willing to accept such a position, obtain confirmation that all relevant terms are contained in the documentation provided.

Of the sub-headings covering specific matters, the first, which refers to contracts of an unusual nature or which were entered into outside the normal course of business, is perhaps the most difficult in that a complex business will inevitably involve contracts which are unusual but were nevertheless entered into for the benefit of the target company concerned. The last sub-clause is in the nature of a sweeping-up provision and should be rejected by the vendors for lack of specificity.

Clauses 4.15.1.2 will extend to many licences of intellectual property rights as these are usually of a long-term nature. The vendors may wish to exclude such agreements from this warranty by inserting the words:

" ... (other than an agreement or arrangement relating to the use of Intellectual Property Rights)"

at the beginning of these provisions, as licences of intellectual property are dealt with in cl.8.7.

4.15.2 The Company has made all payments due under all contracts to 7–127 **which it is a party and [so far as the Vendors are aware] observed and performed all conditions thereof.**

The purchaser is entitled to know that all contractual payments are up to date and that contracts have been complied with. While on the face of it this is a factual warranty which the vendors should be able to check and if necessary disclose against, the vendors would usually wish to limit the warranty to material contracts and, in relation to the observance and performance of all conditions, qualify the warranty by awareness. A purchaser would in any event normally only be concerned with material contracts which were likely to affect the ongoing profitability of the target company and if these were considered fundamental would probably require specific warranties on the relevant contracts. If the warranty at cl.4.4.1 were to be given in the proposed form, this warranty would duplicate it. See comments at cl.4.4.1 for details of the matters which the vendors will need to bear in mind if they are to give the warranty, in particular the position in relation to leases.

4.16 Breach of contract

4.16.1 [So far as the Vendors are aware] no party to an agreement with the 7–128 **Company is in default, being a default which would be material in the context of the Company's financial or trading position; and [so far as the Vendors are aware (but without having made enquiry of any third party)] there are no circumstances likely to give rise to a default.**

While the first part of this warranty should be broadly acceptable to the vendors, it should be amended by the insertion of the qualification in square brackets and careful consideration should be given as to whether the phrase "financial or trading position" is sufficiently specific. The final part of the warranty, referring to circumstances likely to give rise to a default, is extremely wide and is unlikely to be acceptable to the vendors. If the vendors are to give it then they will want to include the wording in square brackets.

4.16.2 [So far as the Vendors are aware] the Company is not, nor will it 7–129 **with the lapse of time become, in default of any obligation and no threat or claim of default under any agreement, instrument or arrangement to which it is a party has been made [so far as the Vendors are aware] and there is nothing whereby any such agreement, instrument or arrangement may be prematurely terminated or rescinded by another party or whereby the terms may be worsened to the Company's detriment.**

This is extremely wide-ranging and to some extent duplicates cl.4.15.2. The vendors would usually wish to limit the warranty by the inclusion of the words in square brackets.

4.17 Outstanding offers

7–130 **4.17.1 No offer or tender [outside of the ordinary and normal course of the Company's business] is outstanding which is capable of being converted into an obligation of the Company by acceptance or some other act of another person.**

The intention of this clause is clear and it would normally only apply to special cases such as tenders in relation to building contracts. Nevertheless, the wording would apply to any case where an order has been placed by the target company but which has not yet been accepted by the other party. It would therefore be appropriate for the vendors to qualify the clause by adding the wording in brackets so that it does not apply to offers and the like in the ordinary and proper course of business (see cl.4.1.1.1 in relation to the use of a reference to "ordinary course of business" only). The purchaser should treat any such amendment with caution if it is in the ordinary course of the activities of the target company to make sizeable tenders. In such a case, a qualification of the warranty so that it applies to offers in the ordinary course of business could also be subject to a further qualification that any one offer must not involve an expenditure of more than a specified sum.

4.18 Defective products

7–131 **4.18.1 The Company has not manufactured, sold or supplied products which were, are or will become, in a material respect faulty or defective, or which did or do not comply in a material respect with warranties or representations expressly or impliedly made by it or all applicable regulations, standards and requirements in respect thereof.**

This is potentially an extremely onerous warranty for the vendors, particularly because of the absolute liability imposed by the Consumer Protection Act 1987 upon manufacturers, own-branders and importers in respect of defective products. The scope of the provision should accordingly be a matter for specific negotiation between the parties. The problem will be reduced if, as will often be the case, the target company has limited its liability for product defects by way of exclusions in its normal terms of sale although liability under the Act for damage caused by defective products, that is products whose safety is not such as persons generally are entitled to expect, cannot be excluded. Additionally, there may be product liability insurance which would cover most claims. Subject to these qualifications, however, the parties should consider very carefully precisely what liability is covered by the warranty and where the risks should lie. It is particularly difficult to allocate risk in relation to future defects as, although the original owners may have permitted the existence of the circumstances creating the defect, the purchaser would normally accept business risks as from completion.

7–132 **4.18.2 The Company has not received notification that any products supplied by it are defective or unfit and no circumstances exist which could give rise to such a claim.**

To some extent this warranty covers the same ground as cl.4.18.1 but its purpose is to help to elicit disclosure of notifications to the target company in respect of alleged defective or unfit products where the target company does not necessarily accept the circumstances give rise to a breach of cl.4.18.1.

4.18.3 The Company has not received a prohibition notice, a notice to warn or a suspension notice under the Consumer Protection Act 1987.   7–133

A prohibition notice may be served upon a company to prohibit it from supplying, or offering to supply, goods which are considered to be unsafe. A notice to warn requires the recipient to publish at his own expense, in a formal manner and on occasions specified in the notice, a warning that specified goods are considered to be unsafe. A suspension notice prohibits the recipient, for a specified period, from supplying or offering specified goods and can be issued where the enforcement authority for consumer safety has reasonable grounds for suspecting that safety provisions have been contravened in relation to the goods.

The importance of these obligations is obvious and, as they involve a simple question of fact for the vendors, they should have no difficulty in giving the warranty.

4.19 Service and product warranty liabilities

4.19.1 The Company is not obliged (save as implied by law) to repair, maintain, take back or otherwise do or not do anything in respect of goods that have been, or will be [pursuant to existing agreements], delivered by it.   7–134

This warranty essentially involves merely questions of fact but, to avoid extensive disclosures, the vendors may wish to amend the warranty so that it does not apply to obligations undertaken in the normal course of business or warranties, guarantees or other similar matters contained in its standard terms of sale. Furthermore, liability in respect of future deliveries should be restricted, for example, by adding the words in square brackets, to those which are the result of agreements subsisting at the date of the sale agreement.

4.20 Purchases and sales from or to one party

4.20.1 The Company does not obtain or make more than [25 per cent] of the aggregate amount of its purchases from, and not more than [25 per cent] of the aggregate amount of its sales to, the same supplier or customer [(including a person connected with the supplier or customer)][; and no material source of supply to the Company, or material outlet for the sales of the Company, is in jeopardy].   7–135

The part of this warranty which quantifies purchases and sales from or to a specific supplier or customer will not involve difficulty unless a target company exceeds or is close to the specified percentages. In that case, the vendors should consider carefully how the quantities in question are to be identified. In particular, they may wish to specify more clearly how the amount of the purchases or sales is valued and over what period the relevant figures are calculated. The reference to "connected" parties is likely to be unacceptable to the vendors as without asking the relevant suppliers or customers or undertaking specific investigations they are unlikely to know the position. The last part of the warranty, referring to the sources of supply or outlets being in jeopardy, is a different question involving matters of judgment and, unless the vendors are quite clear as to whether in fact the warranty may be breached, they should resist giving it. If they are compelled to give the warranty, the vendors should seek to have it subject to their knowledge and it should be made clear that in determining what the vendors are deemed to know for the purposes of it they are not obliged to make enquiry of any customers or suppliers or to undertake any other specific investigation.

7–136   **4.20.2 During the six months preceding the date of this Agreement there has been no substantial change in the basis or terms on which any person (including any supplier) is prepared to enter into contracts to do business with the Company (apart from normal price changes) [and no such change is likely].**

The warranty in its unaltered form is unlikely to be acceptable to most vendors as it would require an extensive review of all supplier or customer relationships in order to ascertain what disclosures are required. At the very least the vendors will want to impose some level of materiality into the wording of the warranty probably by defining what amounts to a material customer or supplier of the target company's business. For consistency, the same percentages as utilised in cl.4.20.1 might be an appropriate starting point. In addition, the last few words in brackets imposes a forward looking obligation on the vendors which is likely to be unacceptable save on a "so far as aware basis" and then subject to a further caveat that actual enquiry of such suppliers and customers has not actually been made as to do so would be commercially damaging to the target company.

7–137   **4.20.3 No person who is, or who has during the last two years been, a substantial customer or supplier of goods or services to the Company has ceased, or has threatened or indicated an intention to cease trading with or supplying the Company or has reduced, or is likely to reduce, substantially its trading with or supply to the Company.**

For consistency it would be wise to define a substantial customer or supplier in the same way for all of these relevant warranties. This requires a substantial "look back" over the last two years and depending on the nature of the target company's business may impose a considerable burden on the vendors. The purchaser will on the other hand want to ensure that the loss of a key customer or supplier is not one of the reasons that has motivated a sale and also whether any such loss is in fact a sign of a business trend.

4.20.4 The loss of any single supplier to or customer of the Company   7–138
would not have a material effect on its business, and during the financial
year ended on the Balance Sheet Date or in the period since then not more
than [ten per cent] of the goods purchased by the Company were derived
from the same supplier, and not more than [ten per cent] of the goods sold
by the Company were purchased by the same customer and for the purpose
of this paragraph groups of companies shall be deemed a single person.

This warranty covers similar ground but with a slightly different focus. Most
vendors will be keen to avoid repetition in terms of warranty cover. Again, it
would be usual for all materiality thresholds to be consistent.

4.21 Data protection

4.21.1 The Company has, if so required by law, a current entry in the   7–139
register maintained by the Information Commissioner under the Data
Protection Act 1998 which complies with the requirements of that Act, and
particulars of the entry are set out in the Disclosure Letter.

The Data Protection Act 1998 requires data controllers to notify details of their
processing of personal data to the Information Commissioner unless they fall
within one of the exemptions from notification. The application for notification
must state the purposes for which the data is used as well as other information,
including those places outside the European Economic Area to which data is
transferred. The notification entry must be accurate and it must be kept up to date.
Failure to notify or to notify properly is a criminal offence and it is, therefore,
reasonable for the purchaser to seek confirmation of compliance.

4.21.2 The Company has complied with the data protection principles   7–140
applicable to all the processing of personal data carried out by it and
collected, processed and disclosed personal data only in accordance with the
terms of a privacy policy, which is attached to the Disclosure Letter.

The Data Protection Act contains eight principles which are contained in Sch.1,
Pt I of the Act and cover a range of obligations set out in Schs 1 to 4. The target
company will be obliged to comply with these principles, even if it is exempt
from notification as set out in the previous warranty. The principles include
requirements for the data controller to collect personal information fairly, to use
it lawfully, to ensure it is adequate, relevant and not excessive, not kept longer
than necessary, kept up to date and to maintain proper security. The highest areas
of risk relate to security breaches, often linked to the data controller holding
excessive amounts of personal information.

One or more of the specific warranties at cll.4.21.3, 4.21.4, 4.21.5 and 4.21.6
could be employed in addition to the general warranty in this clause to cover
these risks. The specific warranties serve to direct the vendors' minds to the
specific requirements in relation to data quality, data retention, compliance with
security obligations and restrictions on overseas transfers, these being key areas
of risk.

If there is non-compliance with any of the principles the Commissioner can impose a monetary penalty of up to £500,000 or serve an enforcement notice which may prohibit particular uses of data or require the data controller to amend its processing. Alternatively, individuals who suffer financial loss, and in some circumstances, distress because of the breach of principles may claim compensation. The data protection principles are wide-ranging and are broadly stated. It is therefore difficult for a data controller to be certain that no infringement has occurred. As such, the vendors should be cautious about accepting the general warranty in cl.4.21.2 and could suggest the following as an alternative:

7–141   **4.21.3 The Company has not been served with a warrant under Sch.9 of the Data Protection Act 1998 nor has the Company received any statutory notice from the Information Commissioner.**

A warrant under Sch.9 would grant the Information Commissioner powers of entry and inspection to the target company's premises where he had reasonable grounds for suspecting there had been a breach of the principles or an offence had been committed. The statutory notices may be information notices/special information notices, requiring further information, or monetary penalty or enforcement notices described above. The vendors will know whether such a warrant or notice has been received or not and should have no difficulty giving the warranty.

7–142   **4.21.4 The Company has taken measures to ensure personal data are adequate, relevant, not excessive and not kept longer than necessary in relation to the purpose for which they are processed, that they are accurate and where necessary, kept up to date. The Company's data retention policy is attached to the Disclosure Letter.**

Poor data management often underlies security breaches. This warranty requires the vendors to disclose any shortcomings.

7–143   **4.21.5 The Company has taken technical and organisational measures to ensure compliance with the seventh data protection principle in relation to the processing of personal data in manual and in computerised systems (including portable devices) and has taken steps to ensure the reliability of its employees that have access to personal data. The Company has not suffered a security breach that required notification to the Information Commissioner in accordance with the Information Commissioner's guidance.**

This warranty covers the target company's security measures in relation to its own paper-based and computerised systems and the steps it takes to ensure the reliability of its staff. In the wake of high profile security breaches by data controllers, the Information Commissioner has set out in clear terms what he expects by way of security, including that any portable devices holding personal information are encrypted, that personal information is locked up at night and that paper waste and obsolete computer equipment are disposed of securely.

In the absence of breach notification legislation, the Information Commissioner has introduced guidance on when data controllers need to notify him of security breaches. Any breaches by the target company requiring notification indicates a serious problem with the target company's security measures.

4.21.6 Where the Company uses a data processor to carry out the processing of personal data, the processor has provided sufficient guarantees in relation to security measures and compliance with those measures and there is in existence a written contract between the Company and the data processor which complies with the requirements of Sch.1, Pt II, paras 11–12 of the Data Protection Act 1998.   7–144

As part of its own compliance with the seventh data protection principle on security, the target company must ensure any contractor or "data processor" it uses to process personal data on its behalf, for example to send out mailshots to customers, complies with equivalent obligations to those imposed on the target company by the seventh principle. As data processors have no liability under the Act, the target company is required to take steps to secure the personal data. This includes ensuring the data processor has provided sufficient security guarantees and has agreed to comply with the security principle in a contract which is made or evidenced in writing and under which the data processor is to act only on instructions from the target company. Failure to obtain sufficient guarantees or to have such a contract in place is a breach of the Act which may ultimately amount to a criminal offence. On a more practical level, contractors are often the source of security breaches. Moreover, if individuals suffer financial loss as a result of the breach, they will be entitled to claim compensation from the target company. The target company should be able to recover that compensation from the data processor if there is a contract. As such the purchaser is justified in seeking the inclusion of such a warranty. As to whether or not there is a contract in place that complies with the applicable requirements is a question of fact for the vendors and so they should have little difficulty in confirming the position and giving the warranty.

Where the target company does not use a data processor for the processing of personal data it should consider amending the warranty to read:

"The Company does not use a data processor to carry out the processing of personal data".

4.21.7 The Company does not transfer personal data to jurisdictions outside the European Economic Area.   7–145

Under the eighth data protection principle, personal data may not be transferred outside the EEA unless the destination country or territory ensures an adequate level of protection for the rights and freedoms of individuals in relation to the processing of personal data. There are various means of compliance with the eighth principle, including use of the European Commission's model contracts between the target company and the organisation in the destination country. If the target company does transfer personal data outside the EEA, the purchaser will want to amend the warranty so as to provide confirmation of compliance with applicable requirements. An appropriate form of warranty would be:

"Where the Company transfers personal data to jurisdictions outside the European Economic Area it complies with the requirements of Sch.1 Pt II paras 13–15 of the Data Protection Act 1998."

The vendors should have little difficulty with either form of the warranty as they require confirmation of the factual position which the vendors can check. Note that any use by the target company of "cloud computing", such as online data storage facilities, may involve a transfer of personal data to servers located outside the EEA.

7–146   **4.21.8 No individual has claimed or taken, or [so far as the Vendors are aware] has a right to claim compensation or take, action for breach of his rights under the Data Protection Act 1998, against the Company. The Company has not received any notice, letter or complaint alleging a breach of the Data Protection Act 1998.**

Individuals have rights to compensation if they suffer financial loss as a result of a breach of the data protection principles by the data controller. In such a case they may also claim for associated distress. Individuals may also take court action for breach of their right to subject access, to object to automated processing of data, to object to direct marketing or automated decision making or to seek rectification and other remedies where personal information is shown to be inaccurate. In cases where the use of personal information involves the special purposes of journalistic, artistic and literary endeavours, compensation may be claimed for distress without damage having been suffered. The warranty covers both potential claims for compensation and potential claims for breach of the other individual rights.

The warranty is reasonable from the vendors' perspective in so far as it relates to claims which have been made but is onerous to the extent that it covers possible claims. By giving such a warranty the vendors would effectively be warranting on an absolute basis that the target company had complied with all data protection requirements. They will need to ensure that the terms of this warranty are not more onerous than the warranty that they agree to give at cl.4.21.2. If the vendors are to accept this part of the clause they would be acting reasonably in requiring it to be subject to their knowledge.

7–147   **4.21.9 The Company has complied with the Privacy and Electronic Communications (EC Directive) Regulations 2003 in respect of all electronic forms of direct marketing carried out by the Company or on its behalf.**

Breach of these regulations entitles non-corporate recipients of electronic forms of direct marketing such as text, email, telephone or fax to bring a claim for compensation for damage suffered. Breach may also lead to enforcement action by the Information Commissioner. The purchaser will accordingly have a legitimate interest in obtaining such confirmation from the vendors. In circumstances where the company has not engaged in such activities the vendors should consider amending the warranty to read:

"The Company has not carried out (and has not had carried out on its behalf) any form of direct marketing that falls within the provisions of the Privacy and Electronic Communications (EC Directive) Regulations 2003."

4.21.10 [So far as the Vendors are aware] the Company has complied with all other requirements of the Data Protection Act 1998 and all subordinate legislation, guidance and codes of practice.   7–148

This warranty is in the way of a sweeper warranty for anything not caught by the prior specific ones. The vendors would usually seek to qualify this by awareness by adding the wording in brackets, particularly when the prior specific warranties are given in absolute terms, or to argue that the warranty is not necessary given the protection afforded to the purchaser by the preceding clauses.

4.22 Guarantees and indemnities

4.22.1 There is no subsisting guarantee or agreement for indemnity or suretyship given by [the Company as security for the obligations of a third party], or [given by a third party] for the accommodation of, the Company.   7–149

This warranty is to some extent similar to cl.3.4.5. A guarantee is normally to be distinguished from an indemnity by the fact that a guarantee is a collateral contract to be responsible for the default of another party. A guarantee is thus ancillary or subsidiary to another contract. An indemnity is a contract by which the party giving the indemnity undertakes an original and independent obligation. Whilst not the intention of the warranty, it is arguable on its drafting that it would catch, for example, indemnities contained in hire purchase and similar contracts. To clarify the position the vendors should consider adding the wording in brackets.

4.23 Connected persons contracts

4.23.1 The Company is not, nor has it during the past three years been, a party to an agreement or arrangement (whether legally binding or not) in which a Vendor, or Associate of a Vendor, or director of the Company, or Associate of a director of the Company, is or has been interested.   7–150

The essential purpose of this warranty is as a check to establish whether any insider contracts have in the recent past been entered into or are currently subsisting. If any such contracts are brought to light, the purchaser will wish to ensure that the terms are satisfactory notwithstanding the interest of the vendors or the directors. The vendors would not normally have any reasonable ground for objecting to this warranty but they should ensure that its scope is clearly understood. In particular, the reference to "arrangement" is vague and essentially unnecessary. The vendors may wish, in addition, to provide that interests are deemed to be relevant for this warranty only if they are such that, if they involved a director, they would have to be disclosed for the purpose of CA 2006 s.182 and will need to consider carefully, if the vendors are not the only directors of the target company, whether it is appropriate to extend the warranty to cover "Associates" of the non-vendor directors. It would also be appropriate for the vendors to exclude obvious agreements such as employment contracts.

7–151   **4.23.2 The Company is not a party to, and its profits and financial position during the past three years have not been affected by, an agreement or arrangement (whether legally binding or not) which is not of an arm's length nature.**

The precise wording of this warranty is unsatisfactory for the vendors in a number of respects. In the first place, the purchaser should be interested only in transactions which have artificially either increased the profits or improved the apparent financial position of the target company or which have given rise to excessive liabilities. In addition, contracts may not be at arm's length but may be on fully commercial terms. The vendors should also consider whether the word "arrangement" is acceptable and the reference to "financial position" lacks clarity. Unless the warranty is amended to exclude gifts, it will be necessary for the vendors to disclose all charitable and similar donations made by the target company.

7–152   **4.23.3 None of the Company's assets have been acquired for a consideration other than market value (at the time of acquisition).**

This is a related warranty to cl.4.23.2 in the sense that it seeks disclosure of any transaction which involved the acquisition of an asset at less than market value. It is difficult to see how the purchaser could suffer loss as a result of any breach except in the limited circumstances where the transaction could be set aside by a liquidator or trustee in bankruptcy of the seller of the relevant asset.

4.24 Anti-corruption

7–153   **4.24.1 No officer or employee [so far as the Vendors are aware (but without having made any actual enquiry of any employee)] has made or received any Sensitive Payment in connection with any contract or otherwise.**

This warranty should be used pending the implementation of the BA 2010. Upon its implementation, this warranty should be deleted and replaced with cll.4.24.2 to 4.24.5.

Vendors will usually be reluctant to give the warranty unless caveated by their knowledge and the fact that no actual enquiry has been made of any relevant employees. Given the nature of the warranty and the likely confidential nature of the transaction it will not usually be feasible for enquiry to be made of the employees. This assumes, however, that the officers are a part of and/or involved in the transaction. If this is not the case, the caveat should also include that no enquiry has been made of the officers.

Bribery Act 2010

BA 2010 received royal asset on April 8, 2010 and was provisionally due to **7–154** come into force in April 2011. That implemetation date has now been delayed until the Ministry of Justice produces its final guidance regarding the procedures which commercial organisations can put in place to prevent bribery. Once the guidance is published there will be a three month notice period before the BA 2010 will come into force. At the time of writing, there has been no indication as to when the guidance is expected to be published. Upon implementation, the BA 2010 will replace all existing bribery laws, both statutory and common, and will be, subject to any final amendments prior to its implementation, one of the most stringent anti-corruption laws in the world. BA 2010 is not retrospective and therefore will apply only to bribery and/or corruption that takes place post its implementation.

The BA 2010 creates the following offences:

(1) offering, promising or giving a bribe (BA 2010 s.1) ("Offence 1");

(2) requesting, agreeing to receive or accepting a bribe (BA 2010 s.2) ("Offence 2");

(3) bribing a foreign public official (BA 2010 s.6) ("Offence 3"); and

(4) commercial organisations failing to prevent bribery by those acting on their behalf, where the bribery was intended to retain a business advantage for the commercial organisations (BA 2010 s.7) ("Offence 4").

Offences 1 to 3 apply to incidents both in the UK and outside the UK (if the act would constitute an offence if carried out in the UK) providing there is a close connection (as defined in BA 2010 s.12(4)) between the person offering, promising or giving the bribe and the UK. Offence 4 is a strict liability offence and applies to commercial organisations incorporated in the UK or foreign companies carrying out business in the UK, however minor that may be.

The implementation of the BA 2010 will therefore impact on companies who carry out business, particularly in international jurisdictions where bribery is or has historically been common practice but will also become applicable in the UK with regards to corporate entertaining and other inducements used as part of a company's sales and marketing programme.

The potential consequences of being convicted of bribery for both commercial organisations and individuals are criminal penalties. Commercial organisations can receive an unlimited fine whilst individuals can receive up to 10 years' imprisonment and/or an unlimited fine (BA 2010 s.11).

Guidance has yet to be published regarding the likely levels of fines but a recent Crown Court judgement, relating to a company that had been accused of bribing foreign public officials in Indonesia, stated that fines should be in the order of tens of millions of pounds or more (*R. v Innospec Ltd* [2010] Lloyd's Rep. F.C. 462). That said, this case involved the accused paying substantial amounts to many of the senior officials in Indonesia over a long period of time. It does, however, provide an indication of judicial thinking in this regard. Any director convicted under the BA 2010 is also likely to be disqualified from holding a position as a director for up to 15 years pursuant to the Company Directors Disqualification Act 1986.

Whilst the concept of successor liability is not included in the BA 2010, there are risks for a purchaser in acquiring a target company which has been linked to or been involved in bribery or corruption prior to completion; for example, this may impact on its value, senior management may be lost as a result of criminal prosecutions or disqualification and there will be internal costs in remedying corrupt practices and introducing adequate policies and procedures.

The following warranties should be included with effect from the implementation of the BA 2010. Share sale agreements have not historically provided specifically for anti-corruption and instead reliance has been placed on the sensitive payments warranty (see cl.4.24.1). The fundamental purpose of the following warranties is to elicit disclosure. Where specific incidents of corruption or bribery come to light through due diligence or disclosure and depending on the liability uncovered, the purchaser may seek to renegotiate the fundamental terms of the transaction or seek an indemnity.

Great care needs to be taken in seeking to address incidents of anti-corruption or bribery through indemnities since common law indicates that an indemnity against criminal liability is generally unenforceable (*Askey v Golden Wine Co Ltd* [1948] 2 All E.R. 35). This principle therefore is likely to extend to any fines a target company may receive as a result of a breach of the BA 2010. Notwithstanding this common law principle, if the purchaser insists that an indemnity is included care should be taken to ensure that this is drafted in favour of the purchaser as opposed to the target company for tax reasons (see para.1–06 for further discussion on this) and to avoid the indemnity being held to be unenforceable by the courts pursuant to the principle of ex turpi causa; any losses incurred by the purchaser as a result of the purchaser committing the same offence through the target company post-completion should be excluded.

To avoid the uncertainty surrounding indemnities, well-advised purchasers should instead seek a price adjustment in situations where the offence committed is not considered to be serious. Where a serious offence has been committed, consideration should be given to either restructuring the transaction to become an asset deal or delay completion of the transaction until such time as the liability has crystallised in the target company.

7–155   **4.24.2 [So far as the Vendors are aware] neither the Company nor any of its officers or employees is or has at any time engaged in any activity, practice or conduct which would constitute an offence under BA 2010 ss.1, 2 and 6.**

Offences 1 to 3 are covered by this warranty, being, cross-jurisdictional offences of bribing another person, receiving a bribe and bribing a foreign public official. Offence 4 is covered in cl.4.24.3.

Vendors will be reluctant to give this warranty unless caveated by their knowledge. A purchaser will be more likely to accept that the warranty is qualified if a thorough due diligence exercise has revealed that the target company has anti-corruption policies and procedures and has taken steps to implement them and review compliance thereto. If it is clear that the target company has no such policies and procedures in place, the purchaser will expect that the risk is covered in absolute terms.

4.24.3 No Associated Person of the Company has bribed another person (within the meaning given in BA 2010 s.7(3)) intending to obtain or retain business or obtain or retain an advantage in the conduct of business for the Company.

This warranty relates to Offence 4. It will be inherently difficult to ascertain, through due diligence, incidents of bribery by third parties. Well-advised purchasers therefore will insist upon the inclusion of this warranty. Given Offence 4 is a strict liability offence, most purchasers will be unwilling to accept an awareness qualification as that could result in a liability coming to light post-completion which the purchaser has no recourse against the vendors in relation to as a result of the caveat. The BA 2010 provides a defence to Offence 4 in instances where the company has adequate anti-bribery and anti-corruption policies in place (see cl.4.24.4 for further details).

4.24.4 The Company has in place adequate procedures designed to prevent their Associated Persons from bribing another person for the purposes of BA 2010 s.7(3), copies of the Company's anti-corruption policies and procedures are attached to the Disclosure Letter ("Anti-corruption Policies") together with full details of the steps taken to review compliance by the Company and all Associated Persons to the Anti-corruption Policies.

The purpose of this warranty is to elicit disclosure of the target company's anti-corruption policies and procedures and details of the steps taken to review compliance thereto. Depending on the adequacy of the policies and procedures and the ongoing monitoring of compliance thereto, the BA 2010 provides that this can operate as a defence to Offence 4.

4.24.5 Neither the Company nor any of its Associated Persons is or has been the subject of any investigation, inquiry or enforcement proceedings by any governmental, administrative or regulatory body or any customer regarding any offence or alleged offence under the BA 2010 or any anti-bribery or anti-corruption legislation in any other jurisdictions in which the Company operates, and no such investigation, inquiry or proceedings have been threatened or are pending and there are no circumstances likely to give rise to any such investigation, inquiry or proceedings.

Well-advised vendors may resist this warranty on the basis that cl.1.13.1 provides the purchaser with sufficient comfort regarding investigations and enquiries and therefore this is duplication. This can, however, be defended on the basis that this warranty goes further, providing the purchaser with greater comfort and also requires the vendors to focus on this particular area in eliciting disclosure of pertinent matters.

4.25 Consultants' reports

7–156   **4.25.1 No financial or management consultants have, within the past three years, given a report in relation to the Company.**

The purchaser will be interested in any management reports which have been obtained by the target company in that they will highlight problems that have arisen and solutions that have been proposed. The vendors might feel that such a report could prejudice their negotiations with the purchaser and should resist producing it. If any such reports are to be provided the vendors should review their contents before disclosing them and ensure that any potential problem areas have been addressed with the purchaser in an appropriate manner in advance.

5 Environmental

7–157   The most common way of dealing with environmental risks in any transaction is to try to allocate responsibility for that risk between the parties through the use of warranties or indemnities.

There is no standard approach to the allocation of environmental risk and so risk is apportioned on a case by case basis which is usually relative to the bargaining power between the parties. Liability for environmental matters usually arises due to a failure to comply with a statute or a permit issued under a statute, the presence of a pollutant in, on or under land requiring clean up or under common law (negligence, nuisance, etc.). The vendors would usually be reluctant to accept full environmental responsibility, particularly when they have only recently bought the site or when they have a leasehold interest only. Current convention is to require the purchaser to undertake a full environmental survey and to only provide environmental warranties which relate to pollution actually caused by the target company.

In the sample warranties provided in this Ch.7, environmental matters are dealt with separately from health and safety ones. However, in practice it is becoming increasingly common for health and safety matters to be incorporated within the definition of "environment" and, where this is done, care should be taken to ensure that, for example, vendors are not agreeing to give warranties which, whilst appropriate in respect of the environment, are not appropriate within the context of health and safety legislation.

Whilst a detailed examination of environmental liabilities is beyond the scope of this book, the following provides a brief explanation of some of the key statutory provisions, relating in particular to contaminated land which is increasingly becoming a highly negotiated part of any transaction.

Part IIA of the Environmental Protection Act 1990 creates a complex regulatory system designed to bring about the remediation of contaminated land, supposedly on the basis of a "polluter pays" principle. The use of "supposedly" is because it would be a mistake to work on the basis that a target company will not be liable for pollution that it has not actually caused. Indeed, the application of Pt IIA can commonly result in the polluter not paying, with the burden falling instead on the current owner or occupier.

Part IIA broadly works as follows. Where a regulator determines that there has been contamination, this triggers a duty on the part of the regulator to serve a remediation notice which sets out the steps that must be taken to clean up the site. Who the regulator is in this instance depends on whether the land is classed as a "special site". Where the land is classed as a "special site" (under the Environmental Protection Act 1990 Pt IIA ss.78A(3) and 78C) the Environment Agency will be the regulator. If the land is not deemed a "special site", the Local Authority will be the regulator. Before serving a remediation notice, the regulator must identify who the "appropriate persons" to be served with the notice are. There are two classes of "appropriate persons", known as Class A and Class B. Class A "appropriate persons" are anyone who has caused or "knowingly permitted" the contaminating substances to be in, on or under the land. Class B "appropriate persons" are the owner or occupier for the time being of the land in question. Class B persons are liable to be served with a remediation notice only where, after reasonable enquiry, no Class A person has been found.

Where there is more than one person in a liability group, then various exclusion tests are applied in turn to determine whether any of the group should be excluded from liability (Defra Circular 01/2006: Environmental Protection Act 1990: Part 2A: Contaminated land). The following example illustrates how the exclusion tests work in practice.

"X Ltd ('X') owned a chemical manufacturing site for many years and as a result the site became contaminated with various pollutants. In 1999, X sold the site to Y ('Y') who ran the site for a number of years but closed the plant in 2005. Before acquiring the site, Y had carried out environmental surveys and discovered an area of hydrocarbon contamination. Y did not clean up the contamination. Y sold the land for residential development in 2007 to Z ('Z') disclosing to them a copy of the 1999 environmental survey. Residents of the newly built homes complained and following an investigation by the local authority, it was established that there was an undiscovered area of heavy metal contamination as well as the previously identified hydrocarbon contamination."

It is clear that all the contamination was caused by X's original operations at the site. In this example, X is a "causer" of the contamination and is a Class A "appropriate person". However, as the hydrocarbon contamination was known to both Y and Z, they may be regarded as "knowing permitters" of the contamination because they knew of its presence, but did nothing to clean it up. They are both Class A persons. As regards the heavy metal contamination, X is the only Class A person since neither Y nor Z were aware of the contamination and therefore could not have knowingly permitted it.

In this example, it will only be possible to establish who is liable for what by a careful review of each transaction in the chain. This is because the various exclusion tests mean that it is possible to conclude that there are a number of different liability scenarios. Thus, as regards the hydrocarbon contamination, the "sold with information" test could apply conceivably at every sale, thereby excluding the vendors in turn from the Class A liability group, until the last "knowing" purchaser. If the 1999 environmental report had also been disclosed to the individual residential purchasers, it is possible that they could each be classed as a Class A person and be themselves liable for that contamination as the last Class A persons in the chain. If the sale documentation has not been effectively drafted, all or any of X, Y and/or Z may have some remediation liability for the hydrocarbon contamination, even though they long ago parted with their legal interest in the site. As regards the heavy metal contamination, if Z as original polluter is the only Class A person, then it will be liable only for the clean up. Unfortunately, as is entirely possible with historic contamination, if Z ceased trading and no longer exists as a legal entity, then there would be no Class A person, and liability would default to whoever is the Class B person—the owner or occupier for the time being.

Whilst the statutory contaminated land regime is complex, the main point to note is that just because a target company does not currently have any "contaminated" sites within its portfolio, and/or has not itself caused any pollution, it does not mean that it is safe to assume that it has no contaminated land liabilities. It could have had liability for known historic contamination passed to it through contract documentation, it could be liable for unknown historic pollution on its current sites as "last man standing" or it could carry liabilities for sites that it previously owned or occupied. "Last man standing" liability is a particular concern where a target company has no knowledge of the state of the land either because environmental surveys were not common practice at the time the site was acquired or where the target company was unable to carry out a proper survey, for example, because of a lack of co-operation from a vendor or landlord.

Environmental liabilities can therefore be a minefield, and it is common to encounter purchasers (especially US companies) who are extremely risk-averse and who will make extraordinary demands in terms of warranty and indemnity protection without which they will be reluctant to assume the risk.

5.1 Required permits

7–158   **5.1.1 The Company has obtained all Environmental Permits which it requires and has complied [in all material respects] with all applicable Environmental Laws and with the [material] terms and conditions of the Environmental Permits and [so far as the Vendors are aware] there is no reason why the Environmental Permits should not continue to be complied with [by the Company if the Company is operated in the same manner and scope after Completion as it was prior to Completion]. True, complete and accurate copies of such Environmental Permits are attached to the Disclosure Letter.**

Protection of the environment has become a key issue within EU and United Kingdom policy and, as a result, there has been a vast amount of legislation (both primary and secondary) introduced into the United Kingdom in the last 20 years. The United Kingdom approach to regulating the environment is by way of permits in order that polluting activities are controlled by way of the issue of appropriate permits. There are various regulatory controls including pollution control, waste management and water that are regulated mainly by environmental permits issued by the Environment Agency but in some situations by the local authority. It is important for the purchaser to ensure that all permits have been complied with in the past and that the target company has the ability to continue to comply with any relevant permits it has. Usually a breach of a condition of a permit is a criminal strict liability offence. Furthermore, under the Regulatory Enforcement and Sanctions Act 2008, the Environment Agency has been given new powers to impose "civil sanctions", including fixed and variable monetary penalties. Using these powers, the Environment Agency can in effect impose fines (and determine the amount) without going through the courts. Other civil sanctions that are open to the Environment Agency include:

(i) issuing compliance notices and stop notices which can affect how and what a company is permitted to do;

(ii) issuing a restoration notice, requiring remedial action to be taken; and

(iii) accepting enforcement undertakings from companies—these are "voluntary" agreements to take corrective actions. Failing to comply with an enforcement undertaking is a criminal offence, hence they are voluntary only in the sense that they are offered voluntarily; once accepted by the Environment Agency, they effectively have the force of law. However, the warranty as drafted is unlikely to be acceptable to the vendors for several reasons. Given the amount of legislation that is now in force it is unlikely that the target company complies with every applicable requirement and the vendors will be concerned to ensure that the purchaser is not in a position where it can effectively improve the business of the Company at their expense. In respect of the latter part of the first sentence, the vendors will rightly be required to disclose any permits that contain change of control provisions but beyond that future compliance is a question of speculation on their part. At the very least they should insist on the inclusion of the words in the fourth set of brackets. The position is to some extent adequately covered by cl.5.2.1 and must be resisted by the vendors on that basis or cl.5.2.1 amended to avoid duplication.

5.2 Breaches

5.2.1 The Company has not received notification or communication from which it appears it is, or may be alleged to be, in violation of any Environmental Laws or Environmental Permits or that any Environmental 7–159

Permits may be subject to modification, suspension, revocation or appeal and [so far as the Vendors are aware] there are no circumstances likely to give rise to violation, modification, suspension, revocation or appeal of any Environmental Permits.

It is important to ensure that not only has there been no breach or violation of a permit or a condition of the permit in the past but also that no regulatory body, for example the Environment Agency, has notified the target company that it is investigating an incident with a view to a possible prosecution. It is also important from the purchaser's perspective to ensure that the relevant regulatory body is not considering modification, suspension, revocation or appeal of any permits as this could affect the operation of the target company going forward. Whilst the vendors should have little difficulty in giving the first part of this warranty (although they will need to ensure that correspondence with enforcement agencies is carefully reviewed to ascertain if there are any relevant matters that need to be disclosed) they may want to seek to make the latter part of the warranty subject to their knowledge by including the wording in brackets. The purchaser is likely to object to such a qualification on the basis that the vendors should be required to disclose any material breaches of such permits (they will be required to in any event against cl.5.1.1) and, whilst any permits would be unlikely to be modified etc. in the event of a minor breach by the company, this is a risk that should lie with the vendors.

5.3 Audits and surveys

7–160   **5.3.1 The Disclosure Letter contains copies of all environmental audits and surveys that the Company has commissioned [or that have been addressed to it] in relation to the Properties or land previously owned or occupied by it [in the last [   ] years].**

It is now commonplace when acquiring a company, particularly if that company's assets include land, to ensure that environmental audits and surveys have been carried out and the results of them made available to the purchaser. Provided the vendors are able to locate copies of relevant audits and surveys and attach them to the disclosure letter then the warranty is unlikely to cause them an issue although they will prefer to delete the wording in the first set of brackets and to limit the period in respect of which reports have to be produced to a reasonable time prior to completion. If there is any doubt as to what reports and surveys are intended to be caught by the warranty the vendors should seek clarification given the potential implications of not disclosing a report that identifies breaches of applicable requirements. (Collecting audit reports for the purposes of this warranty will likely assist the vendors in making disclosure of matters relevant for other warranties in this section as the reports may identify breaches that have occurred.)

Under the contaminated land regime, it is possible for the vendor of land to be excluded from liability if the land was sold with information that would be sufficient to enable the purchaser to be aware of the pollutant and the broad measure of its presence. This is known as the "sold with information test". If a company faces action in respect of land which it no longer owns or occupies but can prove that before the sale took place it provided the purchaser with full information so as to satisfy the sold with information test, it may be able to take advantage of this exclusion and avoid liability. The Secretary of State, in determining an appeal by *Redland Minerals Ltd and Crest Nicholson Residential Plc* (July 22, 2009) has clarified that the purpose of the "sold with information test" is to exclude liability where it would be reasonable that a purchaser should bear liability. Therefore, it seems that a practical approach will be taken as to whether sufficient information was provided in any particular case to enable the vendor to escape liability. A purchaser should seek an appropriate warranty from the vendors if during due diligence it becomes apparent that there has been a prior relevant transaction.

5.4 Prosecutions

5.4.1 The Company has not been prosecuted or the subject of any Civil   7–161
Sanction or notified of a possible prosecution or possible Civil Sanction for a breach of any Environmental Laws.

Whilst duplicating cll.5.1.1 and 5.2.1 it is important to note whether the target company has been prosecuted and in particular if it has been prosecuted or subjected to any civil sanction by the Environment Agency or another regulatory body on a regular basis. The Environment Agency regularly publishes on its website details of companies that have been prosecuted and this can have negative public relations consequences for that company. It is also important to know whether the Environment Agency or another regulatory body are in the process of issuing proceedings or civil sanctions or have issued proceedings but the matter has not yet come to court. In its current form the warranty should be acceptable to the vendors as they will be aware of prosecutions or civil sanctions that have take place or been notified.

5.5 No claims

5.5.1 No Environmental Claims exist against the Company or have been   7–162
made within the previous [   ] years and [so far as the Vendors are aware] there are no circumstances [in existence] which may lead to a claim.

From the purchaser's perspective it is important that any claims against the target company in respect of environmental matters (whether past, present or potential) are dealt with. To a large extent the contents of this warranty have already been covered by cll.5.1.1 and 5.2.1 and as such the vendors might reasonably resist any duplication.

The Vendors will also prefer to replace "may" with "are likely to".

5.6 Hazardous Substances

5.6.1 Neither the Company nor any other person has deposited, used,   7–163
treated, kept, disposed of, released or emitted any Hazardous Substances at,

on, from or under any of the Properties now or previously owned, leased, occupied or controlled by the Company.

This is perhaps the most contentious environmental warranty discussed, as accumulation of the substances contained with the wide definition of "Hazardous Substances" may not have involved a breach of environmental law. On the other hand, it may result in considerably increased risks of contamination and liability.

While this warranty commences with what appears to be a list of unnecessary verbs, it is usual to use such terminology as it tracks that used in environmental legislation and there is case law as to the nuances between the activities identified.

The warranty will usually be unacceptable to the vendors in its current form given that it extends to activities of persons not under the control of the target company and is not just confined to its period of ownership. The vendors will want to replace "other person" with:

" . . . employee or agent of the Company in the course of carrying out their duties for the Company".

Where the vendors have not owned the shares since incorporation of the target company they will prefer to limit the warranty to their period of ownership although, for the reasons mentioned at cl.1.3.2 this is likely to be resisted by the Purchaser.

In most cases the vendors will seek to limit the warranty to positive acts of pollution undertaken as part and parcel of the business rather than the much wider basis embodied in this warranty which could extend to unknown migration of pollutants underneath the building occupied or used by the target company.

5.7 Work carried out under notices

7–164   **5.7.1 No notices under Environmental Laws have been served against the Company and no work has been carried out under such a notice by a regulatory body whereby the Company must reimburse the regulatory body for the costs of the work carried out.**

This would cover, for example, work carried out under notices served under the contaminated land regime as well as anti pollution Works Notices under the Water Resources Act 1991 s.161. The warranty should not be objectionable to the vendors as they should be able to ascertain the position relatively easily.

5.8 Prior use

7–165   **5.8.1 So far as the Vendors are aware [(but without having undertaken or commissioned any environmental audits, surveys or investigations other than those referred to at [cl.5.3.1])] there has not been any potentially contaminative use that has been made of any of the Properties or any land previously owned or occupied by the Company.**

This seeks disclosure from the vendors that, while the target company's property to date has not been used for any contaminative use, there is no possibility that it has been used for something potentially contaminative at another time such that it could fall within any regulatory regime now or at some stage in the future.

This may elicit disclosure of more than would be forthcoming in respect of cl.5.5.1, which deals with past, present or future claims, and the vendors should argue that disclosure of audits and surveys coupled with the warranty given in cl.5.5.1 sufficiently protects the purchaser's interests. Under the contaminated land regime an owner or occupier can be held liable for the clean up of contamination it caused on land it no longer owns or occupies and so the purchaser will want to obtain as much information and cover as it can. For example, in a decision of the Secretary of State (July 27, 2009) in an appeal against a remediation notice, Redlands Minerals Ltd ("RML") and Crest Nicholson Residential Plc ("CNR") were both held liable for contamination caused decades ago to a site that had been developed and sold for flats. The original pollution had been released at a chemical works from the mid 1950s to 1980. RML bought the original chemical company and in 1983 sold the site to CNR. CNR carried out some remediation (which actually made the situation worse) and built 66 flats which it then sold. In 2000, contamination of water resources underlying the site was discovered. The Environment Agency served a remediation notice on both RML and CNR on the basis that both had caused or knowingly permitted contamination (although neither had been responsible for the original releases). Both companies appealed, but their appeal was rejected by the Secretary of State. RML as successor to the original polluter, had inherited it liabilities. CNR through its actions and inactions in developing the site caused contaminants that would otherwise have been removed to remain and had also caused contaminants to be flushed deeper and faster into the ground. Subsequent to the Secretary of State's decision letter, CNR were refused leave to seek judicial review (*R. (on the application of Crest Nicholson Ltd) v Secretary of State for the Environment, Food and Rural Affairs* [2010] EWHC 561). If the vendors are obliged to give the warranty they should seek to include the wording in brackets so as to make it clear that to satisfy their obligation of enquiry in relation to it they are not required to commence any new investigations or environmental surveys but can instead rely on information that they have already obtained. In most cases vendors will be exceedingly reluctant to offer wide ranging environmental warranties and will require the purchaser to undertake its own assessments or survey.

6 Employment

6.1 Employees, terms of employment and status

6.1.1 The Disclosure Letter contains anonymised accurate and complete details of the dates of birth, dates of commencement of employment or appointment to office, and terms of employment or appointment of all the employees and officers of the Company, including details of all remuneration (including pensions, whether to be delivered by occupational or personal schemes) and other benefits, such as profit sharing, commission and bonus   7–166

arrangements (whether or not contractual), sufficient to allow the financial obligations of the Company to be ascertained.

Normally the purchaser will want to pay close attention to the terms and conditions of employment of all the employees and will require as much detail as possible. However, if the target company has an unusually large number of employees it may not be realistic for the terms of employment of all of them to be included in the disclosure letter. It may therefore be appropriate either to exclude from the warranty employees whose salary is below a certain level or to make the disclosure on the basis of broad categories of employee. This may be appropriate where there are "standard" terms and conditions of employment for certain classes of employee. In either case, it will be necessary to amend the detailed wording of the warranty. There may also be difficulty in identifying and describing discretionary arrangements if no fixed rule or pattern exists for exercising the discretion although, in such a case, the purchaser is less likely to be legally bound by the arrangements.

Information in respect of employees (and other individuals engaged by the target company) should be provided on an anonymised basis so as to avoid disclosure of personal information which is likely to be a breach of applicable data protection requirements. The position is different when dealing with asset-based transactions to which the Transfer of Undertakings (Protection of Employment) Regulations 2006 apply where, in order to comply with the employee liability information provisions in reg.11, the names of the employees must be given.

7–167   **6.1.2 There is no contract of service between the Company and a director or employee for which approval was required but not obtained under CA 2006 s.188.**

Under CA 2006 s.188 the shareholders must approve, in advance, any term of an agreement under which a director is employed to provide services to the company for more than two years and under which the company cannot terminate the employment by notice or can only do so in certain specified circumstances. A failure to obtain the necessary approval renders the term void to the extent of the contravention. The contract being deemed in such circumstances to contain a term enabling the company to terminate it at any time on giving reasonable notice. The reference to "employee" is required because the sections extend not only to a service agreement between a company and one of its directors but also to a service agreement with a subsidiary where the employee is a director of the holding company. It is unlikely that the purchaser would suffer a disadvantage if the section had been contravened and the warranty operates mainly as a reminder to the parties to check whether any infringement may have occurred.

7–168   **6.1.3 There are no contracts for services (including without limitation consultancy agreements) between the Company and any individual.**

One of the effects of employment legislation in recent years has been to considerably narrow the gap between employees and the self-employed.

Nevertheless the distinction remains vital in terms of taxation matters (principally in relation to PAYE and national insurance contributions) and also so far as rights on redundancy and the right to claim unfair dismissal is concerned. This warranty is designed to identify any arrangements which masquerade as "consultancy agreements" or "contracts for services" but which on closer examination are in fact more like employment arrangements. The vendors should be able to identify any such arrangements and as such should be able to accept the warranty as drafted.

6.1.4 No employee of the Company who has or may have a statutory or contractual right to return to work, is absent on maternity leave, paternity leave, parental leave, adoption leave [or other leave of absence]. No employee of the Company is absent on sick leave which has lasted or is expected to last longer than four weeks. 7–169

Employees have statutory rights to maternity, paternity, adoption and parental leave. Broadly speaking, employees returning from such leave have the right to return to the same or a similar job on no less favourable terms and conditions as those that they enjoyed immediately before commencing leave. A failure to afford that right often gives rise to claims for substantial compensation. The vendors should consider and make any necessary disclosures in respect of any employee or officer who is absent on sickness grounds or on other leave of absence and should consider deleting the wording in brackets and requiring the purchaser to specify any other categories of leave that it is interested in.

6.1.5 No employee or former employee of the Company has or may have a right to be reinstated or re-engaged under the Employment Rights Act 1996. 7–170

An employee who has been unfairly dismissed may be entitled to reinstatement (where the employee is treated in all respects as if he had not been dismissed) or re-engagement (where the employee returns to work for the employer but in a different role). An order for reinstatement or re-engagement will not be made where it is not practicable for the employer to comply or where to make it do so would be unjust. In practice these remedies are rarely appropriate and tribunals will make these orders infrequently. The vendors should be in a position to ascertain which of the target company's employees and former employees have either claimed or may be eligible to claim that they have been unfairly dismissed. If the vendors were to accept this warranty, being prudent they should disclose details of all such employees (save where any claims have already been settled and rights of additional action extinguished). If any existing employees of the company are resigning at completion they should be required to sign compromise agreements waiving their rights to make (amongst others) unfair dismissal claims against the Company.

6.1.6 All of the Company's employees (and other persons engaged by the Company) are legally entitled to work in the United Kingdom, the Company 7–171

having complied in all requirements of the Asylum and Immigration Act 1996 and The Immigration, Asylum and Nationality Act 2006.

The Asylum and Immigration Act 1996 made it a criminal offence to employ a person who was subject to immigration control and who has had no permission to work in the United Kingdom or who was working in breach of their conditions of stay in the United Kingdom. Employers could establish a statutory defence against conviction if they carried out specific checks on prospective employees. An employer who employed an illegal worker between January 27, 1997 and February 29, 2008 and did not establish a statutory defence can still be fined up to £5,000 per illegal worker in the magistrates' court or an unlimited fine in the Crown Court.

The Immigration, Asylum and Nationality Act 2006 came into force on February 29, 2008. Under the Act, an employer is liable to a civil financial penalty if they employ a person who is subject to immigration control and who has no permission to work in the United Kingdom or who is working in breach of their conditions of stay in the United Kingdom. Employers can have a statutory excuse against the civil penalty if they carried out specific checks on the prospective employees. Employers will only have the excuse for employees with time-limited leave to be in the United Kingdom if they carried out repeat checks at least once every 12 months. An employer who has employed an illegal worker since February 29, 2008 and does not have an excuse could be liable for a civil penalty of up to £10,000 per illegal worker.

6.2 Claims and potential employee claims

7–172 **6.2.1 There are no outstanding claims nor [so far as the Vendors are aware] are there any potential claims against the Company by any person who is now or has been an officer or employee of the Company and no liability has been incurred and remains undischarged for breach of any employment contract or for a redundancy payment or a protective award or for damages or compensation for wrongful dismissal or unfair dismissal or otherwise or for failure to comply with any order for the reinstatement or re-engagement of any person remains.**

Although there is likely to be a warranty in respect of litigation generally, cl.6.2.1 will elicit specific information regarding employee claims. The vendors may well consider the expansion of the warranty to "potential claims" to be unreasonable and will be most unlikely to accept it without the addition of the wording in square brackets. This should be acceptable to the purchaser as it will at least oblige the vendors to make enquiries as to whether circumstances exist which are likely to give rise to such litigation.

7–173 **6.2.2 There have not within the period of 12 months prior to the date of this Agreement been any claims under the provisions of the Employment Rights Act 1996, the Trade Union Reform and Employment Act 1993, the Health and Safety at Work etc. Act 1974, the Equal Pay Act 1970, the Sex**

Discrimination Act 1975, the Disability Discrimination Act 1995, the Race Relations Act 1976, the Sex Discrimination (Gender Reassignment) Regulations 1999, the Transfer of Undertakings (Protection of Employment) Regulations 2006, the Trade Union and Labour Relations (Consolidation) Act 1992, the Protection from Harassment Act 1997, the Working Time Regulations 1998, the National Minimum Wage Act 1998, the Employment Relations Act 1999, the Part-Time Workers (Prevention of Less Favourable Treatment) Regulations 2000, the Fixed-Term Employees (Prevention of Less Favourable Treatment) Regulations 2002, the Employment Act 2002, *the Employment Equality (Religion or Belief) Regulations 2003, the Employment Equality (Sexual Orientation) Regulations 2003 or the Employment Equality (Age) Regulations 2006* or the Equality Act 2010 relating to any employee or former employee of the Company nor [so far as the Vendors are aware (but without having made enquiry of any employee or former employee of the Company)] are there any circumstances which are likely to give rise to such claims.

The warranty sets out the principal legislative instruments under which employment claims are made. The wording of the first part of the warranty should not cause the vendors too much difficulty as it simply requires disclosure of claims made, however they may well consider the extension of the warranty to "potential claims" to be unreasonable and will be unlikely to accept it without it being subject to their awareness and the obligation to make enquiry of the target company's employees and former employees in such circumstances being excluded by the inclusion of the wording in brackets. It would be reasonable for the purchaser to carve out of the exclusion any of the people that the vendors have agreed to make enquiry of, if relevant. The Acts whose names appear in italics were, subject to transitional arrangements, repealed by the Equality Act 2010 the principal provisions of which came into force on October 1, 2010. The transitional arrangements are not straightforward and it is recommended that warranties continue to refer to the former legislation, at least for the foreseeable future.

6.2.3 None of the offices or employees of the Company have raised any   7–174
grievance or have been issued with any disciplinary warning which remains
current and there are no disciplinary proceedings pending or contemplated
in respect of any such person.

Unlike transactions to which the Transfer of Undertaking (Protection of Employment) Regulations 2006 applies there is no statutory obligation on the vendors to give details of disciplinary matters to the purchaser. The aim of the warranty is to obtain details of any past or ongoing disciplinary issues of which the purchaser should be aware. It is unlikely that the vendors would object to its terms.

6.2.4 The Company has performed all [material] obligations required to   7–175
be performed by it in respect of its officers and employees whether arising

under contract, statute, at common law or in equity including, without limitation under the Working Time Regulations 1998 and under all health and safety legislation. [N.B. This warranty would also cover stakeholder legislation, which is included more specifically in the pensions section.]

Clause 6.2.4 is very broad in its nature, aiming from the purchaser's point of view to prompt disclosure of any breach or non-compliance by the target company with the terms of any contract of employment or employment legislation. It is also designed to elicit details of outstanding liabilities to officers or employees, which to an extent overlaps with cl.6.2.1. However, the vendors are likely to view the wide scope of this warranty as unreasonable and seek to resist its inclusion or, as a minimum, qualify it by awareness and/or materiality. The Working Time Regulations and health and safety legislation are referred to specifically because it is these regulations which by and large give rise to the most frequent instances of non-compliance and here serve as useful reminders for disclosure.

7–176   **6.2.5 The Company has maintained adequate, suitable and up to date records in relation to each of its employees.**

This warranty deliberately extends beyond those records which an employer is obliged to maintain by law. Its principal purpose is to flush out areas in which documentation and records may be less than satisfactory; this is of particular relevance where the absence of the records may make it more difficult to deal with the employees in the future, or where time and effort will have to be spent rectifying the deficiency following completion.

7–177   **6.2.6 The Company has paid to the Taxation Authority all Taxation due in respect of the employment of the employees of the Company.**

The nature and benefit of this warranty is obvious although the vendors might reasonably seek to resist giving it on the basis that it will be duplicated in the tax warranties and any unpaid tax will be covered by the tax covenant.

7–178   **6.2.7 There are no enquiries or investigations existing [or so far as the Vendors are aware], pending or threatened in relation to the Company by the Commission for Equality and Human Rights, the Health and Safety Executive or any similar body.**

The purpose of this warranty is twofold; first to identify any such investigations which may be embarrassing should they proceed and second to identify any potential discrimination claims. This second element will be important particularly where cl.6.2.2 is not extended to cover "potential" claims. The Commission for Equality and Human Rights, which was established by the Equality Act 2006, assumed the functions of the Equal Opportunities Commission, the Commission for Racial Equality and the Disability Rights Commission on October 1, 2007. The vendors will not necessarily know whether enquiries or investigations are existing (as they may be at an early stage and the company not yet notified of them) and as such the vendors should seek to have this element of the warranty caveated by reference to their awareness by adding the wording in brackets.

6.3 Changes in remuneration

6.3.1 During the period to which the Accounts relate and since the Balance Sheet Date or (where employment or holding of office commenced after the beginning of the period) since the commencement date of the employment or holding of office: 7–179

    6.3.1.1   **no change has been made in the rate of remuneration, or the emoluments of employment or pension benefits, of any officer, ex-officer or senior employee of the Company (a senior employee being a person in receipt of remuneration in excess of £[ ] per annum); and**

    6.3.1.2   **no [material] change has been made in the other terms of employment of any officer or senior employee.**

The warranty is limited to changes in remuneration of officers, ex-officers and "senior" employees to avoid extensive disclosures where changes have taken place in relation to employees at a comparatively low salary level. There will of course be occasions where it would be inappropriate to limit the warranty in this way. The insertion of the word "material", as indicated in square brackets, may also help to minimise unnecessary disclosures. This warranty is relevant to the purchaser, even if a warranty equivalent to cl.6.1.1 is given, as it will wish to know what changes have occurred in the payroll which are not fully reflected in the last accounts. As the warranty requires disclosure of factual matters that are easily ascertainable from the target company's records the vendors should be willing to accept the warranty as drafted.

6.3.2 No agreement has been reached with any officers, employees, trade union or other body representing employees that will or may on a future date result in any changes to the terms and conditions of employment of any of the officers or employees of the Company (including without limitation any increase in the rate of remuneration or enhancement of the emoluments of employment or pension benefits of such persons); and no negotiation relating to the terms and conditions of employment of any officer or employee of the Company (including without limitation for any increase in the remuneration or enhancement of the emoluments of employment or pension benefits of such persons) are current or likely to take place within the next six months.   7–180

The purpose of this warranty is to identify commitments which have already been or which might be incurred by the target company by reason of negotiations but which will result in changes only after completion. Whether the vendors would be willing to allow the clause to extend to negotiations which are not current but are merely "likely" would depend upon the nature of the business. Reference to "planned" would be preferable, especially as the vendors will not know with any certainty whether any of the employees may seek to commence negotiations. If the target company is unionised, the timing of negotiations for changes in remuneration is likely to be well understood and capable of disclosure to the purchaser.

6.4 Bonus and share options schemes

7–181 **6.4.1 There are no schemes (whether contractual or discretionary) in operation by or in relation to the Company under which any employee or director of the Company is entitled to any shares in the Company or to any bonus, profit share, commission or remuneration of any other sort (whether calculated by reference to the whole or part of the turnover, profits/losses or sales of the Company or otherwise).**

6.4.2 The Company is not under any legal or moral obligation to make nor is it accustomed to making any bonus payments to or for the benefit of any officer or employee of the Company.

Bonus schemes can be problematic particularly in the case of senior executives (whose bonus packages are often a key part of their remuneration arrangements) who tend to negotiate bonuses on an annual basis and where entitlement is often expressed to be discretionary in some way. These warranties catch both contractual and discretionary schemes as well as those arrangements which are informal and ad hoc but to which an employee might nevertheless be able to establish a contractual right. The purchaser should ensure that it fully understands the target company's commitments in relation to this. Whilst overlapping with cl.6.1.1 the warranty serves a useful purpose in directing the minds of the vendors to focus on bonus and similar arrangements. The vendors cannot reasonably object to such warranties.

6.5 Termination of contracts of employment

7–182 **6.5.1 All subsisting employment contracts to which the Company is a party are determinable at any time on three months' notice or less without compensation (other than compensation for unfair dismissal in accordance with the Employment Rights Act 1996).**

This warranty is designed to flag up those employees with lengthy contractual notice periods who consequently would be expensive to dispense should, for example, a redundancy situation arise. In the ordinary course of events an employee with more than one year's continuous service has the right to bring a claim for unfair dismissal, even where his employment is terminated on proper notice. In certain limited cases (for example where the employee has been dismissed because he has indicated an intention to join a trade union, has raised concerns about health and safety matters or has asserted a statutory right) the right is extended to those with less than one year's service. Compensation for unfair dismissal is based principally on loss of earnings and other benefits, and is awarded in such amount as the employment tribunal considers just and equitable in all the circumstances of the case.

6.5.2 No employee of the Company [who is in receipt of remuneration in excess of £[   ] per annum], and no officer of the Company has given or received notice terminating his employment, except as expressly contemplated in this Agreement, and no such employee or officer will be entitled or[, so far as the Vendors are aware [(but without having made enquiry of any employee or officer of the Company)], is likely to leave his employment or office prematurely, nor to receive any payment from the Company as a result of the sale of the Shares.   7–183

The main purpose of this warranty is to identify senior employees who are still with the target company but under notice of termination. The circumstances of the target company may make it desirable, from the purchaser's point of view, to extend the warranty to all employees, regardless of seniority. The second part of the clause would be more acceptable to vendors if it covered cases where the employee "will" leave rather than being "likely" to leave and if the wording in brackets were inserted given the content of the warranty (in particular in circumstances where it does extend to all employees of the target company). It would not be appropriate for fairly obvious reasons to ask the individual employees. The reference to employees leaving "prematurely" relates to contracts which give the employee a right to leave if there is a change in the control of the employer. In the absence of express provision, there would be no specific right of termination simply by reason of a change of control. The position is different where the transaction proceeds by way of asset sale (rather than share sale). In those circumstances the Transfer of Undertakings (Protection of Employment) Regulations 2006 apply. Those regulations include the specific right for an employee to resign because he "objects" to being employed by the new owner.

6.6 Industrial relations

6.6.1 The Company does not recognise any trade unions, works or staff councils or associates of trade unions and there are no collective agreements or other agreements (whether or not legally binding and whether in writing or arising by virtue of custom or practice) between the Company and any trade union or other body representing employees.   7–184

If the target company's employees are represented by one or more trade unions it will be important for the purchaser to have full disclosure of all arrangements which have been entered into with the unions and the extent to which each union has been recognised. A variety of other arrangements may be in place for the purposes of informing, consulting or negotiating with the workforce, including staff and works councils. The purchaser should also bear in mind that in the case of certain trades and industries remuneration, holidays and other terms and conditions of employment may be regulated at industry level by a bargaining mechanism involving a panel of unions' and employers' representatives.

7–185   6.6.2 The Company has not done anything which might be construed as recognition of a trade union and has not received an application for recognition from a trade union.

Recognition of a trade union for collective bargaining purposes can occur by agreement or, where the business has 21 or more employees, following a request by an independent trade union for recognition by an employer. Recognition requests are considered by the Central Arbitration Committee who in the vast majority of cases will order that a ballot takes place. Recognition will in broad terms follow where both a majority of voters and at least 40 per cent of all workers in the appropriate bargaining unit support recognition. Where a trade union is recognised, an employer will be committed to collective bargaining in respect of matters such as pay, hours and holidays. Although this warranty serves a useful function in bringing out information which could be of considerable commercial relevance to a purchaser, it is not clear how the purchaser would be able to easily establish loss for breach.

7–186   6.6.3 Neither the Company nor any of its employees is or has been in the last two years involved in an industrial dispute and so far as the Vendors are aware there is nothing which might suggest that there may be an industrial dispute involving the Company, or that this Agreement may give rise to such a dispute.

The importance of this clause depends on the nature of the businesses of the target company. If the target company is unionised it will be imperative to know whether there are existing industrial disputes. The purchaser will also want to know something of the industrial relations history of the target given that the future profitability of it could be affected by poor industrial relations, and will be anxious to be informed of any circumstances which are likely to result in a dispute although the vendors may feel that the wording of the second half of this warranty is too broad. If they are to give a warranty as to the possibility of future industrial disputes, the vendors might wish to limit the warranty so that it applies only to disputes that are "likely" to occur. The closing words of the clause, relating to disputes which could arise from the sale of the target company, are unlikely to be acceptable to the vendors as they may reasonably feel in most cases that the purchaser would have at least as clear an idea as they do as to whether such disputes would arise by reason of the change in ownership of the target company. This part of the warranty might alternatively be included in the items covered by cl.4.3.1.

7–187   6.6.4 The Company has not received any request for an information and consultation agreement pursuant to the Information and Consultation of

Employees Regulations 2004 and the Company is not party to any negotiations for such an agreement.

The Information and Consultation of Employees Regulations 2004 currently apply to all businesses with 50 or more employees. The regulations provide for the setting up of internal arrangements for informing and consulting employees in relation to the company's economic position, employment prospects and decisions likely to lead to substantial changes in work organisation or contractual relations. Failure to comply with the regulations can result in the application of a cumbersome "default" model for informing and consulting as well as the complaints to the Central Arbitration Committee which has the power to order the employer to remedy breaches. Where a breach has occurred the complainant can apply to the Employment Appeal Tribunal for an order requiring the employer to pay a fine which can be as much as £75,000. As such the purchaser will be acting reasonably in requesting disclosure of details of the position in the target company. The vendors should be willing to accept the warranty as they will be able to disclose the existence of any relevant request or negotiation.

6.7 Redundancies

6.7.1 No employee of the Company will become redundant and be entitled to a redundancy payment as a result of this Agreement.   7–188

If the agreement specifically provides for redundancies, or if redundancies are a clear and inevitable consequence of the sale of the target company, then the warranty is incorrect and inappropriate. The implications of redundancies should be specifically considered in the course of the sale negotiations and the risk and cost allocated between the parties. In any other case there is no particular reason why the vendors should make a representation on this question. The presence of the warranty often serves as a reminder so that the possibility of redundancies is not overlooked.

This clause could, as an alternative to being a separate warranty, be included in cl.4.3.1.

6.7.2 There is no plan, scheme or commitment or established practice relating to the termination of employment affecting an employee or officer of the Company which is more generous than the statutory redundancy entitlement or such sum as may be properly payable by way of damages for breach of contract.   7–189

The purchaser will want to know if the target company operates an enhanced redundancy scheme or is morally obliged to make an ex gratia payment to an employee or officer on termination of his or her employment. This will be especially relevant if the purchaser envisages job losses following the acquisition of the target company. The vendors cannot reasonably object to giving such a warranty.

7 Pensions

7–190   Pension schemes are often complex arrangements, each with potentially a number of difficult issues that need to be identified. Then, the monetary value of the risks involved must be estimated, which in most cases is not a straightforward exercise, and in so far as possible the risks need to be apportioned between the parties by way of appropriate indemnities and warranties or mitigated by post-completion actions. The warranties in this section are designed to elicit as much information as possible in relation to any present or historic pension arrangements.

Historic pension arrangements, such as final salary schemes that are closed to new entrants or occupational schemes that are in the process of winding-up or have completed their winding-up, tend to be overlooked as they no longer have any day to day relevance to the target company, but they may still conceal significant liabilities that attach to the target company and become "live" once more many years after the closure or winding-up.

The warranties are listed in the following order:

(a) warranties 7.1.1 to 7.1.6 relate to pension liabilities of the target company that may not be ascribed to any existing scheme;

(b) warranties 7.2.1 to 7.3.1 that are applicable to all categories of pension arrangements;

(c) warranties 7.4.1, 7.5.1, 7.8.1, 7.9.1 and 7.10.1 that are applicable only to defined benefit (often referred to as final salary) arrangements; and finally

(d) warranties 7.6.1 and 7.7.1 that are applicable only to defined contribution (often referred to as money-purchase) arrangements.

Pension schemes are rarely presented in standard form. Each one will have its own specific issues arising from events occurring over a number of years. Each individual warranty should therefore be tailored according to the results of the due diligence process to relate to what has been disclosed and to the apportionment of risk that has been agreed between the parties.

The quantification of pension issues in monetary terms is difficult due to the complex nature of the arrangements, especially where defined benefit arrangements are concerned. Other professional advice may be required, in particular actuarial and other pensions consultancy advice, in order to fully understand the deficits or other potential or unfunded liabilities revealed by the due diligence process, that need to be addressed through a price reduction, an indemnity or a combination of these.

Aside from the technical issues affecting the schemes themselves and the obvious cost of resolving these issues, making changes to any pension arrangements as a result of or as part of a corporate transaction can give rise to employment contract disputes where pension rights are explicitly written into the employment contract, and human relations issues where the provision of defined pension benefits is not a contractual right. The effect on staff morale or productivity is often difficult to quantify and usually impossible to recover through any warranty claim given that the "loss" will usually arise as a result of actions taken by the purchaser after completion and there is usually a warranty limitation which will "carve out" any losses arising in such circumstances. A properly crafted indemnity can address the issue. The negotiation of an appropriate risk apportionment basis, in all but the most straightforward of cases, is not usually a quick process. The warranties below are not intended to specifically deal with target companies involved with public sector pension arrangements and, when dealing with target companies in this category, bespoke warranties would be required. Such companies would include companies that have undertaken outsourcing contracts for public authorities in consequence of which they may have:

(a) set up pension schemes that are broadly comparable to public sector schemes (such information would be elicited by warranty 7.1 below); or

(b) become participating employers ("admitted bodies") in the Local Government Pension Scheme (such information would be elicited by warranty 7.1, below); or

(c) may retain an obligation to fund, guarantee or indemnify pensions liabilities in connection with a public sector pension scheme (such information would be elicited by warranty 7.2.3, below)

7.1 No other pension arrangements (always include)

7.1.1 Save in respect of the Scheme, the Company has no legal obligation to provide or cause to be provided to any person benefits: 7–191

7.1.1.1 under a "pension scheme", as defined by s.150(1) of the FA 2004; or

7.1.1.2 under an "employer-financed retirement benefits scheme", as defined by s.393B of the IT(EP)A 2003; or

7.1.1.3 under a superannuation fund to which s.15(3) of the ICTA 1988 applies;

7.1.1.4 that are "retirement or death benefits" for the purposes of s.307 of the IT(EP)A 2003 and do not fall under the categories referred to in 7.1.1.1–7.1.1.3 above; or

7.1.1.5 that are "excluded benefits" for the purposes of s.393B of the IT(EP)A 2003 and do not fall under the categories above.

This is the most fundamental of the pensions-related warranties. It prompts disclosure of all known arrangements that may give rise to any pensions-related liabilities attaching to the target company which will then subsequently be defined in the definition of "Scheme" and for the purposes of this warranty will then serve to elicit disclosure of any other pension arrangements. The warranty is deliberately very wide in scope, covering all arrangements currently in operation and also any arrangements operated or participated in by the target at any time in the past under which any pension rights (and hence liabilities) may still exist.

7.2 Other company liabilities (always include)

7–192   **7.2.1 The Company is not subject to a contribution notice or a financial support direction or similar notice, order or direction under the Pensions Act 2004 nor [so far as the Vendors are aware] are there any circumstances which are likely to lead to such notices, orders or directions being imposed upon the Company.**

This warranty is concerned with liabilities that may attach to the target company independent of any pensions arrangements as a result of any action taken by the Pensions Regulator or the Pensions Protection Fund. The first part of this warranty is factual and should be straightforward for the vendors to disclose against. The second part of this warranty is more complex as the circumstances that may lead to action by the Pensions Regulator are many and varied. Consequently, the vendors may resist the second part of the warranty or prefer to qualify it by awareness.

7–193   **7.2.2 The Company has not entered into any agreement with either the trustees or the administrators of any pension arrangement or with any member of the same or any of its past or present employees or with any other party including any regulatory authority in respect of any potential or actual pension-related liability.**

This warranty is concerned with liabilities that may attach to the target company independently of any existing pensions arrangement as a result of agreements or compromises relating to the target company's previous pension arrangements or as a result of agreements and compromises relating to pension arrangements that were not operated by the target company but by third parties connected to the target company. It also covers any agreements or compromises reached with the Pensions Regulator or the Pensions Protection Fund.

7–194   **7.2.3 The Company has not entered into any agreement with any party to fund, indemnify or guarantee any potential or actual pension-related liability.**

This warranty is concerned with liabilities that may attach to the target company independently of any existing pensions arrangements as a result of agreements entered into to fund, indemnify or guarantee the pensions liabilities of third parties.

7.3 Additional member's rights

7–195   **7.3.1 No employee has at any time transferred to the Company under the provisions of the Transfer of Undertakings (Protection of Employment)**

Regulations 1981 or the Transfer of Undertakings (Protection of Employment) Regulations 2006.

7.3.2 If any such employee has transferred there are no circumstances in which such employee may have retained any pension rights from previous employment that do not fall within the categories of benefits relating to old age, survivorship or ill health and which have not been fully and appropriately provided for under the Company's pension arrangements.

These warranties are concerned with liabilities that may attach to the target company independent of any existing pensions arrangements as a result of the case law of the European Court of Justice beginning with the case of *Beckmann v Dynamco Whicheloe Macfarlane* [2002] All E.R. (EC) 865. The case law has established that occupational pension rights that do not relate to old age, survivorship and ill-health transfer to a purchaser in a TUPE transfer. These rights are generally known as "Beckmann" rights. As Beckmann rights are defined negatively, i.e. by reference to what they are not (namely not relating to old age, survivorship and ill-health), they form an open-ended category of rights. Consequently, such rights taken out of the context of their original pension arrangement (which did not pass under TUPE) are very difficult to identify, to quantify and to administer and can also give rise to complex employment disputes. They may include, for example, provisions providing for enhanced benefits on early retirement or on redundancy.

The first warranty seeks to identify factual circumstances in which Beckmann rights may potentially arise, and should be straightforward for the vendors to disclose against. The second warranty goes further in that it also covers circumstances where employees with Beckmann rights may have TUPE transferred to the target company and the vendors may be unaware of the Beckmann rights attaching to these individuals. Consequently, the vendors may resist the second part of the warranty or prefer to qualify it by awareness.

Should disclosures give rise to any likelihood of Beckmann rights being present an indemnity to cover the potential liabilities may be appropriate.

7.4 Stakeholder Compliance (always include)

7.4.1 The Company has at all times complied with all the requirements of s.3 of the Welfare Reform and Pensions Act 1999 in relation to the duty of employers to facilitate access to stakeholder pension schemes. 7–196

This warranty is concerned with liabilities that may attach to the target company independent of any existing pensions arrangements as a result of its failure to comply with its statutory obligations in relation to provision of stakeholder pension schemes. Whilst the obligation is to provide a stakeholder scheme in practice there is often little employee take up of such schemes and therefore the risks associated with non-compliance are usually insignificant. In practice, stakeholder issues rarely lead to the imposition of maximum fines (currently £50,000) and, in any event, the Pensions Regulator has adopted a practice of allowing new owners to resolve stakeholder issues provided this is done within a short time following completion.

The statutory requirement to facilitate access to a stakeholder pension scheme is due to fall away in October 2012, at which time employers will be required to auto-enrol employees into either the National Employment Savings Trust, a qualifying occupational pension scheme or a qualifying Workplace Personal Pension.

7.5 Full and accurate particulars (always include)

7–197 **7.5.1 Full, accurate and up to date particulars of the Scheme are set out in the Disclosure Letter, including (without limitation):**

7.5.1.1   all constitutional documents in relation to the Scheme including, where applicable, the trust deeds and rules together with any amendments and any related agreements;

7.5.1.2   all explanatory literature including, where applicable, booklets currently in force and any subsequent communications to members or employees who are or may become members of the Scheme;

7.5.1.3   evidence that the Scheme was an exempt approved scheme for the purposes of ICTA prior to April 6, 2006 and is a Registered Pension Scheme for the purposes of s.153 of the FA 2004 and have been registered with the Pensions Regulator for the purposes of s.59 of the Pensions Act 2004;

7.5.1.4   details of all active, deferred, pensioner and prospective members (including dates of birth, sex, age at joining the Scheme, and current pensionable pay, and name of employer);

7.5.1.5   details of all employee and all employer contributions in the last five years (including any statutory schedules of contributions or payments);

7.5.1.6   any insurance policies, schedules and certificates and details of all premiums paid in the last five years;

7.5.1.7   any correspondence with the Pensions Advisory Service or with regulatory authorities including, without limitation, the Occupational Pensions Regulatory Authority ("OPRA"), the Pensions Regulator, the Pensions Ombudsman, the Financial Services Authority or the Board of the Pension Protection Fund in relation to the Scheme;

7.5.1.8   details of all contracting-out certificates (including any schedules thereto) issued to the Company relating to the Scheme;

7.5.1.9   all letters or agreements for the appointment of professional advisers pursuant to s.47 of the Pensions Act 1995 and all

agreements with persons providing services of any nature in connection with the Scheme including, without limitation, administration and data processing services;

7.5.1.10   details of arrangements for the selection of trustees or directors of a trustee company in accordance with s.241 or s.242 of the Pensions Act 2004, including copies of any notices to members;

7.5.1.11   details of all past and present participating employers and copies of any compromise, apportionment or withdrawal agreements;

7.5.1.12   the latest actuarial valuation together with any subsequent correspondence with the Scheme's actuary, accounts and annual trustee report which together give a true and fair view of the state and method of funding of the Scheme and do not contain any material errors or omissions;

7.5.1.13   the statement of funding principles, the statement of investment principles and all investment agreements; and

7.5.1.14   the FRS17 or IAS19 disclosures in the Company's accounts for the last five years.

This warranty is concerned with obtaining all the information necessary for the purchaser to continue operating the pension arrangements of the target company post-completion. The ideal situation would be a seamless transition but this is rarely the case, often because of problems with the pension arrangements in existence prior to completion.

Warranty 7.5.1 requires full particulars as partial disclosure will likely lead to administrative errors and other practical difficulties. It requires accurate and up to date particulars in anticipation of there being problems with the pension arrangements in existence prior to completion. This warranty applies to all types of schemes.

Warranty 7.5.1.1 is concerned with obtaining the formal documentation of the pension arrangements whilst warranty 7.5.1.2 is concerned with establishing what the expectations of the employees may be and what custom and practice may have become. Both of these are important for resolving any disputes that may arise. This warranty applies to all types of scheme.

Warranty 7.5.1.3 is concerned with compliance with the tax regimes governing **7–198** pension schemes. This warranty applies to all types of scheme.

Warranties 7.5.1.4, 7.5.1.5 and 7.5.1.6 are concerned with gathering information about the immediate costs of running the scheme: the contributions normally payable. Warranty 7.5.1.6 is concerned mainly with insured occupational schemes, which tend to be final salary in nature, whilst the other two apply to all types of scheme.

Warranty 7.5.1.7 is concerned with eliciting any regulatory correspondence that may indicate existing or future compliance problems. This warranty applies to all types of scheme.

Warranty 7.5.1.8 is concerned with eliciting the contracted-out status of the scheme. This warranty applies to all types of scheme.

Warranties 7.5.1.9 and 7.5.1.10 are concerned with all occupational pension schemes rather than personal pension arrangements. These are intended to elicit factual matters relevant to the continued operation of the schemes.

Warranties 7.5.1.11 to 7.5.1.14 relate to occupational final salary arrangements only and are intended to elicit information concerning the longer-term liabilities of the scheme.

Whilst these warranties appear burdensome at first sight, it should be fairly straightforward for the vendors to disclose the relevant information having made appropriate enquiries of the target company's advisors. Some of the information may be held by the trustees of any occupational schemes. Difficulties may arise if the trustees have not been informed of the proposed transaction and if they are not meant to be informed. Maintaining confidentiality may make disclosure impossible. In such cases, comprehensive indemnities would be appropriate.

7.6 Member details (always include)

7–199   **7.6.1 [So far as the Vendors are aware] the membership data in respect of the Scheme is complete, accurate and up to date in all material respects and is stored safely.**

This warranty is designed to flush out practical issues in relation to membership data which often constitute a source of dispute between the various parties involved in pension arrangements. Where membership data is incomplete, significant issues may arise that take considerable expense, financially and in terms of management time, to resolve. Vendors might, with some justification, be reluctant to warrant all details as membership data is as a rule dealt with by third parties such as trustees of pension schemes and scheme administrators. At the very least they might wish to make the warranty subject to their awareness.

7.7 Taxation Status (always include)

7–200   **7.7.1 The Scheme was an exempt approved scheme between the date of establishment of the Scheme and April 5, 2006 inclusive, within the meaning of Ch.I Pt XIV ICTA 1988 (as was in force from time to time) and is, since April 6, 2006, a Registered Pension Scheme for the purposes of s.153 of the FA 2004 and have also been registered with the Pensions Regulator for the purposes of s.59 of the Pensions Act 2004 and [so far as the Vendors are aware] there is no reason why such exempt approved status or registered status may be lost or withdrawn.**

This warranty aims to confirm that the target company's pension arrangements have been registered with the appropriate regulatory authorities for the purpose of tax efficiency and compliance. Non-registered arrangements may give rise to complex tax issues due to the lack of a comprehensive compliance regime. The vendors should be able to establish the factual status of the schemes with some ease. The latter part of the warranty is more problematic and in most cases will be beyond the vendors' knowledge. Most vendors would therefore wish to qualify the latter part by their awareness. Assuming that the obligations on the vendors, as far as satisfying any "awareness" requirement, include the need to make enquiry of relevant advisers, then the purchaser should be prepared to accept the qualification.

7.8 Proposed amendments to the Scheme (always include)

7.8.1 No proposal has been announced by the Company either: 7–201

    7.8.1.1   **to modify, amend, alter or improve the Scheme that does not form part of the Scheme's constitutional documents as at Completion; or**

    7.8.1.2   **regarding the continuation of the Scheme, or its closure to new members, or its closure to new benefit accruals, or its discontinuance or winding-up.**

7.8.2 Since the Balance Sheet Date the Scheme has not been modified, amended, altered or improved and no closure to new members, cessation or accruals or commencement of winding-up in relation to the Scheme has been prepared or commenced.

This warranty aims to identify any changes to the target company's pension arrangements which have occurred since the Balance Sheet Date perhaps with a view to grooming the target company for sale, and which may directly or indirectly increase the liabilities of the pension arrangements or of the target company. This warranty is particularly important where the pension arrangements are occupational and defined benefit in nature, although it remains relevant for defined contribution schemes if an increase in employer's contributions has been announced.

7.9 Trustees (always include)

7.9.1 The trustees of the Scheme have all been properly appointed and have   7–202
at all times administered the Scheme properly and in accordance with all relevant laws and regulations.

7.9.2 The persons named in the Disclosure Letter as the trustees of the Scheme are all its present trustees and not less than one third of the trustees are member-nominated trustees (or member-nominated directors of a corporate trustee) appointed in accordance with either s.241 or s.242 of the Pensions Act 2004 and regulations made thereunder.

This warranty concerns only occupational pension schemes and not contract-based pension schemes. It is intended to produce a general statement of compliance with the detailed and complex legislation governing pension schemes. It is likely that vendors would seek to resist such a wide-ranging warranty as very few schemes have complied with all the legislation all the time. This warranty is also designed to identify the trustees and to ensure they have fulfilled their obligations, including that the member-nominated trustee provisions of the Pensions Act 2004 s.241 have been complied with. If the trustee is a body corporate then reference instead should be made to the member-nominated director provisions of the Pensions Act 2004 s.242.

7.10 Appointments (always include)

7–203   **7.10.1 The trustees of the Scheme have made written appointments of an auditor, an actuary, a fund manager, a legal adviser and any other professional adviser whose appointment is required to be made under s.47 of the Pensions Act 1995 and they do not rely upon the advice of an adviser not so appointed by them in relation to the Scheme.**

This warranty concerns only occupational pension schemes and not contract-based pension schemes. It aims to confirm that appropriate appointments of advisers are in place, the lack of which may indicate that the target company's pension arrangements may have undiagnosed problems.

7.11 No disputes (always include)

7–204   **7.11.1 No claim or investigation has been threatened or made against the Company or the trustees or administrators of the Scheme (other than routine claims for benefits) or against any other person whom the Company is or the said trustees or administrators are or may be liable to pay, indemnify or compensate in respect of any matter arising out of or in connection with the Scheme, nor are there any circumstances which may give rise to any such claim.**

7.11.2 No civil or criminal penalty, fine or sanction has been imposed on the Company or on the trustees or administrators of the Scheme in relation to the Scheme and there are no circumstances which might give rise to any such penalty.

This warranty concerns both occupational pension schemes and contract-based pension schemes and is designed to identify potential disputes. It is reasonable for the purchaser to be made aware of these matters and the vendors should be willing to give this warranty. The vendors may only express reluctance to warrant that "there are no circumstances which might give rise" to any penalty fine or sanction, as this is a very wide provision. Most well-advised vendors would qualify this warranty with their awareness.

7.12 Scheme operated properly (always include)

7–205   **7.12.1 The Scheme has been operated at all times in accordance with all applicable laws, regulations and requirements of any competent governmental body or regulatory authority and its governing documentation and any notifiable events and material breaches of the law have been appropriately notified to the Pensions Regulator or the appropriate regulatory authority, or if not material, all breaches of the law have been appropriately recorded and rectified.**

This warranty concerns both occupational pension schemes and contract-based pension schemes. It is a very wide ranging warranty which in most cases the vendors will be reluctant to provide on an unqualified basis. Where the trustees of the scheme are independent of the company enquiry should be made of them. In most cases a qualified warranty coupled with an obligation on the vendors to make appropriate enquiry should be sufficient for the purchaser.

7.13 Contracting Out (always include)

7.13.1 Where the Scheme is contracted out a fully up to date and correct contracting-out certificate (including schedules thereto) has been properly obtained and maintained.   7–206

This warranty concerns occupational pension schemes and not contract-based pension schemes where contracting-out operates (if at all) on an entirely individual basis. This warranty aims to confirm that the correct contracting-out certificates have been obtained in respect of the target company's pension arrangements. If the contracting-out of any pension arrangement has not been correctly put in place then tax issues may arise with HMRC and retrospective National Insurance contributions may be reclaimed by HMRC and penalties imposed. In most cases the vendor should be able to establish the factual basis to enable this warranty to be given.

It is to be noted that contracting-out for the purposes of defined contribution schemes is due to be abolished in October 2012.

7.14 Non discrimination (always include)

7.14.1 No discrimination on ground of sex, disability, marital status, hours of work, fixed-term or temporary agency workers, sexual orientation, religion or belief is, or has at any stage been, made in the provision of pension, lump sum, death, ill-health, disability or accident benefits by the trustees or administrators of the Scheme or by the Company.   7–207

This warranty mainly concerns occupational pension schemes but also applies to contract-based schemes. It aims to confirm that there is no risk of any discrimination claims arising in relation to the target company's pension arrangements. The vendors will usually seek to negate the absolute risk of this warranty by qualifying it by awareness and relying on the advice of the pension advisers.

7.15 Insurance (always include)

7.15.1 All lump sums held in relation to the Scheme (other than normal pension benefits) are securely and fully insured with a reputable insurance company and all premiums due in respect of such insurance has been paid.   7–208

This warranty mainly concerns occupational pension schemes and not contract-based schemes. It aims to confirm that all liabilities for which it is appropriate to seek insurance cover are fully insured. If no or inappropriate cover is in place an unexpected liability may fall on the target company.

7.16 Fees and charges (always include)

7–209   **7.16.1 All actuarial, consultancy, legal and other charges and fees in respect of the Scheme, whether payable by the Company or by the trustees or administrators of the Scheme, have been paid and no services have been rendered in respect of the Scheme in relation to which an account or other invoice has not been rendered.**

This warranty mainly concerns occupational pension schemes but also applies to contract-based schemes. It aims to confirm that there are no outstanding fees payable to service providers. In most cases this will just involve the vendors checking the position and providing appropriate disclosures.

7.17 Employer related investments (defined benefit schemes only)

7–210   **7.17.1 The assets of the Scheme are held securely and do not include employer-related investments (as defined in s.40 of the Pensions Act 1995).**

This warranty concerns only occupational pension schemes and not contract-based schemes. Section 40 prohibits over-investment in property or shares related to the employer. The mischief which s.40 seeks to address is that if the Scheme holds employer-related assets and the employer suffers an event such that, for example, its shares become worthless, pension scheme members may suffer a double disadvantage. In the case of insolvency, for example, they lose their employment and suffer because the asset holding under the pension scheme has become less valuable. The sanctions for breach of s.40 include the imposition of fines and, in certain circumstances, imprisonment. In limited circumstances, employer-related investments are allowed and the vendors should reasonably be required to disclose any permissible employer-related investments against this warranty.

7.18 Scheme surpluses and refunds (defined benefit schemes only)

7–211   **7.18.1 No refunds of surplus have been made to and no contribution holidays have been taken for the benefit of the Company or any other person in relation to the Scheme.**

This warranty concerns only defined benefit occupational pension schemes and not contract-based schemes. It aims to identify any refunds of surplus to the target company and any contribution holidays that the target company may have taken. This information will enable the purchaser to assess whether the target company has historically borne the true cost of pension provision and whether its financial performance has been enhanced either by a refund of surplus or a holiday from contribution. In certain circumstances, the funding history of the arrangement may be pertinent when considering the likelihood of the imposition of a contribution notice or a financial support direction by the Pensions Regulator under the Pensions Act 2004.

7.19 Discretions and powers (always include)

7.19.1 No discretion or power has been exercised under the Scheme in respect of a member (whether active, deferred or a pensioner) (or a beneficiary claiming through or under a member) to augment any of the benefits provided by the Scheme; admit to membership of the Scheme a director or employee who would not otherwise have been eligible for admission to membership; provide in respect of a member a benefit which would not otherwise be provided under the Scheme in respect of the member or pay a contribution to it which would not otherwise have been paid.   7–212

7.19.2 No undertaking, assurance or intimation has been given to any person pursuant to which such a discretion or power will or may be exercised.

These warranties concern only defined benefit occupational pension schemes and not contract-based schemes. They are designed to identify special treatment for certain categories of members and to flush out any assurances made, even if not properly recorded, as these could give rise to industrial relations problems, if unfulfilled, or greater funding requirements. Again the vendors should be able to give the warranty by checking the terms of it with their pension advisers.

7.20 Contributions paid (always include)

7.20.1 All contributions payable by the Company and every other participating employer in accordance with the terms of the Scheme or under the relevant contractual obligations to the employees in order to secure or provide for the benefits for and in respect of members (including pensioners, deferred members and other persons prospectively or contingently entitled to benefit under it) have been duly paid to the Scheme in good time and to the proper parties who should receive them.   7–213

This warranty concerns both occupational pension schemes and contract-based pension schemes. If there is a history of non-payment of contributions the purchaser should be made aware of this. Non-payment may have led to employment disputes and may have been notified to the Pensions Regulator. Non-payment, or even late or incorrect payment, can lead to particular problems in respect of money purchase schemes, so for those schemes this warranty is of added importance.

7.21 Benefits payable (defined benefit schemes only)

7.21.1 The benefits payable under the Scheme consist exclusively of money-purchase benefits as defined in s.152(4) of the FA 2004 and no assurance, promise or guarantee (whether oral or written) has been made or given to   7–214 any employee of any particular level or amount of benefits (other than insured lump sum death in service benefits) to be provided for or in respect of him or her under the Scheme on retirement, death or leaving service.

This warranty concerns both occupational pension schemes and contract-based pension schemes. The purpose of this warranty is to obtain confirmation of the nature of the scheme. In particular, it seeks to flush out defined benefit schemes by asking the Vendors to confirm that the scheme or schemes are defined contribution in nature. Whether a scheme is "money purchase" for the purposes of applicable legislation is a matter that has given rise to a number of complex cases before the courts. Schemes that are apparently "money purchase" can have obscure characteristics such as ancillary promises based on targets or salary levels that would prevent the scheme from being categorised as a pure money-purchase scheme. Where this happens, debt on an employer may be triggered in the same way as with a final salary arrangement.

7.22 Assets sufficient (defined benefit schemes only)

7–215   **7.22.1 The assets, investments and insurance policies held by the trustees or administrators of the Scheme are sufficient to satisfy the liabilities and obligations (both actual and contingent) of the Scheme as at Completion [on the basis or bases adopted in the latest actuarial valuation of the Scheme] [on the basis of purchase of deferred annuity policies on a full buy-out basis].**

This warranty only applies to defined benefit arrangements and seeks to confirm that the assets are sufficient to meet the arrangements' liabilities. It would be an unusual defined benefit arrangement, in the current climate, that would satisfy this criteria and the vendors should be very cautious about giving such assurance. In preference, the vendors should produce and warrant factual information regarding the value of the scheme, on such basis as would allow the purchaser and its actuary to be able to reach their own conclusions on the ability of the scheme to satisfy the required liabilities.

7.23 Debts arising (defined benefit schemes only)

7–216   **7.23.1 No debt on the employer obligations have arisen on the Company (nor are there any circumstances likely to create the conditions under which such obligations will arise) under s.75 of the Pensions Act 1995 or under s.222 of the Pensions Act 2004.**

This warranty only applies to defined benefit arrangements and is designed to identify whether or not there is any possibility of a debt on employer liability under s.75 arising. Such a debt could result from its previous participation in an arrangement which later winds up in deficit. Since the warranty deals with the possibility of a debt arising, the vendors might seek to qualify it by awareness.

7.24 Bulk transfers (defined benefit schemes only)

**7.24.1 There are no individual or bulk payments due to the trustees or   7–217
administrators of the Scheme which have not, at Completion been received
by the trustees or administrators of the Scheme.**

This warranty applies in the relatively rare and specialised circumstances where
a transaction involves a bulk transfer between pension arrangements. Practical
difficulties are often encountered when such payments are delayed by
administrative issues, such difficulties being much more difficult to resolve after
completion as the control of the pension arrangements may have altered.

8 Assets

8.1 Ownership of assets

**8.1.1 All assets included in the Accounts or acquired by the Company since   7–218
the Balance Sheet Date and all [tangible] assets owned by the Company
are:**

> **8.1.1.1   legally and beneficially owned by the Company free from any
> Encumbrance;**
>
> **8.1.1.2   in the possession or under the exclusive control of the
> Company;**
>
> **8.1.1.3   situated in the United Kingdom; and**
>
> **8.1.1.4   where subject to a requirement for a Licence, duly licensed or
> registered in the sole name of the Company.**

The vendors should consider whether the properties owned by the target
company should be excluded from this clause, as normally separate extensive
warranties will apply in relation to them (see Ch.6). Furthermore, it is possible
that many assets as shown in the last accounts will be subject to reservation of
title clauses in view of the guidance statement issued by the Consultative
Committee of Accountancy Bodies in September 1976. This recommended that,
where the circumstances indicate that the reservation of title is regarded by the
parties as having no practical relevance except in the event of insolvency, it
would prevent the accounts showing a true and fair view if the stock subject to
reservation of title were omitted from the balance sheet of the purchasing
customer. Normally a note in the accounts would explain the position. Another
relevant point is that equipment leased on finance leases will usually be shown
as assets under SSAP 21.

The vendors should consider separately each asset appearing in the last
accounts to determine whether this warranty can fairly be given in respect of it.
They should be alert to the possibility of property being occupied by a company
but owned by trustees of a directors' pension arrangement. As debts are normally
covered by a separate group of warranties, it would be preferable for the vendors
to exclude them from this clause and, indeed, to amend the wording by the
inclusion of the word "tangible" so that intangible assets generally are not
included.

8.2 Assets sufficient for the business

7–219   **8.2.1 The assets owned by the Company, together with the Intellectual Property Rights owned or validly licensed to and assets held under the hire purchase, leasing and rental agreements in each case listed in the Disclosure Letter, comprise all assets necessary for the continuation of its business [for a period of [   ] from Completion in substantially the same manner] as now carried on [and on the assumption that it was carried on by the Vendors], and no assets are shared with another person.**

The first part of this clause involves matters of judgment, and its accuracy will be tested only by the conduct of the business of the target company after completion. The vendors would therefore normally be reluctant to accept it and, if they did so, they will wish to insert the wording in brackets. The final part is concerned with matters of fact and ought not pose a difficulty to the vendors.

8.3 Stocks and work in progress

7–220   **8.3.1 The stocks of raw materials, packaging materials and finished goods held by the Company are not [in the Vendors' opinion] excessive and are adequate in relation to its current trading requirements and [so far as the Vendors are aware], save where written down or provided for, none of such stock is obsolete, slow moving, unusable, in poor condition, defective, unmarketable or inappropriate or of limited value in relation to the current business of the Company.**

As with cl.8.2.1, this provision is largely subjective and its accuracy will be tested only once the purchaser has control of the target company. The vendors should accept the warranty only in so far as the matters covered have been taken into account in the negotiations determining the consideration paid for the target company, save in circumstances where there is a stock valuation mechanism included in the sale agreement pursuant to which the quality and quantity of stock is to be determined by the parties (or representatives of them), in which case warranties such as this and that at cl.8.3.3 will generally be inappropriate (as the matters that they cover will be addressed as necessary in the stock valuation procedure).

If the vendors are required to give the warranty then they should seek to include the wording in brackets:

7–221   **8.3.2 [So far as the Vendors are aware] the work in progress of the Company is adequate to maintain cash flow and profitability at a level not less than that Disclosed.**

The precise wording of this warranty will depend upon the form of any cash flow and profit projections which have been produced to the purchaser. If the terms of the acquisition have been negotiated on the basis of projections, both the purchaser and the vendors will wish to consider carefully what representations should be warranted in relation to them. This clause deals only with a limited aspect and might serve as a pointer to a suitable warranty. If projections have not been made or, if made, have not formed a basis for negotiating terms, the vendors should resist giving the warranty.

8.3.3 The stock in trade of the Company is in good condition and is   7–222
capable of being sold by it in the normal course of its business in accordance
with its current price list, without rebate or allowance to a purchaser.

Again, this is a subjective question and the vendors would generally prefer the purchaser to satisfy itself by inspection. See also comments at cl.8.3.1. As drafted, the warranty will in all normal circumstances be far too onerous to be acceptable without substantial qualification.

8.4 Insurance

8.4.1 All the assets of the Company of an insurable nature are, and have at   7–223
all material times [since the Balance Sheet Date] been, insured in amounts
representing their full replacement or reinstatement value against fire and
other risks normally insured against by persons carrying on similar
businesses or owning property of a similar nature.

The interest of the purchaser is to ensure that no loss of assets has occurred since the balance sheet date which is not fully covered by insurance. It would therefore be appropriate for this warranty to relate only to circumstances since that date by including the wording in brackets. The vendors might have difficulty in satisfying themselves as to what is the full replacement or reinstatement value of assets and what risks are normally covered by insurance by persons carrying on similar businesses. An alternative approach to this warranty, therefore, is for the vendors to produce particulars of all insurance to the purchaser with a warranty that the particulars are correct and that the policies are in force. Provided that the purchaser has sufficient time to review the policies, it would be reasonable to accept this alternative. In such circumstances the following wording would be appropriate:

"True, complete and accurate particulars of all insurance and indemnity
policies in respect of which the Company has an interest are attached to the
Disclosure Letter; all the insurances are in force [and will be maintained in
force without alteration pending completion] and all premiums have been
paid on time."

The wording in square brackets would be appropriate if exchange of contracts and completion were not going to be simultaneous.

8.4.2 The Company is, and has at all material times been, adequately   7–224
insured against accident, damage, third party loss (including product
liability), loss of profits and other risks normally insured against by persons
carrying on the same type of business as that carried on by it.

This is an extension of cl.8.4.1 and similar comments apply. Given the subjective nature of this warranty most vendors would be reluctant to provide it on an unqualified basis. In most cases the levels of insurance will have been determined by a combination of advice received, premiums payable and the vendors' appetite for risk. The warranty ought to be tailored to reflect this.

7–225   **8.4.3 Nothing has been done or omitted or has occurred which could make a policy of insurance taken out by the Company void or voidable or which is likely to result in an increase in premium.**

An insurance contract will generally be void if there is a fundamental mistake of fact relating to the contract (such as the non-existence of the asset purportedly insured), if the contract is illegal, if the contract is in the nature of a gaming contract or if the insured has no insurable interest. A policy is voidable if it is obtained by misrepresentation or non-disclosure of material facts. While it would normally be reasonable for the vendors to accept responsibility for the policies not being void or voidable, it is generally unreasonable for them to be required to warrant that nothing has occurred which could lead to a rise in premium. If the purchaser insists on the inclusion of this wording, the vendors might restrict the warranty to circumstances where the insurance company has intimated that an increase of premium will result from events which have occurred.

7–226   **8.4.4 None of the insurance policies is subject to special or unusual terms or restrictions or to the payment of a premium in excess of the normal rate.**

This clause involves matters of judgment and the vendors cannot readily satisfy themselves as to whether the position stated in the warranty is correct. They should decline to give the warranty and instead ask the purchaser to inspect the policies and determine for itself whether the terms of them are unusual or the premiums excessive.

7–227   **8.4.5 No claim is outstanding, threatened or may be made, under any of the policies and [so far as the Vendors are aware] no circumstances exist which could give rise to a claim.**

On the face of it this is a reasonable warranty to request and give, although it may not be easy for the vendors to be sure what circumstances fall within the scope of the second half of the warranty. They might therefore wish to include the wording in brackets. Nevertheless, it is unclear as to what disadvantage the purchaser would suffer if the warranty were breached. So long as the insurance cover is satisfactory, there will be no financial loss. Any inconvenience caused to the business of the target company in the circumstances giving rise to a claim will generally be covered by other warranties.

8.5 Leased assets

7–228   **8.5.1 The Company is not a party to or liable under a lease or hire, hire purchase, credit sale or conditional sale agreement. Nothing has occurred**

[or is likely to occur] in relation to an asset held by the Company, under a lease or similar agreement, whereby the rental payable has been[, or is likely to be,] increased.

It is customary for finance leases of plant and equipment to include a tax adjustment clause providing for an increase in the rental in certain circumstances. The main events normally giving rise to an increase are a change in the corporation tax rate or in the extent of the capital allowances and accordingly the warranty should be acceptable in relation to past events. The vendors should delete the words in brackets.

8.6 *Plant in working order*

8.6.1 The plant, machinery, vehicles and other equipment used in connection with the business of the Company: 7–229

8.6.1.1   are [subject to normal wear and tear] in a good and safe state of repair and satisfactory working order [taking into account their age, use and value] and have been properly serviced and maintained;

This clause, even when qualified by the words in the first set of square brackets, is onerous. With the addition of the words in the second set of square brackets it becomes less onerous and the vendors will be more inclined to give it. Whether the vendors will be obliged to give the warranty will depend upon the circumstances of the transaction and the bargaining position of the parties. It is usually desirable from the point of view of both parties that the purchaser should inspect the premises of the target company and satisfy itself, so far as possible, as to the state of repair and condition of the equipment.

8.6.1.2   are not surplus to requirements;   7–230

The purchaser cannot reasonably object to surplus plant unless the purchase price is based upon the asset value of the target company. In any case, it is likely to be a difficult matter of judgment to decide whether plant is surplus at any given moment and the vendors will generally find this clause unacceptable. It is difficult to see how the purchaser could suffer loss in most cases.

8.6.1.3   are in the possession and control of, and are the absolute unencumbered property of, the Company, except for those items the subject of the hire purchase, leasing or rental agreements listed in the Disclosure Letter, and in respect of each of which the outstanding payments do not exceed £[   ]; and   7–231

This warranty is largely a question of fact and the vendors should, in principle, have no difficulty with giving it.

7–232   **8.6.1.4   [So far as the Vendors are aware and on the assumption that the Company carries on its business in the same manner as carried on prior to Completion] are not expected to require replacements or additions at a cost in excess of £[   ] within the next six months.**

It is difficult for the vendors to satisfy themselves in connection with this warranty and they should take into account the fact that any need to replace or add to equipment after completion will largely be within the control of the purchaser. The vendors are likely to find this clause acceptable only if the value of the plant has been taken into account in determining the purchase consideration for the shares being sold. With the inclusion of the words in brackets the warranty becomes more acceptable from the vendors' perspective although even with the awareness qualification the vendors ought to consider a disclosure against this warranty that they have not arranged an inspection or survey of the relevant plant and equipment (or to seek to make it clear that their obligation to make enquiry into the subject matter of the warranty does not include an obligation to inspect or survey the relevant plant and equipment by adding after "So far as the Vendors are aware" the words:

" . . . **(but without having undertaken or commissioned any inspection or survey of the relevant plant and equipment)"**)

if in fact that is the case.

7–233   **8.6.2 There are maintenance contracts with independent specialist contractors in respect of all assets of the Company for which it is normal or prudent to have maintenance agreements and in respect of all assets which the Company is obliged to maintain or repair under a lease or similar agreement.**

This warranty can be dealt with more satisfactorily from the vendors' point of view by producing copies of all maintenance contracts to the purchaser and warranting that they are in force. An appropriate warranty in such circumstances would be:

"Copies of all maintenance contracts in place in respect of the assets of the Company are attached to the Disclosure Letter and all such contracts are in force."

Alternatively the warranty could be amended to make it clear that the company has maintenance agreements in force for those assets which the vendors consider it prudent or necessary to do so taking account of the age, condition and value of the relevant assets and the use to which they are put.

8.7 Assets Register

8.7.1 The asset register of the Company attached to this Disclosure Letter comprise a true, complete and accurate record of all plant, machinery, equipment and vehicles owned, held or used by the Company. 7–234

The purpose of this warranty is to elicit disclosure of the target company's asset register. This is usually a request which can be easily satisfied whether it is provided directly by the target company or its accountants.

8.8 Intellectual Property Rights

In seeking intellectual property warranties, the purchaser has two primary objectives. First, to ensure that it understands fully the strength of the intellectual property portfolio (such as the technical and geographical scope of the rights, their validity and enforceability, whether or not the rights may be subject to attack and the strength of competing third party registered rights). Secondly, to understand fully the existing potential liabilities which have been or may be incurred by the target company as a result of the past and continued use of the intellectual property rights. 7–235

If the value of the intellectual property rights of the target company are particularly significant to the purchaser (for example, in the case of technology companies), the purchaser may require more extensive and comprehensive intellectual property warranties including specific warranties pertinent to particular intellectual property rights. In such circumstances the purchaser might also consider it appropriate to undertake its own assessment as to the technical and commercial value of the intellectual property rights.

If applications for registered intellectual property rights have significant potential commercial value the purchaser may also wish to extend the warranties relating to such applications.

8.8.1 Full details of all Intellectual Property Rights owned by the Company are set out in the Disclosure Letter and are complete and accurate. The Intellectual Property Rights are: 7–236

    8.8.1.1   **used exclusively in the business of the Company;**

    8.8.1.2   **legally and beneficially owned by the Company and not held jointly or in common with any other person;**

    8.8.1.3   **valid, subsisting and enforceable and nothing has been done or omitted to be done by which they may cease to be valid and enforceable;**

    8.8.1.4   **not subject to infringement, challenge, opposition or attack or the subject of any claim for ownership or compensation by any third party or competent authority and the Vendors know of no reason why any of them may be subject to challenge, opposition or attack or claim; and**

    8.8.1.5   **where capable of registration are registered in the name of the Company in all jurisdictions relevant to its business.**

This warranty is intended to deal with all intellectual property rights owned by the target company, whether or not registered, rather than any third party intellectual property rights which are licensed to the target company and which are dealt with in cl.8.8.4. The definition of intellectual property rights is very wide and as such the vendors may wish to limit their obligations to registered intellectual property rights and material unregistered intellectual property rights.

The purchaser will want assurance that all intellectual property rights owned by the target company are valid. However, this is an onerous warranty which many vendors will refuse to give. They will argue that they are not in a position to say whether or not intellectual property rights may be invalid for technical or other reasons and so will seek the deletion of cl.8.8.1.3. However, the vendors will normally agree to warrant that intellectual property rights have not been subject to any challenge or attack and that they know of no reason why they should be. They are, however, likely to object to the inclusion of cl.8.8.15 on the basis that in order to be able to give the warranty (or alternatively make appropriate disclosures) they would have to undertake an assessment of which, if any, of the target company's intellectual property rights are capable of registration, and determine which jurisdictions they need to be registered in. The vendors will argue that they will have to disclose under cl.8.8.1 details of the intellectual property rights that the company has and identify which of them are registered and that, armed with this information, the purchaser will be able to assess the position for itself.

7–237   **8.8.2 The renewal and registration fees for the protection of the registered Intellectual Property Rights have been paid [and all other steps required for their prosecution, maintenance and protection have been taken].**

If intellectual property rights are particularly valuable to the purchaser then this clause could be expanded to cover specific types of intellectual property. For example, in respect of patent applications, the warranty could state that there has been no prior disclosure of the claimed invention except under obligations of confidence, or, in relation to trade marks, that the trade marks have not lost their distinctiveness and are therefore not liable to attack. The vendors may resist the inclusion of the wording in brackets on the basis that such steps are already adequately covered by cl.8.8.7.

7–238   **8.8.3 The Vendors are not aware of any factors which would cause any applications for registration of any Intellectual Property Rights to be unacceptable to any body to whom the application is being made.**

The vendors will wish to restrict this warranty to specific actual applications to specific bodies, and to disclose any and all known problems. If the purchaser does not wish to bear the risk that the applications will not succeed for reasons unknown to the vendors, this warranty may be made absolute rather than subject to the vendors' knowledge, although the vendors are likely to object to that.

8.8.4 Copies of the licences of Intellectual Property Rights owned by third parties which have been granted to the Company are attached to the Disclosure Letter. The Company is not in breach of any of the licences and the Vendors are not aware of and have no reason to believe that there is cause for a licence to come to an end or be restricted. 7–239

The vendors will want to limit this warranty solely to licences expressly granted to the target company, rather than to any implied licence of intellectual property rights such as those granted in relation to goods which embody protected rights. The purchaser will resist this if the target company is in fact using third party intellectual property rights where the licence ought to be express but, for example, the target company has no written evidence of the grant. Even if restricted to express licences only, the warranty may still extend to a significant number of agreements, that are not material in the context of the transaction, such as standard packaged software licences. In large transactions the vendors may wish to limit the obligation to disclose licences to those which are "material" to the business. In such a case materiality should extend not only to the amount of fees or licence payments but also to licences of low monetary value, the enjoyment of which is critical to the business of the target company. The vendors may also wish to exclude from the warranty off-the-shelf software licences, which may be dealt with as a separate category under the computer systems warranties.

The vendors may find it difficult to be sure that the target company is not in breach of all licence agreements and may, therefore, seek to limit the clause such that the target company has not received any notice or claim of any breach of any such agreements.

8.8.5 Copies of the licences of Intellectual Property Rights owned by the Company which have been granted to third parties are attached to the Disclosure Letter. The Company is not in breach of any of the licences and the Vendors are not aware and have no reason to believe that there is cause for a licence to come to an end or be restricted. 7–240

Again, the vendors may wish to limit this warranty to material licences, and also to those which are subsisting.

8.8.6 The Intellectual Property Rights referred to in clause [8.8.1] and detailed in the Disclosure Letter and the third party Intellectual Property Rights referred to in clause [8.8.4] are all the Intellectual Property Rights necessary for the Company to carry on its business [(on the assumption that the Company carries on its business in the same manner as carried on in the 12 month period prior to Completion)] and the Company has not charged or encumbered or created any equity, lien or other adverse interest over any of them or agreed to grant an option, right licence, sub-licence or other adverse right over any of them to any other person and is not obliged to do the same. 7–241

If not all licences of intellectual property are disclosed, the purchaser may want this clause extended by the inclusion of the words:

"None of the licences of third party Intellectual Property Rights referred to in clause [8.8.4] is subject to a restriction or right of termination".

The vendors will prefer to see the inclusion of the wording in brackets so as to make it clear that the warranty is confined to intellectual property rights that the company has used during the last 12 months and not any intellectual property rights that it might ever have used or required. If this wording is accepted by the purchaser, it will probably want to insert the words:

" . . . and to satisfy all existing obligations and arrangements of the Company"

after the end of the vendors' wording so as to ensure that the warranty extends to intellectual property rights that are required to satisfy existing contracts.

7–242   **8.8.7 [So far as the Vendors are aware] none of the activities of the Company, its products, business methods, processes or services infringe third party Intellectual Property Rights. In the past six years the Company has not been a party or received a threat of litigation or a claim relating to Intellectual Property Rights or passing off. The Vendors are not aware and have no reason to believe that a third party is infringing the Intellectual Property Rights of the Company or that the Company has acquiesced to an infringement.**

This warranty is very far reaching and it is likely that the vendors will, as a minimum, wish to have the first sentence made subject to their knowledge by inclusion of the wording in brackets, if not deleted. The third element of the clause is effectively similarly qualified but the vendors should ensure that the wording is no broader than any definition agreed in respect of "awareness". To ascertain whether the company is infringing third party intellectual property rights, or a third party is infringing the company's, the vendors would need to undertake investigations, for example searching for names similar to those of the target company at the Companies House Registry, in the phone book and on the internet. Even then they may not be able to identify an infringement. In reality, the vendors are not going to want to be under an obligation to undertake searches and accordingly they are likely to want to limit their obligation to make enquiry in the context of this warranty such that they do not have to do so.

7–243   **8.8.8 No licences of Intellectual Property Rights will terminate or become capable of termination or otherwise be adversely affected by this Agreement.**

This clause deals with the potential termination of intellectual property rights. In most cases the main benefit of the warranty is one of reminder for the vendors to address the issue and check its relevance.

8.8.9 There are no pending or outstanding claims against the Company for   7–244
compensation under the Patents Act 1977 s.40.

The Patents Act 1977 s.40 provides for compensation to be payable if an
employee makes an invention which is of outstanding benefit to his employer.
Whilst awards of compensation have been extremely rare, if the vendors are in
any doubt as to whether or not this warranty could apply they should seek to
include a suitable disclosure in the disclosure letter.

8.8.10 The Confidential Business Information which has been developed   7–245
by or acquired by the Company has been kept secret and has not been
disclosed to or used by another person except under obligations of
confidentiality. The Vendors are not aware and have no reason to believe
that a third party is in breach of any confidentiality obligations.

The first sentence of this clause is far reaching given the definition of
"Confidential Business Information". The vendors may wish to exclude
information which is over a certain age, perhaps which is more than five years
old, on the basis that such information is unlikely to be of significant commercial
value and is likely to have entered the public domain. However, where some or
all of the matters encompassed by the definition are particularly valuable, this
exclusion would be inappropriate and should be resisted by the purchaser. The
vendors may also want to exclude any information required to be disclosed to
professional advisers or by law or regulatory authority. Where the target
company contracts with the public sector, there is a risk that confidential
information held by the public body may be disclosed pursuant to a request under
the Freedom of Information Act 2000. In such circumstances, the purchaser may
wish to extend the warranty to provide:

"The Company has taken all reasonable steps to ensure the non-disclosure
of Confidential Business Information supplied to any public authority
subject to the Freedom of Information Act 2000".

8.8.11 The Company is not a party to a secrecy agreement or other   7–246
agreement or arrangement which restricts the use or disclosure of
confidential information.

The vendors may wish to exclude from the warranty restrictions within the
commercial agreements of the target company which have already been disclosed
to the purchaser so as to reduce the disclosure burden.

8.8.12 [So far as the Vendors are aware] all moral rights in respect of the   7–247
Intellectual Property Rights have been waived in favour of the Company.

Under English law, moral rights consist of the right to be identified as the author
of a work (paternity right), the right to not have a work subjected to derogatory
treatment (integrity right), the right not to have a work falsely attributed to

another person (right against false attribution) and the right to privacy of photographs and films commissioned for private and domestic purposes (privacy right). Moral rights may be infringed unless the right-holder has consented to the act, waived his rights by a signed instrument in writing, or the act is permitted under the relevant provisions of the Copyright Designs and Patents Act 1988. Moral rights subsist for the duration of the copyright in the work, except for the right against false attribution which subsists for 20 years following the right-holder's death. Moral rights may not be assigned but are transmitted on death, except for the right of non-attribution which is actionable for its duration by the right-holder's personal representatives.

This warranty is of particular importance to the purchaser where individuals have been contracted by the target company to create certain types of copyright works on its behalf. The vendors will usually wish to qualify this warranty by reference to their knowledge by inserting the wording in brackets.

8.9 Computer Systems

7–248   Many companies are heavily reliant on the use of information technology, and, where this is the case, specific warranties will normally be required in relation to it. The purchaser will want to ensure that during its due diligence it has fully understood what computer systems are used by the target company, how they are used and their robustness and functionality. It will need to understand whether those systems are shared with anyone, whether it will be necessary to separate them and whether it is practical to do so. Furthermore, the purchaser will wish to establish whether it will require the use of any computer systems retained by the vendors on a transitional basis following completion. Finally, it will want to ensure that it is aware of all the software licences and the provision, support, maintenance and other services provided by third parties in respect of the computer systems (such as telecommunications services, outsourcing, managed services, collocation, escrow and facilities management services). The purchaser's aim will be to ensure that it is aware of the terms of all material agreements so that it can establish whether it can transfer and separate the computer systems or whether new licences and other arrangements need to be put in place. If the purchaser intends to link its own systems to those of the target company post-completion, consideration should be given to covering that with separate warranties. (If the purchaser does intend to do this, it will require substantial planning and the parties will need to understand and agree the cost of any transition and separation issues and the apportionment of such costs).

7–249   **8.9.1 The Computer Systems:**

8.9.1.1   are used exclusively by the Company and under its sole control;

The purpose of this clause is to elicit information as to the extent that the target company may be dependent upon shared use of computer systems or third party services, and, if so, on what terms. It should not pose any difficulties for the vendors. If the target company makes significant use of third party services, from collocation of servers and "software as service" to data warehousing or use of cloud computing facilities, specific warranties covering those services will need to be obtained.

8.9.1.2   are, in respect of the hardware, handheld devices, firmware,   7–250 peripherals, networking and other equipment comprised in those Computer Systems, legally and beneficially owned by the Company;

The purpose of the clause is to elicit information as to ownership of hardware, in so far as this is not already covered by the earlier asset warranties. As this will be a question of fact for the vendors, giving the warranty should not pose any difficulties for them.

8.9.1.3   are in full working order and performing the functions for   7–251 which they were acquired efficiently and without material errors or downtime;

The vendors will need to disclose any known problems with or limitations of the systems and may wish to qualify or replace the broad subjective phrase "performing the functions for which they were acquired" by references to reasonableness, specific intended functions and actual performance. It is unlikely that the vendors will know whether the computer systems are "in full working order" without commissioning an audit of them and as such they may prefer to limit this part of the warranty by reference to their knowledge (without having undertaken any assessment of the systems).

8.9.1.4   have not, within the two years immediately preceding   7–252 Completion, unduly interrupted or hindered the operation of the business of the Company;

The normal warranties as to the condition of plant, machinery, vehicles and other equipment are not appropriate for computer systems which by their nature may include many minor errors or "bugs" which do not materially adversely affect performance. The purchaser may seek to extend the warranty to include a statement that there are no defects in the computer systems, whereas the vendors will wish to avoid such a warranty or limit it to material defects and by reference to their knowledge and awareness.

8.9.1.5   have adequate capacity for the Company's present and (taking   7–253 into account the extent to which the Computer Systems are expandable) future needs;

This clause assures the purchaser that the computer systems are suitable and have sufficient capacity for the anticipated growth of the target company. However, the vendors are unlikely to underwrite the future performance or needs of the target company; they will, as a minimum, seek to qualify the target company's future needs as those which are "foreseeable" or limit them to those occurring in a short specified period following completion, and would not be acting unreasonably were they to seek to delete the second half of the warranty in its entirety.

7–254   **8.9.1.6   have been satisfactorily and appropriately maintained and supported and have the benefit of appropriate maintenance and support agreements (copies of which are attached to the Disclosure Letter), which agreements include emergency support;**

This clause may be inserted in support of cl.8.9.1.3.

The vendors are likely to resist the breadth of this warranty and will look to restrict it to a factual statement only that certain specified agreements are actually in place, and on the terms disclosed. Software support agreements are the normal means of obtaining "bug fixes" and upgrades, and the purchaser will want to check the scope of the target company's entitlement under these as well as under any service level agreements, particularly where these form part of the emergency support provision. Where the support and maintenance function is provided in-house, the purchaser will want to extend the warranty to require the vendors to disclose details of internal service levels. For example, the target company may have in-house first line support with second line support available from a third party if required; and in-house support may be in respect of only certain functions. The more business-critical the function which is supported in-house, the more details the purchaser is likely to want to know.

7–255   **8.9.1.7   [so far as the Vendors are aware] have not been used in such a way as would invalidate any manufacturer's or supplier's guarantee or warranty or entitle the provider of maintenance or support for the Computer Systems to exclude, suspend or terminate those services;**

This clause is intended to highlight problems with cover for hardware and for proprietary and bespoke software, rather than standard packaged software which is usually only warranted for around 90 days from purchase. The vendors will wish to qualify the warranty by inclusion of the wording in brackets. However, the purchaser will resist this, wanting a clear indication of whether it can expect additional costs of repairing or replacing hardware and software which is no longer covered by guarantee or contract. Certain types of hardware maintenance performed by anyone not authorised by the manufacturer to do so, for example by employees of the target company, are likely to invalidate any guarantee or breach the applicable maintenance agreement; so may failure to comply with the manufacturer's instructions—for example, some types of hardware may be required to be kept in a clean environment or within a certain temperature range. Software guarantees and support contracts may also be invalidated or breached by failure to use the software in accordance with its licence terms. If the target company's computer systems contain systems which are key to the successful operation of the business then the purchaser should consider whether it would be appropriate to take specific warranties in respect of those items.

**8.9.1.8   have, in conjunction with the support and maintenance   7–256
agreements referred to in clause [8.9.1.6], adequate security
measures, back-up systems, disaster recovery arrangements,
measures to protect them from viruses and other harmful code
and trained personnel to ensure that so far as reasonably
practicable:**

The scope of this warranty is wide, and the vendors will wish to restrict it to a statement of specified measures that the target company has taken.

**8.9.1.8.1   the authenticity, integrity and confidentiality of all   7–257
data held by or transmitted by the Computer
Systems are preserved;**

The vendors will wish to qualify this clause by reference to knowledge, to limit it to confidential, sensitive or material data, and to restrict "transmitted" to categories of sensitive material sent by the target company. They will need to disclose failure to take appropriate measures, for example to have in place and enforce a rigorous information security policy, if that is the case.

**8.9.1.8.2   no more than one day's data would be lost in the   7–258
event of a failure of the Computer Systems;**

The target company's back-up systems will normally be designed to enable this, with real-time backup of data now commonplace. The vendors should ensure that back-up data can, in practice, be retrieved and restored. Any problems will need to be disclosed.

**8.9.1.8.3   breaches of security, errors and breakdowns are   7–259
kept to a minimum and that in the event of the
occurrence of any such event there will not [so far as
the Vendors are aware] be a material disruption to
the Company;**

The vendors will seek either to delete the second half of this warranty or to qualify it by reference to knowledge.

**8.9.1.9   enable all records and data stored by electronic means which   7–260
relate to the Company to be readily accessible by appropriate
personnel; and**

This warranty is wide in scope and few vendors will accept it as drafted. They will seek either to delete it or to qualify it by reference to knowledge, or to specified "material" records and data. The vendors will need to disclose problems with the speed of data delivery, whether due to load on the system or to system design. If certain systems do not permit the setting of appropriate access levels to information, that will also need to be disclosed.

7–261   **8.9.1.10   will correctly carry out all calculations relating to or in connection with the Euro and display all symbols adopted by any government or European body in connection with the Euro.**

A purchaser will wish to know about non-compliant systems if either the target company currently trades in the Euro or makes calculations or conversions by reference to the Euro, or if the purchaser intends that the target company will do so post completion. There will be a cost for the purchaser in making computer systems Euro-compliant, and this clause is intended to highlight any such issue.

7–262   8.9.2 All software used or stored or resident in the Company:

The vendors may wish to reduce the scope of this warranty by removing the words "stored or resident", thereby restricting the following clauses to software actually used in the target company. The purchaser will resist this, as software which is stored but unlicensed is a potential liability. The vendors may be prepared to include software which is stored or resident in the target company in relation to specific warranties, for example the warranty on unlawful copying, but are unlikely to be willing to accept it in relation to all of the following warranties.

7–263   **8.9.2.1   [so far as the Vendors are aware] is free from any defect or feature which may adversely affect its performance [or the performance of any other software in the future];**

The vendors will be very unlikely to agree to the second half of this warranty as it relates to matters outside of their control. They will normally seek to restrict the first half of the warranty to their knowledge by including the wording in brackets.

7–264   8.9.2.2   performs in accordance with its specification;

This warranty is inappropriate for standard packaged software, where the licensee will rarely have access to the specification. However, a purchaser should insist on the warranty for any bespoke software which has been written or commissioned by the target company.

7–265   **8.9.2.3   [so far as the Vendors are aware] has been (if copied) lawfully copied;**

The vendors may seek to restrict this warranty by reference to knowledge by including the wording in brackets. The purchaser should resist this, given the serious consequences if unlawful copying has taken place. Unlicensed software is a matter which the vendors should rectify pre-completion.

8.9.2.4   is lawfully held and [so far as the Vendors are aware] does not   7–266 infringe the Intellectual Property of any person;

The first half of this warranty should not pose any difficulties for the vendors, but they will want to qualify the second half by reference to knowledge by including the wording in brackets, or remove it altogether.

8.9.2.5   as to the copyright therein: 7–267

Copyright is the main intellectual property right which protects software.

8.9.2.5.1   in the case of software written or commissioned by   7–268 the Company, is owned solely by the Company, no other person has rights therein or rights to use or make copies of the software or source codes;

This warranty is of fundamental importance to the purchaser and as such it would be unlikely to accept any qualification by the vendors by reference to knowledge. If the target company licenses software to third parties, or has developed or commissioned software which is important to the business, the purchaser will normally wish to seek further appropriate warranties.

8.9.2.5.2   in the case of standard packaged software   7–269 purchased outright, is validly licensed to the Company in perpetuity (other than in the event of breach or insolvency) on written terms which do not require the Company to make any further payments, and no licences will terminate on change of control; and

This warranty puts the onus on the vendors to check standard licence terms, which can be a laborious task if the target company's use of software is extensive. The mechanisms for software licensing are no longer restricted to a single one-off fee for use in perpetuity and increasingly are on the basis of an annual or other fee. The vendors may seek to shift the risk back to the purchaser by replacing this warranty by a statement that the licence terms are as disclosed.

8.9.2.5.3   in the case of all other software, is licensed to the   7–270 Company on the terms of a written licence which requires payment by the Company of a fixed annual licence fee the terms of which are set out in the Disclosure Letter.

The vendors will need to remove this warranty if it not relevant, or to make suitable disclosures. For example, the target company may need to disclose its use of software which is provided through monthly or per-usage subscription to a service supplied over the internet, so called "software as a service" or "SaaS".

7–271   8.9.3 No software owned by or licensed to the Company is licensed or sub-licensed by the Company to (or otherwise used by) any other person.

This clause is wide and its purpose is to elicit information about any and all third party use of the target company's software. Unless these activities constitute the target company's business, the vendors should be able to give this warranty without too many difficulties. The purchaser will resist any attempt by the vendors to qualify the clause by reference to their knowledge, particularly in relation to software sub-licensed to or by the target company, as sub-licensing will normally be a breach of the licensor's terms.

7–272   8.9.4 No action will be necessary to enable the Company to continue to use any software currently used by it to the same extent and in the same manner as it has been used prior to Completion.

Some licence terms require the target company to give notice of change of control, although this is more frequently the case where the software is transferred to a new owner in a business sale. As with cl.8.9.2.5.2, this clause will require the vendors to check the licence terms. The vendors will argue this is properly part of the purchaser's due diligence and will wish to replace the warranty by a reference to disclosed licence terms.

7–273   8.9.5 [So far as the Vendors are aware] the terms of all software licences have been complied with and no notices of breach or termination have been served on the Company in respect of any such licence.

The vendors may wish to qualify the target company's compliance by reference to knowledge by including the wording in brackets, particularly if the licence terms are not in writing or cannot be located. The purchaser should resist this.

7–274   8.9.6 Details of all Company domain names and websites are set out in the Disclosure Letter. The Company is the registrant and beneficial owner of those domain names and is [so far as the Vendors are aware] the legal and beneficial owner of all Intellectual Property in the websites.

This clause is intended to elicit information which the vendors will normally be able to provide without qualification. However, commissioned websites are rarely developed from scratch and may well include a licence of the developer's underlying platform, content management system and specific software tools. Moreover, if the websites are particularly complex or large and have been developed over a number of years, the vendors may not be able to give an absolute assurance on ownership, and will seek to qualify the warranty by reference to knowledge by inserting the wording in brackets. The purchaser will wish to know if any domain names have been registered in the name of a third party, commonly an employee or hosting company, rather than the target company, and to require these to be transferred to the target company pre-completion, so that it can exercise effective control over them. If intellectual property rights in parts of the website, for example photographs or other artwork, are owned by a third party rather than the target company, the purchaser will need to establish the terms on which those rights may be used.

8.9.7 Details of all Social Media are set out in the Disclosure Letter. [So far   7–275
as the Vendors are aware] the Company's use complies with each Social
Media provider's terms.

Companies increasingly use social media to promote their businesses, particularly but by no means exclusively, where the goods/services are aimed at consumers. The use carries a higher degree of legal risk than traditional advertising: content is informal and customer feedback is public and often immediate. The purchaser will need to know from the vendors what forms of social media are being used for promotional purposes so it can assess the risks and arrange to take over operation post-completion. As a minimum, the purchaser will wish to establish that use has been in accordance with the providers' terms, which may restrict types of promotional activity or set out levels of acceptable use. The vendors may be reluctant to give anything other than restricted warranties due to the lack of control over the social media providers that are often outside the jurisdiction of England and Wales.

8.9.8 [So far as the Vendors are aware] all websites operated by the   7–276
Company comply with the Electronic Commerce (EC Directive) Regulations
2002 and, if the Company sells online to consumers, the Consumer
Protection (Distance Selling) Regulations 2000. Each website is accessible in
compliance with the requirements set out in Pt III of the Disability
Discrimination Act 1995 (as amended or superseded).

Websites operated by the target company should be legally compliant and contain all relevant information; failure to ensure this puts the target company at risk of action by consumers and regulators.

The vendors will almost certainly want to qualify the warranty on awareness. A well-advised purchaser is unlikely to accept this and instead will require that the warranty is given on an absolute basis.

8.10 Money laundering

8.10.1 The Company's assets do not include any Criminal Property and   7–277
neither the Company nor [so far as the Vendors are aware] any of its
directors or officers have committed any offence pursuant to the Proceeds of
Crime Act 2002 s.327.

This is a wide-ranging warranty designed to identify any money laundering offences committed by the target company or its directors and officers and whether any of the target company's assets constitute "Criminal Property". In most cases the vendors will only be prepared to give the latter part of the warranty on an awareness basis by inclusion of the wording in brackets.

CHAPTER 8

Warranties and Indemnities on the Sale of a Business

INTRODUCTION

The sale of a business by way of its assets and undertaking (usually on a going concern basis) is different from the sale of shares of the target company as it involves the transfer of defined assets and the assumption, by way of express contractual provision between the vendor and the purchaser, of certain defined liabilities with generally any undefined liabilities or risks remaining with the vendor. In a share sale there is no "cherry picking" of assets and liabilities as they remain with the target company that is sold, and liability and risk can only be apportioned through warranties and indemnities. An assets based deal will usually involve the sale or transfer of: **8–01**

(1) assets such as stock, machinery, equipment, motor vehicles and computer systems, some of which may be subject to finance or leasing agreements;

(2) freehold or leasehold properties;

(3) intangible assets (including the goodwill of the business, and commonly the benefit (subject to the burden) of customer and supply contracts, know-how and confidential business information, the customer and employee databases and intellectual property rights); and

(4) rights relating to the business such as to the current order book or the vendor's rights against third parties.

Although book debts will usually be an asset of the business in most deals they are excluded and retained by the vendor. Where the vendor is not retaining any accounting or administrative function the purchaser may agree to collect them on the vendor's behalf and account to the vendor on receipt. In these cases the purchaser may seek to levy a charge for this collection function. If there is a sensitivity to the vendor having any continuing contact with the suppliers or customers of the business a further variation on this is for the purchaser (if collecting the book debts on the vendor's behalf) to use the receipts from the book debts to discharge defined creditors on behalf of the vendor.

The transaction will not normally involve the purchaser taking over liabilities and these will not generally pass unless there is an express contractual agreement by the purchaser (for example in respect of contracts) to do so. This broad principle needs, however, to be qualified in a number of respects:

 (1) liabilities in relation to properties may run with the land and accordingly automatically bind the purchaser when it acquires the property;

 (2) pursuant to the Transfer of Undertakings (Protection of Employment) Regulations 2006 ("TUPE") on the transfer of "an economic entity which retains its identity" (which will include most businesses and parts of businesses) responsibility for the contracts of employment of those persons employed in the business immediately before the transfer is automatically assumed by the purchaser who may neither, except in certain very limited circumstances, change their terms and conditions of employment nor dismiss the employees by reason of the transfer or for a reason connected with it;

 (3) with land and buildings, liability for environmental contamination can pass to the purchaser, many vendors will actively seek to include wording designed to achieve this, in order to make a clean break with the property. Vendors often include wording which aims to trigger the "sold with information" and/or the "payments for remediation" exclusion tests under Pt IIA Environment Protection Act 1990 contaminated land regime. Where effective, these provisions will exclude the vendor from liability for clean up works under a remediation notice, as between the purchaser and vendor;

 (4) partly completed goods, the manufacture of which is completed by the purchaser, will give rise to a liability on the purchaser if they prove to be defective even though the defect arises from work done by the vendor; and

 (5) whilst strictly not a liability that passes to the purchaser there is often a practical need for the purchaser to perform warranty or remedial work on goods or services sold or provided by the vendor prior to sale in order to preserve customer goodwill. For this reason it is usually a good idea to agree a specific mechanism to deal with this to ensure that the cost of this sort of work is fairly apportioned between the vendor and the purchaser.

8–02 Despite these exceptions, the general rule is that the purchaser does not take over any liabilities of the business for which it does not wish to be responsible. This significantly affects the scope of the warranties and indemnities which the purchaser will seek and, broadly, a number of the warranties on share sales dealing with potential liabilities, and in particular those concerning taxation, will largely be unnecessary. Nevertheless, not all potential liabilities are irrelevant in determining whether the purchaser has acquired what it thought it was buying. Accordingly, the purchaser will wish to be sure that:

(1) the vendor owns the assets to be transferred to the purchaser absolutely, that there are no encumbrances over any of them, that they are in appropriate working order and comply with any legal requirements that might be relevant to them;

(2) there are no potentially significant environmental liabilities associated with any of the vendor's land or buildings;

(3) there has been no breach or default by the vendor in respect of any of the contracts to be transferred to the purchaser, or, in so far as there has been, the purchaser does not assume responsibility for such breach or default;

(4) the vendor has complied with its obligations to inform (and possibly also consult) the employees in accordance with reg.13 of TUPE;

(5) it has the benefit of full employee warranties as to identity, terms and conditions of employment, disputes and claims made;

(6) the accounts of the vendor correctly reflect the profitability of the business and that liabilities reducing the profits are fully taken into account so as to give a true reflection of the profitability or trading of the business; and

(7) there are no disputes with suppliers and customers or in respect of any of the intellectual property rights of the business as these could adversely affect the goodwill of the business and the ability of the purchaser to carry it on in succession to the vendor.

It is usual in the case of a business sale for the purchaser to seek indemnities rather than warranties from the vendor in respect of the few areas where liability may pass from the vendor to the purchaser. The most notable example of this is in relation to employment matters, where the operation of TUPE means that the purchaser becomes liable for the acts and omissions of the vendor. Here the appropriate indemnities will provide the purchaser with comfort that if it acquires more employment liabilities than it was led to believe then the cost or losses incurred can be recovered from the vendor through the indemnities given. Similarly there will often be mutual indemnities between the vendor and the purchaser to ensure that their intentions in respect of liabilities and profits and losses before and after the deal remain where they were intended to fall or benefit. The wording of this sort of indemnity needs to be consistent with the usual apportionments clause which will seek to apportion any accruals, prepayments and sometimes even profits for any matters that relate to or bridge periods falling both before and after completion. Another area where indemnities may commonly be sought is in relation to unresolved contaminated land issues. A purchaser may require the comfort of appropriate indemnities in relation to any contamination issues which are known to exist prior to completion. The vendor, if willing to offer such an indemnity, will usually want to impose time and quantum limits on the indemnity, and may wish to obtain a cross-indemnity from the purchaser in relation to contamination occurring post-completion. It should be remembered that indemnities are only as good as the entity or person giving them when the relevant indemnified event or action occurs. Usually with known contamination it is difficult to be prescriptive as to who is liable for which part of the contamination when the contamination may be continuing. It often makes more sense for the matter to be addressed by the parties prior to any deal taking place rather than relying on indemnities to provide a satisfactory resolution in these circumstances. Indemnities are more usual in this area to apportion theoretical risk rather than a known liability.

Defined Terms

8–03 To facilitate the drafting of the warranties and indemnities it is normal to make use of a number of defined terms. Examples of the definitions used in the warranties and indemnities on the sale of a business are contained in Pt 1 of Appendix 5. Paragraph 4–02 provides a commentary on a number of these definitions (which apply to both a share sale and a business sale) highlighting particular points that should be borne in mind on a business sale. However, there are also a number of additional definitions set out in Appendix 5 which are only relevant to the warranties and indemnities on a business sale. Where these definitions require any special consideration they are discussed below.

Scope of Indemnities

8–04 The areas detailed below will generally be the areas in which the purchaser has a legitimate interest in receiving indemnities.

(1) As already discussed an indemnity against all losses, liabilities, obligations and outgoings of the business prior to completion. Legally these liabilities would not ordinarily pass to the purchaser but a "sweeping" indemnity often catches minor liabilities which pass as part of another obligation. There will usually be a "mirror" indemnity in favour of the vendor for any such obligations arising after completion.

(2) Against any pre-completion breach of a contract to be transferred to the purchaser or any default, negligence or misrepresentation concerning any such contract by the vendor. It is also usual for the vendor to require that the purchaser provide a similar indemnity in respect of the purchaser's performance of the obligations it has agreed to perform under contracts following completion.

(3) That the vendor has complied with the information and consultation requirements of TUPE in relation to all affected employees and that there are no other employees entitled to transfer to the purchaser other than those known to the purchaser and that the full terms of their employment have been disclosed. (The transferring employees are

commonly listed by name in a schedule to the sale agreement with detailed terms of employment being set out in replies to enquiries or the disclosure letter.) In return, the vendor will usually require that the purchaser warrants and/or provides an indemnity that it has complied with its TUPE obligations by providing all relevant information in respect of any "measures" it anticipates taking in respect of the transferring employees.

(4) Against any pre-completion act or omission by the vendor in relation to the contract of employment of any transferring employee. Again it is usual for the purchaser to grant a reciprocal indemnity to the vendor to cover any post-completion acts or omissions by the purchaser.

(5) Against any of the employees having any pension rights not relating to old age, survivorship or ill health.

(6) Against any contaminated land liabilities arising as a result of anything in existence prior to completion.

Depending on the particular circumstances of a transaction and the nature of the business there may be other specific indemnities that a purchaser may legitimately require; for example, in respect of compliance with the data protection principles and eprivacy legislation on the transfer of a customer database.

CONSIDERATION OF INDIVIDUAL INDEMNITIES

As discussed above, specific indemnities are designed to cover the key areas of risk for a purchaser on a business sale without having to rely upon the need to prove loss as a result of a breach of warranty. The indemnities will also be supported by warranties but these will be subject to any negotiated warranty protection provisions, any financial deductibles or de minimis and the need to prove loss. Examples of suitable indemnities are given below and repeated in Pt 2 of Appendix 5 and are briefly discussed below. Operative clauses from a standard form business sale agreement have been included, where relevant, in order to give meaning to the indemnities. **8–05**

Creditors and liabilities

1.1 Subject to the other provisions of this Agreement: **8–06**

1.1.1 **all profits and receipts of the Business and all losses, liabilities, obligations and outgoings of the Business up to Completion belong to and are for the account of the Vendor;**

1.1.2 **the Vendor shall promptly discharge the Creditors and the Liabilities (at the latest by the expiry of any agreed or statutory credit or payment periods);**

1.1.3 **notwithstanding Completion the Vendor shall be responsible for all debts payable by and claims (whether contingent or**

otherwise) **outstanding against it at Completion or that primarily relate to any fact or matter occurring prior to Completion or anything done or omitted to be done on or prior to Completion by the Vendor including, without limitation, all wages, sums payable in respect of Taxation, rent and other expenses or any failure by the Vendor in the performance of any of its obligations falling due on or before Completion in relation to the Business or which relate to any of the Excluded Assets; and**

1.1.4   the Vendor shall indemnify the Purchaser in respect of any breach in whole or part of this sub-clause by the Vendor.

1.2 Subject to the other provisions of this Agreement all profits and receipts of the Business and all losses, liabilities, obligations and outgoings of the Business (to the extent that they are transferred to the Purchaser under this Agreement or relate to, or otherwise arise after the date of Completion) belong to and must be paid and discharged by the Purchaser. Accordingly, and without prejudice to its rights under the Warranties and subject to the other provisions of this Agreement, the Purchaser shall indemnify the Vendor against:

1.2.1   all liabilities, obligations and outgoings relating to the Assets to the extent that they are referable to the period after the date of Completion; and

1.2.2   all costs, claims, proceedings, damages and expenses in connection with them.

It is a widely accepted principle of a business sale that the liabilities and outgoings of the business up to completion are the responsibility of the vendor and, to the extent that they are transferred to the purchaser, that following completion they are the responsibility of the purchaser. Clauses 1.1 and 1.2 provide indemnities between the vendor and the purchaser to ensure that such a clean break is achieved.

The wording of the indemnities makes reference to "subject to the other provisions of this Agreement". This is designed to make it clear that there may be provisions which are inconsistent with these, as is often the case when liabilities are expressly agreed to be assumed. Clause 1.1 is the basic indemnity in favour of the purchaser. Clause 1.2 is a more limited "mirror" indemnity in favour of the vendor. To avoid potential arguments as to which other provisions of the Agreement are inconsistent with these general indemnities it is sometimes made even clearer by the use of the words "express" after "other" and before "provisions" in the introduction to the indemnities and the words "to the contrary" inserted after "Agreement". This would then require any contrary provisions to be expressly referred to in the balance of the agreement.

The indemnities, as in cl.1.1.4, simply refer to indemnifying against any breach. It is good practice to define how far the indemnity is to go by defining the extent of the indemnity obligations by use of an appropriate definition.

Contracts

2.1 In so far as the benefit of any of the Contracts may be effectively assigned   8–07
by the Vendor to the Purchaser without the consent of a third party:

2.1.1   the Vendor hereby agrees to assign and transfer with effect from
Completion all the benefit of them to the Purchaser;

2.1.2   the Purchaser shall perform all of the Vendor's obligations
thereunder save any such obligations that were under the terms
of the relevant Contract to be performed prior to Completion or
any obligations that the Vendor is in breach of as at Completion;
and

2.1.3   the Purchaser shall indemnify the Vendor in respect of any
breach of this sub-clause by it.

2.2 In so far as the benefit of any of the Contracts may not be effectively
assigned by the Vendor to the Purchaser without the consent of a third party
then:

2.2.1   the Vendor and the Purchaser shall each use their reasonable
endeavours to procure a novation of those Contracts or consent
to assignment (as the Purchaser may require) and that those
Contracts are novated or assigned, provided that:

2.2.1.1   the Purchaser shall not be obliged to make any
payment, give any security or provide any guarantee as
the basis for, or in connection with, any such
assignment or novation; and

2.2.1.2   nothing contained in this Agreement shall or shall be
deemed to operate, so far as concerns any third party,
as such an assignment or novation as would or might
give rise to any termination or forfeiture of any benefit,
right or interest of any person in any of the Contracts
in question;

2.2.2   unless and until any such Contracts (but excluding the Supply
Contracts) shall be so novated or assigned:

2.2.2.1   the Vendor shall, in so far as may be permissible and
lawful, give to the Purchaser the benefit of them as if
the same had already been novated to or assigned to the
Purchaser;

2.2.2.2   the Purchaser shall after Completion as the Vendor's
sub-contractor (or in any way or capacity reasonably
open to the Purchaser) perform on behalf of the Vendor
all of the Vendor's obligations thereunder arising after
Completion save any obligations of the Vendor that
under the terms of any of the Contracts were to be

> performed prior to Completion or any obligations that the Vendor is in breach of as at Completion; and
>
> 2.2.2.3   the Purchaser shall indemnify the Vendor in respect of any breach of this sub-clause;

2.2.3   the Vendor shall hold all Supply Contracts in trust for the Purchaser and:

> 2.2.3.1   as required by the Purchaser all goods to be delivered or services to be provided thereunder shall be delivered or provided as the Purchaser may direct;
>
> 2.2.3.2   the Vendor shall permit the Purchaser to have the use of any assets or rights whose use by the Vendor is authorised by any such Supply Contract; and
>
> 2.2.3.3   the Purchaser shall, in respect of the period during which the provisions of this sub-clause are followed and to the extent that such Supply Contracts permit (and save in so far as they are not inconsistent with the provisions hereof), perform the obligations of the Vendor and make payments due thereunder (but only in so far as such obligations and payments do not relate to a breach of any of the Vendor's obligations thereunder on or prior to Completion);

2.2.4   in respect of the Contracts to which sub-clauses 2.2.1 and 2.2.2, apply the Vendor shall not do any act in respect of such Contracts without the consent of the Purchaser and shall keep the Purchaser fully and properly informed of all communications and any other relevant information concerning such Contracts; and

2.2.5   in the event of the actions referred to in sub-clauses 2.2.1 and 2.2.2 being unlawful or in breach of the terms of any of the Contracts, all liabilities and obligations relating to such Contracts shall remain with the Vendor which shall indemnify the Purchaser in respect of the loss of profit to the Purchaser in not being able to complete such Contracts and obtain the benefit thereof.

2.3 The Vendor shall indemnify the Purchaser in respect of any default by the Vendor under the Contracts or negligence or misrepresentation concerning all or any of the Contracts.

2.4 The Vendor shall perform all obligations in the Contracts that the Purchaser has not hereunder agreed to perform.

The purchaser has the following concerns in respect of the contracts it is agreeing to take over from the vendor:

(1) that the vendor is not in breach of its obligations under any of the contracts at completion;

(2) that a contract may not be capable of being effectively assigned or novated and as a result remains with the vendor causing a loss of profit for the purchaser;

(3) that the vendor has not been negligent or made any misrepresentation in respect of the contracts; and

(4) that the purchaser is aware of all the obligations it will assume under the contracts.

It is legitimate for the purchaser to expect to be indemnified in respect of matters (1) to (3) above. These matters are covered in cll.2.1 to 2.3. It is, however, normal practice for the purchaser to be expected to rely upon its due diligence supported by limited warranties in respect of (4). Any contracts that the purchaser is assuming will be defined in the definition of "Contracts", which is separately broken down into "Customer Contracts", "Finance Agreements" and "Supply Contracts".

In return for providing the indemnities in cll.2.1 to 2.3 it would be reasonable for the vendor to expect to receive an indemnity back from the purchaser in respect of the purchaser's performance of the contracts following completion, again to reflect the clean break principle of a business sale. This indemnity is covered in cl.2.2.2.

Employees

3.1 The parties agree that the sale and purchase to be effected pursuant to this Agreement will amount to a relevant transfer for the purposes of the Regulations and that accordingly the contracts of employment of the Employees will be transferred to the Purchaser upon Completion in accordance with the Regulations.   8–08

3.2 The Vendor shall indemnify the Purchaser against each and every cost, claim, liability, expense or demand relating to or arising out of any act or omission by the Vendor or any other event or occurrence before the date of Completion and incurred by the Purchaser in relation to any contract of employment or collective agreement concerning the Employees and former employees of the Vendor or the Business or under statute pursuant to the Regulations, including without limitation any such matter relating to or arising out of:

3.2.1 the Vendor's rights, powers, duties and liabilities under or in connection with any such contract of employment or collective agreement or under statute, which rights, powers, duties and liabilities transfer to the Purchaser in accordance with the Regulations;

3.2.2 anything done or omitted before the date of Completion by or in relation to the Vendor in respect of any contract of employment

or collective agreement or any person employed in the Business which is deemed to have been done or omitted by or in relation to the Purchaser in accordance with the Regulations;

3.2.3   the Vendor's failure to pay to any of the Employees any sums due in respect of the period before Completion; and

3.2.4   any claim by any trade union, staff association or staff body recognised by the Vendor in respect of all or any of the Employees arising out of the Vendor's failure to comply with its legal obligations to such trade union, staff association or body.

3.3 If any contract of employment of any person who is not an Employee has effect as if originally made between the Purchaser and such person, whether as a result of the provisions of the Regulations or otherwise;

3.3.1   the Purchaser may, within [14] days of learning of the existence of such contract terminate it; and

3.3.2   the Vendor shall indemnify the Purchaser against each and every cost, claim, liability, expense or demand;

3.3.2.1   by reason of, on account of or arising out of such termination; or

3.3.2.2   arising from such contract prior to the date on which such termination takes place.

3.4 The Purchaser shall indemnify the Vendor against each and every cost, claim, liability, expense or demand arising from;

3.4.1   any claim or allegation by any of the Employees that as a result of the sale of the Business to the Purchaser there have been or will be a substantial change in the Employee's working conditions to his detriment contrary to the Regulations;

3.4.2   any act or omission of the Purchaser in relation to any of the Employees occurring after the date of Completion, and any claim for redundancy payments or protective awards, and any liability for wrongful dismissal or unfair dismissal or otherwise in connection with the transfer of the employment of the Employees to the Purchaser;

3.4.3   any failure by the Purchaser to provide retirement or death in service benefits for or in respect of any of the Employees in accordance with the Transfer of Employment (Pension Protection) Regulations 2005; and

3.4.4   any claim arising from the failure or delay of the Purchaser to notify the Vendor pursuant to reg.13(4) of the Regulations of the measures the Purchaser envisages taking in relation to the Employees.

TUPE will apply to the sale or other transfer of "an undertaking, business or part of an undertaking or business situated immediately before the transfer in the United Kingdom to another person where there is the transfer of an economic entity which retains its identity". It will therefore apply to virtually all transfers of businesses or parts of businesses. TUPE does not apply to share transactions but care should be taken in circumstances where, following completion, there is integration by way of transfer of the target company's business into the purchaser's group as this can trigger the application of TUPE even where there is no formal hive-up or reorganisation; see *Millam v The Print Factory (London) 1991 Ltd* [2007] EWCA Civ 322. This is often the case following the acquisition of a group of companies by an existing company with its own business or divisional structure. TUPE also applies in the vast majority of outsourcing and contracting situations, including the bringing back in-house of functions and services previously provided by external contractors. The question of precisely when TUPE does or does not apply is perhaps the most vexed question in employment law. Specialist advice in this area should be obtained early in the course of the transaction; especially where it is proposed to proceed upon the basis that TUPE does not apply.

Where TUPE applies, the contracts of employment of those persons who were employed in the business immediately before the transfer will be deemed to have been made with the purchaser with effect from the moment of completion. The effect of this is that employees' continuous service is preserved and they transfer across to the purchaser on the same terms and conditions of employment. Any change to the contracts of employment of any transferring employee and which is to the detriment of that employee is void, even where it is made with the agreement of the employee concerned, see *Power v Regent Security Services Ltd* [2007] EWCA Civ 1188. As such, the purchaser will almost invariably take over responsibility for all employees and this, depending of course on the size of the business and number of employees, can give rise to a sizeable liability.

The other crucial aspect of TUPE is that where an employee is dismissed by reason of the transfer then his dismissal is automatically unfair. Similarly, if the reason for the dismissal is not the transfer itself but is a reason connected with the transfer, then the dismissal will be automatically unfair unless an "economic, technical or organisational reason entailing a change in the workforce" can be established. This protection extends to employees who are dismissed either before or after the transfer takes place.

It is becoming increasingly common for vendors with more than one trading division or those who are selling only part of their business to exclude or "cherry pick" certain employees from the transfer. These employees may serve a multi-functional role across a number of the vendor's businesses or the vendor may simply want to transfer a skilled employee of the transferring business to one of its other businesses. Conversely it is not unknown for a vendor to try to palm off unsatisfactory or expensive employees on the purchaser upon the premise that they are actually based in the part of the business being sold, where that is not strictly the case. In order to resolve these issues it is necessary to look precisely at which "organised grouping" the employee is assigned to. This is a difficult issue which needs to be addressed in the course of the due diligence exercise.

Alternatively, TUPE allows employees to formally object to being transferred **8–09** to the purchaser, with the effect that their employment terminates and they are deemed to have resigned with effect from completion. Where, as in *New ISG Ltd* *v Vernon* [2007] EWHC 2665, the employee does not ascertain the identity of his new employer until after the transfer has taken place, he can nevertheless validly object upon finding out and the objection is backdated to the point of transfer.

It is normal practice for the agreement to include a list of the transferring employees (defined as the "Employees") and, for the avoidance of doubt, a list of the employees specifically excluded from the transfer (defined as the "Excluded Employees"). The purchaser will normally insist upon an indemnity from the vendor in respect of any liability accruing to it under TUPE in connection with the "Excluded Employees".

Regulation 13 has been mentioned above. It sets out a framework for informing affected employees of the transfer, the reasons for it, the implications of it and whether the vendor or purchaser intend taking any "measures" in connection with it. Although it is commonly thought that the only affected employees are those whom it is intended to transfer, this is not the case. Either party may well have employees who are "affected" by the transfer, for example, if the acquisition of the new business will lead to a redundancy situation or changes in terms of employment of the existing workforce. Such people are equally entitled to be informed in accordance with reg.13.

8–10   So far as transferring employees are concerned, the vendor should formally ask the purchaser whether it intends taking any "measures" in respect of them. "Measures" are not defined but a sensible starting point is to consider whether any dismissals or significant changes in working practices are contemplated. Under the Pensions Act 2002 measures include any replacement measures that might be contemplated for pension purposes. The purchaser is obliged to answer this question by giving details of the measures contemplated or, if no such measures are contemplated, by confirming that to be the case.

Where an employer contemplates taking "measures" then a secondary duty of consultation is triggered. Typically this will be a matter for the purchaser, as it is rare that vendors (other than insolvent ones) will want to take any steps in connection with the employees before the transfer takes place. The aim of the consultation exercise is to reach agreement with the employees as to the measures proposed. Consultation must obviously be completed before the measures take effect. A very important limitation on the duty to consult was established in *Amicus v Glasgow City Council* [2009] I.R.L.R. 253; TUPE does not require any consultation with the transferring employees after the transfer has actually taken place.

Where consultation is necessary, regs 13 and 14 set out how—and with whom—it should be carried out. The rules are complicated and specialist advice will normally be required.

An employer who fails to comply with its information and (where appropriate) consultation obligations risks Employment Tribunal claims which can give rise to awards of compensation of up to 13 weeks' gross pay per employee. Opportunities for defending such claims are extremely limited.

8–11   TUPE makes it clear that liability for failure to inform and/or consult is joint and several as between vendor and purchaser. In connection with transferring employees it is common to apportion this liability between the two parties so that the vendor remains liable for its failure to inform and (where appropriate) consult and the purchaser remains liable for any liability arising from its failure to provide details of proposed measures.

Even where the absence of any proposed "measures" means that the statutory duty to consult is not triggered, a transferor must be alive to the possibility of voluntary consultation as to the transfer and the situation generally. This means that the required information must be given to the employer representatives long enough before the transfer date to enable voluntary consultation to take place; the previously widespread practice of delaying the issue of the information until very shortly before the transfer date must now be considered unsafe; see *Cable Realisation Ltd v GMB Northern* [2009] All E.R. (D) 179. For the reasons discussed above, the potential employee liability is usually the largest risk for a purchaser on a business sale. The purchaser will therefore wish to be comfortable on a number of areas of key concern in order to ensure that it can quantify the obligations it proposes to assume. Commonly the purchaser will want comfort that:

(1) the vendor has complied with TUPE regs 11, 13 and 14;

(2) the vendor has not done anything or omitted to do anything before the date of completion in respect of any contract of employment which could give rise to a liability;

(3) the vendor has not failed to pay any sum due to the transferring employees prior to completion;

(4) the vendor has not breached any obligation to any trade unions;

(5) there are no persons entitled to transfer to the purchaser other than the listed employees; and

(6) the purchaser is fully informed as to the terms of employment of the transferring employees.

It is legitimate for the purchaser to expect to be indemnified in respect of matters (1) to (6). The indemnities in cll.3.1.1 to 3.1.6 cover these matters.

In return for providing the indemnities in cll.3.1.1 to 3.1.6 it would be reasonable for the vendor to expect to receive indemnities from the purchaser in respect of the following matters:

(1) any claim against the vendor by a transferring employee that the transfer of his employment to the purchaser amounted to a substantial detrimental change to his conditions of employment;

(2) any liability for post-transfer acts or omissions of the purchaser in respect of any transferring employee; and

(3) any liability under TUPE reg.13 arising from the failure or delay of the purchaser to notify the vendor of the "measures" the purchaser envisaged taking in relation to the transferring employees following

completion (to allow the vendor comply with its own obligations under TUPE reg.13).

These indemnities from the purchaser to the vendor are covered in cl.3.2.

Pensions

8–12   **4.1 The Vendor shall indemnify the Purchaser against:**

4.1.1   **any claim for any Benefit in respect of any scheme other than the Scheme referable to any period up to and including Completion, including without limitation any order made by any court, tribunal or regulator in respect of such claim and any payment made by the Purchaser to any such person to settle any such claim; and**

4.1.2   **any claim in respect of the Scheme relating to any benefits other than those relating to old age, invalidity or survivors or relating to any output target on benefits referable to pensionable service in the period up to and including Completion.**

This indemnity is worded in very broad terms and may need tailoring to the circumstances of the transaction. Clause 4.1.1 aims to capture all liabilities that may transfer to the purchaser that relate to non-disclosed schemes. In particular this would include "Beckmann" liabilities (namely liabilities which do not relate to old age, invalidity or survivorship) but would cover any other liability of any kind that would not be covered by the warranties. Clause 4.1.2 is narrower in scope and aims to cover any Beckmann liabilities that would attach to the Scheme. Although the operation of TUPE normally excludes parts of an employment contract relating to pensions from transferring to the Purchaser, where the employment contracts contain an express right to membership of a pension scheme of a defined benefit design (for example, final salary or career average benefits), it may be useful to also include an indemnity against any contractual claims arising from such an express right. This depends on the due diligence, however, and is likely to be forcefully resisted by the vendor.

The following warranties are taken from Ch.7 (except cl.10) as they are also applicable for asset transactions. Although the liability for occupational pension schemes does not transfer to the purchaser in an asset transaction, the purchaser has the three following areas of potential liability:

(1) rights to employer contributions to contract based arrangements such as personal pension plans, stakeholder pension schemes, group life schemes and group personal pension plans must be honoured, usually by replicating these contributions;

(2) where the vendor operated an occupational pension scheme, the purchaser will be under an obligation, set out in the Pensions Act 2004 ss.257 and 258 and the Transfer of Employment (Pension Protection)

Regulations 2005 to provide a replacement pension as prescribed by this legislation; and

(3) liability for Beckmann rights, as discussed in Ch.7 will transfer to the purchaser. This is usually the main pension related concern of any purchaser of a business.

The following warranties have been amended to refer to the Employees (defined by reference to those transferring to the purchaser), as the liabilities of the purchaser (if any) will only relate to those persons. Other than this, the comments set out in Ch.7 are relevant here also, but are not repeated.

1. No other pension arrangements

Save in respect of the Scheme, the Vendor has no legal obligation to provide   8–13
or cause to be provided to any Employees benefits under a "pension scheme", as defined by s.150(1) of the Finance Act 2004, under an "employer-financed retirement benefits scheme", as defined by s.393B of the Income Tax (Earnings and Pensions) Act 2003, under a superannuation fund to which s.615(3) of the Income and Corporation Taxes Act 1988 applies, that are "retirement or death benefits" for the purposes of s.307 of the Income Tax (Earnings and Pensions) Act 2003 and do not fall under the categories above, or that are "excluded benefits" for the purposes of s.393B of the Income Tax (Earnings and Pensions) Act 2003 and do not fall under the categories above.

2. Other liabilities

The Vendor is not subject to a contribution notice or a financial support direction or similar notice, order or direction under the Pensions Act 2004 nor are there any circumstances which are likely to lead to such notices, orders or directions being imposed upon the Vendor.

3. Additional member's rights

3.1 None of the Employees have at any time transferred to the Vendor under the provisions of the Transfer of Undertakings (Protection of Employment) Regulations 1981 and 2006.
   3.2 If any such Employees have transferred there are no circumstances in which such Employees may have retained any pension rights from previous employment that do not fall within the categories of benefits relating to old age, survivorship or ill health and which have not been fully and appropriately provided for under the Vendor's pension arrangements.

4. Full and accurate particulars

4.1 Full, accurate and up to date particulars of the Scheme are set out in the Disclosure Letter, including (without limitation):

    4.1.1   all constitutional documents in relation to the Scheme including, where applicable, the trust deeds and rules together with any amendments and any related agreements;

    4.1.2   all explanatory literature including, where applicable, booklets currently in force and any subsequent communications to members or Employees who are or may become members of the Scheme;

    4.1.3   details of all Employees who are active, deferred, pensioner and prospective members (including dates of birth, sex, age at joining the Scheme, date on which a prospective member would become eligible to join the Scheme had the transfer not taken place and current pensionable pay, and name of employer);

    4.1.4   in relation to the Employees, details of all employee and all employer contributions in the last five years (including any statutory schedules of contributions or payments); and

    4.1.5   any insurance policies, schedules and certificates and details of all premiums paid in the last five years.

5. Member details

The membership data in respect of the Employees is complete, accurate and up to date in all material respects and is stored safely.

6. Proposed amendments to the Scheme

6.1 No proposal has been announced by the Vendor either:

    6.1.1   to modify, amend, alter or improve the Scheme that does not form part of the Scheme's constitutional documents as at Completion; or

    6.1.2   regarding the continuation of the Scheme, or its closure to new members, or its closure to new benefit accruals, or its discontinuance or winding-up.

6.2 Since the Balance Sheet Date the Scheme has not been modified, amended, altered or improved and no closure to new members, cessation or accruals or commencement of winding-up in relation to the Scheme has been prepared or commenced

This warranty aims to identify any changes to the target company's pension arrangements which have occurred since the Balance Sheet Date, perhaps with a view to grooming the target company for sale.

7. No disputes

8–14   **No claim or investigation has been threatened or made against the Vendor or the trustees or administrators of the Scheme (other than routine claims for benefits) or against any other person whom the Vendor is or the said**

trustees or administrators are or may be liable to pay, indemnify or compensate in respect of any matter arising out of or in connection with the Scheme, nor are there any circumstances which may give rise to any such claim.

8. Contracting-Out

Where the Scheme is contracted out a fully up to date and correct contracting-out certificate (including schedules thereto) has been properly obtained and maintained.

9. Insurance

All lump sums held in relation to the Scheme (other than normal pension benefits) are securely and fully insured with a reputable insurance company and all premiums due in respect of such insurance has been paid.

10. Employer related investments

The Assets do not include any assets owned by a pension arrangement retained by the Vendors.

This warranty aims to confirm whether any of the transferring assets (mainly property) were owned in part or in full by a pension arrangement prior to a transaction as this may cause complications of a practical nature in relation to the transfer of ownership.

Scope of Warranties

In addition to the specific indemnities and warranties discussed above the matters detailed below will generally be the areas in which the purchaser has a legitimate interest in receiving warranties.   **8–15**

    (1) The accounts of the business will be warranted. The form of these warranties will closely follow those that are sought by the purchaser of shares of a company. The primary purpose of the warranties is to enable the purchaser to have a claim if the value which it attributes to goodwill, and which in practice will have been greatly influenced by the accounts, was excessive because the accounts were inaccurate. This is not so straightforward in circumstances where part only of the business is being purchased. In such circumstances the accounts of the enlarged business may not be much help and a more detailed warranty which relates to the part of the business being sold will be more appropriate. Often a standalone set of "financials" will have been produced for the part of the business and this is usually what should be warranted in these circumstances. The definition of "Accounts" should be adjusted to suit the precise circumstances.

(2) The assets, including stock, information technology systems, debtors (where these are to be assigned to the purchaser) and intellectual property rights, will usually be covered by appropriate warranties.

(3) Most of the warranties relating to the trading activities of the business will correspond to those adopted on a share sale.

(4) The purchaser will only assume responsibility for those contracts it elects to do so and any breach or default by the vendor under the contracts will be covered by the specific indemnities at cll.2.1 to 2.3 of Pt 2 of Appendix 5. As such not all of the warranties included in a share purchase agreement in relation to contracts will be relevant. However, some basic warranty cover on the nature, terms and performance of the contracts should be sought, partly to back up any due diligence exercise and partly to elicit disclosure of any issues in respect of the contracts.

(5) As discussed above the rights of employees will be important both commercially and legally. The employment and pensions indemnities at cll.3 and 4 of Pt 2 of Appendix 5 will be supported by fairly long form warranties confirming the accuracy of the details and terms of employment for each employee and any disputes or other potential liabilities.

(6) The purchaser will wish to be sure that the vendor has all necessary and desirable licences and permits in respect of the business (so as to ensure it can arrange for the transfer of these where possible or the application for any new ones when they are not transferable), has carried the business on in accordance with applicable laws and that there are no statutory restrictions on the business as these factors could effect the value the purchaser has attributed to goodwill and its ability to carry on the business following completion. The transfer of environmental permits requires the joint application or notification of both the holder and the proposed transferee. The transfer of a permit for stand-alone water discharge or groundwater activities cannot take effect until at least 20 business days after the joint notification is given.

(7) The taxation warranties—to the extent any taxation warranties are included—will largely be restricted to capital allowances in respect of the transferring assets, value added tax and PAYE and national insurance deductions in respect of the transferring employees.

(8) The purchase of any properties will be dealt with in accordance with normal conveyancing practice. As, however, there may be factors relating to the properties which affect the value of the goodwill of the business but which would not normally be relevant on a property purchase which is unrelated to a business purchase, a few of the warranties that are included in a share purchase agreement may be relevant. Depending on the nature of the business the purchaser may

also seek either full or modified environmental warranties or indemnities when a property is included as part of the deal although usually a vendor would expect a purchaser to rely on its own surveys or investigations.

OMITTED WARRANTIES

The warranties, other than in relation to properties, which are suitable for a **8–16** business sale are set out in Pt 3 of Appendix 5 and closely follow those for a share sale which are discussed in para.7–03. These that merit particular discussion are repeated below for ease of reference. The warranties omit a number of categories which are adopted on a share sale. These include the following:

> *Preliminary*—The warranties dealing with the information regarding the share capital of the company and its directors will not be relevant.

> *Accounts*—The clauses dealing with liabilities will be irrelevant except in so far as they affect the profits shown in the accounts on the basis of which the purchaser has valued the goodwill of the business.

> *Finance*—The purchaser will not need to be satisfied about the financial facilities available to the vendor for running the business as it would be most unusual for it to take these over. The warranties in this section relating to book debts are dealt with as part of the warranties concerning the assets which are being acquired.

> *Trading and contracts*—The aspects of the business which merely give rise to liabilities will not concern the purchaser except in so far as they affect the contracts which are to be transferred or are relevant in valuing its goodwill.

> *Employees*—Liabilities to former employees will rarely be taken over by the purchaser.

CONSIDERATION OF INDIVIDUAL WARRANTIES

The commentary which follows deals only with those aspects of the warranties **8–17** in Pt 3 of Appendix 5 which give rise to special considerations in the case of a business sale. In considering whether the warranties are satisfactorily worded or need amendment, regard should be given to the comments in para.7–03 (which are not repeated here). The numbering of some of the warranties below reflects that of Ch.7, whereas others do not. This is due to the subject matter of the particular warranty and its relevance to comments made in Ch.7.

Information disclosed to the Purchaser

8–18 **1.14 Information disclosed to the Purchaser**

  1.14.1 **All information given by the Vendor, the Vendor's Solicitors or the Vendor's Accountants to the Purchaser, the Purchaser's Solicitors or the Purchaser's Accountants relating to the Business and the Assets was when given and is on Completion true, accurate and complete in all respects and opinions, expectations and beliefs included in the information are honestly held and have been arrived at on a reasonable basis after full enquiry.[1]**

  1.14.2 **There are no material circumstances in relation to the Business or the Assets which have not been Disclosed and which, if Disclosed, might reasonably have been expected to affect the decision of the Purchaser to enter into this Agreement.**

  1.14.3 **The information contained in Schedule[s] [ ] of this Agreement is true, complete and accurate.**

The primary purpose of warranty 1.14.1 is to give the purchaser comfort that the legal, financial or commercial due diligence information that has been provided is warranted as true and accurate. Warranty 1.14.2 is a "catch all" which requires the vendor to second guess what may or may not be material to the purchaser. In most cases the vendor should be very reluctant to give this.

In addition the asset sale agreement will usually contain a number of schedules some or all of which are likely to contain information that the purchaser is relying upon being correct. The asset schedule will likely include the value of the assets, the employee schedule should include the identities of each employee, the contracts schedule will usually contain a list of contracts, and the intellectual property rights schedule will contain a list of the registered and unregistered intellectual property rights used by the business. The purchaser will have a legitimate interest in requesting that the accuracy of these schedules be warranted so that it can properly assess the assets it is acquiring and the potential liabilities for employees and contracts it is assuming. The warranties will usually require specific details in relation to those schedules to be spelt out in the disclosure letter.

Accounts

8–19 **2.1 The Accounts**

  2.1.1 **The Accounts were prepared in accordance with the historical cost convention and with the requirements of all relevant statutes and generally accepted accounting principles; and the bases and policies of accounting, adopted for the purpose of**

---

[1] Please see comments at para.7–30 in relation to this warranty and the alternative form of wording that a well-advised vendor is likely to insist on.

preparing the Accounts, were the same as those adopted in preparing the audited accounts of the Vendor in respect of the preceding three accounting periods.

2.1.2   The Accounts:

2.1.2.1   give a true and fair view of the assets and liabilities of the Business at the Balance Sheet Date and its profits for the financial period ended on that date;

2.1.2.2   comply with the requirements of the Companies Acts;

2.1.2.3   comply with all current Accounting Standards;

2.1.2.4   are not affected by extraordinary, exceptional or non-recurring items; and

2.1.2.5   properly reflect the financial position of the Vendor as at the Balance Sheet Date [including reflecting any events or matters that are discovered after the Balance Sheet Date which, if known at the Balance Sheet Date, would have been included in the Accounts.]

This warranty is likely to be unacceptable to the vendor as the purchaser's legitimate interest should only be with the element of the business which is being purchased and not any part of it which is being retained by the vendor. Following the *Macquarie Internationale Investments Ltd v Glencore UK Ltd* [2010] EWCA Civ 697 decision, well-advised purchasers may wish to consider including the wording in brackets in order to seek to impose liability on the vendor where applicable. Whilst it might be prudent to include the wording in brackets, as can be seen from the *Macquarie* case, clarifying wording such as this may not of itself be sufficient to impose liability. Please refer to para.7–33 for a discussion of the *Macquarie* decision.

The Last Accounts

2.1.3   The amount included in the Accounts in respect of each asset,   8–20
whether fixed or current, did not exceed its purchase price or production cost or (in the case of current assets) its net realisable value at the Balance Sheet Date.

2.2 Valuation of stock in trade and work in progress

2.2.1   In the Accounts and in the accounts of the Vendor for the three preceding financial years, stock in trade and work in progress was valued at the lowest cost or net realisable value, cost represents materials and appropriate proportions of direct labour and overheads.

2.2.2   In the Accounts slow moving stock in trade was written down as appropriate and redundant, obsolete, obsolescent and defective stock was wholly written off and the value attributable to any other stock did not exceed the lower of cost and net realisable value at the Balance Sheet Date.

The approach adopted is that the purchaser has an interest in the profit and loss accounts for recent periods as these will have influenced its valuation of the goodwill of the business. The warranties relating to the financial position of the vendor and to the provisions for liabilities are omitted. These are really only appropriate in their full format in circumstances where the whole of the business is being acquired on a going concern basis. Where there is a sale of part or an insignificant amount of consideration is being paid for goodwill the full format of these warranties will need to be substantially reduced or modified to fairly reflect something more appropriate.

The Management Accounts

8–21 2.3 Management Accounts

> **2.3.1 The Management Accounts have been prepared in accordance with accounting policies consistent with those used in the preparation of the Accounts with all due care and on a basis consistent with the management accounts of the Vendor prepared in the preceding year.**

Again, the same comments apply in relation to the management accounts as the full accounts warranties and great care needs to be taken to ensure the warranties only cover matters within the legitimate interests of the purchaser.

Books and records

8–22 2.4 Books and records

> **2.4.1 The accounting and other records of the Business:**
>
> > **2.4.1.1 have been fully, properly and accurately prepared and have at all times been fully, properly and accurately maintained and are properly written up to date in each case, as required by law, and will be so kept to Completion;**
> >
> > **2.4.1.2 are accurate in all material respects;**
> >
> > **2.4.1.3 in respect of the accounting records, show a true and fair view of its trading transactions and its financial, contractual and trading position; and**
> >
> > **2.4.1.4 are in the possession or under the control of the Vendor.**

The purchase agreement will often provide for the books of the business to be transferred to the purchaser, in which case the purchaser will require reassurance that they are accurate. This warranty will also be appropriate if the purchaser has inspected the books during the pre-contract investigation of the business and if the vendor is to retain the books after completion, perhaps because they relate to more than one business, with the purchaser being granted a right of access to them.

Assets

Ownership of assets

3.1 Ownership of assets 8–23

3.1.1 Apart from current assets acquired or realised by the Vendor in the ordinary course of the Business, the Assets are the same as the assets shown in the Accounts.

3.1.2 The Vendor legally and beneficially owns the Assets free from Encumbrances except for those items the subject of Finance Agreements listed in the Disclosure Letter.

3.1.3 None of the Assets is subject to, and there is no agreement to create, an Encumbrance.

3.1.4 None of the Assets were purchased by the Vendor on terms that provided for a reservation of title by the seller.

3.1.5 There has been no exercise or purported exercise of or claim under any Encumbrance over any of the Assets and there is no dispute directly or indirectly relating to any of the Assets.

The warranties relating to the vendor having good title to the assets and it being free from security interests or other encumbrances will be redundant if the vendor is expressed to sell with full title guarantee (see para.4–08), however, it is not unusual for there to be warranties which cover the same points.

Fixed assets

3.3 Fixed Assets 8–24

3.3.1 The Fixed Assets:

    3.3.1.1 are in a good and safe state of repair and satisfactory working order and have been properly serviced and maintained;

    3.3.1.2 are not surplus to requirements;

    3.3.1.3 would not be expected (if the sale of the Business had not taken place) to require replacement or additions at a cost in excess of £[ ] within the next six months; and

    3.3.1.4 are used exclusively in connection with the Business.

3.3.2 There are maintenance contracts with independent specialist contractors in respect of all the Fixed Assets for which it is normal or prudent to have maintenance agreements and in respect of all the Fixed Assets which the Vendor is obliged to maintain or repair under a leasing or similar agreement.

3.3.3 Nothing has occurred or is likely to occur in relation to any of the Fixed Assets under a lease or similar agreement whereby the rental payable has been, or is likely to be, increased.

In most cases a vendor will be reluctant to give the warranties contained in 3.3.1 and will usually expect the purchaser to rely on their own investigation and survey. However much depends on the circumstances of the transaction and in particular whether significant value has been placed upon their value. The purchaser does not have a direct interest in the existence of maintenance contracts except in the event of its taking over and retaining those contracts—in which case the agreements will be included in the "Contracts" and will be covered by the warranties in cl.4. But if the fixed assets include leased equipment and the purchaser is taking over the leases, it will need to be satisfied that the lease covenants have been satisfied. However, from a commercial perspective, if the purchaser is paying more than net book value for the assets it will be concerned to ensure that the assets it is acquiring have been properly maintained.

Debts

8–25   3.5 Debts

> **3.5.1   None of the Debts is overdue by more than 12 weeks, or has been released on terms that the debtor pays less than the full book value of his debt, or has been written off or is regarded by the Vendor as wholly or partly irrecoverable.**
>
> **3.5.2   The Debts will be recoverable in full, in the normal course of the Business, and in any event not later than 12 weeks after Completion; and none of them is subject to a right of counter-claim or set-off or withholding or other deduction.**
>
> **3.5.3   All charges securing any of the Book Debts have (if appropriate) been registered in accordance with the provisions of the Companies Acts.**

It is unusual for the purchaser to acquire the book debts of the business although it often adopts the convenient role of collecting the debts for the benefit of the vendor. In such cases, the purchaser will not be concerned as to the value of the debts and these warranties can be omitted. If, however, the debts are acquired by the purchaser, it is likely that the price paid for them will be determined, at least in part, by the amount they realise on collection. The relevance of these warranties in such circumstances may again be minimal.

Insurance

8–26   3.6 Insurance

> **3.6.1   All the Assets which are of an insurable nature are [and have at all material times been] insured in amounts representing their full replacement or reinstatement value against fire and other risks normally insured against by persons carrying on the same type of business as the Business.**

3.6.2   The Business and the Assets are and have at all material times been adequately covered against employee's liability, public liability, professional liability and accident, damage, injury, third party loss, loss of profits (including product liability) and other risks normally covered by insurance.

3.6.3   A list of all current insurance and indemnity policies (the "Insurance Policies") relating to the Business and the Assets are contained in the Disclosure Letter.

3.6.4   Nothing has been done or omitted or has occurred which could make any of the Insurance Policies void or voidable or which is likely to result in an increase in premium.

3.6.5   None of the Insurance Policies is subject to special or unusual terms or restrictions or to the payment of a premium in excess of the normal rate.

3.6.6   The details set out in the Disclosure Letter give all relevant information relating to and the status of all claims by the Vendor under any of its Insurance Policies in the period of two years prior to Completion.

Risk in relation to assets passes to the purchaser on the signing of the contract unless there is express provision to the contrary. The purchaser will accordingly need to have insurance cover in place at the time contracts are exchanged even if there is to be a gap between contracts and completion. In rare cases the purchaser may seek to take over the vendor's existing policies although this is increasingly exceptional. The purpose of these warranties are to protect the purchaser in such rare cases. The only other legitimate interest arises in relation to employee personal injury or similar claims which transfer under TUPE. In such cases the purchaser has an interest in ensuring the adequacy of relevant insurance as claims can be made against the vendor's policy. This is particularly apparent in cases where the transferring employees have been subject to contamination, for example, from exposure to asbestos which could lead to disease claims. In instances such as this, the purchaser will want to ensure that it will have the benefit of the vendor's employer's liability insurance in place at the relevant time. If this is the sole concern the vendor should ensure that the warranties are substantially amended so as to be restricted to this area. The vendor might reasonably resist giving the warranties on the basis that the purchaser should either make its own insurance arrangements or inspect the policies before contracts to satisfy itself that they are in order. Adequacy or otherwise of insurance is very subjective and in most cases the vendor would be unwilling to offer a high degree of comfort on this.

Intellectual property rights

3.8 Intellectual property rights   8–27

3.8.1   Full details of all the Business Intellectual Property Rights and IP Licences are set out in Schedule [   ]. All such Business

Intellectual Property Rights are used, enjoyed and exploited exclusively in connection with the Business.

3.8.2   Except in respect of any Business Intellectual Property Rights which are the subject of a valid and enforceable IP Licence which has been granted to the Vendor are listed in Schedule [ ], the Vendor is the sole legal and beneficial owner of all Business Intellectual Property Rights (including the subject matter of them) free from all claims, liens, equities, Encumbrances, licences and adverse rights of any description. No Business Intellectual Property Rights are held jointly or in common with any other person.

3.8.3   None of the Business Intellectual Property Rights are subject to any challenge or attack by a third party or competent authority. All renewal and registration fees for the protection of the registered Business Intellectual Property Rights have been paid.

3.8.4   All IP Licences are valid and enforceable. There are no other outstanding agreements or arrangements whereby a licence, sub-licence or other permission to use has been granted to or by, or is obliged to be granted to or by, the Vendor in respect of any of the Business Intellectual Property Rights.

3.8.5   Neither the Vendor nor any other party is in breach of any IP Licence and all such licences are in full force and effect and will not terminate or be capable of termination by reason of the execution and performance of this Agreement.

3.8.6   None of the activities involved in the conduct of the Business infringe or have infringed any Intellectual Property of any third party, or constitute or have constituted any breach of confidence, passing off or actionable unfair competition in any jurisdiction. No such activities give or have given rise to any obligation to pay any royalty, fee, compensation or any other sum whatsoever.

3.8.7   The Vendor is not, and has not within the six years preceding the date of this Agreement been, party to or threatened with any legal proceedings relating to any Intellectual Property of any third party and the Vendor is not aware of (and has not acquiesced in) any infringement of any Business Intellectual Property Rights by a third party or any breach of confidence, passing off or actionable unfair competition in any jurisdiction.

3.8.8   There are no outstanding or potential claims against the Vendor under any contract or under s.40 of the Patents Act 1977, for employee compensation in respect of any Intellectual Property of any third party.

3.8.9   The Business Intellectual Property Rights set out in Schedule [ ] constitute all the Intellectual Property necessary to carry on the Business.

These will frequently constitute a significant element of the assets which are being acquired. If, however, no material part of the purchase price is allocated to the rights, there may be difficulty for the purchaser in making an effective claim for damages in the event of a breach of the warranties relating to them. This question is discussed in para.3–06.

Many of the warranties such as 3.8.3 and 3.8.6, ought if appropriate to be given on an awareness basis only, as otherwise they amount to guarantees often beyond the control of the vendor.

Confidential Business Information

3.9 Confidential Business Information   8–28

3.9.1   The Confidential Business Information is in the Vendor's lawful possession and under its control. No licences or other agreements have been granted or entered into in respect thereof and no circumstances exist under which the Vendor or any of its predecessors in title have granted any rights or interest to any third party or any third party has acquired any rights or interest in connection with the Confidential Business Information.

3.9.2   No disclosure has been made or agreed to be made to any person (other than the Purchaser) of any of the Confidential Business Information or confidential information of any customer or client of the Business and the Vendor has not entered into any agreement for the use by any third party of any Confidential Business Information or other Business Intellectual Property Rights held by the Vendor, other than pursuant to written obligations of confidence which have been set out in the Disclosure Letter.

Confidential business information or know-how is an intangible asset which is increasingly being treated separately to goodwill. Whether these warranties are appropriate will depend on the nature of the business being acquired. If this warranty is to be utilised a comprehensive definition of confidential business information will be required to be inserted into the sale agreement.

Information technology

3.10 Information Technology   8–29

All Computer Systems:

3.10.1   are used exclusively by the Vendor and under its sole control or are otherwise used on the terms detailed in the Disclosure Letter.

3.10.2   are, in respect of the hardware, handheld devices, firmware, peripherals, networking and other equipment comprised in those Computer Systems, legally and beneficially owned by the Vendor.

3.10.3   are in full working order and performing the functions for which they were acquired efficiently and without material errors or downtime.

3.10.4   have not, within the two years immediately preceding Completion, unduly interrupted or hindered the operation of the Business.

3.10.5   have adequate capacity for the Business' present and (taking into account the extent to which the Computer Systems are expandable) future needs.

3.10.6   have been satisfactorily and appropriately maintained and supported and have the benefit of appropriate maintenance and support agreements (copies of which are attached to the Disclosure Letter), which agreements include emergency support.

3.10.7   [so far as the Vendor is aware] have not been used in such a way as would invalidate any manufacturer's or supplier's guarantee or warranty or entitle the provider of maintenance or support for the Computer Systems to exclude, suspend or terminate those services.

3.10.8   have, in conjunction with the support and maintenance agreements referred to in clause [3.10.6], adequate security measures, back-up systems, disaster recovery arrangements, measures to protect them from viruses and other harmful code and trained personnel to ensure that so far as reasonably practicable:

    3.10.8.1   the authenticity, integrity and confidentiality of all data held by or transmitted by the Computer Systems are preserved;

    3.10.8.2   no more than one day's data would be lost in the event of a failure of the Computer Systems;

    3.10.8.3   breaches of security, errors and breakdowns are kept to a minimum and that in the event of the occurrence of any such event there will not [so far as the Vendor is aware] be a material disruption to the Vendor;

    3.10.8.4   enable all records and data stored by electronic means which relate to the Vendor to be readily accessible by appropriate personnel; and

    3.10.8.5   will correctly carry out all calculations relating to or in connection with the Euro and display all symbols adopted by any government or European body in connection with the Euro.

3.10.9   all software used or stored or resident in the Vendor:

    3.10.9.1   [so far as the Vendor is aware] is free from any defect or feature which may adversely affect its performance [or the performance of any other software in the future];

3.10.9.2   performs in accordance with its specification;

3.10.9.3   [so far as the Vendor is aware] has been (if copied) lawfully copied;

3.10.9.4   is lawfully held and [so far as the Vendor is aware] does not infringe the Intellectual Property of any person.

3.10.10   as to the copyright therein:

3.10.10.1   in the case of software written or commissioned by the Vendor, is owned solely by the Vendor, no other person has rights therein or rights to use or make copies of the software or source codes;

3.10.10.2   in the case of standard packaged software purchased outright, is validly licensed to the Vendor for use in the Business in perpetuity (other than in the event of breach or insolvency) on written terms which do not require the Vendor to make any further payments, and no licences will terminate on change of control; and

3.10.10.3   in the case of all other software, is licensed to the Vendor on the terms of a written licence which requires payment by the Vendor of a fixed annual licence.

3.10.11   no software owned by or licensed to the Vendor is licensed or sub-licensed by the Vendor to (or otherwise used by) any other person.

3.10.12   no action will be necessary to enable the Vendor to continue to use any software currently used by it to the same extent and in the same manner as it has been used prior to Completion.

3.10.13   [so far as the Vendor is aware] the terms of all software licences have been complied with and no notices of breach or termination have been served on the Vendor in respect of any such licence.

3.10.14   details of all domain names and websites are set out in the Disclosure Letter. The Vendor is the registrant and beneficial owner of those domain names and is [so far as the Vendor is aware] the legal and beneficial owner of all Intellectual Property in the websites.

3.10.15   details of all Social Media are set out in the Disclosure Letter. [So far as the Vendor is aware] the Business' use complies with each Social Media provider's terms.

3.10.16   [so far as the Vendor is aware] all websites operated by the Business comply with the Electronic Commerce (EC Directive) Regulations 2002. The websites are accessible in compliance with the requirements set out in Pt III of the Disability Discrimination Act 1995 (as amended or superseded).

Many businesses are heavily reliant on information technology to run all aspects of their business, and as such computer systems are often a significant asset. If there are any problems with these systems following completion then this could cause expense and loss of profit/goodwill to the purchaser in having to rectify the problems and/or replace any equipment or software not operating correctly. The purpose of these warranties is to provide comfort to the purchaser that the computer systems are in operating order and fulfil the purpose for which they were acquired, have adequate capacity, that there are no potential issues in respect of security breaches, failure, breakdown or breaches of software licences or other intellectual property rights. In a business where the computer systems are not critical or where the purchaser is not paying above net book value for the computer systems then it is likely that the vendor might reasonably resist giving the warranties or may only be prepared to give more limited warranties, usually qualified in respect of knowledge. In such circumstances the purchaser will need to assess the potential liabilities if the information technology systems do not operate correctly and should consider whether to carry out an information technology audit as part of its due diligence process.

Contracts

Nature of contracts

8–30   4.1 The Contracts

> **4.1.1   The Contracts, true copies of which are annexed to the Disclosure Letter or the full terms of which are set out in the Disclosure Letter, constitute all the contracts and other engagements, whether written or oral, referable to the Business and Assets to which the Vendor is now a party, apart from the contracts of employment of the employees.**
>
> **4.1.2   All of the Contracts are assignable by the Vendor to the Purchaser without the consent of any other party.**
>
> **4.1.3   The performance of this Agreement will not relieve any other party to any Contract from its obligations or enable it to determine any of them.**
>
> **4.1.4   No steps have been taken by any party to the Finance Agreements to terminate the Finance Agreements.**

4.2 Nature of the contracts

> **4.2.1   None of the Contracts:**
>
> > **4.2.1.1   was entered into in any way otherwise than in the ordinary and normal course of the Business bona fide on an arm's-length basis; or**
> >
> > **4.2.1.2   is of a loss-making nature; or**

4.2.1.3   **cannot readily be fulfilled or performed by the Vendor on time without undue expenditure or application of money, effort or personnel; or**

4.2.1.4   **involves, or is likely to involve, other obligations or liabilities which ought reasonably to be made known to an intending purchaser of the Business; or**

4.2.1.5   **is of an unusual, abnormal or onerous nature; or**

4.2.1.6   **is of a long term nature (that is to say incapable of performance in accordance with its terms within six months after the date on which it was entered into or undertaken); or**

4.2.1.7   **involves payment by reference to fluctuations in the index of retail prices, or other index, or in the rate or exchange for a currency; or**

4.2.1.8   **involves an aggregate outstanding expenditure by the Vendor of more than £[   ]; or**

4.2.1.9   **is for the supply of goods and services by or to the Vendor on terms under which retrospective or future discount, price reduction or other financial incentives are given; or**

4.2.1.10   **involves, or is likely to involve, the supply of goods or services the aggregate sales value of which will be more than 10 per cent of its turnover for the preceding financial year; or**

4.2.1.11   **involves the payment by the Vendor of any commission, finder's fee, royalty or the like.**

The contracts taken over by a purchaser will generally represent a combination of work in progress and customer contracts, supply contracts and finance agreements (and accordingly the definition of "Contracts" is broken down into these elements). The sale agreement will usually provide that except for the obligations arising from a default on the part of the vendor, the purchaser will duly perform the contracts. If this approach is adopted, the purchaser will usually require the protection of the indemnities contained in cll.2.1 to 2.3 in respect of any post completion breach or omission by the vendor in respect of the contracts and any negligence or misrepresentation concerning them. The purchaser will also require the protection of these warranties concerning the nature of obligations it is taking on under the contracts. However, the vendor may resist these warranties on the basis that the purchaser is likely to review the terms of the contracts it is taking on during due diligence. Whether the vendor is prepared to give these warranties will depend on the circumstances, what other options the vendor has to discharge the obligations under the contract following completion and whether the purchaser needs the benefit of the contracts to allow it to operate the business going forward. If the purchaser is paying more than a nominal sum for the contracts in order to buy the benefit of profitable customer contracts, then appropriate additional warranties should be included in respect of the continuation of these contracts and/or their profit or revenue stream.

Defaults and agreements concerning the business

8–31　4.3 Defaults

> **4.3.1** **None of the parties to the Contracts is in default, being a default which would be material in the context of the financial or trading position of the Business; and there are no circumstances likely to give rise to a default and none of the parties to the Contracts have given notice of its intention to terminate, or has sought to repudiate or disclaim, such agreement, arrangement or obligation.**
>
> **4.3.2** **No event has occurred, is subsisting or is likely to arise which, with the giving of notice and/or lapse of time will constitute or result in a default or the acceleration of any obligation of the Vendor under any agreement or arrangement which it has entered into for the purpose of, or which is used in the operation of, the Business and Assets.**

The purchaser would normally expect to receive the indemnity contained in cl.2.1 from the vendor in respect of any default or omission by the vendor under any of the contracts and therefore there is an overlap between this indemnity and the warranties. However, these warranties also cover default by a third party under the contracts and will be used by the purchaser to illicit disclosure of any issues in respect of the business' contracts or agreements which ought to be of concern to it. The latter warranty is designed to be wider in scope than simply relating to the contracts or agreements which will be acquired by the purchaser. Consequently, this warranty is likely to be resisted by the vendor on the basis that it is not appropriate.

Defective products

8–32　4.4 Defective products

> **4.4.1** **The Vendor has not, in the course of carrying on the Business, manufactured, sold or supplied products which were, are or will become, in a material respect, faulty or defective, or which do not comply in a material respect with warranties or representations expressly or impliedly made by it and all applicable regulations, standards and requirements in respect hereof.**
>
> **4.4.2** **The Vendor has not received a prohibition notice, a notice to warn or a suspension notice under the Consumer Protection Act 1987.**

As previously discussed the purchase agreement will commonly provide that the purchaser assumes responsibility for rectifying defects in products of the business sold by the vendor. This will be because of the practical difficulty which the vendor would otherwise experience in dealing with these once the business has been sold. The agreement will generally provide a mechanism for compensating the purchaser if this obligation proves to be unduly onerous and the warranties need to be reviewed in parallel with any other terms of the agreement which deal with this. The purchaser will also be concerned about defects in products sold by the vendor, apart from any obligation it has accepted to remedy them, because customer dissatisfaction with the products could reduce the value of the goodwill of the business. Warranties can be used to elicit appropriate disclosure.

Service liabilities

4.6 Service liabilities   8–33

4.6.1   The Vendor is not obliged to repair, maintain, take back or otherwise do or not do anything in respect of goods sold in the course of carrying on the Business.

The vendor might reasonably adopt the position that the purchaser is entitled to this warranty only if it takes over the responsibility for discharging the vendor's obligations. However, from the purchaser's perspective it is important to identify possible causes of customer dissatisfaction and the need to protect goodwill may necessitate the purchaser accepting responsibilities to the vendor's customers which it does not have legally.

Trading

Vendor's other interests

5.1 Vendor's other interests   8–34

5.1.1   The Vendor and its Associates are not, directly or indirectly, interested in businesses which are or are likely to be competitive with the Business, apart from interests in securities listed on the London Stock Exchange's market for listed securities, or traded in on the AIM (its alternative investment market of the London Stock Exchange), and in respect of which the Vendor, with its Associates, is interested in less than three per cent of any class of the securities in that company.

The purchaser will wish to protect the goodwill of the business by identifying—and then, if possible, restricting, competing activities of the vendor. The vendor will argue that this warranty is unnecessary and that the purchaser should obtain whatever protection is reasonable by the covenants restricting future activities of the vendor which will feature in almost every sale agreement.

Joint ventures and partnerships

8–35 5.3 Joint venture and partnerships

> **5.3.1 The Vendor is not, and has not agreed to become, a party to or member of a joint venture, consortium, partnership or other unincorporated association.**

This warranty has information value only and it is difficult to see how the purchaser can suffer loss if it is breached. On that basis the vendor might reasonably take the position that it is willing to provide the information but not to warrant it.

Undertakings restricting the business

8–36 5.5 Undertakings restricting the Business

> **5.5.1 The Vendor is not subject to an undertaking or assurance which it has given to a court or government agency in relation to the Business.**

The purchaser is entitled to this warranty only in relation to undertakings which are likely to affect it as successor to the business and which are not purely personal to the vendor.

Unfair trade and restrictive practices

8–37 5.6 Unfair trade and restrictive practices

> **5.6.1 The Vendor is not, nor has it been in relation to the Business, a party to or concerned in any agreement, practice or arrangement (whether legally binding or not) which is or was:**
>
> **5.6.1.1 in contravention of the Trade Descriptions Act 1968;**
> **5.6.1.2 in contravention the Fair Trading Act 1973 Pt XI as amended by the Trading Schemes Act 1996;**
> **5.6.1.3 in contravention of the Consumer Credit Act 1974 (as amended);**
> **5.6.1.4 in contravention of or invalidated (in whole or in part) by the Competition Act 1998;**
> **5.6.1.5 in contravention of the Enterprise Act 2002;**
> **5.6.1.6 in contravention of [arts 101 and 102 of] Treaty on the Functioning of the European Union; or**
> **5.6.1.7 in contravention of any other anti-trust, anti-monopoly or anti-cartel legislation or regulation.**
>
> **5.6.2 The Vendor has not, in relation to the Business, received notice of any breach by it of any competition, anti-trust, anti-restrictive trade practices or consumer protection law, rule or regulation**

> anywhere in the world or of any investigation, inquiry, report or order by any regulatory authority under any such law, rule or regulation.

The reason for the purchaser requiring the above warranties is that it will need to know if the ability of the business to achieve the anticipated results is to any extent dependent on practices which are potentially illegal or likely to attract an attack from the authorities.

Litigation, disputes and winding-up

5.7 Litigation and winding-up   8–38

5.7.1 The Vendor is not engaged (nor at any time has been engaged) in connection with the Business in any litigation, arbitration, mediation, prosecution or any other legal proceedings or claims with any person (including any customers of the Business). No injunction or order for specific performance has been granted against the Vendor in respect of any activity or potential activity of the Business and the Vendor has not given any undertaking to any prospective claimant or defendant or any other governmental or administrative body or court in connection with the Business or any of the Assets. There is no circumstance which might give rise to the same and there are no circumstances which may give rise to any claims against the Vendor or litigation or arbitration in relation to the Business.

5.7.2 There are no outstanding claims against the Vendor on the part of customers or other parties in respect of defects in quality or delays in delivery or completion of contracts or deficiencies of design or performance or otherwise relating to liability for goods or services sold or supplied by the Vendor in the course of the Business. No such claims are threatened and there is no matter or fact in existence in relation to goods or services sold or supplied by the Vendor in the course of the Business which might give rise to the same.

5.7.3 There are no outstanding claims against the Vendor by suppliers of goods or services to the Vendor in respect of the Business, or disputes between the Vendor and suppliers. There are no such claims by the Vendor against such suppliers and there is no matter or fact in existence which may give rise to any such claims or disputes.

5.7.4 Full details of all material claims, complaints or returns relating to the Business that have occurred during the 12 months preceding the date of this Agreement are set out in the Disclosure Letter.

    5.7.5   **The Vendor is not insolvent or unable to pay its debts within the meaning of the Insolvency Act 1986 s.123 (the references in that section to proving to the satisfaction of the court being disregarded).**

    5.7.6   **No order has been made, petition presented or resolution passed for the winding-up of the Vendor; no distress, execution or other process has been levied and remains undischarged in respect of the Assets; and there is no outstanding judgment or court order against the Vendor in relation to the Business or the Assets.**

    5.7.7   **No meeting of its creditors, or any class of them, has been held or summoned and no proposal has been made for a moratorium, composition or arrangement in relation to any of its debts, or for a voluntary arrangement under Pt 1 of the Insolvency Act 1986.**

    5.7.8   **No floating charge created by the Vendor has crystallised over the Business or Assets or any of them and there no circumstances likely to cause such an event.**

    5.7.9   **No event analogous to those described in clauses 5.8.4 or 5.8.5 has occurred outside England.**

The interest of the purchaser in litigation relating to the business is limited to cases that affect the assets which it is acquiring or the goodwill of the business. The solvency of the vendor is a concern if there is any possibility that the sale is not on arm's length terms or that it might constitute a preference in relation to the purchaser as one of the creditors of the vendor. These circumstances would be unusual and, although the vendor should have no difficulty in checking the facts underlying the warranties contained in these warranties, it might reasonably object to giving them as a matter of principle. Furthermore, the purchaser will derive some protection from the warranty in cl.1.12.

Compliance with statutes

8–39   5.8 Compliance with statutes

    5.8.1   **The Vendor has not done or omitted to do anything in relation to the Business and/or the Assets, the doing or omitting of which is, or could be, in contravention of a statute, regulation or the like giving rise to a penalty, default proceedings or other liability.**

A default by the vendor in relation to the statutory obligations applicable to the business could affect the purchaser's prospects of getting any permits or other statutory authorities it requires—although this is more specifically covered by the warranties in cl.5.11. The warranty in cl.5.11 is, however, so widely drawn that the vendor will normally be justified in refusing to give it unless it is made much more specific.

Branches

5.11 Branches   8–40

> 5.11.1 The Vendor does not carry on any part of the Business outside the United Kingdom through a branch, agency or other place of business. The Disclosure Letter contains full particulars of all telephone and fax numbers and all other electronic addresses and codes used by the Business at or in the 12-month period prior to Completion.

This warranty is unlikely to serve any other function than that of providing information. Although the vendor should have no difficulty in deciding whether the warranty is factually correct, it may reasonably consider that there is no reason why it should commit itself to a warranty.

Employment

Employees and terms of employment

6.1 Employees and terms and conditions   8–41

> 6.1.1 Full and accurate details are given in Schedule [   ] of the Employees' full names, addresses, national insurance numbers, tax codes, rates of remuneration (or methods of calculating remuneration) (including overtime pay), benefits, bonuses, commissions, dates of birth, commencement dates, periods of notice, pensions, voluntary pensions, annuities and rights under any retirement benefit, life assurance or hospital or medical insurance scheme of the Vendor in respect of the Business and all other benefits (including share option schemes and pre-requisites of any nature) of each of the Employees. Copies of any communication to staff concerning any such matters have been supplied to the Purchaser and are attached to the Disclosure Letter.
>
> 6.1.2 The details shown in Schedule [   ] together with the information contained in the Disclosure Letter (including, without limitation, any staff handbook) give full, complete and accurate details of all the terms and conditions of employment of each of the Employees.
>
> 6.1.3 There are no loans outstanding from the Vendor to any of the Employees.
>
> 6.1.4 There are no employees of the Vendor or any other person engaged or employed in the Business or in carrying on the Business except the Employees.
>
> 6.1.5 No past employee of the Vendor has a right to return to work or may have a right to be reinstated or re-engaged under the Employment Rights Act 1996.

6.1.6   No offers of employment have been made to any persons other than the Employees nor any agreements made for any person to become an employee of the Vendor.

6.1.7   All of the Employees are employed by the Vendor, are wholly and exclusively engaged in carrying on the Business and have been so engaged for at least 12 months prior to Completion.

6.1.8   All contracts of employment between the Vendor and the Employees are terminable on not more than three months' notice without compensation, other than compensation payable in accordance with the Employment Rights Act 1996.

6.1.9   All of the Employees are legally entitled to work in the United Kingdom.

6.1.10   The Vendor is not bound (whether legally or morally) to vary any of the terms and conditions of any of the Employees and has not offered any new contract of employment to any of the Employees.

6.1.11   The Vendor is not in breach of any of the terms of the contracts of employment of any of the Employees nor any other duties or obligations owed to the Employees (or any of them) nor (so far as the Vendor is aware) is any Employee in breach of his contract of employment.

6.1.12   None of the Employees is absent on maternity leave, paternity leave, adoption leave, parental leave or other leave of absence. None of the Employees is absent on sick leave which has lasted or is expected to last longer than four weeks.

6.1.13   There are not in existence and the Vendor has neither proposed nor is proposing to introduce any bonus, profit sharing, share option or share incentive scheme or any other scheme or arrangement (whether contractual or discretionary) under which the Employees or any of them are or is or would be entitled to participate in the profits of the Business.

The reasons why it is imperative for the purchaser to have full and accurate details of all the transferring employees and their terms and conditions of employment are, having regard to the operation of TUPE, fairly obvious. The purchaser should ask the vendor to warrant that all employees have been employed exclusively in the business (or part being transferred) for the previous 12 months to ensure that the vendor has not reassigned underperforming or troublesome employees from its other business or divisions in order that the obligations in respect of such employees pass to the purchaser.

Changes in remuneration

8–42   6.2 Changes in remuneration

6.2.1   Since the Balance Sheet Date or (where employment commenced after the Balance Sheet Date, since the date of commencement of employment) no change has been made in the rate of remuneration, emoluments, pension benefits or, without limitation, any other terms or conditions of employment of any of the Employees.

6.2.2   No negotiations for any increase in remuneration or benefits or any other changes in the terms and conditions of employment of any of the Employees are current or due within a period of six months from Completion.

The purchaser is legally bound only by the actual terms of employment but, from a commercial point of view, it will wish the employees to be supportive of the sale. For this reason it will want to be informed about the employees' expectations but the vendor will need to ensure that the warranty (cl.6.2) relates to factual questions which are easily verified.

Of course, under TUPE, if the vendor has promised a pay rise to take effect at some point following completion—perhaps with effect from the end of the financial year—then the purchaser will be bound to honour that promise. The same applies where the expectation of a pay rise arises by custom and practice.

Termination of contracts of employment and redundancies

6.3 Termination of contracts of employment and redundancies   8–43

6.3.1   No liability has been incurred by the Vendor and not yet been discharged for:

6.3.1.1   breach of any contract of service or employment or for redundancy payments (including protective awards);

6.3.1.2   damages or compensation for wrongful dismissal or unfair dismissal or otherwise;

6.3.1.3   failure to comply with any order for reinstatement or re-engagement of any Employee engaged in connection with the Business; or

6.3.1.4   for the actual or proposed termination or suspension of employment or variation of any contract of employment of any present or former director or employee of the Vendor employed in connection with the Business.

6.3.2   None of the Employees have given or been given notice of termination of his employment nor is any of the Employees engaged in any grievance or disciplinary procedure, nor within the period of 12 months prior to Completion has the Vendor been engaged in relation to the Business or any of the Employees in any dispute, litigation or claim arising out of or relating to the provisions of the Employment Rights Act 1996, the Trade Union Reform and Employment Act 1993, the Health and Safety at

Work Act 1974, the Equal Pay Act 1970, the Sex Discrimination Act 1975, the Disability Discrimination Act 1995, the Race Relations Act 1976, the Sex Discrimination (Gender Reassignment) Regulations 1999, the Regulations, the Trade Union and Labour Relations (Consolidation) Act 1992, the Protection from Harassment Act 1997, the Working Time Regulations 1998, the National Minimum Wage Act 1998, the Employment Relations Act 1999, the Part-Time Workers (Prevention of Less Favourable Treatment) Regulations 2000, the Fixed-Term Employees (Prevention of Less Favourable Treatment) Regulations 2002, *the Employment Act 2002, the Employment Equality (Religion or Belief) Regulations 2003, the Employment Equality (Sexual Orientation) Regulations 2003, the Employment Equality (Age) Regulations 2006* or the Equality Act 2010 or any other law statute or regulation relating to the Employees (or any of them), and there is no matter or fact in existence which can be reasonably foreseen as likely to give rise to the same.

6.3.3   **No employees currently or previously employed in the Business have received or been given notice of dismissal during the period of twelve months prior to Completion.**

6.3.4   **None of the Employees as a result of this Agreement will be entitled to terminate their contracts of employment or will become redundant and be entitled to a redundancy payment.**

As the purchaser will assume liabilities for the employees (including any claims for unfair, wrongful or constructive dismissal or for redundancy payments) it will be reasonable for the vendor to warrant (cl.6.3) that no employees have given notice or been given notice of termination or have any dispute or grievance with the business and that there are no reasonably foreseeable circumstances likely to give rise to such a matter.

The Acts whose names appear in italics were, subject to transitional arrangements, repealed by the Equality Act 2010 the principal provisions of which came into force on October 1, 2010. The transitional arrangements are not straightforward and it is recommended that warranties continue to refer to the former legislation, at least for the foreseeable future.

Industrial agreements, disputes and negotiations

8–44 **6.4 Industrial agreements disputes and negotiations**

6.4.1   **The Vendor does not in respect of the Business recognise any trade unions, works or staff councils or associates of trade unions and there are in force no collective agreements (whether or not legally binding and whether in writing or arising by virtue of customs and practice) relating to any of the Employees.**

6.4.2   **The Vendor has not, in relation to the Business or the Employees, done anything which might be construed as** recognition of a trade union and has not, in respect of the Business or the Employees received an application for recognition from any trade union.

6.4.3 At no time during the period of two years immediately prior to Completion has the Vendor or any of the Employees been involved in an industrial dispute in relation to the Business and so far as the Vendor is aware there is nothing which might suggest that there may be an industrial dispute involving the Business or any of the Employees, or that this Agreement may give rise to such a dispute.

6.4.4 There is no dispute between the Vendor and any trade union or any of the Employees existing or pending at the date of this Agreement and there are no circumstances (including without limitation the entry into and carrying out of this Agreement) which may give rise to a dispute with any of the Employees.

6.4.5 The Vendor has not in relation to the Business received any request for an information and consultation agreement pursuant to the Information and Consultation of Employees Regulations 2004 and the Vendor is not, in relation to the Business, a party to such an agreement.

6.4.6 There are no enquiries or investigations existing, pending or threatened into the Vendor in relation to the Business by the Commission for Equality and Human Rights, the Health and Safety Executive or any similar body.

In law the purchaser is not affected by disputes involving the vendor but in practice these are likely to have a significant impact on the purchaser's relations with its new employees. It must be remembered that rights and duties under collective agreements will be binding on the purchaser following completion.

Compliance with laws

6.5 Compliance with laws   8–45

6.5.1 The Vendor has complied in all material respects with all:

6.5.1.1 obligations imposed on it by all statutes, regulations and codes of conduct and practice (including without limitation the Working Time Regulations 1998 and any obligations under any health and safety legislation or any legislation relating to the environment);

6.5.1.2 collective agreements and customs and practices for the time being dealing with relations between the Vendor and the Employees or any relevant trade union and the terms and conditions of service of the Employees; and

6.5.1.3 relevant orders, declarations and awards made under any relevant statute, regulation or code of conduct and

> **practice affecting the conditions of service of any of the Employees.**

The purchaser will wish to receive fairly wide warranties from the vendor that it has met all contractual obligations and complied with all relevant legislation and codes of practice in respect of the employees. These are contained in cl.7.5.

Sub-contractors, agency workers and the self-employed

8–46   6.6 Sub-contractors, agency workers and the self-employed

> **6.6.1   Full, complete and accurate details are set out in the Disclosure Letter of the terms on which all consultants, sub-contractors, self-employed persons and other independent contractors are engaged in the Business. The Taxation Authority has confirmed in writing that it does not consider any such person to be an employee of the Vendor.**
>
> **6.6.2   The Vendor has paid to the Taxation Authority all taxes, national insurance contributions and other levies payable prior to Completion in respect of the Employees.**

The purchaser will need to scrutinise the terms on which all consultants, sub-contractors, agency workers and other self-employed personnel are engaged in the business in order to be sure that there is no risk of them asserting that they are in fact employees and therefore availing themselves of the protection afforded by TUPE. It is usual for the purchaser to expect to receive a fairly wide warranty to cover this.

Taxation

8–47   7.1 VAT and PAYE

> **7.1.1   The Vendor has duly deducted all amounts from any payments from which tax falls to be deducted at source under the PAYE system and national insurance contributions and any other sums required by law to be deducted from wages, salaries or other benefits and the Vendor has duly paid or accounted for such amounts and all other sums due in respect of any benefits that are subject to taxation or similar contributions to a Taxation Authority.**
>
> **7.1.2   There have been no investigations made by a Taxation Authority within three years prior to the date hereof into or affecting the payment of tax on benefits in cash or otherwise paid by the Vendor to its employees or persons alleged by a Taxation Authority to be employees.**
>
> **7.1.3   In respect of the Business, the Vendor has complied with the provisions of VATA 1994 and with all statutory requirements, regulations, orders, provisions, directions or conditions relating**

to VAT, including the terms of any agreement reached with a Taxation Authority in respect of the Business and has maintained full, complete, correct and up to date records, invoices and other documents (as the case may be) appropriate or requisite for the purposes thereof and has preserved such records, invoices and other documents in such form and for such periods as are required by the relevant legislation.

7.1.4 The Disclosure Letter contains full details of all current agreements or arrangements between the Vendor and a Taxation Authority relating to VAT.

7.1.5 The Vendor is not liable to any abnormal or non-routine payment, or any forfeiture, penalty, interest or surcharge, or to the operation of any penal provision, in relation to VAT.

7.1.6 The Vendor has not been required by a Taxation Authority to give security for payment of VAT.

7.1.7 There has been no investigation by a Taxation Authority within three years prior to the date hereof into or affecting the payment of VAT in respect of the Business.

7.1.8 The Disclosure Letter contains details (including the cost and percentage of input tax claimed on the item in the first interval as defined in the VAT Regulations reg.114) of all land and other capital items which are used in the course of furtherance of the Business to which VAT Regulations reg.115 could apply. No such adjustment as is referred to in the VAT Regulations regs 112–116 has been made or should have been made in respect of the current interval in relation to any such capital items.

7.1.9 No election under VATA 1994 Sch.10, para.2 to waive exemption from VAT in respect of the grant of any interest in or right over land owned or occupied by the Vendor which is to be transferred to the Purchaser under the terms of this Agreement has been made by the Vendor or by any person making such a grant to the Vendor.

7.1.10 The Vendor has not made exempt supplies such, or of such amount, that it is unable to obtain full credit for input tax paid or suffered by it.

7.1.11 The Disclosure Letter contains details in respect of:

7.1.11.1 such of the Property as is leasehold; all fixtures, within the meaning of CAA 2001 s.173, which are treated pursuant to that section as belonging to the Vendor;

7.1.11.2 such of the Property as is freehold; all fixtures, so defined, that are treated pursuant to the said s.173 as belonging to a person other than the Vendor.

7.2 Inheritance tax

7.2.1 The Assets hereby agreed to be sold are not subject to a Taxation Authority charge as it mentioned in IHTA 1984 s.237 nor is any unsatisfied liability to inheritance tax attached to or attributable to any of the Assets.

7.2.2 No person is liable to inheritance tax attributable to the value of the Assets hereby agreed to be sold in such circumstances that such person has the power under IHTA 1984 s.212 to raise the amount of such tax by the sale or mortgage or by a terminable charge on the said assets.

Except in the rare case of the purchaser taking over the vendor's VAT registration, tax liabilities will not transfer to the purchaser. As the purchaser is not taking over any liabilities, the vendor may resist giving any taxation warranties. However, the purchaser will usually want taxation warranties to get information both as to how the business has been run and any potential tax problems.

A number of the suggested taxation warranties relate to PAYE and VAT compliance. As noted, it can be argued that these warranties are irrelevant as the purchaser does not take over any liabilities to which they relate. However, the purchaser will be interested in the compliance record, as a poor record may indicate that there will need to be investment in systems and training to ensure future compliance. (A poor record may also indicate that HMRC will continue to take a strict line on compliance matters despite the change in ownership.) Where these warranties are given it is difficult to see how a claim for breach of these warranties would provide any recovery of expenses incurred as a result of any new investment required. If as a result of disclosure the purchaser has a concern it should address this directly in negotiations or seek a more direct warranty on the point.

The other warranties give information to the purchaser so that it can plan its tax affairs and be aware of any inherent tax problems. These include information regarding assets held under the capital goods scheme, electing to charge VAT on supplies of property, irrecoverable input tax and the capital allowances position.

Finally, as noted in para.5–103, in certain circumstances a charge in respect of unpaid inheritance tax may attach to the assets of the business. Although any problems are likely in any event to be caught under the general warranties as to title, it may be worth in appropriate circumstances having a specific warranty so that the vendor specifically addresses the issue.

CHAPTER 9

Disclosure Letters

PURPOSE

It has long been the custom that, in contrast to the practice in relation to **9–01** purchases of land, the first draft of an agreement for the purchase of the shares or business of a company is prepared by the solicitors for the purchaser. This arises from the fact that a major part of the document consists of the warranties and the purchaser's solicitors will wish to prepare the first draft of these. If the draft is sent out too early, that is to say before receipt of legal due diligence, the document will often have been prepared by somebody who has comparatively little information about the target company or the business that is being acquired. In these circumstances the warranties will often extend to areas that are of little or no relevance to the target company or business and will require amendment to comply with the actual circumstances of it.

The information which is specific to the target company or the business falls into two broad categories. In the first place, there is information which is the subject of express warranties (which for convenience is referred to as "warranted items"). An example is a warranty that the listed names of the employees and their terms of employment are accurate and comprehensive. Secondly there is information which operates in derogation of a warranty (referred to as "excepted items"). An example might arise in the case of a warranty that no employee is entitled to more than one month's notice—the warranty would have to be modified so as to exclude named employees who were in fact entitled to longer notice.

Warranted items will normally be dealt with by listing the relevant details **9–02** either in a schedule to the sale agreement or, more often, in the disclosure letter. Where the warranty concerned is very rigorous, the details to be provided in relation to the warranted items may be extremely extensive and of comparatively little relevance to the transaction as a whole. It is therefore common to reduce the extent to which warranted items have to be listed by qualifying the warranties so as to remove from their scope items of a trivial nature. Thus, for example, the warranty referred to above with regard to employees might be qualified by specifying that the warranty applies only to employees receiving a salary in excess of a particular amount.

So far as the excepted items are concerned, the warranties can either be expressly qualified by suitable amendments or, as is now convention, left in absolute terms with the qualifications collected together in the disclosure letter. The agreement will contain a clause that the warranties are to apply "save as [fully, fairly and accurately disclosed] [fairly disclosed] [set out] in the

Disclosure Letter" or "save as Disclosed" (if the defined term of Disclosed is being used, as is assumed for the purposes of this Chapter). See para.4–06, cl.3C for a more detailed discussion of these points. To the extent that any of the disclosures do not meet the agreed standard of disclosure, the purchaser will have a potential warranty claim, which, if successful and subject to being able to demonstrate loss, will result in a retrospective adjustment to the purchase price.

9–03   It is usual practice to attach to the disclosure letter a bundle of documents (referred to as the disclosure bundle) which comprises copies of all documents which are either required to be provided for the purposes of giving information in connection with warranted items, for example, the warranted copies of the memoranda and articles of association, or provided in support of disclosures of qualifications to the excepted items. Two copies of the disclosure letter and bundle should be prepared; one to be delivered to the purchaser and one to be retained by the vendors. In all bar exceptional circumstances, the bundles will be compared to ensure they are identical and each party's will be initialled by representatives of the other as evidence of that. The production and agreement of the contents of the disclosure bundle avoids arguments about which documentation was or was not included in it and is designed to remove the doubt that could arise if a warranty relates to a document "which has not been attached".

It is sometimes suggested that the main purpose and function of the disclosure letter is to bring together all relevant information which might affect the purchaser in making an evaluation of the target company. While this is certainly an important aspect from the purchaser's perspective as it enables it to have a full picture of the target company prior to it becoming legally obliged to complete the acquisition, of arguably more importance to both the parties is the effect of the disclosures in relation to excepted items, namely to transfer to the purchaser the commercial risks which arise from the matters disclosed. If the purchaser is not willing to accept the disclosures, its general approach will be to amend the sale agreement so that, notwithstanding the disclosures, the risk of any loss resulting from them is clearly re-imposed on the vendors. This is normally done by way of a specific indemnity or, less frequently, by a negotiation of a reduction in the price. If the disclosure is of a very significant issue the purchaser may instead decide not to proceed with the transaction.

EFFECT OF DISCLOSURES

9–04   The function of a disclosure letter is therefore to set out the details that are required in relation to the warranted items and to specify how the warranties need to be qualified to deal with excepted items. While in the case of the warranted items the details required will generally only be relevant to the particular warranty that calls for their production, this is not usually the case in respect of the excepted items as warranties have developed in their scope and operation such that with a full set of warranties it will usually be the case that the relevant excepted item will be the subject of several of them. For example, if a claim against the target company is disclosed, it can affect separately the warranties relating to the accounts, liabilities and litigation. See para.9–26 for a discussion of how the risk of not disclosing a certain matter against all of the relevant warranties is typically addressed.

The vendors and the purchaser will have the following concerns in relation to the disclosure letter.

(1) The vendors will wish to ensure that a disclosure of an excepted item is effective to remove liability in relation to that item under any of the warranties which could be applicable, that a disclosure of a warranted item accurately contains all relevant information, and that all relevant matters are disclosed (even if the vendors know that the purchaser is fully aware of the relevant matter or where the vendors are unsure whether technically it needs to be disclosed), otherwise the vendors may be subject to warranty claims that should have been avoided.

(2) The vendors will wish to pass to the purchaser the burden of understanding the implication of all disclosures made so that if, for example, a complex agreement is disclosed to the purchaser, there cannot subsequently be a complaint by the purchaser that the full effect and repercussions of it were not understood.

(3) The purchaser will wish to ensure that disclosures are fairly made and that the vendors do not avoid a liability which they have apparently accepted by swamping the purchaser with large amounts of disclosure information which cannot readily be absorbed and the implications of which cannot easily be appreciated.

(4) The purchaser will sometimes wish to ensure that, by accepting a disclosure, it does not reduce its prospective right to damages if the associated warranty is breached. The general position is that the purchaser will have difficulty in proving loss if it entered into the contract in the knowledge that deficiencies existed (see para.4–25). While it would seem that this is a perfectly fair result as between the parties if the purchaser has all the details—either through its own investigations or as a result of the disclosure process—which it needs to evaluate the problem, the position will be less clear if the information it receives or which is available is not sufficient to permit this. An example would be if the purchaser was aware that there might be problems in relation to land contamination but the existence or scope of the risk could not realistically be determined. The vendors will take the view that the purchaser is accepting the risk by deciding to proceed with the transaction once the potential problem has been identified; the purchaser will maintain that the vendors must accept responsibility for a problem existing at the time of the sale if there are no realistic means available to the purchaser to carry out a full investigation. The outcome of the argument will depend upon the relative bargaining strengths of the parties but, if the purchaser's

approach is adopted, the usual way to deal with the issue given the historical uncertainty on the effect of knowledge in relation to disclosure is for the purchaser to cover the issue by way of a specific indemnity.

TIMING OF DELIVERY OF THE DISCLOSURE LETTER

9–05 Given its importance and the potential implications of any errors, the disclosure letter requires very careful drafting and consideration by both the vendors and the purchaser. The vendors should be persuaded to provide an early draft of the disclosure letter and associated disclosure bundle so that their contents can be properly considered and reviewed. In practice this often does not happen, the bundle in particular regularly being delivered only a short period (sometimes hours) before the intended completion time. As discussed below in para.9–20 at sub-para.(e), the purchaser should ensure that it allows itself sufficient time to review any last minute bulk or general disclosure of masses of documents made by the vendors.

SOLICITORS AS PARTIES TO THE DISCLOSURE LETTER

9–06 If the disclosure letter is sent by the vendors' solicitors and addressed to the purchaser's solicitors, as is occasionally the case (this is not convention and is increasingly uncommon), the solicitors should take care to avoid any professional responsibility in relation to the disclosures and to state that they are making the disclosures to the purchaser on the instructions of the vendors.

IS THE DISCLOSURE LETTER PART OF THE SALE AGREEMENT?

9–07 In the vast majority of cases the disclosure letter will not form part of the sale agreement, save where a US purchaser is involved when it may seek to incorporate the disclosure letter as a specific schedule (this being convention in the US). In the United Kingdom, the disclosure letter is usually a separate letter addressed by the vendors to the purchaser.

Where the disclosure letter is a document which is physically separate from the sale agreement, the question may arise as to whether it is nevertheless part of the agreement. This will be relevant where, for example, documents are made available for inspection under the rules of the Stock Exchange. It is suggested that a disclosure letter does not form part of the sale agreement if the disclosures are of a normal routine nature. If, however, the disclosures are so fundamental that they render the sale agreement misleading on its face, it is considered that it would be wrong to treat the sale agreement as being complete unless the disclosure letter is attached.

PRECEDENT

A reasonably balanced form of first draft disclosure letter from the vendors is set out in Appendix 10, with a more comprehensive form, incorporating common provisions that might be seen in a first draft, set out below: **9–08**

From: [*Insert names and addresses of the Vendor(s)*]

To: [*Insert name and address of the Purchaser*]

Dear Sirs,

[Sale of the entire issued share capital of] [Sale of the business and assets of] [   ] Limited ("the Company")

This letter is the Disclosure Letter as defined in an agreement [for the sale and purchase of the entire issued share capital of the Company] [relating to the sale and purchase of the [   ] business of the Company] to be entered into today between (1) [   ] (the "Vendor[s]") and (2) [   ] (the "Purchaser") ("the Agreement").

All words and expressions defined in the Agreement shall, unless the context otherwise requires, have the same respective meanings in the Disclosure Letter.

Other than in circumstances where there is a split exchange and completion   **9–09** (where it is common for one disclosure letter to be provided at exchange (the date of the sale agreement) and a second, supplementary disclosure letter, dealing with changes since exchange, provided at completion), the disclosure letter will almost always be dated the same date as the sale agreement. In the context of a business sale where only part of the business is being sold it would be usual to refer to the relevant part of the business, so the last set of brackets would read "the [   ] business of the Company".

The adoption of the definitions contained in the sale agreement is useful but requires care. Although the definitions in para.4–02, which are used in the following paragraphs, will not cause difficulty, this will not always be the case. For example, some sale agreements adopt wholesale the definitions appearing in certain statutes—a procedure which is not to be encouraged—and as a result apparently innocuous phrases can be given quite unexpected meanings. Where definitions from the sale agreement are being incorporated, care should be taken when drafting and reviewing the disclosure letter to ensure that from the vendors' perspective the disclosures are as intended, and from the purchaser's perspective that the scope of them is fully appreciated.

The disclosure letter is normally divided into two parts, namely, "general disclosures" and "specific disclosures". The general disclosures are usually much shorter than the specific disclosures and take effect so as to disclose certain matters which appear in public records (or are such that the purchaser ought to be aware of them on the basis of searches which have been or are normally carried out) or that have otherwise been made available to the purchaser during the course of negotiations. The purchaser should ensure that before accepting general disclosure of any matters it has undertaken the relevant searches and/or received the relevant information and has actual knowledge of the matters disclosed. The fact that information is available on the public record does not mean that the purchaser has to accept it as being generally disclosed and it would be open to it to seek to raise an argument on that basis. Certainly, if the vendors seek to disclose all matters on the public record the purchaser should resist this—please see comments at para.9–24 sub-para.(j) for a discussion of this point. If there are warranties on specific areas, for example intellectual property, it would be reasonable for the vendors to seek general disclosure of the results of relevant searches at the applicable registries. The usual area for debate is where the vendors are seeking to generally disclose the results of searches that the purchaser has not undertaken. The vendors will rightly argue that the purchaser has had the opportunity to undertake the relevant searches and as such it should not be able to rely on the fact that it has chosen not to do so as an argument for not accepting disclosure of the results of them. The purchaser's position will be that it has not undertaken the relevant searches and, as such, cannot accept general disclosure of them, often on the basis that there is now no time to undertake the searches in any event. To try to avoid the purchaser adopting such a position, the vendors should raise the fact that they intend making general disclosure of certain searches at an early stage in negotiations, at a time when the purchaser will have time to undertake relevant searches and as such will not be in a position to raise that argument. The purchaser may still decline to accept general disclosures of such matters but at least that will become apparent in sufficient time to allow the vendors to carry the searches out and prepare relevant specific disclosure.

The specific disclosures disclose matters which if they were not disclosed would constitute a breach of warranty.

9–10   Where there is any inconsistency between the contents of the documents referred to at (a) to [   ] below and the factual statements contained in this Disclosure Letter, then the provisions and contents of these documents shall prevail. Neither the Vendors nor any of their representatives or agents are liable to the Purchaser to the extent that a loss which arises as a result of any such inconsistency or any failure to specifically refer to any of the documents referred to in (a) to [   ] below.

The documents referred to are those that are referred to in the specific disclosures and contained in the disclosure bundle. The intention of the first part of the provision is to protect the vendors from potential claims in circumstances where, for example, a mistake has been made by their solicitors in transposing information from the documents in the disclosure bundle into the disclosure letter, for example, a typographical error that states that the term of an agreement is 12 and not 13 months or that the salary of an employee is £5,000 per annum instead of £50,000 per annum. The purchaser will usually argue that it is relying on the disclosure letter and that it is not for it to check that every piece of information that has been taken from a document in the disclosure bundle is correct, that is the responsibility of the vendors. The vendors' position will usually be that the purchaser should not be able to make a claim in circumstances where it is obvious that a mistake has been made or where the purchaser has had the opportunity to review the disclosures and the disclosure bundle and will know what the correct position is. This is a reasonable position for the vendors to take where the purchaser has had sufficient opportunity to review the documentation but less so in circumstances where the relevant documentation has been provided on a last minute basis.

The disclosure of any matters or documents in this Disclosure Letter shall not imply any representation, warranty or undertaking not expressly given in the Agreement nor shall any disclosure be taken to extend the scope of any such representation, warranty or undertaking.   9–11

The inclusion of this clause should be acceptable to the purchaser since it is confirming that the vendors are not deemed to have represented, warranted or undertaken any matters or documents which are not expressly stated in the sale agreement.

The disclosures contained in this Disclosure Letter are not to be taken as any admissions that all or any of the matters call for disclosure, but are merely made for such purposes as they may serve as representing matters which might arise from the wording of the Warranties.   9–12

Although this wording is commonly found in disclosure letters its worth is questionable as it attempts, to some extent, to re-write the contractual standard of "disclosure" contained in the sale agreement. It will always be a question of fact as to whether each disclosure meets the required contractual standard. If the disclosure fails to meet the contractual standard, the disclosure will have no affect against the respective warranty and so that warranty will remain valid. Most well-advised purchasers will therefore delete this clause to avoid any ambiguity. If the purchaser adopts this approach the vendors will find it difficult to justify its inclusion.

Where brief particulars of a matter are set out or referred to in this Disclosure Letter or a document is referred to but not attached, or reference is made to a particular part only of such document, full particulars of the matter and the full contents of the document are deemed to be Disclosed and it is assumed that the Purchaser does not require further particulars.   9–13

The purchaser should resist any attempt to achieve disclosures which are more extensive in their impact than appears on the face of them. If the vendors wish to qualify a warranty, they should be required to state expressly the way in which the qualification is to operate—this is a determination for them to make. Normally a clause in this form would be resisted by the purchaser on the basis it does not meet the required standard of fair disclosure (here by reference to the definition of "Disclosed").

9–14   **For ease of reference, the majority of disclosures are made under paragraph numbering which refers to particular paragraphs of Schedule [ ] of the Agreement and, subject to the proviso below or as expressly provided elsewhere in this Disclosure Letter, they are numbered accordingly. Such numberings are for convenience only. Accordingly, if the information disclosed [is capable of applying] [could be fairly said to apply] in respect of any of the other Warranties, such information shall be deemed to be Disclosed where [it is capable of applying] [that is the case] and the Purchaser shall not be entitled to claim that any fact or matter has not been disclosed to it because it is not specifically related to any particular clause of the Agreement or paragraph of any schedule.**

The vendors' position will usually be that the purchaser should not be able to make a claim in circumstances where it is obvious that the same disclosure should have been made against another warranty in addition to the warranty it has been disclosed against, but a mistake has been made. This is a reasonable position for the vendors to take where the purchaser has had sufficient opportunity to review the documentation but less so in circumstances where the relevant documentation has been provided on a last minute basis. The purchaser may argue that it is relying on the disclosure letter and that it is not for it to check that every piece of information has been correctly disclosed against each warranty, that is the responsibility of the vendors. If the purchaser adopts this approach, depending on each party's bargaining position, the purchaser may insist on striking out this provision or softening it by replacing the wording in the first set of brackets with the wording in the second set of brackets or by insisting that disclosures shall only be effective against the other warranties to the extent it satisfies the defined basis of disclosed.

9–15   **This Disclosure Letter shall be deemed to include, and there are hereby incorporated into it, the following matters, [but no warranty is given as to the accuracy of the matters or the information deemed to be Disclosed in sub-paras (a) to [ ] save where the matters and documents referred to are specifically warranted in the Warranties]:**

In circumstances where a disclosure letter does not contain a provision in the form set out in para.9–11 then a more restricted basis of such wording, given it only applies to general disclosures, is provided for in the wording in brackets in this paragraph. If the wording in para.9–11 is included then there is no need to include the wording in brackets.

9–16   **(a) any matter [contained in and all matters to be inferred from] [reasonably apparent from] [provided for, noted or evident from] the accounts of the Company [the Vendor] [for [all][the last [ ]] financial periods up to the Balance Sheet Date] or [which are attached to this Disclosure Letter as documents [ ]];**

While it is fair and reasonable for the vendors to expect the purchaser to give careful consideration to the contents of the published accounts, nevertheless the purchaser should not be expected to deduce from items appearing in the accounts matters which would not normally flow from the disclosures as made nor to assess the impact of historical accounts. The purchaser should seek to have the disclosure limited to the accounts that it has relied on. The vendors will reasonably expect to generally disclose the accounts that they have been required to warrant in the sale agreement. The purchaser will want to delete the words in the first set of brackets as being too wide-ranging and vague (the relevant matters will not have been brought specifically to its attention). The result of accepting them would be to shift the burden of understanding the implications of the contents of the accounts to it. The purchaser will prefer to have the wording in the last set of brackets as this would restrict matters that were deemed disclosed to those in respect of which there was either a specific provision or note in the accounts, matters that someone without an understanding of accounts or the reading of them would be able to identify by reading the text of them. As the purchaser will in almost all circumstances have had the accounts reviewed by its accountants this is not an approach that most vendors will accept and they would not be acting unreasonably in doing so. The wording in the middle set of brackets is a fair compromise as it would catch matters that the purchaser's advisers would reasonably have been expected to have identified and brought to the attention of the purchaser.

See para.9–32 for a discussion of the courts' interpretation of the effectiveness of generally disclosing documents such as the accounts and why the wording "all matters to be inferred from" is preferable to, for example, "all matters referred to in". Even where the contents of the accounts are generally disclosed, the safest approach for the vendor will be to identify all relevant matters in the disclosure letter and cross-refer to specific parts of the accounts as necessary, for example, so that any issues are brought specifically to the purchaser's attention prior to completion (and can, if necessary, be resolved without the need to engage in litigation after the event) and so that there can be no arguments about whether a particular matter was, or was not "reasonably apparent".

(b) the contents of the Agreement and all transactions referred to therein and documents to be entered into pursuant thereto;

9–17

The purpose of this disclosure is to avoid the need to have to disclose any of the transactional arrangements that constitute exceptions to the warranties and which the parties will already be aware of as they will have been negotiated between them. There is clearly logic in this. However, a large amount of the contents of the transaction documents will not be relevant to the warranties, and it would in any event seem illogical for a court to uphold a claim for breach of warranty in circumstances where the breach arose as a result of matters provided for in the terms of the transaction documentation. Notwithstanding this, given the move towards reliance on the strict terms of the sale agreement that has been seen in recent case law (see para.9–32 for a discussion of this), in circumstances where the sale agreement limits the purchaser's knowledge to matters disclosed in the disclosure letter it will be prudent for the vendors to include such a provision. In most instances this should not cause an issue for the purchaser (assuming that there are relevant arrangements in the transaction documents), although before accepting it, it should check that it has assessed the potential implications of the arrangements that are being entered into.

The use of the defined term "Disclosed" in the introduction to the general disclosures seeks to erode any argument the purchaser may have that the general disclosures do not satisfy the required contractual standard of disclosure. If the purchaser wishes to preserve the opportunity to debate this point then an alternative phrase should be used.

9–18   **(c) any matters appearing on the file at the Companies House Registry [in respect of the previous two years in respect of the Company as at the close of business on the day prior to the date of this Disclosure letter] [during the period [   ] to [   ]].**

The purchaser would be expected to make searches of the Companies House Registry and it is fair for the vendors to exclude liability for matters which would appear from those searches. The parties should, however, bear in mind that the file may not, in practice, be fully up-to-date in view of the inevitable interval which occurs between lodging and registration of documents. It would be usual to have a date on which the disclosure was deemed to apply to ensure that last minute filings are excluded. This would be achieved by using the wording in the second set of brackets. Often the search itself will be attached to the disclosure letter (and in the interests of certainty it would be preferable from the purchaser's perspective that only the contents of the search that are attached are disclosed).

Furthermore, if the target company or business is old, there will be a vast amount of material at the Companies House Registry and it may be almost impossible to evaluate it all in the context of the warranties. In such circumstances it would be reasonable for the purchaser to require that the disclosure is restricted to entries made within a specified prior period, for example, the last six years. This would be achieved by using the wording in the first set of brackets.

This general disclosure would be unlikely to be relevant in the context of a business sale.

9–19   **(d) the contents of[, and all matters referred to in,] the documents in the bundle of documents annexed to this Disclosure Letter and numbered 1 to [   ] an index to which is attached to this Disclosure Letter;**

As noted at para.9–05, it is, unfortunately, not unusual for vendors to deliver to the purchaser, sometimes only shortly before the signing of the sale agreement, large bundles of documents which cannot be fully assimilated and analysed by the purchaser without inordinate effort. If the vendors do attempt to do this then the purchaser should either refuse to accept the documentation disclosed and require the vendors to specifically disclose any relevant information in it, amend the sale agreement to provide for a more limited basis of disclosure to apply to such documents, or delay completion until such time as it has been able to review and assess the implications of it. It is generally preferable for the purchaser to be aware of all potential issues prior to completion so that it has the opportunity to address them, for example, by negotiating amendments to the sale agreement, rather than having to rely on making a claim for breach of warranty after completion (as this will be likely to incur substantial management time and the warranty limitation provisions will apply). The purchaser may also be faced with an argument from the vendors that it has to disclose the relevant information as otherwise it may lose the protection of the warranty limitation provisions as a result of, for example, deliberate non-disclosure, or could face criminal sanctions under the Financial Services and Markets Act 2000 or the Fraud Act 2006 (see para.9–35 for a more detailed discussion of the issues surrounding a failure to make disclosure of relevant matters).

The purchaser should delete the wording in brackets so as to avoid uncertainty as to what documents have or have not been disclosed. It should not accept general disclosure of documents that it has not seen. If any are relevant then the vendors should be required to include copies in the disclosure bundle.

> (e) **the Vendors' replies to the legal due diligence questionnaire** 9–20
> **(including the documentation attached to them) sent to the**
> **Purchaser[, the financial [and commercial] due diligence report on**
> **[the Company] [the Business] prepared by [   ]][and the contents of**
> **and matters referred to in all correspondence between the**
> **Purchaser or the Purchaser's advisers and the Vendors or the**
> **Vendors' advisers];**

Where the purchaser's advisers have undertaken due diligence on the target for the purposes of reporting to the purchaser and/or its funders their understanding of the target's position in relation to the matters covered by the warranties is likely to be better than the vendors', in particular, as the vendors are unlikely to have had specialist advisers review all of the information and documentation that has been provided to the purchaser during the due diligence process. Accordingly, vendors will generally seek to argue that matters contained in the legal due diligence replies and in any reports that have been prepared should be deemed to be generally disclosed. The purchaser typically resists this, in respect of the legal due diligence replies on the basis that they are not a substitute for the disclosure letter and it is for the vendors to identify relevant matters and bring them specifically to the purchaser's attention in that document, and, in respect of any reports, that they are confidential to it. The purchaser will also generally argue that it does not know anything about the target's business that the vendors should not themselves be aware of or able to ascertain. As to whether the replies are ultimately generally disclosed will usually come down to whether or not the vendors have agreed to provide a warranty in respect of them (see para.7–30 for a discussion of this). If the replies have been warranted it would be reasonable for the vendors to insist on their general disclosure.

Whether the reports are ultimately disclosed will depend on the bargaining position of the parties. It is suggested that the vendors should strongly argue for their general disclosure even on a "deemed" basis, that is without sight of them. Wherever possible the vendors should try and obtain a copy of the purchaser's financial due diligence report, particularly so, where the vendors' accountants have not been actively involved in the financial due diligence process or otherwise engaged to assess the target company's financial position as they are unlikely to be aware of all of the potential areas for claim that the purchaser's advisers have identified. In a deal where completion accounts are relevant the report is likely to detail potential areas of concern which might give rise to potential provisions being made. With knowledge of these areas the vendors' advisers can protect against these by writing specific wording to the contrary in the completion accounts schedule. For obvious reasons the purchaser will be reluctant to disclose the contents of the reports.

In respect of the wording in the last set of brackets, there will no doubt be a large volume of information outside of that contained in the legal due diligence replies and due diligence reports that has passed between the parties during the course of negotiations, the vast majority of which will not have been regarded by either the vendors or the purchaser as having been given or received for the purposes of qualifying the warranties. It is likely that the vendor will have strongly resisted the giving of a warranty in respect of the accuracy of such information (see the discussion at para.7–30) and, if the purchaser has accepted that, the purchaser could reasonably refuse to accept the disclosure. If the purchaser is to accept such a disclosure then it should ensure that any correspondence that is to be generally disclosed is compiled by the vendors and included in the disclosure bundle. Irrelevant documents, for example, former drafts of the disclosure letter, should be excluded.

9–21   **(f) the contents of the statutory books of the Company all of which have been made available for inspection by the Purchaser's Solicitors prior to Completion;**

As with other information, the purchaser should only accept general disclosure of the contents of the statutory books if it has had the opportunity to review them. If the target company is old then the purchaser may wish to decline to review the books (given the amount of time that will be spent in doing so), instead putting the onus on the vendors to make disclosure of relevant breaches, or to impose a time limit on the entries that are accepted as generally disclosed. As with the results of company searches this disclosure is unlikely to be relevant in the context of a business sale.

9–22   **(g) all matters which are [in] [apparent from] the deeds of the Properties which have been made available for inspection by [the Vendors'] [the Vendor's] Solicitors to the Purchaser's Solicitors or which would have been revealed in relation to the Properties by the following searches and enquiries:**

      (i) a search on form LLC1 (Local Land Charges Rules 1977) and enquiries of the [   ] local authority for the areas in which each

of the Properties are located on Oyez Form CON29 1 and 2 (2002 Edition) [   ];

   (ii) searches on the registers of Common Land and Town and Village Greens kept by the relevant local authority for the areas in which the Properties are located;

   (iii) a search of the information retained by The Coal Authority in relation to past, present and future mining operations in proximity to each of the Properties;

   (iv) a search of HM Land Registry and the Land Charges Department against each of the Properties as at the date of this Disclosure Letter;

   (v) a search of the information retained by the relevant water and sewerage undertakings for the areas in which the Properties are located;

   (vi) a phase 1 desktop environmental search for the areas in which the Properties are located;

   (vii) a search of the information retained by the relevant electricity provider for the areas in which the Properties are located;

   (viii) a search of the information retained by Transco in relation to the gas infrastructure for the areas in which the Properties are located;

   (ix) all information or matters relating to the Properties which have been provided to the Purchaser or the Purchaser's Solicitors or other advisers in correspondence;

   (x) any information contained in the replies to the enquiries and requisitions that the Purchaser's Solicitors have made in connection with their investigation of title; and

   (xi) the asbestos surveys carried out at the Properties copies of which are attached at document [   ];

(h) all matters which are apparent from the surveys of the Properties, copies of which are attached at document [   ] or physical inspection of the Properties (the Purchaser and its agents having been given facilities for the inspection of them).

The effect of this disclosure is largely to nullify many of the warranties in relation to the properties owned by the target company or which are included in the business assets which are being purchased. As discussed in Ch.6, the parties must decide whether property warranties are to be given or whether the purchaser is to rely on its own investigation or a certificate of title. In the former case the first part of the disclosure, relating to title deeds and searches, is inappropriate (although notwithstanding this vendors will generally seek to disclose the results of standard property searches) and in the latter there will be effectively no warranties to which that part of the disclosure relates. As mentioned in para.9–09, it is sensible to agree at the outset which, if any, searches are to be generally disclosed and the purchaser should where possible include copies of the agreed searches in the disclosure bundle.

The rest of the disclosure which relates to matters apparent from a physical inspection is likely to be unacceptable to the purchaser because it is unlikely that it could realistically be conducted by all personnel and advisors who might appreciate what they see. Also, evidentially, it may be unclear what would or should be apparent from any inspection. The only situation where this may be acceptable, however, is if it has been agreed between the parties that the purchaser will obtain, and rely upon, a survey of the properties, in which case it would be usual to refer to the actual surveyor's report so as to obtain certainty in relation to the scope of this disclosure. However, in circumstances where a survey has been undertaken it is likely that the purchaser will have resisted giving warranties about the structure of the target's properties and as such the contents of the report are likely to be of limited relevance. The risk for the purchaser in accepting a wider disclosure is that whilst the surveyor will have taken into account matters relevant to the preparation of its report (principally the structure of the properties), a thorough inspection that would reveal all matters relevant to the warranties is unlikely to have been undertaken by all the parties that could have been in a position to appreciate their relevance. The purchaser will also be opening itself up to arguments by the vendors about what was or was not apparent from a physical inspection of the properties. If the purchaser is to accept such a disclosure it should ensure that it applies only to the property warranties (so as to avoid arguments that breaches of non-property warranties would have been apparent from an inspection of the properties. Undoubtedly any physical inspection that has been carried out will not have been done with a view to identifying matters that might constitute such a breach and it would be extremely difficult to do so).

Where environmental warranties are given and the target company's or business' manufacturing process involves the use of hazardous substances or the properties are located on an industrial area the general disclosure of the phase 1 desktop environmental survey is unlikely to be sufficient. In such a situation, the purchaser is likely to have undertaken a more detailed environmental search such as, for example, bore hole sampling and in that case the more detailed survey should also be generally disclosed. Environmental issues are usually dealt with by way of indemnity as opposed to warranty protection and so the general disclosure of such surveys will negate warranty claims but will not impact on the indemnities given.

9–23   **(i)   anything which would be apparent from inspection of the plant, books of account and records of [the Company] [the Business] (the Purchaser and its agents having been given facilities for the inspection of them);**

To an extent this overlaps with the general disclosure of matters apparent from a physical inspection of the properties. Where the target company or the business has been the subject of a detailed investigation, the vendors would wish to exclude matters which have been disclosed in the course of the investigation or which would be apparent to the purchaser and its agents. The purchaser, on the other hand, would be concerned to ensure that there is certainty as to what items are covered by this disclosure and, while the principle may not be unacceptable to the purchaser, the wording is much too wide. As suggested above in relation to properties, if faced with this qualification, the purchaser should insist upon the identification of the particular items which the parties agree will have been disclosed by the inspection. More often the contents of any due diligence reports that have been produced as a result of such investigations by the purchaser's financial and/or legal advisers will be deemed to be disclosed instead. This is the approach that reflects current convention. It would be unusual now for the vendors to include a provision such as this and, if they did, it would usually be resisted by the purchaser.

(j) everything which is in the public domain; and

9–24

This disclosure is particularly appealing from the vendors' perspective where it is required to warrant, for example, that there has been no change in the financial position or prospects of the target company or business (see cl.4.1.1.2 in para.7–78). The purpose of the disclosure is to avoid the warranty being breached by reason of circumstances or events of general application (such as changes in interest or tax rates) as opposed to those relating specifically to the target company or business. The disclosure nevertheless should not be accepted by the purchaser, even if confined in its application to those warranties where it is most appropriate, as the purchaser cannot be expected to be aware of everything in the public domain and might not be aware of, or may have overlooked, information regarding the target company or business which has been made public but in a low-key manner. The purchaser should require the vendors instead to make specific disclosure of any pertinent events (it would be reasonable for the vendors to have the risk of them) or, if the vendors are not willing to accept this, to include appropriate limitations in the share sale agreement, for example as per the amendments suggested at para.7–78.

(k) all matters which would be revealed by a search of the registers and documents maintained by the Office of Fair Trading, the Consumer Credit Registry, the Trade Marks Registry of the Intellectual Property Office in respect of the [Company] [Business].

9–25

Following the principle that the vendors should disclose everything of relevance to the sale to qualify the warranties, the prudent approach for the vendors would be to maintain this disclosure in its widest form.

However, as with the general disclosure of matters apparent from a physical inspection of any property, the purchaser will be concerned to ensure that the items covered by this disclosure are precise and limited. If the purchaser is prepared to accept this disclosure they will, as a minimum, insist upon certain amendments limit it in scope.

Particularly, a prudent purchaser should narrow the scope of the search to specify which types of intellectual property are included, state that the search is against specific trade mark numbers or registered proprietors as listed, and include a list of search terms which will be used in completing the search. This extends to avoiding searches for a "similar type" of mark or design. A search of all registers and documents maintained by the Intellectual Property Office in respect of the target company would be extremely vast and time consuming.

Additionally the search should be confined to registers and documents held online and available on a certain specified date.

9–26   **We wish also to make the following specific disclosures and for convenience only reference is made to particular paragraphs in Schedule [ ] of the Agreement. Each item disclosed is nevertheless deemed to be Disclosed [(to the extent Disclosed)] in respect of all of the Warranties and is not limited to the paragraph which is referred to below.**

The detailed disclosures will normally specify the principal warranty to which each disclosure most particularly relates. In view of the extensive nature of the warranties, it will be difficult in practice, as previously stated, for the vendors to ensure that all the warranties affected by each disclosure are expressly indicated and the vendors will therefore wish to protect themselves by general wording of the kind set out above. Although this may seem to be fair and is generally accepted by most purchasers a problem arises if the relevance of a disclosure to any other warranty is not apparent. If, for example, a licence agreement is disclosed and it contains a provision that a large minimum royalty is to be paid for a considerable number of years, the vendors might disclose it in relation to a warranty which relates only to licence agreements. This disclosure would, by virtue of the general words, also qualify a warranty, for example, that there are no outstanding liabilities under subsisting contracts of more than a specified amount (for example cl.4.15.1.7 in para.7–126). It would be unreasonable for the vendors to achieve a disclosure in this oblique manner. The problem can be dealt with in part by the warranty suggested below at cl.9A to the effect that the disclosures have disclosed every matter to which they relate to the agreed standard of "Disclosed". The words in square brackets achieve a similar position. (Where a defined term of "Disclosed" is not being used the wording "but subject always to the provisions of clause [ ] of the Agreement" should be inserted by the purchaser at the end of the last sentence. The wording is intended to cross-refer to the clause in the sale agreement which sets the standard that disclosures will have to meet to be effective.) The purpose of the wording is to avoid the fact that disclosures should only be effective to the extent that they meet the agreed standard being overridden by the first part of the sentence to which the words are added. If this is the case then it is in the interests of the vendors to ensure that as much cross-referencing as is possible to each relevant warranty is undertaken.

The specific disclosures which are made in practice, including in particular the disclosure of excepted items, vary so greatly that it is not possible to provide a comprehensive precedent or detailed guidance for all of them, although some examples of specific disclosures that might be made against the warranties in Ch.7 and the issues that the purchaser should consider in relation to them are given below. What is of the utmost importance, however, is that the vendors and the purchaser should realise that the drafting of the disclosure letter, in relation both to the opening general paragraphs and the specific disclosures themselves, should be treated with as much care and attention as the sale agreement itself. In so far as the disclosure letter contains excepted items, it operates to reduce the scope and impact of the warranties and both parties should understand the extent to which this occurs. With this in mind, the purchaser should not be reluctant to request additional information or clarification if it feels that any of the details provided in relation to any of the disclosures are not sufficiently clear and should, if appropriate, supplement the warranties to provide it with the required amount of cover. (If the vendors will not agree to the inclusion of additional issue specific warranties, the purchaser will need to seek to amend the terms of the specific disclosures so that their terms are clear and they contain all pertinent information.)

Specific disclosures

[1.10.1] Copies of the memorandum and articles of association of the Company are attached at document [ ]. 9–27

This is a factual disclosure of a warranted item. The vendors will need to check that any relevant resolutions that should be attached to the memorandum or articles are and, to the extent they are not, make a relevant disclosure. Provided the purchaser checks that it is satisfied with the contents of the documents that are attached then it should not have any issue with accepting the disclosure.

[3.8.2] The dividend shown in the Accounts has been paid [and an additional dividend in the sum of [ ] has been paid and approved]. 9–28

The warranty requires disclosure of distributions made in breach of the target company's articles of association, the Companies Acts and any other agreements or arrangements that are in place governing the payment or declaration of dividends. The disclosure made does not disclose any exceptions to the warranty, just the fact that dividends have been paid. The purchaser will need to clarify whether in fact the distributions were made in breach of any applicable requirements and have the vendors amend or delete the disclosure as necessary. (The disclosure, however, would be relevant in respect of cl.3.8.1.)

[3.9.1] The Company has received two government grants in the last six years. 9–29

Whilst constituting a disclosure of an excepted item, the disclosure does not provide sufficient details from the purchaser's perspective. The purchaser will want details of the terms of the grants (in particular any potential repayment obligations), confirmation of compliance with them and details of any amounts received in respect of them to be provided. In such circumstances it would be prudent for the purchaser to seek to replace cl.3.9.1 with warranties that covered these and any other matters relating to the grants that it considered relevant.

We acknowledge receipt of the Disclosure Letter and copies of the documents numbered 1 to [ ] attached to the Disclosure Letter [and confirm our acceptance of its terms]. 9–30

Whilst the purchaser will have no issue in accepting receipt of the disclosure letter, it will be reluctant to confirm acceptance of the terms of it. The reason for this is that it is arguable that in confirming acceptance of the terms, the purchaser is confirming that it accepts all of the disclosures that are purported to be made in it meet the agreed standard and are effective for negating all of the relevant warranties. The purchaser will not want to prejudice its position in respect of seeking to argue that a particular disclosure had not met the required standard by giving such an acknowledgement and would usually decline to do so.

PREPARATION OF DISCLOSURES

9–31 The preparation of the material to be covered by the disclosures can be an extremely onerous task for the vendors' solicitors who will need to work closely with the appropriate executives of the target company/business to undertake a thorough review of the warranties. When the sale agreement is received by the vendors' solicitors, it is generally unrealistic for them to send the agreement to the vendors with a bare request for comments on the warranties as, unless the vendors are experienced in dealing with the disclosure process, it will normally be impossible for them to appreciate the meaning and implications of the warranties without expert guidance.

Throughout the transaction and, in particular, whilst preparing the due diligence replies and the disclosure letter, the vendors' solicitors are obliged to report all instances where the target company/business has committed money laundering offences to the Serious Organised Crime Agency ("SOCA"). Money laundering offences include where the target company/business has committed any criminal offences or other "technical breaches" which have resulted in a financial benefit; for example, where it has allowed its employees to work in excess of 48 hours per week without signing "opt outs" from the working time regulations. The effect of reporting such offences may be that consent may be required from SOCA to proceed with the transaction. If the vendors' solicitors fail to report they would themselves potentially commit a criminal offence.

STANDARD OF DISCLOSURE

9–32 It is in the interests of the purchaser and the vendors that all disclosures made are fair. The purchaser will want as accurate a picture of the target company as possible prior to completion, at a time when the terms of the transaction are still in the course of negotiation, and the vendors will want to obviate the risk of a later claim for breach of warranty. Last minute "bad news" disclosures are generally not a good idea from the point of view of the vendors as they risk the purchaser walking away from the deal at a stage when significant professional costs will have been expended.

As mentioned above, it is common for the sale agreement to provide that the warranties given are qualified by matters "fairly disclosed" in the disclosure letter. In such circumstances, if the disclosure is not precise enough, a court may find that it is insufficient to prevent a successful claim for breach of warranty (see, for example, *Levison v Farin* [1978] 2 All E.R. 1149) and, if it is not specific and accurate, it might not constitute a fair disclosure. What amounts to fair disclosure has been considered in the case of *Daniel Reeds Ltd v EM ESS Chemists Ltd* [1995] C.L.C. 1405 and the Scottish case of *New Hearts Ltd v Cosmopolitan Investments Ltd* [1997] 2 B.C.L.C. 249. In the first of these cases, the vendor warranted that the target company had valid product licences for its products. This was not the case and the vendor sought to argue that because it had positively disclosed all existing licences it had in effect disclosed that the licence to which no reference had been made did not exist. The court did not regard this as a fair disclosure of the missing licence. In the latter case, the court cast doubt upon the practice of making deemed disclosure of all matters "set out in or referred to" in the accounts and concluded that simply referring to a complex body of information would not be a fair disclosure, even if a diligent reader might be able to identify relevant information. This point was discussed further in the case of *MAN Nutzfarhrzeuge AG v Freightliner Ltd* [2005] EWHC 2347.[1] In that case it was noted obiter that for disclosure of matters that could be ascertained from documentation that had been generally disclosed to be fair, the sale agreement would need to specially provide for such a construction. Words such as "matters that could be inferred from" would need to be included in the sale agreement such that it was clear that such matters were to be treated as disclosed. The parties will need to give careful consideration to the wording of the sale agreement to ensure in light of the above decisions that so far as possible the intended position in relation to what matters will or will not be regarded as disclosed is achieved. It will always be the safest approach from the vendors' perspective to disclose matters as fully, clearly and fairly as possible, whatever the standard in the sale agreement is.

WARRANTING THE DISCLOSURE LETTER

The purchaser will sometimes seek to include in the sale agreement a warranty relating to the disclosure letter in the following terms, it being assumed that "Disclosure Letter", "Disclosed" and "Warranties" are defined terms (see para.4–02): **9–33**

[9A] Disclosures accurate

The disclosures contained in the Disclosure Letter [and the details contained **9–34**
in the disclosure bundle] are [true] and accurate [in all respects] and not misleading and have Disclosed every matter to which they relate [and the Warranties which are affected][; and there are no other matters which have not been Disclosed and which may render the disclosures incomplete, inaccurate or misleading].

---

[1] This decision has been affirmed by the Court of Appeal in *MAN Nutzfarhrzeuge AG v Freightliner Ltd* [2007] EWCA Civ 910.

The vendors will need to consider carefully whether they are prepared to give the warranty which in simple terms warrants the accuracy of the disclosures and the contents of the disclosure bundle. The vendors may argue that if, as is usual, the sale agreement sets the standard by reference to which disclosures will be effective, if the relevant disclosure fails to satisfy the agreed standard then the disclosure against the relevant warranty fails, leaving the original warranty intact and the purchaser with a claim for breach of warranty. The purpose of the disclosure letter is to provide the vendors with a mechanism of negating liability they would otherwise have in respect of the warranties, not to provide another potential head of claim for the purchaser. The purchaser will usually argue that it has relied on the disclosures contained in the disclosure letter as being accurate and not misleading in evaluating the warranties and the risk that it is prepared to assume. If therefore the disclosures are inaccurate and as a result it suffers loss it ought to be able to claim for such loss. Ultimately, whether the warranty is given will depend upon the bargaining position of the parties, although current convention is for such a warranty not to be given. If the vendors are prepared to accept the warranty, which in most cases would be unlikely, they should consider carefully whether they are willing to accept the burden, which it imposes upon them, of stating clearly which specific warranty is qualified, and in what respects, by each disclosure of the excepted items. They may also reasonably consider that the second half of the clause, which contains a representation that there are no other matters which should be disclosed, is unduly wide and burdensome and not acceptable. Finally, the vendors should seek to have the warranty limited to the narrative of the specific disclosures in the disclosure letter and not to the contents of the general disclosures and the disclosure bundle (or any other matters that are deemed to be disclosed), as these are not matters that it is appropriate for the vendors to warrant given their nature.

DELIBERATE NON-DISCLOSURE

9–35   A practical problem can arise where vendors who are extremely anxious to effect a sale of the target company know that a breach of warranty will arise if an adverse circumstance—such as the existence of outstanding litigation—is not disclosed, but are apprehensive about making a disclosure in case it causes the purchaser to withdraw. The vendors might be quite happy to compensate the purchaser in due course and might therefore consider that there is no question of fraud, arising from deliberate concealment, as there is every intention to make the purchaser's position good. Nevertheless, in the context of a share sale, the purchaser will have been induced to enter into the sale agreement by a deliberate misrepresentation or concealment—and this in general terms would constitute fraud. Under the Fraud Act 2006 ss.2 and 3 it is a criminal offence (fraud) for a person to dishonestly make a false representation, or dishonestly fail to disclose to another person information which he is under a legal duty to disclose, with the intention of making a gain for himself or another, causing loss to another, or exposing another to a risk of loss. The offence can carry an unlimited fine and/or up to 10 years' imprisonment. Shareholders, directors, managers and other similar officers can be liable as well as the company committing the offence in circumstances where they have consented to or connived in the commission of the offence. It is likely that a deliberate non-disclosure against warranties will be caught by this offence. Advisors need to be wary of this given that they may be accused of consenting to or conniving in the commission of an offence where they continue to act in the transaction in circumstances where the vendors refuse to disclose a relevant matter or circumstance against a warranty.

It is also a criminal offence under the Financial Services and Markets Act 2000 s.397(1) for a person knowingly or recklessly to make a false statement (or one that is deceptive in a material particular) or to dishonestly conceal any material facts for the purpose of inducing another person to enter into an investment agreement—in this context, the sale agreement. The offence carries an unlimited fine and/or seven years' imprisonment. While there is no civil remedy available for a purchaser under the section (although an action for civil remedies can be brought by the Financial Services Authority under the Act), the purchaser may be able to bring an action for deceit if any of the disclosures constitute fraudulent misrepresentations of the actual position that induced the purchaser to complete the transaction (*Bottin (International) Investments Ltd v Venson Group Plc* [2006] EWHC 3112).

The vendors' solicitors could also be ordered by a court to pay compensation to a purchaser who suffered loss as a result of the vendors' breach of s.397(1) if they were "knowingly concerned" in such breach (see the Court of Appeal's decision in *Securities and Investments Board v Pantell SA (No.2)* [1992] 3 W.L.R. 896 which related to the Financial Services Act 1986 s.47(1), the predecessor to s.397(1)).

If the vendors decide to remain silent regarding a problem, then, since there is **9–36** no general duty to disclose relevant facts, this would not constitute a misrepresentation under general law, as total non-disclosure does not amount to misrepresentation (*Percival v Wright* [1902] 2 Ch. 421). However, if the silence of the vendors distorts a positive representation, the vendors would not be entitled to keep quiet. Therefore, if a warranty requires disclosure for it to be accurate and not misleading, non-disclosure would constitute misrepresentation.

Where a warranty constitutes a misrepresentation of a material fact, it is considered that the only correct way to proceed is either to amend the warranty, so as to eliminate the misrepresentation, or to make a full disclosure of the relevant circumstances.

CHAPTER 10

Tax Covenant and Tax Limitations

INTRODUCTION

10–01 As indicated in para.1–06, the original idea of indemnities, as distinguished from warranties, was to provide the target company with a means of recovering tax for which it had only a secondary liability without a statutory right of recovery from the person primarily liable. This narrow concept is still occasionally accepted, with the tax covenant being confined to cases where, although the primary liability is not that of the company, a secondary liability is imposed upon it by statute.

The clear principle upon which tax deeds were originally based became eroded with the introduction of the corporation tax regime and the development of the practice of adding additional statutory provisions to which the indemnity would expressly relate. Eventually, tax deeds became of inordinate length with a large number of specific provisions set out in the body of them.

The next stage of development of the form of the tax deed was when an attempt was made to shorten the document by having a blanket indemnity against any taxation liability. The scope of the indemnity was spread even further by an increasingly wide definition of the kinds of taxation covered by the indemnity (considered in more detail below). Then came the case of *Zim Properties Ltd v Procter (Inspector of Taxes)* [1985] 58 T.C. 371 after which ESC D33 was issued (as described in paras 3–18 and 3–19). Following this, as a payment to the target company could be taxable whereas a payment to the purchaser was unlikely to be taxable, the tax deed was redrafted as a deed of covenant under which a covenant was given directly to the purchaser. This is the most common approach today, with only the vendors and the purchaser being parties (although the target company is occasionally a party for specific purposes, such as conduct of claims). It is technically inaccurate to refer to this as a tax indemnity as an indemnity is not given to the target company.

10–02 Thereafter it became the norm to incorporate the provisions that would have been contained in a tax deed in a schedule to the sale agreement. In this form it was usually known as a tax covenant.

The most recent development has been to put all matters relating to tax—definitions, warranties, covenant, limitation and administrative provisions—in a single schedule within the sale agreement. This approach has the following advantages.

(1) It avoids repetitions and inconsistencies—for example, "Taxation" would often be defined in both the sale agreement and the tax deed, though not always with the same definition.

(2) It ensures that the same limitations apply to a claim for taxation, whether that claim is brought under the tax deed/covenant or the tax warranties. Previously tax warranties would usually be subject to the general warranty limitations. With the result that, for example, there might be different conduct of claims provisions that applied depending on whether the claim was brought under the tax warranties or the tax deed, with resultant confusion if the claim was brought under both.

(3) On a practical level, it makes negotiation of the tax provisions easier as the tax advisers can remove a discrete portion of the sale agreement to negotiate between themselves, rather than having to review the whole sale agreement to find the relevant tax bits (with the risk that some tax issues could be overlooked).

Although separate tax deeds or tax covenants are still occasionally seen, the current convention is to have a single schedule dealing with all tax matters. This is the approach adopted in this edition.

The modern tax covenant will generally raise numerous complex and obscure questions. Normally the purchaser's solicitors will make use of a standard comprehensive form and the vendors' solicitors will face the task of providing amendments which reflect the liabilities which the vendors should reasonably expect to accept. This task has been to some extent simplified by the recent trend for first drafts of the tax provisions to be more balanced with the purchaser's solicitors including many of the amendments which the vendors' solicitors would historically have been expected to make. The tax covenant given here is a reasonably balanced draft although some of the provisions in favour of the vendors may not be appropriate in every case.

Summary of Tax Schedule

The tax schedule is typically divided into four or five parts as follows: **10–03**

Part 1—Tax Definitions
Part 2—Tax Warranties
Part 3—Tax Covenant
Part 4—Limitations
Part 5—General and administrative provisions

The tax warranties are discussed in Ch.5 and are not further considered in this chapter.

Summary of Covenant

10–04 The definitions and covenant together reflect the core of the traditional tax deed or covenant.

Before giving detailed consideration to the contents of a typical tax schedule, it is helpful to summarise the main points which will or should be dealt with in the tax covenant. Those that will typically need addressing are listed below.

(1) The covenant will generally be in favour of the purchaser for the reasons set out above. If for any reason the covenant is in favour of the target company, this will generally be unacceptable to the vendors.

(2) The covenant will cover unexpected liabilities to taxation which relate to events or transactions prior to completion.

(3) The covenant may cover the loss of an expected right to a tax repayment, it being a matter for negotiation as to whether the vendors should accept this liability.

(4) The purchaser may seek a covenant against the withdrawal of anticipated tax reliefs. It is, however, a complex matter to determine whether this particular covenant is appropriate and, if so, how the covenant should operate.

(5) Subject to which matters are covered by the covenant, a payment by the vendors will be required:

(a) when the unexpected liability, or loss of expected relief, results in a payment of tax;

(b) when the expected repayment would have been received;

(c) when a payment of tax occurs which would have been avoided if an expected relief had not been withdrawn; and

(d) when a payment of tax would have occurred but for the availability of other reliefs.

(6) The covenant will not normally extend to liabilities which result in no net loss to the target company, for example because of the availability or otherwise of unclaimed reliefs which could be called upon to shelter the liability.

Detailed Consideration

10–05 A typical form of the tax schedule is set out in Appendix 6 and considered below clause by clause.

As indicated in para.2–20, although the vendors will usually be all the vendors, in special cases—for example, where the vendors include trustees—some of the vendors may be excluded. The purchaser will usually not object as long as it has joint and several covenants from a number of vendors who have the means to meet potential claims.

Given the modern structure of a tax covenant any payment which is made under the tax covenant would not normally be taxable in the hands of the purchaser and with the vendors receiving an adjustment to the amount of the purchase consideration which is brought into account for capital gains tax purposes to the extent of any payments made to the purchaser, whether pursuant to the warranties or under the tax covenant.

Part 1: Taxation definitions

As noted above, Pt 1 usually comprises definitions. Appendix 6 contains the full definitions. Not all of them have been repeated here as many of them are self-explanatory. The commentary below only discusses those definitions that have been repeated here and require comment. **10–06**

In this Schedule [3]: **10–07**

1.1 Words and expressions defined in the Agreement shall except where otherwise provided or expressly defined below have the same meaning.

It is clearly convenient to adopt the definitions contained in the main body of the sale agreement and the provisions dealing with construction and interpretation without setting them out again in full. The parties must take care to ensure that these provisions and the definitions are equally appropriate for the tax covenant. The comments on the definitions in para.4–02 should be borne in mind.

1.3 "Claim for Taxation" includes any notice, demand, assessment, determination, letter or other document issued, or action taken, by or on behalf of a Taxation Authority and whether issued before or after Completion, whereby it appears that the Company is, or may be, subject to a Liability to Taxation (whether or not it is primarily payable by the Company and whether or not the Company has a right of reimbursement). **10–08**

Although the basic indemnity (contained in Pt 3, cl.1.1.1) is against any liability to taxation, as defined, Pt 4, cl.1.1.4 contains a covenant relating to the costs of dealing with claims for taxation. Further, the conduct of claims provisions in Pt 4, cl.2 are triggered by a "Claim for Taxation". Accordingly, the purchaser will wish the definition to be drawn as widely as possible while the vendors will seek to restrict its scope. The parties will therefore need to give particular consideration to the phrase "whereby it appears that the Company is or may be subject to a Liability to Taxation", the vendors at the very least preferring "may be" to be replaced by "will be" or "likely to be".

1.6 "Event" any event whatsoever, including but not limited to any disposition, action or omission (whether or not the Company or the Purchaser is a party), the earning, accrual or receipt of any income, profits or gains, the declaration, payment or making of any dividend or other **10–09**

distribution (in each case whether actual or deemed) on or before Completion and includes any events which are deemed to have occurred for any Taxation purpose.

The primary covenant contained in Pt 3, cl.1 operates by reference to events on or before completion. The purchaser will want this definition to be drafted as wide as possible. In practice, this definition is rarely subject to substantial amendment; the main issues tend to occur on the so called "combined events wording" contained at Pt 1, cl.1.18 (see para.10–17 below).

10–10   **1.10 "Liability to Taxation" includes:**

> **1.10.1   any liability of the Company to make an actual payment in respect of or in the nature of Taxation;**
>
> **1.10.2   the set-off or utilisation of a Pre-Completion Relief or a Purchaser's Relief against a liability of the Company to make an actual payment of or in respect of Taxation where but for the set-off or utilisation a liability would have arisen under paragraph 1.10.1 above;**
>
> **1.10.3   the loss, disallowance, counteracting or clawing back of a Pre-Completion Relief which would otherwise have been available to the Company other than as set out in paragraph 1.10.2;**
>
> **1.10.4   the loss, qualifying disallowance cancellation or set-off of a right to repayment of Taxation which would otherwise have been available to the Company;**

This is one of the key definitions as the primary covenant contained in Pt 3, cl.1.1.1 turns on the definition of "Liability to Taxation".

One of the principal issues that arises on the definition of "Liability to Taxation" is the extent to which the vendors will compensate the purchaser for the non-availability of tax reliefs of the target company. The circumstances of the transaction as negotiated between the parties will generally reveal whether or not the consideration paid by the purchaser has been influenced by the expected availability of relief. If, for example, the purchase price reflects the value of carry-forward losses then the purchaser would expect to have a claim if the losses were not available to the extent anticipated, whether or not this gives rise to an immediate taxation liability. It should be noted that even in such cases a fair level of compensation may be less than a full indemnity. If, on the other hand, the purchaser is not paying for expected losses, the vendors can reasonably argue that the purchaser should not be compensated if any reliefs are unavailable.

The definition contained here represents a middle approach which is often adopted. It allows the purchaser to recover only where certain reliefs which the purchaser could reasonably expect to be available prove to be unavailable.

The three situations in which the loss of a relief may give rise to a liability are:

> (1) the use of a purchaser's relief;

(2) the loss or use of a pre-completion relief; and

(3) the loss of a right to repayment of tax. (Although a right to repayment of tax is strictly speaking not a relief as normally understood, it is often treated as such for the purposes of the tax schedule.)

Purchaser's reliefs and pre-completion reliefs are dealt with under their respective definitions below and at para.10–12. As regards the right to repayment of taxation (cl.1.10.4) the vendors would usually seek to restrict this to rights of repayment which are contained in the accounts (or completion accounts where completion accounts are to be prepared) on the basis that, if a right to repayment did not appear in the accounts (or completion accounts), the purchaser could not be expecting the repayment, would not have paid for it and so should not be compensated if it is not available.

and the amount of the Liability to Taxation shall be, in the case of: **10–11**

1.10.5   **paragraph 1.11.1 the amount of Taxation payable;**
1.10.6   **paragraph 1.11.2 the amount of Taxation which would have been payable but for such set-off or utilisation;**
1.10.7   **paragraph 1.11.3 the value attributed in the Accounts to the Pre-Completion Relief so lost, counteracted or clawed back; and**
1.10.8   **paragraph 1.11.4 the amount of repayment which would otherwise have been available.**

Although when the liability to taxation constitutes an actual payment of taxation, the amount which the vendors are liable to pay is fairly obvious, it is less clear where the liability to taxation is a loss of a relief and accordingly these clauses are necessary.

In the case of a loss of a purchaser's relief or the loss of a pre-completion relief by way of set-off, it is usual for the vendors' liability to be the amount of tax that would have been saved by the use of the purchaser's relief or pre-completion relief. In the case of loss of pre-completion relief in any other circumstances, it is sometimes proposed by the purchaser that the vendors' liability should be the amount of the relief lost. This is difficult because it raises issues such as what rate of corporation tax is to be assumed when putting a value on the relief lost and whether or not it is fair for the vendors to have to pay if, in practice, it is most unlikely that the target company would within a reasonable time be in a position to use the relief. It is also suggested that such an approach is conceptually wrong. The approach that has been adopted in the clause is that it is fair for pre-completion losses to be included because they have been given a value in the accounts. If those reliefs are lost, therefore, the appropriate level of compensation is the amount by which the assets of the company would have been less if the loss of the reliefs had been known when the accounts were prepared.

The reference to "Accounts" in cl.1.4.7 will need to be changed to the defined term used in the sale agreement for completion accounts if such accounts are to be prepared.

10–12   1.11 "Pre-Completion Relief" any Relief which arises as a result of or by reference to any Event occurring on or before Completion and which has either been treated as an asset in the Accounts or is taken into account in computing (and so reducing or eliminating) a provision for deferred taxation which appears in the Accounts or which would have appeared in the Accounts but for the presumed availability of the Relief.

The concept behind pre-completion reliefs is that it is fair for the vendors to give a covenant in respect of such reliefs since they are reliefs which were taken into account in the balance sheet in the accounts and therefore the purchaser can be assumed to have taken the availability of those reliefs into account in setting the purchase price.

In practice, it is rare for a tax relief to be given a value in the accounts of a company and therefore the first part of the definition will not often be relevant. The position in relation to deferred taxation is more difficult. A provision for deferred taxation may be reduced or eliminated on the basis that when the tax liability becomes actual there will be available to the company some relief, such as carry forward losses or capital allowances, to off-set against the tax liability. If those assumed reliefs prove to be unavailable, the provision for deferred taxation should have been greater and consequently the net assets of the company would have been less. The purchaser will seek compensation on that basis. The vendors may argue that it is unreasonable to expect them to compensate the purchaser in respect of a liability that may never arise—deferred taxation is, by its very nature, not an actual liability and may never become an actual liability. If an actual tax liability does subsequently arise, the vendors may argue that the purchaser should recover at that stage either under the tax covenant (if such tax liabilities are covered under the tax covenant) or under an appropriate warranty (for example, a warranty that adequate provision for tax is made in the accounts).

Again, reference to "Accounts" will need to be changed to the defined term used in the sale agreement for completion accounts if such accounts are to be prepared.

10–13   1.12 "Purchaser's Relief" any Relief of the Company which arises as a result or by reference to an Event occurring after the Balance Sheet Date [or any Relief of any company within the Purchaser's Group].

It is usual to exclude from the scope of the tax covenant any tax liabilities arising in the normal course of trading after the balance sheet date (see Pt 4 cl.1.1.2). On that basis, any tax reliefs occurring after the balance sheet date should also be for the benefit of the purchaser. If those reliefs are lost by being used to reduce another tax liability of the target company then the purchaser should be able to recover from the vendors.

Purchaser's Relief also, as here, often refers to reliefs of companies other than the target company which can include reliefs that are available to companies within the purchaser's group. This is to ensure that if a relief which belonged to the purchaser's group was used to reduce a liability of the target company that should be properly compensated by way of the definition being extended to include the wording in brackets. If the wording in brackets is included "Purchaser's Group" needs to be separately defined.

1.13 "Relief" includes any relief or allowance, exemption, set-off or   10–14
deduction from or credit available from, against or in relation to Taxation or
in the computation of income, profits or gains for a Taxation purpose.

This definition is of considerable significance if the covenant is extended to cases which, while not giving rise to immediate liability to make a tax payment, involve a loss of relief. The kinds of relief covered are:

(1) Relief as such—for example, group relief or relief from stamp duty;

(2) Allowances—such as capital allowances;

(3) Exemption—for example, the exemption from capital gains tax enjoyed by investment trusts;

(4) Set-off—which occurs, for example, in relation to set-off of losses in succeeding accounting periods under CTA 2010 s.45 and by a claimant company in respect of group relief under CTA 2010 ss.99 et seq.;

(5) Deduction—which arises most commonly in computing taxable profits or gains; and

(6) Credit—for example under CTA 2010 s.1109, which confers a tax credit for certain recipients of qualifying distributions, and credits for foreign tax.

1.14 "Saving" a reduction of any liability of the Company to Taxation by   10–15
virtue of the set-off against the liability or against any income, profits or
gains of any Relief arising as a result of a Liability to Taxation in respect of
which the Vendors have made a payment under Part 3 of this Schedule 6.

Sometimes a liability to taxation can give rise to a corresponding saving in taxation of the target company. This can arise because of timing issues. For example, if a deduction has been claimed in one tax period which should have been claimed for a later tax period, there will be a liability to taxation in respect of the earlier period. However, the taxation for the later period may be reduced as the deduction is allowable for the later period. Therefore, the only loss the target company suffers is in respect of penalties and interest for having claimed the deduction in the wrong period. In other cases, payment of one form of taxation may lead to a deduction in payment of another form of taxation. For example, stamp duty may be deductible when calculating chargeable gains. Where there is a group of companies, sometimes deductions may be claimed in the wrong company with the result that the tax liability of one group company increases, but the tax liability of the group company in which the deduction should properly have been claimed is reduced. These matters are dealt with in Pt 4 para.5.

10–16   **1.15 "Taxation" shall have the meaning as in clause [ ] of the Agreement.**

As noted above, it is preferable to avoid having two possibly conflicting definitions of "Taxation" in the sale agreement. The definition is better left in the main definition provisions as the term "Taxation" will usually be used more widely than the tax schedule. However, this definition is included here to remind the tax specialists reviewing the tax provisions to check the definition.

The definition in para.4–08 is very wide. Nonetheless, a wide definition is usually accepted by the vendors. However, issues do sometimes arise, particularly in relation to the following matters.

(1) Rates—it is often argued that rates should not be covered by the tax covenant. They will, in any case, normally be dealt with fully under the non-taxation warranties.

(2) National Insurance Contributions—these are not strictly speaking tax. However, it is usual to treat them in the same way as tax.

(3) Stamp Duty, Stamp Duty Reserve Tax and SDLT—including stamp duty within the tax covenant can cause problems, particularly as stamp duty (unlike stamp duty reserve tax or SDLT) is effectively an optional tax. Further, an indemnity against stamp duty may be ineffective under the Stamp Act 1891 s.117. Such considerations do not apply in relation to Stamp Duty Reserve Tax and SDLT because of their compulsory nature. A specific provision is sometimes included providing that if any document requires stamping the stamp duty shall be treated as a liability to taxation.

It is often found in practice that the definition of "Taxation" includes taxes which are almost certainly of historical interest only but which, if there has been fraudulent evasion of a tax assessment, may remain a theoretical possibility indefinitely. A note of certain taxes which are no longer in force (and of some taxes which are of limited relevance) is included in para.5–106. The vendors will find it difficult to insist on the deletion of specific taxes on the grounds of irrelevance since the purchaser may reasonably argue that any risk of a liability, however slight, should fall on the vendors.

10–17   **1.18 References to any Event occurring on or before Completion include a combination of two or more Events the first of which occurred or is deemed to have occurred on or before Completion.**

This is often a controversial provision. The purchaser will not want its claim defeated on the basis that some part of the event which gave rise to the claim arose after completion of the sale. For example, if there was a contract which had been largely performed prior to completion the fact that payment was received after Completion should not prevent a claim. Secondly, there are a number of specific tax situations where a later act combined with an earlier act can give rise to a tax charge, for example, a charge under TCGA 1992 s.179 (see para.5–62) or a claw back of stamp duty or SDLT relief (see para.5–101). However, the vendors will argue that the clause as drafted is far too wide; for example, this wording may leave the vendors liable for capital gains tax in respect of a disposal of an asset acquired before completion if that acquisition is combined with the subsequent disposal. This clause also does not address the position where there has been something "unusual" in tax terms about the original acquisition, for example where the asset was not acquired on arm's length terms, or an earlier gain was rolled over into the asset. The vendors will therefore usually try to either delete this clause or qualify it by wording such as:

" . . . provided that the Event occurring on or before Completion occurred outside the ordinary course of business of the Company and the Event occurring after Completion occurred in the ordinary course of business of the Company."

Alternative wording which favours the purchaser more is:

" . . . provided that the Event occurring after Completion occurred either (a) pursuant to a binding contract entered into on or before Completion or (b) in the ordinary course of business after Completion."

Part 2: Taxation Warranties

These are discussed in detail in Ch.5 and not repeated here.   **10–18**

Part 3: Taxation Covenant

1.1 Subject as provided below, the Vendors jointly and severally covenant to   **10–19**
pay to the Purchaser an amount equal to the amount of:

The vendors will normally be required to accept joint and several liability and, in the absence of express contrary provision, they will ultimately bear the liability amongst themselves in proportion to their rights in the total consideration. For further discussion of this point see para.3–15.

1.1.1   any Liability to Taxation which has arisen or arises as a result of   **10–20**
or in connection with an Event which occurred on or before
Completion whether or not such liability has been discharged on
or before Completion;

This is the basic covenant, the scope of which depends to a large extent on the definition of "Liability to Taxation".

10–21   **1.1.2   any Liability to Taxation which arises on, before or after Completion as a result of the non-payment of Taxation by a Vendor or any person (other than the Company) which is or has been connected (within the meaning of ITA 2007 ss.993 and 994) with a Vendor and for which that person is primarily liable;**

A Company may sometimes be secondarily liable when a connected party, such as another group company or a controlling shareholder fails to pay a tax liability, for example for capital gains under TCGA 1992 s.190. In such cases, it could be argued that the event which gives rise to the Company's liability is the failure to pay by the connected party which is primarily liable. If that event occurs after Completion it would not be caught by the general indemnity in cl.1.1.1. This clause makes it clear that such a liability is covered.

10–22   **1.1.3   any liability of the Company to make a payment in respect of Taxation under any indemnity, covenant, guarantee or charge (including any payment in respect of a surrender of group relief) entered into on or before Completion;**

This is potentially wide-ranging and the vendors need to consider the matter carefully before they give the covenant. It covers not only situations where there is a statutory right of reimbursement (see the examples set out at para.5–23) but also where there is a contractual right. For example, if the target company had previously sold a subsidiary, it could cover any continuing liability under the tax covenant given at that time. The vendors may want to argue that it is inappropriate that those types of arrangements are dealt with in the tax covenant.

The clause also covers payments for the surrender of group relief. As noted at para.5–58, a company to whom group relief is surrendered normally pays to the surrendering company an amount equal to the tax saved. The purchaser can argue, therefore, that a payment made in order to reduce the tax liability of the target company should be treated in the same way as a tax liability. The wording in brackets will clearly only be of relevance where the target company is or has been a member of a group.

10–23   **1.1.4   the costs and expenses reasonably incurred by the Company or the Purchaser in respect of any Liability to Taxation or Claim for Taxation arising as a result of or in connection with an Event which occurred on or before Completion or in taking or defending any action under this Part 3 of Schedule [   ];**

The purchaser will normally wish to ensure that the covenant to pay costs covers not only liabilities to tax in respect of which the vendors are liable but also all claims for taxation, even if the relevant tax authority's claim is subsequently found to be groundless. The justification for this is that any claim for tax will arise as a result of a problem created by the vendors and therefore they should be responsible for the costs of dealing with it.

The vendors should ensure that this clause only relates to liabilities to taxation and claims for tax to the extent that they arise from events on or before completion. The vendors may also want to seek to limit the clause to liabilities and claims for which they are liable.

1.1.5 any depletion in or reduction of value of the assets of the 10–24
Company or an increase in its liabilities as a result of inheritance
tax which:

1.1.5.1 is at Completion a charge on any of the Shares or the
assets of the Company or gives rise to a power to sell,
mortgage or charge any of the Shares or the assets of
the Company; or

1.1.5.2 after Completion becomes a charge on or gives rise to a
power to sell, mortgage or charge any of the Shares or
the assets of the Company which arises as a result of a
transfer of value occurring or being deemed to occur on
or before Completion (whether or not in conjunction
with the death of any person whenever occurring);

provided that any right to pay by instalments shall be
disregarded and the provisions of IHTA 1984 s.213 shall not
apply to payments to be made under this Covenant;

As set out in para.5–100, in certain circumstances a charge can arise over the
shares in or the assets of the target company in respect of unpaid inheritance tax.
It is reasonable for the vendors to give this covenant.

1.1.6 any liability which arises at any time of the Company to account 10–25
for income tax or national insurance contributions in respect of
an option or other right to acquire securities granted prior to
Completion by the Company or by any other person (other than
the Purchaser or any person connected with the Purchaser or
acting on its behalf) or in respect of the exercise of such option
or right or in respect of any acquisition, disposal or any other
event in relation to employment related securities (as defined for
the purposes of Pt 7 IT(EP)A):

1.1.6.1 acquired at any time on or before Completion or at any
time after Completion pursuant to the exercise of any
right or option (in either case whether conditional or
otherwise) granted on or before Completion [but for
the avoidance of doubt not including the consideration
shares]; or

1.1.6.2 acquired (before Completion) in replacement or
exchange for or derived from any employment related
securities (as defined for the purposes of Pt 7 IT(EP)A
acquired as mentioned in paragraph 1.1.6.1 above;

If shares and/or options have been granted to employees before completion and the shares/options survive completion, events after completion may give rise to tax for which the target company may be liable to account under PAYE and pay national insurance contributions. In most cases, employee share schemes or options will not survive completion so this is unnecessary. However, care may need to be taken with options as sometimes these are not technically capable of exercise until after completion. This type of provision is now reasonably standard.

Other covenants may sometimes be included in Pt 3. Examples include the following.

(1) Specific covenants against identified issues—although any such issues are usually covered by the general wording in cl.1.1.1 in any event, they may be included both to avoid any doubt as to whether they are intended to be covered and because the purchaser may adopt the approach that certain limitations should not apply to known problems.

(2) As noted at para.10–26, it is usual to include an indemnity against liability in respect of shares and options in the target company issued or granted prior to completion. Where the consideration includes the issue of shares in the purchaser, the purchaser may seek an indemnity against any tax liabilities arising from the issue of the consideration above. This could arise if HMRC seek to argue that the issue of shares is not true consideration, but disguised employment income—an issue that is particularly relevant with earn-outs.

In principle, it is hard for the vendors to object to such a provision as any tax on the sale proceeds should be for the vendors. However, where the purchaser insists on a provision that makes employment—income treatment more likely—for example, requiring an earn-out payment to be dependent on continued employment—the vendors may have grounds to amend or delete such an indemnity.

(3) Where property and/or shares are major assets of the target company, covenants relating to stamp duty and SDLT. In the case of stamp duty, this is to avoid arguments on share acquisitions and pre-SDLT land acquisitions that stamp duty is a "voluntary tax" and therefore never payable. In the case of land transactions to which SDLT applies, events occurring after completion may give rise to the requirement to file a further SDLT returns and pay additional SDLT.

Part 4: Limitations

1 Limitations on claims

10–26   In a tax covenant, the limitations have two roles:

(a) To establish what the true loss is. Like with an indemnity, there is no need to establish loss under a tax covenant. For example, if the purchaser can show that there is a liability to Taxation as defined, it can, in the absence of limitations, recover that amount from the vendors even if the purchaser or the target company has already recovered an amount in respect of that liabilities, whether, for example, from the vendors under a different provision of the sale agreement or from a third party such as an employee.

(b) To apportion risk. For example, is the risk of a change in law one which the vendors or the purchaser should properly bear?

This distinction should be borne in mind in considering the limitations. It may be perfectly proper to argue which party should bear a particular risk, but it will usually not be reasonable for a purchaser to argue against a limitation designed to prevent double recovery.

1.1 The Tax Covenant and any claim under the Tax Warranties shall not apply to any Liability to Taxation: 10–27

As noted above, the limitations apply to both the covenant and the tax warranties to ensure consistent treatment.

1.1.1 to the extent that specific provision or reserve or allowance in respect thereof has been made in the Accounts; 10–28

If the vendors have provided management accounts for periods subsequent to the balance sheet date which contain provisions for taxation on the profits shown, the clause should extend to also include those accounts. If there are to be completion accounts, this clause should refer to the completion accounts rather than the last statutory accounts.

The purchaser cannot fairly complain about a liability which arises after completion where a specific provision or reserve was made in the accounts, although a note in the accounts may not of itself provide a quantification of the anticipated liability.

Deferred taxation needs careful consideration. If no reference is made to deferred taxation, the vendors will normally not be liable if it becomes an actual liability as this will be the result of post-completion events (although there may be liability if the adequacy of the deferred taxation is as a result of the loss of a pre-completion relief). The purchaser should specifically consider the nature of any deferred tax provision to see if it is acceptable for the liability, if it arises, to be outside the scope of the tax covenant. It is not unusual for the purchaser to seek to exclude provisions for deferred tax from this exclusion.

The vendors will often seek to delete "specific" on the grounds that if the provision or reserve for tax is sufficient in aggregate to cover all the tax liabilities, it should not matter whether the provision or reserve has been allocated to a specific liability.

1.1.2 for which the Company is, or may become, liable wholly or primarily as a result of transactions in the usual course of its business after the Balance Sheet Date; 10–29

A general exclusion for liabilities arising from transactions in the usual course of the company's business is fair having regard to the broad principle that the indemnities should relate to unexpected liabilities and that the purchaser is effectively getting the benefit of profits earned in that period. Furthermore, the purchaser has the protection of the warranties. This exclusion is not appropriate if there are to be completion accounts and cl.1.1.1 has been amended to include reference to completion accounts as any liability should be picked up by way of provision in the completion accounts. The purchaser may want clarification on what is and is not usual course of business. For example, distributions should be excluded.

10–30   **1.1.3   to the extent that it would not have arisen or been increased but for a change in the rate of Taxation or change in legislation or published administrative practice made after Completion, or change after Completion in any extra statutory concession or published practice previously made by any Taxation Authority;**

Until 1984, the corporation tax rate was fixed annually in arrears and it has become established practice for the purchaser to accept the risk of an increased liability and, conversely, for the vendors to allow the purchaser the benefit of a reduction in the tax rate (though in practice retrospective changes of this nature are unlikely).

The part of this clause relating to changes in the law will not be necessary if the definition of relevant statutory provisions is limited to those which are in force at the date of the sale agreement or result from a mere consolidation. However, if the definition allows for future changes in the law then it is a matter for negotiation between the parties as to whether retrospective liability imposed upon the target company should be borne by the vendors or by the purchaser. The purchaser should bear in mind that provisions in Finance Acts are often retrospective, at least to the date of the budget speech. Where taxation avoidance is involved, for example in relation to employee remuneration, the Government has indicated that it may impose retrospective legislation. The purchaser may want to consider whether this limitation is appropriate if the target company has been involved in matters which run a greater risk of retrospective legislation, such as aggressive tax avoidance.

The vendors may wish to try to extend the exclusion to avoid a liability which results, for example, from a recognised interpretation of the law being reversed by the ruling of a higher court.

10–31   **1.1.4   to the extent that the Liability to Taxation arises as the result of the change after Completion in any accounting policy, any Taxation or accounting practice or the length of any accounting period for tax purposes of the Company;**

If a change in accounting policy after the purchaser acquires control of the target company gives rise retrospectively to a taxation liability which would not otherwise relate to the pre-completion period, the vendors might reasonably consider that they should not be required to meet that liability. For example, treatment of an asset as a fixed asset rather than trading stock could affect the deductibility of expenditure incurred on the asset.

There is a considerable subjective element involved in quantifying timing differences and the vendors should not be penalised if a change of treatment taking place after the sale of the target company results in an unexpected liability.

A purchaser will often qualify this exclusion to exclude changes in accounting policy that are necessary because the target company's accounts have not previously been prepared in accordance with accounting standards. The vendors cannot reasonably object to this.

1.1.5 to the extent of any recovery by the Purchaser under the Non Tax Warranties in respect of, or arising from, the same Liability to Taxation;

10–32

This clause adopts the definition of "Non Tax Warranties" which appears in the sale agreement (see para.4–02). In principle it should not be objectionable as its aim is to avoid double recovery. The purchaser will generally want to bring a claim under the tax covenant to the extent that it is able to give a better basis for recovery unless warranty claims are to be quantified on an indemnity basis as discussed in para.3–06.

1.1.6 to the extent that a Relief other than a Pre-Completion Relief or a Purchaser's Relief is available to reduce such Liability to Taxation;

10–33

As discussed at para.10–10, the position adopted in this tax covenant is that the purchaser should only be entitled to the benefit of reliefs if the availability of those reliefs was assumed in deciding the purchase price. If the availability or otherwise of such reliefs is not reflected in the purchase price, then it is fair that the vendors should have the benefit of them to reduce any potential claim under the tax covenant. This exclusion would cover a situation where, for example, there was a liability to taxation but there were carry-forward losses to offset against that liability.

The purchaser may want to limit this to reliefs that are actually used, rather than just being available.

1.1.7 if it results from the cessation of the trade of the Company after Completion;

10–34

Cessation of a trade will usually result in the crystallisation of various tax liabilities, some of which might be caught under the tax covenant. The vendors can fairly argue that, unless it is expressly contemplated at the time of entering into the sale agreement, cessation of trade is outside the reasonable contemplation of the parties and therefore the vendors should not be liable for the consequences of it.

The exclusions set out above are ones which it is considered reasonable for a purchaser to include in a first draft. The vendors may want to include other exclusions, as set out below.

10–35   **1.1.8   to the extent that it has been made good or otherwise compensated for by the Purchaser or the Company;**

In certain circumstances, particularly where there is a corporate vendor, a liability may be counteracted by making retrospective claims for relief. If this can be achieved without cost to the purchaser or the target company, then it is fair that the vendors should benefit from any saving that is made. Similarly, tax paid under PAYE and national insurance may be recovered from employees, resulting in no net loss to the target company.

10–36   **1.1.9   which is attributable to the Company ceasing to be entitled to the small companies' rate of corporation tax as a result of the purchase of the Shares by the Purchaser;**

If the taxable profits of a company do not exceed a maximum amount as fixed by Parliament from time to time, a reduced rate of corporation tax applies under CTA 2010 ss.18 et seq. This maximum is allocated equally among "associated" companies (that is, companies under common control) and accordingly the acquisition of the target company by a corporate purchaser could reduce the maximum applicable to the target company. If this results in loss of the small companies' relief, it is unreasonable that the vendors should be penalised.

10–37   **1.1.10   to the extent Disclosed in the Disclosure Letter;**

It is unusual to have a disclosure letter which affects the tax covenant. In general it is better practice to detail the exclusions that are agreed.

10–38   **1.1.11   which would not have arisen, or been increased but for a voluntary act or omission of the Company or the Purchaser [which could reasonably have been avoided] carried out, or occurring, after the date of this Agreement, otherwise than in the ordinary and proper course of business, [and which the Purchaser or the Company was, or ought reasonably to have been, aware could give rise to a Liability to Taxation]; or**

On the face of it, it would appear fair that the vendors should not be responsible for a liability which arises as a result of voluntary acts on the part of the target company after completion. An example of this that could arise where the target company was a member of a group of companies is where there has been a transfer of assets within the target group and, during the period of six years after the transfer, the transferee ceases to be a member of the group. In that event, a tax charge arises retrospectively to the date at which the group transfer took place (TCGA 1992 s.179) (as amended). Unless the transaction was one that was specifically contemplated at the time of the purchase of the target group, it is unreasonable for the purchaser to expect the vendors to be responsible for this liability. The purchaser would often accept this clause with the inclusion of the words in brackets.

It is to be noted that the exception, even without the bracketed amendments, applies only to transactions effected outside of the usual course of business as the purchaser cannot be expected to absolve the vendors from liabilities that arise from activities carried out in the ordinary course. The parties may wish to clarify the effect on this clause of post-completion changes in the nature of the target company's business, for example by excluding liability which results from a change in the nature of, or manner of conducting, the business.

> **1.1.12 if the Company fails, after due warning, to act in accordance   10–39
> with the reasonable instructions of the Vendors in conducting a
> dispute (as referred to in paragraph 2 of this Part 4 of Schedule
> [   ]) in respect of a Claim for Taxation of claim for breach of the
> Tax Warranties;**

It is of considerable importance to the vendors that they should control the conduct of negotiations and litigation with HMRC in accordance with para.2. The clause itself provides no special sanction if the target company fails to comply with its obligations. The vendors will therefore sometimes seek to exclude from the scope of the covenant liability which arises in circumstances where they have not been responsible for the negotiations but, from the purchaser's point of view, this sanction may be considered to be excessive. Paragraph 2 contains contrary wording of the type the purchaser will often want. The purchaser will also need to consider what effect there will be if one of the vendors complains that the consultation clause has not been properly observed in relation to him or her while the others have been consulted. In that event, there is no reason why those vendors who have been consulted should be released from liability simply because of failure to consult another one of the vendors. The position of the vendor who has not been consulted may be different, but complex questions will then arise as to the impact on the joint and several liability of the vendors if one of them is released from liabilities. See also the discussion of this question in para.3–15.

All of the limitations on liability under the tax covenant and the tax warranties can be set out in the tax schedule itself. Alternatively certain limitations can be included by incorporating the appropriate provisions in the limitation provisions in the sale agreement. The matters that are typically dealt with in the limitation provisions in the sale agreement follow.

> (1) Time limits: it is usual to provide that claims under the tax covenant
> must be brought within a time period of between six and seven years
> from completion. This equates to the six year period in which, in
> normal circumstances, HMRC can raise an enquiry.

(2) Overall cap: it is usual for claims under the tax covenant to be included in the overall cap on claims of, usually, the amount of consideration received by the vendors. (See comments at para.11–07 for further discussion of this point.) The purchaser may argue that where there are specific known tax problems, these should be excluded from the cap.

(3) Small claims: a purchaser will often argue that there should be no small claims exclusions in terms of either a "de minimis" or "floor" for claims under the tax covenant on the basis that the tax covenant should provide a straight pound for pound indemnity. The vendors may argue that there is no logical reason why claims under the tax covenant should be treated differently from claims under the warranties. This is usually a matter of commercial negotiation. (See comment at para.11–05 for further discussion of this point.)

The position adopted in this draft is to have these matters dealt with in the limitation schedule. See Ch.11 for details.

2 Conduct of Claims

10–40 **2.1 The Purchaser shall as soon as reasonably practicable notify the Vendors in writing of any Claim for Taxation which comes to its notice, whereby it appears that the Vendors are, or may become, liable to pay the Purchaser under the Tax Covenant or in respect of a claim under the Tax Warranties [provided that the giving of such notice will not be a condition precedent to the liability of the Vendors under the Tax Covenant or Tax Warranties].**

Careful consideration needs to be given to the following points.

(1) The clear identification of items which require notification to the vendors. In this context, the target company will wish to avoid a constant correspondence with the vendors but the vendors are entitled to ensure that no significant matter is dealt with without their having an opportunity to intervene.

(2) Where there is more than one vendor, it is desirable to have a simple system for giving notice and for ensuring that a collective decision is reached and is communicated to the target company. It may be helpful to appoint a representative for this purpose.

(3) The vendors may wish to insert a time period in which they must be notified to enable the vendors to consult together, take advice and reach a view well before any time limit for contesting the claim with the relevant tax authority could lapse.

(4) All parties should bear in mind that a variety of liabilities not normally thought of as "taxation" may fall within that term as defined.

(5) The wording in brackets is important for the purchaser to ensure that it does not lose the right to recover from the vendors because it failed

to give notice—see also para.11–10. The vendors may seek to delete it. (See also the discussion at para.10–39).

2.2 The Purchaser shall ensure that a Claim for Taxation to which paragraph 2.1 of this Part 4 of Schedule [ ] applies is, so far as reasonably practicable, dealt with separately from claims to which it does not apply. 10–41

To minimise some of the potential complexities, the purchaser is expressly required to attempt to deal with matters which can be the subject of a claim under the tax covenant separately from the target company's general tax affairs. This should also in principle suit the target company as it will not want the vendors to have access to information regarding its taxation affairs generally by reason of the right of the vendors to have the conduct of claims.

2.3 Provided that the Vendors indemnify and secure the Company and the Purchaser to the reasonable satisfaction of the Purchaser against all losses, costs, damages and expenses (including interest on overdue Taxation) which may be incurred thereby, the Purchaser will procure that the Company at the Vendors' cost and expense takes such action and gives such information and assistance in connection with its Taxation affairs as the Vendors may reasonably and promptly request to dispute, appeal, settle or compromise any Claim for Taxation. This obligation will not apply where a Taxation Authority alleges dishonest or fraudulent conduct by the Vendors or by the Company before Completion. 10–42

The basic proposition that the vendors should have control of negotiations with and litigation against HMRC or other taxation authorities is often unobjectionable, though the purchaser may want to impose additional restrictions. This clause as drafted does not explicitly allow the vendors conduct of the claim, that is the ability to conduct negotiations on behalf of the target company. Rather, the vendors are limited to instructing the target company to do certain things. In practice, the purchaser may be prepared to allow the vendors to deal direct with the tax authorities, but it is unusual for the purchaser to concede this point in the sale agreement.

The vendors should consider whether it would be helpful when entering into the tax covenant to make it clear among themselves as to how liability for costs should be apportioned. It might well be, for example, that in a particular case one vendor would wish to agree to a certain settlement with the relevant taxation authority while another would prefer to litigate. In that case, several possible choices exist. A basis of majority votes could determine whether or not the settlement should be accepted, the majority being determined either purely on numbers of persons or on amounts of sale consideration received. Another possibility is that a vendor prepared to accept a compromise could pay his contribution into a suspense account on the basis that such payment would then discharge him from any subsequent liability. If the ultimate liability from a contest of the claim was less than the amount paid into the suspense account, the vendor who made the payment into that account would receive back only the net amount after deducting an appropriate contribution to the costs incurred. Alternatively, the vendor willing to accept a settlement could pay his proportion of the amount of the settlement into a common fund the benefit of which would accrue to those vendors contesting the claim and any surplus would be handed back to the vendor.

It is nevertheless unusual to spell out these provisions in detail but, where there are vendors who have distinctly different interests and it is known that a tax liability might arise, it is desirable for these points to be resolved from the start. The purchaser should be aware that litigation can involve heavy demands on executive time and, especially in any case where there is a likelihood of disputes arising, it would be desirable to have a clear understanding as to whether a charge for time is to be made in this respect and, if so, on what basis.

Purchasers occasionally seek to extend the final sentence to cover allegations of negligent conduct. This is unreasonable. It is easy for HMRC to allege negligence whenever a mistake in calculating tax has been made, even if only as a negotiating technique.

10–43   **2.4 The Purchaser shall procure that the Vendors (and their advisers) are given reasonable access to all relevant documents, records and personnel of the Company and the Purchaser and its advisers to enable the Vendors promptly and effectively to evaluate, dispute and enforce their rights under this paragraph 2.**

The vendors will, in practice, often require documentary and executive assistance in handling claims. In principle the purchaser should not object as long as the demands are not excessive. If litigation requires the attendance of employees of the target company at court, there could be considerable costs involved and as such it might be fair for the vendors to pay a suitable attendance fee.

10–44   **2.5 In connection with the conduct of a dispute relating to a Claim for Taxation to which the Tax Covenant or the Tax Warranties apply:**

> **2.5.1   the Vendors and the Purchaser shall keep the other parties informed of all relevant matters and shall promptly forward or procure to be forwarded copies of all material correspondence and other written communications [other than those which have been prepared by the Purchaser or its professional advisers with a view to assessing the merits of any such claim or which are otherwise subject to legal professional privilege];**

Again, where there is more than one vendor, it would be advisable for them to provide a mechanism for reaching decisions amongst themselves so that one vendor cannot be penalised for a failure in co-operation on the part of another. The purchaser will want to include the wording in brackets so that it is not obliged to disclose privileged documents or those that might prejudice its ability to make claims against the vendors to the vendors.

2.5.2 the Vendors shall not settle or compromise the dispute, or agree **10–45** anything in its conduct which is likely to affect the amount involved or the future Liability to Taxation of the Company, or the Purchaser, without the prior approval of the Purchaser, such approval not to be unreasonably withheld or delayed;

Although in principle the target company and the purchaser are unlikely to be concerned about the terms of a settlement or compromise, nevertheless they do have a legitimate interest in case the compromise affects any of their other taxation affairs. For example, the target company may have agreed procedures with HMRC in relation to such matters as determination of disallowed expenses which it would not wish to be disturbed by the disputed matters. The purchaser will also be concerned to ensure that the vendors are able to discharge the agreed liability.

2.5.3 if a dispute arises between the Purchaser and the Vendors as to **10–46** whether a Claim for Taxation should be settled in full or contested, the dispute shall be referred to the determination of a senior tax counsel of at least 10 years standing ("Counsel"), appointed by agreement between the Purchaser and the Vendors, or (if they do not agree) upon the application by either party to the President for the time being of the Law Society, whose determination shall be final. Counsel shall be asked to advise whether, in his opinion, an appeal against the Claim for Taxation would, on the balance of probabilities, be likely to succeed. Only if his opinion is in the affirmative shall that Claim for Taxation be contested. Any further dispute arising between the Vendors and the Purchaser as to whether a further appeal should be pursued following determination of an earlier appeal (whether or not in favour of the Vendors) shall be resolved in a similar manner.

The purchaser may wish to impose some restraint on the freedom of the vendors in relation to the conduct of claims. This clause as drafted substantially limits the rights of the vendors. In practice, this provision will often be amended so that the vendors can contest the claim up to a certain level, often to the First-tier Tribunal and the procedure in this paragraph will only apply if the vendors want to appeal the matter further.

2.6 Nothing contained in this paragraph 2 shall require the Purchaser to **10–47** **prevent the Company from making a payment of Taxation at the time necessary to avoid incurring a fine, penalty or interest in respect of unpaid Taxation.**

Self explanatory.

2.7 If the Vendors fail promptly (and in any event within 20 Business Days **10–48** of the Purchaser giving notice requiring the Vendors to do so) to inform the

Purchaser of any action which the Vendors wish the Purchaser to procure the Company to take under paragraph 2.3, the Purchaser will be entitled to procure that the Company settles or compromises any Claim for Taxation on such terms as it determines in its absolute discretion.

This clause allows the purchaser complete discretion over the settlement of any claim if the vendors do not take the opportunity to give instructions regarding it. This can work harshly against the vendors as under a claim under the tax covenant (unlike a claim under the taxation warranties) the purchaser is not under a duty to mitigate its loss and get the best settlement possible with the tax authority. However, it is hard to counter the argument that if the vendors are concerned about this, they should exercise their right to defend the claim in accordance with the agreed procedure.

3 Dates for payments

10–49   **3.1 This paragraph applies solely for determining the date on which payments are to be made by the Vendors under the Tax Covenant.**

It might be thought that there would be no need to provide for the time at which payments under the tax covenant are made. However, special provision is required given the fact that the tax covenant may cover not only the actual payments of tax but also loss relief.

10–50   **3.2 The Vendors shall make a payment to the Purchaser in cleared funds on the date falling five clear Business Days after the date on which the Purchaser has notified the Vendors of the amount of the payment required to be made or, if later:**

This states the general rule and is amplified by cll.3.2.1 to 3.2.3.

10–51   **3.2.1   in any case involving a liability of the Company to make an actual payment (whether or not of Taxation) three clear Business Days prior to that date on which the Company is required to make such payment; or**

This deals with the simple case where the target company makes an actual taxation payment.

10–52   **3.2.2   in any case involving the set-off or utilisation of a Pre-Completion Relief or a Purchaser's Relief pursuant to paragraph 1.11.2 of Part 1 of this Schedule [   ], three clear Business Days before the date on which the payment of Taxation is or would have been required to be made but for such set-off or utilisation; or**

This deals with the situation where a relief which the purchaser was expecting is used to reduce a taxation liability of the target company. The logical date for payment in those circumstances is the date on which the tax which has been saved would have been payable.

3.2.3 in any case involving the loss, nullifying, disallowance, cancellation or set-off or a right to repayment of Taxation, three clear Business Days after such repayment of Taxation would have been received by the Company. 10–53

Note that there is no specific provision dealing with the position where a pre-completion relief is lost otherwise than by being used to reduce another tax liability. The result is that where there is a claim for the loss of a pre-completion relief of this nature this will fall within the general wording in cl.3.2 and will be payable within five days of notification.

3.3 If any payment by the Vendors under the Tax Covenant or the Tax Warranties is not made on the date referred to in paragraph 3.2 it shall carry interest from the due date of payment at the rate of [   ] per cent above the base rate from time to time of [ ] Bank Plc until payment is received by the Purchaser. 10–54

This is a standard interest clause and should reflect the equivalent clause, if any, in the sale agreement.

3.4 Disputes in relation to the provisions of paragraphs 3.2 and 3.3 may be referred by the Purchaser or the Vendors to the auditors of the Company, acting as experts and not as arbitrators, whose certificate shall in the absence of manifest error be final. 10–55

In view of the complexity of circumstances that can arise in practice and the difficulty that exists in many cases of identifying clearly the taxation liabilities which are covered by a specific payment, it is considered sensible to provide for a simple method of determination. While the purchaser will be happy to rely on the certificate of the auditors of the target company, the vendors may wish to ensure that the auditors are a firm of sufficient standing and independence to carry out the determination competently and fairly. Although in relation to taxes, such as stamp duty and rates the auditors might not be the appropriate experts, it is to be expected that they would obtain suitable professional advice in resolving the matter.

4 Deduction from Payments and Right of Set-off

4.1 Except as required by law payments under the Tax Covenant shall be made gross, free of rights of counterclaim or set-off and without any deductions or withholdings of whatever nature. 10–56

This excludes the vendors' right of set-off. Although usually accepted, this could potentially cause problems for the vendors. If the purchaser's wording in para.2.1

of this part is accepted, the purchaser's failure to follow the conduct of claims procedure does not reduce the vendors' liability—it only allows them to bring a claim against the purchaser for breach of contract. Under the wording of this para.4.1 the purchaser could claim that the vendors' breach of contract claim cannot be offset against amounts due to the purchaser.

10–57   **4.2 If a deduction or withholding is required by law to be made from a payment by the Vendors under the Tax Covenant, there shall be paid to the Purchaser such additional amount as is necessary to ensure that the net receipt by the Purchaser is equal to the amount which it would have received and retained had the payment in question not been subject to deduction or withholding.**

In practice this is limited to very few situations, mainly tax related, where there is an obligation on the payer to make a deduction at source. An example is payment of interest to persons overseas in certain circumstances. In circumstances where this does apply, the vendors should consider amending the clause to ensure that any corresponding benefit to the purchaser (for example a tax credit) is taken into account.

10–58   **4.3 If the Purchaser or the Company is liable to Taxation in respect of a payment under the Tax Covenant (or would have been liable but for the availability of Relief or a right to repayment of Taxation), there shall be paid to the Purchaser an additional amount as if the Taxation had been a deduction or withholding from the payment and paragraph 4.2 shall apply accordingly to the payment.**

This is a fairly standard tax gross-up clause. It is usually accepted by the vendors where, as is normally the case, payments are made to the purchaser. ESC D33 clarifies that in most cases, such payments will not be taxable in the hands of the purchaser and so the clause is largely academic. If, for whatever reason, payments are to be made to the target company or there is a real risk that ESC D33 will not apply, the vendors should consider amending or deleting this clause.

5 Savings

10–59   **5.1 If (at the request and expense of the Vendors) the auditors of the Company certify that the Company or the Purchaser has obtained a Saving, the Purchaser shall as soon as reasonably practicable repay to the Vendors the lesser of:**

> **5.1.1   the amount of the Saving less costs incurred in obtaining it (as certified by the Company's auditors); and**
> **5.1.2   the amount paid by the Vendors to the Purchaser pursuant to the Tax Covenant or under the Tax Warranties.**

5.2 If the amount referred to in paragraph 5.1.1 exceeds that referred to in paragraph 5.1.2, the excess shall be carried forward to be set-off against (and so as to reduce or eliminate) the future liability of the Vendors under the Tax Covenant or the Tax Warranties.

As noted above (see para.10–14) in certain circumstances a tax liability may give rise to a saving of tax in the target company. In those circumstances it is fair for the vendors to have the benefit of that saving. However, the benefit will only be by way of repayment of claims already paid or a reduction in future liabilities—it does not give rise to a net cash payment to the vendors.

The purchaser may object to cl.5.2 on the grounds that the benefit of a saving should only relate to the liability to taxation which gave rise to the saving.

**5.3 If the Company or the Purchaser becomes aware that the Company or   10–60
the Purchaser has obtained or may obtain a Saving, the Purchaser shall as soon as reasonably practicable give notice of that fact to the Vendors. Provided that the Vendors have paid the Purchaser in respect of the Liability to Taxation which gave rise to the Saving, the Purchaser shall take and procure the taking by the Company of reasonable steps to obtain the Saving.**

5.4 In certifying a Saving under paragraph 5.1, the Company's auditors shall act as experts and not as arbitrators and their certificate shall in the absence of manifest error be final.

In practical terms, the problem for the vendors will be in finding out whether the target company has made a saving. Clause 5.3 is therefore important from the vendors' perspective, although in practice it may be difficult to enforce.

6 Recovery from Third Party

**6.1 If the Company or the Purchaser recovers or becomes aware that it is   10–61
entitled to recover from a third party (including but not limited to a Taxation Authority) an amount which is referable to a Liability to Taxation in respect of which the Vendors have made a payment to the Purchaser, the Purchaser shall as soon as reasonably practicable give notice of that fact to the Vendors and shall take or procure that the Company takes (at the Vendors' expense and provided that the Vendors indemnify and secure the Purchaser and the Company to the reasonable satisfaction of the Purchaser against all losses, expenses and Taxation relating to that recovery) such reasonable action necessary to effect the recovery as the Vendors reasonably request in writing.**

If the target company or the purchaser has the right to be reimbursed by a third party in relation to a liability which is discharged by the vendors, it is appropriate to give the vendors the benefit of this right by accounting for sums received or by assigning the right. This clause covers not only recovery from taxation authorities but also, for example, recovery where the target company has a right of reimbursement. An example of a statutory right of reimbursement is TCGA 1992 s.190 where corporation tax on a chargeable gain accruing to a group company may be recovered from the principal company in the group. The principal company, which has only a secondary liability, has a right of reimbursement against the group company which is primarily liable.

There may also be a right to recover from employees in respect of amounts due under PAYE and in respect of National Insurance Contributions. The purchaser may, however, object to being obliged to take action against people who may, after completion, be its own employees and specifically exclude recovery from employees from the scope of this clause.

10–62   **6.2 The Purchaser shall repay to the Vendors the lesser of:**

         6.2.1   the amount so recovered together with any interest (net of Taxation) or repayment supplement received in respect of it (net of any losses, costs, damages, expenses and tax relating to the amount recovered not previously recovered from the Vendors); and

         6.2.2   the amount paid by the Vendors under the Tax Covenant in respect of the Liability to Taxation or Claim for Taxation in question.

     6.3 If the amount provided for under paragraph 6.2.1 exceeds that under paragraph 6.2.2, the excess shall be set against, and so reduce or eliminate, any liability of the Vendors under the Tax Covenant which arises after the recovery.

The same considerations apply here as in para.10–59 above. As with cl.5.2 the purchaser may object to cl.6.3.

Part 5: Purchaser's Covenant and Administrative Matters

10–63   As its heading suggests, Pt 5 of the tax schedule deals mainly with any covenants that are to be provided by the purchaser relating to tax and administrative matters. Set out below is the general tax covenant that a purchaser will often be prepared to give and provisions relating to the preparation, submission and agreeing of any outstanding corporation tax returns. If the target company is being sold out of a group, this part of the tax schedule may contain more extensive provisions dealing with, for example, leaving the VAT group and surrender of group relief.

1 Purchaser's Covenant

10–64   **1.1 The Purchaser covenants with the Vendors that, to the extent that the Vendors or any person connected with the Vendors are assessed to Taxation pursuant to CTA 2010 ss.713–715, it shall pay the Vendors an amount equal to such liability.**

1.2 The covenant in paragraph 1.1 of this Part 5 of Schedule [   ] shall not apply to a Liability to Taxation to the extent that:

    1.2.1 if that Liability to Taxation were to be discharged by the Company then a liability would arise for the Vendors under the Tax Covenant; and

    1.2.2 the Vendors have not paid an amount to the Purchaser equal to and in respect of that Liability to Taxation.

1.3 The provisions of paragraphs 3 (Dates for payments) and 4 (Deduction from Payments and Right of Set-off) of Part 4 of this Schedule [   ] shall apply to any payment due under this paragraph 1 mutatis mutandis.

Under CTA 2010 ss.713–715 (formerly ICTA 1988 s.767AA) it is possible for the vendors to become secondarily liable in circumstances where certain corporation tax liabilities of the target company are not discharged after completion. This provision provides some protection for the vendors against such liability. Whilst there is a right of reimbursement from the target company, this is likely to be of no value. This type of provision is not usually objectionable to the purchaser.

Where capital gains are an issue, TCGA ss.189 and 190 provide for other group companies and shareholders to be secondarily liable. Consideration should be given by the vendors to extending the scope of the purchaser's covenant to cover these provisions in circumstances where the detailed provisions of these sections may be satisfied.

2 Corporation Tax Returns

2.1 In this paragraph 2.1:   10–65

    2.1.1 the "Agents" means [the Vendors' Accountants or] such [other] firm of chartered accountants as may be appointed by the Vendors for the purposes of this paragraph 2;

    2.1.2 "Relevant Returns" means the corporation tax returns and computations of the Company in respect of periods ended on or before [   ]; and

    2.1.3 "Relevant Correspondence" means all documents, correspondence and communications relating to the Relevant Returns which shall be received from or sent to the Taxation Authority.

2.2 The Vendors shall each use their reasonable endeavours to procure that the Agents shall (to the extent not done before Completion):

    2.2.1 prepare the Relevant Returns; and

    2.2.2 submit drafts of the same to the Vendors and the Company as soon as reasonably practicable.

This provision is designed to deal with the situation where at completion there are corporation tax returns which have either not yet been submitted or submitted but not finally agreed as there may be an issue as to who deals with such returns. (If "Vendors' Accountants" is not a defined term then the wording in brackets should be deleted.) From the vendors' perspective:

(1) as the vendors are likely to be liable under the tax covenant if there are any tax problems, they have an interest in ensuring the returns are dealt with as they want and by their accountant;

(2) the vendors and their accountant will have a better understanding of what happened before completion and therefore be in a better position to deal with any queries raised; and

(3) if the vendors' accountant deals with the returns, the vendors will have to bear the costs.

From the purchaser's perspective:

(1) it may be reluctant for any tax affairs of a group company to be dealt with by anyone other than the group's tax advisers (especially where the purchaser is part of a large group); and

(2) there may be a suspicion that the vendors' accountants will try to settle the tax affairs in a manner which minimises any claims against the vendors, rather than in the best interests of the target company.

This clause is drafted on the basis that the vendors' accountants deals with tax returns. It can easily be changed so that it is the purchaser's accountants dealing if that is required.

The Purchaser may by notice in writing to the Vendors and the Agents comment on or suggest amendments to the Relevant Returns.

10–66   **2.3 The Purchaser shall procure that the Relevant Returns shall be authorised and signed by or on behalf of the Company and be submitted to the Taxation Authority without amendment or with such amendments as the Purchaser reasonably requests provided that neither the Purchaser nor the Company shall be obliged to authorise, sign or submit any Relevant Return unless the Purchaser reasonably believes that it is true and accurate in all material respects.**

The Vendors and the Purchaser shall procure that the Agents have conduct of all Relevant Correspondence but subject always to paragraph 2 of Part 4 of this Schedule [   ].

If the vendors' accountants deal with returns, the interaction between this paragraph and cl.2 and the conduct of claims provisions is not always clear.

2.4 The Vendors shall procure that:

  2.4.1 all reasonable steps are taken to ensure that the Relevant Returns are prepared, submitted and agreed with the Taxation Authority as soon as practicable;

  2.4.2 the Purchaser and the Company are kept fully informed of all matters relating to the submission, negotiation and agreement of the Relevant Returns; and

  2.4.3 the costs of the Agents in carrying out their functions under this paragraph 2.4.2 of this Part 5 of Schedule [   ] shall be borne by the Vendors.

The purchaser will usually require that the vendors' accountants' costs are borne by the vendors even though they are, in effect, performing work for the company. The vendors are normally willing to accept this as a compromise for giving their accountants the right to prepare the returns (given that this is usually in the vendors' interest).

CHAPTER 11
Limitations and Risk Transfer

11–01   Whilst the purchaser would ideally like there to be no limitations on the vendors' liability in respect of warranty claims (preferring to rely on the position under statute and at common law which favours it), this is a position that the purchaser is unlikely to be able to secure other than in circumstances where the vendors are ill advised or the purchaser has an extremely dominant bargaining position. Current convention is for the purchaser to offer some limitations to the vendors in its first draft of the sale agreement, as a minimum in relation to the time periods during which claims can be made and the value of claims. These limitations are discussed in this chapter, along with a number of other limitations that the vendors might wish to seek to include in the sale agreement.

Appendix 7 contains a precedent set of clauses which the vendors are likely to find of assistance in their first mark-up of the sale agreement prepared by the purchaser or its advisors (and on the assumption it is a share sale).

Whilst historically certain limitations to the tax deed were dealt with as part of the warranty limitation provisions, these are now principally contained in the schedule of the sale agreement that contains the tax covenant and tax warranties—see Ch.10 for details. Those that are still customarily dealt with in the limitation provisions that apply to the non-tax warranties are, as noted in Ch.10, the time limits and, to the extent that they are to apply to the tax covenant and/or the tax warranties, the financial thresholds and limits. The structure adopted in this book follows that approach.

This chapter will also briefly consider warranty and indemnity insurance which both vendors and purchasers are increasingly turning to, in appropriate circumstances, to cover risk that for one reason or another is not covered by the other party.

PERIODS OF LIMITATION

11–02   The normal period of limitation within which an action must be brought is six years, if the right arises under a document which is not a deed, and 12 years if there is a deed. It is current convention for the period to be reduced to two or three years in respect of the non-taxation warranties on a share sale and to six or seven years for the tax warranties and the tax covenant. The underlying principle is that one or two audits of the target company should identify most defects which existed at the time of the sale but, as the statutory limitation period for certain taxation matters (in particular corporation tax returns) is six years from the end of the relevant accounting period (Finance Act 1998 Sch.18, Pt 5) (in the absence of special factors such as fraud), a six-year period from the end of the relevant accounting period should apply to the tax covenant and the tax warranties.

Sometimes a purchaser may seek to differentiate between limitation periods for different types of warranties, for instance environmental, where a longer period than the two or three years normally requested may be sought. It will be a matter for negotiation in each particular case whether these matters should be dealt with differently than claims based on other warranties but, as a matter of drafting, it is possible to specify different limitation periods for any of the warranties. More often, if a purchaser has a particular concern it will request an indemnity rather than a warranty and the limitations, if any, that apply to that will be a matter for negotiation.

Where there is a distinction under the sale agreement between the limitations to apply to the tax warranties and those that apply to the tax covenant the vendors will normally prefer claims which can be brought under either heading to be based on the warranties (see para.1–09). As such the vendors are unlikely to object to the limitation period in respect of claims under the tax warranties being the same length as that in respect of claims under the tax covenant. A suitable clause dealing with this aspect in relation to the warranties on a share sale is as follows:

[11A] Time limit for Warranty claims

A claim shall not be brought by the Purchaser in respect of a breach of the Warranties unless notice of the claim (specifying in reasonable detail the circumstances which give rise to the claim[, the breach that results and the amount claimed]) has been given to the Vendors before the expiration of the appropriate period. [The claim shall be deemed to have been withdrawn (if it has not been previously satisfied, settled or withdrawn) six/nine/twelve months after the expiration of the appropriate period, unless proceedings in respect of it have commenced by being issued and served on [all of] [any of] the Vendors prior to then.] For the purpose of this clause, the "appropriate period":   11–03

> **[11A.1] in respect of claims which arise under the Tax Warranties or the Tax Covenant is seven years from the Balance Sheet Date;**

> **[11A.2] in respect of claims which arise under clauses [   ] or [   ] of Schedule [   ] is [   ] years from Completion; and**

> **[11A.3] in respect of other claims is [two years from Completion].**

The vendors might reasonably require that the period specified in cl.11A.1 should be six years from the end of the last complete accounting period but, if the tax covenant relates also to liabilities of the current period, it is logical that the six years should run from the end of the current period.

Clause 11A.2 would be used where specific warranties have been identified as having a longer limitation period, for example, it is often agreed that if there are any environmental issues with the target company or business that given their nature may not materialise or be disclosed until some time after completion such that the limitation period for claims in respect of such matters should be extended. This in the vast majority of circumstances is likely to be unacceptable to the vendors.

Apart from imposing a time limit for claims, a major purpose of this clause from the vendors' perspective is to ensure that the purchaser cannot maintain an open position by giving a general notice of claims at the end of the period. To prevent this, the vendors will want to include the wording in the second set of brackets. The purchaser would not usually offer such wording in its initial draft.

The vendors are justified in requiring a claim to be made in sufficiently specific terms to ensure that it is bona fide. The purchaser cannot reasonably object to this although it will want to ensure that it is not having to provide large amounts of detail at this early stage given the burden that this is likely to impose.

The purchaser will need to be careful to ensure that, when a claim is made, the precise procedure specified in this clause (and in any other conduct related limitations, see for example cl.11D) is followed.

MINIMUM LEVEL OF LIABILITY

11–04 To avoid the inconvenience of trivial claims, it has been custom for the vendors to require, and for the purchaser to accept, that small claims are completely excluded and that claims should not be brought unless their values exceeds a specified floor. Trivial claims are usually referred to as de minimis and the floor as a "threshold" or "basket". There is no absolute convention as to whether, once the minimum level is exceeded, the claim can relate to the full amount or only to the excess. More often than not it will be the full amount, as, if the rationale for having a floor is the avoidance of small claims, once claims exceed the minimum the liability should be for the full amount. An alternative view is that the floor operates as a kind of margin of error allowed to the vendors, on which basis only the excess liability should be discharged.

A clause which takes the second approach is as follows:

[11B] Exclusion of small claims

11–05 **The Vendors shall not be liable in respect of a claim brought by the Purchaser for a breach of the Warranties unless their liability for all claims would exceed in aggregate £[ ] and in that event they shall be liable only for the excess.**

If the first approach is adopted, it would suffice to omit the last part of this clause commencing with the words "and in that event … ". It is preferable, however, for the purchaser to make the position absolutely clear by substituting for those words the following:

" . . . and in that event they shall be liable for the whole of the claims and not merely the excess."

If the vendors wish all small claims to be disregarded, even if claims in aggregate exceed the agreed floor, the clause should read as follows: **11–06**

The Vendors shall not be liable in respect of a claim brought by the Purchaser for a breach of the Warranties where the liability would not exceed £[   ]. The Vendors shall not be liable in respect of other claims unless their liability for all the other claims would exceed in aggregate £[   ] and, in that event, they shall be liable only for the excess. [For the purpose of this clause, all claims arising from a particular set of circumstances shall be treated as one claim.]

The purchaser would wish to add the last sentence so as to avoid the possibility that a series of claims, which while individually small are large in aggregate, could be excluded even though arising from the same cause. An example would be if there were a large number of small claims made against the target company as a result of defects in goods manufactured by it.

It should be noted that neither version of cl.11B will necessarily be effective in protecting the vendors from being involved in claims which the purchaser genuinely believes will exceed the floor even if, in the event, the liability is held to be for a lesser amount and the vendors are accordingly absolved. An unscrupulous purchaser could with relative ease claim an amount in excess of the floor in the belief that the vendors, to avoid the nuisance of litigation, would be prepared to make a payment in settlement even though the liability is in fact likely to be below the minimum level of the floor.

A similar clause can be used in the tax covenant, although the more common approach adopted by the purchaser is that it would normally be appropriate for the vendors to be liable under it for the full amount of the claim on a pound for pound basis without any financial deductibles. Sometimes the purchaser may be persuaded to agree a "floor" to apply to the tax covenant but rarely any de minimis. There is little logic to this position although the usual justification is that a tax liability is an actual liability which the target company will need to pay rather than a loss of some element of "bargain" as might be the case in a warranty claim. However, often the distinction is not clear cut, for example where a tax relief which was not treated as an "asset" by the purchaser has been lost and gives rise to an indemnity payment under the tax covenant. The purchaser would in any event wish any financial limit to be in the aggregate, and not to apply separately to claims under the warranties and the tax covenant. This would be achieved by adding "or by the Purchaser under the Tax Covenant" after the words "by the Purchaser for a breach of the Warranties" in cl.11B and by making an appropriate cross-reference to that clause in the tax covenant. This wording will not be appropriate if the vendors and parties giving the tax covenant are not identical and in that event separate floors would have to be agreed.

If the purchaser agrees to a floor for claims or individual de minimis, this could affect its view on amendments which the vendors might wish to make to the warranties. It is frequently suggested by the vendors that certain warranties should be amended so that they apply only to "material" matters (see, for example, cl.1.14 in para.7–30). However, from the purchaser's point of view such a qualification would provide a double margin of error for the vendors if there is also a de minimis clause in the sale agreement.

MAXIMUM LEVEL OF LIABILITY

11–07 The vendors commonly seek a ceiling (or "cap") on their liability under the warranties and tax covenant. This is usually fixed at the amount of the consideration paid for the target company or business. Some vendors find it extraordinarily hard to accept that they could be in the unenviable position of having sold their company, there being a substantial warranty or other claim (such that they have to hand back all or a substantial part of the consideration they have received) and yet at no point do they get their company back. Arguments as to the asset (usually the shares) being worth less as a result of the claim do not offer much comfort.

Sometimes the purchaser may be persuaded to agree a lower ceiling on claims although there usually needs to be special circumstances which might justify this, such as advantageous pricing for the acquisition or in an auction situation where the bid documents provide for this. Often a purchaser will seek to support, usually for some or all of the reasons outlined below, that the ceiling ought to be set at a higher amount than the full purchase price. The vendors conversely will argue for a much lower ceiling. In practice the debate will usually be settled by the ceiling being set at the full purchase price.

Reasons why a purchaser may argue for a higher ceiling follow:

(1) In many cases the real consideration given by the purchaser is not only the price actually paid but also any further sums specifically provided for at the time of the purchase, for example sums required to repay loans made to the target company by the vendors or to obtain the release of guarantees given by the vendors.

(2) The purchaser will normally provide funds for the subsequent development of the target company or business, thereby increasing the total amount invested by it.

(3) If the vendors had retained the target company and liabilities materialised which effectively gave the group a negative value, the vendors could not necessarily have avoided the obligation to make up the difference by allowing the group to be wound up. If the vendors are individuals, there will frequently be personal guarantees outstanding and, if there is a corporate vendor, the insolvent liquidation of a subsidiary could result in an event of default under financial and other agreements.

11–08 It is sometimes suggested, by way of justification for the ceiling, that at worst the purchaser could recover from the vendors the cost of its purchase and avoid any further liability by allowing the target company or business to be liquidated. This, however, is rarely a real choice open to a purchaser for reasons similar to those mentioned in para.(3). In particular, in the case of the purchase of a business, the purchaser would only be able to contemplate a liquidation if it was established purely for the purpose of carrying on the acquired business and had no other activities. In the case of a share sale, it is sometimes the case that the consideration paid for the shares is minimal since the purchaser will be incurring the liabilities of the target company. If, post-completion, the liabilities turn out to be more than expected then a ceiling set at the purchase price does not provide the purchaser with a suitable remedy. In situations such as this, it may be appropriate to increase the ceiling on claims to mirror the target company's liabilities. As with many of the questions relating to the scope of warranties, it is ultimately a question for the parties as to where the residual risk of unexpected problems should lie which will depend on their respective bargaining positions.

The simplest form of a clause imposing a ceiling on claims, which would have to be included in both the sale agreement and the tax covenant, is:

[11C] Ceiling on claims

The total liability of the Vendors, arising by reason of claims under the Warranties or the Tax Covenant, shall not exceed £[   ].   11-09

The purchaser will ideally want to be able to recover the aggregate of the purchase price and all other sums laid out by it at the time of the acquisition. However, a ceiling which exceeds the purchase price payable for the shares or business—because, for example, it includes the amount of loans repaid to the vendors at completion or obligations of the business for which the purchaser accepts responsibility—will not necessarily give the purchaser the automatic right to take those additional amounts into account in determining its entitlement to damages (see para.3–06 for the reasons for this).

If the agreed limit is to be the purchaser's total investment, cl.11C could be expanded by replacing the reference to "£[   ]" by:

"... an amount equal to the aggregate of £[   ] and the amounts which the Purchaser provides for the Company to enable it to discharge its liabilities to the Vendors and any other expenditure reasonably incurred by the Purchaser in consummation of the transactions contemplated in this Agreement."

The advantage of stating a specific sum is clarity but if the purchase price is not quantifiable at the date of the sale agreement (for example, because there is additional consideration payable according to future profits) it might be appropriate to replace the reference to a specific sum by:

"... an amount equal to the total consideration paid for [the Shares] [the Business]."

The above formulations are adequate, in principle, where there is a cash purchase. However, if the consideration consists wholly or partly of shares or loan stock of the purchaser, it might be fairer, though complex, to fix the ceiling at the value of the consideration securities at the date of claim.

CONDUCT OF CLAIMS

11–10   It has been common practice for the conduct of claims in relation to matters arising under the tax covenant to be given to the vendors (see the tax covenant discussion in para.10–44). Following the move towards dealing with all tax matters in a separate schedule to the sale agreement (see Ch.10 for details) it has also become common practice to treat claims in respect of the tax warranties in the same manner. This is normally acceptable to the purchaser as taxation matters can generally be dealt with separately from the other affairs of the target company.

The position is less simple in relation to the non-tax warranties as matters which are the subject of them can have considerable importance in relation to the goodwill of the target company and litigation to enforce third party rights could be very harmful. Additionally, it is more difficult to treat individual commercial problems separately from the general business activities of the target company. The purchaser is therefore unlikely to agree to the vendors having conduct of general warranty claims. However, a balance needs to be struck as the vendors will, not unreasonably, want to be in a position where, so far as possible, they are made aware of claims at an early stage and are able to ensure that rights against third parties are pursued properly and not treated as being of secondary importance on the basis that the liability can simply be passed on to them. The vendors will typically seek to include a clause similar to the following (which is not dissimilar to the conduct of claims provision in the tax covenant (see para.10–40)):

[11D] Conduct of Claims

11–11   **In the event that the Purchaser shall be aware or become aware of any fact, matter or event [which might constitute or give rise to a claim for breach of the Non Tax Warranties] [whereby it appears that the Vendors are, or may become, liable to pay the Purchaser under the Non Tax Warranties] the Purchaser shall:**

> **[11D.1] [as soon as is reasonably practicable][promptly] notify in writing the Vendors giving [reasonable][full] details of any such fact matter or event so far as practicable [and consult with the Vendors in respect of the matter];**

> **[11D.2] thereafter keep the Vendors informed of all relevant matters and shall [as soon as reasonably practicable][promptly] forward or procure to be forwarded to the Vendors copies of all [material]**

correspondence and other written communications relating to the claim [(other than those which have been prepared by the Purchaser or its professional advisors with a view to assessing the merits of any claim for breach of the Non Tax Warranties or are otherwise subject to legal professional privilege)];

[11D.3] not settle or compromise the potential claim or do anything in its conduct which is likely to affect the amount involved or the future liability of [the Company, or] the Purchaser, without prior approval of the Vendors [such approval not to be unnecessarily withheld or delayed,] and take such action as the Vendors may [reasonably] request to dispute, appeal, settle or compromise the claim (or any event or fact which has or may give rise to it) provided that:

[11D.3.1] the Vendors indemnify and secure [the Company and] the Purchaser to the reasonable satisfaction of the Purchaser against all losses, costs, damages and expenses which may be incurred thereby; and

[11D.3.2] [nothing in this clause 11D shall require the Purchaser [or the Company] to take any action (or omit to take any action) if in the [reasonable] opinion of the Purchaser it would be [materially] harmful to the goodwill of the [Company] [Business] to do so];

[11D.4] procure that the Vendors (and their advisors) are given reasonable access to all relevant documents, records and personnel of [the Company] and the Purchaser and its advisors to enable the Vendors promptly and effectively to evaluate, dispute and enforce their rights under this clause clause 11D;

The vendors will want to ensure that the purchaser is informing them as soon as possible of any matters that might constitute breaches of the non-tax warranties so that they have the opportunity of seeking to address them at an early stage (when the likely costs of resolving them are lower) and to avoid the purchaser notifying them of numerous claims at the end of the agreed time period for the making of claims, a particular concern in circumstances where there is deferred consideration due for payment at the end of that period that the purchaser has the ability to set-off against. This should not be an issue for the purchaser provided that the obligation to notify the vendors only arises in appropriate circumstances (the purchaser will not want to be subject to an obligation that requires it to notify the vendors every time something occurs that could possibly give rise to a warranty claim as this is likely to result in it being obliged to make numerous meaningless notifications). The purchaser will generally prefer to include the wording in the second set of brackets where the obligation is linked to a likely payment liability.

In respect of cll.11D.1 and 11D.2 the purchaser will want to include references to reasonableness and materiality and, so as not to find itself in the position of potentially having to disclose documentation that would otherwise be privileged or that might prejudice its position in any claim against the vendors, to include the wording in the last set of brackets in cl.11D.2. See also comments at paras 10–40 and 10–44, some of which are relevant and should be considered in the context of the conduct provisions in relation to general warranty claims.

If the general confidentiality obligations in the sale agreement do not cover the disclosure to the vendors of such information, the purchaser should consider "and subject to obligations of confidentiality" although the vendors will usually be concerned as to the potential effect of this.

In the absence of a clause similar to cl.11D.3, the vendors will have no control over how the purchaser handles claims—the purchaser will be under an obligation to take reasonable steps to mitigate the loss, the vendors would not usually have the ability in such circumstances to say that the purchaser should have taken a particular course of action that would have resulted in a smaller loss. Whilst the purchaser will be wary about fettering its ability to handle third party claims as it sees fit, and may in some instances refuse to give the vendors control over such matters, most purchasers will, provided they have the benefit of a suitable indemnity (for example that in cl.11D.3.1), and that they are not obliged to do anything that they consider will be harmful to the business acquired or its existing business, agree to be subject to an obligation to take such action as the vendors reasonably request in relation to the conduct of claims. The precise terms of this will usually be a matter for negotiation. The vendors will ideally want to be consulted and involved from the outset and to have the ability to require the purchaser to take such action as they see fit, regardless of the purchaser's perception of the effect that this might have in the business and as such will prefer to include the wording in the first set of brackets in cl.11D.1 and to exclude cl.11D.3.2. If it is to be included the vendors will want it to operate by reference to the purchaser acting reasonably (or preferably by reference to an objective purchaser) and for the purchaser only to have a veto in respect of matters that are materially harmful to the business. The purchaser will want cl.11D.3.2 to be as subjective and favourable to it as possible. The purchaser will want to include the wording in the second set of brackets in cl.11D.3 to make sure that the target company's position is not adversely affected by delay on the part of the vendors.

The vendors will, in practice, often require documentary and administrative assistance in assessing and deciding how they want the purchaser to handle claims and so will want to include cl.11D.4. In principle, where the purchaser is willing to allow the vendors some input on the conduct of claims, the purchaser should not object as long as the demands imposed upon it are not excessive.

and the Purchaser shall not be entitled to make a claim in respect of a Non Tax Warranty if it fails to comply with the provisions of this clause [11D].

The wording at the end of the clause is likely to be unacceptable to the purchaser and will not be readily agreed to. If the purchaser fails to perform its obligations the vendors will in any case be entitled to appropriate compensation for the breach. The sanction imposed is too onerous and inflexible. The purchaser will prefer to replace the wording with the following:

" . . . provided that compliance by the Purchaser with this [clause 11D] shall not be a condition precedent to the liability of the Vendors under the Non Tax Warranties."

See also comments at para.10–39.

In the context of a business sale, the references to "the Vendors" will need to be changed to "the Vendor" and remove the references to "the Company" in square brackets. It is also likely that limitations to the tax warranties will be dealt with in the limitations to the non-tax ones, rather than being in a separate tax schedule. As such, references to "Non Tax Warranties" should be changed to "Warranties".

THIRD PARTY RECOVERY

In some circumstances on a share sale where there is a liability under the warranties or indemnities, the target company will have a right of recovery from a third party.

11–12

In an ideal world the vendors will wish the target company to pursue its rights of recovery or reimbursement to the full before making a claim. A suitable clause for dealing with this is as follows:

[11E] Obligation to effect third party recovery

Where the Company is entitled to recover from a third party or claim reimbursement of all or part of a sum in respect of which it has a claim or potential claim under the Non Tax Warranties, the Purchaser shall procure that it takes all possible steps to enforce the recovery or reimbursement before making a claim under the Non Tax Warranties.

11–13

This clause is unlikely to be acceptable to the purchaser as it imposes a severe restriction on it, not least given the difficulties that there may be in identifying and taking "all possible steps" and the fact that the agreed time limits for making a claim under the warranties may expire before all such steps against the third party have been completed. If the purchaser were willing to accept the clause, (which is considered unlikely) it would wish to replace "all possible" with "reasonable". A more acceptable approach is for the purchaser to procure the transfer of the debt or right of reimbursement to the vendors once they have discharged the liability, although a provision to this effect is rarely sought these days. The more common approach and one that reflects a sensible compromise is to include provision to the effect that in the event that the vendors have made payments to the purchaser in settlement of warranty claims and the purchaser subsequently receives a payment from a third party in respect of those matters, the purchaser will repay the relevant amount to the vendors (after deducting any costs incurred in effecting the recovery). A suitable clause dealing with this is:

[11F] Third party recovery

11–14 **If the Vendors pay to the Purchaser an amount in respect of a breach of the Warranties and the Purchaser subsequently receives from a third party a sum which is referable to that matter the Purchaser shall forthwith repay to the Vendors an amount equal to whichever is the lesser of that sum and the amount paid by the Vendors to the Purchaser in respect of such breach of Warranty, after deducting (in either case) all reasonable costs and charges and expenses incurred by the Purchaser [or the Company] in obtaining that payment and in recovering that sum from the third party.**

The purchaser will want to ensure that on the drafting of the clause there is not an obligation imposed on it to seek recovery from third parties in circumstances where it has a right to do so. It will already have succeeded in making recovery pursuant to a warranty claim (which could have been a costly and time consuming process) and will, as part of that process, have had to mitigate its loss.

In the context of a business sale the purchaser's rights against third parties will be a lot more limited. In a share sale the target company will be the party that has, for example, contracted with third parties, and that has the benefit of rights against them, in a business sale the purchaser will only have those rights that have been transferred to it under the sale agreement. The clauses will need amending in the same manner as noted at para.11–10 where they are to be used.

LIMITATION OF CLAIMS

11–15 There are a number of specific circumstances in respect of which the vendors will want the purchaser's ability to make claims to be limited. The vendors will commonly seek to include provisions that prevent the purchaser from being able to make claims:

(1) If they arise as a result in a change of law, interpretation of law or administrative practice after the date of the sale agreement that have retrospective effect. It is likely that the sale agreement will already contain a provision similar to cl.3B (as amended—see para.4–04) that prevents either party's position under it being adversely affected by such matters and it is reasonable for the vendors to request such a position as the parties will have negotiated and agreed the terms of the sale on the basis of the law applicable and administrative practices at that time. If a clause such as cl.3B (as amended) is included then the limitation is not strictly necessary.

(2) If they arise as a result of acts or omissions of the purchaser or, in the case of a share sale, the target company after completion. There are some acts that the purchaser will be bound by and in respect of which the vendors cannot reasonably expect it to be precluded from bringing

a claim, for example acts required in order to comply with contracts that the company has entered into prior to completion. It is customary for these to be carved out in the manner proposed at cl.11G.2. The purchaser will want to include the wording in brackets at the end of the clause although the vendors may object to this as the exception will only apply if the purchaser does something that is outside of the usual course of business and not done in order to comply with law or any obligation that the target company has entered into whilst under the vendors' control.

(3) If the relevant matter has been effectively disclosed in the disclosure letter (see Ch.9 for further details of this). If a clause similar to cl.3C is included in the sale agreement then it is not strictly necessary to include this limitation, although the vendors usually will.

(4) The claim is based on a liability that is contingent. The issue for the vendors will be that they will not want the purchaser to be able to make claims until such time as the liability to which the claim relates has crystallised. It may never do so. The purchaser will be concerned to ensure that if there are contingent liabilities that have been identified, the time periods for bringing claims do not expire prior to the purchaser being able to notify the claim. A suggested compromise is to amend the limitations such that the purchaser is entitled to notify the claim whilst it is contingent, the relevant time periods within which proceedings then have to be issued being extended until an agreed period after the liability has crystallised. The vendors will generally be reluctant to accept such a position given it could significantly extend the time period during which the prospect of warranty claims will be hanging over them. The vendors are likely to argue that if a claim has not crystallised during the agreed time limitation periods then it is not a claim that they should be responsible for.

(5) Where the purchaser or the company has already been compensated in respect of the claim or has the ability to effect recovery against a third party relatively easily, for example, under the company's insurance policies. If the purchaser or the Company have already been compensated for the relevant breach then they should not be entitled to effect double-recovery by also making a claim against the vendors in respect of the same loss. However, there is likely to have been a cost to the purchaser and/or the target company in taking relevant mitigating action and, to the extent that there has been, the purchaser will not want to be precluded from seeking damages from the vendors. The purchaser will accordingly want to add "but after deducting costs incurred by the Purchaser or the Company directly as a result of doing so" to the end of the clause. The purchaser is also likely to object to the wording in square brackets at the end of the clause. It will be obliged to mitigate its loss and will not want to be subject to any obligations that might impose further requirements on it, for example

seeking to make an insurance claim prior to claiming against the vendors.

(6) Where the relevant issue has been provided for or taken into account in the last statutory accounts (and maybe management accounts where the vendors have provided them for periods subsequent to the balance sheet date and they contain relevant accountancy provisions) of the company or, where they are being prepared, completion accounts (defined as "Completion Accounts" for the purpose of this clause). Usually the purchaser cannot fairly complain about a liability which arises after completion where a specific provision or reserve was made in the accounts. (A note in the accounts may not in itself provide a quantification of the anticipated liability and the net assets will not have taken account of the liability) and as such the purchaser would usually wish to exclude them from the limitation. The vendors will sometimes seek to delete "specific" on the grounds that if there is a general provision which might cover a liability that should be sufficient, it should not matter whether the provision or reserve has been allocated to a specific liability. The purchaser is likely to resist this. Under UK GAAP provisions should generally only be made on a specific basis so in most cases the arguments are somewhat academic.

[11G] Limitation of claims

11–16 **The Purchaser shall have no claim whatsoever against the Vendors in respect of any breach of any of the [Non Tax] Warranties if and to the extent that:**

> **[11G.1] the claim would not have arisen or been increased but for a change in legislation or the interpretation of the law or published administrative practice of any government, governmental department, agency or regulatory body made after Completion;**
>
> **[11G.2] the claim would not have arisen or been increased but for a voluntary act or omission the Purchaser [which could reasonably have been avoided] carried out, or occurring, after the date of this Agreement, otherwise then in the ordinary and proper course of the business as required by law or pursuant to a legally binding obligation of the Company created prior to Completion, and which the Purchaser [or the Company] was, or ought reasonably to have been, aware could give rise to a claim];**
>
> **[11G.3] the fact, omission, circumstance or occurrence giving rise to or forming the basis of the claim has been Disclosed;**
>
> **[11G.4] the claim is based on a liability which is contingent only unless and until such contingent liability becomes an actual liability and is due and payable;**

[11G.5] the claim relates to a loss or liability in respect of which the Buyer [or the Company] has already received damages or otherwise obtained reimbursement, or restitution [or is indemnified by insurance];

[11G.6] specific provision, reserve, allowance [or note] in respect thereof has been made in the Accounts, the Management Accounts or the Completion Accounts.

The amendments discussed in respect of cl.11D.1 will need to be made to this clause where used in the context of a business sale.

Exclusion of Fundamental Warranties from Limitation Provisions

It is generally accepted that warranties as to title to shares (in the context of a **11–17** share sale) and assets (in the context of a business sale) should, given their fundamental nature, be given on an absolute basis, without the benefit of any of the limitation provisions that apply in respect of the other warranties. It is also convention for warranties as to the capacity of the vendors to enter into the sale agreement and associated documents and be bound by their terms to be treated in the same manner. The vendors should not usually have any difficulty in giving the warranties on this basis. A suitable clause dealing with the exclusion of these fundamental warranties from the limitation provisions is as follows:

[11H] Disapplication of limitation provisions in respect of fundamental Warranties

Clauses [   ] to [   ] (inclusive) will not apply in respect of a claim for breach of the Non Tax Warranties contained in clauses [1.1] to [1.2.5] of Schedule [   ].

Fraud and Similar Offences

It is a well established principle that parties are not entitled to seek to exclude or **11–18** limit liability in circumstances where they have been fraudulent (*Thomas Witter Ltd v TBP Industries Ltd* [1996] 2 All E.R. 573). See para.3–03 for further details. A clause that deals with this in the context of the limitation is as follows:

[11I] Fraud and [similar offences]

Notwithstanding any other provision of this Agreement, clauses [   ] to [   ] 11–19 (inclusive) will not apply to exclude or limit the liability of the Vendors to the extent that any claim for breach of the [Non Tax] Warranties arises by

reason of any fraud [dishonesty, wilful or negligent misstatement or omission] by [or on behalf of] the Vendors.

The clauses referred to are those containing the limitation provisions (cll.11A–H in this book). The purchaser will normally seek to include the wording in the first set of brackets on the basis that the vendors should not receive the benefit of the limitations in circumstances where they have been dishonest or deliberately or negligently misstated a position or not made a disclosure. The vendors' only obligation in respect of the warranties is to make disclosure of relevant items and as such they will often argue that the limitations should only fall away if they have failed to do this, that is where they have deliberately not disclosed a relevant matter against the Warranties. They will prefer to replace the wording at the first set of brackets with "wilful non-disclosure against the Warranties". If they do include such wording the vendors should take care to ensure that they are not caught by the limitation as a result of, for example, deciding not to disclose something that they considered not to be relevant.

The vendors should ensure that the limitation only applies "to the extent that any claim . . . arises" so that in the event if wilful non-disclosure, the limitations only cease to apply to the "extent" of the matters affected by the wilful non-disclosure as opposed to all of the limitation provisions ceasing to apply in respect of all warranty claims.

See comments at para.11–10 for details of amendments required to be made to the clause in the context of a business sale.

BOXING LIMITATIONS

11–20   In view of the usual extensive nature of warranties it is not uncommon for an issue to be covered by numerous warranties, including those that at first sight do not appear to relate to the subject matter in question. Often this will give rise to an unintended result for the vendors in terms of the standard of warranty they thought they had agreed in relation to a particular subject matter.

The usual way for this to be addressed by the vendors is by the use of a "boxing limitation" which would normally be inserted in the operative part of the sale agreement following the clause that makes the warranties operative. Appropriate wording would be:

[11J] Boxing Limitations

11–21   **The only Warranties given in respect of Properties are those set out in paragraph [   ] (Properties) of Schedule [   ] (Warranties) and the other Warranties shall be deemed not given in relation to Properties.**

The wording limits the extent of warranty cover on the subject matter, in this case property, to the specific warranty section that is meant to address that. As far as the vendors are concerned the principle is fair in that the relevant warranty section contained all the relevant property warranties they were prepared to give.

Conversely the purchaser may have preferred the wide ranging approach that exists without the "boxing limitation". Ultimately the inclusion or otherwise of such a limitation will depend upon the extent of warranty cover offered in a particular area (the subject of the intended limitation), the extent to which other relevant information may be pertinent (for instance replies to enquiries) and how that is addressed (by warranties outside of the particular section) as well as the bargaining position of the parties.

Taken to its logical conclusion "boxing limitations" could be applied to all of the various subject headings of the warranties but such an approach is likely to be unacceptable to the purchaser.

SUBSEQUENT DISPOSALS OF THE TARGET COMPANY

The vendors may be willing to rely on the various provisions set out in this chapter being observed, even though no security is provided by the purchaser, provided that the purchaser retains control of the target company. To deal with possible future disposals, the vendors might request the following undertaking: **11–22**

[11K] Undertakings from a future purchaser of the Company

The Purchaser shall not, whilst any of the provisions of [this Schedule] are applicable or capable of taking effect, cease to control the Company without procuring from the person acquiring control an enforceable undertaking, in favour of the Vendors to be bound by those provisions, so far as they affect the Company, to the same extent as the Purchaser is bound. **11–23**

This draft assumes that all the relevant provisions are contained in a separate schedule. Although this clause may give comfort to the vendors, its value is in fact limited. The purchaser will in any case remain bound by the obligations even if it ceases to control the target company and, as a matter of prudence, it should anyway oblige the new owners to observe the outstanding obligations. If the purchaser fails to comply with its obligations under this clause, it is not clear that the vendors would be entitled to damages simply by reason of this failure. Furthermore, even though the clause has little real effect, the purchaser might object to a clause which imposes, however modestly, a fetter on its free right to dispose of the target company.

WARRANTY AND INDEMNITY INSURANCE

Although warranty and indemnity insurance has been around since the early 1980s it did not start to grow in popularity until the latter part of the 1990s. This was in the main due to a decrease in premiums, increasingly litigious purchasers, insurance companies adopting a more commercial and flexible approach in terms of the policy wording and lawyers beginning to realise that insurance can, in some cases, help to overcome an impasse in negotiations which would otherwise result in the transaction not proceeding. **11–24**

An insurance broker or underwriting agency should be contacted when putting in place warranty and indemnity insurance and this should be done as early as possible in the transaction. Ideally this would be at the outset of the transaction, but often the reality is that it is left till fairly late in the day as a possible means of bridging an impasse between the vendors and the purchaser.

The mainstream policies that are usually available are:

(1) *Vendors' policies*—these are designed to protect and indemnify the vendors against liability arising from a breach of warranty claim or under an indemnity together with associated professional fees involved in defending such a claim. Whilst such a policy significantly reduces the likelihood of the vendors having to give back part or all of the sale proceeds this does not absolve them from any future involvement in defending such claims as the policy will be conditional on their assistance. To assist in this process, it is advisable that the vendors develop a working relationship with their insurers.

(2) *Purchaser's policies*—these are designed to protect a purchaser in situations where the vendors have capped the warranty and/or indemnity cover at less than the potential liability and/or the purchaser has doubts as to the ongoing financial position of the vendors. A purchaser can either insure against any shortfall in terms of the vendors' liability or alternatively against the actual warranty or indemnity claims themselves. The latter obviously avoids the need for the purchaser to claim against the vendors.

In order to assess risk, the insurers will need to be fully briefed on the transaction which includes providing them with an explanation of the disclosure and due diligence process together with the most recent versions of the sale agreement and disclosure letter and details of the negotiations which have taken place in relation to the warranties and indemnities. Once the insurers have "picked" through the transaction documentation, in particular focusing on the negotiated tax covenant, warranties, warranty protection provisions and the disclosure letter, they will generally wish to meet with the vendors/purchaser and their respective professional advisors to discuss the outcome of their review. Most insurers employ experienced corporate lawyers (at the insured's cost) who are adept in reviewing transactions quickly and effectively and are willing to work to tight timescales.

The draft policy should be reviewed in detail to ensure that the exclusions are drafted on a reasonable basis as in some cases the more obvious warranties that might give rise to warranty claims are excluded making the policy not economic or worthwhile.

The premium itself will depend on what view the insurers and their lawyers take of "the risk" following their review. At the time of writing, premiums are generally between one per cent and two per cent of the sum insured for larger transactions and between three per cent and four per cent for smaller transactions. The premium is payable in full on the commencement of the policy for the full duration of the period. Insurance premium tax of five per cent is also payable on the total premium. Insurers typically require the insured to bear at least one per cent of the sum insured in the form of an excess.

Although warranty and indemnity insurance can be of benefit in certain circumstances as described, in the majority of cases, if the vendors' advisors have negotiated a balanced set of warranties, undertaken a rigorous disclosure exercise and produced a full disclosure letter, then the risk of successful post-completion warranty claims is usually fairly minimal.

CHAPTER 12

Completion Accounts

PURPOSE IN THE CASE OF SHARE PURCHASES

12–01   Completion accounts are a set of non-statutory accounts drawn up shortly following completion which are used to "test" the price to be paid for the target company, usually by reference to levels of profit and/or net assets existing at completion. They do so by adjusting the price paid after completion if the target levels have not been met either on a £1 for £1 basis for net assets and/or on a multiplier of profit for any diminution in the level of anticipated profit.

The appropriateness or otherwise of these adjustments can usually be determined by reference to how the target company was valued and whether the vendors and the purchaser are able to reach agreement on the suggested basis of their preparation. Often the vendors will not know how the purchaser has valued the target company and should be very reluctant to agree specific adjustment mechanisms which are based upon unknown valuation criteria.

WHEN ARE THEY USED?

12–02   The most common use for completion accounts is where the last set of audited accounts are historic or the business of the target company has changed substantially since them. Sometimes they are also used to make a share transaction reflect an assets based deal, particularly in the case of property based transactions where the target company has been used as a vehicle to "house" the assets.

Where the transaction has been negotiated around agreed levels of profit (or more commonly earnings before interest, tax, depreciation and amortisation "EBITDA") and/or levels of net assets or some element of the latter (by reference to "cash free" and "debt free" deals), some form of completion accounts will be used to provide a contractual price adjustment mechanism that will operate to give the purchaser certainty and comfort on price. Such a mechanism will always be a better option for the purchaser rather than having to rely on a claim for breach of warranty, as to bring a successful warranty claim loss will have to be proved and, more often than not, various layers of warranty protection surpassed before there is any actual price adjustment. In contrast, completion accounts provide a certain contractual adjustment.

ADVANTAGES AND DISADVANTAGES

12–03   From a purchaser's perspective, the provision of completion accounts will almost invariably be of advantage to it and in the most extreme cases will allow it to artificially reduce the price based upon its own subjective accounting treatment. While the purchaser will usually have the benefit of meaningful warranties on the last set of audited accounts (and in terms of consistency at least the two prior sets of audited accounts), financial deterioration warranties (covering the period from the last accounts date to completion) and maybe also a "soft" warranty on management accounts, such warranties will often provide limited comfort for the purchaser in ensuring that it is getting the target company in at least as good financial shape as was reflected in the last audited accounts. Completion accounts allow the purchaser to ensure that the value that it acquires the target company by reference to is based on up-to-date financial information.

From the vendors' perspective completion accounts will rarely result in an increase in the price to be paid and at the very least will require the vendors to expend accounting and legal fees (sometimes significant) in ensuring that the mechanisms contained in the sale agreement are fair and in having their accountants review and agree the completion accounts after completion. Given the subjectivity that exists in the implementation of many of the accounting standards there is very little comfort for the vendors in simply referring to consistency with the latest set of audited accounts of the target company as this will leave scope for the purchaser to interpret the accounting standards in a manner which favours its position. The vendors should not agree to proceed on this basis but should instead insist that separate accounting policies (which restrict and if possible prevent the manipulation of the position by the purchaser) are included in the sale agreement.

In the context of the provision of warranties and indemnities by the vendors, completion accounts are often overlooked by lawyers (who believe that responsibility for these aspects should be the province of the vendors' accounting advisers) with the result that a risk that the purchaser had agreed to accept (either by way of fair disclosure against the relevant warranty or on the basis of a provision of an appropriate indemnity in its favour) then causes an actual price adjustment to be made through the completion accounts so that the vendors effectively end up paying for the issue. To understand how this works it is necessary first to look at some standard completion accounts provisions.

ANALYSIS OF COMPLETION ACCOUNTS PROVISIONS

Sample wording for a completion accounts mechanism which adjusts the price **12–04** paid for the target company by reference to both the level of net assets and EBITDA is set out below. The following definitions are used (other defined terms having the meanings set out in para.4–02):

"Completion Accounts Procedure" the procedure set out in clause [   ] and Schedule [   ] governing the preparation of the Completion Balance Sheet, and Profit and Loss Account and the issue of the Net Asset and EBITDA Statement.

This is a consolidating definition which brings together the completion accounts mechanisms in the main body of the sale agreement with the particular accounting requirements or adjustments set out in the relevant schedule to the sale agreement.

"Completion Balance Sheet" the statement of assets and liabilities of the Company as at Completion prepared in accordance with the Completion Accounts Procedure.

"EBITDA" the Operating Profit before interest, tax, depreciation, amortisation, exchange gains or losses and management fees of the Company for the financial period following the Balance Sheet Date up to and including the date of Completion calculated in accordance with the Completion Accounts Procedure.

Sometimes the purchaser will take the view that depreciation should be deducted from earnings as a true cost of running the business. In such circumstances the definition simply excludes depreciation and becomes "EBITA". Sometimes in keeping with the acronym, "Operating Profit" is defined as "Earnings" but it amounts to the same thing.

"Net Asset and EBITDA Statement" the statement to be prepared as part of the Completion Accounts Procedure and being the statement showing the Net Asset Value and EBITDA.

"Net Asset Value" the net assets of the Company as shown in the Completion Balance Sheet calculated in accordance with the Completion Accounts Procedure.

Given the nature of the specific accounting obligations or practices that can be included in the schedule, the net asset value calculated in accordance with this will often bear little resemblance to the actual net assets of the target company or business.

"Operating Profit" the operating profit of the Company computed in accordance with the accounting principles adopted in the Accounts.

"Profit and Loss Account" the profit and loss account of the Company reflecting the Operating Profit of the Company for the period commencing on the day after the Balance Sheet Date and ending on the Completion Date.

"The Purchaser's Accountants" [   ].

"The Vendors' Accountants" [   ].

The definitions would usually be inserted at the definitions section of the sale agreement rather than seeking to define these matters in the clause itself.

COMPLETION ACCOUNTS PROCEDURE

After Completion the Vendors and the Purchaser shall procure that the Net 12–05 Asset Value and EBITDA are determined in accordance with the Completion Accounts Procedure.

The Vendors shall [procure that the Vendors' Accountants] prepare and deliver to the [Purchaser [and the] [Purchaser's Accountants] within [60] Business Days of Completion, drafts of the Completion Balance Sheet and Profit and Loss Account together with a draft Net Asset and EBITDA Statement.

This clause is drafted such that the vendors' accountants will prepare the first draft of the completion accounts (on the basis that they will usually be more familiar with the target company's accounting). A more aggressive approach by the purchaser may substitute the purchaser's accountants as preparing the first draft. The latter approach will usually favour the purchaser as the vendors' accountants will not necessarily be able to identify all of the adjustments to conventional accounting that the purchaser's accountants have made when preparing the draft accounts. (Conversely the vendors' accountants will be able to identify any adjustments that are made by the purchaser's accountants to their drafts once they receive the purchaser's accountants' comments back.) Sometimes the completion accounts will be dealt with solely between the respective accountants. Where the purchaser or vendors have significant internal accounting resources they may wish to have a more active involvement. These options are catered for by inclusion in this and the subsequent clauses of the purchaser as well as the purchaser's accountants and the vendors as well as the vendors' accountants.

If the [Purchaser or the] [Purchaser's Accountants] shall notify the 12–06 [Vendors or the] [Vendors' Accountants] in writing within [30] Business Days of receipt of the draft Completion Balance Sheet, Profit and Loss Account and the Net Asset and EBITDA Statement that they do not accept the terms thereof and specify in reasonable detail the nature of the objection or disagreement the parties shall then use their reasonable endeavours to reach agreement on any disputed items within a further [10] Business Days of receipt of any such notice. If the [Purchaser or the] [Purchaser's Accountants] do not so notify the [Vendors or the] [Vendors' Accountants] within the said period then the Purchaser shall be deemed to accept the correctness of the draft Completion Balance Sheet, the Profit and Loss Account and the Net Asset and EBITDA Statement which shall become the Completion Balance Sheet, the Profit and Loss Account and the Net Asset and EBITDA Statement for the purposes of this Agreement and shall be final and binding on the parties (in the absence of manifest error).

Obviously the time periods within these provisions are flexible and should be tailored to suit the particular transaction. This clause provides for the completion accounts to be deemed to have been agreed if no objections are received. If the completion accounts are not agreed to by the purchaser/the purchaser's accountants then they must ensure that the vendors and their accountants are notified of the disagreement within the prescribed period and that the notice that is given specifies the grounds for objection.

12–07   **If the parties are unable to reach agreement within [20] Business Days following the notification of objections by [the Purchaser or] [the Purchaser's Accountants] to [the Vendors or] [the Vendors' Accountants] the matter in dispute may be referred on the application of either party to an independent chartered accountant to be appointed by agreement or (in default of nomination by agreement) on application by either party by the President for the time being of the Institute of Chartered Accountants in England and Wales. In giving his decision such independent accountant shall state what adjustments (if any) are necessary to the draft Completion Balance Sheet, Profit and Loss Account and the Net Asset and EBITDA Statement in order to comply with the requirements of this Agreement. The draft Completion Balance Sheet, Profit and Loss Account and the Net Asset and EBITDA Statements as so adjusted or not (as the case may be) shall become the Completion Balance Sheet, Profit and Loss Account and the Net Asset and EBITDA Statement for the purposes of this Agreement and shall be final and binding on the parties (in the absence of manifest error) upon the giving of such decision to the Vendors and the Purchaser.**

This clause provides for a short period in which the parties may be able to agree the outstanding points between themselves without the need for a referral to an independent accountant. If a referral is necessary it can be initiated by either party.

12–08   **Any determination by an independent accountant appointed pursuant to clause [   ] shall be given by him as an expert and not as an arbitrator and the Arbitration Act 1996 shall not apply. The expenses of the independent accountant shall be borne as determined by the independent accountant having regard to the relevant merits of each party's position in relation to the matter or matters in dispute, failing which equally between the Vendors and the Purchaser.**

This sets out the basis upon which the independent accountant will be appointed. It is important to ensure that the appointment is as an expert and not an arbitrator and that there is a fall back provision on costs if the independent accountant does not wish to make a costs award based on the relative merits of the parties. Without these provisions it is unlikely that an independent accountant would be prepared to act and that could frustrate the completion accounts mechanism.

12–09   **The Vendors and the Purchaser shall procure to the extent within their respective powers that the Vendors' Accountants, the Purchaser's Accountants and the independent accountant (as the case may be) shall have**

full access to all relevant papers, documents, records and personnel and shall be provided with such access and information upon request together with all reasonable assistance and information (as necessary) including the right to make copies and take extracts of such books, records and working papers (as necessary) for the purpose of preparing or agreeing or determining the Completion Balance Sheet, Profit and Loss Account and the Net Asset and EBITDA Statement.

This provision provides extensive rights of access. It does not however change the basis of the determination of the completion accounts, which must be in accordance with the agreed completion accounts procedure.

Each party shall be entitled to make written representations concerning the matter or matters in dispute to any such independent accountant appointed pursuant to clause [   ]. 12–10

Self explanatory.

Subject to clause [   ] the Vendors and the Purchaser shall each bear their own costs and expenses incurred pursuant to this clause [   ]. For the avoidance of doubt the Purchaser shall be responsible for the cost and expenses of the Purchaser's Accountants and the Vendors shall be responsible for the costs and expenses of the Vendors' Accountants. 12–11

This provision is designed to make it clear that the costs of each party's accountants are borne by them. It is only the independent accountant's costs which are shared equally or as he otherwise directs. Care needs to be taken where the vendors' accountants are also the target company's auditors to ensure that costs are correctly apportioned between those of the target company for any audit work and those of the vendors in relation to the preparation of the completion accounts to avoid potential issues of impropriety.

If following the agreement or determination of the Net Asset Value under this clause [   ] the Net Asset Value is lower than £[   ] the Consideration shall be reduced by the amount of such shortfall on a £1 for £1 basis. Any payment required to be made by the Vendors to the Purchaser as a result of there being such a shortfall shall be paid within seven days of agreement or determination of the Net Asset Value. 12–12

The target amount of net assets agreed by the parties will need to be inserted in the first set of brackets. If the targeted levels of net assets should fairly include the profit since the last accounts date then the target levels should be uplifted to reflect this. When there is a separate EBITDA adjustment as in these provisions then that would result in an unfair adjustment, given any profit diminution would be caught on a £1 for £1 basis on the net asset adjustment and on a multiplier basis on the EBITDA adjustment. Where there are both it would usually be appropriate to strip out the profit from the net asset target and leave profits to be dealt with under the EBITDA adjustment. The vendors will need to be careful to ensure that they are not potentially going to be paying twice for the same loss as a result of duplication between the agreed definitions of net assets and EBITDA.

12–13   **If following the agreement or determination of the EBITDA under this clause the EBITDA is lower than £[   ] the Consideration shall (in addition to any adjustment required to the Consideration pursuant to clause [   ]) be reduced by a sum equating to £[   ] for each £1 of shortfall of EBITDA below £[   ]. Any payment required to be made by the Vendors to the Purchaser as a result of their being such a shortfall shall be paid within seven days of agreement or determination of the EBITDA.**

The target amount of EBITDA agreed by the parties will need to be inserted in the first and last set of brackets and the appropriate multiplier inserted in the third set. (The clause cross-referred to will be the one at para.12–12 dealing with the adjustment to the consideration by reference to the value of net assets.)

The mechanism works by reference to the mechanics set out in the preceding clauses and the general and specific accounting requirements which, as mentioned previously, are usually set out in a separate schedule.

The provisions provide for drafts of the various financial statements to be produced within a set timeframe and agreed, or, in the event of disagreement, determined by an independent accountant. In all cases the financial statements have to be prepared by reference to the accounting requirements of the schedule, an example of which is set out below. Following agreement or determination in accordance with the contractual mechanisms the price is then adjusted by reference to the target levels of net assets and/or EBITDA. In the example wording above the adjustments are only in favour of the purchaser, as no additional consideration is payable for any excess of either net assets or EBITDA over the targeted levels. Where the target company has been valued by reference to assumed levels of these it would usually be fair to provide for an upwards adjustment as well in the event that the target levels are exceeded. A suitable clause dealing with this in relation to net assets (which would replace the clause at para.12–12 is as follows:

"If following the agreement or determination of the Net Asset Value under this clause the Net Asset Value is lower than £[   ] the Consideration shall be reduced by the amount of such shortfall on a £1 for £1 basis and if the Net Asset Value is higher than £[   ] the Consideration shall be increased by the amount of such excess on a £1 for £1 basis. Any payment required to be made by the Vendors to the Purchaser (or vice versa) as a result of their being any such shortfall or excess shall be paid within seven days of agreement or determination of the Net Asset Value."

Similar amendments would need to be made to para.12–13.

Where there is a concern that there could be a significant adjustment to the price as a result of the completion accounts mechanism it is usual to provide for some of the purchase price to be paid into a retention account (controlled by the vendors' solicitors and the purchaser's solicitors), the terms of which will provide for automatic payments to be made once the target levels of net assets and/or EBITDA have been agreed or determined.

Schedule [   ]   12–14

The Completion Balance Sheet, Profit and Loss Account and the Net Asset and EBITDA Statement shall be prepared consistently with the Accounts but only to the extent that they comply with the Accounting Standards or, to the extent they do not, in accordance with the Accounting Standards subject to the following specific adjustments or practices in respect of the Net Asset and EBITDA Statement which shall override both prior bases:

(1) **Profits or losses of a capital nature arising on the disposal of, or on the revaluation of, assets or investments by the Company shall be deducted or added back.**

(2) **No value shall be attributed to goodwill or any other intangible asset.**

(3) **No value shall be attributed to any computer equipment not used by the Company as at Completion.**

(4) **Provision shall be made for the cost of remedial works required pursuant to the recommendations of [   ] in connection with the Company's obligations under the Control of Asbestos at Work Regulations 2002 to the extent that such recommendations require the immediate removal of any asbestos found.**

These are a few examples of some of the matters that might be dealt with in the specific accounting mechanisms. There are numerous other matters that could either be protected or altered in favour of the purchaser. To ensure that all relevant matters are addressed a careful analysis of the balance sheet and/or profit and loss account of the target company or business should be undertaken in conjunction with accountancy advisers.

The wording works by firstly providing for consistency with the Accounts (which will have been warranted by the vendors) but then provides for an exception to such consistency where the Accounts do not comply with applicable accounting standards (essentially UK GAAP) and then a further exception to both prior bases by reference to the specific adjustments or practices listed.

It is usually in the specific accounting requirements where the vendors will either protect their position or where the purchaser will provide for specific adjustments or practices that suit its purposes. A few examples which illustrate some of the issues from both viewpoints are discussed below.

The vendors seek to disclose a potential litigation liability against the relevant   **12–15**
warranty in the sale agreement. The purchaser views the disclosure and concludes that it is happy to accept the risk and does not require an indemnity or, alternatively, that it is not happy to accept the risk and requests a specific

indemnity in its favour in respect of it. The relevant transaction has been negotiated by reference to a target level of net assets and the sale agreement contains a similar mechanism to the one outlined above. In the former case where the purchaser has accepted the risk, the vendors would need to ensure that the completion accounts did not provide for the liability disclosed by inserting a specific provision to that effect in the specific accounting principles. In the latter case the purchaser could still require a provision for the liability in the completion accounts notwithstanding the provision of the indemnity in its favour. In those circumstances, if the liability crystallised there would be nothing to stop the purchaser seeking redress under the indemnity, even though a provision had already been made in the completion accounts and the price been adjusted through the relevant diminution in the target net asset value.

The only way for the vendors to ensure that no provision is made is to note the matter as a specific adjustment or practice in the schedule. Suitable wording for these purposes would be as follows:

"No provision shall be made in respect of the litigation detailed at [ ] of the Disclosure Letter."

Using the same example but where there was less probability in terms of the litigation liability, for example where perhaps a note to the accounts (rather than an actual provision) would suffice for UK GAAP (specifically by reference to FRS 12), an unscrupulous purchaser might seek to modify UK GAAP or even consistency with the Accounts by requiring a specific adjustment along the following lines:

"Full provision shall be made for any liabilities disclosed in the Disclosure Letter."

This phrase potentially overrides FRS 12 and requires a provision to be made where in the ordinary accounting course it would not need to be.

More obvious examples of specific adjustments overriding normal accounting on either a consistent basis or by reference to UK GAAP might be in relation to bad or doubtful debts. For example, a disclosure is made against the relevant warranty in the sale agreement by reference to a schedule detailing the aged debtors with a view to escaping any liability pursuant to the warranty. Given the subjective interpretation of doubtful or bad debts the purchaser decides that a specific adjustment ought to be made in the completion accounts as follows:

"Full provision shall be made for all debts over [60] [90] [120] days."

In those circumstances, far from the vendors escaping liability by reference to the relevant matters in the disclosure letter, the purchaser is able to adjust the price to take account of its preferred policy of provision for aged debtors rather than the target company's prior practice. To protect themselves, the vendors might provide an alternative to ensure that the accounting is in line with the target company's usual practice by effectively reversing the wording to make it clear that no provision will be made for any aged debt unless it exceeds a certain age.

The most common areas (in addition to trade debtors or contingent liabilities) where interpretation issues arise on UK GAAP are in relation to fixed assets and stock and work in progress. Great care needs to be taken to achieve certainty in relation to these areas. The vendors' legal advisors should always ensure that they work hand in hand with the target company's auditors or, when different, the vendors' accountants, so that between them the disclosure process, the due diligence process and the negotiation of indemnities do not give rise to any unforeseen adjustments to the price by reference to a completion accounts mechanism where no such adjustment had either been intended or contemplated.

Careful consideration should be given to whether an issue is best addressed through completion accounts or an indemnity. One of the main influencing factors will typically be when it is considered likely that a relevant liability will crystallise as often it will not be possible to provide in full for a liability at the time when completion accounts are drawn up either because the full extent of the liability is not known at that time or the liability is too contingent for a provision to be made. In such a case an indemnity (supported by appropriate security where relevant) may be a better option.

Chapter 13

Valuation

Relevance in the Context of Warranties and Indemnities

13–01 In order to understand the use of warranties and indemnities in the context of the sale and purchase of companies and businesses it is necessary to have an understanding of the way that such businesses are valued, as without this the negotiation of the warranties and indemnities will be undertaken in a vacuum. It is often the case that the purchaser's legal advisers are instructed after valuation or pricing issues have been addressed but without obvious reference being made to the basis of them in any heads of terms or letter of offer. It is crucial that the purchaser's legal advisors understand the valuation basis that has been used or they will not be able to ensure that likely losses to the purchaser (which affect the valuation of the target company or business) have been properly addressed in their drafting of the sale agreement. From the vendors' perspective, it will be important to ensure that an unscrupulous purchaser cannot gain from artificial adjustments to the price through warranties and indemnities or by the use of a completion accounts adjustment mechanism where such adjustments bear no relevance to the purchaser's valuation of the target company or business. Insight into and an understanding of the valuation mechanism that has been used is therefore important to ensure that these issues are properly and fairly addressed.

Basic Concepts

13–02 This chapter is by no means intended to be a complete guide to how companies or businesses are valued. Reference should be made to any of the established works in the area for a more detailed analysis. Instead this chapter is intended to give the practitioner a useful insight into the more common methodologies that are likely to have been used in valuing trading companies.

The three most common bases are by reference to the net assets of the target company or business, a multiple of historical earnings, usually by reference to EBITDA (earnings before interest, taxation, depreciation and amortisation), or future earnings on a discounted cashflow basis.

The Net Assets Basis

13–03 This is one of the simplest methods and simply looks at the difference between the total assets and total liabilities as recorded in the accounts or books of the target company or business. Often this methodology is only appropriate for the smallest of businesses and even then will in most cases need adjustment to reflect the value of any intangible assets and to take account of the extraction of cash and other assets for the owner's use. It is very rare for any business or target company to be worth significantly less than its net asset value on anything other than an insolvency valuation. Where a business has been valued by reference to its net assets then any adjustments to the price either by reference to warranty claims, indemnity claims or through a completion accounts mechanism should follow suit.

MULTIPLE OF HISTORIC EARNINGS

The most common method of valuation is by reference to a multiplier of **13–04** EBITDA or occasionally EBITA (where in the latter case the valuer believes that depreciation should be treated as a cost to be deducted from the earnings). The earnings are arrived at by looking at historical earnings over the last two or three years and then combining them with some element of future earnings, either for the current or following year, calculating an average of those and then multiplying that by reference to an appropriate multiplier.

The multiplier will usually be based upon a sector average PE ratio (derived from public company sector indices) discounted by as much as 60 per cent to reflect the fact that the target company or business is a private one. That gives an enterprise value for the target company from which is then deducted any debt and added any excess cash in the target company or business (over and above that required for ordinary working capital purposes). What is included in debt and cash is always the subject of much debate and can significantly affect the net price. For this type of valuation it would normally be appropriate to ensure that any price adjustment mechanism, whether through warranty, indemnity or completion accounts, relates to the earnings of the target company and by reference to the actual multiplier used to arrive at the enterprise value, as slightly adjusted by the impact of the netting off of any debt or the addition of any cash.

DISCOUNTED CASH FLOW BASIS

The generally accepted definition of the value of any business interest (whether **13–05** in shares in a company or by ownership of a business) is that it must equal the future benefits, usually cash, that attach or will accrue to that business interest discounted back to a present value at an appropriate discount rate.

A discounted cashflow valuation follows this definition and involves three steps. The first is determining the period over which cashflow should be forecast. As in most valuation matters there are no hard and fast rules, although there are sector norms which can be obtained and used as a benchmark. The second stage in the process involves the preparation of a cashflow forecast which will take account of economic assumptions throughout the forecast period and then sales, purchases, payroll and other operating expenditure, capital and financing costs and tax costs for the entity projected forward over the forecast period. The final stage involves discounting that by an appropriate discount rate. The rate should reflect the anticipated level of return on alternative investments with comparable risk. Once again there are established rates for different categories of investment but these will need to be tailored to reflect the perceived risk rather than the industry standard.

If this method of valuation has been used then any price adjustment mechanism should follow the valuation methodology to match the loss with the value actually paid.

AN EXAMPLE

13–06 "Target Co Ltd", an active trading company in the print and packaging sector, has net assets of £3.8m, EBITDA of £1.2m, debt of £1m and surplus cash (over and above working capital requirements) of £350k.

On a multiple of historic earnings basis (this being an appropriate valuation method used for companies in this sector) an appropriate multiplier is six times EBITDA. Using the key financial information provided for Target Co Ltd and assuming that any offer made for the company would be on a "debt and cash free" basis gives a value for Target Co Ltd of £6.55m (being six times £1.2m, less £1m debt plus £350k of surplus cash).

A purchaser would usually structure any offer on terms that required EBITDA on completion of no less than £1.2m, net assets of £3.8m and phrase its offer by reference to a "debt and cash free" basis.

It would be difficult for the vendors' advisers to resist completion accounts which adjusted the actual price paid by reference to these elements by simply suggesting that these matters were warranted as this would not give the purchaser the contractual certainty that it would want in such circumstances. Care would need to be taken to ensure that an adjustment to the price based upon any diminution in the EBITDA level was not caught twice, once as part of the net assets and once as part of the multiplier adjustment (which in this case would be £6 for every £1 of diminution).

By comparison, a net assets based valuation for target co ltd would give an indicative valuation of £3.8m which amounts to a substantial discount on the likely open market value of the company.

From the information provided it is not possible to produce a discounted cashflow valuation for target co ltd but it is likely that such a valuation would fall somewhere between a net assets valuation and that derived from the historic earnings basis.

SUMMARY

13–07 While these valuation methodologies can give an insight into how a purchaser may have approached its valuation of the target company or business, the actual price paid may well have been determined by external commercial factors such as the target company or business operating in a niche sector, which could result in higher or lower pricing, significant interest being shown in the target company or business, which would usually result in a higher than desktop price being paid, or simply a strategic purchaser, where the value of the target company or business represents to that particular purchaser far more than any desktop valuation would ever suggest.

Where a transaction involves completion accounts with a specific adjustment mechanism, perhaps by reference to the levels of net assets and a multiple of earnings as in the example provided in Ch.12, then if there is a breach of warranty it is likely that the courts will use the adjustment basis in the completion accounts as a basis for determining the loss for breach of warranty. The completion accounts mechanism in such circumstances will be taken as evidence as to how the parties valued the target company.

Legal Due Diligence Enquiries

This legal due diligence questionnaire is designed to be of general application to most companies. However, before using it consideration should be given as to whether any of the enquiries should be removed and, in particular, whether any Competition, Accounts and Taxation enquiries are to be included. More usually Accounts and Taxation enquiries will be dealt with as part of the financial due diligence. Short form Accounts and Taxation enquiries which may be useful are included in clauses 17 and 18. The Competition enquiries are included in clause 16 so that they can easily be deleted if not required (as will often be the case). With effect from the implementation of the Bribery Act 2010, the Anti-Corruption enquiries at clauses 19.2 to 19.6 should be included and 19.1 should be deleted.

Acquisition of [ ] Limited (the "Company")

Please supply full details/copies of all the items specified below including, where documents are requested, accurate and up to date copies of those documents. (Where a full understanding of the position cannot be obtained from the copy document(s) alone please also provide an explanation.)

In the event that items are not applicable to the Company please state so.

Please identify replies using the same numerical reference system.

All references to "the Company" include references to its subsidiaries (if any). Please therefore reply to each enquiry for the Company and all of its subsidiaries.

1 Incorporation and statutory matters

1.1 The current Memorandum and Articles of Association of the Company (with any amending resolutions).

1.2 Certificate of incorporation and any certificate on change of name of the Company.

1.3 Registered office and other trade addresses.

1.4 The Company's registers of members, directors (and register of directors' residential addresses), charges and minute books (both for board and committee minutes and shareholder meetings).

1.5 All shareholder resolutions passed in the last five years.

2 Share capital

2.1 The authorised and issued share capital of the Company (including details of classes of shares and number of shares in each class), together with names and addresses of all registered shareholders in the Company, showing numbers of shares held and whether held beneficially or otherwise.

2.2 All shareholder agreements, pre-emption rights, conversion rights or agreements under which any person may acquire the right to subscribe for or purchase shares in the Company.

2.3 All buy-backs or redemptions of the Company's share capital (and all agreements to buy back or redeem any of the Company's share capital) and of all financial assistance given by the Company.

2.4   All shareholder agreements, pre-emption rights, conversion rights or agreements under which any person may acquire the right to subscribe for or purchase shares in the Company.

2.5   All buy-backs or redemptions of the Company's share capital (and all agreements to buy back or redeem any of the Company's share capital) and of all financial assistance given by the Company.

2.6   Details of all and any encumbrances on or affecting the shares of the Company.

2.7   Details of any options, contracts, warrants, schemes, rights, interests over the share capital of the Company.

2.8   Details of any provision for entrenchment (as defined in s.22 of the Companies Act 2006) contained in the articles. If there are such provisions please confirm that all required filings at Companies House have been made in respect of such provisions.

3 Subsidiaries

3.1   All subsidiaries of the Company and the Company's interests in other companies, partnerships or businesses together with particulars of such shareholdings or interests.

3.2   An organisational chart showing the group structure.

3.3   Details of any branch, agency or place of business both within and outside the United Kingdom.

4 Officers

4.1   Names and addresses of all directors and the secretary (if any) of the Company, stating job title, whether or not they are employed by the Company and any other directorships.

4.2   Service agreements/contracts of employment with officers of the Company. (Where no written documentation exists please supply details of the officer's obligations and duties, date of commencement, remuneration and benefits, unexpired term of office and applicable notice periods.)

4.3   All benefits currently provided to or if not currently provided, provided in the last five years to officers of the Company whether contractual or discretional.

4.4   Arrangements between the Company and its officers or former officers (or any other person connected with such an officer within the meaning of s.252 of the Companies Act 2006) which relate to or affect the capital, business, property, assets or liabilities of the Company and/or its group undertakings.

4.5   Loans or other indebtedness granted by the Company and/or any group undertaking to any of the Company's directors or former directors (or any person connected with such a director within the meaning of s.252 of the Companies Act 2006), and/or vice versa.

5 Employees

5.1   Anonymised details of all employees (including overseas employees) of the Company specifying position, age, date of commencement of employment, normal hours of work (including number of hours worked and when those hours are worked with details of any shift patterns and identifying any part time employees), contractual notice period (on either side), length of any fixed term contracts, place of work, current salary and other contractual and non-contractual benefits (including holiday pay, sick pay, bonuses, company car, medical insurance, car allowance, permanent health insurance, redundancy payment, enhanced maternity/paternity/adoption pay, overtime pay, shift allowances and allowances for working anti-social hours).

5.2 The standard contract of employment (or contracts) for all employees (including overseas employees). If there is more than one standard contract please indicate which contract applies to which employee(s).

5.3 All variations to employees' contracts of employment and a summary of any oral variations.

5.4 Anonymised contracts of all key employees; or employees whose contract is not terminable on [three] months' notice or less; or employees with non-standard contracts.

5.5 Anonymised details of any employee of the Company who will not pass to the Purchaser on completion of the proposed purchase.

5.6 Staff handbooks, policies, procedures and/or circulars (including disciplinary and grievance procedures).

5.7 Next pay review date and negotiations currently in progress or due for implementation in the next 12 months.

5.8 All share option, share incentive, profit sharing, commission or bonus arrangements, with details of all outstanding entitlements and all bonuses paid in the last 12 months.

5.9 Ex gratia payments made in the last 12 months and all current arrangements for the making of ex gratia payments to current or former employees. All current or former employees to whom the directors consider the Company to be under a moral obligation to provide ex gratia payments or to provide retirement, death, accident or sickness disability benefits.

5.10 Holiday arrangements, including the basis of calculation of holiday pay and the date on which the holiday year commences.

5.11 Systems in place to record/confirm compliance with the Working Time Regulations 1998 (including copies of any agreements to opt-out of reg.4(1) of the Working Time Regulations 1998, details of any "night workers" and means by which the time worked by employees, rest breaks provided, holiday taken or holiday pay received is recorded together with sample records).

5.12 Systems in place to record/confirm compliance with the National Minimum Wage Regulations 1999 (including agreements entered into in connection with the Regulations).

5.13 Particulars/copies of pre-employment checks carried out in respect of all employees employed since February 29, 2008 and the process(es) in place for monitoring these checks.

5.14 Job offers made/about to be made and job vacancies currently being advertised.

5.15 Employees on/about to go on leave and nature of leave (e.g. sick, maternity etc.).

5.16 Resignations/dismissals in the last 12 months (including the reason for dismissal/resignation and details of any unexpired notice periods).

5.17 Company redundancy policy and details of any significant redundancy/ lay-off/short-time working programmes in the last three years.

5.18 Transfers of employees which took place during the last five years and which were relevant transfers for the purposes of the Transfer of Undertakings (Protection of Employment) Regulations 2006 or (where appropriate) the Transfer of Undertakings (Protection of Employment) Regulations 1981 to which the Company or the Vendors (or any predecessor or owner of part of or all of its business) was a party, which affected any employee currently or previously employed by the Company, including details of:

5.18.1   any variation to any employee's contract of employment which was by reason of, or connected with, such transfer;

5.18.2   any dismissal connected to such a transfer whether made by the Company, the Vendors or another party to the relevant transfer; and

5.18.3   any failure to comply with obligations to inform or consult in connection with such a transfer or any redundancy.

5.19   All agreements or arrangements with trade unions or employee associations (including recognition agreements, collective agreements and any agreement for the information and consultation of employees (whether made in accordance with the Information and Consultation of Employees Regulations 2004 or otherwise)) and details of all labour disputes within the last five years, details of any trade union seeking recognition and details of the current state of any ongoing negotiations with such bodies.

5.20   Anonymised details of all consultants, self-employed persons and sub-contractors retained/engaged by the Company and anonymised copies of agreements with them (or if not available a summary of the agreed terms (including termination provisions, whether they have provided a tax indemnity and whether they are subject to the Commercial Agents (Council Directive) Regulations 1993)).

5.21   Anonymised details of all agency workers engaged by the Company together with details of the terms and conditions on which they are supplied.

5.22   Training schemes/qualifications that employees are required to undertake/have.

5.23   All disciplinary or grievance procedures taken against/taken by any current employee in the last two years.

5.24   All disputes, claims or legal proceedings within the last two years between the Company and any current employees, former employees, trade unions, works council or any other organisation formed for a similar purpose including matters already referred to an employment tribunal or Court or anticipated to be so referred or settled by payment of money.

5.25   Details of any loans or guarantees provided to any employee.

5.26   Details of any employee who has received or has given notice or is likely to give notice to terminate their contract, whether in connection with the sale of the Company or otherwise, including details of the reasons for such notice.

5.27   Details of any employee who has been absent due to sickness for a period of [20] days or more (whether or not consecutive) in any [six] month period within the last [two] years, including details of the reason(s) for the absence.

5.28   Any employee who is on secondment, sabbatical, long-term sick, maternity or other leave.

6   Pensions

The following enquiries are deliberately kept as short as possible in order to obtain a first view of the documents relating to any pensions arrangements. Depending on the issues that arise from the replies to these preliminary enquiries, subsequent enquiries of a much more technical and detailed nature will need to be made to establish the liabilities that may arise from each issue uncovered.

6.1 Please supply details of all pension schemes effected by the Company or in which the Company or any of its current or former directors or employees have or have had an interest.

6.2 Please supply a copy of all Trust Deeds and rules (including any amendments) and all other documents affecting the governance of the pension schemes.

6.3 Please supply a copy of all announcements issued to employees and all explanatory booklets or leaflets distributed to members.

6.4 Please supply a copy of all insurance policies (for insured schemes).

6.5 Please supply a copy of the two most recent valuation reports and details of any actuarial advice or certificates received.

6.6 Please supply a list of the scheme's active members at the annual review date, including their sex, date of birth, pensionable salary and the date upon which each such member joined the scheme.

6.7 Please provide details of all employees who are not yet members of the pension schemes but will in future become eligible for membership, together with the expected date of eligibility.

6.8 Please provide details of all employees who joined the Company as a result of a relevant transfer for the purposes of TUPE.

7 Finance and Grants

7.1 Name and branch address of all banks in which the Company has an account.

7.2 All financial facilities and accounts (including facility letters, account numbers, current balances and all existing bank mandates).

7.3 All legal charges, debentures, mortgages and other financial or security documents affecting the Company.

7.4 Details or copies of all guarantees or indemnities given by or for the benefit of the Company, including intra-group arrangements.

7.5 Loans made to or by the Company including all inter-company loans and all loans to or from the Company's officers.

7.6 All off-balance sheet commitments.

7.7 Copies of debt facilities (including loan notes) issued by or to the Company.

7.8 All dividends and other distributions of the Company made or declared since the date of the last audited accounts or any bonus issues or repayments of capital on, before or after that date (including details of the amount of dividend payable in respect of each class of shares, how such dividends are calculated and when they are payable).

7.9 All grants or subsidies (including investment, employment, local authority and central government grants) paid or awarded to the Company with all associated agreements and documentation.

7.10 Confirmation that no notice requiring repayment has been served and that the Company has not breached any covenant contained in, any charge, debenture or guarantee, loan agreement facility letter or similar document.

8 Properties[1] and Environmental

8.1 All properties owned by, leased to, licensed to or otherwise used by the Company (or in which the Company has any interest) specifying tenure

---

[1] As with the pensions enquiries, the property enquiries are designed to obtain preliminary information with a view to any required pre-contract property enquiries following.

and providing title deeds, any relevant leases or licences and plans for the purposes of making searches.

8.2   Property transactions in the course of negotiation/to be completed before completion.

8.3   Leasehold properties previously occupied by the Company where contingent liabilities may exist.

8.4   All insurance policies, planning permissions, planning restrictions, building regulation consents, approvals, licences, permits and certificates relating to any of the Company's properties.

8.5   All mortgages, deeds of trust, security agreements and the like over any of the Company's properties.

8.6   Existing use of the Company's properties.

8.7   Details of Company properties or other facilities shared or used in common with other persons (including all relevant agreements and other documentation relating to the same).

8.8   Notices relating to the Company's properties which have been served upon or received by the Company.

8.9   Non-domestic rateable value of the Company's properties.

8.10   Major works of repair in the last three years or anticipated (with copies of any building contract, certificate, guarantee, insurance policy etc. relating to the design or construction of the properties or any subsequent works).

8.11   All valuations, reports and appraisals in the last five years of any of the Company's properties.

8.12   All environmental and health and safety audits, surveys and reports carried out by or on behalf of the Company or in respect of the Company's operations.

8.13   Non-compliance with environmental and/or health and safety laws (for the purposes of this paragraph including all statutes, regulations, instruments, judgments, by-laws or decrees pertaining to occupational health and safety or the environment); disputes with/outstanding recommendations from agencies regarding compliance with environmental or health and safety law; pending or threatened administrative, judicial or civil investigations, proceedings or actions with respect to environmental or health and safety law; and all notices served on the Company alleging breach of environmental or health and safety law (including details of any potential costs).

8.14   The Company's environmental and health and safety policies.

8.15   All hazardous substances, polluted or contaminated materials that have been or are used, stored, generated, treated, handled, released or disposed of, including off-site, by the Company and all documents, transfer notes, consignment notes and registered carriers certificates relating to such hazardous substances including their use, treatment and disposal.

8.16   All permits, licences, registrations, notices, approvals, consents, certifications, contingency plans, certificates of destruction and other authorisations of the Company relating to environmental law.

8.17   All emission monitoring or sampling test results pertaining to the Company or property owned by it at any time.

8.18   All pollution control equipment used by the Company.

8.19   All PCBs, asbestos, toxic substances or other contaminated materials present in equipment, structures or premises that the Company owns or operates, or has owned or operated, along with all inspection reports or surveys.

8.20   Maintenance and inspection programmes relating to environmental compliance or control, including all spill or release reports, pertaining to the Company.

8.21   All contracts involving the handling, treatment, storage, transportation, recycling, reclamation or disposal of substances subject to regulation.

8.22   Complaints or claims by owners or occupiers of neighbouring land in respect of activities carried on by the Company or in respect of the condition of land currently or previously owned, occupied, used or held by the Company.

8.23   Confirmation that the Company does not need to register under the Producer Responsibility Obligations (Packaging Waste) Regulations 1997.

8.24   All risk assessments, standard operating procedures and health and safety manuals/documents as well as accident and "near miss" statistics in relation to all the Company activities/operations and premises.

9   Trading Matters and Contracts

9.1   All licences or consents, agreements or arrangements (including hire purchase, leasing, credit sale or deferred payment, maintenance, agency, distribution or factoring agreements or arrangements) to which the Company is party specifically identifying in the replies those which:

9.1.1   involve a capital commitment or annual expenditure or receipts of £[5,000] or more; or

9.1.2   have an unexpired term in excess of six months; or

9.1.3   cannot be terminated on 60 days' notice or less without payment of compensation; or

9.1.4   are onerous or unusual; or

9.1.5   are loss making; or

9.1.6   are material to the business of the Company; or

9.1.7   involves payment by the Company by reference to fluctuations in the index of retail prices or any other index or in the rate of exchange for any currency.

9.2   A summary of the terms of all verbal agreements, arrangements, commitments or understandings which would fall within paragraph 9.1 above and details of all proposals or negotiations which may if accepted or concluded result in a written or verbal agreement, arrangement, commitment or understanding which if already entered into would fall within that paragraph.

9.3   Company brochures/pamphlets giving details of products/services and principle activities.

9.4   All standard terms of business issued by the Company and details of how and when such terms and conditions are used.

9.5   All standard terms of business issued by third parties and which affect the Company and details of how and when such terms are used.

9.6   If the Company deals with any customer or third party on a non-standard basis, details of all significant agreements/arrangements currently in place.

9.7   All agreements, arrangements or transactions to which the Company has been a party in the last six years for either the transfer of assets at an undervalue or which were not at arm's length.

9.8   All trading arrangements between the Company and the Vendors or any member of the Company's group.

9.9   All contracts relating to the acquisition or disposal of shares in the Company, its business or major assets since incorporation.

9.10 All outstanding quotations or tenders made by or to the Company of a value of £[ ] or over.

9.11 All credit arrangements in favour of a customer of the Company granting more than [30] days terms of payment or providing for special discounts.

9.12 Registrations necessary or desirable to conduct the Company's business and confirmation/copies of those which the Company has.

9.13 All Government or trade regulations applicable to the Company together with all significant correspondence and details of all recent regulatory visits.

9.14 All trade associations of which the Company is a member and all rules or codes of conduct with which the Company is expected to comply.

9.15 All agreements or arrangements by which the Company is a member of a joint venture, buying group, consortium, partnership or incorporated or unincorporated association (other than a trade association).

9.16 All non-competition agreements or arrangements/agreements or arrangements with competitors (whether legally enforceable or not) to which the Company is a party and all documentation relating to the same.

9.17 Products in the course of development and expected launch date (whether the new products represent a new product range or modification of an existing range).

9.18 The Company's quality assurance controls in terms of its own services/products and those applied in the procurement of the services/products of others.

9.19 All after sales services and potential liability under warranties, guarantees or recourse arrangements.

9.20 Major suppliers and customers of the Company (i.e. those accounting for more than [10] per cent of goods or materials purchased or sold) and the value of purchases from or sales to each in the last three years.

9.21 All rebate arrangements with suppliers in the last three years.

9.22 Details of all suppliers or customers where the relationship is likely to change with or because of the sale of the Company or for other reasons (including full details of the last 12 months' purchases or sales and orders in hand with such suppliers or customers).

9.23 All significant capital or reserve commitments.

9.24 All existing powers of attorney granted by the Company.

10 Plant, Equipment and Stock

10.1 All machinery, equipment (including fixtures and fittings), plant, tooling and motor vehicles used by the Company in its business differentiating between those which are owned by the Company and those which are subject to lease, hire purchase, conditional sale or similar arrangements and providing copies of any such agreements.

10.2 Material assets of the Company to be disposed of prior to completion or excluded from the sale.

10.3 All notices or directions issued in respect of the safety or operation of any plant, equipment or Company premises.

10.4 The Company's obsolescence policy or other policy dealing in whole or in part with the valuation of stock.

10.5 Inventory of current stock and work-in-progress and confirmation that it is sufficient for the normal requirements of the Company.

10.6 Details of the use of any assets owned or facilities provided by the Vendors which are not being acquired by the Purchaser.

10.7   Details of the relevant import quota restrictions and licences for imported stock, including whether the quota has ever been exceeded in respect of each category of goods and how much of the quota has been used in the current quota period.

10.8   Details of any asset which is not:

10.8.1   adequate and fit for the purposes of the business of the Company; or

10.8.2   in good repair and condition; or

10.8.3   in satisfactory working order; or

10.8.4   properly served and regularly maintained; or

10.8.5   used exclusively for the business of the Company.

11 Litigation

11.1   All litigation, arbitration claims, or judgments existing, pending, threatened or taking place in the last [five] years with amounts involved.

11.2   All general or special provisions made by the Company in relation to the recovery of outstanding book debts.

11.3   All investigations existing, pending or threatened by the Commission for Equality and Human Rights.

11.4   All outstanding complaints or disputes involving the Company in relation to any materials or goods (or class of materials or goods) supplied by the Company, all services (or class of services) rendered by the Company and/or any other aspect of the business of the Company.

11.5   Details of all accidents that have occurred which could give rise to a claim against the Company and/or criminal proceedings. Please supply the Company's accident book and/or RIDDOR reports.

11.6   All insolvency proceedings (whether threatened or actual) including any bankruptcy, liquidation, winding up, receivership, administration, arrangement or scheme with creditors or members affecting the Company or its assets (including any distress, charging order, garnishee order, execution or other process that has been levied or applied for).

11.7   Any circumstances which have given or may give rise to any of the insolvency proceedings against the Company referred to in paragraph 11.6.

11.8   Details of any actual or threatened proposed enforcement action or criminal proceedings against the Company by any regulatory body including but not limited to the Health and Safety Executive, Environment Agency, relevant local authorities, the police and any government agency and/or department. Please supply any prohibition, improvement, food hygiene notices or other similar enforcement notice served on the Company discharged or not.

12 Intellectual Property and Information Technology

12.1   All intellectual property rights vested in, or used by, the Company whether registered or not and including all trade marks, trade names, brand names, patents, design rights, registered designs, copyrights, database rights and domain names, rights in get-up, rights in goodwill or to sue for passing off, patents, rights to inventions, design rights, registered designs, topography rights, copyrights, moral rights, rights in confidential information (including know-how and trade secrets) and database rights ("IPR").

12.2   All certificates (including registration and renewal certificates) for all registered IPR vested in the Company.

12.3   All agreements, licences or arrangements to which the Company is a party affecting IPR vested in, or used by, the Company (or where such agreements, licences or arrangements are not in writing a summary of their terms, including the names of the parties, commencement date, termination date and termination provisions).

12.4   Confirmation that all fees payable by the Company to third parties in relation to intellectual property have been paid including details of the annual costs of maintenance of all registered IPR (including any agents' fees) and receipts for payment of all renewal and registration fees for the protection of registered IPR.

12.5   Details of IPR which the Company owns jointly or in common with any other person or which are shared intra-group.

12.6   Details of any prohibition on assignment of any IPR or any provision in an agreement between the Company and a third party relating to IPR which will terminate or be capable of termination by reason of the purchase of the Company by the Purchaser.

12.7   Details of any claims, liens, equities, encumbrances, licences and adverse rights of any description affecting the IPR.

12.8   Details of any disputes, complaints, objections, challenges or claims for infringement, subsistence, validity or ownership of IPR or any legal proceedings threatened or brought in relation to the IPR.

12.9   Details of any existing, suspected or alleged infringement of third party intellectual property rights by the Company and any obligation on the Company to pay any royalty, fee, compensation or any other sum whatsoever in respect of that infringement.

12.10   Details of any outstanding or potential claims against the Company, under any contract or relevant legislation, for employee compensation in respect of any IPR.

12.11   Confirmation that the Company has in its exclusive possession and control all information, know-how and techniques used, enjoyed or exploited by the Company (or held with a view to such use, enjoyment or exploitation).

12.12   Details of any confidentiality undertakings, except in the ordinary course of business or with its employees, that the Company has entered into with any third party in relation to IPR.

12.13   Details of the Company's computer system ("Computer System") including:

12.13.1 facilities and other information technology hardware or system (including make, model, specification and capacity) in the possession of and/or used by the Company in the operation of its business specifying which is owned by the Company, which is subject to hire purchase, leasing, rental or deferred payment agreement, and which is otherwise provided by a third party or outsourced (together with copy agreements and/or documentation);

12.13.2 all communications facilities (wireless or otherwise) owned or used by the Company including those for landline, mobile and ISP services (together with copy agreements and/or documentation);

12.13.3 all software owned or used by the Company (including nature, description, number of copies licensed, author (where an employee or contractor) or licensor and details of any source code escrow arrangements for software used under licence) and all licences or agreements; and

12.13.4 all website(s) owned or used by the Company.

12.14 All agreements for the supply, development, commissioning, financing, hosting, colocation or support and maintenance of any part of the Computer System.

12.15 Confirmation that all licence fees have been paid and that there is no underlicensing of software used by the Company.

12.16 Details of any element of the Computer System for which the Company owns the IPR, including details of the author of that element of the Computer System, whether the author was an employee or consultant and the terms of employment or consultancy contract with the author.

12.17 Details of any elements of the Computer System that are shared intra-group.

12.18 Details of any recurring technical problems with the Computer System.

12.19 Details of any disputes between the Company and any third party in respect of any matter relating to the Computer System or between the supplier of any element of the Computer System and a third party which may affect the continued use of that element by the Company.

12.20 Company rules, policies and procedures concerning intellectual property rights and use of the Computer System including but not limited to, installation of software, security, backup, disaster recovery and use of portable devices, email and the Internet.

12.21 Details of the Company's policy and practice in the disposal of portable media and hardware elements of the Computer System.

12.22 Details confirming the extent to which the Computer System is able to perform its monetary functions in the euro and in all national currencies necessary for the carrying on of the Company's business.

13 Data Protection

In this section the terms "personal data", "data subject", "data processor", "data controller", "fair processing" and "processing" have the meanings ascribed to them in the Data Protection Act 1998 (the "Act").

13.1 The Company's entry in the Information Commissioner's register of data controllers.

13.2 The Company's internal data protection policy for officers and employees.

13.3 Purposes for which data subjects' personal data are used by the Company (the "Purposes").

13.4 All fair processing notices given by the Company to third parties from whom it collects personal data (including without limitation from its employees and customers), including all website privacy policies, cookie statements, notices on application forms, telephone scripts and any other form of notice.

13.5 All direct marketing opt-in or opt-out notices used to collect and update data subjects' direct marketing preferences stating by which method direct marketing is undertaken by the Company (fax, email, telephone, post, SMS, other) and whether the direct marketing is in relation to the Company's own products and services, group products and services and/or third party products and services, providing a separate description for each of these categories of products and services.

13.6   All mailing lists bought by the Company from, or exchanged with, any third party including a copy of all contracts with those third parties or, if none, details of those third parties and mailing lists.

13.7   Steps taken by the Company to enable data subjects to access their personal data, update their records/profiles and change their preferences, the frequency of this, all standard wording or forms used and all other steps taken by the Company to ensure its records are adequate, relevant, not excessive in relation to the Purposes, accurate, up to date and not kept longer than is necessary for the Purposes.

13.8   Steps taken by the Company to ensure compliance with the seventh data protection principle on security including whether the Company's policy is to encrypt all portable media and devices, and details of any security breaches by the Company or its contractors.

13.9   Details of all data processing arrangements and all data processing contracts entered into between the Company and data processors that process personal data on its behalf, including, without limitation, all arrangements with payroll providers, mailing houses and hosting companies.

13.10   Transfers of personal data outside the European Economic Area (the EU member states, Norway, Iceland and Liechtenstein) and steps taken to ensure an adequate level of protection for the rights and freedoms of data subjects in relation to the processing of personal data in the recipient country.

13.11   All complaints made by or notices received from data subjects and/or the Information Commissioner regarding the Company's processing of personal data and confirmation that the Company has processed personal data in accordance with data subjects' rights under Pt II of the Act.

13.12   Details of any tenders that the Company has submitted for contracts, or arrangements that the Company has entered into, with any entities which are public authorities within the meaning of the Freedom of Information Act 2000 ("FOIA").

13.13   Does the Company hold any information on behalf of a public authority within the meaning of the FOIA? Has the Company received any request to assist in responding to a request for information under the FOIA?

13.14   Details of any communications from the Advertising Standards Authority regarding the Company's advertising practices.

14 Insurance

14.1   All insurance policies currently in effect and owned by or providing coverage to the Company, its directors, officers and employees, in each case giving details of the renewal date, annual premium, risk covered, name of insurance company and policy number.

14.2   All claims filed during the last [three] years under all insurance policies which would fall within paragraph 14.1 with a description of the claim (including claimant, amount claimed, current status and expected settlement date).

14.3   Insurance coverages cancelled or not renewed during the last [five] years.

14.4   All proposals or requests for insurance in the last six years which were declined or which were accepted subject to the imposition of special terms/payment of a high premium.

14.5   Confirmation of payment of all insurance premiums for current policies and the name and address of the Company's insurance brokers.

15 Miscellaneous

15.1   All consents the shareholders must obtain prior to completion.

15.2   All consents the Company must obtain, or permits or licences that will expire consequent upon the change of ownership of the Company.

15.3   All agreements to which the Company is a party which contain change of control provisions.

15.4   All brokers or finders agreements.

15.5   Details of any products manufactured, sold or distributed by the Company which are or may become defective or do not comply with any express or implied warranties given by the Company.

15.6   Details of any confidentiality undertakings given by the Vendors or by the Company and whether these undertakings will be breached by providing the information required in this questionnaire.

[16 Competition

For the purposes of this section "competition law" shall mean all directly or indirectly effective competition legislation governing the conduct of the Company in the jurisdictions in which it operates.

16.1   The Company's main products and geographic markets.

16.2   Market share per product and turnover of the Company within the United Kingdom and within each country in which the Company operates.

16.3   The Company's main competitors in each geographic market in which it operates and their market shares.

16.4   All infringements or notices or allegations of infringement of competition law.

16.5   All actual or potential investigations by any competition authority, government body, agency or court in relation to the Company's actual or potential breach of competition law.

16.6   All actual or potential complaints by any third party alleging that the Company is breaching/has breached competition law.

16.7   All agreements or arrangements to which the Company is a party and which it is believed may infringe competition law.]

[17 Accounts

17.1   Audited accounts and directors' reports of the Company for the last five financial years.

17.2   Most recent management accounts of the Company.

17.3   Current accounting reference date of the Company and all changes which have been made within the last three years.

17.4   Operating projections (including profit and loss and cash flow forecasts) for the next [12] months including all planned or required capital expenditure.

17.5   Current debtors, period of debt and amount and current creditors, period of credit and amount.

17.6   Details of any changes in accounting policies, both in respect of the audited accounts and the management accounts, in the last five financial years.]

[18 Taxation

18.1   All agreements with HMRC as to the latest tax computations of the Company.

18.2   All corporation tax outstanding and due to HMRC.

18.3   All deferred taxation provisions, including any rollover relief claimed in respect of corporation tax on capital gains relating to the last set of audited accounts.

18.4   Confirmation of whether the Company is or has been a close company and if it is or has been a close company confirmation that it is not and has not been a close investment company.

18.5   All tax clearances obtained and all tax indemnities taken.

18.6   Particulars of VAT group registrations.

18.7   The last [six] tax computations and returns for the Company and any correspondence with HMRC in relation thereto.

18.8   Dates to which tax returns have been settled.

18.9   Dates to which tax has been deducted under PAYE/VAT and been accounted for and paid over.

18.10   PAYE: All recent or ongoing audits or investigations in relation to employee taxes and potential exposures in this respect.

18.11   VAT: All recent or ongoing audits or investigations in relation to VAT, sales taxes and customs duties, and potential exposures in this respect.

18.12   All correspondence with HMRC concerning shortfall assessments or apportionment of income.

18.13   All stamp duty or stamp duty land tax exemptions in which the Company may have been involved within the last [five] years.

18.14   Capital allowances claimed.

18.15   Disputes with HMRC and unagreed assessments.

18.16   Confirmation of tax losses, if any, available for carrying forward.

18.17   Intra-group dividends and group relief structures or group income and management fee arrangements for the last [six] years (including associated documentation).

18.18   All covenants entered into since April 6, 1965 for annual payment of any nature.

18.19   Analysis of the tax provision in the latest audited accounts with explanation of key components and calculation of deferred tax.

18.20   All special arrangements with, or dispensations by, any tax authority.

18.21   All overseas trading via non-statutory entities or agents, and details of controls and procedures for compliance with overseas filing requirements.

18.22   Details of all employment related securities (as defined in ITA 2003 Pt 7) or agreements relating to the issue or transfer of employment related securities.]

19 Anti-corruption[2]

19.1   Details of all assessments carried out by the Company to ensure compliance with the Bribery Act 2010 (when brought into force) and any policies or procedures to be implemented by the Company in connection with the Bribery Act 2010.

[19.2   A copy of the Company's anti-bribery and anti-corruption policy (the "Policy") and, save as set out in the Policy, please provide:

19.2.1   details as to who is responsible for bribery/corruption risk within the Company;

---

[2] For a discussion of the Bribery Act 2010 and its implementation please refer to paras 4–02 and 7–153. With effect from the implementation of the Act, clauses 19.2 to 19.6 should be inserted and 19.1 should be deleted.

19.2.2 details as to what extent senior management are involved in enforcing the Policy; and

19.2.3 details of how the Policy is published.

19.3 Details of steps taken by the Company to (i) implement and (ii) monitor and ensure compliance with the Policy and the Bribery Act 2010 as regards its officers and employees.

19.4 Details of the Company's distributors, agents, joint venture partners, sub-contractors and other parties associated with the Company ("Third Parties") and the extent to which the Company carries out due diligence in relation to their appointment and, save to the extent set out in Policy, details of the steps taken by the Company to monitor and ensure compliance by Third Parties to the Policy and the Bribery Act 2010.

19.5 Details of any reporting mechanisms pursuant to the Policy for the Company's officers, employees or Third Parties to report incidents of bribery or corruption and copies of any reports made pursuant thereto.

19.6 In respect of the Company, or any of its officers, employees or Third Parties, details of:

19.6.1 any actual or potential violation of the Policy;

19.6.2 any investigations which have been or are being carried out by law enforcement agencies in relation to incidents of bribery and/or corruption; and

19.6.3 any incidents which have given rise to prosecutions or convictions under the Bribery Act 2010 or anti-bribery or corruption legislation in any other jurisdiction.]

APPENDIX 2

Restrictions on Activities Prior to Completion

[See paras 3–04, 4–14 and 4–16]

Note: For the purposes of this Appendix, the definitions in para.4–02 are used.

The suggested restrictions are fairly comprehensive and of generic application to most companies but consideration should be given as to the suitability of them in relation to the target company and as to whether additional specific restrictions would also be appropriate.

Pending Completion the Vendors undertake to procure that save with the prior written consent of the Purchaser:

1.1 the business of the Company is carried on in the ordinary and normal course in all respects in the same manner as prior to today's date without alteration to its location or operations which would or might in the reasonable opinion of the Purchaser materially prejudice its trade;

1.2 the Purchaser is informed as soon as reasonably practicable of any matter of which the Vendors become aware which [may] [is likely to] [will] materially adversely affect the business of the Company and is consulted with thereon;

1.3 they will use their best endeavours to procure that the employees and customers of the Company do not cease to be employed by or have dealings with the Company;

1.4 the Purchaser is consulted in advance on all material decisions taken in relation to the Company;

1.5 the Company keeps proper accounting records and makes true and complete entries in such records of all of its dealings and transactions;

1.6 the Company shall not:

1.6.1 create or issue, or agree to create or issue, any securities, or agree to grant, any rights in respect of its share or loan capital;

1.6.2 repay or redeem or agree to repay or redeem any of its share capital or reduce any of its share capital;

1.6.3 enter into any agreement or arrangement whereby another company becomes its Subsidiary;

1.6.4 enter into any loan [outside of the ordinary and normal course of business];

1.6.5 borrow any monies or give or allow to exist any Encumbrance over its assets or undertaking except for Encumbrances existing as at today's date (on the same terms as at today's date) [or arising in the ordinary and normal course of its business and operation of bank overdrafts and facilities within existing limits as required in the ordinary and normal course of business];

1.6.6 give any financial guarantees for any purpose whatsoever;

1.6.7 prematurely repay any loans, borrowings or other form of funding;

1.6.8 declare, make or pay a dividend or other distribution;

1.6.9 enter or agree to enter into any long-term or abnormal contract or other agreement outside of the ordinary and normal course of business;

1.6.10 enter or agree to enter into any contract involving capital expenditure or a capital commitment of a value in excess of £[   ] in any one case or £[   ] in aggregate;

1.6.11 pass a resolution of its members;

1.6.12 appoint new auditors;

1.6.13 change (save as required by law) the terms and conditions of employment (whether contractual or not) of any of the officers of the Company or any of the Company's employees;

1.6.14 appoint or dismiss any officers or employees [on salaries in excess of £[   ]];

1.6.15 appoint any directors in addition to the current directors of the Company;

1.6.16 acquire or agree to acquire assets on hire purchase or deferred sale terms, otherwise than in the ordinary and normal course of business;

1.6.17 sell, transfer or otherwise dispose of or agree to dispose of its business, undertaking or assets or any material part thereof;

1.6.18 commence, compromise or discontinue any disputes or legal or arbitration proceedings or claims (other than routine debt collection and price negotiations in the ordinary and normal course of business);

1.6.19 write off or release any debts [of a value of £[   ] or over] or deal with any of its debtors or creditors in an inconsistent manner to how it has dealt with them in the period from the Balance Sheet Date to today's date; or

1.6.20 knowingly permit any of its insurance policies to lapse or do anything to make any insurance policy void or voidable, cause any increase in the insurance premium payable in respect of any insurance policy or prejudice the ability of the Company to effect insurance (on the same or better terms) in the future (save that this shall not prevent the notification to insurers of claims and/or circumstances which might give rise to claims under any of the current insurance policies in accordance with their relevant terms provided that the Vendors inform the Purchaser of any notification to insurers at or before the time that it is made).

APPENDIX 3

Warranties Relating to the Purchaser

[See para.1–05]

Note: save as otherwise defined in this Appendix, the definitions in para.4–02 are used. Reference should be made to the comments in Ch.7 on equivalent warranties to those included in this Appendix for details of the issues that the purchaser should bear in mind when reviewing these warranties and the amendments that it should consider making.

1 The audited balance sheets and profit and loss accounts of the Purchaser and its Subsidiaries, consolidated where applicable, ("the Accounts") for the year ended [ ] ("the Balance sheet Date") have been properly prepared on a consistent basis in accordance with generally accepted accounting principles, standards and practices so as to give at the Balance Sheet Date a true and fair view of the then state of affairs of the Purchaser and its Subsidiaries and of their profit and losses for the period ended on that date.

2 The Accounts contain either provisions adequate to cover, or particulars and notes of, all liabilities (whether quantified or contingent) and all capital commitments of the Purchaser and its Subsidiaries at the Balance Sheet Date.

3 Since the Balance Sheet Date:

   3.1 the Purchaser and its Subsidiaries have carried on their respective businesses in the normal and proper course;

   3.2 there has been no material adverse change in the financial or trading position or prospects of the Purchaser or any of its Subsidiaries;

   3.3 neither the Purchaser nor any of its Subsidiaries has entered into a contract or commitment otherwise than in the normal course of business; and

   3.4 no dividends or other distributions have been declared, made or paid by the Purchaser.

4 The Purchaser and its Subsidiaries have good title to all of their fixed assets as shown in the Accounts, subject only to disposals in the normal course of business.

5 No order has been made, petition presented or resolution passed for the winding up of the Purchaser or any of its Subsidiaries; no distress, execution or other process has been levied in respect of the Purchaser or any of its Subsidiaries during the past three years; there are no outstanding or unsatisfied judgments or court orders against the Purchaser or any of its Subsidiaries; and there has been no material delay by the Purchaser or any of its Subsidiaries in the discharge of any monetary obligation due to be discharged by it.

6 Neither the Purchaser nor any of its Subsidiaries nor a person for whom any of them is or may be liable, vicariously or otherwise, is engaged in or affected by criminal or civil litigation or arbitration proceedings which, individually or collectively, are or are likely to be of material importance, and no proceedings are threatened or pending.

7 There is no material fact or circumstances known or which, on reasonable enquiry, would be known to the Purchaser which, if disclosed to the Vendors, might have influenced them in determining whether to accept the allotment of shares of the Purchaser in satisfaction of the whole or part of the consideration for the Shares.[1]

---

[1] Please see comments at para.7–31 in relation to this warranty which is the infamous "sweeping up" warranty which is likely to be strongly resisted by the purchaser.

APPENDIX 4

Full Commercial Warranties

PART 1: TAXATION WARRANTIES

[See para.5–03]

Note: for the purpose of this Appendix, the definitions in para.4–02 and Ch.10 are used.

Before using this precedent consideration should be given as to whether or not the warranties should be tailored to meet the specifics of the transaction (the warranties currently reflect a comprehensive "hard" purchaser's first draft) and whether all of the warranties are applicable. For example, the warranties at cll.7, 16 and 17 of Pt 1 would only be relevant when the target company has been or is part of a group of companies. Reference should be made to the commentaries on the individual warranties in Chs 5, 6 and 7 in connection with this.

There is an element of overlap in certain areas between the warranties in Pts 1, 2 and 3, for example the insurance warranties at cl.7 of Pt 2 and cl.8.4 of Pt 3. The vendors may resist the inclusion of both sets of warranties on the basis that they duplicate each other.

In relation to the tax warranties, reference has been made to the current legislation as opposed to including the current and former legislation as set out in Ch.5.

Whilst the warranties are up to date as at the time of writing, there will inevitably be developments in a number of areas that will necessitate changes to them. Care should be taken to ensure that the warranties are up to date.

1 Returns and Clearances

1.1 All returns, notifications, computations and payments which should have been made or given by the Company for a Taxation purpose were made or given within the requisite periods and were up-do-date, correct and on a proper basis; and none of them is, or is likely to be, the subject of a dispute with HMRC or other Taxation Authorities.

1.2 All particulars furnished to the Taxation Authorities, in connection with an application for consent or clearance on behalf of the Company, or affecting the Company, fully and accurately disclosed everything material to their decision; the consent or clearance is valid and effective; and the transactions for which the consent or clearance was obtained have been carried into effect (if at all) only in accordance with the terms of the application and the consent or clearance.

1.3 The Company has not taken any action which has had, or might have, the result of altering or prejudicing for a period commencing after the Balance Sheet Date an arrangement or agreement which it has with a Taxation Authority.

1.4 There has been no determination under FA 1998 Sch.18, Pt V (Revenue determinations and assessments) of the amount of tax payable by the Company.

1.5 The Company is not obliged to pay corporation tax in quarterly instalments under the provisions of Corporation Tax (Instalment Payments) Regulations 1998 (SI 1998/3175) and TMA 1970 s.59E.

1.6 The Company has not entered into any group payment arrangements under TMA 1970 ss.59F–59H.

2 PAYE and other deductions at source

2.1 The Company has properly operated the PAYE system, by duly deducting tax from all payments made, or treated as made, to its employees or former employees, and accounting to HMRC for all tax deducted by it and for all tax chargeable on benefits provided for its employees or former employees.

2.2 The Company has complied fully with all its obligations relating to Class 1 and Class 1A National Insurance Contributions, both primary and secondary.

2.3 The Company has made all deductions and retentions of or on account of Taxation as it was obliged or entitled to make and has made all such payments of or on account of Taxation as should have been made to any Taxation Authority in respect of such deductions or retentions.

2.4 The Company is not and has not been a contractor for the purposes of FA 2004 Pt 3, Ch.3 (Construction Industry Scheme).

2.5 No liability to National Insurance Contributions or obligation to account for income tax under the PAYE system could fall on the Company as a result of a chargeable event (within the meaning of IT(EP)A 2003 Pt 7), before, at or after Completion in respect of securities and interests in securities made available or securities options granted to an employee or director prior to Completion.

2.6 No officer or employee of the Company participates in any scheme approved under IT(EP)A 2003 Schs 2 (Approved share incentive plans), 3 (Approved SAYE option schemes) or 4 (Approved CSOP schemes) or has any unapproved options (whether under IT(EP)A 2003 Sch.5 (Enterprise Managing Incentives) or otherwise).

3 Penalties

3.1 The Company has not paid or, since the Balance Sheet Date, become liable to pay a penalty or interest under any statute relating to Taxation.

3.2 The Company has not been the subject of an investigation, discovery or access order by or involving a Taxation Authority and there are no circumstances which make it likely that an investigation, discovery or order will be made.

4 Claims, elections, liabilities and reliefs

4.1 The Disclosure Letter contains full details of all matters relating to Taxation in respect of which the Company (either alone or jointly with another person) is, or at Completion will be, entitled:

4.1.1 to make a claim (including a supplementary claim) for, disclaimer of or election for relief under any statute relating to Taxation;

4.1.2 to appeal against an assessment to or a determination affecting Taxation;

4.1.3 to apply for the postponement of Taxation.

4.2 The Company has not made a claim under TCGA 1992 s.24(2) (Disposals where assets lost or destroyed, or become of negligible value) or exercised an option to pay tax by instalments under s.280 (Consideration payable by instalments).

4.3 The Company is not, nor will it become, liable to pay, or to reimburse or indemnify another person in respect of Taxation in consequence of the failure by any other person (not being the Company) to discharge the Taxation, where the Taxation relates to a profit, income or gain arising or deemed to have arisen or anything occurring or deemed to have occurred (whether wholly or partly) prior to Completion.

4.4 No relief from Taxation has been claimed by or given to the Company, or taken into account in determining the provision for Taxation in the Accounts, which could be withdrawn, postponed or restricted as a result of anything occurring after Completion which is not a deliberate act or omission, or a circumstance deliberately created, by the relevant Company after Completion for the purpose of effecting the withdrawal, postponement or restriction.

5 Unremittable income and capital gains

5.1 The Company has not received or become entitled to income which is "unremittable income" within the meaning of CTA 2009 s.1274 (Unremittable income: introduction) or a gain to which TCGA 1992 s.279 (Foreign assets: delayed remittances) could apply and which has not been remitted to the United Kingdom.

6 Tax avoidance

6.1 The Company has not, since the Balance Sheet Date, engaged in, or been a party to, a scheme or arrangement of which the main purpose, or one of the main purposes, was the avoidance of, or a reduction in liability to, Taxation.

6.2 The Company has not been a party to, or otherwise involved in, a transaction to which any of the following could apply:

- ICTA 1988 s.56 (Transactions in deposits with and without certificates or in debts);
- CTA 2010 s.52 (Dealing in commodity futures);
- CTA 2010 s.53 (Leasing contracts and company reconstructions), s.154 (Arrangements for transfer of group of companies etc.), s.960 (Restrictions on use of reliefs) and s.961 (Non-trading profit and losses);
- CTA 2010 Pt 16 Ch.1 (Transfers of Income Streams);
- CTA 2010 Pt 16 Chs 2 and 3 (Finance Arrangements);
- CTA 2010 Pt 17 Chs 2 to 4 (Manufactured Dividends);
- CTA 2009 Pt 6 Ch.10 (Repos);
- CTA 2010 ss.710 and 713 (Recovery of Unpaid Corporation Tax);
- ICTA 1988 s.774 (Transactions between dealing company and associated company);
- CTA 2010 ss.834 et seq. (Payments connected with transformed land);
- CTA 2010 ss.870 et seq. (Leased Assets: Capital Sums);
- CAA 2001 Pt 2, Ch.17, ss.218, 221–224, 232(1), 241–243 or 246(1) (Anti Avoidance);
- CAA 2001 s.5 (When capital expenditure is incurred); and
- TCGA 1992 s.29 (Value shifting: General provisions).

6.3 The Company has not, since the Balance Sheet Date, been a party to a transaction to which any of the following provisions have been, or could be, applied other than transactions in respect of which all necessary consents or clearances were obtained:

- CTA 2010 ss.731–751 (Transactions in Securities);
- CTA 2010 ss.815–833 (Transactions in Land);
- TCGA 1992 ss.135–138 (Company reconstructions); or
- TCGA 1992 s.139 (Reconstruction involving transfer of business).

7 Depreciatory transactions and value shifting

7.1 No allowable loss, which may accrue on the disposal of an asset by the Company, is likely to be reduced by reason of TCGA 1992 s.176 (Depreciatory transactions within a group) or s.177 (Dividend stripping).

7.2 No chargeable gain or allowable loss arising on a disposal by the Company is likely to be adjusted under TCGA 1992 s.30 (Tax-free benefits).

7.3 No reduction in the value of the shares of the Company has occurred as a result of:

7.3.1 the payment of a dividend after March 13, 1989 out of chargeable profits within the meaning of TCGA 1992 s.31 (Distributions within a group followed by a disposal of shares) as extended by TCGA 1992 s.31A (Asset-holding company leaving the group); or

7.3.2 a transfer of an asset in circumstances within TCGA 1992 s.32(2) (Disposals within a group followed by a disposal of shares).

8 Disallowance of deductions

8.1 No rents, interest, annual payments or other sums of an income nature paid, or payable, since the Balance Sheet Date by the Company or which the Company is under an obligation to pay are, or may be, wholly or partially disallowable as deductions in computing profits or as charges on income, for the purposes of corporation tax.

9 Transactions not at arm's length

9.1 The Company has not since the Balance Sheet Date carried out, or been engaged in, a transaction or arrangement to which TIOPA 2010 Pt 4 (Transfer Pricing) has been or may be applied.

9.2 The Company has not disposed of or acquired an asset in such circumstances that TCGA 1992 s.17 (Disposals and acquisitions treated as made at market value) could apply.

10 Disallowance of losses

10.1 There has not been in the past three years a major change in the nature or conduct of the trade or business of the Company such as might prevent the carry forward or back of trading losses or excess management expenses by reason of the application of CTA 2010 s.674 (Disallowance of trading losses) or CTA 2010 ss.679–684 (Restrictions on relief).

11 Loan relationships

11.1 The Company is not a party to a loan relationship (within the meaning of CTA 2009 s.302 ("loan relationship", "creditor relationship", "debtor relationship"):

    11.1.1 where there is or was previously a connected companies relationship between the parties as defined in CTA 2009 s.348 (Introduction: meaning of "connected companies relationship");

    11.1.2 to which CTA 2009 s.344 (Transactions not at arm's length: general) applies or may apply; or

    11.1.3 to which CTA 2009 Pt 6, Ch.6A (Shares accounted for as liabilities) or Ch.7 (Shares with guaranteed returns etc.) applies.

11.2 The Company is not subject to a restriction as to the amount of the loss that it may bring into account in respect of a loan relationship by virtue of CTA 2009 s.327 (Disallowance of imported loses etc.).

11.3 The Company has not acquired or disposed of rights or liabilities in respect of a loan relationship where the company from which it made the acquisition or to which it made the disposal was a member of the same group of companies within the meaning of CTA 2009 s.336 (Transfer of loans on group transactions).

11.4 The Company has not been a party to a loan relationship which had an unallowable purpose within the meaning of CTA 2009 s.442 (meaning of "unallowable purpose".

12 Distributions

12.1 The Company has not repaid, or agreed to repay, or redeemed, or agreed to redeem, any of its shares, or capitalised, or agreed to capitalise, in the form of redeemable shares or debentures, any profits or reserves.

12.2 No security, within the meaning of CTA 2010 s.1117 ("Other Interpretation") of the Company was issued in such circumstances that the interest payable on it, or any other payment in respect of it, falls to be treated as a distribution under CTA 2010 s.1000 (meaning of "distribution").

12.3 The Company has not received a capital distribution to which TCGA 1992 s.189 (Capital distribution of chargeable gains: recovery from shareholder) could apply.

13 Close companies

13.1 The Company is not, nor was it at any time during the six years ended on the Balance Sheet Date, a close company as defined in CTA 2010 s.439 ("Close Company").

13.2 No distribution within CTA 2010 s.1064 (Certain expenses of close companies treated as distribution) has been made by the Company.

13.3 No loan or advance within CTA 2010 Pt 10, Ch.3 (Charge to tax in case of loan to participator) has been made and remains outstanding, or agreed to, by the Company and the Company has not, since the Balance Sheet Date, released or written off the whole or part of the debt in respect of such a loan or advance.

14 Sale and leaseback of land

14.1   The Company has not, since the Balance Sheet Date, entered into a transaction to which the provisions of CTA 2010 ss.850–862 (New Lease of Land after assignment or surrender) have been, or could be, applied.

15 Intangible assets

15.1   No election has been made by the Company pursuant to CTA 2009 s.730 (Writing down at fixed rate: election for fixed rate basis).

15.2   The Company has not made a claim for relief under CTA 2009 ss.754–763 (Rollover relief in case of realisation and reinvestment).

15.3   No intangible fixed asset of the Company was acquired on a tax neutral basis pursuant to CTA 2009 s.775 (Transfers within a group).

15.4   No intangible fixed asset of the Company was transferred to the Company by a related party within CTA 2009 s.845 (Transfers between company and related party treated as being at market value).

15.5   The Company has not within the last six years acquired any intangible fixed asset from another company at a time when that other company was a member of the group of companies (as defined in CTA 2009 Pt 8, Ch.1) of which the Company is, or was within the last six years, a member.

16 Group relief and group surrenders

16.1   The Group Companies comprise a group for the purposes of CTA 2010 s.99 (Surrendering of losses and other amounts) and there is nothing in CTA 2010 s.154 or s.155 (Arrangements for transfer of companies) which precludes a Group Company from being regarded as a member of the group.

16.2   The Company has not, since the Balance Sheet Date, made or agreed to make, otherwise than to or from another Group Company a surrender of, or claim for, group relief under CTA 2010 Pt 5 (Group Relief).

16.3   No Group Company is liable to make or entitled to receive a payment for group relief otherwise than to or from another Group Company.

16.4   The Company has not made or received a payment for group relief (otherwise than to or from another Group Company), which may be liable to be refunded in whole or in part.

16.5   If any member of the Group Company only became a member after the Balance Sheet Date, the apportionment of profits and losses will be made under CTA 2010 ss.138–142 (General limitation on amount of group relief given) on a time basis according to the respective lengths of the component accounting periods.

16.6   The Company is not restricted in relation to the surrendering of group relief by CTA 2010 s.109 (Restriction on losses etc. surrenderable by dual resident).

16.7   The Company has not agreed to surrender, otherwise than to another Group Company, any right to receive a tax refund under CTA 2010 s.963 (Power to surrender tax refund).

17 Acquisitions from group members

17.1   The Company does not own an asset which was acquired from another company not being a Group Company, which was, at the time, a member of the same group of companies (as defined in TCGA 1992 s.170 (Groups of companies: interpretation of ss.170–181)) as the relevant Group Company, and which owned that asset otherwise than as trading stock within TCGA 1992 s.173 (Transfers within a group: trading stock).

17.2   The execution or completion of this Agreement will not result in profit or gain being deemed to accrue to the Company for Taxation purposes, whether under TCGA 1992 s.179 (Company ceasing to be member of group: post-appointed day cases) or otherwise.

18   Demergers and purchase of own shares

18.1   The Company has not been engaged in, or been a party to, any of the transactions set out in CTA 2010 ss.1073–1099 (Demergers) nor has it made or received a chargeable payment as defined in CTA 2010 s.1088 (meaning of "chargeable payment").

18.2   The Company has not redeemed, repaid or purchased or agreed to redeem, repay or purchase, any of its own shares.

19   Stock dividends

19.1   The Company has not issued share capital to which the provisions of CTA 2010 s.1049 (Stock Dividends) or TCGA s.142 (Capital gains on stock dividends) could apply and the Company does not own any such share capital.

20   Capital allowances

20.1   All expenditure which the Company has incurred or may incur under a subsisting commitment on the provision of machinery or plant has qualified or will qualify (if not deductible as a trading expense of a trade carried on by the Company) for writing-down allowances under CAA 2001 Pt 2, Ch.5 (Allowances and charges).

20.2   No event has occurred since the Balance Sheet Date which may be treated as a notional sale by the Company of machinery or plant pursuant to CAA 2001 ss.61 (Disposal events and disposal values) or 72 (Disposal values).

20.3   No capital allowances made or to be made to the Company in respect of capital expenditure already incurred or to be incurred under a subsisting commitment arise from special leasing (as defined in CAA 2001 s.19) or qualifying non-trade expenditure (as defined in CAA 2001 s.469) on patents.

20.4   Since the Balance Sheet Date the Company has not done, or omitted to do, or agreed to do, or permitted to be done, an act as a result of which a balancing allowance or a balancing charge may be brought into account for capital allowances purposes, or there may be a recovery of excess relief under CAA 2001 s.111 (Excess allowances: standard recovery mechanism).

20.5   The Company is not in dispute with any person as to any entitlement to capital allowances under CAA 2001 Pt 2, Ch.14 (Fixtures) and at the date of this Agreement as far as the Vendors are aware there are no circumstances which might give rise to such a dispute.

21   Base values and acquisition costs

21.1   If each of the capital assets of the Company was disposed of at Completion for a consideration equal to its book value in, or adopted for the purpose of, the Accounts, no liability to corporation tax on chargeable gains and, on the assumption that the expenditure on each asset was incurred for the purpose of a separate trade, no balancing charge under CAA 2001 would arise; and, for the purpose of determining the liability to corporation tax on chargeable gains, there shall be disregarded reliefs and allowances available to the Company other than amounts falling to be deducted under TCGA 1992 s.38 (Acquisition and disposal costs, etc.).

21.2 The Company has not made an election under TCGA 1992 s.35 (Assets held on March 31, 1982 (including assets held on April 6, 1965)) for capital gains and losses on all the assets held by it on March 31, 1982 to be computed by reference only to their market value on that date.

21.3 The Company has not since the Balance Sheet Date engaged in a transaction in respect of which there may be substituted, for Taxation purposes, a different consideration for the actual consideration given or received by it.

21.4 In determining the liability to corporation tax on chargeable gains in respect of any asset which has been acquired by the Company, or which the Company has agreed to acquire (whether conditionally, contingently or otherwise):

21.4.1 the sums allowable as a deduction will be determined solely in accordance with TCGA 1992 ss.38 (Acquisition and disposal costs, etc.) and 53 (The indexation allowance and interpretative provisions);

21.4.2 the amount or value of the consideration, determined in accordance with s.38(1)(a), will not be less than the amount or value of the consideration actually given by the Company for the asset; and

21.4.3 the amount of any expenditure on enhancing the value of that asset, determined in accordance with s.38(1)(b) will not be less than the amount or value of all expenditure actually incurred by the Company on the asset.

21.5 No asset owned, or agreed to be acquired, by the Company (other than plant and machinery in respect of which it is entitled to capital allowances) is a wasting asset within TCGA 1992 s.44 (meaning of "wasting asset").

21.6 The Company has not joined in the making of a claim under TCGA 1992 s.140A (Transfer of a UK trade) in relation to the transfer to it of the whole or part of a trade carried on within the United Kingdom.

22 Replacement of business assets

22.1 The Company has not made a claim under TCGA 1992 ss.23 (Receipt of compensation and insurance money not treated as a disposal), 152 (Replacement of business assets: Roll-over relief), 153 (Assets only partly replaced), 154 (New assets which are depreciating assets), 175 (Replacement of business assets by members of a group) or 247 (Roll-over relief on compulsory acquisition) which would affect the amount of the chargeable gain or allowable loss which would, but for the claim, have arisen on a disposal of any of its assets.

23 Chargeable gains: special cases

23.1 The Company is not owed a debt (not being a debt on a security), upon the disposal or satisfaction of which a liability to corporation tax on chargeable gains will arise under TCGA 1992 s.251 (Debts: General provisions).

23.2 The Company has not claimed nor is it entitled to claim under TCGA 1992 ss.253 (Relief for loans to traders) that an allowable loss has accrued in respect of a loan made by it.

23.3 The Company does not own rights, or an interest in rights, under a policy of assurance or contract for a deferred annuity on the life of any person of which it is not the original beneficial owner.

23.4 No part of the consideration given by the Company for a new holding of shares (within the meaning of TCGA 1992 s.126 (Reorganisation or reduction of share capital: Application of ss.127–131) will be disregarded by virtue of s.128(2) (Consideration given or received by holder).

23.5 No asset owned by the Company has been the subject of a deemed disposal under TCGA 1992 Sch.2 (Assets held on April 6, 1965), so as to restrict the extent to which the gain or loss, over the period of ownership, may be apportioned by reference to straightline growth.

24 Capital losses

24.1 The Company has not incurred a capital loss to which TCGA 1992 s.18(3) (Transactions between connected persons) is applicable.

25 Gifts involving group companies

25.1 The Company has not received assets by way of gift as mentioned in TCGA 1992 s.282 (Recovery of tax from donee).

26 Foreign businesses

26.1 The Company has not made a claim under TCGA 1992 s.140 (Postponement of charge on transfer of assets to non-resident company) or s.140C (Transfer of a non-UK trade) in relation to the transfer of the whole or part of a trade which it carried on outside the United Kingdom through a branch or agency.

26.2 No notice under ICTA 1988 s.747 (Imputation of chargeable profits and creditable tax of controlled foreign companies) has been received by the Company, no application has been made under ICTA 1988 s.751A (Reduction in chargeable profits for certain activities of EEA business establishments) and no circumstances exist which would entitle HMRC to apportion profits of a controlled foreign company to the Company under ICTA 1988 s.752 (Apportionment of chargeable profits and creditable tax) as extended by ICTA 1988 ss.752A (Relevant interests), 752B (s.752(3): the percentage of shares which a relevant interest represents) and 752C (Interpretation of apportionment provisions).

27 Residence

27.1 The Company is and has at all times been resident in the United Kingdom for the purposes of all Taxation laws and has not at any time been resident outside the United Kingdom or had a permanent establishment outside the United Kingdom for the purposes of any Taxation law or any double Taxation arrangement. The Company has never paid tax on income profits or gains to any Taxation Authority in any other country.

28 Value added tax

28.1   In relation to value added tax the Company:

    28.1.1 has duly registered and is a taxable person;

    28.1.2 has complied, in all material respects, with all statutory requirements, orders, provisions, directions and conditions;

    28.1.3 maintains complete, correct and up-to-date records as required by the applicable legislation;

    28.1.4 has not been required by HMRC to give security;

    28.1.5 has not applied for treatment as a member of a group which includes another company; and

    28.1.6 is not, nor has it agreed to become, an agent (for the purposes of VATA 1994 s.47 (Agents, etc.)) for the supply of goods for a person who is not a taxable person.

28.2   The Disclosure Letter sets out accurate and complete particulars of claims for bad debt relief which have been made and remain outstanding, or which may be made, by the Company under VATA 1994 s.36 (Bad debts) and of any debts which, if written off, would give a right to claim relief.

28.3   The Company has not, during the past 12 or 24 months respectively, received a surcharge liability notice under VATA 1994 s.59 (The default surcharge) nor may it be liable to a penalty under FA 2007 Sch.24 (Penalties for Errors).

28.4   No option to tax in relation to any of the Properties has been made by the Company or a predecessor in title under VATA 1994 Sch.10, para.2 (Election to waive exemption).

29 Inheritance tax

29.1   The Company has not made a transfer of value (as defined in IHTA 1984 s.3 (Transfers of value)).

29.2   No HMRC charge for unpaid inheritance tax (as provided by IHTA 1984 s.237 (Imposition of charge) and s.238 (Effects of purchases) exists over an asset of the Company or in relation to shares in the capital of the Company.

30 Stamp duty and stamp duty land tax

30.1   The Company has not within the past three years made a claim for relief or exemption under FA 1930 s.42 (Relief from transfer stamp duty in case of transfer of property as between associated companies), FA 1995 s.151 (Leases etc. between associated bodies corporate) or FA 1986 ss.75–77 (Acquisitions: reliefs).

30.2   All documents in the possession of the Company, or which the Company is entitled to require the production of, and which confer any right upon the Company or are necessary to establish the title of the Company to any asset, have been stamped and any applicable stamp duties or charges in respect of such documents have been accounted for and paid, and no such documents which are outside of the United Kingdom would attract stamp duty if they were brought into the United Kingdom.

30.3   Stamp duty land tax has been paid in full in respect of all estates or interests in land acquired on or after December 1, 2003 by the Company. The Company has not made any application to defer payment of stamp duty land tax pursuant to FA 2003 s.90 and there are no contingent liabilities or requirements to submit a further land transaction return in relation to:

30.3.1 properties acquired as a going concern for the purposes of VATA s.49 (Taxation of going concerns);

30.3.2 unascertainable future consideration;

30.3.3 transactions capable of being treated as linked for the purposes of FA 2003 s.108 (Linked transactions);

30.3.4 turnover leases;

30.3.5 leases subject to a rent review within five years of grant;

30.3.6 leases the assignment of which would be deemed to be the grant of a new lease; or

30.3.7 any other arrangement capable of giving rise to a further charge to stamp duty land tax.

30.4 The Company has not claimed relief from stamp duty land tax under FA 2003 Sch.7, Pts 1 or 2 (Stamp Duty Land Tax: group relief and reconstruction and acquisition reliefs) in relation to any estate or interest in land that has been transferred to it.

31 Disclosure requirements

31.1 The Company has not entered into any notifiable arrangement for the purposes of FA 2004 Pt 7, any notifiable contribution arrangement for the purpose of the National Insurance (Application of Pt 7 of the Finance Act 2004) Regulations 2007 (SI 2007/785) or any notifiable schemes for the purposes of VATA 1994 Sch.11A and there are no circumstances in which any such disclosure should have been made by the Company.

PART 2: PROPERTY WARRANTIES

[See para.6–16]

1 Title

1.1 The Properties comprise all the properties owned, occupied or otherwise used by the Company in connection with its business and the Company does not have any right of ownership, rights of use, rights options, rights of first refusal or obligations to purchase or take purchase or acquire, or any other legal or equitable estate or interest in or in relation to any land or buildings other than the Properties.

1.2 Those of the Properties which are occupied or otherwise used by the Company in connection with its business are occupied or used by right of ownership or under lease or licence, the terms of which permit the occupation or use.

1.3 The Company is the sole legal and beneficial owner of the Properties and, where any of the Properties are leasehold, the unexpired residue of the term granted by each lease is vested in the Company and is valid and subsisting against all persons, including any person in which any superior estate or interest is vested.

1.4 The information contained in Schedule [   ] as to the tenure of each of the Properties, the principal terms of the leases or licences held by the Company and the principal terms of the tenancies and licences subject to and with the benefit of which the Properties are held, is true, complete and accurate.

1.5   The Company has a good and marketable title to each of the Properties.

1.6   [The Company is the proprietor of the Properties registered at the Land Registry with absolute title.] [None of the Properties are registered at the Land Registry.]

1.7   Each lease of the Properties granted for more than seven years is either registered at the Land Registry with absolute title or not registered because it was not registerable at the time of grant and no event has occurred in consequence of which first registration of title should have been effected.

1.8   The Company is in possession and actual and exclusive occupation of the whole of each Property and no third party has acquired or is in the course of acquiring any rights to occupy or enjoy any of the Properties nor has the Company granted, or agreed to grant, any right of occupation or enjoyment in respect of any of the Properties to any third party.

1.9   All replies given by or on behalf of the Vendors or their solicitors in response to any enquiries raised by or on behalf of the Purchaser or its solicitors in relation to the Properties were true, complete and accurate when given and remain so.

1.10   The Company has in its possession and control and has disclosed copies of all the title deeds and documents necessary to prove good and marketable title to the Properties and (where any of the Properties are leasehold) have further disclosed in relation to each lease evidence of the reversioner's title to the lease, all consents required under the lease, copies of all assignments of the lease and evidence of the current annual rent payable under the lease and the documents of title to be delivered to the Purchaser at Completion shall be the original documents, properly stamped with stamp duty and registered, where required.

1.11   Where title to any of the Properties is not registered at the Land Registry, there is no caution against first registration of title and [to the best of the knowledge and belief of the Vendors] no event has occurred in consequence of which a caution against first registration of title could be effected.

1.12   There is no circumstance that could render any transaction affecting the title of the Company to any of the Properties liable to be set aside under the Insolvency Act 1986.

2   Encumbrances

2.1   The Properties are free from mortgages, debentures, charges, rent charges, liens or other encumbrances.

2.2   The Properties are not subject to outgoings, other than business rates, water and sewage charges and insurance premiums and additionally, in the case of leasehold properties, rent and service charges.

2.3   The Properties are free of restrictive covenants, stipulations, easements, profits à prendre, wayleaves, licences, grants, restrictions, overriding interests or other similar rights vested in third parties or other encumbrances (whether of a private or public nature and whether legal or equitable) which restrict or conflict or which may resist or conflict with the existing use of the Properties or are of an onerous or unusual nature or affect the value of the Properties.

2.4   Where any of the matters referred to in clauses [2.1, 2.2 and 2.3] are disclosed in the Disclosure Letter, the obligations and liabilities imposed and arising under them have been performed and discharged, no payments in respect of them are outstanding and no notice of any alleged breach or failure to perform or discharge any of them has been received by the Company.

2.5   The Properties are free of options, estate contracts or rights of preemption.

2.6   There are no local land charges, land charges, cautions, inhibitions or notices registered against the Properties and there is nothing which is capable of registration against them.

3   Planning matters

3.1   Each of the Properties are used by the Company only for the specific purposes set out in Schedule [   ] and the use of each of the Properties is the permitted use for the purposes of the Planning Acts.

3.2   Planning permission has been obtained, or is deemed to have been granted, for the purpose of the Planning Acts with respect to all development at and of the Properties; no planning permission has been suspended or revised and no application for planning permission has been called in or is otherwise awaiting a decision; no planning permission is temporary or personal and there is no planning permission which is subject to conditions any of which are not fully satisfied.

3.3   Building regulation and all other statutory consents and certificates have been obtained (including without limitation a building regulations final completion certificate) with respect to all development of and alterations and improvements to the Properties.

3.4   The Company has complied and is complying with all planning permissions and statutory consents orders and regulations with respect to and applicable to the Properties.

3.5   The Company has complied and is complying with all agreements and all obligations made in respect of the Properties under s.52 of the Town and Country Planning Act 1971, s.106 of the Town and Country Planning Act 1990, s.18 of the Public Health Act 1936, s.104 of the Water Industry Act 1991, s.33 of the Local Government (Miscellaneous Provisions) Act 1982 and any other legislation relating to the condition and use of the Properties or any services or access servicing or adjoining the Properties.

3.6   None of the Properties is listed as being of special historic or architectural importance or located in a conservation area.

4   Statutory obligations

4.1   The Company has complied and is complying with all applicable statutory and by-law requirements with respect to the Properties including the Public Health Acts, the Occupiers Liability Act 1957, the Offices, Shops and Railway Premises Act 1963, the Fire Precautions Act 1971, the Health and Safety at Work etc. Act 1974, the Environmental Protection Act 1990, the Sunday Trading Act 1994, the Construction (Design and Management) Regulations 1994, the Environment Act 1995, the Disability Discrimination Act 1995, the Control of Asbestos Regulations 2006, the Regulatory Reform (Fire Safety) Order 2005, the Construction (Design and Management) Regulations 2007 and any other legislation current or previous currently affecting the Properties and any other relevant orders, regulations, rules or directions and delegated legislation of a competent authority affecting the Properties.

4.2   There is no outstanding or unperformed obligation with respect to the Properties, compliance with which is necessary to satisfy the requirements (whether formal or informal) of a competent authority exercising statutory or delegated powers.

4.3   No licences are required in relation to any of the Properties.

5   Adverse orders

5.1   There are no compulsory purchase notices, orders or resolutions affecting the Properties and there are no circumstances likely to lead to any being made.

5.2   There are no closing, demolition or clearance orders, enforcement notices or stop notices affecting the Properties and there are no circumstances likely to lead to any being made.

6   Condition of the properties

6.1   The buildings and other structures on the Properties are in good and substantial repair and fit for the purposes for which they are used.

6.2   No structure on the Properties has been affected by structural damage or electrical defects or by timber infestation or disease.

6.3   No structure at the Properties contains any materials which do not comply with relevant regulations, standards and codes of practice of which are generally regarded as deleterious to health, safety or the durability of buildings or structures.

6.4   There are no disputes with a neighbouring owner with respect to boundary walls and fences, or with a third party with respect to easements or rights over or benefiting the Properties.

6.5   The principal means of access to the Properties are over roads which have been taken over by the local or other highway authority and which are maintainable at the public expense, and such roads immediately abut the boundary of the legal title to the Properties at each of them where access is granted, and no means of access to the Properties is shared with another party or subject to rights of determination by another party.

6.6   Each of the Properties enjoys the mains services of water, drainage, electricity and gas.

6.7   None of the Properties is located in an area or subject to circumstances particularly susceptible to flooding.

6.8   The Properties are not subject to rights of common.

6.9   None of the Properties is subject to registration as a town or village green and there are no circumstances which could give rise to the registration of any of the Properties as a town or village green.

6.10   The Properties are not affected by mining activity.

7   Insurance

7.1   The Properties are covered by insurance of a type usually available in the United Kingdom insurance market against a comprehensive range of risks (including subsidence and terrorism) in their full reinstatement values and against third party and public liabilities and professional fees to an adequate extent and, where any of the Properties are let, for not less than three years' loss of rent or such greater period as may be specified in the tenancies affecting the Properties.

7.2   All premiums due in respect of insurance policies relating to the Properties have been duly paid and, where the Properties are let, the premiums are recoverable in full from the tenants pursuant to the tenancies affecting the Properties and nothing has arisen which would vitiate the policies or permit the insurers to avoid them.

7.3   The information in the Disclosure Letter with respect to insurance policies is complete and accurate.

8   Leasehold properties

8.1   The Company has paid the rent and performed the covenants on the part of the tenant and the conditions contained in any leases (which expression in this clause [8] includes underleases) under which the Properties are held, the last demands for rent (or receipts, if issued) were unqualified and all the leases are in full force.

8.2   All licences, consents and approvals required from the landlords and any superior landlords under leases of the Properties have been obtained, and the tenant's covenants therein have been performed.

8.3   There are no rent reviews in progress under leases of the Properties held by the Company and no rent can be reviewed for at least a year after Completion.

8.4   No obligation necessary to comply with a notice or other requirement given by the landlord under a lease of any of the Properties is outstanding and unperformed.

8.5   There is no obligation to reinstate any of the Properties by removing an alteration made to it by the Company or a predecessor in title to the Company and all such alterations are to be disregarded on any review of the rent payable under each lease of the Properties.

8.6   The Company has not entered into an authorised guarantee agreement under the Landlord and Tenant (Covenants) Act 1995 s.16 in respect of any property.

8.7   The Company has not had the right to call for an overriding lease of any property under the Landlord and Tenant (Covenants) Act 1995 s.19.

8.8   The Company has not entered into an agreement with the lessor of any of the Properties specifying circumstances in which it would be reasonable for the lessor to withhold its consent to an assignment in accordance with the Landlord and Tenant Act 1927 s.19(1A).

9   Tenancies

9.1   The Properties are held subject to and with the benefit of the tenancies (which expression in this clause [9] includes subtenancies) as set out in Schedule [   ] and no others.

9.2   With respect to the tenancies, the Disclosure Letter contains particulars of:

9.2.1   the rent and any rent reviews and, with respect to rent reviews, the date for giving notice of exercise of the reviews and the operative review date;

9.2.2   the term and rights to break or renew the term;

9.2.3   the obligations of the landlord and tenant in respect of outgoings, repairs, insurance, services and service charges;

9.2.4   options or pre-emption rights;

9.2.5   the user required or permitted;

9.2.6   the entitlement of a tenant of the Properties to compensation either on quitting the premises, for improvements or otherwise;

9.2.7   any unusual provisions; and

9.2.8   short particulars of subtenancies derived out of the tenancies.

9.3   The Vendors are not aware of a material or persistent breach of covenant by a tenant of the Properties.

9.4   The Company has not at any time:

9.4.1   surrendered any lease, licence or tenancy to the landlord without first satisfying itself that the landlord had good title to accept such surrender and without receiving from the landlord an absolute release from all liability arising under such lease, licence or tenancy;

9.4.2   assigned, or otherwise disposed of, any lease, licence or tenancy without receiving a full and effective indemnity from the assignee or transferee in respect of its liability under such lease, licence or tenancy;

9.4.3   been a guarantor of a tenant's liability under any lease, licence or tenancy or otherwise given a guarantee or indemnity for any liability relating to any of the Properties, any property or other land or buildings previously owned; or

9.4.4   assigned or otherwise disposed or dealt with or held any property in such a way that it retains any other residual liability (whether actual or contingent) in respect thereof.

PART 3: COMMERCIAL WARRANTIES

[See para.7–03]

1 Preliminary

1.1 Capacity and authority of Vendors

1.1.1   Each of the Vendors has the necessary power and authority to enter into and perform this Agreement and all other documents to be executed by them at or before Completion in accordance with this Agreement which constitutes or will when executed constitute binding and enforceable obligations, on each of the Vendors.

1.2 Ownership of Shares

1.2.1   The Shares are fully paid or credited as fully paid and will, at Completion, constitute the whole of the issued and allotted share capital of the Company.

1.2.2   The Vendors have the right to transfer to the Purchaser (without the consent of any third party) and will on Completion transfer the legal and beneficial title to the Shares.

1.2.3   There is not now existing nor is there any agreement to create any Encumbrance on or affecting the Shares or any unissued shares, or securities of the Company.

1.2.4   None of the Shares was, or represents assets which were, the subject of a transfer at an undervalue (within the meaning of the Insolvency Act 1986 ss.238 or 339) within the past five years.

1.2.5   None of the Shares was allotted at a discount.

1.3   Share capital

1.3.1   No share or loan capital has been issued or allotted or agreed to be issued or allotted by the Company since the Balance Sheet Date.

1.3.2   The Company has not at any time repaid, redeemed or purchased any of its own shares, reduced its share capital or capitalised any reserves or profits (or agreed to do the same).

1.3.3   The Company has not at any time provided financial assistance pursuant to CA 1985 ss.151 and 158 or CA 2006 ss.678 or 679.

1.4   Details of the Company

1.4.1   The information relating to the Company in Schedule [   ] is accurate and complete [in respect of the matters dealt with].

1.5   Directors and shadow directors

1.5.1   The Company has no liability to a former member, officer or shadow director of any person nor are there any circumstances in which such liability could arise.

1.5.2   No person is or has been a shadow director (within the meaning of the Companies Acts) of the Company but not treated as one of its directors for all the purposes of the Companies Acts.

1.6   Subsidiaries and branches

1.6.1   The Company:

1.6.1.1   is not the holder or beneficial owner of, nor has it agreed to acquire share or loan capital of a body corporate; and

1.6.1.2   has not outside the United Kingdom a branch, agency or place of business, or a permanent establishment (as that expression is currently defined in the relevant double taxation relief order).

1.7   Options over the Company's capital

1.7.1   Apart from this Agreement, there are no agreements or arrangements which provide for the issue, allotment or transfer of, or grant a right (whether conditional or otherwise) to call for the issue, allotment or transfer of share or loan capital of the Company. No claim has been made by any person to be entitled to any of the foregoing.

1.8   Commissions

1.8.1   No one is entitled to receive from the Company a finder's fee, brokerage or other commission in connection with the sale and purchase of the Shares under this Agreement.

1.9   Written resolutions

1.9.1   The Company has not passed an elective resolution under CA 1985 s.379A.

1.10   Constitutional documents, statutory books and resolutions

1.10.1   The copy of the memorandum and articles of association of the Company attached to the Disclosure Letter is accurate and complete and has embodied in it, or attached to it, a copy of every resolution and agreement required to be annexed to or incorporated in these documents by any applicable laws.

1.10.2 The register of members and other statutory books of the Company have been properly kept in accordance with all applicable laws and contain an accurate and complete record of the matters with which they should deal.

1.10.3 No notice or allegation has been received that the statutory books of the Company are incorrect or should be rectified.

1.10.4 Since the Balance Sheet Date, no alteration has been made to the articles of association of the Company and no resolution has been passed by its shareholders.

1.11 Documents filed

1.11.1 All returns, particulars, resolutions and documents required by CA 2006 or other legislation to be filed with the Registrar of Companies or other authority in respect of the Company have been duly filed and were accurate and complete.

1.11.2 All charges in favour of the Company have (if appropriate) been registered in accordance with the provisions of the Companies Acts.

1.12 Possession of documents

1.12.1 All the title deeds relating to the assets of the Company, an executed copy of all agreements to which the Company is a party and the original copies of all other documents which are in force or otherwise relevant to the Company and which are owned by, or which ought to be in the possession of, the Company are in its possession. All documents are, where relevant, stamped with the correct amounts of stamp duty.

1.12.2 There is no document held outside the United Kingdom which, if brought within the United Kingdom, would result in the Company incurring a liability to pay stamp duty.

1.13 Investigations

1.13.1 No investigation or enquiry by, or on behalf of, a governmental or other body in respect of the affairs of the Company is taking place or pending and the Vendors are not aware of any fact or matter that could lead to any such investigation or enquiry.

1.14 Information disclosed to Purchaser correct

1.14.1 All information given by any of the Vendors or any director of the Company, the Vendors' professional advisors or the Company's auditors to the Purchaser, the Purchaser's solicitors or the Purchaser's accountants in the course of negotiations leading to this Agreement and relating to the business, affairs, assets and liabilities of the Company was and is true, accurate and complete and not misleading and opinions, expectations and beliefs included in the information are honestly held and have been arrived at on a reasonable basis after full enquiry.[1]

1.14.2 There are no material facts or circumstances in relation to the assets, business or financial condition of the Company which

---

[1] Please see comments at para.7–30 in relation to this warranty and the alternative form of wording that well-advised vendors are likely to insist on.

have not been Disclosed and which, if Disclosed, might
reasonably have been expected to affect the decision of the
Purchaser to enter into this Agreement on the terms set out
herein.[2]

2   Accounts

2.1   The Accounts

2.1.1   The Accounts were prepared in accordance with the historical
cost convention and with the requirements of all relevant
statutes and Accounting Standards; and on the same bases and
policies of accounting as adopted for the purpose of preparing
the audited accounts of the Company in respect of the
preceding three accounting periods.

2.1.2   The Accounts:

2.1.2.1   give a true and fair view of the assets and liabilities
and state of affairs of the Company at the Balance
Sheet Date and the profits or losses [and cash flow]
of the Company for the period ended on that
date;

2.1.2.2   comply with the requirements of CA 2006;

2.1.2.3   comply with current Accounting Standards;

2.1.2.4   are not affected by extraordinary, exceptional or
non-recurring items;

2.1.2.5   fully disclose all the assets of the Company on the
Balance Sheet Date;

2.1.2.6   provide or reserve in full for all liabilities and
capital commitments of the Company outstanding
at the Balance Sheet Date, including contingent,
unquantified or disputed liabilities; and

2.1.2.7   provide or reserve, in accordance with the
principles set out in the notes included in the
Accounts, for all Taxation liable to be assessed on
the Company, or for which it may be accountable,
in respect of the period ended on the Balance Sheet
Date.

2.1.3   The amount included in the Accounts in respect of each asset,
whether fixed or current, does not exceed its purchase price or
production cost or (in the case of current assets) its net
realisable value at the Balance Sheet Date.

2.2   Valuation of stock in trade and work in progress

2.2.1   In the Accounts and in the accounts of the Company the stock
in trade and work in progress of the Company was valued at
the lowest of cost or net realisable value. Cost represents
materials and appropriate proportion of direct labour and
overheads.

2.2.2   In the Accounts slow-moving stock in trade was written down
as appropriate and redundant, obsolete, obsolescent and
defective stock was wholly written off.

---

[2] Please see comments at para.7–31 in relation to this warranty which is the infamous "sweeping-up"
warranty which is likely to be strongly resisted by the vendors.

2.2.3　In valuing work in progress in the Accounts no value was attributed in respect of eventual profit and adequate provision was made for such losses as were at the time of signature of the Accounts by the directors of the Company foreseeable as arising or likely to arise on completion and/or realisation thereof.

2.3　Depreciation of fixed assets

2.3.1　In the Accounts the fixed assets of the Company were depreciated in accordance with FRS 15.

2.4　Deferred Taxation

2.4.1　Full provision or reserve of all Taxation which has been or may be assessed or for which the Company may become accountable in respect of any act, omission or event (whether of the Company or any other person) up to and including the Balance Sheet Date and for any contingent or deferred liability provided for in the Accounts.

2.5　Accounting reference date

2.5.1　The accounting reference date of the Company is, and has always been, [　].

2.6　Management Accounts

2.6.1　The Management Accounts have been prepared [in accordance with accounting policies consistent with those used in the preparation of the Accounts,] with all due care and on a basis consistent with the management accounts of the Company prepared in the preceding [year].

2.7　Books and records

2.7.1　The accounting and other records of the Company:

2.7.1.1　are in its exclusive ownership and direct control;
2.7.1.2　have been fully, properly and accurately kept and completed;
2.7.1.3　are accurate in all material respects; and
2.7.1.4　show a true and fair view of its trading transactions and its financial, contractual and trading position.

3　Finance

3.1　Capital commitments

3.1.1　No commitments on capital account were outstanding at the Balance Sheet Date and, since then, the Company has not made, or agreed to make capital expenditure, incurred or agreed to incur capital commitments, or disposed of or agreed to dispose of capital assets (or any interest in them).

3.2　Bank and other borrowings

3.2.1　Particulars of all money borrowed by the Company are set out in the Disclosure Letter. The Company does not have any bank borrowings which exceed applicable overdraft limits (and has not had any that have done so during the last 12 months).

3.2.2　The total amount borrowed by the Company (as determined in accordance with the provisions of the relevant documents) does not exceed any limitation on borrowing powers contained in its articles of association or in a debenture or other document to which it is subject.

3.2.3 The Company does not have outstanding nor has it agreed to create or issue any loan capital nor has it factored or discounted its debts or engaged in financing of a type which would not require to be shown or fully reflected in the Accounts.

3.2.4 The Company has not since the Balance Sheet Date repaid or become liable to repay any loan or other indebtedness in advance of its stated maturity.

3.2.5 The Company has not received notice (whether formal or informal) from any lenders of money, requiring repayment or intimating the enforcement of security which it holds over assets of the Company; and there are no circumstances likely to give rise to such a notice.

3.3 Bank accounts

3.3.1 Statements of all the bank accounts of the Company, showing their balances as at a date not more than day before today's date, have been supplied to the Purchaser.

3.3.2 Since the date of each statement, there have been no payments out of the account to which the statement relates, except for payments in the normal course of business; and the balances on current accounts are not substantially different from the balances shown in the statements.

3.4 Continuation of facilities

3.4.1 The Disclosure Letter sets out full details of (and there are attached to it accurate copies of all documents relating to) all debentures, acceptance credits, loans or other financial facilities outstanding or available to the Company (referred to in this clause as the "Facilities") and of any limits or restrictions to which they are subject.

3.4.2 There has been no contravention of, or non-compliance with, the terms of the Facilities.

3.4.3 No steps for the early repayment of sums outstanding under the Facilities have been threatened or taken and no circumstances have occurred which give rise to an obligation to make, or would permit the calling for, early repayment.

3.4.4 There have not been and are no circumstances known to the Vendors whereby the continuation of any of the Facilities might be prejudiced or their terms altered.

3.4.5 None of the Facilities is dependent on the guarantee or indemnity of, or security provided by, a third party.

3.5 Debts

3.5.1 No part of the amounts included in debtors in the Accounts, or subsequently recorded in the books of the Company as owing by a debtor, is overdue by more than 90 days, or, has been released on terms that the debtor pays less than the full book value of his debt, or, has been written off, or has had a credit issued against it or has proved to be, or is regarded as, wholly or partly irrecoverable.

3.5.2 The amounts due from debtors as at Completion will be recoverable in full, in the normal course of business, and in any event not later than 60 days after Completion; and none of the debts is subject to a right of counterclaim or set-off, or withholding on other deduction except to the extent of the provision or reserve.

3.5.3 Complete and accurate details, including repayment terms and maturity dates, of loans made by the Company which remain outstanding at, and immediately after, Completion are set out in the Disclosure Letter and all the loans will be repaid in full by their maturity dates.

3.5.4 The Company has not made a loan or quasi-loan or entered into a credit transaction (as defined in CA 2006 s.202) to a director of the Company or any holding company or persons connected to such directors contrary to the Companies Acts.

3.5.5 The Company has not made a loan, which remains outstanding, on terms entitling it to receive either a rate of interest varying with, or a share of, the profits of a business.

3.6 Liabilities

3.6.1 The Company has no outstanding liabilities (including disputed or contingent liabilities) other than the liabilities disclosed in the Accounts or incurred, in the normal course of business, since the Balance Sheet Date.

3.6.2 The Company has not been at any time the tenant of, or a guarantor in respect of, a leasehold property which is not one of the Properties.

3.6.3 There has been no exercise, purported exercise or claim for any Encumbrance over any of the assets of the Company and there is no dispute directly or indirectly relating to any assets.

3.7 Working capital

3.7.1 Having regard to the Facilities (as defined in clause [3.4.1]), the Company has sufficient working capital to carry on its business, in its present form and at its present level of turnover, for 18 months after Completion and to carry out, in accordance with their terms, all outstanding commitments.

3.8 Dividends and distributions

3.8.1 Since the Balance Sheet Date, no dividend or other distribution (as defined in ICTA 1988 Pt VI and s.418) has been, or is treated as having been, declared, paid or made by the Company.

3.8.2 All dividends and distributions declared, made or paid by the Company were declared, made or paid in accordance with its articles of association and the applicable provisions of the Companies Acts and in accordance with any agreements or arrangements between the Company, its shareholders or any third party regulating the payment or declaration of dividends.

3.9 Government grants

3.9.1 No Group Company has in the last six years applied for, or received, a grant, subsidy or financial assistance from any government department or agency, or a local or other authority.

4 Trading and contracts

4.1 Changes in business activities and financial position since the Balance Sheet Date

4.1.1 Since the Balance Sheet Date:

4.1.1.1 the business of the Company has been continued in its normal course with a view to maintaining the businesses as a going concern and without entering into any transaction assuming any liability or making any payment which is not provided for in the Accounts or which is not in the normal course of its business;

4.1.1.2 there has been no deterioration in the turnover, or financial or trading position or prospects, of the Company;

4.1.1.3 the Company has not by doing, or omitting to do, anything prejudiced its goodwill;

4.1.1.4 the Company has not entered into any capital transaction as seller, purchaser, lessor or lessee or otherwise undertaken any material commitment on its capital account;

4.1.1.5 of the plant, machinery, fixtures, fittings, equipment, vehicles, furniture, property, materials and other assets (not being included in the current assets) included in the Accounts or acquired by the Company since the Balance Sheet Date:

4.1.1.5.1 none has been sold or disposed of at a figure lower than book value or an open market arm's length value whichever is the higher; and

4.1.1.5.2 none has been or has been agreed to be let on hire or hire purchase or sold on deferred terms.

4.1.1.6 the Company has paid its creditors in accordance with their respective credit terms; and there are no amounts owing by it which have been due for more than [60] [90] days.

4.1.2 The value of the net realisable assets of the Company is not less than at the Balance Sheet Date.

4.2 Vendors' other interests and liabilities

4.2.1 The Vendors and their Associates are not, directly or indirectly, interested in any business, other than that now carried on by the Company, which is or is likely to be competitive with the business of the Company, apart from interests in securities listed on the Official List of the UK Listing Authority and admitted to trading on the main market of the London Stock Exchange Plc, or dealt in on its Alternative Investment Market, and in respect of which the Vendors, with their Associates, are interested in less than three per cent of any class of the securities in that company.

4.2.2 None of the Vendors, or their Associates, is indebted to the Company.

4.3   Effect of sale of Shares

4.3.1   The Vendors are not aware, and have no grounds for believing, that after Completion (whether by reason of an existing agreement or arrangement or as a result of the acquisition of the Company by the Purchaser):

4.3.1.1   a supplier for the purposes of this warranty being a supplier that in the 12 months prior to Completion dealt with or supplied the Company of the Company will cease, or be entitled to cease, supplying it or may substantially reduce its level of supplies;

4.3.1.2   a customer for the purposes of this warranty being a customer that in the 12 months prior to Completion dealt with or was supplied with goods or services by the Company of the Company will cease, or be entitled to cease, to deal with it or may substantially reduce its level of business;

4.3.1.3   a supplier or customer (as defined in warranty 4.3.1.1 or 4.3.1.2) of the Company will seek to impose or negotiate materially different terms of trading from those currently enjoyed by the Company;

4.3.1.4   the Company will lose a right of benefit which it enjoys; or

4.3.1.5   any officer or senior employee of the Company will leave its employment.

4.3.2   Compliance with this Agreement will and the documents referred to in it will not:

4.3.2.1   breach or constitute a default under an agreement or arrangement to which the Company is a party or any undertaking or order of any court or governmental agency or regulatory body or any provision of the memorandum or articles of association of the Company, or any security interest, lease, contract or order, judgment, award, injunction, regulation or other restriction or obligation of any kind affecting the Company;

4.3.2.2   relieve any person from any obligation to the Company (whether contractual or otherwise), or enable any person to determine any such obligation or any right or benefit enjoyed by the Company, or to exercise a right in respect of the Company;

4.3.2.3   result in any present or future indebtedness of the Company becoming, or becoming capable of being declared, due and payable prior to its stated maturity or loan facilities being withdrawn;

4.3.2.4   result in the creation, imposition, crystallisation or enforcement of any Encumbrance on any of the assets of the Company; or

4.3.2.5   result in a breach of a Licence or result in losing the benefit of a Licence.

4.4   Business conducted lawfully

4.4.1   The Company has carried on business and conducted its affairs in compliance with the Companies Acts, the terms of any Licences, its memorandum and articles of association, and all other documents to which it is, or has been, a party and all other statutory obligations applicable to it.

4.4.2   The Company has the power and authority to carry on business in all jurisdictions in which it carries on business.

4.5   Joint ventures and partnerships

4.5.1   The Company is not, nor has it agreed to become, a party in or member of a joint venture, consortium, partnership or other unincorporated association or other profit or income sharing arrangement.

4.6   Agency agreements and agreements restricting business

4.6.1   The Company is not a party to an agency, distributorship, marketing, purchasing, manufacturing or licensing agreement or arrangement, or a restrictive agreement or arrangement, under which part of its business is carried on or which restricts its freedom to carry on its business as it thinks fit.

4.6.2   The Company is not subject to any order, judgment, undertaking or assurance which it has given to a court or government agency which is still in force.

4.7   Unfair trade and restrictive practices

4.7.1   The Company is not nor has it been a party to or concerned in any agreement, practice or arrangement (whether legally binding or not) which is or was:

4.7.1.1   in contravention of the Trade Descriptions Act 1968;

4.7.1.2   in contravention of the Fair Trading Act 1973 Pt XI as amended by the Trading Schemes Act 1996;

4.7.1.3   in contravention of the Consumer Credit Act 1974 (as amended);

4.7.1.4   in contravention of or invalidated (in whole or in part) by, the Competition Act 1998;

4.7.1.5   in contravention of the Enterprise Act 2002;

4.7.1.6   in contravention of [arts 101 and 102 of] the Treaty on the Functioning of the European Union; or

4.7.1.7   in contravention of any regulations, orders, notices or directions made thereunder, or otherwise registerable, unenforceable or void or renders the Company or any of its officers or employees liable to administrative, civil or criminal proceedings under any anti-trust, anti-monopoly or anti-cartel, trade regulation or similar legislation or regulation in any jurisdiction where the Company carries on business.

4.8   Litigation

4.8.1   Neither the Company nor any person for whose acts or defaults the Company is or may be vicariously liable are engaged in litigation, mediation, arbitration, administrative or criminal proceedings or other proceedings or hearings before any statutory or governmental body, department, board or agency [except for debt collection in the normal course of business]; there are no proceedings pending or threatened, either by or against the Company or such persons; and [so far as the Vendors are aware] there is nothing which is likely to give rise to such proceedings.

4.8.2 The Company is not subject to any order or judgment given by any court or governmental agency (local or national).

4.8.3 There are no claims pending or threatened or capable of arising against the Company by an employee or workman or third party in respect of any accident or injury.

4.8.4 There is no dispute with any government (local or national) or agency or body acting on behalf of such government or other authority in the United Kingdom or elsewhere in relation to the affairs of the Company and [so far as the Vendors are aware] there are no facts or circumstances which may give rise to such a dispute.

4.8.5 Neither the Company nor any current or former employee, officer or agent of the Company has been convicted of an offence in relation to the Company and [so far as the Vendors are aware] no employee or officer has been convicted of an offence that reflects upon the reputation of the Company or their suitability for holding the position that they hold in the Company.

4.9 Winding-up

4.9.1 The Company is not insolvent or unable to pay its debts within the meaning of the Insolvency Act 1986 s.123 (the references in that section to proving to the satisfaction of the court being disregarded).

4.9.2 No order has been made, petition presented or resolution passed for the winding-up of the Company; no distress, execution or other process has been levied and remains undischarged in respect of the Company; and there is no outstanding judgment or court order against the Company in connection with the same nor has any application been made for the making of an administration order or notice of intention to appoint an administrator been filed at court, or served on a creditor with the benefit of a floating charge.

4.9.3 No steps have been taken for the appointment of an administrator or administrative receiver or receiver or liquidator or provisional liquidator over the whole or any part of the Company's assets or undertaking.

4.9.4 No meeting of the Company's creditors, or any class of them, has been held or summoned and no proposal has been made for a moratorium, composition or arrangement in relation to any of the Company's debts, or for a voluntary arrangement in relation to any of its debts, or for a voluntary arrangement under Pt 1 of the Insolvency Act 1986.

4.9.5 In relation to each of the Vendors:

4.9.5.1 no statutory demand has been served or attempted to be served on any of them nor are there any grounds for believing that they are unable to pay any debts within the meaning of the Insolvency Act 1986 s.268 (as amended);

4.9.5.2 no petition has been presented and no order made for the bankruptcy of any of them or for the appointment of a receiver over any of their assets;

4.9.5.3 no Encumbrance has been enforced and no distress, execution or other process has been levied, on or over any of the Shares or any assets held by them; and

4.9.5.4 no proposal has been made in respect of an individual voluntary arrangement, or interim order applied for the purpose of making a proposal of an individual voluntary arrangement pursuant to the Insolvency Act 1986 (as amended).

4.9.6 No event analogous to those described in clauses [4.9.2] or [4.9.3 or 4.9.5] has occurred outside England.

4.9.7 No floating charge created by the Company has crystallised and there are no circumstances likely to cause such a floating charge to crystallise

4.10 Compliance with statutes

4.10.1 Neither the Company nor any of its officers, agents or employees (during the course of their duties), have done or omitted to do anything, the doing or omitting of which is, or could be, in contravention of a statute, regulation or the like giving rise to a penalty, default proceedings or other liability.

4.11 Business names

4.11.1 The Company does not make use of any name other than its corporate name.

4.12 Transactions involving directors

4.12.1 The Company has not been a party to a transaction to which CA 1985 ss.320 or 330 or CA 2006 ss.190 or 197 might apply.

4.13 Powers of attorney and authorities

4.13.1 No powers of attorney or authorities (express or implied) by which a person may enter into a contract or incur an obligation on behalf of the Company are subsisting.

4.14 Licences and consents

4.14.1 The Company has all necessary Licences required for the proper carrying on of its business in the manner in which the business is now carried on (short particulars/copies of each such licence being set out in the Disclosure Letter).

4.14.2 The Company is not in breach of any of the terms and conditions of any Licence; all Licences are effective and there is nothing that might prejudice the continuation or renewal of a Licence on the same terms as currently held.

4.14.3 The Company does not carry on investment business or regulated activities within the meaning of the Financial Services and Markets Act 2000.

4.15 Subsisting contracts

4.15.1 The Company is not party to any agreement or arrangement which:

4.15.1.1 is of an unusual nature or was entered into outside the normal course of business;

4.15.1.2   is of a long term nature (that is unlikely to have been fully performed, in accordance with its terms, within six months after the date on which was entered into);

4.15.1.3   is incapable of termination by it in accordance with its terms on not more than 60 days' notice;

4.15.1.4   is of a loss-making nature;

4.15.1.5   cannot readily be performed by it on time without undue or unusual expenditure or application of money, effort or personnel;

4.15.1.6   involves payment by it by reference to fluctuations in the index of retail prices, or other index, or in the rate of exchange for a currency;

4.15.1.7   involves an aggregated outstanding expenditure by it of more than £[   ];

4.15.1.8   involves, or is likely to involve, the supply of goods or services the aggregate sales value of which will be more than 10 per cent of its turnover for the preceding financial year;

4.15.1.9   is a contract for hire or rent, hire purchase or purchase by way of credit sale or periodical payment;

4.15.1.10 can be terminated as a result of a change in the control of the Company; or

4.15.1.11 involves, or is likely to involve, other obligations or liabilities which ought reasonably to be made known to an intending purchaser of the Shares.

4.15.2   The Company has made all payments due under all contracts to which it is a party and observed and performed all conditions thereof.

4.16   Breach of contract

4.16.1   No party to an agreement with the Company is in default, being a default which would be material in the context of the Company's financial or trading position; and there are no circumstances likely to give rise to a default.

4.16.2   The Company is not, nor will it with the lapse of time become, in default of any obligation and no threat or claim of default under any agreement, instrument or arrangement to which it is a party has been made and there is nothing whereby any such agreement, instrument or arrangement may be prematurely terminated or rescinded by another party or whereby the terms may be worsened to the Company's detriment.

4.17   Outstanding offers

4.17.1   No offer or tender is outstanding which is capable of being converted into an obligation of the Company by acceptance or some other act of another person.

4.18   Defective products

4.18.1   The Company has not manufactured, sold or supplied products which were, are or will become, in a material respect faulty or defective, or which did or do not comply in a material respect with warranties or representations expressly or impliedly made by it or all applicable regulations, standards and requirements in respect thereof.

4.18.2 The Company has not received notification that any products supplied by it are defective or unfit and no circumstances exist which could give rise to such a claim.

4.18.3 The Company has not received a prohibition notice, a notice to warn or a suspension notice under the Consumer Protection Act 1987.

4.19 Service and product warranty liabilities

4.19.1 The Company is not obliged (save as implied by law) to repair, maintain, take back or otherwise do or not do anything in respect of goods that have been, or will be, delivered by it.

4.20 Purchases and sales from or to one party

4.20.1 The Company does not obtain or make more than [25 per cent] of the aggregate amount of its purchases from, and not more than [25 per cent] of the aggregate amount of its sales to, the same supplier or customer (including a person connected with the supplier or customer); and no material source of supply to the Company, or material outlet for the sales of a the Company, is in jeopardy.

4.20.2 During the six months preceding the date of this Agreement there has been no substantial change in the basis or terms on which any person (including any supplier) is prepared to enter into contracts to do business with the Company (apart from normal price changes) and no such change is likely.

4.20.3 No person who is, or who has during the last two years been, a substantial customer or supplier of goods or services to the Company has ceased, or has threatened or indicated an intention to cease trading with or supplying the Company or has reduced, or is likely to reduce, substantially its trading with or supply to the Company.

4.20.4 The loss of any single supplier to or customer of the Company would not have a material effect on its business, and during the financial year ended on the Balance Sheet Date or in the period since then not more than [10 per cent] of the goods purchased by the Company were derived from the same supplier, and not more than [10 per cent] of the goods sold by the Company were purchased by the same customer and for the purpose of this paragraph groups of companies shall be deemed a single person.

4.21 Data protection

4.21.1 The Company has, if so required by law, a current entry in the register maintained by the Information Commissioner under the Data Protection Act 1998 which complies with the requirements of that Act, and particulars of the entry are set out in the Disclosure Letter.

4.21.2 The Company has complied with the data protection principles applicable to all the processing of personal data carried out by it and collected, processed and disclosed personal data only in accordance with the terms of a privacy policy, which is attached to the Disclosure Letter.

4.21.3 The Company has not been served with a warrant under Sch.9 of the Data Protection Act 1998 nor has the Company received any statutory notice from the Information Commissioner.

4.21.4 The Company has taken measures to ensure personal data are adequate, relevant, not excessive and not kept longer than necessary in relation to the purpose for which they are processed, that they are accurate and where necessary, kept up to date. The Company's data retention policy is attached to the Disclosure Letter.

4.21.5 The Company has taken technical and organisational measures to ensure compliance with the seventh data protection principle in relation to the processing of personal data in manual and in computerised systems (including portable devices) and has taken steps to ensure the reliability of its employees that have access to personal data. The Company has not suffered a security breach that required notification to the Information Commissioner in accordance with the Information Commissioner's guidance.

4.21.6 Where the Company uses a data processor to carry out the processing of personal data, the processor has provided sufficient guarantees in relation to security measures and compliance with those measures and there is in existence a written contract between the Company and the data processor which complies with the requirements of Sch.1, Pt II, paras 11–12 of the Data Protection Act 1998.

4.21.7 The Company does not transfer personal data to jurisdictions outside the European Economic Area.

4.21.8 No individual has claimed or taken, or has a right to claim compensation or take action for breach of his rights under the Data Protection Act 1998, against the Company. The Company has not received any notice, letter or complaint alleging a breach of the Data Protection Act 1998.

4.21.9 The Company has complied with the Privacy and Electronic Communications (EC Directive) Regulations 2003 in respect of all electronic forms of direct marketing carried out by the Company or on its behalf.

4.21.10 The Company has complied with all other requirements of the Data Protection Act 1998 and all subordinate legislation, guidance and codes of practice.

4.22 Guarantees and indemnities

4.22.1 There is no subsisting guarantee or agreement for indemnity or suretyship given by [the Company as security for the obligations of a third party], or [given by a third party] for the accommodation of, the Company.

4.23 Connected persons contracts

4.23.1 The Company is not, nor has it during the past three years been, a party to an agreement or arrangement (whether legally binding or not) in which a Vendor, or Associate of a Vendor, or director of the Company, or Associate of a director of the Company, is or has been interested.

4.23.2 The Company is not a party to, and its profits and financial position during the past three years have not been affected by, an agreement or arrangement (whether legally binding or not) which is not of an arms' length nature.

4.23.3 None of the Company's assets have been acquired for a consideration other than market value (at the time of acquisition).

4.24   Anti-corruption

4.24.1   No officer or employee [so far as the Vendors are aware (but without having made any actual enquiry of any employee)] has made or received any Sensitive Payment in connection with any contract or otherwise.[3]

4.24.2   [[So far as the Vendors are aware] neither the Company nor any of its officers or employees is or has at any time engaged in any activity, practice or conduct which would constitute an offence under BA 2010 ss.1, 2 and 6.[4]

4.24.3   No Associated Person of the Company has bribed another person (within the meaning given in BA 2010 s.7(3)) intending to obtain or retain business or obtain or retain an advantage in the conduct of business for the Company.

4.24.4   The Company has in place adequate procedures designed to prevent their Associated Persons from bribing another person for the purposes of BA 2010 s.7(3), copies of the Company's anti-corruption policies and procedures are attached to the Disclosure Letter ("Anti-corruption Policies") together with full details of the steps taken to review compliance by the Company and all Associated Persons to the Anti-corruption Policies.

4.24.5   Neither the Company nor any of its Associated Persons is or has been the subject of any investigation, inquiry or enforcement proceedings by any governmental, administrative or regulatory body or any customer regarding any offence or alleged offence under the BA 2010 or any anti-bribery or anti-corruption legislation in any other jurisdictions in which the Company operates, and no such investigation, inquiry or proceedings have been threatened or are pending and there are no circumstances likely to give rise to any such investigation, inquiry or proceedings.]

4.25   Consultants' reports

4.25.1   No financial or management consultants have, within the past three years, given a report in relation to the Company.

5   Environmental

5.1   Required permits

5.1.1   The Company has obtained all Environmental Permits which it requires and has complied with all applicable Environmental Laws and with the terms and conditions of the Environmental Permits and there is no reason why the Environmental Permits should not continue to be complied with by the Company if the Company is operated in the same manner and scope after Completion as it was prior to Completion. True, complete and accurate copies of such Environmental Permits are attached to the Disclosure Letter.

---

[3] Warranty 4.24.1 should be deleted with effect from the implementation of the BA 2010.
[4] Warranties 4.24.2 to 4.24.5 should be included with effect from the implementation of the BA 2010.

5.2   Breaches

5.2.1   The Company has not received notification or communication from which it appears it is, or may be alleged to be, in violation of any Environmental Laws or Environmental Permits or that any Environmental Permits may be subject to modification, suspension, revocation or appeal and there are no circumstances likely to give rise to violation, modification, suspension, revocation or appeal of any Environmental Permits.

5.3   Audits and surveys

5.3.1   The Disclosure Letter contains copies of all environmental audits and surveys that the Company has commissioned or that have been addressed to it in relation to the Properties or land previously owned or occupied by it.

5.4   Prosecutions

5.4.1   The Company has not been prosecuted or the subject of any Civil Sanction or notified of a possible prosecution or possible Civil Sanction for a breach of any Environmental Laws.

5.5   No claims

5.5.1   No Environmental Claims exist against the Company or have been made within the previous [   ] years and there are no circumstances which may lead to a claim.

5.6   Hazardous Substances

5.6.1   Neither the Company nor any other person has deposited, used, treated, kept, disposed of, released or emitted any Hazardous Substances at, on, from or under any of the Properties now or previously owned, leased, occupied or controlled by the Company.

5.7   Work carried out under notices

5.7.1   No notices under Environmental Laws have been served against the Company and no work has been carried out under such a notice by a regulatory body whereby the Company must reimburse the regulatory body for the costs of the work carried out.

5.8   Prior use

5.8.1   So far as the Vendors are aware there has not been any potentially contaminative use that has been made of any of the Properties or any land previously owned or occupied by the Company.

6   Employment

6.1   Employees, terms of employment and status

6.1.1   The Disclosure Letter contains anonymised accurate and complete details of the dates of birth, dates of commencement of employment or appointment to office, and terms of employment or appointment of all the employees and officers of the Company, including details of all remuneration (including pensions, whether to be delivered by occupational or personal schemes) and other benefits, such as profit sharing, commission and bonus arrangements (whether or not contractual), sufficient to allow the financial obligations of the Company to be ascertained.

6.1.2 There is no contract of service between the Company and a director or employee for which approval was required but not obtained under or CA 2006 s.188.

6.1.3 There are no contracts for services (including without limitation consultancy agreements) between the Company and any individual.

6.1.4 No employee of the Company who has or may have a statutory or contractual right to return to work, is absent on maternity leave, paternity leave, parental leave, adoption leave [or other leave of absence]. No employee of the Company is absent on sick leave which has lasted or is expected to last longer than four weeks.

6.1.5 No employee or former employee of the Company has or may have a right to be reinstated or re-engaged under the Employment Rights Act 1996.

6.1.6 All of the Company's employees (and other persons engaged by the Company) are legally entitled to work in the United Kingdom, the Company having complied in all respects with the requirements of the Asylum and Immigration Act 1996 and The Immigration, Asylum and Nationality Act 2006.

6.2 Claims and potential employee claims

6.2.1 There are no outstanding claims nor are there any potential claims against the Company by any person who is now or has been an officer or employee of the Company and no liability has been incurred and remains undischarged for breach of any employment contract or for a redundancy payment or a protective award or for damages or compensation for wrongful dismissal or unfair dismissal or otherwise or for failure to comply with any order for the reinstatement or re-engagement of any person remains.

6.2.2 There have not within the period of 12 months prior to the date of this Agreement been any claims under the provisions of the Employment Rights Act 1996, the Trade Union Reform and Employment Act 1993, the Health and Safety at Work etc. Act 1974, the Equal Pay Act 1970, the Sex Discrimination Act 1975, the Disability Discrimination Act 1995, the Race Relations Act 1976, the Sex Discrimination (Gender Reassignment) Regulations 1999, the Transfer of Undertakings (Protection of Employment) Regulations 2006, the Trade Union and Labour Relations (Consolidation) Act 1992, the Protection from Harassment Act 1997, the Working Time Regulations 1998, the National Minimum Wage Act 1998, the Employment Relations Act 1999, the Part-Time Workers (Prevention of Less Favourable Treatment) Regulations 2000, the Fixed-Term Employees (Prevention of Less Favourable Treatment) Regulations 2002, the Employment Act 2002, the Employment Equality (Religion or Belief) Regulations 2003, the Employment Equality (Sexual Orientation) Regulations 2003 or the Employment Equality (Age) Regulations 2006 or the Equality Act 2010 relating to any employee or former employee of the Company nor are there any circumstances which are likely to give rise to such claims.[5]

6.2.3 None of the offices or employees of the Company have raised any grievance or have been issued with any disciplinary warning which remains current and there are no disciplinary proceedings pending or contemplated in respect of any such person.

6.2.4 The Company has performed all obligations required to be performed by it in respect of its officers and employees whether arising under contract, statute, at common law or in equity including, without limitation under the Working Time Regulations 1998 and under all health and safety legislation.

6.2.5 The Company has maintained adequate, suitable and up to date records in relation to each of its employees.

6.2.6 The Company has paid to the Taxation Authority all Taxation due in respect of the employment of the employees of the Company.

6.2.7 There are no enquiries or investigations existing, pending or threatened in relation to the Company by the Commission for Equality and Human Rights, the Health and Safety Executive or any similar body.

6.3 Changes in remuneration

6.3.1 During the period to which the Accounts relate and since the Balance Sheet Date or (where employment or holding of office commenced after the beginning of the period) since the commencement date of the employment or holding of office:

6.3.1.1 no change has been made in the rate of remuneration, or the emoluments of employment or pension benefits, of any officer, ex-officer or senior employee of the Company (a senior employee being a person in receipt of remuneration in excess of £[ ] per annum); and

6.3.1.2 no change has been made in the other terms of employment of any officer or senior employee.

6.3.2 No agreement has been reached with any officers, employees, trade union or other body representing employees that will or may on a future date result in any changes to the terms and conditions of employment of any of the officers or employees of the Company (including without limitation for any increase in the remuneration or enhancement of the emoluments of employment or pension benefits of such persons); and no negotiation relating to the terms and conditions of employment of any officer or employee of the Company (including without limitation for any increase in the rate of remuneration or enhancement of the emoluments of employment or pension benefits of such persons) are current or likely to take place within the next six months.

---

[5] See the discussion of this warranty in relation to the introduction of the Equality Act 2010 at para.7–173.

6.4   Bonus and share option schemes

6.4.1   There are no schemes (whether contractual or discretionary) in operation by or in relation to the Company under which any employee or director of the Company is entitled to any shares in the Company or to any bonus, profit share, commission or remuneration of any other sort (whether calculated by reference to the whole or part of the turnover, profits/losses or sales of the Company or otherwise).

6.4.2   The Company is not under any legal or moral obligation to make nor is it accustomed to making any bonus payments to or for the benefit of any officer or employee of the Company.

6.5   Termination of contracts of employment

6.5.1   All subsisting employment contracts to which the Company is a party are determinable at any time on three months' notice or less without compensation (other than compensation for unfair dismissal in accordance with the Employment Rights Act 1996).

6.5.2   No employee of the Company [who is in receipt of remuneration in excess of £[   ] per annum], and no officer of the Company has given or received notice terminating his employment, except as expressly contemplated in this Agreement and no such employee or officer will be entitled or is likely to leave his employment or office prematurely, nor to receive any payment from the Company as a result of the sale of the Shares.

6.6   Industrial relations

6.6.1   The Company does not recognise any trade unions, works or staff councils or associates of trade unions and there are no collective agreements or other agreements (whether or not legally binding and whether in writing or arising by virtue of custom or practice) between the Company and any trade union or other body representing employees.

6.6.2   The Company has not done anything which might be construed as recognition of a trade union and has not received an application for recognition from a trade union.

6.6.3   Neither the Company nor any of its employees is or has been in the last two years involved in an industrial dispute and so far as the Vendors are aware there is nothing which might suggest that there may be an industrial dispute involving the Company, or that this Agreement may give rise to such a dispute.

6.6.4   The Company has not received any request for an information and consultation agreement pursuant to the Information and Consultation of Employees Regulations 2004 and the Company is not party to any negotiations for such an agreement.

6.7   Redundancies

6.7.1   No employee of the Company will become redundant and be entitled to a redundancy payment as a result of this Agreement.

6.7.2   There is no plan, scheme or commitment or established practice relating to the termination of employment affecting an employee or officer of the Company which is more generous than the statutory redundancy entitlement or such sum as may be properly payable by way of damages for breach of contract.

7 Pensions

7.1 No other pension arrangements

7.1.1 Save in respect of the Scheme, the Company has no legal obligation to provide or cause to be provided to any person benefits:

7.1.1.1 under a "pension scheme", as defined by s.150(1) of the FA 2004; or

7.1.1.2 under an "employer-financed retirement benefits scheme", as defined by s.393B of the IT(EP)A 2003; or

7.1.1.3 under a superannuation fund to which s.15(3) of the ICTA 1988 applies;

7.1.1.4 that are "retirement or death benefits" for the purposes of s.307 of the IT(EP)A 2003 and do not fall under the categories referred to in cll.7.1.1.1–7.1.1.3 above; or

7.1.1.5 that are "excluded benefits" for the purposes of s.393B of the IT(EP)A 2003 and do not fall under the categories above.

7.2 Other Company liabilities

7.2.1 The Company is not subject to a contribution notice or a financial support direction or similar notice, order or direction under the Pensions Act 2004 nor [so far as the Vendors are aware] are there any circumstances which are likely to lead to such notices, orders or directions being imposed upon the Company.

7.2.2 The Company has not entered into any agreement with either the trustees or the administrators of any pension arrangement or with any member of the same or any of its past or present employees or with any other party including any regulatory authority in respect of any potential or actual pension-related liability.

7.2.3 The Company has not entered into any agreement with any party to fund, indemnify or guarantee any potential or actual pension-related liability.

7.3 Additional member's rights

7.3.1 No employee has at any time transferred to the Company under the provisions of the Transfer of Undertakings (Protection of Employment) Regulations 1981 or the Transfer of Undertakings (Protection of Employment) Regulations 2006.

7.3.2 If any such employee has transferred there are no circumstances in which such employee may have retained any pension rights from previous employment that do not fall within the categories of benefits relating to old age, survivorship or ill health and which have not been fully and appropriately provided for under the Company's pension arrangements.

7.4   Stakeholder compliance

7.4.1   The Company has at all times complied with all the
requirements of s.3 of the Welfare Reform and Pensions Act
1999 in relation to the duty of employers to facilitate access to
stakeholder pension schemes.

7.5   Full and accurate particulars

7.5.1   Full, accurate and up to date particulars of the Scheme are set
out in the Disclosure Letter, including (without limitation):

7.5.1.1   all constitutional documents in relation to the
Scheme including, where applicable, the trust
deeds and rules together with any amendments and
any related agreements;

7.5.1.2   all explanatory literature including, where
applicable, booklets currently in force and any
subsequent communications to members or
employees who are or may become members of
the Scheme;

7.5.1.3   evidence that the Scheme was an exempt approved
scheme for the purposes of ICTA prior to April 6,
2006 and is a Registered Pension Scheme for the
purposes of s.153 of the FA 2004 and have been
registered with the Pensions Regulator for the
purposes of s.59 of the Pensions Act 2004;

7.5.1.4   details of all active, deferred, pensioner and
prospective members (including dates of birth, sex,
age at joining the Scheme, and current pensionable
pay, and name of employer);

7.5.1.5   details of all employee and all employer
contributions in the last five years (including any
statutory   schedules   of   contributions   or
payments);

7.5.1.6   any insurance policies, schedules and certificates
and details of all premiums paid in the last five
years;

7.5.1.7   any correspondence with the Pensions Advisory
Service or with regulatory authorities including,
without limitation, the Occupational Pensions
Regulatory Authority ("OPRA"), the Pensions
Regulator,   the   Pensions   Ombudsman,   the
Financial Services Authority or the Board of the
Pension Protection Fund in relation to the
Scheme;

7.5.1.8   details of all contracting-out certificates (including
any schedules thereto) issued to the Company
relating to the Scheme;

7.5.1.9   all letters or agreements for the appointment of
professional advisers pursuant to s.47 of the
Pensions Act 1995 and all agreements with
persons providing services of any nature in
connection with the Scheme including, without
limitation, administration and data processing
services;

7.5.1.10   details of arrangements for the selection of
trustees or directors of a trustee company in

accordance with s.241 or s.242 of the Pensions Act 2004, including copies of any notices to members;

7.5.1.11 details of all past and present participating employers and copies of any compromise, apportionment or withdrawal agreements;

7.5.1.12 the latest actuarial valuation together with any subsequent correspondence with the Scheme's actuary, accounts and annual trustee report which together give a true and fair view of the state and method of funding of the Scheme and do not contain any material errors or omissions;

7.5.1.13 the statement of funding principles, the statement of investment principles and all investment agreements; and

7.5.1.14 the FRS17 or IAS19 disclosures in the Company's accounts for the last five years.

7.6 Member details

7.6.1 The membership data in respect of the Scheme is complete, accurate and up to date in all material respects and is stored safely.

7.7 Taxation and Status

7.7.1 The Scheme was an exempt approved scheme between the date of establishment of the Scheme and April 5, 2006 inclusive, within the meaning of Ch.I of Pt XIV of ICTA 1988 (as was in force from time to time) and is, since April 6, 2006, a Registered Pension Scheme for the purposes of s.153 of the FA 2004 and have also been registered with the Pensions Regulator for the purposes of s.59 of the Pensions Act 2004 and there is no reason why such exempt approved status or registered status may be lost or withdrawn.

7.8 Proposed amendments to the Scheme

7.8.1 No proposal has been announced by the Company either:

7.8.1.1 to modify, amend, alter or improve the Scheme that does not form part of the Scheme's constitutional documents as at Completion; or

7.8.1.2 regarding the continuation of the Scheme, or its closure to new members, or its closure to new benefit accruals, or its discontinuance or winding-up.

7.8.2 Since the Balance Sheet Date the Scheme has not been modified, amended, altered or improved and no closure to new members, cessation or accruals or commencement of winding-up in relation to the Scheme has been prepared or commenced.

7.9 Trustees

7.9.1 The trustees of the Scheme have all been properly appointed and have at all times administered the Scheme properly and in accordance with all relevant laws and regulations.

7.9.2 The persons named in the Disclosure Letter as the trustees of the Scheme are all its present trustees and not less than one third of the trustees are member-nominated trustees (or member-nominated directors of a corporate trustee) appointed in accordance with either s.241 or s.242 of the Pensions Act 2004 and regulations made thereunder.

7.10 Appointments

7.10.1 The trustees of the Scheme have made written appointments of an auditor, an actuary, a fund manager, a legal adviser and any other professional adviser whose appointment is required to be made under s.47 of the Pensions Act 1995 and they do not rely upon the advice of an adviser not so appointed by them in relation to the Scheme.

7.11 No disputes

7.11.1 No claim or investigation has been threatened or made against the Company or the trustees or administrators of the Scheme (other than routine claims for benefits) or against any other person whom the Company is or the said trustees or administrators are or may be liable to pay, indemnify or compensate in respect of any matter arising out of or in connection with the Scheme, nor are there any circumstances which may give rise to any such claim; and

7.11.2 No civil or criminal penalty, fine or sanction has been imposed on the Company or on the trustees or administrators of the Scheme in relation to the Scheme and there are no circumstances which might give rise to any such penalty.

7.12 Scheme operated properly

7.12.1 The Scheme has been operated at all times in accordance with all applicable laws, regulations and requirements of any competent governmental body or regulatory authority and its governing documentation and any notifiable events and material breaches of the law have been appropriately notified to the Pensions Regulator or the appropriate regulatory authority, or if not material, all breaches of the law have been appropriately recorded and rectified.

7.13 Contracting out

7.13.1 Where the Scheme is contracted out a fully up to date and correct contracting-out certificate (including schedules thereto) has been properly obtained and maintained.

7.14 Non discrimination

7.14.1 No discrimination on ground of sex, disability, marital status, hours of work, fixed-term or temporary agency workers, sexual orientation, religion or belief is, or has at any stage been, made in the provision of pension, lump sum, death, ill-health, disability or accident benefits by the trustees or administrators of the Scheme or by the Company.

7.15 Insurance

7.15.1 All lump sums held in relation to the Scheme (other than normal pension benefits) are securely and fully insured with a reputable insurance company and all premiums due in respect of such insurance has been paid.

7.16 Fees and charges

7.16.1 All actuarial, consultancy, legal and other charges and fees in respect of the Scheme, whether payable by the Company or by the trustees or administrators of the Scheme, have been paid and no services have been rendered in respect of the Scheme in relation to which an account or other invoice has not been rendered.

7.17 Employer related investments

7.17.1 The assets of the Scheme are held securely and do not include employer-related investments (as defined in s.40 of the Pensions Act 1995).

7.18 Scheme surpluses and refunds

7.18.1 No refunds of surplus have been made to and no contribution holidays have been taken for the benefit of the Company or any other person in relation to the Scheme.

7.19 Discretions and powers

7.19.1 No discretion or power has been exercised under the Scheme in respect of a member (whether active, deferred or a pensioner) (or a beneficiary claiming through or under a member) to augment any of the benefits provided by the Scheme; admit to membership of the Scheme a director or employee who would not otherwise have been eligible for admission to membership; provide in respect of a member a benefit which would not otherwise be provided under the Scheme in respect of the member or pay a contribution to it which would not otherwise have been paid.

7.19.2 No undertaking, assurance or intimation has been given to any person pursuant to which such a discretion or power will or may be exercised.

7.20 Contributions paid

7.20.1 All contributions payable by the Company and every other participating employer in accordance with the terms of the Scheme or under the relevant contractual obligations to the employees in order to secure or provide for the benefits for and in respect of members (including pensioners, deferred members and other persons prospectively or contingently entitled to benefit under it) have been duly paid to the Scheme in good time and to the proper parties who should receive them.

7.21 Benefits payable

7.21.1 The benefits payable under the Scheme consist exclusively of money-purchase benefits as defined in s.152(4) of the FA 2004 and no assurance, promise or guarantee (whether oral or written) has been made or given to any employee of any particular level or amount of benefits (other than insured lump sum death in service benefits) to be provided for or in respect of him or her under the Scheme on retirement, death or leaving service.

7.22 Assets sufficient

7.22.1 The assets, investments and insurance policies held by the trustees or administrators of the Scheme are sufficient to satisfy the liabilities and obligations (both actual and contingent) of the Scheme as at Completion [on the basis or bases adopted in the latest actuarial valuation of the Scheme] [on the basis of purchase of deferred annuity policies on a full buy-out basis].

7.23 Debts arising

7.23.1   No debt on the employer obligations have arisen on the Company (nor are there any circumstances likely to create the conditions under which such obligations will arise) under s.75 of the Pensions Act 1995 or under s.222 of the Pensions Act 2004.

7.24 Bulk transfers

7.24.1   There are no individual or bulk payments due to the trustees or administrators of the Scheme which have not, at Completion been received by the trustees or administrators of the Scheme.

8 Assets

8.1 Ownership of assets

8.1.1   All assets included in the Accounts or acquired by the Company since the Accounts Date and all assets owned by the Company are:

8.1.1.1   legally and beneficially owned by the Company free from any Encumbrance;

8.1.1.2   in the possession or under the exclusive control of the Company;

8.1.1.3   situated in the United Kingdom; and

8.1.1.4   where subject to a requirement for a Licence, duly licensed or registered in the sole name of the Company.

8.2 Assets sufficient for the business

8.2.1   The assets owned by the Company, together with the Intellectual Property Rights owned or validly licensed to and assets held under the hire purchase, leasing and rental agreements in each case listed in the Disclosure Letter, comprise all assets necessary for the continuation of its business as now carried on, and no assets are shared with another person.

8.3 Stocks and work in progress

8.3.1   The stocks of raw materials, packaging materials and finished goods held by the Company are not excessive and are adequate in relation to its current trading requirements and, save where written down or provided for, none of such stock is obsolete, slow moving, unusable, in poor condition, defective, unmarketable or inappropriate or of limited value in relation to the current business of the Company.

8.3.2   The work in progress of the Company is adequate to maintain cash flow and profitability at a level not less than as Disclosed.

8.3.3   The stock in trade of the Company is in good condition and is capable of being sold by it in the normal course of its business in accordance with its current price list, without rebate or allowance to a purchaser.

8.4   Insurance

8.4.1   All the assets of the Company of an insurable nature are, and have at all material times been, insured in amounts representing their full replacement or reinstatement value against fire and other risks normally insured against by persons carrying on similar businesses or owning property of a similar nature.

8.4.2   The Company is, and has at all material times been, adequately insured against accident, damage, third party loss (including product liability), loss of profits and other risks normally insured against by persons carrying on the same type of business as that carried on by it.

8.4.3   Nothing has been done or omitted or has occurred which could make a policy of insurance taken out by the Company void or voidable or which is likely to result in an increase in premium.

8.4.4   None of the insurance policies is subject to special or unusual terms or restrictions or to the payment of a premium in excess of the normal rate.

8.4.5   No claim is outstanding, threatened or may be made, under any of the policies and no circumstances exist which could give rise to a claim.

8.5   Leased assets

8.5.1   The Company is not a party to or liable under a lease or hire, hire purchase, credit sale or conditional sale agreement. Nothing has occurred or is likely to occur in relation to an asset held by the Company, under a lease or similar agreement, whereby the rental payable has been, or is likely to be, increased.

8.6   Plant in working order

8.6.1   The plant, machinery, vehicles and other equipment used in connection with the business of the Company:

8.6.1.1   are in a good and safe state of repair and satisfactory working order and have been properly serviced and maintained;

8.6.1.2   are not surplus to requirements;

8.6.1.3   are in the possession and control of, and are the absolute unencumbered property of, the Company, except for those items the subject of the hire purchase, leasing or rental agreements listed in the Disclosure Letter, and in respect of each of which the outstanding payments do not exceed £[   ]; and

8.6.1.4   are not expected to require replacements or additions at a cost in excess of £[   ] within the next six months.

8.6.2   There are maintenance contracts with independent specialist contractors in respect of all assets of the Company for which it is normal or prudent to have maintenance agreements and in respect of all assets which the Company is obliged to maintain or repair under a lease or similar agreement.

8.7 Assets register

8.7.1 The asset register of the Company attached to this Disclosure Letter comprise a true, complete and accurate record of all plant, machinery, equipment and vehicles owned, held or used by the Company.

8.8 Intellectual Property Rights

8.8.1 Full details of all Intellectual Property Rights owned by the Company are set out in the Disclosure Letter and are complete and accurate. The Intellectual Property Rights are:

8.8.1.1 used exclusively in the business of the Company;

8.8.1.2 legally and beneficially owned by the Company and not held jointly or in common with any other person;

8.8.1.3 valid, subsisting and enforceable, and nothing has been done or omitted to be done by which they may cease to be valid and enforceable;

8.8.1.4 not subject to infringement, challenge, opposition or attack or the subject of any claim for ownership or compensation by any third party or competent authority and the Vendors know of no reason why any of them may be subject to challenge, opposition or attack or claim; and

8.8.1.5 where capable of registration are registered in the name of the Company in all jurisdictions relevant to its business.

8.8.2 The renewal and registration fees for the protection of the registered Intellectual Property Rights have been paid [and all other steps required for their prosecution, maintenance and protection have been taken].

8.8.3 The Vendors are not aware of any factors which would cause any applications for registration of any Intellectual Property Rights to be unacceptable to any body to whom the application is being made.

8.8.4 Copies of the licences of Intellectual Property Rights owned by third parties which have been granted to the Company are attached to the Disclosure Letter. The Company is not in breach of any of the licences and the Vendors are not aware of and have no reason to believe that there is cause for a licence to come to an end or be restricted.

8.8.5 Copies of the licences of Intellectual Property Rights owned by the Company which have been granted to third parties are attached to the Disclosure Letter. The Company is not in breach of any of the licences and the Vendors are not aware and have no reason to believe that there is cause for a licence to come to an end or be restricted.

8.8.6 The Intellectual Property Rights referred to in clause [8.8.1] and detailed in the Disclosure Letter and the third party Intellectual Property Rights referred to in clause [8.8.4] are all the Intellectual Property Rights necessary for the Company to carry on its business and the Company has not charged or encumbered or created any equity, lien or other adverse interest over any of them or agreed to grant an option, right, licence, sub-licence or other adverse right over any of them to any other person and is not obliged to do the same.

8.8.7 None of the activities of the Company, its products, business methods, processes or services infringe third party Intellectual Property Rights. In the past six years the Company has not been a party or received a threat of litigation or a claim relating to Intellectual Property Rights or passing off. The Vendors are not aware and have no reason to believe that a third party is infringing the Intellectual Property Rights of the Company or that the Company has acquiesced to an infringement.

8.8.8 No licences of Intellectual Property Rights will terminate or become capable of termination or otherwise be adversely affected by this Agreement.

8.8.9 There are no pending or outstanding claims against the Company for compensation under the Patents Act 1977 s.40.

8.8.10 The Confidential Business Information which has been developed by or acquired by the Company has been kept secret and has not been disclosed to or used by another person except under obligations of confidentiality. The Vendors are not aware and have no reason to believe that a third party is in breach of any confidentiality obligations.

8.8.11 The Company is not a party to a secrecy agreement or other agreement or arrangement which restricts the use or disclosure of confidential information.

8.8.12 All moral rights in respect of the Intellectual Property Rights have been waived in favour of the Company.

8.9 Computer Systems

8.9.1 The Computer Systems:

8.9.1.1 are used exclusively by the Company and under its sole control;

8.9.1.2 are, in respect of the hardware, handheld devices, firmware, peripherals, networking and other equipment comprised in those Computer Systems, legally and beneficially owned by the Company;

8.9.1.3 are in full working order and performing the functions for which they were acquired efficiently and without material errors or downtime;

8.9.1.4 have not, within the two years immediately preceding Completion, unduly interrupted or hindered the operation of the business of the Company;

8.9.1.5 have adequate capacity for the Company's present and (taking into account the extent to which the Computer Systems are expandable) future needs;

8.9.1.6 have been satisfactorily and appropriately maintained and supported and have the benefit of appropriate maintenance and support agreements (copies of which are attached to the Disclosure Letter), which agreements include emergency support;

8.9.1.7 have not been used in such a way as would invalidate any manufacturer's or supplier's guarantee or warranty or entitle the provider of maintenance or support for the Computer Systems to exclude, suspend or terminate those services;

8.9.1.8 have, in conjunction with the support and maintenance agreements referred to in clause [8.8.1.6], adequate security measures, back-up systems, disaster recovery arrangements, measures to protect them from viruses and other harmful code and trained personnel to ensure that so far as reasonably practicable:

8.9.1.8.1 the authenticity, integrity and confidentiality of all data held by or transmitted by the Computer Systems are preserved;

8.9.1.8.2 no more than one day's data would be lost in the event of a failure of the Computer Systems;

8.9.1.8.3 breaches of security, errors and breakdowns are kept to a minimum and that in the event of the occurrence of any such event there will not be a material disruption to the Company;

8.9.1.9 enable all records and data stored by electronic means which relate to the Company to be readily accessible by appropriate personnel; and

8.9.1.10 will correctly carry out all calculations relating to or in connection with the Euro and display all symbols adopted by any government or European body in connection with the Euro.

8.9.2 All software used or stored or resident in the Company:

8.9.2.1 is free from any defect or feature which may adversely affect its performance [or the performance of any other software in the future];

8.9.2.2 performs in accordance with its specification;

8.9.2.3 has been (if copied) lawfully copied;

8.9.2.4 is lawfully held and does not infringe the Intellectual Property of any person;

8.9.2.5 as to the copyright therein:

8.9.2.5.1 in the case of software written or commissioned by the Company, is owned solely by the Company, no other person has rights therein or rights to use or make copies of the software or source codes;

8.9.2.5.2 in the case of standard packaged software purchased outright, is validly licensed to the Company in perpetuity (other than in the event of breach or insolvency) on written terms which do not require the Company to make any further payments, and no licences will terminate on change of control; and

8.9.2.5.3 in the case of all other software, is licensed to the Company on the terms of a written licence which requires payment by the Company of a fixed annual licence fee the terms of which are set out in the Disclosure Letter.

8.9.3   No software owned by or licensed to the Company is licensed or sub-licensed by the Company to (or otherwise used by) any other person.

8.9.4   No action will be necessary to enable the Company to continue to use any software currently used by it to the same extent and in the same manner as it has been used prior to the Completion.

8.9.5   The terms of all software licences have been complied with and no notices of breach or termination have been served on the Company in respect of any such licence.

8.9.6   Details of all Company domain names and websites are set out in the Disclosure Letter. The Company is the registrant and beneficial owner of those domain names and is the legal and beneficial owner of all Intellectual Property in the websites.

8.9.7   Details of all Social Media are set out in the Disclosure Letter. The Company's use complies with each Social Media provider's terms.

8.9.8   All websites operated by the Company comply with the Electronic Commerce (EC Directive) Regulations 2002 and, if the Company sells online to consumers, the Consumer Protection (Distance Selling) Regulations 2000. Each website is accessible in compliance with the requirements set out in Pt III of the Disability Discrimination Act 1995 (as amended or superseded).

8.10   Money Laundering

8.10.1 The Company's assets do not include any Criminal Property and neither the Company nor any of its directors or officers have committed any offence pursuant to the Proceeds of Crime Act 2002 s.327.

APPENDIX 5

Warranties and Indemnities on the Sale of a Business

[See paras 8–03, 8–05, 8–12, 8–15, 8–16, 8–17, 8–30 and 8–31]

PART 1: DEFINITIONS

In this Agreement, the following expressions have the meanings stated namely:

"Accounts" the audited financial statements of the Vendor as at the Balance Sheet Date including the balance sheet, profit and loss account together with the notes on them, the cash flow statement and the auditor's and directors' reports.

"Accounting Standards" SSAPs, FRSs, UITF Abstracts, SORPs and all other generally accepted accounting practices applied to a United Kingdom company [at the date hereof] [at the Balance Sheet Date] (excluding International Accounting Standards and International Financial Reporting Standards issued by the International Accounting Standards Board).

"Agreement" this agreement [and the Schedules hereto] for the sale and purchase of the Business and Assets.

"Assets" all the assets and rights of the Business to be purchased by the Purchaser as described in clause [ ].

"Associate" in relation to any person, a person who is connected with that person within the meaning of CTA 2010 s.1122.

"Associated Person" in relation to a company, a person (including an employee, agent or Subsidiary) who performs or has performed services for or on that company's behalf.

"Balance Sheet Date" 200[ ] (being the date as at and to which the Accounts were prepared).

"Benefit" any pension, lump sum, gratuity or other like benefit given or to be given on retirement or on death, or in anticipation of retirement, or after retirement or death, or to be given on or in anticipation of or in connection with any change in the nature of the service of the employee in question, including (without limitation) the termination of the employment of the employee, or given or to be given on or in connection with the illness, injury or disability of, or suffering of any accident by, an employee.

"Business" the business of [ ] carried on by the Vendor at Completion from the Property under the Name and, where the context so admits, includes the Assets and the Goodwill.

"Business Intellectual Property Rights" all Intellectual Property Rights owned, used, enjoyed, exploited or held for use by the Vendor in, or in connection with, the Business (including those specified in Schedule [ ]).

"CA 1985" the Companies Act 1985.

"CAA 2001" the Capital Allowances Act 2001.

"Companies Acts" CA 2006 and CA 1985, as amended, and in each case, in so far as the same are in force at the date of this Agreement or in force at the time of the relevant event for the purposes of the Warranties.

"Completion" completion of the sale and purchase of the Business and Assets.

"Computer Systems" all hardware, handheld devices, firmware, peripherals, communication links, storage media, backup systems, networking equipment and other equipment used by or on behalf of the Business together with all software [and all source, object and executable codes], databases and websites used by or on behalf of the Business.

"Confidential Business Information" all or any information relating to the following (details of which are not in the public domain) existing in any form:

(1) the business methods, corporate plans, management systems, finances, new business opportunities or development projects of the Vendor;

(2) the marketing or sales of any present or future product of the Vendor including, without limitation, customer names and lists and other details of customers, prospects, sales targets, sales statistics, pricing information, market research reports and surveys and advertising or other promotional material; and

(3) any trade secrets or other information relating to the provision of any product or services of the Vendor which is of a confidential nature or in respect of which the Vendor owes an obligation of confidence to any third party.

"Contracts" the Customer Contracts, the Supply Contracts and the Finance Agreements but not the contracts with employees.

"Creditors" the aggregate amount owed (whether or not due in accordance with any credit terms) by the Vendor in connection with the Business to or in respect of trade or other creditors and accrued costs, expenses and charges as recorded in the books of account of the Business at Completion.

"Customer Contracts" those orders, engagements or contracts entered into prior to Completion by or on behalf of the Vendor with customers for the sale of goods or provision of services by the Vendor in connection with the Business which remain (in whole or in part) to be performed by the Vendor (other than in relation to warranty or guarantee obligations or commitments of the Vendor) details of which are set out in Schedule [   ].

"Debts" the trade and other debts owing to the Vendor in connection with the Business (whether or not due and payable and whether or not invoiced) at Completion.

"Disclosure Letter" the disclosure letter (together with all documents attached or appended to it), having the same date as this Agreement, from the Vendor to the Purchaser and delivered to the Purchaser immediately prior to execution of this Agreement.

"Employees" the persons listed in Part 1 of Schedule [   ].

"Encumbrance" any mortgage, charge, debenture, assignment or assignment by way of security, option, right of conversion, pledge, declaration of trust, lien, right of set off or counterclaim, combination of accounts, retention of title arrangement, third party right or equity or any other security interest, encumbrance or preferential arrangement whatsoever, howsoever created or arising and any agreement or arrangement to create and of the above.

"Excluded Assets" any assets of the Business not comprised in the Assets which are to be purchased by the Purchaser under this Agreement including for the avoidance of doubt those assets listed in Schedule [   ].

"Excluded Employees" the employees listed in Part 2 of Schedule [   ].

"Finance Agreements" hire purchase, conditional sale, hire, rental, leasing or other agreements of a similar type the details of which are set out in Schedule [   ].

"Fixed Assets" all plant, machinery, tools, equipment, motor vehicles, fixtures and fittings, fixed IT equipment and other chattels on the Property or otherwise owned by the Vendor at Completion for the purposes of the Business listed in Schedule [   ].

"FRS" a financial reporting standard adopted or issued by the Accounting Standards Board Limited or such other body or bodies as are prescribed for the purposes of CA 2006 s.464.

"Goodwill" the goodwill of the Vendor in relation to the Business, together with the exclusive right for the Purchaser or its assignee so far as the Vendor can confer it but excluding the right to use the Name to represent itself as carrying on the Business in succession to the Vendor.

"IHTA 1984" the Inheritance Tax Act 1984.

"Intellectual Property" all copyright and related rights, moral rights, design rights, registered designs, database rights, semiconductor topography rights, patents, rights to inventions, utility models, business names, trade marks, service marks, trade names, domain names, rights in get up, know-how, trade secrets and rights in confidential information, rights to goodwill or to sue for passing off or unfair competition, and any other intellectual property rights or rights of a similar nature (in each case whether or not registered) and all applications for any of them which may subsist anywhere in the world.

"IP Licences" any licences, authorisations and permissions in any form whatsoever whether express or implied, pertaining to the use, enjoyment and exploitation of the Business Intellectual Property Rights.

"Liabilities" means the liabilities whether actual or contingent of the Business (other than the Creditors) incurred or outstanding at Completion and without limitation all other liabilities of the Vendor.

"Management Accounts" the unaudited balance sheet of the Vendor as at [ ] and the unaudited profit and loss account of the Vendor for the period ended on [ ] copies of which are attached to the Disclosure Letter.

"Name" [ ].

"Pension Schemes" [ ].

"Property" the [freehold/leasehold] property owned by the Vendor described in Schedule [ ].

"Purchaser's Accountants" [ ].

"Purchaser's Solicitors" [ ].

"Regulations" the Transfer of Undertakings (Protection of Employment) Regulations 2006.

"Social Media" all social networking sites, blogs, microblogs, wikis or other forms of social media used by or on behalf of the Vendor for business purposes.

"Software" all software products together with all related object executable and source codes and databases used or owned by the Vendor in connection with the Business.

"SSAP" a Statement of Standard Accounting Practice published by the Accounting Standards Committee of CCAB Limited and adopted by the Accounting Standards Board Limited.

"Stocks" the stocks owned or used by the Vendor at Completion for the purpose of or in connection with the Business including without limitation, spare parts, accessories, goods or other assets purchased for resale, raw materials, consumables and components, Work in Progress, partly finished and finished goods, finished but uninvoiced work and including items which although subject to reservation of title by the seller are under the control of the Vendor.

"Subsidiary" a subsidiary undertaking as defined in CA 2006 s.1162 save that a company shall be treated, for the purposes of the membership requirement contained in subs.1162(2), as a member of another company even if its shares in that other company are registered in the name of (a) another person (or its nominee) whether by way of security or in connection with the taking of security, or (b) its nominee.

"Supply Contracts" the orders, engagements or contracts entered into prior to Completion by or on behalf of the Vendor with suppliers for the supply of goods or services in connection with the Business which remain (in whole or in part) to be performed by the supplier details of which are set out in schedule [ ].

"Taxation or Tax" all forms of taxation, duties, imposts, government charges (whether international, national or local) and levies whatsoever and whenever created, enacted or imposed and whether of the United Kingdom or elsewhere and without prejudice to the generality of that expression includes:

(1) income tax, corporation tax, capital gains tax, capital transfer tax, inheritance tax, stamp duty, stamp duty reserve tax, stamp duty land tax rates, VAT, customs and

other import duties, insurance premium tax, national insurance contributions, amounts for which the Vendor is liable to account under PAYE and any payments whatsoever which the Vendor may be or become bound to make to any Taxation Authority or any other person as a result of any enactment relating to taxation and any other taxes, duties or levies supplementing or replacing any of the above; and

(2) all costs, charges, interests, fines, penalties and expenses incidental or relating to any taxation, duties, imposts, charges and levies whatsoever (including without limitation any such described above).

"Taxation Authority" HM Revenue & Customs, any predecessor of HM Revenue & Customs including without limitation the Inland Revenue, HM Customs and Excise and the Department of Social Security or any statutory or governmental authority or body (whether in the United Kingdom or elsewhere) involved in the collection or administration of Taxation.

"UITF Abstract" an abstract issued by the Urgent Issues Task Force of the Accounting Standards Board Limited or such other body or bodies as are prescribed for the purposes of CA 2006 s.464.

"VAT" value added tax chargeable under VATA and any similar replacement or additional tax.

"VATA 1994" the Value Added Tax Act 1994.

"VAT Regulations" the Value Added Tax Regulations 1995 (SI 1995/2518).

"Vendor's Accountants" [   ].

"Vendor's Solicitors" [   ].

"Warranties" the warranties[, representations and undertakings] of the Vendor contained in [this Agreement] [clause [   ] and] [Schedule [   ]] and "Warranty" means anyone of them.

"Work in Progress" services partially performed by the Vendor on behalf of the Business but not completed as at the close of business on the date of Completion (whether performed by the Vendor or by a subcontractor of the Vendor) including the parts, accessories and consumables used in the performance of said services.

PART 2: INDEMNITIES

1   Creditors and liabilities

1.1   Subject to the other provisions of this Agreement:

    1.1.1   all profits and receipts of the Business and all losses, liabilities, obligations and outgoings of the Business up to Completion belong to and are for the account of the Vendor;

    1.1.2   the Vendor shall promptly discharge the Creditors and the Liabilities (at the latest by the expiry of any agreed or statutory credit or payment periods);

    1.1.3   notwithstanding Completion the Vendor shall be responsible for all debts payable by and claims (whether contingent or otherwise) outstanding against it at Completion or that primarily relate to any fact or matter occurring prior to Completion or anything done or omitted to be done on or prior to Completion by the Vendor including, without limitation, all wages, sums payable in respect of Taxation, rent and other expenses or any failure by the Vendor in the performance of any of its obligations falling due on or before Completion in relation to the Business or which relate to any of the Excluded Assets; and

1.1.4   the Vendor shall indemnify the Purchaser in respect of any breach in whole or part of this sub-clause by the Vendor.

1.2   Subject to the other provisions of this Agreement all profits and receipts of the Business and all losses, liabilities, obligations and outgoings of the Business (to the extent that they are transferred to the Purchaser under this Agreement or relate to, or otherwise arise during the period after the date of Completion) belong to and must be paid and discharged by the Purchaser. Accordingly, and without prejudice to its rights under the Warranties and subject to the other provisions of this Agreement, the Purchaser shall indemnify the Vendor against:

1.2.1   all liabilities, obligations and outgoings relating to the Assets to the extent that they are referable to the period after the date of Completion; and

1.2.2   all costs, claims, proceedings, damages and expenses in connection with them.

2 Contracts

2.1   In so far as the benefit of any of the Contracts may be effectively assigned by the Vendor to the Purchaser without the consent of a third party:

2.1.1   the Vendor hereby agrees to assign and transfer with effect from Completion all the benefit of them to the Purchaser;

2.1.2   the Purchaser shall perform all of the Vendor's obligations thereunder save any such obligations that were under the terms of the relevant Contract to be performed prior to Completion or any obligations that the Vendor is in breach of as at Completion; and

2.1.3   the Purchaser shall indemnify the Vendor in respect of any breach of this sub-clause by it.

2.2   In so far as the benefit of any of the Contracts may not be effectively assigned by the Vendor to the Purchaser without the consent of a third party then:

2.2.1   the Vendor and the Purchaser shall each use their reasonable endeavours to procure a novation of those Contracts or consent to assignment (as the Purchaser may require) and that those Contracts are novated or assigned, provided that:

2.2.1.1   the Purchaser shall not be obliged to make any payment, give any security or provide any guarantee as the basis for, or in connection with, any such assignment or novation; and

2.2.1.2   nothing contained in this Agreement shall or shall be deemed to operate, so far as concerns any third party, as such an assignment or novation as would or might give rise to any termination or forfeiture of any benefit, right or interest of any person in any of the Contracts in question;

2.2.2   unless and until any such Contracts (but excluding the Supply Contracts) shall be so novated or assigned:

2.2.2.1   the Vendor shall, in so far as may be permissible and lawful, give to the Purchaser the benefit of them as if the same had already been novated to or assigned to the Purchaser;

2.2.2.2 the Purchaser shall after Completion as the Vendor's sub-contractor (or in any way or capacity reasonably open to the Purchaser) perform on behalf of the Vendor all of the Vendor's obligations thereunder arising after Completion save any obligations of the Vendor that under the terms of any of the Contracts were to be performed prior to Completion or any obligations that the Vendor is in breach of as at Completion; and

2.2.2.3 the Purchaser shall indemnify the Vendor in respect of any breach of this sub-clause;

2.2.3 the Vendor shall hold all Supply Contracts in trust for the Purchaser and:

2.2.3.1 as required by the Purchaser all goods to be delivered or services to be provided thereunder shall be delivered or provided as the Purchaser may direct;

2.2.3.2 the Vendor shall permit the Purchaser to have the use of any assets or rights whose use by the Vendor is authorised by any such Supply Contract; and

2.2.3.3 the Purchaser shall, in respect of the period during which the provisions of this sub-clause are followed and to the extent that such Supply Contracts permit (and save in so far as they are not inconsistent with the provisions hereof), perform the obligations of the Vendor and make payments due thereunder (but only in so far as such obligations and payments do not relate to a breach of any of the Vendor's obligations thereunder on or prior to Completion);

2.2.4 in respect of the Contracts to which sub-clauses 2.2.1 and 2.2.2, apply the Vendor shall not do any act in respect of such Contracts without the consent of the Purchaser and shall keep the Purchaser fully and properly informed of all communications and any other relevant information concerning such Contracts; and

2.2.5 in the event of the actions referred to in sub-clauses 2.2.1 and 2.2.2 being unlawful or in breach of the terms of any of the Contracts, all liabilities and obligations relating to such Contracts shall remain with the Vendor which shall indemnify the Purchaser in respect of the loss of profit to the Purchaser in not being able to complete such Contracts and obtain the benefit thereof.

2.3 The Vendor shall indemnify the Purchaser in respect of any default by the Vendor under the Contracts or negligence or misrepresentation concerning all or any of the Contracts.

2.4 The Vendor shall perform all obligations in the Contracts that the Purchaser has not hereunder agreed to perform.

3 Employees

3.1 The parties agree that the sale and purchase to be effected pursuant to this Agreement will amount to a relevant transfer for the purposes of the Regulations and that accordingly the contracts of employment of the Employees will be transferred to the Purchaser upon Completion in accordance with the Regulations.

3.2   The Vendor shall indemnify the Purchaser against each and every cost, claim, liability, expense or demand relating to or arising out of any act or omission by the Vendor or any other event or occurrence before the date of Completion and incurred by the Purchaser in relation to any contract of employment or collective agreement concerning the Employees and former employees of the Vendor or the Business or under statute pursuant to the Regulations, including without limitation any such matter relating to or arising out of:

3.2.1   the Vendor's rights, powers, duties and liabilities under or in connection with any such contract of employment or collective agreement or under statute, which rights, powers, duties and liabilities transfer to the Purchaser in accordance with the Regulations;

3.2.2   anything done or omitted before the date of Completion by or in relation to the Vendor in respect of any contract of employment or collective agreement or any person employed in the Business which is deemed to have been done or omitted by or in relation to the Purchaser in accordance with the Regulations;

3.2.3   the Vendor's failure to pay to any of the Employees any sums due in respect of the period before Completion; and

3.2.4   any claim by any trade union, staff association or staff body recognised by the Vendor in respect of all or any of the Employees arising out of the Vendor's failure to comply with its legal obligations to such trade union, staff association or body.

3.3   If any contract of employment of any person who is not an Employee has effect as if originally made between the Purchaser and such person, whether as a result of the provisions of the Regulations or otherwise;

3.3.1   the Purchaser may, within [14] days of learning of the existence of such contract terminate it; and

3.3.2   the Vendor shall indemnify the Purchaser against each and every cost, claim, liability, expense or demand;

3.3.2.1   by reason of, on account of or arising out of such termination; or

3.3.2.2   arising from such contract prior to the date on which such termination takes place.

3.4   The Purchaser shall indemnify the Vendor against each and every cost, claim, liability, expense or demand arising from;

3.4.1   any claim or allegation by any of the Employees that as a result of the sale of the Business to the Purchaser there have been or will be a substantial change in the Employee's working conditions to his detriment contrary to the Regulations;

3.4.2   any act or omission of the Purchaser in relation to any of the Employees occurring after the date of Completion, and any claim for redundancy payments or protective awards, and any liability for wrongful dismissal or unfair dismissal or otherwise in connection with the transfer of the employment of the Employees to the Purchaser;

3.4.3   any failure by the Purchaser to provide retirement or death in service benefits for or in respect of any of the Employees in accordance with the Transfer of Employment (Pension Protection) Regulations 2005; and

any claim arising from the failure or delay of the Purchaser to notify the Vendor pursuant to reg.13(4) of the Regulations of the measures the Purchaser envisages taking in relation to the Employees.

4 Pensions

4.1 The Vendor shall indemnify the Purchaser against:

4.1.1 any claim for any Benefit in respect of any scheme other than the Scheme referable to any period up to and including Completion, including without limitation any order made by any court, tribunal or regulator in respect of such claim and any payment made by the Purchaser to any such person to settle any such claim; and

4.1.2 any claim in respect of the Scheme relating to any benefits other than those relating to old age, invalidity or survivors or relating to any output target on benefits referable to pensionable service in the period up to and including Completion.

Part 3: Warranties

1 Preliminary

1.1 Capacity and authority of Vendor

1.1.1 The Vendor has the power and authority to enter into and perform this Agreement, which constitutes a binding obligation on the Vendor in accordance with its terms.

1.2 Investigations

1.2.1 No investigations or enquiries by, or on behalf of, a governmental or other body in respect of, or which might affect, the Business are taking place or pending.

1.3 Information disclosed to the Purchaser

1.3.1 All information given by the Vendor, the Vendor's Solicitors or the Vendor's Accountants to the Purchaser, the Purchaser's Solicitors or the Purchaser's Accountants relating to the Business and the Assets was when given and is on Completion true, accurate and complete in all respects and opinions, expectations and beliefs included in the information are honestly held and have been arrived at on a reasonable basis after full enquiry.[1]

1.3.2 There are no material circumstances in relation to the Business or the Assets which have not been Disclosed and which, if Disclosed, might reasonably have been expected to affect the decision of the Purchaser to enter into this Agreement.

1.3.3 The information contained in Schedule[s] [ ] of this Agreement is true, complete and accurate.

---

[1] Please see comments at para.7–30 in relation to this warranty and the alternative form of wording that a well-advised vendor is likely to insist on.

2   Accounts

2.1   The Accounts

2.1.1   The Accounts were prepared in accordance with the historical cost convention and with the requirements of all relevant statutes and generally accepted accounting principles; and the bases and policies of accounting, adopted for the purpose of preparing the Accounts, were the same as those adopted in preparing the audited accounts of the Vendor in respect of the preceding three accounting periods.

2.1.2   The Accounts:

2.1.2.1   give a true and fair view of the assets and liabilities of the Business at the Balance Sheet Date and its profits for the financial period ended on that date;

2.1.2.2   comply with the requirements of the Companies Acts;

2.1.2.3   comply with all current Accounting Standards;

2.1.2.4   are not affected by extraordinary, exceptional or non-recurring items; and

2.1.2.5   properly reflect the financial position of the Vendor as at the Balance Sheet Date.

2.1.3   The amount included in the Accounts in respect of each asset, whether fixed or current, did not exceed its purchase price or production cost or (in the case of current assets) its net realisable value at the Balance Sheet Date.

2.2   Valuation of stock in trade and work in progress

2.2.1   In the Accounts and in the accounts of the Vendor for the three preceding financial years, stock in trade and work in progress was valued at the lowest cost or net realisable value, cost represents materials and appropriate proportions of direct labour and overheads.

2.2.2   In the Accounts slow moving stock in trade was written down as appropriate and redundant, obsolete, obsolescent and defective stock was wholly written off and the value attributable to any other stock did not exceed the lower of cost and net realisable value at the Balance Sheet Date.

2.3   Management Accounts

The Management Accounts have been prepared in accordance with accounting policies consistent with those used in the preparation of the Accounts with all due care and on a basis consistent with the management accounts of the Vendor prepared in the preceding year.

2.4   Books and records

2.4.1   The accounting and other records of the Business:

2.4.1.1   have been fully, properly and accurately prepared and have at all times been fully, properly and accurately maintained and are properly written up to date in each case, as required by law, and will be so kept to Completion;

2.4.1.2   are accurate in all material respects;

2.4.1.3   in respect of the accounting records, show a true and fair view of its trading transactions and its financial, contractual and trading position; and

2.4.1.4   are in the possession or under the control of the Vendor.

3   Assets

3.1   Ownership of assets

3.1.1   Apart from current assets acquired or realised by the Vendor in the ordinary course of the Business, the Assets are the same as the assets shown in the Accounts.

3.1.2   The Vendor legally and beneficially owns the Assets free from Encumbrances except for those items the subject of Finance Agreements listed in the Disclosure Letter.

3.1.3   None of the Assets is subject to, and there is no agreement to create, an Encumbrance.

3.1.4   None of the Assets were purchased by the Vendor on terms that provided for a reservation of title by the seller.

3.1.5   There has been no exercise or purported exercise of or claim under any Encumbrance over any of the Assets and there is no dispute directly or indirectly relating to any of the Assets.

3.2   Assets sufficient for the Business and location

3.2.1   The Assets comprise all assets necessary for the satisfaction of the Vendor's obligations under the Contracts and for the continuation of the Business as now carried on (which without limitation shall include the continuation of the Business in the same scale and manner).

3.2.2   All of the Assets are currently being used exclusively in the Business.

3.2.3   Any of the Assets which are not situated at the Property at Completion are specified together with their actual location in the Disclosure Letter and are clearly identified as assets of the Vendor at such specified locations.

3.3   Fixed Assets

3.3.1   The Fixed Assets:

3.3.1.1   are in a good and safe state of repair and satisfactory working order and have been properly serviced and maintained;

3.3.1.2   are not surplus to requirements;

3.3.1.3   would not be expected (if the sale of the Business had not taken place) to require replacement or additions at a cost in excess of £[   ] within the next six months; and

3.3.1.4   are used exclusively in connection with the Business.

3.3.2   There are maintenance contracts with independent specialist contractors in respect of all the Fixed Assets for which it is normal or prudent to have maintenance agreements and in respect of all the Fixed Assets which the Vendor is obliged to maintain or repair under a leasing or similar agreement.

3.3.3   Nothing has occurred or is likely to occur in relation to any of the Fixed Assets under a lease or similar agreement whereby the rental payable has been, or is likely to be, increased.

3.4   Stock and Work in Progress

3.4.1   The Stock is not excessive and is adequate in relation to the current trading requirements of the Business and to perform the Contracts.

3.4.2   The Work in Progress included in the Stock is adequate to maintain current cash flow and profitability of the Business at a level not less than as disclosed in the Disclosure Letter.

3.4.3   The Stock is in good condition and is capable of being sold in the normal course of the Business in accordance with the Vendor's current price list, without rebate or allowance to a purchaser.

3.5   Debts

3.5.1   None of the Debts is overdue by more than 12 weeks, or has been released on terms that the debtor pays less than the full book value of his debt, or has been written off or is regarded by the Vendor as wholly or partly irrecoverable.

3.5.2   The Debts will be recoverable in full, in the normal course of the Business, and in any event not later than 12 weeks after Completion; and none of them is subject to a right of counter-claim or set-off or withholding or other deduction.

3.5.3   All charges securing any of the Book Debts have (if appropriate) been registered in accordance with the provisions of the Companies Acts.

3.5.4   The Vendor is not and has not agreed to become a party to any factoring or discounting arrangements in respect of such debts

3.5.5   All amounts due from the Vendor and included amongst the Creditors relate exclusively to the Business, were properly incurred in the ordinary and usual course of business, are not subject to dispute and are now due, owing and payable.

3.6   Insurance

3.6.1   All the Assets which are of an insurable nature are insured in amounts representing their full replacement or reinstatement value against fire and other risks normally insured against by persons carrying on the same type of business as the Business.

3.6.2   The Business and the Assets are and have at all material times been adequately covered against employee's liability, public liability, professional liability and accident, damage, injury, third party loss, loss of profits (including product liability) and other risks normally covered by insurance.

3.6.3   A list of all current insurance and indemnity policies (the "Insurance Policies") relating to the Business and the Assets are contained in the Disclosure Letter.

3.6.4   Nothing has been done or omitted or has occurred which could make any of the Insurance Policies void or voidable or which is likely to result in an increase in premium.

3.6.5   None of the Insurance Policies is subject to special or unusual terms or restrictions or to the payment of a premium in excess of the normal rate.

3.6.6   The details set out in the Disclosure Letter give all relevant information relating to and the status of all claims by the Vendor under any of its Insurance Policies in the period of two years prior to Completion.

3.7   Documents

3.7.1   All the title deeds relating to the Assets will be delivered to the purchaser at Completion.

3.7.2   All documents which affect the title or interest of the Vendor to or in the Assets or which relate to contracts included in the Assets have been duly stamped within the requisite period for stamping.

3.8   Intellectual property rights

3.8.1   Full details of all the Business Intellectual Property Rights and IP Licences are set out in Schedule [   ]. All such Business Intellectual Property Rights are used, enjoyed and exploited exclusively in connection with the Business.

3.8.2   Except in respect of any Business Intellectual Property Rights which are the subject of a valid and enforceable IP Licence which has been granted to the Vendor are listed in Schedule [   ], the Vendor is the sole legal and beneficial owner of all Business Intellectual Property Rights (including the subject matter of them) free from all claims, liens, equities, Encumbrances, licences and adverse rights of any description. No Business Intellectual Property Rights are held jointly or in common with any other person.

3.8.3   None of the Business Intellectual Property Rights are subject to any challenge or attack by a third party or competent authority. All renewal and registration fees for the protection of the registered Business Intellectual Property Rights have been paid.

3.8.4   All IP Licences are valid and enforceable. There are no other outstanding agreements or arrangements whereby a licence, sub-licence or other permission to use has been granted to or by, or is obliged to be granted to or by, the Vendor in respect of any of the Business Intellectual Property Rights.

3.8.5   Neither the Vendor nor any other party is in breach of any IP Licence and all such licences are in full force and effect and will not terminate or be capable of termination by reason of the execution and performance of this Agreement.

3.8.6   None of the activities involved in the conduct of the Business infringe or have infringed any Intellectual Property of any third party, or constitute or have constituted any breach of confidence, passing off or actionable unfair competition in any jurisdiction. No such activities give or have given rise to any obligation to pay any royalty, fee, compensation or any other sum whatsoever.

3.8.7   The Vendor is not, and has not within the six years preceding the date of this Agreement been, party to or threatened with any legal proceedings relating to any Intellectual Property of any third party and the Vendor is not aware of (and has not acquiesced in) any infringement of any Business Intellectual Property Rights by a third party or any breach of confidence, passing off or actionable unfair competition in any jurisdiction.

3.8.8 There are no outstanding or potential claims against the Vendor under any contract or under s.40 of the Patents Act 1977, for employee compensation in respect of any Intellectual Property of any third party.

3.8.9 The Business Intellectual Property Rights set out in Schedule [   ] constitute all the Intellectual Property necessary to carry on the Business.

3.9   Confidential Business Information

3.9.1 The Confidential Business Information is in the Vendor's lawful possession and under its control. No licences or other agreements have been granted or entered into in respect thereof and no circumstances exist under which the Vendor or any of its predecessors in title have granted any rights or interest to any third party or any third party has acquired any rights or interest in connection with the Confidential Business Information.

3.9.2 No disclosure has been made or agreed to be made to any person (other than the Purchaser) of any of the Confidential Business Information or confidential information of any customer or client of the Business and the Vendor has not entered into any agreement for the use by any third party of any Confidential Business Information or other Business Intellectual Property Rights held by the Vendor, other than pursuant to written obligations of confidence which have been set out in the Disclosure Letter.

3.10   Information Technology

All Computer Systems:

3.10.1 are used exclusively by the Vendor and under its sole control or are otherwise used on the terms detailed in the Disclosure Letter.

3.10.2 are, in respect of the hardware, handheld devices, firmware, peripherals, networking and other equipment comprised in those Computer Systems, legally and beneficially owned by the Vendor.

3.10.3 are in full working order and performing the functions for which they were acquired efficiently and without material errors or downtime.

3.10.4 have not, within the two years immediately preceding Completion, unduly interrupted or hindered the operation of the Business.

3.10.5 have adequate capacity for the Business' present and (taking into account the extent to which the Computer Systems are expandable) future needs.

3.10.6 have been satisfactorily and appropriately maintained and supported and have the benefit of appropriate maintenance and support agreements (copies of which are attached to the Disclosure Letter), which agreements include emergency support.

3.10.7 [so far as the Vendor is aware] have not been used in such a way as would invalidate any manufacturer's or supplier's guarantee or warranty or entitle the provider of maintenance or support for the Computer Systems to exclude, suspend or terminate those services.

3.10.8   have, in conjunction with the support and maintenance agreements referred to in clause [3.10.6], adequate security measures, back-up systems, disaster recovery arrangements, measures to protect them from viruses and other harmful code and trained personnel to ensure that so far as reasonably practicable:

    3.10.8.1   the authenticity, integrity and confidentiality of all data held by or transmitted by the Computer Systems are preserved;

    3.10.8.2   no more than one day's data would be lost in the event of a failure of the Computer Systems;

    3.10.8.3   breaches of security, errors and breakdowns are kept to a minimum and that in the event of the occurrence of any such event there will not [so far as the Vendors are aware] be a material disruption to the Vendor;

    3.10.8.4   enable all records and data stored by electronic means which relate to the Vendor to be readily accessible by appropriate personnel; and

    3.10.8.5   will correctly carry out all calculations relating to or in connection with the Euro and display all symbols adopted by any government or European body in connection with the Euro.

3.10.9   all software used or stored or resident in the Vendor:

    3.10.9.1   [so far as the Vendor is aware] is free from any defect or feature which may adversely affect its performance [or the performance of any other software in the future];

    3.10.9.2   performs in accordance with its specification;

    3.10.9.3   [so far as the Vendor is aware] has been (if copied) lawfully copied;

    3.10.9.4   is lawfully held and [so far as the Vendor is aware] does not infringe the Intellectual Property of any person;

3.10.10   as to the copyright therein:

    3.10.10.1   in the case of software written or commissioned by the Vendor, is owned solely by the Vendor, no other person has rights therein or rights to use or make copies of the software or source codes;

    3.10.10.2   in the case of standard packaged software purchased outright, is validly licensed to the Vendor for use in the Business in perpetuity (other than in the event of breach or insolvency) on written terms which do not require the Vendor to make any further payments, and no licences will terminate on change of control; and

    3.10.10.3   in the case of all other software, is licensed to the Vendor on the terms of a written licence which requires payment by the Vendor of a fixed annual licence;

3.10.11   no software owned by or licensed to the Vendor is licensed or sub-licensed by the Vendor to (or otherwise used by) any other person.

3.10.12　no action will be necessary to enable the Vendor to continue to use any software currently used by it to the same extent and in the same manner as it has been used prior to Completion.

3.10.13　[so far as the Vendor is aware] the terms of all software licences have been complied with and no notices of breach or termination have been served on the Vendor in respect of any such licence.

3.10.14　details of all Company domain names and websites are set out in the Disclosure Letter. The Company is the registrant and beneficial owner of those domain names and is [so far as the Vendor is aware] the legal and beneficial owner of all Intellectual Property Rights in the websites.

3.10.15　details of all Social Media are set out in the Disclosure Letter. The Business' use complies with each Social Media provider's terms.

3.10.16　[so far as the Vendor is aware] all websites operated by the Business comply with the Electronic Commerce (EC Directive) Regulations 2002. The websites are accessible in compliance with the requirements set out in part III of the Disability Discrimination Act 1995 (as amended or superseded).

4　The Contracts

4.1　The Contracts

4.1.1　The Contracts, true copies of which are annexed to the Disclosure Letter or the full terms of which are set out in the Disclosure Letter, constitute all the contracts and other engagements, whether written or oral, referable to the Business and Assets to which the Vendor is now a party, apart from the contracts of employment of the employees.

4.1.2　All of the Contracts are assignable by the Vendor to the Purchaser without the consent of any other party.

4.1.3　The performance of this Agreement will not relieve any other party to any Contract from its obligations or enable it to determine any of them.

4.1.4　No steps have been taken by any party to the Finance Agreements to terminate the Finance Agreements.

4.2　Nature of the contracts

4.2.1　None of the Contracts:

4.2.1.1　was entered into in any way otherwise than in the ordinary and normal course of the Business bona fide on an arms-length basis;

4.2.1.2　is of a loss-making nature; or

4.2.1.3　cannot readily be fulfilled or performed by the Vendor on time without undue expenditure or application of money, effort or personnel; or

4.2.1.4　involves, or is likely to involve, other obligations or liabilities which ought reasonably to be made known to an intending purchaser of the Business; or

4.2.1.5　is of an unusual, abnormal or onerous nature; or

4.2.1.6　is of a long term nature (that is to say incapable of performance in accordance with its terms within six months after the date on which it was entered into or undertaken);

4.2.1.7 involves payment by reference to fluctuations in the index of retail prices, or other index, or in the rate or exchange for a currency; or

4.2.1.8 involves an aggregate outstanding expenditure by the Vendor of more than £[ ]; or

4.2.1.9 is for the supply of goods and services by or to the Vendor on terms under which retrospective or future discount, price reduction or other financial incentives are given; or

4.2.1.10 involves, or likely to involve, the supply of goods or services the aggregate sales value of which will be more than 10 per cent of its turnover for the preceding financial year; or

4.2.1.11 involves the payment by the Vendor of any commission, finder's fee, royalty or the like.

4.3 Defaults

4.3.1 None of the parties to the Contracts is in default, being a default which would be material in the context of the financial or trading position of the Business; and there are no circumstances likely to give rise to a default and none of the parties to the Contracts have given notice of its intention to terminate, or has sought to repudiate or disclaim, such agreement, arrangement or obligation.

4.3.2 No event has occurred, is subsisting or is likely to arise which, with the giving of notice and/or lapse of time will constitute or result in a default or the acceleration of any obligation of the Vendor under any agreement or arrangement which it has entered into for the purpose of, or which is used in the operation of, the Business and Assets.

4.4 Defective products

4.4.1 The Vendor has not, in the course of carrying on the Business, manufactured, sold or supplied products which were, are or will become, in a material respect, faulty or defective, or which do not comply in a material respect with warranties or representations expressly or impliedly made by it and all applicable regulations, standards and requirements in respect hereof.

4.4.2 The Vendor has not received a prohibition notice, a notice to warn or a suspension notice under the Consumer Protection Act 1987.

4.5 Agreements concerning the business

4.5.1 There have been no arrangements or understandings (whether legally enforceable or not) between the Vendor and any person who is, directly or indirectly, a shareholder or the beneficial owner of any interest in the Vendor, or any company in which the Vendor is interested relating to the management of the Business or the ownership or transfer of ownership or the letting of any of the Assets or the provision of finance, goods, services or other facilities to or by the Vendor or otherwise in any way relating to the Business or the Assets.

4.5.2 The Vendor has not been and is not a party to any agency, distributorship, marketing, purchasing, manufacturing, licensing or restrictive trading agreement or arrangement or any agreement or arrangement pursuant to which any part of the Business has been carried on or any agreement or arrangement which in any way has restricted its freedom to carry on the whole or any part of the Business or to use or exploit any of the Assets in any part of the world in such manner as it thinks fit.

4.5.3   Compliance with the terms of this Agreement does not and will not conflict with, result in the breach of or constitute a default under any of the terms, conditions or provisions of any rules or provisions relating to the membership of any association or body or any arrangement, licence agreement or instrument to which the Vendor is now a party or which affects or relates to the Business or the Assets (including without limitation the Contracts), or give rise to a right exercisable by any person other than the Vendor to terminate or in any way vary the terms of any such membership, arrangement, licence agreement or instrument or excuse performance by such party from the whole or part of its obligations under such agreement or instrument.

4.6   Service liabilities

4.6.1   The Vendor is not obliged to repair, maintain, take back or otherwise do or not do anything in respect of goods sold in the course of carrying on the Business.

5   Trading

5.1   Vendor's other interests

5.1.1   The Vendor and its Associates are not, directly or indirectly, interested in businesses which are or are likely to be competitive with the Business, apart from interests in securities listed on the London Stock Exchange's market for listed securities, or traded in on the AIM (its alternative investment market of the London Stock Exchange) and in respect of which the Vendor, with its Associates, is interested in less than three per cent of any class of the securities in that company.

5.2   Effect of sale of the Business

5.2.1   The Vendor is not aware, and has no grounds for believing, that after Completion (whether by reason of an existing agreement or arrangement or as a result of the acquisition of the Business by the Purchaser):

5.2.1.1   a supplier of the Business will cease, or be entitled to cease, supplying it or may substantially reduce its level of supplies;

5.2.1.2   a customer of the Business will cease, or be entitled to cease, to deal with it or may substantially reduce its level of business; or

5.2.1.3   the Business will lose a right or benefit which the Vendor enjoys in relation to it.

5.2.2   Compliance with this agreement will not breach or constitute a default under any agreement or arrangement to which the

Vendor is a party, any provision of its memorandum or articles of association or any other restriction affecting it.

5.3   Joint venture and partnerships

5.3.1   The Vendor is not, and has not agreed to become, a party to or member of a joint venture, consortium, partnership or other unincorporated association.

5.4   Outstanding offers

5.4.1   No offer, tender or the like relating to the Business which is capable of being converted into an obligation of the owner of the Business by an acceptance or other act of some other person, firm or corporation is outstanding.

5.5   Undertakings restricting the Business

5.5.1   The Vendor is not subject to an undertaking or assurance which it has given to a court or government agency in relation to the Business.

5.6   Unfair trade and restrictive practices

5.6.1   The Vendor is not, nor has it been in relation to the Business, a party to or concerned in any agreement, practice or arrangement (whether legally binding or not) which is or was:

5.6.1.1   in contravention of the Trade Descriptions Act 1968;

5.6.1.2   in contravention the Fair Trading Act 1973 Pt XI as amended by the Trading Schemes Act 1996;

5.6.1.3   in contravention of the Consumer Credit Act 1974 (as amended);

5.6.1.4   in contravention of or invalidated (in whole or in part) by the Competition Act 1998;

5.6.1.5   in contravention of the Enterprise Act 2002;

5.6.1.6   in contravention of [arts 101 and 102 of] the Treaty of Rome on the Functioning of the European Union; or

5.6.1.7   in contravention of any other anti-trust, anti-monopoly or anti-cartel legislation or regulation.

5.6.2   The Vendor has not, in relation to the Business, received notice of any breach by it of any competition, anti-trust, anti-restrictive trade practices or consumer protection law, rule or regulation anywhere in the world or of any investigation, inquiry, report or order by any regulatory authority under any such law, rule or regulation.

5.7   Litigation and winding-up

5.7.1   The Vendor is not engaged (nor at any time has been engaged) in connection with the Business in any litigation, arbitration, mediation, prosecution or any other legal proceedings or claims with any person (including any customers of the Business). No injunction or order for specific performance has been granted against the Vendor in respect of any activity or potential activity of the Business and the Vendor has not given any undertaking to any prospective claimant or defendant or any other governmental or administrative body or court in connection with the Business or any of the Assets. There is no circumstance which might give rise to the same and there are no circumstances which may give rise to any claims against the Vendor or litigation or arbitration in relation to the Business.

5.7.2 There are no outstanding claims against the Vendor on the part of customers or other parties in respect of defects in quality or delays in delivery or completion of contracts or deficiencies of design or performance or otherwise relating to liability for goods or services sold or supplied by the Vendor in the course of the Business. No such claims are threatened and there is no matter or fact in existence in relation to goods or services sold or supplied by the Vendor in the course of the Business which might give rise to the same.

5.7.3 There are no outstanding claims against the Vendor by suppliers of goods or services to the Vendor in respect of the Business, or disputes between the Vendor and suppliers. There are no such claims by the Vendor against such suppliers and there is no matter or fact in existence which may give rise to any such claims or disputes.

5.7.4 Full details of all material claims, complaints or returns relating to the Business that have occurred during the 12 months preceding the date of this Agreement are set out in the Disclosure Letter.

5.7.5 The Vendor is not insolvent or unable to pay its debts within the meaning of the Insolvency Act 1986 s.123 (the references in that section to proving to the satisfaction of the court being disregarded).

5.7.6 No order has been made, petition presented or resolution passed for the winding-up of the Vendor; no distress, execution or other process has been levied and remains undischarged in respect of the Assets; and there is no outstanding judgment or court order against the Vendor in relation to the Business or the Assets.

5.7.7 No meeting of its creditors, or any class of them, has been held or summoned and no proposal has been made for a moratorium, composition or arrangement in relation to any of its debts, or for a voluntary arrangement under Pt 1 of the Insolvency Act 1986.

5.7.8 No floating charge created by the Vendor has crystallised over the Business or Assets or any of them and there no circumstances likely to cause such an event.

5.7.9 No event analogous to those described in clauses 5.7.4 or 5.7.5 has occurred outside England.

5.8 Compliance with statutes

5.8.1 The Vendor has not done or omitted to do anything in relation to the Business and/or the Assets, the doing or omitting of which is, or could be, in contravention of a statute, regulation or the like giving rise to a penalty, default proceedings or other liability.

5.9 Business names

5.9.1 The Vendor does not, in relation to the Business, make use of a name other than the Name.

5.10   Licences and consents

5.10.1   The Vendor has, in relation to the Business, all necessary or desirable licences and consents required for carrying it on properly (short particulars of each licence and consent being set out in the Disclosure Letter).

5.10.2   The Vendor is not in breach of any licence or consent; all licences and consents are in full force and effect and there is nothing that might prejudice the continuation or renewal of a licence or consent by the Purchaser without the necessity for any expense or special arrangement.

5.11   Branches

5.11.1   The Vendor does not carry on any part of the Business outside the United Kingdom through a branch, agency or other place of business. The Disclosure Letter contains full particulars of all telephone and fax numbers and all other electronic addresses and codes used by the Business at or in the 12-month period prior to Completion.

5.12   Purchases and sales from or to one party

5.12.1   Not more than 25 per cent of the aggregate amount of all the purchases, and not more than 25 per cent of the aggregate amount of all the sales, of the Business are obtained, or made, from or to the same supplier or customer (including a person connected with the supplier or customer); and no material source of supply to the Business, or material outlet for its sales, is or is likely to be in jeopardy.

5.12.2   The profits of the Business and financial position of the Vendor in relation to it have not been affected during the past three years by an agreement or arrangement which was not at arm's length.

5.13   Management reports

5.13.1   No financial or management consultants have, within the past three years, produced a report in relation to the Business.

5.14   Grants

5.14.1   The Vendor has not received any grants from any national or supranational body or any governmental or public body which would or might become repayable by virtue of the entering into or completing of this Agreement or for any reason after Completion.

6   Employment

6.1   Employees and terms and conditions

6.1.1   Full and accurate details are given in Schedule [   ] of the Employees' full names, addresses, national insurance numbers, tax codes, rates of remuneration (or methods of calculating remuneration) (including overtime pay), benefits, bonuses, commissions, dates of birth, commencement dates, periods of notice, pensions, voluntary pensions, annuities and rights under any retirement benefit, life assurance or hospital or medical insurance scheme of the Vendor in respect of the Business and all other benefits (including share option schemes and pre-requisites of any nature) of each of the Employees. Copies of any communication to staff concerning any such matters have been supplied to the Purchaser and are attached to the Disclosure Letter.

6.1.2   The details shown in Schedule [ ] together with the information contained in the Disclosure Letter (including, without limitation, any staff handbook) give full, complete and accurate details of all the terms and conditions of employment of each of the Employees.

6.1.3   There are no loans outstanding from the Vendor to any of the Employees.

6.1.4   There are no employees of the Vendor or any other person engaged or employed in the Business or in carrying on the Business except the Employees.

6.1.5   No past employee of the Vendor has a right to return to work or may have a right to be reinstated or re-engaged under the Employment Rights Act 1996.

6.1.6   No offers of employment have been made to any persons other than the Employees nor any agreements made for any person to become an employee of the Vendor.

6.1.7   All of the Employees are employed by the Vendor, are wholly and exclusively engaged in carrying on the Business and have been so engaged for at least 12 months prior to Completion.

6.1.8   All contracts of employment between the Vendor and the Employees are terminable on not more than three months' notice without compensation, other than compensation payable in accordance with the Employment Rights Act 1996.

6.1.9   All of the Employees are legally entitled to work in the United Kingdom.

6.1.10   The Vendor is not bound (whether legally or morally) to vary any of the terms and conditions of any of the Employees and has not offered any new contract of employment to any of the Employees.

6.1.11   The Vendor is not in breach of any of the terms of the contracts of employment of any of the Employees nor any other duties or obligations owed to the Employees (or any of them) nor (so far as the Vendor is aware) is any Employee in breach of his contract of employment.

6.1.12   None of the Employees is absent on maternity leave, paternity leave, adoption leave, parental leave or other leave of absence. None of the Employees is absent on sick leave which has lasted or is expected to last longer than four weeks.

6.1.13   There are not in existence and the Vendor has neither proposed nor is proposing to introduce any bonus, profit sharing, share option or share incentive scheme or any other scheme or arrangement (whether contractual or discretionary) under which the Employees or any of them are or is or would be entitled to participate in the profits of the Business.

6.2   Changes in remuneration

6.2.1   Since the Balance Sheet Date or (where employment commenced after the Balance Sheet Date, since the date of commencement of employment) no change has been made in the rate of remuneration, emoluments, pension benefits or, without limitation, any other terms or conditions of employment of any of the Employees.

6.2.2   No negotiations for any increase in remuneration or benefits or any other changes in the terms and conditions of employment of any of the Employees are current or due within a period of six months from Completion.

6.3   Termination of contracts of employment and redundancies

6.3.1   No liability has been incurred by the Vendor and not yet been discharged for:

6.3.1.1   breach of any contract of service or employment or for redundancy payments (including protective awards);

6.3.1.2   damages or compensation for wrongful dismissal or unfair dismissal or otherwise;

6.3.1.3   failure to comply with any order for reinstatement or re-engagement of any Employee engaged in connection with the Business; or

6.3.1.4   for the actual or proposed termination or suspension of employment or variation of any contract of employment of any present or former director or employee of the Vendor employed in connection with the Business.

6.3.2   None of the Employees have given or been given notice of termination of his employment nor is any of the Employees engaged in any grievance or disciplinary procedure, nor within the period of 12 months prior to Completion has the Vendor been engaged in relation to the Business or any of the Employees in any dispute, litigation or claim arising out of or relating to the provisions of the Employment Rights Act 1996, the Trade Union Reform and Employment Act 1993, the Health and Safety at Work Act 1974, the Equal Pay Act 1970, the Sex Discrimination Act 1975, the Disability Discrimination Act 1995, the Race Relations Act 1976, the Sex Discrimination (Gender Reassignment) Regulations 1999, the Regulations, the Trade Union and Labour Relations (Consolidation) Act 1992, the Protection from Harassment Act 1997, the Working Time Regulations 1998, the National Minimum Wage Act 1998, the Employment Relations Act 1999, the Part-Time Workers (Prevention of Less Favourable Treatment) Regulations 2000, the Fixed-Term Employees (Prevention of Less Favourable Treatment) Regulations 2002, the Employment Act 2002, the Employment Equality (Religion or Belief) Regulations 2003, the Employment Equality (Sexual Orientation) Regulations 2003, the Employment Equality (Age) Regulations 2006 or the Equality Act 2010 or any other law statute or regulation relating to the Employees (or any of them), and there is no matter or fact in existence which can be reasonably foreseen as likely to give rise to the same.[2]

6.3.3   No employees currently or previously employed in the Business have received or been given notice of dismissal during the period of twelve months prior to Completion.

6.3.4   None of the Employees as a result of this Agreement will be entitled to terminate their contracts of employment or will become redundant and be entitled to a redundancy payment.

---

[2] See the discussion of this warranty in relation to the introduction of the Equality Act 2010 at para.8–43.

6.4 Industrial agreements disputes and negotiations

6.4.1 The Vendor does not in respect of the Business recognise any trade unions, works or staff councils or associates of trade unions and there are in force no collective agreements (whether or not legally binding and whether in writing or arising by virtue of customs and practice) relating to any of the Employees.

6.4.2 The Vendor has not, in relation to the Business or the Employees, done anything which might be construed as recognition of a trade union and has not, in respect of the Business or the Employees, received an application for recognition from any trade union.

6.4.3 At no time during the period of two years immediately prior to Completion has the Vendor or any of the Employees been involved in an industrial dispute in relation to the Business and so far as the Vendor is aware there is nothing which might suggest that there may be an industrial dispute involving the Business or any of the Employees, or that this Agreement may give rise to such a dispute.

6.4.4 There is no dispute between the Vendor and any trade union or any of the Employees existing or pending at the date of this Agreement and there are no circumstances (including without limitation the entry into and carrying out of this Agreement) which may give rise to a dispute with any of the Employees.

6.4.5 The Vendor has not in relation to the Business received any request for an information and consultation agreement pursuant to the Information and Consultation of Employees Regulations 2004 and the Vendor is not, in relation to the Business, a party to such an agreement.

6.4.6 There are no enquiries or investigations existing, pending or threatened into the Vendor in relation to the Business by the Commission for Equality and Human Rights, the Health and Safety Executive or any similar body.

6.5 Compliance with laws

6.5.1 The Vendor has complied in all material respects with all:

6.5.1.1 obligations imposed on it by all statutes, regulations and codes of conduct and practice (including without limitation the Working Time Regulations 1998 and any obligations under any health and safety legislation or any legislation relating to the environment);

6.5.1.2 collective agreements and customs and practices for the time being dealing with relations between the Vendor and the Employees or any relevant trade union and the terms and conditions of service of the Employees; and

6.5.1.3 relevant orders, declarations and awards made under any relevant statute, regulation or code of conduct and practice affecting the conditions of service of any of the Employees.

6.6 Sub-contractors, agency workers and the self-employed

6.6.1 Full, complete and accurate details are set out in the Disclosure Letter of the terms on which all consultants, sub-contractors, self-employed persons and other independent contractors are engaged in the Business. The Taxation Authority has confirmed in writing that it does not consider any such person to be an employee of the Vendor.

6.6.2   The Vendor has paid to the Taxation Authority all taxes, national insurance contributions and other levies payable prior to Completion in respect of the Employees.

6.7   Pensions

6.7.1   No other pension arrangements

Save in respect of the Scheme, the Vendor has no legal obligation to provide or cause to be provided to any Employees benefits under a "pension scheme", as defined by s.150(1) of the Finance Act 2004, under an "employer-financed retirement benefits scheme", as defined by s.393B of the Income Tax (Earnings and Pensions) Act 2003, under a superannuation fund to which s.615(3) of the Income and Corporation Taxes Act 1988 applies, that are "retirement or death benefits" for the purposes of s.307 of the Income Tax (Earnings and Pensions) Act 2003 and do not fall under the categories above, or that are "excluded benefits" for the purposes of s.393B of the Income Tax (Earnings and Pensions) Act 2003 and do not fall under the categories above.

6.7.2   Other liabilities

6.7.2.1   The Vendor is not subject to a contribution notice or a financial support direction or similar notice, order or direction under the Pensions Act 2004 nor are there any circumstances which are likely to lead to such notices, orders or directions being imposed upon the Vendor.

6.7.2.2   The Vendor has not entered into any agreement with either the trustees or the administrators of any pension arrangement or with any member of the same or any of its past or present employees or with any other party including any regulatory authority in respect of any potential or actual pension-related liability.

6.7.2.3   The Vendor has not entered into any agreement with any party to fund, indemnify or guarantee any potential or actual pension-related liability.

6.7.3   Additional member's rights

6.7.3.1   None of the Employees have at any time transferred to the Vendor under the provisions of the Transfer of Undertakings (Protection of Employment) Regulations 1981 and 2006.

6.7.3.2   If any such Employees have transferred there are no circumstances in which such Employees may have retained any pension rights from previous employment that do not fall within the categories of benefits relating to old age, survivorship or ill health and which have not been fully and appropriately provided for under the Vendor's pension arrangements.

6.7.4 **Full and accurate particulars**

Full, accurate and up to date particulars of the Scheme are set out in the Disclosure Letter, including (without limitation):

6.7.4.1 all constitutional documents in relation to the Scheme including, where applicable, the trust deeds and rules together with any amendments and any related agreements;

6.7.4.2 all explanatory literature including, where applicable, booklets currently in force and any subsequent communications to members or Employees who are or may become members of the Scheme;

6.7.4.3 details of all Employees who are active, deferred, pensioner and prospective members (including dates of birth, sex, age at joining the Scheme, date on which a prospective member would become eligible to join the Scheme had the transfer not taken place and current pensionable pay, and name of employer);

6.7.4.4 in relation to the Employees, details of all employee and all employer contributions in the last five years (including any statutory schedules of contributions or payments); and

6.7.4.5 any insurance policies, schedules and certificates and details of all premiums paid in the last five years.

6.7.5 **Member details**

The membership data in respect of the Employees is complete, accurate and up to date in all material respects and is stored safely.

6.7.6 **Proposed amendments to the Scheme**

6.7.6.1 No proposal has been announced by the Vendor either:

6.7.6.1.1 to modify, amend, alter or improve the Scheme that does not form part of the Scheme's constitutional documents as at Completion; or

6.7.6.1.2 regarding the continuation of the Scheme, or its closure to new members, or its closure to new benefit accruals, or its discontinuance or winding-up.

6.7.6.2 Since the Balance Sheet Date the Scheme has not been modified, amended, altered or improved and no closure to new members, cessation or accruals or commencement of winding-up in relation to the Scheme has been prepared or commenced.

6.7.7 **No disputes**

No claim or investigation has been threatened or made against the Vendor or the trustees or administrators of the Scheme (other than routine claims for benefits) or against any other person whom the Vendor is or the said trustees or administrators are or may be liable to pay, indemnify or compensate in respect of any matter arising out of or in connection with the Scheme, nor are there any circumstances which may give rise to any such claim.

6.7.8 Contracting-Out

Where the Scheme is contracted out a fully up to date and correct contracting-out certificate (including schedules thereto) has been properly obtained and maintained.

6.7.9 Insurance

All lump sums held in relation to the Scheme (other than normal pension benefits) are securely and fully insured with a reputable insurance company and all premiums due in respect of such insurance has been paid.

6.7.10 Employer related investments

The Assets do not include any assets owned by a pension arrangement retained by the Vendors.

7 Taxation

7.1 VAT and PAYE

7.1.1 The Vendor has duly deducted all amounts from any payments from which tax falls to be deducted at source under the PAYE system and national insurance contributions and any other sums required by law to be deducted from wages, salaries or other benefits and the Vendor has duly paid or accounted for such amounts and all other sums due in respect of any benefits that are subject to taxation or similar contributions to a Taxation Authority.

7.1.2 There have been no investigations made by a Taxation Authority within three years prior to the date hereof into or affecting the payment of tax on benefits in cash or otherwise paid by the Vendor to its employees or persons alleged by a Taxation Authority to be employees.

7.1.3 In respect of the Business, the Vendor has complied with the provisions of VATA 1994 and with all statutory requirements, regulations, orders, provisions, directions or conditions relating to VAT, including the terms of any agreement reached with a Taxation Authority in respect of the Business and has maintained full, complete, correct and up to date records, invoices and other documents (as the case may be) appropriate or requisite for the purposes thereof and has preserved such records, invoices and other documents in such form and for such periods as are required by the relevant legislation.

7.1.4 The Disclosure Letter contains full details of all current agreements or arrangements between the Vendor and a Taxation Authority relating to VAT.

7.1.5 The Vendor is not liable to any abnormal or non-routine payment, or any forfeiture, penalty, interest or surcharge, or to the operation of any penal provision, in relation to VAT.

7.1.6 The Vendor has not been required by a Taxation Authority to give security for payment of VAT.

7.1.7 There has been no investigation by a Taxation Authority within three years prior to the date hereof into or affecting the payment of VAT in respect of the Business.

7.1.8   The Disclosure Letter contains details (including the cost and percentage of input tax claimed on the item in the first interval as defined in the VAT Regulations, reg.114) of all land and other capital items which are used in the course of furtherance of the Business to which VAT Regulations, reg.115 could apply. No such adjustment as is referred to in the VAT Regulations, regs 112–116 has been made or should have been made in respect of the current interval in relation to any such capital items.

7.1.9   No election under VATA 1994 Sch.10, para.2 to waive exemption from VAT in respect of the grant of any interest in or right over land owned or occupied by the Vendor which is to be transferred to the Purchaser under the terms of this Agreement has been made by the Vendor or by any person making such a grant to the Vendor.

7.1.10 The Vendor has not made exempt supplies such, or of such amount, that it is unable to obtain full credit for input tax paid or suffered by it.

7.1.11 The Disclosure Letter contains details in respect of:

7.1.11.1 such of the Property as is leasehold; all fixtures, within the meaning of CAA 2001 s.173, which are treated pursuant to that section as belonging to the Vendor;

7.1.11.2 such of the Property as is freehold; all fixtures, so defined, that are treated pursuant to the said s.173 as belonging to a person other than the Vendor.

7.2   Inheritance tax

7.2.1   The Assets hereby agreed to be sold are not subject to a Taxation Authority charge as it mentioned in IHTA 1984 s.237 nor is any unsatisfied liability to inheritance tax attached to or attributable to any of the Assets.

7.7.2   No person is liable to inheritance tax attributable to the value of the Assets hereby agreed to be sold in such circumstances that such person has the power under IHTA 1984 s.212 to raise the amount of such tax by the sale or mortgage or by a terminable charge on the said assets.

APPENDIX 6

The Tax Schedule

PART 1: DEFINITIONS

1 Definitions

In this Schedule [ ]:

1.1 Words and expressions defined in the Agreement shall except where otherwise provided or expressly defined below have the same meaning;

1.2 "Auditors" the auditors of the Company from time to time;

1.3 "Claim for Taxation" includes any notice, demand, assessment, determination, letter or other document issued, or action taken, by or on behalf of any Taxation Authority and whether issued before or after Completion, whereby it appears that the Company is, or may be, subject to a Liability to Taxation (whether or not it is primarily payable by the Company and whether or not the Company has or may have any right of reimbursement);

1.4 "Company" [details of target company to be inserted];

1.5 "CTA 2010" Corporation Tax Act 2010;

1.6 "Event" any event whatsoever including but not limited to any disposition, action or omission (whether or not the Company or the Purchaser is a party) the earning, accrual or receipt of any income, profits or gains, the declaration, payment or making of any dividend or other distribution (in each case whether actual or deemed) on or before Completion and includes any events which are deemed to have occurred for any Taxation purpose;

1.7 "IHTA 1984" Inheritance Tax Act 1984;

1.8 "ITA" Income Tax Act 2007;

1.9 "IT(EP)A 2003" Income Tax (Earnings and Pensions) Act 2003;

1.10 "Liability to Taxation" includes:

1.10.1 any liability of the Company to make an actual payment in respect of or in the nature of Taxation;

1.10.2 the set-off or utilisation of a Pre-Completion Relief or Purchaser's Relief against a liability of the Company to make an actual payment of or in respect of Taxation where, but for such set off or utilisation, a liability would have arisen under paragraph 1.10.1 above;

1.10.3 the loss, disallowance, counteracting or clawing back of a Pre-Completion Relief which would otherwise have been available to the Company other than as set out in paragraph 1.10.2;

1.10.4 the loss, qualifying, disallowance, cancellation or set-off of a right to repayment of Taxation which would otherwise have been available to the Company;

and the amount of the Liability to Taxation shall be, in the case of:

1.10.5   paragraph 1.10.1 the amount of Taxation payable;

1.10.6   paragraph 1.10.2 the amount of Taxation which would have been payable but for such set-off or utilisation;

1.10.7   paragraph 1.10.3 the value attributed in the Accounts to the Pre-Completion Relief so lost, counteracted, or clawed back; and

1.10.8   paragraph 1.10.4 the amount of repayment which would otherwise have been available;

1.11   "Pre-Completion Relief" any Relief which arises as a result of or by reference to any Event occurring on or before Completion and which has either been treated as an asset in the [Accounts] or is taken into account in computing (and so reducing or eliminating) a provision for deferred tax which appears in the [Accounts] or which would have appeared in the [Accounts] but for the presumed availability of the Relief;

1.12   "Purchaser's Relief" any Relief of the Company which arises as a result of or by reference to any Event occurring after the Balance Sheet Date or any Relief of any company other than the Company which arises at any time;

1.13   "Relief" includes any relief allowance, exemption, set-off, deduction from or credit available from, against or in relation to Taxation or in the computation of income, profits or gains for a Taxation purpose;

1.14   "Saving" a reduction of any liability of the Company to Taxation by virtue of the set off against the liability or against any income profits or gains of any Relief arising as the result of a Liability to Taxation in respect of which the Vendors have made payment under Part 3 of this Schedule 3;

1.15   "Taxation" shall have the same meaning as in clause 1 of the Agreement;

1.16   "Taxation Authority" the HMRC or any statutory or governmental authority or body (whether in the United Kingdom or elsewhere) involved in the collection or administration of Taxation;

1.17   "Tax Covenant" the covenant contained in Part 3 of this Schedule 3;

1.18   References to any Event occurring on or before Completion include a combination of two or more Events the first of which occurred or is deemed to have occurred on or before Completion [provided that the Event occurring on or before Completion occurred outside the ordinary course of business of the Company and the Event occurring after Completion occurred in the ordinary course of business of the Company].

PART 2: TAXATION WARRANTIES

[See Ch.5 and Appendix 4]

[This schedule and various parts within it work by reference to appropriate operative provisions contained in the sale agreement which provides that the Vendors warrant in these terms and provide the covenant contained in Part 3.]

PART 3: COVENANT

1   Covenant

1.1   Subject as provided below, the Vendors jointly and severally covenant to pay to the Purchaser an amount equal to the amount of:

1.1.1 any Liability to Taxation which has arisen or arises as a result of or in connection with an Event which occurred on or before Completion whether or not such liability has been discharged on or before Completion;

1.1.2 any Liability to Taxation which arises on, before or after Completion as a result of the non-payment of Taxation by a Vendor or any person (other than the Company) which is or has been connected (within the meaning of ITA 2007 s.993 and 994) with a Vendor and for which that person is primarily liable;

1.1.3 any liability of the Company to make a payment in respect of Taxation under any indemnity, covenant, guarantee or charge (including any payment in respect of a surrender of group relief) entered into on or before Completion;

1.1.4 the costs and expenses reasonably incurred by the Company or the Purchaser in respect of any Liability to Taxation or Claims for Taxation arising as a result of or in connection with an Event which occurred on or before Completion or in taking or defending any action under this Part 3 of this Schedule 3;

1.1.5 any depletion in or reduction in value of any of the assets of the Company or an increase in its liabilities as a result of any inheritance tax which:

1.1.5.1 is at Completion a charge on any of the shares or the assets of the Company or gives rise to a power to sell, mortgage or charge any of the shares or the assets of the Company; or

1.1.5.2 after Completion becomes a charge on or gives rise to a power to sell, mortgage or charge any of the shares or the assets of the Company which arises as a result of a transfer of value occurring or being deemed to occur on or before Completion (whether or not in conjunction with the death of any person whenever occurring);

provided that any right to pay by instalments shall be disregarded and the provisions of IHTA 1984 s.213 shall not apply to payments falling to be made under this Covenant;

1.1.6 any liability which arises at any time of the Company to account for income tax or national insurance contributions in respect of an option or other right to acquire securities granted prior to Completion by the Company or by any other person (other than the purchaser or any person connected with the purchaser or acting on its behalf) or in respect of the exercise of such option or right or in respect of any acquisition, disposal or any other event in relation to employment related securities (as defined for the purposes of Pt 7 IT(EP)A):

1.1.6.1 acquired at any time on or before Completion or at any time after Completion pursuant to the exercise of any right or option (in either case whether conditional or otherwise) granted on or before Completion but for the avoidance of doubt not including the consideration shares; or

1.1.6.2 acquired (before Completion) in replacement or exchange for or derived from any employment related securities (as defined for the purposes of Pt

7 IT(EP)A) acquired as mentioned in paragraph 1.1.6.1 above.

PART 4: LIMITATIONS

1 Limitations on claims

1.1   The Tax Covenant and any claim under the Taxation Warranties shall not apply to any Liability to Taxation:

1.1.1   the extent that specific provision or reserve or allowance in respect thereof has been made in the [Accounts];

1.1.2   for which the Company is, or may become, liable wholly or primarily as a result of transactions in the usual course of its business after the Balance Sheet Date;

1.1.3   to the extent that it would not have arisen or been increased but for a change in the rate of Taxation or change in legislation or published administrative practice made after Completion, or change after Completion in any extra statutory concession or published practice previously made by any Taxation Authority;

1.1.4   to the extent that the Liability to Taxation arises as the result of the change after Completion in any accounting policy, Taxation or accounting practice or the length of any accounting period for Tax purposes of the Company;

1.1.5   to the extent of any recovery by the Purchaser under the Non-Tax Warranties in respect of, or arising from, the same Liability to Taxation;

1.1.6   to the extent that a Relief other than a Pre-Completion Relief or a Purchaser's Relief is available to reduce such Liability to Taxation;

1.1.7   if it results from the cessation of the trade of the Company after Completion;

1.1.8   to the extent that it has been made good or otherwise compensated for by the Purchaser or the Company but after deducting costs incurred by them directly as a result of doing so;

1.1.9   which is attributable to the Company ceasing to be entitled to the small companies' rate of corporation tax as a result of the purchase of the Shares by the Purchaser;

1.1.10 to the extent Disclosed in the Disclosure Letter;

1.1.11 which would not have arisen, or been increased but for a voluntary act or omission of the Company or the Purchaser [which could reasonably have been avoided] carried out, or occurring, after the date of this Agreement, otherwise that in the ordinary and proper course of business [and which the Purchaser or the Company was or ought reasonably to have been aware could give rise to a Liability to Taxation]; or

1.1.12 if the Company fails, after due warning, to act in accordance with the reasonable instructions of the Vendors in conducting a dispute (as referred to in paragraph 2 of this Part 4 of Schedule 3) in respect of a claim for Taxation for breach of the Tax Warranties.

1.2   The Vendors shall have no liability in respect of a claim under the Tax Covenant or the Tax Warranties unless the Purchaser shall have given notice in writing to the Vendors of such claim pursuant to paragraph 2 of this Part 4 of this Schedule 3 not later than the seventh anniversary of Completion.

2 Conduct of Claims

2.1   The Purchaser shall as soon as reasonably practicable notify the Vendors in writing of any Claim for Taxation which comes to its notice, whereby it appears that the Vendors are, or may become, liable to pay the Purchaser under the Tax Covenant or in respect of a claim under the Tax Warranties [provided that the giving of such notice will not be a condition precedent to the liability of the Vendors under the Tax Covenant or the Tax Warranties].

2.2   The Purchaser shall ensure that a Claim for Taxation to which paragraph 2.1 of this Part 4 of Schedule 3 applies, is, so far as reasonably practicable, dealt with separately from claims to which it does not apply.

2.3   Provided that the Vendors indemnify and secure the Company and the Purchaser to the reasonable satisfaction of the Purchaser against all losses, costs, damages and expenses (including interest on overdue Taxation) which may be incurred thereby, the Purchaser will procure that the Company at the Vendors' cost and expense, takes such action and gives such information and assistance in connection with its Taxation affairs as the Vendors may reasonably and promptly request to dispute, appeal against, settle or compromise any Claim for Taxation. This obligation will not apply where a Taxation Authority alleges dishonest or fraudulent conduct by the Vendors or by the Company before Completion.

2.4   The Purchaser shall procure that the Vendors (and their advisers) are given reasonable access to all relevant documents, records and personnel of the Company and the Purchaser and its advisers to enable the Vendors promptly and effectively to evaluate the dispute and enforce any of their rights under this paragraph 2.

2.5   In connection with the conduct of a dispute relating to a Claim for Taxation to which the Tax Covenant or the Tax Warranties apply:

2.5.1   the Vendors and the Purchaser shall keep the other parties informed of all relevant matters and shall promptly forward or procure to be forwarded copies of all material correspondence and other written communications;

2.5.2   the Vendors shall not settle or compromise the dispute, or agree anything in its conduct which is likely to affect the amount involved or the future Liability to Taxation of the Company, or the Purchaser, without the prior approval of the Purchaser, such approval not to be unreasonably withheld or delayed;

2.5.3   if a dispute arises between the Purchaser and the Vendors as to whether a Claim for Taxation should be settled in full or contested, the dispute shall be referred to the determination of a senior tax counsel of at least 10 years standing ("Counsel"), appointed by agreement between the Purchaser and the Vendors, or (if they do not agree) upon the application by either party to the President for the time being of the Law Society, whose determination shall be final. Counsel shall be asked to advise whether, in his opinion, an appeal against the Claim for Taxation would, on the balance of probabilities, be likely to succeed. Only if his opinion is in the affirmative shall that Claim for Taxation be contested. Any further dispute arising between the Vendors and the Purchaser as to whether a further appeal should be pursued following determination of an earlier appeal (whether or not in favour of the Vendors) shall be resolved in a similar manner.

2.6   Nothing contained in this paragraph 2 shall require the Purchaser to prevent the Company from making a payment of Taxation at the time necessary to avoid incurring a fine, penalty or interest in respect of unpaid Taxation.

2.7   If the Vendors fail promptly (and in any event within 20 Business Days of the Purchaser giving notice requiring the Vendors to do so) to inform the Purchaser of any action which the Vendors wish the Purchaser to procure the Company to take under paragraph 2.3, the Purchaser will be entitled to procure that the Company settles or compromises any Claim for Taxation on such terms as it determines in its absolute discretion.

3   Dates for Payments

3.1   This paragraph applies solely for determining the date on which any payments are to be made by the Vendors under the Tax Covenant.

3.2   The Vendors shall make payment to the Purchaser in cleared funds on the date falling five clear Business Days after the date on which the Purchaser has notified the Vendors of the amount of the payment required to be made or, if later:

3.2.1   in any case involving a liability of the Company to make an actual payment (whether or not of Taxation) three clear Business Days prior to that date on which the Company is required to make such payment; or

3.2.2   in any case involving the set off or utilisation of a Pre-Completion Relief or a Purchaser's Relief pursuant to paragraph 1.11.2 of Part 1 of this Schedule 3, three clear Business Days before the date on which the payment of Taxation is or would have been required to be made but for such set off or utilisation; and

3.2.3   in any case involving the loss, nullifying, disallowance, cancellation or set off or a right to repayment of Taxation, three clear Business Days after such repayment of Taxation would have been received by the Company.

3.3   If any payment by the Vendors under the Tax Covenant or the Tax Warranties is not made on the date referred to in paragraph 3.2 it shall carry interest from the due date for payment at the rate of [3] per cent above the base rate from time to time of [Barclays] Bank Plc until payment is received by the Purchaser.

3.4   Disputes in relation to the provisions of paragraphs 3.2 and 3.3 may be referred by the Purchaser or the Vendors to the Auditors, acting as experts and not as arbitrators, whose certificate shall in the absence of manifest error be final.

4   Deduction from payments and right of set-off

4.1   Except as required by law all payments under the Tax Covenant shall be made gross, free of rights of counterclaim or set-off and without any deductions or withholdings of whatever nature.

4.2　If a deduction or withholding is required by law to be made from a payment by the Vendors under the Tax Covenant, there shall be paid to the Purchaser such additional amount as is necessary to ensure that the net receipt by the Purchaser is equal to the amount which it would have received and retained had the payment in question not been subject to deduction or withholding.

4.3　If the Purchaser or the Company is liable to Taxation in respect of a payment under the Tax Covenant (or would have been liable but for the availability of Relief or a right to repayment of Taxation), there shall be paid to the Purchaser an additional amount as if the Taxation had been a deduction or withholding from the payment and paragraph 4.2 shall apply accordingly to the payment.

5　Savings

5.1　If (at the request and expense of the Vendors) the Company's Auditors certify that the Company or the Purchaser has obtained a Saving, the Purchaser shall as soon as reasonably practicable repay to the Vendors the lesser of:

5.1.1　the amount of the Saving less any costs incurred in obtaining it (as certified by the Company's Auditor); and

5.1.2　the amount paid by the Vendors to the Purchaser pursuant to the Tax Covenant or under the Tax Warranties.

5.2　If the amount referred to in paragraph 5.1.1 exceeds that referred to in paragraph 5.1.2, the excess shall be carried forward to be set-off against (and so as to reduce or eliminate) the future liability of the Vendors under the Tax Covenant or the Tax Warranties.

5.3　If the Company or the Purchaser becomes aware that the Company or the Purchaser has obtained or may obtain a Saving, the Purchaser shall as soon as reasonably practicable give notice of that fact to the Vendors. Provided that the Vendors have paid the Purchaser in respect of the Liability to Taxation which gave rise to the Saving, the Purchaser shall take and procure the taking by the Company of all reasonable steps to obtain the Saving.

5.4　In certifying a Saving under paragraph 5.1, the Company's Auditors shall act as experts and not as arbitrators and their certificate shall in the absence of manifest error be final.

6　Recovery from third parties

6.1　If the Company or the Purchaser recovers or becomes aware that it is entitled to recover from any third party (including but not limited to a Taxation Authority) an amount which is referable to a Liability to Taxation in respect of which the Vendors have made a payment to the Purchaser, the Purchaser shall as soon as reasonably practicable give notice of that fact to the Vendors and shall take or procure that the Company takes (at the Vendors' expense and provided that the Vendors indemnify and secure the Purchaser and the Company to the reasonable satisfaction of the Purchaser against all losses, expenses and Taxation relating to that recovery) such reasonable action necessary to effect the recovery as the Vendors reasonably request in writing;

6.2　The Purchaser shall repay to the Vendors the lesser of:

6.2.1　the amount so recovered together with any interest (net of Taxation) or repayment supplement received in respect of it (net of any losses, costs, damages, expenses and tax relating to the amount recovered not previously recovered from the Vendors); and

6.2.2   the amount paid by the Vendors under the Tax Covenant in respect of the Liability to Taxation or Claim for Taxation in question.

6.3   If the amount provided for under paragraph 6.2.1 exceeds that under paragraph 6.2.2, the excess shall be set against, and so reduce or eliminate, any liability of the Vendors under the Tax Covenant which arises after the recovery.

PART 5: PURCHASER'S COVENANT AND ADMINISTRATIVE MATTERS

1   Purchaser's covenant

1.1   The Purchaser covenants with the Vendors that, to the extent that the Vendors or any person connected with the Vendors are assessed to Taxation pursuant to CTA 2010 ss.713–715, it shall pay the Vendors an amount equal to such liability.

1.2   The covenant in paragraph 1.1 of this Part 5 of Schedule 3 shall not apply to Liability to Taxation to the extent that:

1.2.1   if that Liability to Taxation were to be discharged by the Company then a liability would arise for the Vendors under the Tax Covenant; and

1.2.2   the Vendors have not paid an amount to the Purchaser equal to and in respect of that Liability to Taxation.
The provisions of paragraphs 3 (Dates for Payment) and 4 (Deduction from Payments and Right of Set Off) of Part 4 of this Schedule 3 shall apply to any payment due under this paragraph 1 mutatis mutandis.

2   Corporation Tax Returns

2.1   In this paragraph 2.1:

2.1.1   the "Agents" means the Vendor's Accountants or such other firm of chartered accountants as may be appointed by the Vendor for the purposes of this paragraph 2;

2.1.2   "Relevant Returns" means the corporation tax returns and computations of the Company in respect of periods ended on or before [   ]; and

2.1.3   "Relevant Correspondence" means all documents, correspondence and communications relating to the Relevant Returns which shall be received from or sent to the Taxation Authority.

2.2   The Vendors shall each use their reasonable endeavours to procure that the Agents shall (to the extent not done before Completion):

2.2.1   prepare the Relevant Returns; and

2.2.2   submit drafts of the same to the Vendors and the Company as soon as reasonably practicable.

2.3   The Purchaser shall procure that the Relevant Returns shall be authorised and signed by or on behalf of the Company and be submitted to the Taxation Authority without amendment or with such amendments as the Purchaser reasonably requests provided that neither the Purchaser nor the Company shall be obliged to authorise, sign or submit any Relevant Return unless the Purchaser reasonably believes that it is true and accurate in all material respects.

The Vendors and the Purchaser shall procure that the Agents have conduct of all Relevant Correspondence but subject always to paragraph 2 of Part 4 of this Schedule 3.

2.4   The Vendors shall procure that:

2.4.1   all reasonable steps are taken to ensure that the Relevant Returns are prepared, submitted and agreed with the Taxation Authority as soon as practicable;

2.4.2   the Purchaser and the Company are kept fully informed of all matters relating to the submission, negotiation and agreement of the Relevant Returns; and

2.4.3   the costs of the Agents in carrying out its functions under this paragraph 2 shall be borne by the Vendors.

APPENDIX 7

Limitation Provisions

[See para.11–01]

Note: before using any of the clauses reference should be made to the commentary in Ch.11 which will provide a summary of the purpose of the clause, suitable amendments and, where applicable, arguments for and against them. As commented in Ch.11, the clauses in this Appendix are those which the vendors are likely to (if they are acting reasonably) consider inserting in their first mark-up of the sale agreement as for a sale of shares.

[11A] Time limit for Warranty claims

A claim shall not be brought by the Purchaser in respect of a breach of the Warranties unless notice of the claim (specifying in reasonable detail the circumstances which give rise to the claim, the breach that results and the amount claimed) has been given to the Vendors before the expiration of the appropriate period. The claim shall be deemed to have been withdrawn (if it has not been previously satisfied, settled or withdrawn) six months after the expiration of the appropriate period, unless proceedings in respect of it have commenced by being issued and served on any of the Vendors prior to them. For the purpose of this clause, the "appropriate period":

> [11A.1] in respect of claims which arise under the Tax Warranties or the Tax Covenant is seven years from the Balance Sheet Date;
> [11A.2] in respect of other claims which arise under clauses [ ] or [ ] of Schedule [ ] it is [ ] years from Completion; and
> [11A.3] in respect of other claims is [two years from Completion].

[See para.11–03]

[11B] Exclusion of small claims

The Vendors shall not be liable in respect of a claim brought by the Purchaser for a breach of the Warranties unless their liability for all claims would exceed in aggregate £[ ] and in that event they shall be liable for the excess.
[See para.11–05]

[11C] Ceiling on claims

The total liability of the Vendors arising, by reason of claims under the Warranties or the Tax Covenant, shall not exceed £[ ].
[See para.11–09]

[11D] Conduct of Claims

In the event that the purchaser shall be aware or become aware of any fact matter or event which might constitute or give rise to a claim of breach of the Non Tax Warranties the Purchaser shall:

[11D.1] as soon as reasonably practicable notify in writing the vendors giving reasonable details of any such fact matter or event so far as practicable and consult with the vendors in respect of the matter;

[11D.2] thereafter keep the vendors information of all relevant matters and shall as soon as is reasonably practicable forward or procure to be forwarded to the vendors copies of all material correspondence and other written communications;

[11D.3] not settle or compromise the potential claim or do anything in its conduct which is likely to affect the amount involved or the future liability of [the Company, or] the Purchaser, without prior approval of the Vendors [such approval not to be unnecessarily withheld or delayed,] and take such action as the Vendors may [reasonably] request to dispute, appeal, settle or compromise the claim (or any event or fact which has or may give rise to it) provided that:

    [11D.3.1] the Vendors indemnify and secure [the Company and] the Purchaser to the reasonable satisfaction of the Purchaser against all losses, costs, damages and expenses which may be incurred thereby; and

    [11D.3.2] [nothing in this clause 11D shall require the Purchaser [or the Company] to take any action (or omit to take any action) if in the [reasonable] opinion of the Purchaser it would be [materially] harmful to the goodwill of the [Company] [Business] to do so];

[11D.4] procure that the vendors (and their advisors) are given reasonable access to all relevant documents, records and personnel of the Company and the Purchaser and its advisors to enable the Vendors promptly and effectively to evaluate, dispute and enforce their rights under this clause 11D.

[See para.11–11]

[11E] Obligation to effect third party recovery

Where the Company is entitled to recover from a third party or claim reimbursement of all or part of a sum in respect of which it has a claim or potential claim under the Non Tax Warranties, the Purchaser shall procure that it takes all possible steps to enforce the recovery or reimbursement before making a claim under the Non Tax Warranties.
[See para.11–13]

[11F] Third party recovery

If the Vendors pay to the Purchaser an amount in respect of a breach of the Warranties and the Purchaser subsequently receives from a third party a sum which is referable to that matter, the Purchaser shall forthwith repay to the Vendors an amount equal to whichever is the lesser of that sum and the amount paid by the Vendors to the Purchaser in respect of such breach of Warranty, after deducting (in either case) all reasonable costs and charges and expenses incurred by the Purchaser [or the Company] in obtaining that payment and in recovering that sum from the third party.
[See para.11–14]

[11G] Limitation of claims

The Purchaser shall have no claim whatsoever against the Vendors in respect of any breach of any of the Non Tax Warranties if and to the extent that:

[11G.1] the claim would not have arisen or been increased but for a change in legislation or the interpretation of the law or published administrative practice of any government, governmental department, agency or regulatory body made after Completion.

[11G.2] the claim would not have arisen or been increased but for a voluntary act or omission the Purchaser which could reasonably have been avoided, carried out or occurring after the date of this Agreement, otherwise than in the ordinary and proper course of the business as required by law or pursuant to a legally binding obligation of the Company created prior to Completion, and which the Purchaser [or the Company] was, or ought reasonably to have been, aware could give rise to a claim];

[11G.3] the fact, omission, circumstance or occurrence giving rise to or forming the basis of the claim has been Disclosed;

[11G.4] the claim is based on a liability which is contingent only unless and until such contingent liability becomes an actual liability and is due and payable;

[11G.5] the claim relates to a loss or liability in respect of which the Purchaser or the Company has already received damages or otherwise obtained reimbursement, or restitution or is indemnified by insurance;

[11G.6] specific provision, reserve, allowance or note in respect thereof has been made in the Accounts, the Management Accounts or the Completion Accounts;

[11G.7] not settle or compromise the potential claim or do anything in its conduct which is likely to affect the amount involved or the future liability of the Company, or the Purchaser, without prior approval of the Vendors and take such action as the Vendors may reasonably request to dispute, appeal, settle or compromise the claim (or any event or fact which has or may give rise to it) provided that the Vendors indemnify and secure the Company and the Purchaser to the reasonable satisfaction of the Purchaser against all losses, costs, damages and expenses which may be incurred thereby.

[See para.11–16]

[11H] Disapplication of limitation provisions in respect of fundamental Warranties

Clauses [   ] to [   ] (inclusive) will not apply in respect of a claim for breach of the Non Tax Warranties contained in clauses [1.1] to [1.2.5] of Schedule [   ].
[See para.11–17]

[11I] Fraud and [similar offences]

Notwithstanding any other provision of this Agreement, clauses [   ] to [   ] (inclusive) will not apply to exclude or limit the liability of the Vendors to the extent that any claim for breach of the [Non Tax] Warranties arises by reason of any fraud by the Vendors.
[See para.11–19]

[11J] Boxing Limitations

The only Warranties given in respect of Properties are those set out in paragraph [   ] (Properties) of Schedule [   ] (Warranties) and the other Warranties shall be deemed not given in relation to Properties.
[See para.11–21]

[11K] Undertakings from future purchaser of the Company

The Purchaser shall not, whilst any of the provisions of [this Schedule] are applicable or capable of taking effect, cease to control the Company without procuring from the person acquiring control an enforceable undertaking, in favour of the Vendors to be bound by those provisions, so far as they affect the Company, to the same extent as the Purchaser is bound.

[See para.11–23]

APPENDIX 8

Miscellaneous Clauses

Note: before using any of these clauses reference should be made to the commentary in the body of the book at the paragraph indicated, which will provide a summary of the purpose of the clause, suitable amendments and, where applicable, the arguments for and against them. Where relevant, the drafting of the clauses reflects that which the purchaser is likely to use in its first draft of the sale agreement drafted on the basis that the sale agreement is for a sale of shares—see comments in Ch.4 for details of which of the clauses the purchaser would be likely to include. See Ch.8 for details of other definitions that are likely to be relevant in the context of a business sale.

[1A] Restrictions on distributions by trustee Vendors

The liability of the Trustees under the Warranties is limited to the net value from time to time of the capital of the Trust, after deduction of sums due to the Taxation Authority and costs and fees properly chargeable against the capital of the Trust. The Trustees may not distribute capital of the Trust, other than for the payment of those sums, costs and fees, whilst a claim under the Warranties is outstanding or prior to the expiration of the time limit for making a claim, unless an undertaking in favour of the Purchaser is obtained from a beneficiary, in a form satisfactory to the Purchaser, by which the beneficiary accepts joint and several liability with the Trustees to the extent of the value of the distribution. [See para.2–07]

[1B] No assignment of Warranties

The Purchaser shall not be entitled to assign the Warranties and shall not be taken to hold the benefit of the Warranties for its successors in title to [the Shares] [the Assets]. [See para.2–14]

[1C] Liability of Vendors to assignee

If the benefit of the Warranties is assigned, the liability of the Vendors shall be no greater than it would have been had the Purchaser remained the owner of [the Shares] [the Business] and retained the benefit of the Warranties. [See para.2–15]

[1D] Exclusion of the Contracts (Rights of Third Parties) Act 1999

A person which is not a party to this Agreement has no right under the Contracts (Rights of Third Parties) Act 1999 to enforce any of its terms but this does not affect the rights or remedies of a third party which exist or are available apart from or pursuant to that Act. [See para.2–17]

[1E] Sharing of liability between Vendors

Without affecting their joint and several liability under this Agreement, the Vendors agree that, as between themselves, any one person shall bear only his appropriate part of a liability which arises in relation to the Warranties. For this purpose "appropriate part" means:

[1E.1]   in the case of a liability which is fairly attributable to, or which arises by reason of, income or benefits received by, or the act or default of, that person or persons connected with him (not themselves being any of the Vendors): the whole liability; and

[1E.2]   in any other case that proportion of the liability that the number of the Shares sold by him bears to the total number of the Shares.

[See para.2–21]

[2A] Right to rescind prior to Completion

The Purchaser may rescind this Agreement by notice in writing to the Vendors or the Vendors' solicitors if prior to Completion:

[2A.1]   it appears that the Warranties were not or have ceased to be accurate; or

[2A.2]   an act or event occurs which, had it occurred on or before today's date, would have had the effect that there would have been a breach of the Warranties; or

[2A.3]   there is a breach or non-fulfilment of the Warranties which (being capable of remedy) is not remedied prior to Completion.

[See para.3–05]

[2B] Purchaser's loss on breach of Warranty

If a Warranty does not relate to the value, or to anything affecting the value, of the Assets other than the Goodwill, the loss suffered by the Purchaser as a result of a breach of the Warranty shall be determined as if the value of each of the Assets (other than the Goodwill) was not that stated in clause [   ] but the lesser value that they would have had if the sale of the Business had been a forced sale and the reduction in the value of those Assets was additional consideration given for the Goodwill. If the parties are unable to agree to the adjustments to be made under this clause, the matter shall be referred to an independent firm of accountants nominated by the President of the Institute of Chartered Accountants in England and Wales for their determination as independent experts and, in the absence of manifest error, their determination shall be final.
[See para.3–07]

[2C] Measure of damages for breaches of Warranty

Without limiting the rights of the Purchaser or its ability to claim damages on any basis if there is a breach of Warranty or any of the Warranties is untrue or misleading, if [the Company incurs and becomes subject to a liability or an increase in any liability which it would not have incurred or been subject to had the breach not occurred or][1] the value of any asset of the Company is less or becomes less than the value would have been had the breach not occurred then the Vendor[s] undertake to the Purchaser to pay to the Purchaser (as the Purchaser elects) in cash on demand a sum equal to the [liability or increased liability, or the] reduction in the value of the asset [(as appropriate), or the reduction in the value of the Shares caused by the breach].
[See para.3–08]

---

[1] The words in square brackets will not be relevant and "undertake" will need to be changed to "undertakes" in the case of the purchase of a business.

[2D] Credit for improvements

The liability of the Vendors under the Warranties shall be reduced by:

[2D.1]   an amount equal to the value or additional value of any fixed assets (apart from the Properties and goodwill) owned at Completion which were not included in the Accounts or were included at less than market value after deducting (in the case of assets acquired after the Balance Sheet Date) their costs of acquisition;

[2D.2]   the amount of or by which Taxation for which the Company is accountable is extinguished or reduced as a result of the claim giving rise to the liability;

[2D.3]   the amount by which a provision for Taxation, bad or doubtful debts or contingent or other liabilities contained in the Accounts proves after Completion to have been excessive, except by reason of a reduction in Taxation rates after Completion;

[2D.4]   the amount of debts paid which had been previously written off;

[2D.5]   the amount of credits, recoveries or other benefits which have been or will be received or obtained by the Company by reason of the matters giving rise to the liability.

[See para.3–11]

[3A] Definitions

In this Agreement, the following expressions have the meanings stated namely:

"Accounts" the audited financial statements of the Company as at and to the Balance Sheet Date including the balance sheet, profit and loss account together with the notes on them, the cash flow statement and the auditor's and directors' reports.

"Accounting Standards" SSAPs, FRSs, UITF Abstracts, SORPs and all other generally accepted accounting principles applied to a United Kingdom [at the date hereof] [at the Balance Sheet Date].

"Agreement" this agreement [and the Schedules hereto] for the sale and purchase of the Shares.

"Associate" in relation to any person, a person who is connected with that person within the meaning of CTA 2010 s.1122.

"Associated Person" in relation to a company, a person (including an employee, agent or Subsidiary) who performs or has performed services for or on that company's behalf.[2]

"Balance Sheet Date" [   ] 200[   ] (being the date as at and to which the Accounts were prepared).

"BA 2010" the Bribery Act 2010.[3]

"Business Day" 9.00 am to 5.00 pm on the day other than Saturdays and Sundays and bank holidays during which clearing banks are open for business in the City of London.

"CA 1985" the Companies Act 1985.

"CA 2006" the Companies Act 2006.

"Civil Sanction" means any of the sanctions referred to in the Regulatory Enforcement and Sanctions Act 2008 s.36(1).

---

[2] This definition should be included with effect from the implementation of the BA 2010.
[3] This definition should be included with effect from the implementation of the BA 2010.

"Companies Acts" CA 2006 and CA 1985, as amended, and in each case, in so far as the same are in force at the date of this Agreement or in force at the time of the relevant event for the purposes of the Warranties.

"Completion" completion of the sale and purchase of [the Shares] [the Business].

"Computer Systems" all hardware, handheld devices, firmware, peripherals, communication links, storage media, backup systems, networking equipment and other equipment used by or on behalf of the Company together with all software [and all source, object and executable codes], databases and websites used by or on behalf of the Company.

"Confidential Business Information" all or any information relating to the following (details of which are not in the public domain) existing in any form:

(1) the business methods, corporate plans, management systems, finances, new business opportunities or development projects of the Company;

(2) the marketing or sales of any present of future product of the Company including, without limitation, customer names and lists and other details of customers, prospects, sales targets, sales statistics, pricing information, market research reports and surveys and advertising or other promotional material; and

(3) any trade secrets of other information relating to the provision of any product or services of the Company which is of a confidential nature or in respect of which the Company owes an obligation of confidence to any third party.

"Control" has the same meaning as in ITA 2007 s.995.

"Criminal Property" shall be defined by reference to the Proceeds of Crime Act 2002 s.340(3) (but disregarding paragraph (b) of that section).

"Disclosed" disclosed with sufficient information or particularity in the Disclosure Letter to enable a reasonable purchaser to make an informed assessment of the impact upon the Company of the matter disclosed after taking appropriate advice upon the matter and the relevant disclosure.

"Disclosure Letter" the disclosure letter (together with all documents attached or appended to it), having the same date as this Agreement, from the Vendors to the Purchaser and delivered to the Purchaser immediately prior to execution of this Agreement.

"Encumbrance" any mortgage, charge, debenture, assignment or assignation by way of security, guarantee, indemnity, hypothecation, restriction, right to acquire, right of pre-emption, option, right of conversion, pledge, declaration of trust, lien, right of set off or counterclaim, combination of accounts, retention of title arrangement, third party right or equity or any other security interest, encumbrance or preferential arrangement whatsoever, howsoever created or arising and any agreement or arrangement to create any of the above.

"Environment" includes any or all of the following media: air, water and land and the medium of air includes the air within buildings and the air within other natural or man-made structures above or below ground and the medium of water includes ground water and aquifers.

"Environmental Claim" any actual, pending or threatened claim, notice of violation, prosecution, demand, action, official warning, abatement or other order or notice (conditional or otherwise) relating to any Environmental Matters or Environmental Liabilities and any other notification or order requiring compliance with the terms of any Environmental Permit or Environmental Laws.

"Environmental Damage" any pollution, contamination, degradation, damage or injury caused by, related to or arising from or in connection with the presence, generation, use, handling, processing, treatment, storage, transportation, disposal or release of any Hazardous Substance.

"Environmental Laws" any Official Requirements relating to the protection of the Environment or the control or prevention or remedying of Environmental Damage or the control of Hazardous Substances.

"Environmental Liabilities" any liabilities, responsibilities, claims, losses, costs (including remedial, removal, response, abatement, clean-up, investigative and/or monitoring costs), damages, expenses, charges, assessments, liens, penalties and fines which are incurred by, asserted against or imposed upon a person as a result of or in connection with any violation of or non-compliance with Environmental Laws (including the failure to procure or violation of any Environmental Licence required by Environmental Laws); or any Environmental Damage.

"Environmental Matters" means any of the following:

(1) any generation, deposit, keeping, treatment, transportation, transmission, handling or manufacture of any Hazardous Substances;

(2) damage to property, nuisances, noise, defective premises, health and safety at work or elsewhere;

(3) the carrying out of a development (as defined in the Town and Country Planning Act 1990 s.55(1)); and

(4) the pollution, conservation or protection of the Environment whether relating to man or any living organisms supported by the Environment or any other matter whatsoever affecting the Environment or any part of it.

"Environmental Permit" any permit, licence, authorisation, consent, registration, exemption or other approval obtained or which ought to have been obtained pursuant to any Environmental Laws at any time by either the Company and/or in relation to the business carried on by the Company.

"FA" the Finance Act.

"FRS" a financial reporting standard adopted or issued by The Accounting Standards Board Limited or such other body or bodies as are prescribed for the purposes of CA 2006 s.464.

"Hazardous Substances" any solid, liquid, gas, noise and any other substance or thing which causes or may cause harm (alone or in combination with any other substance) to the Environment or any structure, thing or living organism within the Environment including any substance regulated under any Environmental Laws.

"HMRC" HM Revenue & Customs.

"ICTA 1988" the Income and Corporation Taxes Act 1988.

"Intellectual Property" all copyright and related rights, moral rights, design rights, registered designs, database rights, [semi-conductor topography rights,] patents, rights to inventions, [utility models,] business names, trade marks, [service marks,] trade names, domain names, [rights in get-up,] knowhow, trade secrets and rights in confidential information, rights to goodwill or to sue for passing off [or unfair competition,] and any other intellectual property rights or rights of a similar nature (in each case whether or not registered) and all applications for any of them which may subsist anywhere in the world.

"Intellectual Property Rights" all Intellectual Property owned or used by the Company or in relation to its business.

"ITA 1984" the Inheritance Tax Act 1984.

"IT Contracts" all arrangements and agreements under which any third party provides any element of, or services relating to, the Computer Systems, including without limitation leasing, hire purchase, licensing, subscription, supply, escrow, maintenance, support and service agreements.

"IT(EP)A 2003" the Income Tax (Earnings and Pensions) Act 2003.

"LPMPA 1994" the Law of Property (Miscellaneous Provisions) Act 1994.

"Licence" a licence, permit, certificate, consent, approval, filing of notifications, reports and assessments, registrations or authorisations required by law for operation of the Company's business, its ownership, use possession or occupation of any asset or the performance of this Agreement.

"Management Accounts" the unaudited balance sheet of the Company as at [ ] and the unaudited profit and loss account of the Company for the period ended on [ ] copies of which are attached to the Disclosure Letter.

"Non Taxation Warranties" those warranties other than the Taxation Warranties.

"Official Requirement" any law, statute, ordinance, pact, decree, treaty, code, rule, regulation, directive, order, notice or official published plan or policy with legal or actual force in any geographical area and/or for any class of persons.

"Planning Acts" the Town and Country Planning Act 1990, the Planning (Listed Buildings and Conservation Areas) Act 1990, the Planning (Hazardous Substances) Act 1990 (as amended) and the Planning and Compensation Act 1991.

"Political Cause" includes political parties, election committees, party affiliated organisations, party aligned research bodies, pressure and lobby groups.[4]

"Political Contributions" any payments to support a Political Cause which may include, but is not limited to, donations, loans, gifts, provisions of services, advertising and/or promotional expenditure.[5]

"Properties" the [leasehold and freehold] properties briefly described in Schedule [ ] and reference to a "Property" include a reference to each of the individual Properties.

"Schemes" [details of disclosed pension schemes to be inserted].

"Sensitive Payments" (1) Political Contributions; (2) commercial bribes, bribes or kickbacks paid to any person including central or local government officials, trade union officials or employees; (3) amounts received with an understanding that rebates or refunds will be made in contravention of the laws of any jurisdiction either directly or through a third party; (4) payments or commitments (whether made in the form of commissions, payments or fees for goods received or otherwise) made with the understanding or under circumstances that would indicate that all or part thereof is to be paid by the recipient to central or local government officials or as a commercial bribe, influence, payment or kickback; and (5) any payment deemed illegal under the Prevention of Corruption Acts 1889 to 1916.[6]

"Shares" the fully paid up shares in the capital of the Company to be and comprising the whole of the issued and allotted share capital of the Company.

"Social Media" all social networking sites, blogs, microblogs, wikis or other forms of social media used by or on behalf of the Company for business purposes.

"Subsidiary" a subsidiary undertaking as defined in CA 2006 s.1162 save that a company shall be treated, for the purposes of the membership requirement contained in subs.1162(2), as a member of another company even if its shares in that other company are registered in the name of (a) another person (or its nominee) whether by way of security or in connection with the taking of security, or (b) its nominee.

"SORP" a statement of recommended practice issued by The Accounting Standards Board Limited or such other body or bodies as are prescribed for the purposes of CA 2006 s.464.

"SSAP" a statement of standard accounting practice published by the accounting standards committee of CCAB Limited and adopted by The Accounting Standards Board Limited.

"Taxation or Tax" all forms of taxation, duties, imposts, governmental charges (whether international, national or local) and levies whatsoever and whenever created, enacted or imposed and whether of the United Kingdom or elsewhere and without prejudice to the generality of that expression includes:

(1) income tax, corporation tax, capital gains tax, capital transfer tax, inheritance tax, stamp duty, stamp duty reserve tax, stamp duty land tax, rates, value added tax, customs and other import duties, insurance premium tax, national insurance contributions, amounts for which the company is liable to account under PAYE

---

[4] This definition should be deleted with effect from the implementation of the BA 2010.
[5] This definition should be deleted with effect from the implementation of the BA 2010.
[6] This definition should be deleted with effect from the implementation of the BA 2010.

and any payment whatsoever which the Company may be or become bound to make to any Taxation Authority or any other person as a result of any enactment relating to taxation and any other taxes, duties or levies supplementing or replacing any of the above;

(2) all costs, charges, interests, fines, penalties and expenses incidental or relating to any taxation, duties, imposts, charges and levies whatsoever (including without limitation any such described above).

"Taxation Authority" HMRC or any statutory or governmental authority or body (whether in the United Kingdom or elsewhere) involved in the collection or administration of Taxation.

"Tax Covenant" a tax deed in the form set out in Part 3 of Schedule [3].

"Tax Warranties" the warranties in Part B of Schedule [3].

"TCGA 1992" the Taxation of Chargeable Gains Act 1992.

"TMA 1970" the Taxes Management Act 1970.

"UITF Abstract" an abstract issued by the Urgent Issues Task Force of The Accounting Standard Board Limited or such other body or bodies as are prescribed for the purposes of CA 2006 s.464.

"VATA 1994" the Value Added Tax Act 1994.

"Warranties" the warranties[, representations and undertakings] of the Vendors contained in [this Agreement] [clause [ ] and] Schedules [ ] and the Tax Warranties and "Warranty" means any one of them.

"Warranty Claim" any claim made by the Purchaser for breach of any of the Warranties.

[See para.4–02]

[3B] Statutory references

References to any statute, or to any statutory provision, statutory instrument, order or regulation made thereunder, includes that statute, provision, instrument, order or regulation as amended, modified, consolidated, re-enacted or replaced from time to time, whether before or after the date of this Agreement and also includes any previous statute, statutory provision, instrument, order or regulation, amended, modified, consolidated, re-enacted or replaced by such statute, provision, instrument, order or regulation.
[See para.4–04]

[3C] The Warranties

The Vendors [jointly and severally] warrant and [represent] to the Purchaser that, save as Disclosed the Warranties are true in all respects.
[See para.4–05]

[3D] Restriction on implied covenants

The express assurance in clause [ ] as to freedom from encumbrances and the covenants implied in that clause by ss.2 and 3 LPMPA 1994 shall apply to anything falling within the scope of such assurances and covenants notwithstanding that the Vendors do not know or could not reasonably be expected to know about it, or, at the time of transfer, it is within the actual knowledge, or is a necessary consequence of facts then within the actual knowledge of the Purchaser, and the operation of the covenants implied by ss.2 and 3 LPMPA 1994 shall be deemed to be extended so as not to exclude the liability of the Vendors thereunder in any such circumstances.
[See para.4–10]

[3E] Application of Warranties to past events

The Vendors shall not be liable, in relation to a breach of the Warranties, if and to the extent that the breach is primarily attributable to anything which occurred prior to [ ].
[See para.4–12]

[3F] Effect of post-Completion events

The Vendors shall not be liable for a claim under the Warranties which would not have arisen but for anything occurring after Completion.
[See para.4–13]

[3G] Events occurring prior to Completion

[Each of the Vendors] [The Vendor] will promptly disclose in writing to the Purchaser any [material] circumstance which arises, or becomes known to [him] [her] [it], prior to Completion and is inconsistent [in a material respect] with any of the Warranties or the matters Disclosed, [or which might be material to be known by a purchaser for value of [the Shares] [the Business]].
[See para.4–15]

[3H] Conduct of the Company pending Completion

The Vendors shall procure that, save as may be necessary to give effect to this Agreement, the Company shall not, before Completion, without the prior written consent of the Purchaser [knowingly] do, procure or allow anything which might constitute or result in a [material] breach of the Warranties, or make any of them inaccurate or misleading, if they were given at Completion.
[See para.4–17]

[3I] Warranties to apply at Completion

Each of the Warranties shall be deemed to be repeated, with any necessary modification, immediately before the time of Completion, immediately before the time of Completion, with reference to the facts then existing.
[See para.4–18]

[3J] Enquiry by the Vendors

Where a Warranty refers to the knowledge, information, awareness or belief of the Vendors, each of the Vendors undertakes that they have made full enquiry into the subject matter of the Warranty and it shall not be a defence that the Vendors did not appreciate the relevance of any particular matter.
[See para.4–20]

[3K] Knowledge of the Vendor

In determining whether the Vendor has the knowledge referred to in a Warranty it shall be treated as knowing:

[3K.1] anything which is known to any of its directors; and

[3K.2] anything which is known to the persons listed in Schedule [ ] but, in respect of each of the individuals named, only in relation to those of the Warranties which are specified against his name in that Schedule.

[See para.4–22]

[3L] Awareness of one of the Vendors

If one of the Vendors is or could reasonably have been aware that there was a breach of a Warranty which refers to the knowledge, information, awareness or belief of the Vendors, he shall be liable for a fraction of the Purchaser's loss arising from that breach equal to the fraction of the Shares which are sold by him.
[See para.4–23]

[3M] Effect of investigation or waiver of liability

The remedies of the Purchaser in respect of a breach of the Warranties shall not be affected by any investigation made, or to be made, by or on behalf of the Purchaser into [the affairs of the Company] [the Business], or by the Purchaser rescinding, or failing to rescind, this Agreement or anything else other than a specific and duly authorised written waiver or release.
[See para.4–25]

[3N] Ejusdem generis rule

In construing this Agreement the so-called "ejusdem generis rule" does not apply and accordingly the interpretation of general words is not restricted by:

[3N.1]   being preceded by words indicating a particular class of acts, matters or things; or

[3N.2]   being followed by particular examples.

[See para.4–28]

[3O] Overseas companies or businesses

The Warranties apply, with any necessary modification, to [that part of the Company's business as is carried on] [any part of the Business carried on] outside England and Wales, and for the purpose of construction:

[3O.1]   a reference to a statutory provision enacted, or accounting principle applying, in England and Wales includes a reference to the corresponding provision in the local legislation and (where relevant) to a generally accepted accounting principle; and

[3O.2]   a reference to a governmental, or administrative, authority or agency includes a reference to the equivalent local governmental, or administrative, authority or agency.

[See para.4–30]

[3P] Information supplied to Vendors

Information supplied by the Company or its professional advisers to the Vendors, or their agents, representatives or advisers, in connection with the Warranties and the Disclosure Letter, or otherwise in relation to the business and affairs of the Company, is not deemed to be a representation by the Company to the Vendors as to its accuracy, and the Vendors may not make a claim against the Company, its officers or employees or its professional advisers in respect of that information.
[See para.4–33]

[3Q] Warranties independent

Each of the Warranties is independent of other Warranties [and undertakings] and, unless the contrary is expressly stated, no clause in this Agreement limits the extent or application of another clause.
[See para.4–34]

[3R] Warranties to survive Completion

Each of the Warranties, other than a Warranty fully performed at Completion, shall remain in full force and effect notwithstanding Completion.
[See para.4–35]

[3S] Delay in enforcing Warranties

A failure by the Purchaser to exercise, or a delay by it in exercising, a right in respect of a Warranty shall not operate as a waiver of the right or Warranty, and a single or partial exercise of a right shall not preclude another or further exercise of the right or the exercise of another right.
[See para.4–36]

[3T] Purchaser's warranty

The Purchaser has not already formulated, and does not presently have any actual knowledge (save as Disclosed) of any circumstances which it knows would presently entitle it to make, a Warranty Claim.
[See para.4–37]

APPENDIX 9

Short Form Warranties

[See paras 5–01, 6–17 and 7–02]

Note: for the purpose of this Appendix, the definitions in para.4–02 are used.

1 Corporate matters and capacity

1.1 Each Vendor has the necessary power and authority to enter into and perform this Agreement and all other documents to be executed by them at or before Completion in accordance with this Agreement which constitutes, or will when executed constitute, binding and enforceable obligations on each of the Vendors.

1.2 The information relating to the Company in Schedule [ ] is accurate and complete [in respect of the matters dealt with].

1.3 The Shares will at Completion constitute the whole of the issued and allotted share capital of the Company.

1.4 The Vendors are the sole legal and beneficial owners of the Shares.

1.5 Apart from this Agreement, there are no agreements or arrangements which provide for the issue, allotment or transfer of, or grant a right (whether conditional or otherwise) to call for the issue, allotment or transfer of share or loan capital of the Company. No claim has been made by any person to be entitled to any of the foregoing.

1.6 The register of members and other statutory books of the Company have been properly kept [in accordance with all applicable laws] [in accordance with the Companies Acts] and contain an accurate and complete record of the matters with which they should deal; and no notice or allegation that any of them is incorrect or should be rectified has been received.

1.7 All returns, particulars, resolutions and documents required to be filed with the Registrar of Companies in respect of the Company have been duly filed and were correct.

1.8 The Company is not the holder or beneficial owner of, nor has it agreed to acquire, share or loan capital of a body corporate.

2 Possession of documents

2.1 All title deeds relating to the assets of the Company, an executed copy of all [subsisting written] agreements to which the Company is a party and the original copies of all other documents [which are in force or otherwise relevant to the Company] and which are owned by, or which ought to be in the possession of the Company are in its possession [or under its control]. All documents are, where relevant, stamped with the correct amount of stamp duty.

3 Accounting

3.1 The Accounts were prepared in accordance with the historical cost convention and with the requirements of all relevant statutes and

Accounting Standards; and on the same bases and policies of accounting as adopted for the purpose of preparing the audited accounts of the Company in respect of the preceding three accounting periods.

3.2   The Accounts:

      3.2.1   give a true and fair view of the assets and liabilities and state of affairs of the Company at the Balance Sheet Date and the profits or losses [and cash flow] of the Company for the period ended on that date;

      3.2.2   comply with the requirements of CA 2006;

      3.2.3   comply with current Accounting Standards; and

      3.2.4   are not affected by extraordinary, exceptional or non-recurring items.

3.3   All accounting and other records of the Company are in its possession, have been fully, properly and accurately kept and completed and give a true and fair view of its financial contractual and trading position.

3.4   The Management Accounts have been prepared [in accordance with accounting policies consistent with those used in the preparation of the Accounts,] with all due care and on a basis consistent with the management accounts of the Company prepared in the preceding [year].

4   Financial

4.1   Full details of the Company's existing facilities (none of which are dependent on security provided by any third party) ("the Facilities") are set out in the Disclosure Letter. The Facilities provide sufficient working capital for the purposes of the Company continuing to carry on its business in its present form and at its present level of turnover for the period of 12 months after Completion.

4.2   The Company has no outstanding, nor has it agreed to create or issue any, loan capital, nor has it factored or discounted any of its debts or engaged in financing of a type which would not be required to be shown or reflected fully in the Accounts, nor borrowed any money which it has not repaid, save for borrowings not exceeding the amounts shown in the Accounts.

4.3   The Company has not lent any money which has not been repaid to it nor owns the benefit of any debt (whether or not due for payment) other than debts which have arisen in the ordinary and normal course of its business.

4.4   Full details of all grants, subsidies or financial assistance applied for or received by the Company from any governmental department or agency or any local or other authority are set out in the Disclosure Letter and the Company had complied in full with the terms of such grants, subsidies and financial assistance.

5   Business since the Balance Sheet Date

5.1   Since the Balance Sheet Date the Company has:

      5.1.1   not paid, made or declared a dividend or other distribution (as defined in ICTA 1988);

      5.1.2   not repaid, or become liable to repay any indebtedness in advance of its stated maturity;

      5.1.3   paid its creditors in accordance with their respective credit terms;

5.1.4   carried on its business in the ordinary and normal course of business and there has been no adverse change in the Company's financial position or trading position and in particular there has been no reduction in the level of turnover;

5.1.5   not entered into any long-term, substantial or abnormal obligations or transactions (including joint venture, consortium or similar arrangements);

5.1.6   not acquired or set up (or agreed to do so) any new branch or subsidiary; and

5.1.7   not made or agreed to make any capital expenditure or incurred or agreed to incur any capital commitments nor has it disposed of or realised any capital assets or any interest in such assets (and there were no commitments on capital account in respect of the Company outstanding at the Balance Sheet Date).

6   Effect of Sale of Shares

6.1   The Vendors are not aware, and have no grounds for believing, that after Completion (whether by reason of an existing agreement or arrangement or otherwise) or as a result of the proposed acquisition of the Company by the Purchaser any person or third party with whom the Company deals will or will seek to change the manner and/or terms upon which it deals with the Company.

6.2   Compliance with the terms of this Agreement will not so far as the Vendors are aware have a detrimental effect to the Company under the terms of any subsisting contract, agreement, transaction, arrangement, liability, understanding or commitment (howsoever the same may be described) to which it is a party.

7   Liabilities

7.1   The Company has no outstanding liabilities (including disputed or contingent liabilities) other than the liabilities Disclosed or incurred in the ordinary and normal course of trading since the Balance Sheet Date.

7.2   There has been no exercise, purported exercise or claim for any Encumbrance over any of the assets of the Company and there is no dispute directly or indirectly relating to any assets.

7.3   The Company has at all times conducted and is conducting its business in accordance with all applicable Official Requirements and contractual obligations and has obtained all requisite licences, permits and consents and there are no investigations or enquiries in existence or pending in respect of the affairs of the Company and the Vendors have no knowledge of any fact or matter which could lead to such investigations or enquiries.

7.4   The Company is not under any liability in relation to goods sold or services provided by it and the Vendors know of no reason why it may become so liable in the future in respect of goods already sold and services already provided.

8   Guarantees and Indemnities

8.1   There are no subsisting loans, guarantees or agreements for indemnity given by or for the accommodation of the Company.

9   Taxation

9.1   The Accounts make proper provision (taking account of the relevant Accounting Standards) or reserve for all Taxation (including deferred Taxation) which is liable to be assessed on the Company, or for which it may be accountable, in respect of the period ended on the Balance Sheet Date including distributions made down to such date or provided for in the Accounts.

9.2   All returns, notifications, computations and payments which should have been made or given by the Company for a Taxation purpose in the last six years were made or given within the requisite periods and were up to date, correct and on a proper basis.

9.3   There is no material dispute or disagreement outstanding or contemplated at the date of this Agreement with any Taxation Authority regarding liability or any potential liability to any tax or duty (including in each case penalties or interest) recoverable from the Company or regarding the availability of any relief from tax or duty to the Company and so far as the Vendors are aware there are no circumstances which make it likely that any such dispute or disagreement will commence.

10   Litigation and insolvency

10.1   Neither the Company nor any person for whose acts or defaults the Company is or may be vicariously liable are engaged in any litigation, mediation, arbitration, administrative or criminal proceedings or other proceedings or hearings before any statutory or governmental body, department, board or agency; and there are no proceedings pending or threatened or expected by or against such persons or the Company; and there is nothing which is likely to give rise to such proceedings. The Company is not subject to any order or judgment given by any court or governmental agency (whether local or national) nor has it been a party to any undertaking or assurance given to any court, governmental agency or person which is still in force.

10.2   No insolvency event has occurred in relation to the Company and the Vendors are not aware of any circumstances which may lead to such an event.

11   Trading matters

11.1   No authorities (express or implied) by which any person may enter into a contract or commitment to do anything on behalf of the Company are subsisting.

11.2   The Disclosure Letter contains accurate particulars of all subsisting contracts to which the Company is a party at the date of this Agreement and the Vendors know of no breach of or any invalidity, or grounds for determination, rescission, avoidance or repudiation of any such contract or of any allegations of such thing.

11.3   The Company is not a party to, and its profits and financial position during the past three years have not been affected by, a contract or arrangement which is not of an arm's length nature.

11.4   The Company has complied with all Environmental Laws, obtained all relevant Environmental Licences (and complied with the terms of them) and is not subject to any Environmental Liabilities.

12 Property

12.1   The Company has good and marketable title to all of the Properties which comprise all the estate or interest of the Company in land or premises, and [the Company is the proprietor of each of the Properties registered at the Land Registry with absolute title] [particulars of the titles to the Properties are set out in Schedule [   ]].

12.2   The Company has in its possession, or under its control, all duly stamped deeds and documents which are necessary to prove title to each of the Properties.

12.3   There is no option, or agreement for sale, mortgage (whether specific or floating), charge, lien, lease agreement or lease, overriding interest, condition, restrictive covenant, easement or other encumbrance in respect of any of the Properties.

12.4   The Properties are not subject to the payment of any outgoings (except business and water rates).

12.5   The Company has duly and punctually performed and observed all covenants, conditions, agreements, statutory requirements, planning consents, bye-laws, orders and regulations affecting any of the Properties, and no notice of a breach has been received.

12.6   The use of each of the Properties is the permitted use for the purposes of the Town and Country Planning Act 1990 and there is a valid and subsisting planning permission for all development that has taken place in respect of the Properties.

12.7   There are no compulsory purchase notices, orders or resolutions affecting any of the Properties.

12.8   The Properties have at all times been held by the Company as investments and not as trading stock.

13 Employment matters

13.1   Accurate and complete particulars of the identities, dates of commencement of employment or appointment to office and terms and conditions of employment of all the employees and officers of the Company, including without limitation details of all remuneration and other benefits, such as profit sharing, commission and bonus arrangements (whether or not contractual), and details of any outstanding claims or potential claims by any person who is now or has been an officer or employee of the Company (all of which are fully covered by insurance) are fully and accurately set out in the Disclosure Letter.

14 Pensions

14.1   Save in respect of the Scheme, the Company has no legal obligation to provide or cause to be provided to any person benefits under a "pension scheme", as defined by s.150(1) of the FA 2004, or under an "employer-financed retirement benefits scheme", as defined by s.393B of the IT(EP)A 2003, or under a superannuation fund to which s.15(3) of the ICTA 1988 applies, that are "retirement or death benefits" for the purposes of s.307 of the IT(EP)A 2003 and do not fall under the categories referred to above, or that are "excluded benefits" for the purposes of s.393B of the IT(EP)A 2003 and do not fall under the categories above.

15 Asset matters

15.1 Except for assets disposed of by the Company in the ordinary and normal course of business, the Company is the legal and beneficial owner of and has title to all assets included in the Accounts and all assets which have been acquired by the Company since the Balance Sheet Date (save for those items the subject of hire purchase, leasing or rental agreements listed in the Disclosure Letter) and there is not outstanding any Encumbrance (or agreement to grant any Encumbrance) over the whole or any part of the undertaking property or assets of the Company.

15.2 The plant, machinery, vehicles and other equipment used in connection with the business of the Company are in a good and safe state of repair and satisfactory working order and have been properly maintained.

15.3 The Company's stock levels are not excessive and are adequate in relation to current trading requirements, with stock in trade being in good condition and capable of sale in accordance with the Company's current price list, without rebate or allowance to a purchaser.

15.4 All the assets of the Company of an insurable nature are and have at all material times been insured in amounts representing their full replacement or reinstatement value against fire and other risks normally insured against by persons carrying on the same type of business as that carried on by it.

15.5 The Company is, and has at all material times been, adequately covered against accident, damage, third party loss (including product liability), loss of profits and other risks normally insured against by persons carrying on the same type of business as that carried on by it.

15.6 All of the Company's insurance policies are currently fully effective (all premiums having been duly paid to date) and nothing has been done or omitted to be done which could make a policy of insurance void or voidable or which is likely to result in an increase in premium.

15.7 No claim is outstanding, or may be made, under any of the Company's insurance policies and no circumstances exist which are likely to give rise to a claim.

16 Intellectual Property Rights

16.1 The Company is the sole legal and beneficial owner and exclusive user of the Intellectual Property Rights which have been or are being used by the Company or which are necessary for the carrying on of its business as it has been carried on up to Completion (as accurately detailed in the Disclosure Letter).

16.2 All Intellectual Property Rights are valid, subsisting and enforceable (nothing having been done that could affect this), are not subject to any infringement or challenge (and the Vendors know of no reason why they should be) and, where capable of registration, have been registered by the Company in all jurisdictions relevant to its business, with all renewal and registration fees having been paid and all other steps required for the prosecution, maintenance and protection of the Intellectual Property Rights having been taken.

17 Information Technology

17.1 All Computer Systems are owned and used exclusively by the Company, do not infringe the Intellectual Property any third party, are covered by appropriate maintenance and support agreements (details of which are set out in the Disclosure Letter), and are in full working order and performing the functions for which they were acquired without material errors or downtime. The Vendors are not aware of any matters which may interrupt or affect the use of the Computer Systems used by the Company on the same basis as currently used.

17.2 The Computer Systems have adequate capacity for the Company's present needs and adequate security and backup systems to ensure that breaches of security, errors and breakdowns are kept to a minimum and that in the event of a failure of the Computer Systems that no more than one day's data will be lost and there will not be a material disruption to the Company.

17.3 The Company has complied with the Data Protection Act 1998 and the Privacy and Electronic Communications (EC Directive) Regulations 2003.

18 General matters

18.1 All information given by any of the Vendors, the Vendors' Solicitors or the Company's auditors to the Purchaser, the Purchaser's Solicitors or the Purchaser's accountants relating to the business, activities, affairs, or assets or liabilities of the Company was and is accurate and complete and opinions, expectations and beliefs included in the information are honestly held and have been arrived at on a reasonable basis after full enquiry.[1]

18.2 There are no material facts or circumstances in relation to the assets, business or financial condition of the Company which have not been Disclosed to the Purchaser or the Purchaser's Solicitors and which, if disclosed, might reasonably have been expected to affect the decision of the Purchaser to enter into this Agreement.[2]

18.3 No one is entitled to receive from the Company any finder's fee or brokerage or other commission in connection with the sale and purchase of the Shares.

---

[1] Please see comments at para.7–30 in relation to this warranty and the alternative form of wording that well-advised vendors are likely to insist on.

[2] Please see comments at para.7–31 in relation to this warranty which is the infamous "sweeping-up" warranty which is likely to be strongly resisted by the vendors.

APPENDIX 10

Disclosure Letter

Note: as discussed in Ch.9 this precedent represents a reasonably balanced form of first draft from the vendor. Before using this however, reference should be made to the commentary in Ch.9 which provides a summary on a number of the general and specific disclosures used below as well as suitable amendments which can be made. In addition to the amendments found in Ch.9 it is important that the vendors' solicitors tailor this precedent to their particular transaction and in particular that the terms of the disclosures, both general and specific, are drafted in here with the required contractual standard of "fair disclosure" contained in the sale agreement. In this case it does by reference to the defined term "Disclosed".

When different standards may apply or the general disclosure may be one that is likely to be deleted square brackets have been used to identify the relevant ones.

From: [*Insert names and addresses of the Vendor(s)*]

To: [*Insert name and address of the Purchaser*]

Dear Sirs,

[Sale of the entire issued share capital of] [Sale of the business and assets of] [   ] Limited ("the Company")

This letter is the Disclosure Letter referred to in the agreement [for the sale and purchase of the entire issued share capital of the Company] [relating to the sale and purchase of the [   ] business of the Company] to be entered into today between (1) [   ] (the "Vendor[s]") and (2) [   ] (the "Purchaser") ("the Agreement").

All words and expressions defined in the Agreement shall, unless the context otherwise requires, have the same respective meanings in the Disclosure Letter.

Where there is any inconsistency between the contents of the documents referred to at (a) to [ ] below and the factual statements contained in this Disclosure Letter, then the provisions and contents of these documents shall prevail. The disclosure of any matters or documents in this Disclosure Letter shall not imply any representation, warranty or undertaking not expressly given in the Agreement nor shall any disclosure be taken to extend the scope of any such representation, warranty or undertaking. The disclosures contained in this Disclosure Letter are not to be taken as any admissions that all or any of the matters call for disclosure, but are merely made for such purposes as they may serve as representing matters which might arise from the wording of the Warranties. For ease of reference, the majority of disclosures are made under paragraph numbering which refers to Schedule [ ] of the Agreement and, subject to the proviso below or as expressly provided elsewhere in this Disclosure Letter, they are numbered accordingly. Such headings and numberings are for convenience only. Accordingly, if the information disclosed could be fairly said to apply in respect of any of the other Warranties, such information shall be deemed to be Disclosed where that is the case and the Purchaser shall not be entitled to claim that any fact or matter has not been disclosed to it because it is not specifically related to any particular clause of the Agreement or paragraph of any schedule.

This Disclosure Letter shall be deemed to include and there are hereby incorporated into it the following matters, but no warranty is given as to the accuracy of the matters or the information deemed to be Disclosed in sub-paragraphs (a) to [   ] save where the matters and documents referred to are specifically warranted in the Warranties:

(a) any matter provided for, noted or evident from the accounts of the Company [the Vendor] [for [all] [the last [   ]] financial periods up to the Balance Sheet Date] or [which are attached to this Disclosure Letter as documents [   ]];

(b) the contents of the Agreement and all transactions referred to therein and documents to be entered into pursuant thereto;

(c) any matters appearing on the file at Companies House Registry in respect of the previous two years in respect of the Company as at the close of business on the day prior to the date of this Disclosure letter;

(d) the contents of, and all matters referred to in, the documents in the bundle of documents annexed to this Disclosure Letter and numbered 1 to [   ] an index to which is attached to this Disclosure Letter;

(e) the Vendors' replies to the legal due diligence questionnaire (including the documentation attached to them) sent to the Purchaser[, the financial [and commercial] due diligence report on [the Company] [the Business] prepared by [   ]] [and the contents of and matters referred to in all correspondence between the Purchaser or the Purchaser's advisers and the Vendors or the Vendors' advisers];

(f) the contents of the statutory books of the Company all of which have been made available for inspection by the Purchaser's Solicitors prior to Completion;

(g) all matters which are [in] [apparent from] the deeds of the Properties which have been made available by [the Vendors' Solicitors] [the Vendors'] to the Purchaser's Solicitors or which would have been revealed in relation to the Properties by the following searches and enquiries[1]:

(i) a search on form LLC1 (Local Land Charges Rules 1977) and enquiries of the [   ] local authority for the areas in which each of the Properties are located on Oyez Form CON29 1 and 2 (2002 Edition) [   ];

(ii) searches on the registers of Common Land and Town and Village Greens kept by the relevant local authority for the areas in which the Properties are located;

(iii) a search of the information retained by The Coal Authority in relation to past, present and future mining operations in proximity to each of the Properties;

(iv) a search of HM Land Registry and the Land Charges Department against each of the Properties as at the date of this Disclosure Letter;

(v) a search of the information retained by the relevant water and sewerage undertakings for the areas in which the Properties are located;

(vi) a phase 1 desktop environmental search for the areas in which the Properties are located;

(vii) a search of the information retained by the relevant electricity provider for the areas in which the Properties are located;

(viii) a search of the information retained by Transco in relation to the gas infrastructure for the areas in which the Properties are located;

(ix) all information or matters relating to the Properties which have been provided to the Purchaser or the Purchaser's Solicitors or other advisers in correspondence;

---

[1] The property searches which are to be generally disclosed will depend on those which have been undertaken by the purchaser as part of its due diligence. A purchaser will be unwilling to be bound by searches it did not undertake.

(x) any information contained in the replies to the enquiries and requisitions that the Purchaser's Solicitors have made in connection with their investigation of title; and

(xi) the asbestos surveys carried out at the Properties copies of which are attached at document [ ];

(h) all matters which are apparent from the surveys of the Properties copies of which are attached at document [ ] or physical inspection of the Properties (the Purchaser and its agents having been given facilities for the inspection of them);

(i) anything which would be apparent from inspection of the plant, books of account and records of [the Company] [the Business] (the Purchaser and its agents having been given facilities for the inspection of them);

(j) everything which is in the public domain; and

(k) all matters which would be revealed by a search of the registers and documents maintained by the Office of Fair Trading, the Consumer Credit Registry, the Trade Markets registry of the Intellectual Property Office in respect of the [Company] [Business].

[Set out any other documents or information which are deemed to be Disclosed.]

We wish also to make the following specific disclosures and for convenience only reference is made to particular paragraphs in Schedule [ ] of the Agreement. Each item disclosed is nevertheless deemed to be Disclosed in respect of all of the Warranties and is not limited to the paragraph which is referred to below.

[Set out specific disclosures below, one has been included by way of example.]

[1.10.1] Copies of the memorandum and articles of association of the Company are attached at document [ ].

We acknowledge receipt of the Disclosure Letter and copies of the documents numbered 1 to [ ] attached to the Disclosure Letter.

....

Signed by [ ]

Duly authorised for and on behalf of

[ ]

We acknowledge receipt and acceptance of the Disclosure Letter, copies of the Documents numbered 1 to [ ] attached to the Disclosure Letter and copies of the Annexures to the Disclosure Letter numbered 1 to [ ].

....

[ ]

Duly authorised for and on behalf of
[ ]

Index

THE COMPANION CD-ROM
Instructions for Use

Introduction

These notes are provided for guidance only. They should be read and interpreted in the context of your own computer system and operational procedures. It is assumed that you have a basic knowledge of WINDOWS. However, if there is any problem please contact our help line on 020 7393 7266 who will be happy to help you.

CD Format and Contents

To run this CD you need at least:
- IBM compatible PC with Pentium processor
- 8mb RAM
- CD-ROM drive
- Microsoft Windows 95

The CD contains data files of Precedent material. It does not contain software or commentary.

Installation

The following instructions make the assumption that you will copy the data files to a single directory on your hard disk (e.g. C:\SweetandMaxwell\Sinclair on Warranties 8th Edition).

Open your **CD ROM drive,** select and double click on **setup.exe** and follow the instructions. The files will be unzipped to your **C drive** and you will be able to open them up from the new **C:\SweetandMaxwell\Sinclair on Warranties 8th Edition** folder there.

LICENCE AGREEMENT

Definitions

1. The following terms will have the following meanings:
"The PUBLISHERS" means SWEET & MAXWELL LIMITED, incorporated in England & Wales under the Companies Acts (Registered No. 28096) whose registered office is 100 Avenue Road, London NW3 3PF, (which expression shall, where the context admits, include the PUBLISHERS' assigns or successors in business as the case may be) of the other part (on behalf of Thomson Reuters (Professional) UK Limited incorporated in England & Wales under the Companies Acts (Registered No. 1679046) whose registered office and address for service is Aldgate House, 33 Aldgate High Street, London EC3N 1DL).
"The LICENSEE" means the purchaser of the work containing the Licensed Material.
"Licensed Material" means the data included on the disk;
"Licence" means a single user licence;
"Computer" means an IBM-PC compatible computer.

Grant of Licence; Back up copies

2. (1) The PUBLISHERS hereby grant to the LICENSEE, a non-exclusive, non-transferable licence to use the Licensed Material in accordance with these terms and conditions.

(2) The LICENSEE may install the Licensed Material for use on one computer only at any one time.

(3) The LICENSEE may make one back-up copy of the Licensed Material only, to be kept in the LICENSEE's control and possession.

Proprietary Rights

3. (1) All rights not expressly granted herein are reserved.

(2) The Licensed Material is not sold to the LICENSEE who shall not acquire any right, sale or interest in the Licensed Material or in the media upon which the Licensed Material is supplied.

(3) The LICENSEE shall not erase, remove, deface or cover any trademark, copyright notice, guarantee or other statement on any media containing the Licensed Material.

(4) The LICENSEE shall only use the Licensed Material in the normal course of its business and shall not use the Licensed Material for the purpose of operating a bureau or similar service or any online service whatsoever.

(5) Permission is hereby granted to LICENSEES who are members of the legal profession (which expression does not include individuals or organisations engaged in the supply of services to the legal profession) to reproduce, transmit and store small quantities of text for the purpose of enabling them to provide legal advice to or to draft documents or conduct proceedings on behalf of their clients.

(6) The LICENSEE shall not sublicense the Licensed Material to others and this Licence Agreement may not be transferred, sublicensed, assigned or otherwise disposed of in whole or in part.

(7) The LICENSEE shall inform the PUBLISHERS on becoming aware of any unauthorised use of the Licensed Material.

Warranties

4. (1) The PUBLISHERS warrant that they have obtained all necessary rights to grant this licence.

(2) Whilst reasonable care is taken to ensure the accuracy and completeness of the Licensed Material supplied, the PUBLISHERS make no representations or warranties, express or implied, that the Licensed Material is free from errors or omissions.

(3) The Licensed Material is supplied to the LICENSEE on an "as is" basis and has not been supplied to meet the LICENSEE's individual requirements. It is the sole responsibility of the LICENSEE to satisfy itself prior to entering this Licence Agreement that the Licensed Material will meet the LICENSEE's requirements and be compatible with the LICENSEE's hardware/software configuration. No failure of any part of the Licensed Material to be suitable for the LICENSEE's requirements will give rise to any claim against the PUBLISHERS.

(4) In the event of any material inherent defects in the physical media on which the licensed material may be supplied, other than caused by accident abuse or misuse by the LICENSEE, the PUBLISHERS will replace the defective original media free of charge provided it is returned to the place of purchase within 90 days of the purchase date.
The PUBLISHERS' entire liability and the LICENSEE's exclusive remedy shall be the replacement of such defective media.

(5) Whilst all reasonable care has been taken to exclude computer viruses, no warranty is made that the Licensed Material is virus free. The LICENSEE shall be responsible to ensure that no virus is introduced to any computer or network and shall not hold the PUBLISHERS responsible.

(6) The warranties set out herein are exclusive of and in lieu of all other conditions and warranties, either express or implied, statutory or otherwise.

(7) All other conditions and warranties, either express or implied, statutory or otherwise, which relate in the condition and fitness for any purpose of the Licensed Material are hereby excluded and the PUBLISHERS shall not be liable in contract, delict or in tort for any loss of any kind suffered by reason of any defect in the Licensed Material (whether or not caused by the negligence of the PUBLISHERS).

Limitation of Liability and Indemnity

5. (1) The LICENSEE shall accept sole responsibility for and the PUBLISHERS shall not be liable for the use of the Licensed Material by the LICENSEE, its agents and employees and the LICENSEE shall hold the PUBLISHERS harmless and fully indemnified against any claims, costs, damages, loss and liabilities arising out of any such use.

(2) The PUBLISHERS shall not be liable for any indirect or consequential loss suffered by the LICENSEE (including without limitation loss of profits, goodwill or data) in connection with the Licensed Material howsoever arising.

(3) The PUBLISHERS will have no liability whatsoever for any liability of the LICENSEE to any third party which might arise.

(4) The LICENSEE hereby agrees that
(a) the LICENSEE is best placed to foresee and evaluate any loss that might be suffered in connection with this Licence Agreement;
(b) that the cost of supply of the Licensed Material has been calculated on the basis of the limitations and exclusions contained herein; and
(c) the LICENSEE will effect such insurance as is suitable having regard to the LICENSEE's circumstances.

(5) The aggregate maximum liability of the PUBLISHERS in respect of any direct loss or any other loss (to the extent that such loss is not excluded by this Licence Agreement or otherwise) whether such a claim arises in contract or tort shall not exceed a sum equal to that paid at the price for the title containing the Licensed Material.

Termination

6. (1) In the event of any breach of this Agreement including any violation of any copyright in the Licensed Material, whether held by the PUBLISHERS or others in the Licensed Material, the Licence Agreement shall automatically terminate immediately, without notice and without prejudice to any claim which the PUBLISHERS may have either for moneys due and/or damages and/or otherwise.

(2) Clauses 3 to 5 shall survive the termination for whatsoever reason of this Licence Agreement.

(3) In the event of termination of this Licence Agreement the LICENSEE will remove the Licensed Material.

Miscellaneous

7. (1) Any delay or forbearance by the PUBLISHERS in enforcing any provisions of this Licence Agreement shall not be construed as a waiver of such provision or an agreement thereafter not to enforce the said provision.

(2) This Licence Agreement shall be governed by the laws of England and Wales. If any difference shall arise between the Parties touching the meaning of this Licence Agreement or the rights and liabilities of the parties thereto, the same shall be referred to arbitration in accordance with the provisions of the Arbitration Act 1996, or any amending or substituting statute for the time being in force.